W9-ABV-629

DIEV ET MON DROIT.

The Second Charles, Heire of y^e Royall Martyr,
who, for Religion and his Subiects Charter,
spent the best Blood, y^e uniust Sword ere dy'de,
since the rude Souldier pierc'd our Saviours side:
who such a Father had'st; art such a Son;
redeeme thy people and assume thy Owne.   J.O.

Charles II. From an engraving by William Faithorne.

POEMS ON AFFAIRS OF STATE

AUGUSTAN SATIRICAL VERSE, 1660-1

PR
1195
.H5
P623

Anthology of

Poems on Affairs of State

AUGUSTAN SATIRICAL VERSE, 1660–1714

edited by

GEORGE deF. LORD

Salem Academy and College
Gramley Library
Winston-Salem, N.C. 27108

New Haven & London

YALE UNIVERSITY PRESS

1975

Copyright © 1975 by Yale University.
All rights reserved. This book may not be
reproduced, in whole or in part, in any form
(except by reviewers for the public press),
without written permission from the publishers.
Library of Congress catalog card number: 74–29735
International standard book number: (cloth) 0–300–01620–4, (paper) 0–300–01717–0

Designed by John O. C. McCrillis
and set in Baskerville type.
Printed in the United States of America by
The Murray Printing Co., Forge Village, Massachusetts.

Published in Great Britain, Europe, and Africa by
Yale University Press, Ltd., London.
Distributed in Latin America by Kaiman & Polon,
Inc., New York City; in India by UBS Publishers' Distributors Pvt.,
Ltd., Delhi; in Japan by John Weatherhill, Inc., Tokyo.

EDITORS

George deF. Lord, *General Editor*

William J. Cameron

Galbraith M. Crump

Frank H. Ellis

Elias F. Mengel, Jr.

Howard H. Schless

ASSOCIATES

Basil D. Henning

Maynard Mack

James M. Osborn

ADVISORY BOARD

Richard C. Boys

Sir Arthur Bryant

Brice Harris

Wilmarth S. Lewis

J. H. Plumb

Caroline Robbins

James R. Sutherland

James Thorpe

A. Ronald Tree

David M. Vieth

J. Harold Wilson

CONTENTS

THE POPISH PLOT AND THE EXCLUSION CRISIS, 1677–1681

THE TRIAL AND DEATH OF SHAFTESBURY

Salem Academy and College
Gramley Library
Winston-Salem, N.C. 27108

LIST OF ILLUSTRATIONS

xiii

PREFACE

This volume is designed to make available to students and general readers a generous selection from the seven-volume edition of *Poems on Affairs of State*. I have tried to represent the ingenious virtuosity of satirical forms, strategies, and styles in which the period abounded as well as to record the salient political issues and events of a momentous historical era.

In preparing this edition I have eliminated material aimed primarily at the specialist, including the textual apparatus. I have abbreviated headnotes and commentary by eliminating much authenticating detail. I have also modernized and normalized spelling and punctuation throughout.

In addition to the manifold assistance the editors have received and acknowledged in the individual volumes of the series I wish to express deep gratitude to Carola Bradford Lea, Millicent Marcus, Claire McGuire, and Nancy Woodington for help in preparing the manuscript, to Judy Metro for her lynx-eyed copy editing, and to Delight Ansley for making the index.

G.deF.L.

Yale University

INTRODUCTION

The august title *Poems on Affairs of State* hardly prepares the reader for the actual nature of the material involved. This may explain why for the last two hundred years interest in these once extremely popular collections of late seventeenth- and early eighteenth-century political verse has been confined to scholars and specialists. It may well be that the title was first applied in an intentionally sardonic way to those extraordinary lampoons and satires that poured from the press in various quarto editions on the heels of James II's flight from England in 1688. The affairs of state alluded to were comprehensive indeed and included the affairs of kings and actresses, of orange wenches and leaders of the court, as well as more momentous matters of state. The poems were written in a period when there was little compartmentalization in the public life of England, when those who wielded power at court, on the bench, or in Parliament, the church, or the armed forces all knew each other and lived and worked within a few square miles along the Thames between Westminster Hall and the Tower. It was a time when those who influenced British political, ecclesiastical, and social life formed a remarkably small and homogeneous group. With the deterioration of the mystique that had traditionally surrounded men of power, public interest in the private lives of these individuals became intense, and it was fed by thousands of "libels," "lampoons," and "satyrs." Thus we know more about the amours of Charles II with a succession of duchesses and actresses or the unseemly marriage of George Monck, duke of Albemarle, to a vociferous laundress named Nan Clarges, than we do about the devious and secretive foreign policy that Charles pursued in the twenty-five years of his reign or the equally devious and secretive maneuvers by which Monck became the architect of Charles's restoration.

Charles and his brother still clung to the idea that policy in church and state was solely the concern of the king and his ministers, an idea which their grandfather, James I, had forcefully enunciated when he came to the throne and which their father, Charles I, had pursued so intemperately that it led him to that famous scaffold upon which he died with consummate dignity, "While round the armed bands / Did clap their bloody hands." Deviousness and secrecy were thus a Stuart tradition, but after the civil wars and the interregnum, as the respect and awe surrounding monarchy declined, the tradition was increasingly challenged.

In the opening decades of this period the reading public had little in the way of news sources except for the government-sponsored *Gazette,* published twice a week, which printed very little significant information on domestic or foreign affairs. As the reading public increased steadily from the era of the civil wars, so did its appetite for the numerous satirical commentaries on public events hawked about the streets or provided in coffeehouses. In fact, the wide circulation of these commentaries on state secrets so agitated Charles's ministers that in 1675 the government made a vain effort to put an end to them by closing the coffeehouses, regarded as the breeding grounds of sedition. If censorship made circulation of these lampoons and satires in printed form too risky, a kind of manuscript publication was resorted to. A roomful of scribes would make many copies of the most popular pieces, and these would be retailed through various clandestine sources. Many manuscripts of single poems were sent from one reader to another by private messenger, and some stationers seem to have made a specialty of compiling manuscript collections of satires dealing with specific events, public figures, or themes. Thus one finds compilations primarily devoted to court scandal, or to bribery and place-selling in Parliament, or to the exposure of the government's pro-French and Romanist designs. Perhaps as an aid to internal intelligence, James II had such a compilation made toward the end of his reign. The volume, bound in black morocco and stamped with the royal arms, could not have given its owner much pleasure. In almost every poem the coming revolution is implied with implacable hostility and mordant wit.

Clandestine circulation in manuscript helps account for the enormous number of manuscripts that have come down to us, while the widespread employment of professional scribes—for example, in the case of the famous Marvell compilation in the Bodley—helps account for the high level of their textual quality. Censorship appears to have stimulated these underground productions instead of thwarting them, and it unquestionably whetted the political curiosity of an expanding reading public. The phenomenon of the state poems, with their skeptical, profane and pragmatic views on public institutions, seems to be one indication of the watershed between medieval and renaissance England on the one hand and modern England on the other. They helped to introduce a fundamentally secular attitude toward monarchical government.

A keener interest in the private lives of public servants and a corresponding erosion of respect for the whole political establishment from the monarch on down heralded more modern attitudes in the demythologizing of the king, both as God's vicegerent and as defender of the faith. This tendency to degrade divine right and its attendant myths was strengthened by the civil wars and the interregnum, and by the sectarianism which suggested, even to the least rebellious subject, that no institution had a monopoly on religious or political truth. It was accelerated most of all, however, by the very character of the thirty-year-old monarch who was now restored to the throne. Unlike his father, the royal martyr and author of *Ikon Basilike*, Charles II was not a king to hold his office in much awe. The divinity that doth hedge a king tended to evaporate rather rapidly during his reign. And the evaporation of this sustaining monarchist myth was certainly not abetted by aspects of Charles's personal life. The son's unbuttoned ease made a striking contrast to the kingliness of his father, and the proliferation of many well-publicized love affairs with such flamboyant and exigent mistresses as the duchess of Castlemaine, the duchess of Cleveland, Mall Kirke, and Nell Gwynne helped to bring the new regime into disrepute, especially with the more conservative or straitlaced members of the community. Even Charles's wittiest and most eloquent spokesman had to concede the king's personal weaknesses in his brilliant opening to *Absalom and Achitophel*:

> In pious times, ere priestcraft did begin,
> Before polygamy was made a sin;
> When man on many multiplied his kind,
> Ere one to one was cursedly confined:
> When Nature prompted, and no law denied
> Promiscuous use of concubine and bride;
> Then Israel's monarch, after Heaven's own heart,
> His vigorous warmth did variously impart
> To wives and slaves and, wide as his command,
> Scattered his Maker's image through the land.

Those who were willing to overlook the random polyphiloprogenitiveness of their king were unwilling to overlook the brutal and—all too often—fatal pranks of some of his noble courtiers, like Sedley, Rochester, Mulgrave, and Dorset, who are represented in this collection as both authors and objects of satire and whom Milton characterized unforgettably as "the sons of Belial flown with insolence and wine." On the other hand, some of Charles's support came from old Cavaliers and new Tories, who saw him as their champion against the austerity and alleged hypocrisy of Roundheads and Puritans.

In the long run the fate of the monarchy hinged on larger issues than the private life of Charles. His otherwise remarkable fecundity was thwarted by the barrenness of his queen, Catherine de Braganza, whom he refused to divorce. With no prospects of his having a legitimate and Protestant heir, widespread fear of popery and arbitrary government (the phrase became a watchword) built up a clamor for the rejection of the true heir to the throne, Charles's unpopular Catholic brother, James, duke of York. Great pressure was brought to bear on Charles to persuade him to disinherit his brother in favor of his eldest bastard, the Protestant duke of Monmouth. The resulting exclusion crisis in 1678 brought to a head the most bitter political feelings of the whole reign and led to an explosion of plots and recriminations, judicial murders, reprisals, and finally to a repressive reaction against the exclusionist forces of Shaftesbury.

When the problems posed by the succession issue and those arising from Charles's "private" life and his natural deviousness in the conduct of affairs are coupled with his persistent efforts to reign free of ministerial or parliamentary interference, one can readily see why he became a fascinating object for the satirist's scrutiny. To this day historians disagree about the extent to which he seriously intended to fulfill his commitments to Louis XIV in the secret Treaty of Dover (1670) to reimpose the Roman religion on his subjects in return for the subvention that would free him from fiscal dependence on Parliament. After weathering the crisis of 1681, Charles in any event managed, with Louis's help, to keep the royal prerogative untrammeled by parliamentary controls.

The exclusion crisis and its aftermath represent yet another version of the profound constitutional struggle between royal prerogative and parliamentary privilege that had been the central issue of the civil war. Charles's reimposition of his authority with the dissolution of the Oxford Parliament in 1681 could, however, only temporarily arrest the decline in the power of the monarchy. James, who had none of Charles's tact and charm but all his stubbornness and deviousness, so exacerbated his subjects that it took him a mere four years to lose the kingdom that Charles had so shrewdly preserved and passed on to him. James fled the kingdom when the birth of a son in 1688, raising the specter of a Papist dynasty, led to an invitation that brought William and Mary to the throne. James had tried to govern by force and threats; he had violated the law of the land by introducing Catholic officers into the army and into positions of trust; he had employed the threat of Irish troops against his English subjects; and he had flaunted his adherence to the old religion and aroused the slumbering dread of a return to the period of the martyrs under Bloody Mary. And now the birth of a son raised the prospect of an interminable popish tyranny.

With the revolution of 1688 England gained a monarch whose claim to the throne was relatively tenuous—at least while James or his son was alive—and one whose powers, therefore, could be more strictly curbed by Parliament than those of Charles or James. If William of Orange and his wife Mary shared the Stuart passion for absolute power that had characterized their predecessors, they concealed it well, and it is indisputable that they brought to England an unprecedented and badly needed religious toleration. Their reign was marked by the gradual establishment of a modus vivendi that nevertheless failed to reconcile extreme Tories and Jacobites to the Dutchman who was an inveterate and tenacious foe of Louis XIV.

Opposition to William and Mary at first found satirical expression in lampoons treating them as usurpers and virtual parricides, riding over the body of their uncle and father in the royal coach, like Tarquin and Tullia. As long as James and his son, James Edward, were alive, the tenure of James's older daughter and his nephew had to be justified on grounds other than succession, and some fine-spun casuistries were accordingly called into play. But if, from a de jure standpoint, their title was flawed, the energy and tolerance that marked their regime established them as the right de facto rulers for the times. Despite the huge wars that took William away from his kingdom for five or six months each year to campaign against Louis, there was a gradual trend toward stability in England throughout their reign, a trend that accelerated when James's younger daughter, Anne, came to the throne without the stigma of usurpation. Whether one agrees with Trevelyan that it was "the Dutch schoolmaster" William who ushered in the peace of the Augustans, or with Plumb that its "adamantine strength and profound inertia" were established somewhat later with the accession of George I, there is no question that the period was marked by a great increase in party strife and a corresponding decrease in real violence.[1] Conspiracies, plots, and invasions, which had characterized English domestic politics throughout much of the seventeenth century, were now largely a thing of the past.

The peace of the Augustans was to be hailed in one of Alexander Pope's finest early poems, *Windsor Forest,* celebrating the imminent Treaty of Utrecht, which was to put an end to decades of wars with Louis XIV:

> O fact accursed! What tears has Albion shed,
> Heavens! what new wounds, and how her old have bled?
> She saw her sons with purple deaths expire,
> Her sacred domes involved in rolling fire,
> A dreadful series of intestine wars,
> Inglorious triumphs, and dishonest scars.
> At length great Anna said—Let discord cease!
> She said, the world obeyed, and all was peace!

Three-quarters of a century earlier, Marvell had celebrated the phenomenal emergence of Cromwell and his impact upon the youthful poet in *An Horatian Ode:*

> The forward youth that would appear
> Must now forsake his Muses dear,
>   Nor in the shadows sing
>   His numbers languishing,

1. George Macaulay Trevelyan, *England under the Stuarts,* 21st ed. (London, 1949), p. 372; J. H. Plumb, *The Origins of Political Stability: England, 1675–1725* (Boston, 1967), p. xviii.

> 'Tis time to leave the books in dust,
> And oyl the unused armors rust:
>   Removing from the wall
>   The corslet of the hall.

Cromwell appears as an apocalyptic agent destroying the old order:

> Then burning through the air he went,
> And palaces and temples rent:
>   And Caesar's head at last
>   Did through his laurels blast.

In the conclusion to his poem, Pope—imitating Virgil, as Marvell had imitated Horace—brings the curtain down on decades of civil strife and returns to his shadows, his Muses, and his "numbers languishing":

> My humble Muse, in unambitious strains,
> Paints the green forests and the flowery plains,
> Where Peace descending bids her olives spring,
> And scatters blessings from her dovelike wing.
> Even I more sweetly pass my careless days,
> Pleased in the silent shade with empty praise;
> Enough for me, that to the listening swains
> First in the fields I sung the sylvan strains.

Between them, the Puritan poet who supported Cromwell and the Catholic poet who so indefatigably supported the Stuarts embrace the critical period covered by the poems in this volume. They also embrace a whole range of political attitudes from apocalypse to paradise regained. But in hailing a new era Pope was unwittingly erecting a monument to an old (for *Windsor Forest* is one of the last attempts to invoke the traditional, classical, religiously oriented view of monarchy). Certainly Virgil's influence, in the *Georgics* especially, continued to be felt for some time in English poetry, but not with the profundity and passion exhibited in this early poem of Alexander Pope.

The real spokesman for the new age that was emerging after the revolution of 1688 and that prevailed throughout the eighteenth century was not Alexander Pope but Daniel Defoe. A sociopolitical and economic revolution, which steadily increased the power of Whig money-men as against Tory landed gentry, undermined the traditional conservative concept of man and society embodied in "the great chain of being." This myth, with its emphasis on subordination and fixed class structure, was challenged by new notions of social mobility fueled by the expanding wealth of Whig projectors, merchants, and businessmen. Conservative Augustan writers such as Bolingbroke, Pope, Swift, and Gay were appalled by the disintegration of the social ideal to which they had subscribed. At the center of their traditional and conservative ethos was a fervent belief in "the hierarchical ordering of society and nature according to the divinely ordained chain of being" in contradistinction to the Lockean principles of "voluntary contract sponsored by the emerging middle class." Unlike the traditionalists, who tended to be Anglican, Tory, and, by their addiction to the classical writers, champions of the ancients against the moderns, the new man, whose greatest spokesman was Defoe, tended to be low church and Whiggish and to disparage the old order and the humanist culture founded on Greek and Latin learning. He embraced an individualistic concept of man freed from the restrictions of a social hierarchy:

> In both his career and writings Defoe embodied the projecting spirit—the restless and optimistic desire to tinker with and change society and nature. Tradition, the inherited social order, and nature ceased to be sacred before the projector and the tinkerer. His wholly progressive spirit gloried in inventions and newness, in solving traditional problems, in conquering new worlds. His practical and utilitarian spirit enshrined the handy, the useful, the profitable; his was the spirit of self-interest, avarice, and individualism. Projecting man, free of any functional duty to any organic social structure, stood alone, creating and shaping his own world and his own destiny. His was the spirit of Locke's man, of Robinson Crusoe, a necessary ingredient of the capitalist creed.[2]

The growth of Augustan capitalism, hastened by the foundation of the Bank of England, debit financing, the issuance of paper money, and the proliferation of joint-stock companies, enabled a new class to rise to political and social power. Upward social mobility probably contributed to the expansion of a middle class reading public with distinctly unclassical tastes that patronized the popular stage entertainments of Colley Cibber and Rich, supported the rage for opera and the new sentimental drama, and found a mirror of its own values and interests in the novels of Defoe. The time had come when any man who was clever, ambitious, and hardworking could aspire to wealth and power; the aristocratic bias of the old order had been nullified.

While many of the state poems were written in defense of the old order, the total impact, regardless of the political viewpoints they represent, tended to erode that order. In the first place, it was subversive, by traditional standards, to invite public discussion of state secrets. In the second place, these corrosive satires ate away traditional attitudes of awe and respect toward one's betters. In the third place, the predominantly pessimistic and cynical tone of what must have appeared to be a never ending flood of satires undermined confi-

2. This quotation and the two preceding ones are from Isaac Kramnick, *Bolingbroke and His Circle: The Politics of Nostalgia in the Age of Walpole* (Cambridge, Mass., 1967), pp. 214, 193.

dence in institutions and public figures. In a rare attack on satire one anony-
mous poet put the case thus:

> Unhinge not governments except you could
> Supply us better ere you change the old.
> You would have all amended. So would I,
> Yet not deface each piece where faults I spy.
> 'Tis true I could find colors to expose
> Faulty grandees and over-paint a rose,
> But this checks me, that whatso'er is aimed,
> Few such are mended by being proclaimed.
> Public disgrace oft smaller sinners scares,
> But vice with greatness armed no colors fears.
> Besides, the rout grows insolent hereby,
> And slights the once disgraced authority,
> Whence, to paint all our betters' faults would be
> To hang up order in effigie.[3]

The satirists of course failed to heed this advice but continued in their head-
long pursuit of alleged or actual instances of folly and knavery among the
great. The cumulative force of these thousands of state poems was over-
whelmingly antiheroic. The legions of satirists would not permit heroic
virtues to survive, and their disillusionment was generally confirmed by the
behavior of their subjects. Charles II's insouciance was a perennial theme,
but his chief ministers also came under attack. The great Clarendon was
proud and avaricious. Arlington was arrogant and a traitor to boot. Bucking-
ham was a wastrel and a fool. Lauderdale was an overbearing tyrant. Sir
William Coventry was greedy. The duke of York was promiscuous and also a
bigot. His first duchess was unchaste. Their children all died because the duke
had contracted syphilis from the countess of Southesk. Even the upright
William and Mary were not exempt from the satirical lash: she had ridden to
power in a most impious way, over her father's body as it were; William was
a homosexual who filled the government with his Dutch favorites.

Nor was the church free of such attacks. The higher the office the greater
the likelihood of the officeholder's being satirized, and so the chief objects of
satire were bishops and archbishops, such as the concupiscent Sheldon and
Burnet, or the compliant and unprincipled Hoadley.

For a lady to achieve prominence at court was to nominate herself for a
place in various catalogues of ingenious infidelities. The satirist's proclivity
for exaggeration meant that with rare exceptions the malefactors became
undifferentiated monsters: Castlemaine, de Kérouaille, Willis, Hinton,

---

3. *The Answer of Mr. Waller's Painter to His Many New Advisers* (1667), 65–78.

Sedley, Orkney, Marlborough, and Masham are as little individualized as the personae of lust and avarice in a Spenserian allegory.

The net effect of these slashing indictments was to obliterate distinctions essential to a hierarchically ordered society and to introduce a classless society of knaves and rogues and whores. Ambition, greed, and lust were the great levelers. On the other hand it must be emphasized that the effect of the state poems was not always so reductive. One of their more positive achievements was to expose and to help thwart the designs of Charles II and James II to achieve arbitrary power. Charles's stratagems in manipulating Parliament in order to nullify its restraining power over his foreign policy were brought to the public's attention in a great number of effective satires, and James's scheme for overwhelming the English with an Irish army backfired when it was ridiculed in what may well be the most popular political lampoon in history, *Lilliburlero*.

In either case, whether satire is credited with undermining a traditional set of values and the institutions by which they were expressed or with exposing the invasion of freedom by the sovereign under the guise of preserving those old values, the phenomenon of the state poems coincided with, reflected, and in some measure contributed to the destruction of the myth of a hierarchical community ordained by God and replaced it with standards that were individualistic and secular.

If the popularity of the state poems reflected an expanded reading public, it also reflected an expanding society of authors. If one looks for full-time writers of great distinction within the period, only Dryden qualifies. For the remainder, high and low, good and bad, writing was an avocation. One large group, the court wits, whom Pope called "the mob of gentlemen that writ with ease," included Rochester, Dorset, Mulgrave, Sheppard, Sedley, and Etherege. Of these only Rochester produced enough to achieve stature as a satirical poet. The next group would include serious occasional writers outside the court circle, such as Marvell, Ayloffe, Oldham, Prior, Tate, Garth, Tutchin, Shippen, and Swift. Then one perhaps should mention some relatively obscure writers who had written one or two good satires: Caryll (*Naboth's Vineyard*), Freke (*The History of Insipids*), Wharton (*Lilliburlero*). Another group would be comprised of the makers of doggerel: Tom Brown, Durfey, Stephen College, Robert Wild. By far the largest group would yet remain—the flood of satirists whose identity remains undiscovered. It is hard to think of any writer of the period who did not produce at least one satire: as Horace wrote, "Difficile est non satyram scribere."

The generic variety displayed by these satires provides relief from the otherwise ubiquitous occasional poem in heroic couplets. In addition to great numbers of songs and ballads set to popular tunes and often parodying older lyrics, there are mock-litanies, mock-elegies, epistles, and dramatic monologues.

The censorship of the press and other means for the suppression and prosecution of unlicensed printing of "libels" are responsible for the enormous numbers of satires in manuscript that never saw print. The Licensing Act of 1662, which lapsed in 1679, was augmented by the provisions of the Treason Act, the first statute passed by the Cavalier Parliament, aimed at "all printing, writing, preaching, or malicious and advised speaking calculated to compass or devise the death, destruction, injury, or restraint of the sovereign, or to deprive him of his style, honor, or kingly name."

The chief importance of these laws lay in the powers of search and seizure vested in the crown and delegated to the surveyor of the press. Armed with these powers Sir Roger L'Estrange ferreted out the authors and publishers of seditious literature. One of the most frequent offenders was Francis "Elephant" Smith, who published some of the *Advices to a Painter,* which bitterly attacked the government for disastrous miscarriages in the second Dutch war. Smith was repeatedly fined and pilloried. Others suffered harsher punishments. In 1681 one of his authors, Stephen College, a wild supporter of Shaftesbury, was executed for high treason for writing "a scandalous libel called the *Raree Show*" and other lampoons on Charles II. To escape detection satirists often resorted to distribution of manuscript copies. This led to the establishment of well-organized commercial firms that employed batteries of scribes to make copies of single poems and various kinds of manuscript collections. These "scriptoria" became clearinghouses for satire. One of them was run by Robert Julian, facetiously nicknamed "Secretary of the Muses," who was himself lampooned in the following unflattering terms:

> Thou common shore [sewer] of this poetic town,
> Where all our excrements of wit are thrown—
> For sonnet, satire, bawdry, blasphemy
> Are emptied and disburdened all on thee.

In 1684 Julian was fined and pilloried for a poem called *Old Rowley the King,* comparing Charles II to his favorite stallion. There is no evidence that Julian was a printer, so the charge of "making and publishing" here probably refers to manuscript publication. As L'Estrange had observed in 1677 to the Libels Committee of the House of Lords, the legal definition of "libel" should be extended to include manuscript material, "because it is notorious that not one in forty libels ever comes to the press, though by the help of manuscripts they are well-nigh as public." To reduce public access to them the government closed the coffeehouses for a time, perhaps in response to L'Estrange's plea. Charles was reportedly incensed with the proprietors of these establishments, who, "to gain a little money had the impudence and folly to prostitute affairs of state indifferently to the views of those that frequent such houses, some of them of lewd principles, and some of mean birth and education." In these observations Charles was faithful to the principles of his grandfather, James I, who had proclaimed:

> It is atheism and blasphemy to dispute what God can do: good Christians content themselves with His will revealed in His Word: so it is presumption and high contempt in a subject to dispute what a king cannot do, or to say that a king cannot do this or that, but rest with that which is the king's revealed will in his law.

Although it was challenged more and more as time went on, the doctrine of divine right and the attendant notion that affairs of state were of no concern to the king's subjects continued to be supported by conservative writers, especially by Dryden. In 1683 Judge Jeffreys, who was to become infamous in the Bloody Assizes, extended the censorship of unpublished material one ultimate degree further by sending the distinguished Whig statesman, Algernon Sidney, to the block for the mere possession of an allegedly treasonous paper in his holograph. This act of savagery itself became the object of satirical attack in *A New Song for the Times*:

> Algernon Sidney,
> Of commonwealth kidney,
> Composed a damned libel (ay, marry, was it!)
> Writ to occasion
> Ill blood in the nation,
> And therefore dispersed it all over his closet.

The episode suggests the irrepressible vitality of the satirical response to the authoritarianism of the regimes of Charles II and James II.

This spirit of freedom lies behind most of the better opposition satire. Among the many who did not hesitate to take risks Defoe is probably the most famous because of his impudent transformation of what was intended to be a humiliating public punishment into a popular victory, an event commemorated in his *Hymn to the Pillory*. "The indignity of the pillory," Defoe confided to the earl of Nottingham, "was worse to me than death," yet he struck out recklessly against "a merciless as well as unjust ministry," declaring that the punishment was "unjust, exorbitant, and consequently illegal." Defoe anticipates Pope's snide inference in the *Dunciad* that the degrading punishment was appropriate to the victim by reminding his readers:

> But who can judge of crimes by punishment,
> Where parties rule, and law's subservient?

> Justice with change of interest learns to bow,
> And what was merit once is murther now:
> Actions receive their tincture from the times,
> And, as they change, are virtues made or crimes.
>
> [25–30]

The despised mob, who were expected to aggravate Defoe's punishment, instead "expressed their affections by loud shouts and acclamations, when he was taken down."[4] These examples remind us that, despite the venality and cynicism of many party writers, some of them at least could see a crucial question of freedom behind the issues of church doctrine, foreign policy, and the contests of king and Parliament. I do not mean to suggest that infringements of freedom came only from conservatives and royalists: throughout the period that concerns us there was probably no greater threat to domestic order than the Popish Plot, so cynically nurtured by Shaftesbury and the exclusionists. Satires protesting tyranny, whether by a "radical" Defoe or a "conservative" Swift, must have helped to keep freedom alive.

The poems in this selection represent a tiny percentage of the total output, in print and manuscript, produced between 1660 and 1714. Some attempt has been made to reflect the wide variety of subjects and styles used. In addition to poems on what would normally be thought of as affairs of state (primarily political and military matters) questions of ecclesiastical policy were of fundamental importance, from the restrictions on Dissent embodied in the Clarendon Code (1662) to Dr. Sacheverell's jeremiads against Dissenters and his trial in 1710.

With regard to variety of styles, one might begin by making a distinction between mock-heroic on the one hand and such forms as burlesque and invective on the other. Mock-heroic is essentially a conservative style. It judges persons and events by traditional standards. It tends to take the point of view of an insider. This is eminently true of Dryden's attack on Shadwell in *Mac Flecknoe*, where Shadwell is presented as a ludicrous aspirant to the bays of Ben Jonson, while Dryden demonstrates his own matchless competence in deft allusions that assimilate the great literary traditions in an adroit and elegant way. *Absalom and Achitophel*, unquestionably the greatest political satire in English poetry, also assumes a conservative position. A sweeping historical and biblical perspective is provided in terms of which the rebellious aberrations of Shaftesbury's party can be judged and condemned. Even more than in *Mac Flecknoe* the speaker assumes an ironical, sophisticated social tone that helps to authenticate his implicit claim to be spokesman for a rational and traditional politics. Next to *Absalom and Achitophel*, but well

---

4. *POAS*, Yale, *6*, 586.

below it, one should probably rank Marvell's mock-heroic, *The Last Instructions to a Painter,* which lacks the firm control provided by Dryden's historical perspective and his biblical and classical frameworks.

Mock-heroic, though it is responsible for most of the best satirical poetry in English, includes only a very small portion of poems on affairs of state. The paucity of mock-heroic in comparison with other styles such as burlesque and invective may be attributed in large part to the fact that so many of these satires are attacking institutions and traditions. Thus the opposition writers shunned the classical Latin and Greek learning that was the mainstay of conservative writers such as Dryden, Swift, Pope, and Gay. In rejecting the classical education of the nobility and gentry, and promoting the practical training of the merchant, Defoe

> mirrored values of the new age that so frightened men whose sights were set on the past.
>
> He spoke for, and was read by a class totally alien to Bolingbroke, Swift, Pope, and Gay. These brothers of the Scriblerus Club thought Defoe's work socially and intellectually inferior, a fact indicated by its success with the new and bourgeois reading public. They regarded his work as another illustration of the progress of "dullness" that rejected their humanist political, social, and cultural ideals.[5]

Defoe's satirical poems have a utilitarian, journalistic, improvised air about them. They are not allusive or neoclassical and the standards they bring ot political experience are pragmatic. The air of improvisation is characteristic of many of the best opposition satires. As opposed to conservative preoccupation with correctness and form, the more radical writers were primarily concerned with getting a message across in one way or another. Thus they resorted to ballad forms, doggerel, dialogues, mock-litanies, and songs, shunning the more literary and elaborate forms of the animal fable, the mock pastoral, or the advice to the painter. It is significant that after Marvell wrote his last poem defending Charles II against his ministers, he turned from mock-heroic to antiheroic doggerel, to point up his loss of faith in the king. The Charles whom he had compared to the heroic King Minos in *The Last Instructions to a Painter* becomes an unruly and truant apprentice seven years later in *Upon His Majesty's Being Made Free of the City.*

Thus the greatness of Dryden, Swift, and Pope has obscured or misrepresented what really happened in England between 1660 and 1714. "The Peace of the Augustans" was not due to the triumph of traditional social standards or Tory values but to political stability engendered by the Whig magnates. In *Windsor Forest* Pope correctly predicted a period of peace and

5. Kramnick, *Bolingbroke and His Circle,* p. 196.

prosperity, starting with the Treaty of Utrecht (1713), but the architect of this unprecedented political stability was not to be his philosophical friend Bolingbroke and what Kramnick evocatively calls "the politics of nostalgia," but the creative and unprincipled Walpole and political writers such as Marvell and Defoe.

CHRONOLOGY

1660	The Restoration	Pepys begins his *Diary*
		Dryden, *Astraea Redux*
1661	Savoy Conference Corporation Act	
1662		Founding of Royal Society
1663		Butler, *Hudibras* (Part I)
1665	Second Dutch War	
	Great Plague	
	Five Mile Act	
1666	Great Fire of London	
1667	End of second Dutch war	Dryden, *Annus Mirabilis*
		Milton, *Paradise Lost*
1668	Triple Alliance	
1670	Secret Treaty of Dover	Dryden becomes poet laureate
1672	Duke of York becomes an avowed Roman Catholic	
	Third Dutch war	
1673	Test Act	
	Dismissal of Shaftesbury from chancellorship	
1678	Popish Plot	
1681	Prosecution of Shaftesbury thwarted by Ignoramus Grand Jury	Dryden, *Absalom and Achitophel*
1682	Duke of Monmouth's Progress through West of England	Dryden, *The Medal, Mac Flecknoe, Religio Laici*
1683	Rye House Plot	
1685	Charles II dies: succeeded by his brother, James II	
	Monmouth uprising	
1688	Trial of the Seven Bishops	Alexander Pope born
	The Revolution	
1689	William and Mary reign	Dryden loses laureateship to Shadwell
		Quarto editions of *POAS*

1690	Battle of the Boyne	
1693	National Debt originated	
1694	Bank of England founded	
1697	Peace of Ryswick	Dryden's translation of Virgil
1700		Death of Dryden
1702	Anne reigns	
1704	Battle of Blenheim	Swift, *Battle of the Books, Tale of a Tub*
		Defoe, *The Review*
1710	Trial of Sacheverell	
	Fall of the Whigs; Harley and St. John in power	
1711		Steele Addison, et al., *The Spectator*
1713	Treaty of Utrecht	Pope, *Windsor Forest*
1714	Death of Anne	

Anthology of Poems on Affairs of State
1660-1714

ROBERT WILD

Iter Boreale
(1660)

"He is the very Wither of the City: they have bought more editions of his works than would serve to lay under all their pies at the lord mayor's Christmas. When his famous poem first came out in the year 1660, I have seen them reading it in the midst of 'Change time; nay so vehement they were at it, that they lost their bargain by the candles' ends." Thus Eugenius, in Dryden's *Essay of Dramatic Poesy*, testifies to the extraordinary impact of *Iter Boreale,* a poem that was not only the most popular of the innumerable lampoons upon the expelled Rump Parliament, but the most popular of the many effusions in verse that welcomed Charles Stuart back to his kingdom.

Dryden's discussion of popular occasional verse had begun with a reference to the English naval victory over the Dutch on 3 June 1665, the famous Battle of Lowestoft, which was to be an important motif in so much Restoration poetry. Wild, Crites says, is a poet who watches a battle "with more diligence than the ravens and birds of prey," one "whom this victory with both her wings will never be able to escape." Although Wild did not happen to celebrate this occasion in his verses, the spirit of Crites's prophecy is right—few important events, especially in the realm of ecclesiastical affairs, escaped Wild's vigilant pen, and he did turn out a panegyric upon a later engagement with the Dutch fleet. As a Puritan minister and a royalist Wild was always trying to vindicate the loyalty of Charles II's Nonconformist subjects, while he derided both the jealousies and the forms of the Anglicans. In George Monck (1608–70), the great Presbyterian architect of Charles's restoration, he found a subject heaven-sent. *Iter Boreale* relates with gusto and with considerable historical detail the steps by which this shrewd and taciturn hero outmaneuvered both the Rump Parliament and the army faction to engineer this bloodless revolution.

Iter Boreale illustrates clearly the peculiar appeal of minor political verse—its intense contemporary interest, its vivid detail, and its occasional vitality of thought and style. In the person of Crites, the greatest of Restoration satirists remarks that Wild, who was probably the most popular, is addicted to "a certain clownish kind of raillery," and that he is "a very leveler in poetry; he creeps along with ten little words in every line, and helps out his numbers with *for to* and *unto* and all the pretty expletives he can find." The

3

remark is not exactly just, for *Iter Boreale* manages, in its intense Cleveland-esque way, to convey some of the excitement and joy so deeply and widely felt on the eve of the Restoration, as well as some of the popular contempt for the regimes that immediately preceded it.

ITER BOREALE

Attempting Something upon the Successful
and Matchless March of the Lord General
George Monck from Scotland to London in
the Winter, 1659

1.

The day is broke! Melpomene, begone;
Hag of my fancy, let me now alone;
Nightmare my soul no more; go take thy flight
Where traitors' ghosts keep an eternal night;
Flee to Mount Caucasus and bear thy part   5
With the black fowl that tears Prometheus' heart
For his bold sacrilege; go fetch the groans
Of defunct tyrants, with them croak thy tones.
Go see Alecto with her flaming whip,
How she firks Nol and makes old Bradshaw skip.   10
Go make thyself away—thou shalt no more
Choke up my standish with the blood and gore
Of English tragedies: I now will choose
The merriest of the nine to be my Muse,
And, come what will, I'll scribble once again.   15
The brutish sword hath cut the nobler vein
Of racy poetry; our small-drink times
Must be contented and take up with rhymes.
They're sorry toys from a poor Levite's pack,
Whose living and assessments drink no sack—   20
The subject will excuse the verse, I trow;
The venison's fat, although the crust be dough.

10. *firks:* beats. *Nol:* Oliver Cromwell. *Bradshaw:* John Bradshaw (1602–59), president of
the commission that tried Charles I.
12. *standish:* inkstand.
17. *small-drink:* trivial.
19. *Levite:* priest.

George Monck, duke of Albemarle. From an engraving by Loggan.

2.

I, he who whilom sat and sung in cage
My king's and country's ruin by the rage
Of a rebellious rout; who weeping saw   25
Three goodly kingdoms, drunk with fury, draw
And sheathe their swords, like three enraged brothers,
In one another's sides, ripping their mother's
Belly, and tearing out her bleeding heart;
Then, jealous that their father fain would part   30
Their bloody fray and let them fight no more,
Fell foul on him and slew him at his door;
I that have only dared to whisper verses,
And drop a tear by stealth on loyal hearses;
I that enraged at the times and Rump,   35
Had gnawed my goose-quill to the very stump,
And flung that in the fire, no more to write,
But to sit down poor Britain's Heraclite,
Now sing the triumphs of the men of war,
The glorious rays of the bright northern star,   40
Created for the nonce by Heav'n to bring
The wise men of three nations to their king.
Monck! the great Monck! that syllable outshines
Plantagenet's bright name or Constantine's.
'Twas at his rising that our day begun;   45
Be he the morning star to Charles our sun.
He took rebellion rampant by the throat,
And made the canting Quaker change his note.
His hand it was that wrote (we saw no more)
Exit tyrannus over Lambert's door.   50
Like to some subtle lightning, so his words
Dissolvèd in their scabbards rebels' swords.
He with success the sovereign skill hath found
To dress the weapon and so heal the wound.

23–42. While Wild was a royalist throughout his life, there is no evidence that he wrote or suffered imprisonment in the cause of Charles I. The career here described sounds much like that of John Cleveland, whose influence is reflected in the style and opinions of *Iter Boreale*.

38. *Heraclite:* Heraclitus, the "weeping philosopher."

50. *Lambert:* John Lambert (1619–83) commanded the army sent north in November 1659 to oppose Monck's entry into England. His soldiers deserted en masse.

54. A reference to the medical superstition that wounds could be healed by treating the weapon that had inflicted them.

George and his boys, as spirits do, they say,   55
Only by walking scare our foes away.

3.

Old Holofernes was no sooner laid
Before the idol's funeral pomp was paid
(Nor shall a penny e'er be paid for me:
Let fools that trusted his true mourners be),   60
Richard the Fourth just peeping out of squire
(No fault so much as the old one was his sire,
For men believed, though all went in his name,
He'd be but tenant till the landlord came),
When on a sudden, all amazed, we found   65
The seven years' Babel tumbled to the ground,
And he, poor heart, thanks to his cunning kin,
Was soon in cuerpo honest Dick again.
Exit protector. What comes next? I trow,
Let the state-huntsmen beat again. "So ho!"   70
Cries Lambert, Master of the Hounds, "Here sits
That lusty puss, the Good Old Cause, whose wits
Showed Oliver such sport." "That! that!" cries Vane,
"Let's put her up, and run her once again!
She'll lead our dogs and followers up and down,   75
Whilst we match families and take the crown."

57. *Old Holofernes:* Wild refers to Oliver Cromwell by the name of Nebuchadnezzar's tyrannical general. See the Book of Judith in the Old Testament Apocrypha.

58. Cromwell died 3 September 1658. His body lay in state at Somerset House "amid banners, escutcheons, black velvet draperies and all the sombre gorgeousness of the greatest royal funerals . . . and not until the 23rd of November was there an end to these ghastly splendors" (David Masson, *The Life of John Milton Narrated in Connection with the Political, Ecclesiastical, and Literary History of His Time,* 7 vols. [London, 1859–94], *5,* 415).

59. *for me:* on my behalf.

61. *Richard the Fourth:* Richard Cromwell, who succeeded his father as lord protector. *out of squire:* out of square, out of proper order or rule.

67. *cunning kin:* Charles Fleetwood (d. 1692), Richard Cromwell's brother-in-law, a leader of the army or Wallingford House faction, whose ambition to be commander-in-chief released forces that were to topple the new protector (Masson, *Life of Milton, 5,* 425).

68. *in cuerpo:* naked.

71–73. When Richard fell in April 1659, Lambert recovered his old position as chief representative of the army in the negotiations that preceded the restoration of the Rump Parliament. Though not a member of the Wallingford House party, Lambert joined with Fleetwood and John Desborough (1608–80), the leaders of this faction, in restoring the Rump to satisfy public clamor for the Good Old Cause (the pure republican constitution).

73. *Vane:* Sir Henry Vane the younger (1613–62) played a leading part in the restoration of the Rump. After Charles II returned he was among those capitally excepted from pardon as too dangerous to live. He was executed 14 June 1662.

Enter the old members. 'Twas the month of May
These maggots in the Rump began to play.
Wallingford anglers, though they stunk, yet thought
They would make baits by which fish might be caught,   80
And so it proved—they soon by taxes made
More money than the Holland fishing-trade.

4.

Now broke in Egypt's plagues all in a day
And one more, worse than theirs. We must not pray
To be delivered—their scabbed folks were free   85
To scratch where it did itch—so might not we.
That meteor Cromwell, though he scared, gave light,
But we were now covered with horrid night.
Our magistracy was, like Moses' rod,
Turned to a serpent by the angry God.   90
Poor citizens when trading would not do
Made brick without straw and were basted too.
Struck with the botch of taxes and excise,
Servants (our very dust) were turned to lice—
It was but turning soldiers, and they need   95
Not work at all, but on their masters feed.
Strange caterpillars ate our pleasant things,
And frogs croaked in the chambers of our kings;
Black-bloody veins did in the Rump prevail,
Like the Philistines' emrods in the tail.   100
Lightning, hail, fire, and thunder Egypt had,
And England guns, shot, powder (that's as bad).
And that sea-monster Lawson, if withstood,
Threatened to turn our rivers into blood;
And—plague of all these plagues—all these plagues fell   105
Not on an Egypt, but our Israel.

77–78. The Rump was restored on 7 May 1659.

79–80. This rather confusing passage means that the Wallingford House party hoped to enhance their own power by using the Rump, to which they were really opposed.

90. See Exod. 3–4:5.

92. *basted*: cudgeled.

93. *botch*: an eruptive disease.

100. *emrods*: hemorrhoids. For an account of the Philistines' afflictions, see 1 Sam. 5.

103. *Lawson*: Sir John Lawson (d. 1665), commander-in-chief of the fleet in 1659. He finally favored the restoration of Charles II, and his great influence helped bring the navy over to the king.

5.

Sick as her heart can hold the nation lies,
Filling each corner with her hideous cries:
Sometimes rage, like a burning fever, heats,
Anon despair brings cold and clammy sweats;   110
She cannot sleep—or if she doth she dreams
Of rapes, thefts, burnings, blood, and direful themes;
Tosses from side to side, then by-and-by
Her feet are laid there where the head did lie.
None can come to her but bold empirics,   115
Who never meant to cure her but try tricks.
Those very doctors who should give her ease—
God help the patient!—were her worst disease.
The Italian mountebank Vane tells her sure
Jesuits' powder will effect the cure;   120
If grief but makes her swell, Marten and Neville
Conclude it is a spice of the king's evil.
"Bleed her again!" another cries, and Scot
Says he could cure her if 'twas—you know what,
But giddy Harrington a whimsey found   125
To make her head like to his brains run round.
Her old and wise physicians, who before
Had well-nigh cured her, came again to the door,
But were kept out, which made her cry the more,
"Help, help, dear children! Oh, some pity take   130
On her who bore you! help, for mercy sake!
Oh, heart! oh, head! oh, back! oh, bones! I feel
They've poisoned me with giving too much steel!

115. *empirics*: quacks.

120. *Jesuits' powder*: a powdered Peruvian bark used in the treatment of fevers—an allusion to Vane's eclectic religious views or to his tolerant attitude toward Catholics.

121. *Marten*: Henry Marten (1602–80), regicide and member of the Council of State (the assembly elected after Charles I's execution). *Neville*: Henry Neville (1620–94), member of the Council of State and doctrinaire republican.

122. *spice*: kind.

123. *Scot*: Thomas Scot, regicide and staunch republican. Even after the secluded members returned in 1660 he affirmed the justice of Charles I's execution. He was condemned to death and executed on 17 October 1660.

125–26. *Harrington*: James Harrington (1611–77), the well-known republican political theorist. He is reported to have drunk such quantities of guaiac (a stimulating drug like cantharides) that it injured his brain.

127–28. an allusion to the secluded members of the Long Parliament, who were readmitted by Monck's intervention.

133. *steel*: medicine containing iron.

Oh, give me that for which I long and cry—
Something that's sovereign, or else I die!"   135

6.

Kind Cheshire heard and, like some son that stood
Upon the bank, straight jumped into the flood,
Flings out his arms and strikes some strokes to swim.
Booth ventured first and Middleton with him;
Stout Mackworth, Egerton, and thousands more,   140
Threw themselves in and left the safer shore;
Massey, that famous diver, and bold Browne
Forsook his wharf, resolving all to drown
Or save a sinking kingdom; but (O sad!)
Fearing to lose her prey, the 'sea grew mad,   145
Raised all her billows and resolved her waves
Should quickly be the bold adventurers' graves.
Out marches Lambert like an eastern wind
And with him all the mighty waters joined.
The loyal swimmers bore up heads and breasts,   150
Scorning to think of life or interests.
They plied their arms and thighs, but all in vain:
The furious main beat them to shore again,
At which the floating island, looking back,
Spying her loyal lovers gone to wrack,   155

135. *Something that's sovereign*: an especially efficacious remedy.
136 ff. A general rising against the Rump occurred in Cheshire in 1659, but Lambert suppressed it.
139. *Booth*: George Booth, first Lerd Delamere (1622–84), supported the parliamentary party in Cheshire during the civil war. Later he "became one of the leaders of the party of Cromwellian malcontents called 'the new royalists,' who, with the Cavaliers, concocted the 'general plot' for the restoration of Charles II" (*DNB*). He led the Cheshire rising and after its defeat attempted to escape disguised as a woman but was discovered and committed to the Tower. After the Restoration, the House of Commons offered him a reward of £20,000 for his services. *Middleton*: Sir Thomas Middleton (1586–1666), a parliamentary general during the civil war. He took part in Booth's rising, was captured and imprisoned, and was later rewarded by Charles II.
140. *Mackworth*: Sir Francis Mackworth, another participant in the Cheshire rebellion. *Egerton*: Randolph Egerton, another major-general who took part in the rising.
142. *Massey*: Sir Edward Massey (1619?–74?), parliamentary major-general and statesman impeached by the army in 1647. He took service under Charles II as lieutenant-general in the invasion of England in 1651. After Worcester he was brought to London for trial, but he managed to escape to Holland. In 1659 he plotted a rising in Gloucestershire but was betrayed and captured. *Browne*: Sir Richard Browne (d. 1669), parliamentary general expelled by the army from the House of Commons. He joined Booth's rising.
148. Lambert defeated Booth's forces at Winnington Bridge, 19 August 1659.
154. *the floating island*: England. Cf. line 144.

Shrieked louder than before, and thus she cries:
"Can you, ye angry Heav'ns and frowning skies,
Thus countenance rebellious mutineers,
Who, if they durst, would be about your ears?
That I should sink with justice may accord,   160
Who let my pilot be thrown overboard,
Yet 'twas not I, ye righteous Heav'ns do know—
The soldiers in me needs would have it so—
And those who conjured up these storms themselves
And first engaged me 'mongst these rocks and shelves,   165
Guilty of all my woes, have raised this weather,
Fearing to come to land and choosing rather
To sink me with themselves. O cease to frown!
In tears, just Heav'ns, behold, myself I drown!
Let not these proud waves do it; prevent my fears   170
And let them fall together by the ears."

                              7.

    Heav'n heard and struck the insulting army mad;
Drunk with their Cheshire triumphs straight they had
New lights upreared, and new resolves they take,
A single person once again to make.   175
Who shall he be? Oh! Lambert, without rub,
The fittest de'il to be Beelzebub.
He, the fierce fiend cast out of the House before,
Returned and threw the House now out of door;
A legion then he raised of arméd sprites,   180
Elves, goblins, fairies, Quakers, and New Lights,
To be his under-devils; with this rest
He soul and body, church and state, possessed,
Who though they filled all countries, towns, and rooms,
Yet, like that fiend that did frequent the tombs,   185
Churches and sacred grounds they haunted most—
No chapel was at ease from some such ghost.
The priests ordained to exorcise those elves
Were voted devils and cast out themselves—
Bible, or Alcoran, all's one to them;   190
Religion serves but for a stratagem—

174. *New light:* novel doctrines (esp. theological and ecclesiastical), the partisans of which
lay claim to superior enlightenment. I have followed Wild's editor, Hunt, in emending the
text's *appeared* to *upreared.*

175 ff. In the fall of 1659 Lambert blockaded Parliament and prevented members from
entering. It was widely assumed that he intended to make himself lord protector.

The holy charms these adders did not heed;
Churches themselves did sanctuary need.

8.

The church's patrimony and rich store
Alas! was swallowed many years before.   195
Bishops and deans we fed upon before
(They were the ribs and sirloins of the whore);
Now let her legs, the priests, go to the pot
(They have the pope's eye in them—spare them not!)
We have fat benefices yet to eat—   200
Bel and our Dragon army must have meat.
Let us devour her limb-meal, great and small,
Tithe-calves, geese, pigs, the pettitoes and all.
A vicarage in sippets, though it be
But small, will serve a squeamish sectary.   205
Though universities we can't endure,
There's no false Latin in their lands, be sure.
Give Oxford to our Horse and let the Foot
Take Cambridge for their booty and fall to't.
"Christ Church I'll have," cries Vane; Desb'rough swops   210
At Trinity; King's is for Berry's chops;
Kelsey, take Corpus Christi; All Souls, Packer;
Carve Creed St. John's; New College leave to Hacker;
Fleetwood cries, "Weeping Magdalen shall be mine,
Her tears I'll drink instead of muscadine."   215
The smaller halls and houses scarce are big
Enough to make one dish for Hasilrig.
"We must be sure to stop his mouth, though wide,
Else all our fat will be in the fire," they cried,
"And when we have done these, we'll not be quiet—   220

197. *the whore:* the Roman Catholic church.

199. *the pope's eye:* the lymphatic gland surrounded with fat in the middle of a leg of mutton, regarded by some as a tidbit.

201. Bel and the Dragon are voracious Babylonian idols in the apocryphal book of that name. The sectaries wished the Apocrypha included in the authorized Bible.

202. *limb-meal:* piecemeal, obs.

206–17. This plot to despoil the universities is a fiction. Desborough, James Berry (fl. 1665), Thomas Kelsey (d. 1680?), John, Creed Francis Hacker (d. 1660), Charles Fleetwood (d. 1692), and Sir Arthur Hasilrig (d. 1661) were among those senior officers who signed a petition at Derby demanding that Parliament grant vast powers to the army. Monck did not sign the petition and was in consequence appointed commander-in-chief of the parliamentary forces.

210. *swops:* strikes.

Salem Academy and College
Gramley Library
Winston-Salem, N.C. 27108

Lordships' and landlords' rents shall be our diet."
Thus talked this jolly crew, but still mine host
Lambert resolves that he will rule the roast.

9.

    But hark! methinks I hear old Boreas blow.
What mean the north winds that they bluster so? 225
More storms from that black nook? Forbear, bold Scot!
Let not Dunbar and Worcester be forgot.
What! would you chaffer with us for one Charles more?
The price of kings is fallen, give the trade o'er.
"And is the price of kings and kingdoms too, 230
Of laws, lives, oaths, souls, grown so low with you?
Perfidious hypocrites! monsters of men!"
Cries the good Monck, "We'll raise their price again!"
Heav'n said amen! and breathed upon that spark;
That spark, preserved alive in the cold and dark, 235
First kindled and enflamed the British Isle
And turned it all to bonfires in a while.
He and his fuel were so small no doubt
Proud Lambert thought to tread or piss them out.
But George was wary; his cause did require 240
A pillar of a cloud as well as fire:
'Twas not his safest course to flame but smoke—
His enemies he will not burn but choke.
Small fires must not blaze out, lest by their light
They show their weakness and their foes invite; 245
But furnaces the stoutest metals melt,
And so did he, by fire not seen but felt;
Dark-lantern language and his peep-bo play
Will-e-wisped Lambert's New Lights out of the way.
George and his boys those thousands (O strange thing!) 250
Of snipes and woodcocks took by lowbelling;

    227. Cromwell defeated the Scots at Dunbar on 3 September 1650 and exactly one year later routed the Scottish forces of Charles II at Worcester.
    240–51. Monck was extremely cautious in divulging his political intentions. In a letter to Fleetwood, 20 October 1659, he merely declared his intention of upholding the authority of Parliament. Even after he had entered London Monck remained noncommittal. "The ambiguity of his utterances and the contradictions between his words and his actions puzzled the shrewdest observers. Neither Hyde nor the royalist agents in England could guess whether he meant to serve the king or to maintain the Rump in power" (*DNB*).
    248. *Dark-lantern:* cryptic. *peep-bo:* bo-peep, hidden and unpredictable.
    251. *lowbelling:* Lowbells were bells used in fowling at night to stupefy birds.

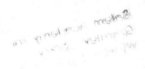

His few Scotch-coal kindled with English fire
Made Lambert's great Newcastle heaps expire.

10.

    Scotland, though poor and peevish, was content
To keep the peacè and (O rare!) money lent.   255
But yet the blessing of their kirk was more—
George had that too—and with this slender store
He and his myrmidons advance. Kind Heaven
Prepared a frost to make their march more even,
Easy, and safe: it may be said, that year,   260
Of the highways Heaven itself was overseer
And made November ground as hard as May.
White as their innocence, so was their way.
The clouds came down in feather-beds to greet
Him and his army and to kiss their feet,   265
The frost and foes both came and went together,
Both thawed away, and vanished God knows whither.
Whole countries crowded in to see this friend,
Ready to cast their bodies down to mend
His road to Westminster, and still they shout,   270
"Lay hold of the Rump and pull the monster out!
A new one or a whole one, good my lord,"
And to this cry the island did accord.
The echo of the Irish hollow ground
Heard England and her language did rebound.   275

11.

    Presto! Jack Lambert and his sprites are gone
To dance a jig with his brother Oberon.
George made him and his cut-throats of our lives
Swallow their swords as jugglers do their knives,
And Carter Desborough to wish in vain   280
He now were wagoner to Charles's Wain.
The conqueror's now come into the south,
Whose warm air is made hot by ev'ry mouth

253. *Newcastle:* the headquarters of Lambert's army.
    257–67. "The going was hard in the very wintry weather, with frost and snow so continuous that, according to Price [Monck's chaplain and biographer], 'I do not remember that ever we trod upon plain earth from Edinburgh to London' " (Godfrey Davies, *The Restoration of Charles II, 1658–1660* [San Marino, Calif.: The Huntington Library, 1955], pp. 265–66).
    280. *Carter:* an allusion to Desborough's former occupation as a small farmer. This term leads to a typical bit of Wild wordplay on *Charles's Wain* (the Big Dipper).

Breathing his welcome and in spite of Scot
Crying, "The whole child, sir, divide it not."   285
 The Rump begins to stink: "Alas!" cry they,
"We've raised a devil which we cannot lay;
I like him not." "His belly is so big.
There's a king in it!" cries furious Hasilrig.
"Let's bribe him," they cry all. "Carve him a share   290
Of our stol'n venison!" Varlets, forbear!
In vain you put your lime-twigs to his hands.
George Monck is for the king, not for his lands.
When fair means would not do, next foul they try:
"Vote him the City scavenger," they cry—   295
"Send him to scour their streets." "Well, let it be;
Your Rumpship wants a scouring too," thinks he.
"That foul house where your worships many years
Have laid your tail sure wants a scavenger.
I smell your fizzle though it make no crack.   300
You'd mount me on the City's galled back
In hopes she'd cast her rider. If I must
Upon some office in the town be thrust,
I'll be their sword-bearer, and to their dagger
I'll join my sword. Nay, good Rump, do not swagger;   305
The City feasts me, and as sure as gun
I'll mend all England's Commons ere I've done."

12.

And so he did. One morning next his heart
He went to Westminster and played his part.
He vamped their boots, which Hewson ne'er could do   310

284. Scot was sent by the Rump to placate Monck, but his mission was unsuccessful.

285. This reference to Solomon's judgment alludes to Monck's insistence on the readmission of the secluded members. Cf. 1 Kings 3:16–28.

292. *lime-twigs:* twigs smeared with birdlime.

295–307. When it was believed that the City refused to pay taxes levied by the Rump, Monck was ordered at Scot's instigation to make the gates of the City indefensible and to arrest a number of leading citizens (9 February 1660). By this device Scot hoped to inflame the citizens against Monck, who was becoming popular. Monck obeyed his orders but explained to the corporation that he had undertaken this disagreeable duty so that it might not be performed more severely by his enemies. The attempt to discredit Monck miscarried and, in fact, led to his alliance with the citizens in a successful demand for the seating of the secluded members. By this stratagem the Rump paved the way for its own dissolution and the election of the Convention Parliament which restored Charles II.

307. *Commons:* (1) the Lower House, (2) daily fare.

310. *vamped:* repaired.

310–11. On 5 December 1659 some apprentices defiantly presented a petition to the Com-

With better leather, made them go upright too.
The restored members, Cato-like, no doubt,
Did only enter that they might go out.
They did not mean within those walls to dwell,
Nor did they like their company so well.   315
Yet Heav'n so blessed them that in three weeks' space
They gave both church and state a better face.
They gave Booth, Massey, Browne, some kinder lots
(The last year's traitors, this year's patriots).
The church's poor remainder they made good   320
And washed the nation's hands of royal blood;
And that a Parliament they did devise
From its own ashes, phoenix-like, might rise.
This done by act and deed that might not fail
They passed a fine and so cut off th' entail.   325

13.

Let the bells ring these changes now from Bow
Down to the country candlesticks below.
Ringers, hands off! The bells themselves will dance
In memory of their own deliverance.
Had not George showed his metal and said nay,   330
Each sectary had borne the bell away.
"Down with them all, they're christened," cried that crew;
"Tie up their clappers and the parson's too;
Turn them to guns, or sell them to the Dutch."
"Nay, hold," quoth George, "my masters, that's too
        much.   335
You will not leap o'er steeples thus I hope—

---

mon Council. In the ensuing disorder a regiment of foot under the regicide Col. John Hewson
fired on the crowd and killed some apprentices. Hewson had been a shoemaker.

312–15. "By the month of March 1660 the position was this—a decayed remnant of
Parliament had been reinvigorated by a transfusion of Presbyterian blood in order to provide
the energy to commit suicide" (Ogg, *Charles II, 1*, 25).

318. Booth was appointed a commissioner to settle the militia. Massey represented London
in the Convention Parliament. Browne, a secluded member, was readmitted to his seat.

321. "Before the dissolution a disorderly and apparently irrelevant debate took place about
the execution of Charles I. John Crew had moved that before they separated for the last time
members should bear their witness against 'the horrid murder.' One after another rose to deny
their concurrence in it. Then Scot bravely defended the execution and hoped he would never
repent of it and desired that on his tombstone might be inscribed: 'Here lies Thomas Scot,
who adjudged to death the late king' " (Davies, *The Restoration of Charles II*, p. 305).

327. *country candlesticks:* country churches. Cf. Rev. 1:20: "the seven candlesticks which
thou sawest are the seven churches."

331. *had borne the bell away:* had won.

I'll save the bells, but you may take the rope."
Thus lay Religion panting for her life,
Like Isaac bound under the bloody knife;
George held the falling weapon, saved the lamb,   340
Let Lambert in the briars be the ram.
So lay the royal virgin, as 'tis told,
When brave St. George redeemed her life of old.
O that the knaves that have consumed our land,
Had but permitted wood enough to stand
To be his bonfires! We'd burn ev'ry stem   245
And leave no more but gallow-trees for them!

14.

March on, great hero! as thou hast begun,
And crown our happiness before thou'st done.
We have another Charles to fetch from Spain;   350
Be thou the George to bring him back again.
Then shalt thou be, what was denied that knight,
Thy prince's and the people's favorite.
There is no danger of the winds at all,
Unless together by the ears they fall   355
Who shall the honor have to waft a king,
And they who gain it while they work shall sing.
Methinks I see how those triumphant gales,
Proud of their great employment, swell the sails;
The joyful ship shall dance, the sea shall laugh,   360
And loyal fish their master's health shall quaff.
See how the dolphins crowd and thrust their large
And scaly shoulders to assist the barge;
The peaceful kingfishers are met together
About the decks and prophesy calm weather;   365
Poor crabs and lobsters have gone down to creep,
And search for pearls and jewels in the deep;
And when they have the booty, crawl before,
And leave them for his welcome to the shore.

338–41. Cf. Gen. 22:1–14. Lambert was not destined to act the part of the sacrificial lamb but died a prisoner in Guernsey in 1683.

350–53. Monck's journey to Breda to fetch Charles II is compared with that of George Villiers, first duke of Buckingham, who accompanied Charles I, then Prince of Wales, to Spain in a vain attempt to make a match with the Infanta. This labored comparison contrasts the popularity of this George with the widespread hatred of Charles I's favorite.

15.

Methinks I see how throngs of people stand,   370
Scarce patient till the vessel come to land,
Ready to leap in, and, if need require,
With tears of joy to make the waters higher.
But what will London do? I doubt Old Paul
With bowing to his sovereign will fall;   375
The royal lions from the Tower shall roar,
And though they see him not, yet shall adore;
The conduits will be ravished and combine
To turn their very water into wine,
And for the citizens, I only pray   380
They may not, overjoyed, all die that day.
May we all live more loyal and more true,
To give to Caesar and to God their due.
We'll make his father's tomb with tears to swim,
And for the son, we'll shed our blood for him.   385
England her penitential song shall sing
And take heed how she quarrels with her king.
If for our sins our prince shall be misled,
We'll bite our nails rather than scratch our head.

16.

One English George outweighs alone, by odds,   390
A whole committee of the heathens' gods;
Pronounce but Monck, and it is all his due:
He is our Mercury, Mars, and Neptune too.
Monck, what great Xerxes could not, proved the man
That with a word shackled the ocean;   395
He shall command Neptune himself to bring
His trident and present it to our king.
Oh, do it then, great admiral! Away!
Let him be here against St. George's day,
That Charles may wear his *Dieu et mon droit,*   400
And thou the noble-gartered *Honi soit.*

378–79. When Charles arrived in London, public fountains did, in fact, flow with wine. See Bryant, p. 81.

399. *Iter Boreale* was published on St. George's day, 23 April. The king did not reach London until 29 May, his birthday.

400. *Dieu et mon droit:* a motto of English kings.

401. *Honi soit [qui mal y pense]:* motto of the Order of the Garter, with which Monck was invested on the day after Charles landed.

And when thy aged corpse shall yield to fate,
God save that soul that saved our church and state.
There thou shalt have a glorious crown, I know,
Who crown'st our king and kingdoms here below,   405
But who shall find a pen fit for thy glory,
Or make posterity believe thy story?

                              Vive St. George!

EDMUND WALLER

Instructions to a Painter
(1665)

To judge from the poetry that celebrates them, the first five years of the Restoration were halcyon ones. Except for one or two inferior squibs on the plight of the Cavaliers, who were bitter about the Restoration settlement in general and felt that the Act of Indemnity and Oblivion in particular was "an act of indemnity for the king's enemies and oblivion for the king's friends," not a breath of criticism survives among all the commendatory verses on the royal family, on Lord Chancellor Hyde, or on Charles's reigning mistress, the countess of Castlemaine.

Early in 1665 England managed to provoke a war with Holland, her commercial rival, after a sneak attack on Dutch merchantmen in the western Mediterranean. The high point of this second Dutch war was the English victory off Lowestoft on 3 June 1665. That night, however, as the Dutch fled eastward, orders were given in the flagship of the duke of York, lord high admiral, to call off pursuit, and the English missed their chance to destroy Dutch sea power. The Dutch fleet revived and in 1667 inflicted on the unprepared English navy the most humiliating defeat it has ever suffered.

The abortive victory of the duke of York is the subject of this panegyric by Waller, whose zeal was intensified, no doubt, by uneasiness over his *Panegyric to My Lord Protector* (1655) and his elegy *Upon the Late Storm and of the Death of His Highness* (1658). Dryden was in a similar plight over his *Heroic Stanzas to the Glorious Memory of Cromwell* and had already paid court to the new regime in *Astræa Redux* (1660), *To His Sacred Majesty, a Panegyric upon His Coronation* (1661), and *To My Lord Chancellor, Presented on New Year's Day* (1662). The duke of York at Lowestoft was to have his turn in the poem in which Dryden dedicated *Annus Mirabilis* (1666) to the duchess.

Instructions to a Painter is modeled upon Giovanni Francesco Busenello's celebration of a Venetian naval victory over the Turks off Candy (Crete) in 1655. This poem (translated in 1658 as *A Prospective of the Naval Triumph of the Venetians*) introduced into English poetry an *ut pictura poesis* device in which the poet instructs the painter in detail how he is to depict the victory. Waller's tribute had a wholly unexpected effect because of the many unfavorable aspects of the engagement that had been excluded. In *The Second Advice to a Painter,* a mock imitation of his poem, some satirist (probably Marvell) hastened to supply the missing details and paint Lowestoft and English naval affairs in 1665 as a masterpiece of mismanagement, greed, and cowardice. *Second Advice* thus helped establish the painter convention in satirical peotry. It was followed by a *Third Advice* (probably also Marvell's), by the *Fourth* and *Fifth Advices* (printed in 1667 with the second and third under the name of Sir John Denham), by Marvell's *Last Instructions* and the *Further Instructions*, and by dozens of other pieces in the same form.* The concentration on visual detail that the painter convention demands made it a singularly effective technique for the satiric poet intent upon the grotesque.

Instructions to a Painter

For the Drawing of the Posture and Progress of His Majesty's
Forces at Sea, under the Command of His Highness-Royal:
Together with the Battle and Victory Obtained over the Dutch
June 3, 1665.

First draw the sea, that portion which between
The greater world and this of ours is seen;
Here place the British, there the Holland fleet,
Vast floating armies, both prepared to meet!
Draw the whole world expecting who shall reign,   5
After this combat, o'er the conquered main.
Make Heav'n concerned and an unusual star
Declare th' importance of th' approaching war.
Make the sea shine with gallantry and all
The English youth flock to their admiral,   10
The valiant duke, whose early deeds abroad.

---

* The authorship of the *Second* and *Third Advices* is discussed in a series of articles in the *Bulletin of the New York Public Library*: George deF. Lord, "Two New Poems by Marvell?" *Bulletin* 62 (1958): 551–70; Ephim G. Fogel, "Salmons in Both, or Some Caveats for Canonical Scholars," *Bulletin* 63 (1959): 223–36, 292–308; and Lord, "Comments on the Canonical Caveat," *Bulletin* 63 (1959): 355–66. The inclusion of these two poems in Bod. MS Eng. poet. d. 49, presumably the manuscript prepared at the direction of William Popple, the poet's nephew, is further evidence in support of Marvell's authorship (see Margoliouth, *1*, xiv–xv).

7. *unusual star*: perhaps the comet reported by Pepys, 6 April 1665.
9. *gallantry*: Many shortcomings of the Restoration navy were attributed to gentlemen captains and noble volunteers.
11. The *valiant duke* is, of course, James, duke of York, lord high admiral. His *early deeds abroad* included service with Turenne against the Fronde in 1652, a second campaign with Turenne in 1653 against Spain and Lorraine, and further service with Turenne in 1654–55 as lieutenant-general.

Such rage in fight and art in conduct showed.
His bright sword now a dearer interest draws,
His brother's glory and his country's cause.
Let thy bold pencil hope and courage spread   15
Through the whole navy, by that hero led;
Make all appear, where such a prince is by,
Resolved to conquer or resolved to die.
With his extraction and his glorious mind
Make the proud sails swell more than with the wind;   20
Preventing cannon, make his louder fame
Check the Batavians and their fury tame.
So hungry wolves, though greedy of their prey,
Stop when they find a lion in their way.
Make him bestride the ocean and mankind   25
Ask his consent to use the sea and wind;
While his tall ships in the barred channel stand,
He grasps the Indies in his armed hand.
Paint an east wind and make it blow away
Th' excuse of Holland for their navy's stay;   30
Make them look pale and, the bold prince to shun,
Through the cold north and rocky regions run.
To find the coast where morning first appears,
By the dark pole the wary Belgian steers,
Confessing now he dreads the English more   35
Than all the dangers of a frozen shore,
While from our arms, security to find,
They fly so far they leave the day behind.
Describe their fleet abandoning the sea
And all their merchants left a wealthy prey.   40
Our first success in war make Bacchus crown
And half the vintage of the year our own.
The Dutch their wine and all their brandy lose,

31–38. In July 1664 a fleet under the command of the earl of Sandwich put to sea to act as
a defense for the rest of the English navy, which was still being made ready for war. The
Dutch were also taking defensive measures at this time and "warned their merchant shipping
to sail round the north of Scotland rather than through the Channel" to avoid Sandwich
(Tedder, p. 104).

34. *Belgian:* a citizen of the Low Countries.

41–46. In November 1664 "Tyddeman and his small squadron had opened the campaign
of attacks on trade which formed the usual preliminaries of a naval war. He opened well on
the 20th by capturing the greater part of the Dutch fleet from Bordeaux laden with French
commodities" (Tedder, p. 111). Among several reports on Dutch prizes taken is the following
(*CSPD*, 6 December 1664): "Capt. Tobias Sackler to the navy commrs. Loss of his boat in
chasing and capturing a Dutch prize from St. Martin's Island, laden with wine and brandy."

Disarmed of that from which their courage grows,
While the glad English, to relieve their toil,   45
In healths to their great leader drink the spoil.
His high command to Afric's coast extend
And make the Moors before the English bend:
Those barbarous pirates willingly receive
Conditions such as we are pleased to give.   50
Deserted by the Dutch, let nations know
We can our own and their great business do,
False friends chastise and common foes restrain,
Which, worse than tempests, did infest the main.
Within those straits make Holland's Smyrna fleet   55
With a small squadron of the English meet:
Like falcons these, those like a num'rous flock
Of fowl which scatter to avoid the shock.
There paint confusion in a various shape:
Some sink, some yield, and flying, some escape.   60
Europe and Africa, from either shore,
Spectators are and hear our cannon roar,
While the divided world in this agree,
Men that fight so deserve to rule the sea.
    But, nearer home, thy pencil use once more   65
And place our navy by the Holland shore.
The world they compassed while they fought with Spain,
But here already they resign the main.

47. In August 1664 "both England and Holland had a squadron preparing to go to Guinea, the latter ostensibly to convoy four West Indiamen there, the former to follow the latter, convoy some Guinea ships" (Tedder, pp. 104–05). The English fleet suffered countless delays in preparation and never got further than Portsmouth, when winter set in.

48–50. These lines probably refer to a treaty negotiated by Sir Thomas Allin with the Algerines in November 1664. If so, they present the treaty in a much too favorable light, although its terms for a while "strengthened English prestige in the Mediterranean, both by admitting to England the freedom of the seas, and by having a chastening effect on two other trade disturbers—Tripoli and Tunis (Tedder, p. 94).

55–64. On 29 December Allin encountered a Smyrna fleet and took two prizes. "Such was the somewhat ignominious action by which the English opened the Dutch war" (Tedder, p. 97). It should be remembered that England had not declared war, but managed by these hostilities to provoke the states into doing so on 14 January 1665. As David Hannay remarks, "Waller greatly exaggerated the British victory" (*A Short History of the Royal Navy, 1217 to 1688* [London, 1898], p. 337).

65–76. Waller's account is especially fanciful here. The British fleet sailed over to the Dutch coast in May 1665. The Dutch fleet was still divided between the harbors at Texel and Vlie. "It was obvious that so long as a united English fleet was cruising between those places the divided Dutch squadrons were not likely to come out to be attacked piecemeal" (Tedder, p. 116). For ten days the English fleet plied up and down the coast without attacking the Dutch. Finally the duke of York was forced to return to port because of the shortage of provisions.

Those greedy mariners, out of whose way
Diffusive nature could no region lay,   70
At home, preserved from rocks and tempests, lie,
Compelled, like others, in their beds to die.
Their single towns th' Iberian armies pressed;
We all their provinces at once invest,
And, in a month, ruin their traffic more   75
Than that long war could in an age before.
    But who can always on the billows lie?
The wat'ry wilderness yields no supply:
Spreading our sails, to Harwich we resort,
And meet the beauties of the British court.   80
Th'illustrious duchess and her glorious train
(Like Thetis with her nymphs) adorn the main.
The gazing sea-gods, since the Paphian queen
Sprung from among them, no such sight had seen.
Charmed with the graces of a troop so fair,   85
Those deathless powers for us themselves declare,
Resolved the aid of Neptune's court to bring
And help the nation where such beauties spring.
The soldier here his wasted store supplies
And takes new valor from the ladies' eyes.   90
    Meanwhile, like bees, when stormy winter's gone,
The Dutch (as if the sea were all their own)
Desert their ports, and, falling in their way,
Our Hamburg merchants are become their prey.
Thus flourish they before th' approaching fight,   95
As dying tapers give a blazing light.
To check their pride, our fleet half-victualed goes,
Enough to serve us till we reach our foes,
Who now appear so numerous and bold,
The action worthy of our arms we hold.   100
A greater force than that which here we find
Ne'er pressed the ocean nor employed the wind.
Restrained a while by the unwelcome night,
Th' impatient English scarce attend the light.
But now the morning (Heav'n severely clear)   105
To the fierce work indulgent does appear,

70. *Diffusive:* dispensing or shedding bountifully.
77–90. The duchess of York began her visit to the fleet at Harwich, 16 May 1665.
91–94. While the English fleet was victualing, the Dutch came out. Cf. *Second Advice,* 49–50.
105. *severely:* with austere plainness or simplicity of style.

And Phoebus lifts above the waves his light,
That he might see, and thus record, the fight.
As when loud winds from different quarters rush,
Vast clouds encountering, one another crush,   110
With swelling sails so, from their several coasts,
Join the Batavian and the British hosts.
For a less prize, with less concern and rage,
The Roman fleets at Actium did engage;
They, for the empire of the world they knew,   115
These for the old contend and for the new.
At the first shock, with blood and powder stained,
Nor heav'n nor sea their former face retained;
Fury and art produce effects so strange,
They trouble nature and her visage change.   120
Where burning ships the banished sun supply,
And no light shines but that by which men die,
There York appears, so prodigal is he
Of royal blood as ancient as the sea,
Which down to him, so many ages told,   125
Has through the veins of mighty monarchs rolled!
The great Achilles marched not to the field
Till Vulcan that impenetrable shield
And arms had wrought, yet there no bullets flew,
But shafts and darts which the weak Phrygians threw.   130
Our bolder hero on the deck does stand
Exposed, the bulwark of his native land:
Defensive arms laid by as useless here
Where massy balls the neighboring rocks do tear.
Some power unseen those princes does protect,   135
Who for their country thus themselves neglect.
    Against him first Opdam his squadron leads,
Proud of his late success against the Swedes,
Made by that action and his high command
Worthy to perish by a prince's hand.   140
The tall Batavian in a vast ship rides,
Bearing an army in her hollow sides,
Yet not inclined the English ship to board,
More on his guns relies than on his sword;

137. *Opdam:* Jacob Wassenaer, baron von Opdam, admiral of the Dutch navy. From 1657
to 1660 the Dutch interfered successfully in the Swedish-Danish war in order to prevent the
entrance of the Baltic from falling into exclusively Swedish control. Opdam took part in these
encounters.

From whence a fatal volley we received: 145
It missed the duke, but his great heart it grieved;
Three worthy persons from his side it tore
And dyed his garment with their scattered gore.
Happy! to whom this glorious death arrives,
More to be valued than a thousand lives!   150
On such a theatre as this to die,
For such a cause, and such a witness by!
Who would not thus a sacrifice be made
To have his blood on such an altar laid?
The rest about him struck with horror stood,   155
To see their leader covered o'er with blood:
So trembled Jacob, when he thought the stains
Of his son's coat had issued from his veins.
He feels no wound but in his troubled thought:
Before for honor, now revenge, he fought.   160
His friends in pieces torn, the bitter news,
Not brought by fame, with his own eyes he views;
His mind at once reflecting on their youth,
Their worth, their love, their valor, and their truth;
The joys of court, their mothers, and their wives,   165
To follow him, abandoned—and their lives!
He storms and shoots, but flying bullets now,
To execute his rage, appear too slow:
They miss, or sweep but common souls away,
For such a loss Opdam his life must pay!   170
Encouraging his men, he gives the word,
With fierce intent that hated ship to board
And make the guilty Dutch, with his own arm,
Wait on his friends, while yet their blood is warm.
His winged vessel like an eagle shows,   175
When through the clouds to truss a swan she goes:
The Belgian ship unmoved, like some huge rock
Inhabiting the sea, expects the shock.
From both the fleets men's eyes are bent this way,
Neglecting all the business of the day.   180

147. *Three worthy persons*: Charles Berkeley, earl of Falmouth, better known as Lord Fitz-harding; Charles MacCarthy, Lord Muskerry (in the Irish peerage); and Richard Boyle, second son of the earl of Burlington, "a youth of great hope, who came newly home from travel, where he had spent his time with singular advantage, and took the first opportunity to lose his life in the king's service" (Clarendon, sec. 643).
148. Pepys mentions "their blood and brains flying in the duke's face, and the head of Mr. Boyle striking down the duke, as some say" (8 June 1665).

Bullets their flight, and guns their noise, suspend;
The silent ocean does th' event attend
Which leader shall the doubtful vict'ry bless
And give an earnest of the war's success,
When Heav'n itself, for England to declare,   185
Turns ship and men and tackle into air.
Their new commander from his charge is tossed,
Which that young prince had so unjustly lost,
Whose great progenitors, with better fate
And better conduct, swayed their infant state.   190
His flight tow'rds Heav'n th' aspiring Belgian took,
But fell, like Phaethon, with thunder strook;
From vaster hopes than this he seemed to fall,
That durst attempt the British admiral.
From her broadsides a ruder flame is thrown   195
Than from the fiery chariot of the sun,
That bears the radiant ensign of the day,
And she, the flag that governs in the sea.
    The duke (ill-pleased that fire should thus prevent
The work which for his brighter sword he meant),   200
Anger still burning in his valiant breast,
Goes to complete revenge upon the rest:
So on the guardless herd, their keeper slain,
Rushes a tiger in the Lybian plain.
    The Dutch, accustomed to the raging sea,   205
And in black storms the frowns of Heav'n to see,
Never met tempest which more urged their fears
Than that which in the prince's look appears.
Fierce, goodly, young! Mars he resembles when
Jove sends him down to scourge perfidious men,   210
Such as with foul ingratitude have paid
Both those that led and those that gave them aid.
Where he gives on, disposing of their fates,

185–86. Opdam's ship, the *Eendracht*, blew up 3 June about 3:00 P.M. Opdam had already died of wounds before the explosion and only five men escaped.

187–88. *that young prince:* evidently the young prince of Orange. The passage seems to refer to the rights and powers traditionally his which were withheld from him by the grand pensionary of Holland, John de Witt. William was proclaimed stadholder, captain- and admiral-general in July 1672. At the time of the Battle of Lowestoft William was only fourteen.

213. *gives on:* makes an assault, obs.

213–20. Waller did not exaggerate York's violent encounters with the Dutch. Cf. "The fighting.at close quarters was furious; man after man was cut down, or his brains were blown out by pistols held only a few feet away" (F. R. Harris, *The Life of Edward Montagu, K.G., First Earl of Sandwich (1625–1672)*, 2 vols. [London: John Murray, 1912], *1*, 304–05).

Terror and death on his loud cannon waits,
With which he pleads his brother's cause so well,   215
He shakes the throne to which he does appeal.
The sea with spoil his angry bullets strow.
Widows and orphans making as they go;
Before his ship fragments of vessels torn,
Flags, arms, and Belgian carcasses are borne,   220
And his despairing foes, to flight inclined,
Spread all their canvas to invite the wind.
So the rude Boreas, where he lists to blow,
Makes clouds above and billows fly below,
Beating the shore, and, with a boist'rous rage,   225
Does Heav'n at once, and earth and sea, engage.
   The Dutch elsewhere did through the wat'ry field
Perform enough to have made others yield,
But English courage, growing as they fight,
In danger, noise, and slaughter takes delight: 230
Their bloody task, unwearied still, they ply,
Only restrained by death, or victory.
Iron and lead, from earth's dark entrails torn,
Like show'rs of hail from either side are borne:
So high the rage of wretched mortals goes,   235
Hurling their mother's bowels at their foes!
Ingenious to their ruin, every age
Improves the arts and instruments of rage.
Death-hast'ning ills Nature enough has sent,
And yet men still a thousand more invent.   240
   But Bacchus now, which led the Belgians on
So fierce at first, to favor us begun;
Brandy and wine (their wonted friends) at length
Render them useless and betray their strength.
So corn in fields, and, in the garden, flowers   245
Revive and raise themselves with moderate showers,
But overcharged with never-ceasing rain,
Become too moist and bend their heads again.
Their reeling ships on one another fall,
Without a foe, enough to ruin all.   250
Of this disorder and the favoring wind
The watchful English such advantage find
Ships fraught with fire among the heap they throw

241–44. Englishmen had long tended to regard drunkenness as a Dutch characteristic. Cf. Donne's "spongy, hydroptic Dutch" (Elegy XVI, *On His Mistress*).

And up the so-entangled Belgians blow.
The flame invades the powder-rooms, and then,   255
Their guns shoot bullets, and their vessels, men.
The scorched Batavians on the billows float,
Sent from their own, to pass in Charon's boat.
   And now our royal admiral success,
With all the marks of victory, does bless;   260
The burning ships, the taken, and the slain
Proclaim his triumph o'er the conquered main.
Nearer to Holland, as their hasty flight
Carries the noise and tumult of the fight,
His cannons' roar, forerunner of his fame,   265
Makes their Hague tremble, and their Amsterdam.
The British thunder does their houses rock,
And the duke seems at ev'ry door to knock.
His dreadful streamer, like a comet's hair,
Threat'ning destruction, hastens their despair,   270
Makes them deplore their scattered fleet as lost
And fear our present landing on their coast.
The trembling Dutch th' approaching prince behold,
As sheep a lion leaping tow'rds their fold.
Those piles which serve them to repel the main   275
They think too weak his fury to restrain.
What wonders may not English valor work,
Led by th' example of victorious York?
Or what defense against him can they make,
Who at such distance does their country shake?   280
His fatal hands their bulwarks will o'erthrow
And let in both the ocean and the foe!
Thus cry the people, and their land to keep,
Allow our title to command the deep,
Blaming their states' ill conduct to provoke   285
Those arms which freed them from the Spanish yoke.
   Painter, excuse me, if I have a while
Forgot thy art and used another style,
For, though you draw armed heroes as they sit,
The task in battle does the Muses fit.   290
They, in the dark confusion of a fight,
Discover all, instruct us how to write,
And light and honor to brave actions yield,
Hid in the smoke and tumult of the field.
Ages to come shall know that leader's toil   295

And his great name on whom the Muses smile.
Their dictates here let thy famed pencil trace,
And this relation with thy colors grace.
    Then draw the Parliament, the nobles met,
And our great monarch high above them set.   300
Like young Augustus let his image be,
Triumphing for that victory at sea,
Where Egypt's queen and eastern kings o'erthrown
Made the possession of the world his own.
Last draw the Commons at his royal feet,   305
Pouring out treasure to supply his fleet;
They vow with lives and fortunes to maintain
Their king's eternal title to the main,
And with a present to the duke approve
His valor, conduct, and his country's love.   310

To the King

Great sir, disdain not in this piece to stand,
Supreme commander both of sea and land!
Those which inhabit the celestial bower
Painters express with emblems of their power:
His club Alcides, Phoebus has his bow,   315
Jove has his thunder, and your navy you.
But your great providence no colors here
Can represent, nor pencil draw that care
Which keeps you waking to secure our peace,
The nation's glory, and our trade's increase.   320
You for these ends whole days in council sit
And the diversions of your youth forget.
Small were the worth of valor and of force,
If your high wisdom governed not their course.

299. Parliament met at Oxford (because of the plague) in October 1665. They rejected a French offer to mediate and thus provoked the threatened breach with France. "The two Houses joined in an address in which they expressed to the king their resolution to assist him with their lives and fortunes against the Dutch, or any others that would assist them" (Ranke, *3*, 433). The large sum of £1,250,000 was voted for the next year.

305–10. For his heroic conduct the House of Commons voted James £120,000 in October 1665 "to be paid him after the £1,250,000 is gathered upon the tax which they have now given the king" (Pepys, 28 October 1665).

321–22. "Shipping and sea affairs . . . seemed to be so much his talent, both for knowledge as well as inclination, that a war of that kind was rather an entertainment than any disturbance to his thoughts. . . . 'Tis certain that no prince was ever more fitted by nature for his country's interest than he was in all his maritime inclinations" (Buckingham, cited by Bryant, p. 171).

You as the soul, as the first mover, you,   325
Vigor and life on ev'ry part bestow:
How to build ships and dreadful ordnance cast,
Instruct the artists and reward their haste.
So Jove himself, when Typhon Heav'n does brave,
Descends to visit Vulcan's smoky cave,   330
Teaching the brawny Cyclops how to frame
His thunder mixed with terror, wrath, and flame.
Had the old Greeks discovered your abode,
Crete had not been the cradle of their god:
On that small island they had looked with scorn   335
And in Great Britain thought the Thunderer born.

ANDREW MARVELL

The Second Advice to a Painter
(1666)

The Second Advice to a Painter mimics the structure, style, attitudes, and substance of Waller's *Instructions*. One finds here absurd similes that mock Waller's insipid analogies from natural history ("So the land crabs, at Nature's kindly call,/ Down to engender at the sea do crawl"), the interspersed mythological references ("One thrifty ferry-boat of mother-pearl/ Sufficed of old the Cytherean girl"), and an envoy to the king alluding to Cretan legend. The poet of *Second Advice* is, if anything, more conscious than Waller of the convention he is using and comments repeatedly on painting techniques

This satire extends the subject matter of Waller's poem to include the entire naval campaign of the first year of war, from Allin's disastrous attack on Dutch merchantmen in December 1664, through the equally disastrous attempt on Bergen in August 1665, to the disgraced Lord Sandwich's embassy to Spain the following spring. It deals in detail with the Battle of Lowestoft and dwells upon the duke of York's failure to pursue the Dutch fleet, which became a subject for parliamentary inquiry. Despite its caustic treatment of politicians and naval officers, *Second Advice* makes a careful distinction in the envoy between the king and his ministers.

Although *Second Advice,* unlike most satirical attacks on the government, was published soon after the event (with its sequel, in 1667), it circulated in manuscript before publication, as noted in the Introduction. On 14 December 1666 Pepys received "sealed up from Sir H. Chumley, the lampoon, or Mock Advice to a Painter, abusing the duke of York and my Lord Sandwich, Penn, and everybody and the king himself, in all matters of the navy and the war." This lampoon was undoubtedly *Second Advice.* As a navy official and a close associate of some of the victims, Pepys was deeply concerned: "I am sorry for my Lord Sandwich's having so great a part in it."

Since the question of the authorship of *Second Advice* is inextricably related to that of *The Third Advice to a Painter* and *The Last Instructions to a Painter,* the reader is referred to the articles cited in the headnote to Waller's *Instructions to a Painter.* Suffice it to say here that the evidence for assigning the *Second* and *Third Advices* to Marvell seems more substantial than what is usually found in such cases of disputed authorship. The use of Denham's name as author in the printed texts and in line 336 ("Denham saith thus, though Waller always so") is clearly a blind to conceal the true author. Denham, a staunch royalist who enjoyed the king's patronage as surveyor-general, would not have put his name to such a piece; he would not have promised a satire on his wife ("Madam l'Edificatresse," line 340) who was the duke of York's mistress; and he was known to be mad in 1666 (see Samuel Butler's *Panegyric upon Sir John Denham's Recovery from His Madness*).

The Second Advice to a Painter

For Drawing the History of Our Naval Business

In Imitation of Mr. Waller.

> navem si poscat sibi peronatus arator
> luciferi rudis, exclamet Melicerta perisse
> frontem de rebus.
> —Persius, Satire 5, 102–04.

London, April 1666

Nay, Painter, if thou dar'st design that fight
Which Waller only courage had to write,
If thy bold hand can, without shaking, draw
What e'en the actors trembled when they saw
(Enough to make thy colors change like theirs   5
And all thy pencils bristle like their hairs)
First, in fit distance of the prospect main,
Paint Allin tilting at the coast of Spain:
Heroic act, and never heard till now,
Stemming of Herc'les' Pillars with his prow!   10
And how two ships he left the hills to waft,
And with new sea-marks Dover and Calais graft.

Epigraph: Translated as follows in Dryden's version:

> The high-shoed plowman, should he quit the land,
> To take the pilot's rudder in his hand
> Artless of stars, and of the moving sand,
> The gods would leave him to the waves and wind
> And think all shame was lost in humankind.

4. *trembled:* trembled at.
6. *pencils:* brushes.
7–12. Before war was declared a British squadron under Sir Thomas Allin made an unsuccessful attack on Dutch merchantmen from Smyrna near the Strait of Gibraltar. Two British warships ran aground, and the poet pretends that Allin left them to waft (convey) the Pillars of Hercules as seamarks between Dover and Calais.

Battaglia Navale tra' Inglesi, et Olandesi Successa
adi 13 di Giugno. 1665.

The Battle of Lowestoft, 3 June 1665. From an engraving by an unknown artist.

Next, let the flaming *London* come in view,
Like Nero's Rome, burnt to rebuild it new:
What lesser sacrifice than this was meet   15
To offer for the safety of the fleet?
Blow one ship up, another thence does grow:
See what free cities and wise courts can do!
So some old merchant, to insure his name,
Marries afresh, and courtiers share the dame;   20
So whatsoe'er is broke, the servants pay't,
And glasses prove more durable than plate.
No mayor till now so rich a pageant feigned,
Nor one barge all the companies contained.
    Then, Painter, draw cerulean Coventry,   25
Keeper, or rather chanc'llor, of the sea;
Of whom the captain buys his leave to die,
And barters or for wounds or infamy;
And more exactly to express his hue,
Ultramarine must do 't, the richest blue.   30
To pay him fees, one's silver trumpet spends;
The boatswain's whistle on his place depends.
Pilots in vain repeat the compass o'er,
Until of him they learn that one point more:
The constant magnet to the pole does hold,   35
Steel to the magnet, Coventry to gold.
Muscovy sells us hemp and pitch and tar,
Iron and copper, Sweden; Münster, war;
Ashley, prize; Warwick, customs; Cart'ret, pay;

13–16. The frigate *London* blew up accidentally in March 1665 and was replaced by a voluntary gift from the merchants of the City.

19–22. The *old merchant* corresponds to the mercantile City, which "insures its name" by giving a new frigate, the *Loyal London,* to replace the lost one. The traditional comic figure of the City merchant cuckolded by courtiers is here applied to the manning of the ship by gentlemen volunteers. The citizens who pay for the ship through "voluntary" subscriptions of silver plate are then in the strange position of servants who must pay for the guests' breakage, and *glasses prove more durable than plate* because exempt from such drives for "contributions."

23–24. The warships are compared to the floats or barges of the various merchant companies in the processions that took place annually in the City on Lord Mayor's Day.

25–40. *cerulean Coventry:* Sir William Coventry (1628–86) was noted for his venality in selling offices in the navy.

38. *Münster:* a bishop with a large mercenary army who signed an alliance with England in return for Dutch territories to which he had a dubious claim.

39. *Ashley:* Antony Ashley Cooper, later first earl of Shaftesbury, was treasurer of prizes. *Warwick:* Sir Philip Warwick, an official in the office of the treasury. *Cart'ret:* Sir George Carteret, treasurer of the navy.

But Coventry sells the whole fleet away.   40
   Now let our navy stretch its canvas wings,
Swoll'n like his purse, with tackling like it strings,
By slow degrees of the increasing gale,
First under sale, and after under sail;
Then in kind visit unto Opdam's gout,   45
Hedge the Dutch in only to let them out.
So huntsmen fair unto the hares give law,
First find them and then civilly withdraw;
That the blind Archer, when they take the seas,
The Hamburg convoy may betray at ease.   50
So that the fish may more securely bite,
The fisher baits the river overnight.
   But, Painter, now prepare, t' enrich thy piece,
Pencil of ermines, oil of ambergris:
See where the duchess, with triumphant tail   55
Of num'rous coaches, Harwich does assail!
So the land crabs, at Nature's kindly call,
Down to engender at the sea do crawl.
See then the admiral, with navy whole,
To Harwich through the ocean caracole.   60
So swallows, buried in the sea, at spring
Return to land with summer on their wing.
One thrifty ferry-boat of mother-pearl
Sufficed of old the Cytherean girl;
Yet navies are but properties, when here   65
(A small sea-masque and built to court you, dear)
Three gooddesses in one: Pallas for art,
Venus for sport, and Juno in your heart.
O duchess! if thy nuptial pomp were mean,
'Tis paid with int'rest in this naval scene.   70
Never did Roman Mark within the Nile

45–46. *Opdam:* Jacob Wassenaer, baron von Opdam, commander of the Dutch fleet.

49–50. British merchantmen from Hamburg were captured by the Dutch through the carelessness of the convoy commander, Captain Archer.

55–58. A burlesque account of the duchess of York's visit to the fleet at Harwich in May.

61–62. An allusion to the discredited theory that swallows are torpid in winter.

63–64. After her birth from sea foam Venus was borne on a seashell to the island of Cytherea.

65. *properties:* stage properties.

69. The duchess, the former Anne Hyde, daughter of Lord Chancellor Clarendon, was pregnant when she was secretly married in her father's house on 3 September 1660.

71–72. Compare the refrain to Cleveland's *Mark Antony* (1647): "Never Mark Antony / Dallied more wantonly / With the fair Egyptian queen."

So feast the fair Egyptian Crocodile,
Nor the Venetian duke, with such a state,
The Adriatic marry at that rate.
    Now, Painter, spare thy weaker art, forbear   75
To draw her parting passions and each tear;
For love, alas! has but a short delight:
The winds, the Dutch, the king, all call to fight.
She therefore the duke's person recommends
To Brouncker, Penn, and Coventry, as friends: 80
Penn much, more Brouncker, most to Coventry;
For they, she knew, were all more 'fraid than she.
Of flying fishes one had saved the fin,
And hoped with these he through the air might spin;
The other thought he might avoid his knell   85
In the invention of the diving bell;
The third had tried it, and affirmed a cable
Coiled round about men, was impenetrable.
But these the duke rejected, only chose
To keep far off and others interpose   90
    Rupert, that knew not fear, but health did want,
Kept state suspended in a chaise-volante;
All save his head shut in that wooden case,
He showed but like a broken weatherglass;
But, armed in a whole lion cap-a-chin,   95
Did represent the Hercules within.
Dear shall the Dutch his twinging anguish know,
And feel what valor whet with pain can do.
Cursed in the meantime be the trait'ress Jael
That through his princely temples drove the nail!   100
    Rupert resolved to fight it like a lion,

73–74. The ritual wedding of Venice to the Adriatic on Ascension Day still commemorates that city's maritime importance.

80. *Brouncker:* William, second Lord Brouncker, a navy commissioner. *Penn:* Sir William Penn, a navy commissioner and admiral of the duke of York's flagship. He was severely criticized for taking refuge in a coil of cable during the battle.

83. A virtuoso habit. See Butler's satire on Brouncker and other members of the Royal Society, *The Elephant in the Moon.*

86. The diving bell was introduced into England from Sweden in 1661. See Evelyn, 19 July 1661 and *CSPD,* 1660–61, pp. 320, 490.

91. *Rupert:* Prince Rupert, count palatine of the Rhine and duke of Bavaria, had been a distinguished royalist officer in the civil wars. He was ill at the time (of venereal disease, the poem suggests) and used a *chaise-volante,* some type of enclosed and suspended chair.

95. *lion:* the symbol of the palatine; Hercules wore the skin of the Nemean lion he had slain, *cap-a-chin:* head-to-chine (chine = backbone).

99. *Jael:* slew Sisera by driving a nail into his head while he slept. See Judges 4.

But Sandwich hoped to fight it like Arion:
He, to prolong his life in the dispute
And charm the Holland pirates, tuned his lute,
Till some judicious dolphin might approach   105
And land him safe and sound as any roach.
Hence by the gazetteer he was mistook,
As unconcerned as if at Hinchingbrooke.
    Now, Painter, reassume thy pencil's care;
It hath but skirmished yet, now fight prepare   110
And draw the battle terribler to show
Than the Last Judgment was of Angelo.
    First, let our navy scour through silver froth,
The ocean's burden and the kingdom's both,
Whose very bulk may represent its birth   115
From Hyde and Paston, burdens of the earth:
Hyde, whose transcendent paunch so swells of late
That he the rupture seems of law and state;
Paston, whose belly bears more millions
Then Indian carracks and contains more tuns.   120
    Let shoals of porpoises on every side
Wonder, in swimming by our oaks outvied,
And the sea fowl, at gaze, behold a thing
So vast, more strong and swift, than they of wing,
But, with presaging gorge, yet keep in sight   125
And follow for the relics of a fight.
    Then let the Dutch, with well-dissembled fear,
Or bold despair, more than we wish, draw near,
At which our gallants (to the sea but tender,
More to the fight) their queasy stomachs render,   130
With breasts so panting that at every stroke
You might have felt their hearts beat through the oak,
While one concerned most, in the interval
Of straining choler, thus did cast his gall:

        "Noah be damned and all his race accursed,   135
        That in sea brine did pickle timber first!
        What though he planted vines! He pines cut down—

102. *Sandwich:* Edward Montagu, earl of Sandwich, admiral of the blue squadron at the Battle of Lowestoft. *Arion* was a Greek poet of the 7th century B.C. who was supposed to have been rescued at sea by a dolphin.
    116. *Hyde:* Edward Hyde, Lord Chancellor Clarendon. *Paston:* Sir Robert Paston, M.P. from Norfolk, who on 9 February 1665 moved the unprecedented sum of £2,500,000 for the war.

He taught us how to drink and how to drown.
He first built ships and in that wooden wall,
Saving but eight, e'er since endangers all.   140
And thou Dutch necromantic friar, be damned,
And in thine own first mortar-piece be rammed!
Who first invented cannon in thy cell,
Nitre from earth and brimstone fetched from hell.
But damned and treble damned be Clarendine,   145
Our seventh Edward, and his house and line!
Who, to divert the danger of the war
With Bristol, hounds us on the Hollander;
Fool-coated gownman! sells, to fight with Hans,
Dunkirk; dismantling Scotland, quarrels France;   150
And hopes he now hath bus'ness shaped and power
T' outlast his life or ours and 'scape the Tower;
And that he yet may see, ere he go down,
His dear Clarinda circled in a crown."

By this time both the fleets in wrath dispute,   155
And each the other mortally salute.
Draw pensive Neptune, biting of his thumbs,
To think himself a slave whos'e'er o'ercomes,
The frighted nymphs retreating to the rocks,
Beating their blue breasts, tearing their green locks.   160
Paint Echo slain: only th' alternate sound
From the repeating cannon does rebound.
Opdam sails in, placed in his naval throne,
Assuming courage greater than his own,
Makes to the duke and threatens him from far   165
To nail himself to 's board like a petar,
But in the vain attempt takes fire too soon

141. *Dutch necromantic friar:* Berthold Schwartz, a 14th-century German, who helped to develop gunpowder and adapt it to military uses.

146. The poet sarcastically places the earl of Clarendon as seventh in England's royal line of Edwards.

147–48. The earl of Bristol brought a charge of treason against Clarendon in the House of Lords in 1663, Bristol was banished for two years.

149. *gownman:* a civilian as distinguished from a soldier. *Hans:* a Dutchman.

149–50. In 1662 Clarendon negotiated the sale of Dunkirk to France on the grounds that it was inadequate as a harbor and that its continued possession might provoke a war with France. He then dismantled forts that Cromwell had built in Scotland and in 1665 rejected France's attempted mediation between England and Holland.

153–54. Clarendon was often charged by satirists with dynastic ambitions in promoting his daughter's marriage to the duke of York.

166. *petar:* a petard, a small explosive charge for breaching walls or gates, etc.

And flies up in his ship to catch the moon.
Monsieurs like rockets mount aloft and crack
In thousand sparks, then dancingly fall back.   170
Yet ere this happened, Destiny allowed
Him his revenge, to make his death more proud:
A fatal bullet from his side did range
And battered Lawson—O too dear exchange!
He led our fleet that day too short a space,   175
But lost his knee, died since in Glory's race;
Lawson, whose valor beyond fate did go
And still fights Opdam through the lakes below.
    The duke himself(though Penn did not forget)
Yet was not out of danger's random set.   180
Falmouth was there (I know not what to act—
Some say 'twas to grow duke, too, by contact);
An untaught bullet in its wanton scope
Quashes him all to pieces and his hope.
Such as his rise such was his fall, unpraised: 185
A chance shot sooner took than chance him raised.
His shattered head the fearless duke distains
And gave the last-first proof that he had brains.
    Berkeley had heard it soon and thought not good
To venture more of royal Harding's blood;   190
To be immortal he was not of age
And did e'en now the Indian prize presage,
But judged it safe and decent (cost what cost)
To lose the day, since his dear brother's lost.
With his whole squadron straight away he bore,   195
And, like good boy, promised to fight no more.
    The Dutch *Urania* fairly on us sailed,
And promises to do what Opdam failed.
Smith to the duke does intercept her way
And cleaves t' her closer than the remora.   200

174. *Lawson:* Sir John Lawson, a vice-admiral who died of wounds.
181. *Falmouth:* Charles Berkeley, earl of Falmouth, Lord Fitzharding, whose death deeply affected the king and the duke of York. Cf. Waller's *Instructions to a Painter*, 147–48 and *n.*
189. *Berkeley:* William Berkeley, second Viscount Fitzharding, Falmouth's younger brother. His conduct in the battle was condemned as cowardly.
192. That is, anticipate the capture and illegal sharing of prizes from the captured Dutch East Indiaman as described in lines 295–310.
197. Captain Sebastian Senten commanding the *Urania* had sworn to board the duke of York's ship, but Capt. Jeremy Smith intervened and captured the *Urania* and 200 men. Smith was knighted for this exploit.
200. *remora:* a sucking fish that attaches itself to larger fish.

The captain wondered and withal disdained,
So strongly by a thing so small detained,
And in a raging brav'ry to him runs;
They stab their ships with one another's guns;
They fight so near it seems to be on ground,   205
And e'en the bullets meeting bullets wound.
The noise, the smoke, the sweat, the fire, the blood,
Are not to be expressed nor understood.
Each captain from the quarterdeck commands;
They wave their bright swords glitt'ring in their hands.   210
All luxury of war, all man can do
In a sea-fight, did pass betwixt them two,
But one must conquer, whosoever fight:
Smith took the giant and is since made knight.
    Marlb'rough, that knew and dared, too, more than all,   215
Falls undistinguished by an iron ball:
Dear Lord! but born under a star ingrate,
No soul so clear, and no more gloomy fate.
Who would set up war's trade that meant to thrive?
Death picks the valiant out, the cow'rds survive.   220
What the brave merit th' impudent do vaunt,
And none's rewarded but the sycophant;
Hence all his life he against Fortune fenced,
Or not well known or not well recompensed.
But envy not this praise to 's memory: 225
None more prepared was or less fit to die.
    Rupert did others, and himself, excel:
Holmes, Tyddiman, Myngs; bravely Sansum fell.
What others did let none omitted blame;
I shall record, whos'e'er brings in his name.   230
But (unless after stories disagree)
Nine only came to fight, the rest to see.
    Now all conspires unto the Dutchman's loss:
The wind, the fire, we, they themselves, do cross,
When a sweet sleep the duke began to drown   235
And with soft diadem his temples crown.
But first he orders all beside to watch,
That they the foe (whilst he a nap) might catch.

215. James Ley, 3d earl of Marlborough, expressed his strong presentiment of death in a letter to a friend written aboard the *James* near the coast of Holland 27 May, 1665.

227–28. *Holms, Tyddiman, Myngs:* naval captains. Robert *Sansum,* rear-admiral of Prince Rupert's squadron, was killed in the battle.

But Brouncker, by a secreter instinct,
Slept not, nor needs it; he all day had winked.   240
The duke in bed, he then first draws his steel,
Whose virtue makes the misled compass wheel:
So ere he waked, both fleets were innocent,
And Brouncker member is of Parliament.
    And now, dear Painter, after pains like those,   245
Twere time that thou and I too should repose.
But all our navy 'scaped so sound of limb
That a small space served to refresh it trim,
And a tame fleet of theirs does convoy want,
Laden with both the Indies and Levant.   250
Paint but this one scene more, the world's our own;
The halcyon Sandwich does command alone.
    To Bergen now with better maw we haste,
And the sweet spoils in hope already taste,
Though Clifford in the character appears   255
Of supercargo to our fleet and theirs,
Wearing a signet ready to clap on
And seize all for his master Arlington.
    Ruyter, whose little squadron skimmed the seas
And wasted our remotest colonies,   260
With ships all foul returned upon our way.
Sandwich would not disperse, nor yet delay,
And therefore (like commander grave and wise)
To 'scape his sight and fight, shut both his eyes,
And, for more state and sureness, Cuttance true   265
The left eye closes, the right Montagu,
And even Clifford proffered (in his zeal

239–42. While the duke was napping after the engagement and the Dutch were fleeing toward their coasts, Henry Brouncker, confidant of the duke of York, gave orders to Harman, the flagship's captain, to shorten sail. Harman, accepting the orders as authorized by the duke, allowed the enemy to escape. Brouncker seems to have been terrified of another battle. After a parliamentary investigation he was expelled from his recently won seat in the House of Commons.

249–50. *tame fleet:* rich Dutch merchantmen returning from the East Indies that the English intended to capture or destroy.

253. Sir Gilbert Talbot, English envoy at Copenhagen, was negotiating with the king of Denmark a joint attack on the Dutch merchantmen that had taken refuge in neutral Danish harbors. *better maw:* better appetite.

255. *Clifford:* Sir Thomas Clifford, confidential agent of Arlington, the secretary of state, who was involved in the scheme to attack the Dutch ships at Bergen.

259–70. The Dutch admiral Michael de Ruyter, homeward bound from harrying the English in Guinea, managed to elude a fleet under the command of Sandwich (and Cuttance, his captain) by hugging the Danish coast.

To make all safe) t' apply to both his seal.
Ulysses so, till he the Sirens passed,
Would by his mates be pinioned to the mast. 270
   Now may our navy view the wished port;
But there too (see the fotune!) was a fort.
Sandwich would not be beaten nor yet beat:
Fools only fight, the prudent use to treat.
His cousin Montagu (by court disaster 275
Dwindled into the wooden horse's master)
To speak of peace seemed among all most proper,
Had Talbot then treated of nought but copper,
For what are forts, when void of ammunition?
With friend or foe what would we more condition? 280
Yet we three days (till the Dutch furnished all—
Men, powder, cannon, money) treat with Wall.
Then Teddy, finding that the Dane would not,
Sends in six captains bravely to be shot,
And Montagu, though dressed like any bride, 285
Though aboard him too, yet was reached and died.
   Sad was this chance, and yet a deeper care
Wrinkles our membranes under forehead fair:
The Dutch armada yet had the impudence
To put to sea to waft their merchants hence; 290
For, as if all their ships of walnut were,
The more we beat them, still the more they bear;
But a good pilot and a fav'ring wind
Bring Sandwich back and once again did blind.
   Now, gentle Painter, ere we leap on shore, 295

275–82. Edward Montagu, Sandwich's cousin, dismissed from his post as Master of the Horse to the queen, now Master of the Wooden Horse, contrived against the Dutch at Bergen. The Bod. MS has a marginal note: "Montagu was Master of the Horse to the queen. One day, as he led her, he tickled her palm. She asked the king what that meant. The king by this means getting knowledge of it, turned Montagu out of his place."
   The rest of this difficult passage seems to mean that if Talbot had not prolonged negotiations by insisting on a Dutch declaration of war the Dutch ships could have been captured while there were no arms or ammunition to defend them. *Wall* personifies Danish intransigence. *Teddy:* Sir Thomas Tyddiman, commander of the British squadron.
291–92. An allusion to the old saying, "A woman, ass, and walnut tree, the more you beat the better be."
295–304. A violent storm early in September dispersed the heavily laden East Indiamen. Sandwich was criticized for his failure to attack and win a decisive victory, although this would have entailed a night battle in rough weather on a lee shore. He contented himself with distributing prizes from the *Phoenix* and *Slothony* among his officers. Because the distribution was made without a warrant from the prize commission, Sandwich was removed from his command and sent on an embassy to Spain.

With thy last strokes ruffle a tempest o'er,
As if in our reproach the winds and seas
Would undertake the Dutch while we take ease.
The seas their spoils within our hatches throw,
The winds both fleets into our mouths do blow,   300
Strew all their ships along the coast by ours,
As easy to be gathered up as flow'rs.
But Sandwich fears for merchants to mistake
A man of war, and among flow'rs a snake.
Two Indian ships, pregnant with eastern pearl   305
And diamonds, sate the officers and earl.
Then warning of our fleet, he it divides
Into the ports, and he to Oxford rides,
While the Dutch, reuniting to our shames,
Ride all insulting o'er the Downs and Thames.   310
    Now treating Sandwich seems the fittest choice
For Spain, there to condole and to rejoice;
He meets the French, but, to avoid all harms,
Slips to the Groin (embassies bear not arms!)
There let him languish a long quarantine   315
And ne'er to England come till he be clean,
    Thus having fought we know not why, as yet,
We've done we know not what nor what we get:
If to espouse the ocean all the pains,
Prince unite and will forbid the bains;   320
If to discharge fanatics, this makes more,
For all fanatic turn when sick or poor;
Or if the House of Commons to repay,
Their prize commissions are transferred away;
But for triumphant checkstones, if, and shell   325
For duchess' closet, 't has succeeded well.
If to make Parliaments all odious pass;
If to reserve a standing force, alas!
Or if, as just, Orange to reinstate,
Instead of that, he is regenerate;   330
And with four millions vainly giv'n as spent,
And with five millions more of detriment,

314. En route to Spain, Sandwich was forced by a storm to take shelter in Corunna (the
"Groin") where, in violation of his diplomatic mission, he seized a Dutch merchantman.
320. *bains:* banns.
325–26. The duchess of York, the poet suggests, was one of the few beneficiaries of this
costly naval war. *checkstones:* counters used in a children's game. *shell:* cant word for money.

Our sum amounts yet only to have won
A bastard Orange for pimp Arlington!
   Now may historians argue con and pro: 335
Denham saith thus, though Waller always so;
But he, good man, in his long sheet and staff,
This penance did for Cromwell's epitaph.
And his next theme must be o' th' duke's mistress:
Advice to draw Madam l'Édificatresse.   340
     Henceforth, O Gemini! two dukes command:
Castor and Pollux, Aumarle, Cumberland.
Since in one ship, it had been fit they went
In Petty's double-keeled *Experiment*.

To the King

Imperial prince, king of the seas and isles,   345
Dear object of our joys and Heaven's smiles:
What boots it that thy light does gild our days
And we lie basking in thy milder rays,
While swarms of insects, from thy warmth begun,
Our land devour and intercept our sun?   350
Thou, like Jove's Minos, rul'st a greater Crete
And for its hundred cities count'st thy fleet.
Why wilt thou that state-Daedalus allow,
Who builds thee but a lab'rinth and a cow?
If thou art Minos, be a judge severe   355
And in 's own maze confine the engineer;
Or if our sun, since he so near presumes,
Melt the soft wax with which he imps his plumes

334. *bastard Orange:* Arlington was married to the daughter of Louis of Nassau, illegitimate son of Prince Maurice. As *pimp* he induced Louise de Kéroualle, later duchess of Portsmouth, to become Charles's mistress.

335–40. *Denham:* The poet pretends that the poem was written by Sir John Denham, who was known at this time to be insane. Denham's friend, Edmund Waller, had written an elegy on Cromwell. "Denham's" next assignment will be to write a poem about the duke of York's mistress who happened to be the wife of the royal architect, the real Sir John Denham (hence her title *Madam l' Édificatresse*). The subject is in contrast to Waller's fulsome eulogy on the duke's wife in *Instructions to a Painter*.

342. *Aumarle:* George Monck, duke of Albemarle, the remarkable soldier, sailor, and statesman who was the architect of the Restoration. *Cumberland:* Prince Rupert, who also held the title of duke of Cumberland.

344. Sir William Petty designed a double-keeled ship, the *Experiment*.

353–54. *state-Daedalus:* refers to Clarendon, the chief architect of English policy, and the lines parody Waller's comparison of Charles to Minos at the end of *Instructions to a Painter*. Where Daedalus built a labyrinth for the Minotaur, Clarendon, by his evil policies, had confined Charles himself in a labyrinth and provided him with a cow (the barren queen?).

And let him, falling, leave his hated name
Unto those seas his war hath set on flame.   360
From that enchanter having cleared thine eyes,
Thy native sight will pierce within the skies
And view those kingdoms calm of joy and light,
Where's universal triumph but no fight.
Since both from Heav'n thy race and power descend,   365
Rule by its pattern, there to reascend:
Let justice only draw and battle cease;
Kings are in war but cards: they're gods in peace.

368. In war kings are but playing cards, powerless instruments of their ministers.

ANDREW MARVELL

The Third Advice to a Painter
(1666)

With the removal of Sandwich, command of the navy was vested jointly in the versatile Monck, now duke of Albemarle, and the aging, ailing Prince Rupert. Late in May 1666 a squadron of twenty ships under Rupert was detached to attack some French warships under the duc de Beaufort, reported to be near Belle-Île in the Bay of Biscay. With the remainder of the English fleet Albemarle encountered a superior Dutch force on 1 June 1666 between the North Foreland and Dunkirk. In the Four Days' Battle (1–4 June) Albemarle's ships were battered and total defeat was avoided only by Rupert's last-minute reunion with the main fleet.

The division of the fleet was investigated by Parliament in October 1667 just as the Commons were exploring methods of impeaching Clarendon. A study based upon new evidence (Fraser, *Intelligence of the Secretaries of State*, 1956) puts the chief blame on the joint commanders. It now appears that Albemarle and Rupert, after the miscarriage, fell in with Clarendon's desire to lay the blame on Sir William Coventry and the earl of Arlington, who had initiated the movement to impeach the chancellor. Rupert and Albemarle testified that Arlington's intelligence service had falsely reported Beaufort at Belle-Île when he was in the Mediterranean and had failed to learn of the advanced readiness of the Dutch fleet. They also testified that Coventry had failed to send the order recalling Rupert with due dispatch.

Fraser shows that these allegations are false and that Albemarle's engagement of the powerful Dutch fleet without Rupert's forces was intentional:

> Rupert sailed with the morning tide on the 29th. The same day Albemarle received advice from a ship that the Dutch fleet had sailed. He made no attempt to recall the prince, who was then only ten miles distant, but was confident that he could engage the Dutch alone. . . . On his way to the station he had chosen between the Downs and the Gunfleet, Albemarle ran into the Dutch fleet. His note to Coventry, written at 11 A.M. on I June reveals that he was neither surprised nor disinclined to a combat (p. 83).

Though *Third Advice* implicates Arlington and Coventry as the chief culprits, it assigns Albemarle a share of the blame in lines 31–34.

Third Advice was first published without license in 1667 under a Breda imprint together with *Second Advice* and some other items. It was written after the outbreak of the great fire (2 September 1666). Pepys saw a manuscript in January 1667: "I took it home with me and will copy it, having the former, being also mightily pleased with it."

THE THIRD ADVICE TO A PAINTER

London, October 1st, 1666

Sandwich in Spain now, and the duke in love,
Let's with new gen'rals a new painter prove:
Lely's a Dutchman, danger in his art;
His pencils may intelligence impart.
Thou, Gibson, that among thy navy small   5
Of marshaled shells commandest admiral
(Thyself so slender that thou show'st no more
Than barnacle new-hatched of them before)
Come, mix thy water-colors and express,
Drawing in little, how we do yet less.   10
    First paint me George and Rupert, rattling far
Within one box, like the two dice of war,
And let the terror of their linked mane
Fly through the air like chain-shot, tearing fame.
Jove in one cloud did scarcely ever wrap   15
Lightning so fierce, but never such a clap!
United gen'rals! sure the only spell
Wherewith United Provinces to quell.
Alas, e'en they, though shelled in treble oak,
Will prove an addle egg with double yolk.   20
And therefore next uncouple either hound
And loo them at two hares ere one be found.
Rupert to Beaufort hollo, "Ay there, Rupert!"

1. Sandwich was in Spain from May 1666 to September 1668. The duke of York was in love with the young woman whom Sir John Denham had married in May 1665.
2. *gen'rals:* commanding officers at sea.
3. *Lely:* Sir Peter Lely, a famous court painter.
5. *Gibson:* Richard Gibson, a dwarf who painted miniatures.
11. *George:* Albemarle.
18. *United Provinces:* the Dutch Republic.
23–28. In May 1666 a squadron of twenty ships under Rupert was detached to attack French warships commanded by the duc de Beaufort that were reported to be in the Bay of Biscay. Beaufort was actually still in the Mediterranean.

Like the fantastic hunting of St. Hubert
When he, with airy hounds and horn of air,   25
Pursues by Fontainebleau the witchy hare—
Deep providence of state that could so soon
Fight Beaufort here ere he had quit Toulon!
So have I seen, ere human quarrels rise,
Foreboding meteors combat with the skies.   30
　　But let the prince to fight with Rumor go;
The gen'ral meets a more substantial foe.
Ruyter he spies, and full of youthful heat,
Though half their number, thinks his odds too great.
The fowler, so, watches the wat'ry spot,   35
And more the fowl, hopes for the better shot.
Though such a limb were from his navy torn,
He found no weakness yet, like Sampson shorn,
But swoll'n with sense of former glory won,
Thought Monck must be by Albemarle outdone.   40
Little he knew, with the same arm and sword,
How far the gentleman outcuts the lord.
　　Ruyter, inferior unto none for heart,
Superior now in number and in art,
Asked if he thought, as once our rebel nation,   45
To conquer theirs too by a declaration?
And threatens, though he now so proudly sail,
He shall tread back his *Iter Boreale*.
This said, he the short period, ere it ends,
With iron words from brazen mouths extends.   50
Monck yet prevents him ere the navies meet
And charges in, himself alone a fleet,
And with so quick and frequent motion wound
His murd'ring sides about, the ship seemed round,
And the exchanges of his circling tire   55
Like whirling hoops showed of triumphal fire.
Single he does at their whole navy aim
And shoots them through a porcupine of flame.
He plays with danger and his bullets trolls
(As 'twere at trou-madam) through all their holls.   60
In noise so regular his cannon met
You'd think that thunder were to music set.

48. *Iter Boreale:* the northern journey which Monck took from Scotland which led to the restoration of Charles II.
60. *trou-madam:* a game in which balls were rolled into holes.

Ah, had the rest but kept a time as true,
What age could such a martial consort shew?
The list'ning air unto the distant shore   65
Through secret pipes conveys the tunéd roar,
Till, as the echoes vanishing abate,
Men feel a deaf sound like the pulse of Fate.
If Fate expire, let Monck her place supply:
His guns determine who shall live or die.   70
     But Victory does always hate a rant:
Valor her brave, but Skill is her gallant.
Ruyter no less with virtuous envy burns
And prodigies for miracles returns.
Yet she observed how still his iron balls   75
Bricoled in vain against our oaken walls,
And the hard pellets fell away as dead,
Which our enchanted timber fillippéd.
"Leave then," said she, "th' invulnerable keel;
We'll find their foible, like Achilles' heel."   80
     He, quickly taught, pours in continual clouds
Of chained dilemmas through our sinewy shrouds.
Forests of masts fall with their rude embrace;
Our stiff sails, mashed, are netted into lace,
Till our whole navy lay their wanton mark,   85
Nor any ship could sail but as the Ark.
Shot in the wing, so, at the powder's call
The disappointed bird does flutt'ring fall.
Yet Monck, disabled, still such courage shows
That none into his mortal gripe durst close.   90
So an old bustard, maimed, yet loth to yield,
Duels the fowler in Newmarket field.
But soon he found 't was now in vain to fight
And imps his plumes the best he may for flight.
     This, Painter, were a noble task, to tell   95
What indignation his great breast did swell
Not virtuous men unworthily abused,
Not constant lovers without cause refused,
Not honest merchant broke, not skillful player
Hissed off the stage, not sinner in despair,   100

76. *Bricoled*: recoiled.
78. *fillippéd*: struck smartly.
88. *disappointed*: unprepared.
91. *bustard*: a large bird.

Not losing rooks, not favorites disgraced,
Not Rump by Oliver or Monck displaced,
Not kings deposed, not prelates ere they die,
Feel half the rage of gen'rals when they fly.
    Ah, rather than transmit our scorn to fame,   105
Draw curtains, gentle artist, o'er this shame.
Cashier the mem'ry of Du Tell, raised up
To taste, instead of death's, His Highness' cup.
And if the thing were true, yet paint it not,
How Berkeley (as he long deserved) was shot,   110
Though others that surveyed the corpse so clear
Say he was only petrified with fear;
And the hard statue, mummied without gum,
Might the Dutch balm have spared and English tomb.
Yet, if thou wilt, paint Myngs turned all to soul,   115
And the great Harman charked almost to coal,
And Jordan old, thy pencil's worthy pain,
Who all the way held up the ducal train.
But in a dark cloud cover Ayscue when
He quit the *Prince* t' embark in Lowestein,   120
And wounded ships, which we immortal boast,
Now first led captive to a hostile coast.
But most with story of his hand or thumb
Conceal (as Honor would) His Grace's bum,
When the rude bullet a large collop tore   125
Out of that buttock never turned before.

102. *Rump:* the remnant of the Long Parliament after Pride's Purge of leading Presbyterians in 1648. The Rump was dissolved by Cromwell in 1653 and restored after the fall of Richard Cromwell only to be displaced a second time by Monck, who restored the members expelled by Pride.

107. *Du Tell:* a Frenchman dismissed by Albemarle because, in the words of Lady Albemarle, he "fired more shot into the prince's ship and others of the king's ships than of the enemy." The duke of York employed him as cupbearer.

110. *Berkeley:* William Berkeley, censured for cowardice at the Battle of Lowestoft. Cf. *Second Advice,* 189–96.

115. *Myngs:* Sir Christopher Myngs, leading the van, was shot in the throat on the fourth day of the battle. He stopped the wound with his fingers and continued to give orders. He died a few days after the battle.

116. *Harman:* Sir John Harman, rear-admiral of the White. The Dutch set fire to his ship, many of his men deserted him, and he was pinned by a falling mast, but nevertheless managed to extinguish the fire and refit during the night.

117. *Jordan:* Capt. Sir Joseph Jordan, knighted for his bravery at Lowestoft, commander of the *Royal Oak,* covered Albemarle's retreat.

119–20. Sir George Ayscue, admiral of the White, ran the *Royal Prince* aground on Galloper Sands. He was captured by the Dutch, who treated him ignominiously and imprisoned him in the castle of Lowestein.

Fortune, it seemed, would give him by that lash
Gentle correction for his fight so rash,
But should the Rump perceiv't, they'd say that Mars
Had now revenged them upon Aumarle's arse.   130
    The long disaster better o'er to veil,
Paint only Jonah three days in the whale,
Then draw the youthful Perseus all in haste
From a sea-beast to free the virgin chaste
(But neither riding Pegasus for speed,   135
Nor with the Gorgon shielded at his need);
For no less time did conqu'ring Ruyter chaw
Our flying gen'ral in his spongy jaw.
So Rupert the sea dragon did invade,
But to save George himself and not the maid,   140
And so arriving late, he quickly missed
E'en sails to fly, unable to resist.
    Not Greenland seamen, that survive the fright
Of the cold chaos and half-eternal night,
So gladly the returning sun adore   145
Or run to spy their next year's fleet from shore,
Hoping yet once within the oily side
Of the fat whale again their spears to hide,
As our glad fleet with universal shout
Salute the prince and wish the second bout;   150
Nor winds, long pris'ners in earth's hollow vault,
The fallow seas so eagerly assault,
As fi'ry Rupert with revengeful joy
Does on the Dutch his hungry courage cloy,
But soon unrigged lay like a useless board   155
(As wounded in the wrist men drop the sword)
When a propitious cloud betwixt us stepped
And in our aid did Ruyter intercept.
Old Homer yet did never introduce,
To save his heroes, mist of better use.   160
Worship the sun who dwell where he does rise:
This mist does more deserve our sacrifice.
    Now joyful fires and the exalted bell
And court-gazettes our empty triumph tell.
Alas, the time draws near when overturned   165
The lying bells shall through the tongue be burned;

165–68. An allusion to the great fire of London, which broke out in September.

Paper shall want to print that lie of state,,
And our false fires true fires shall expiate.
    Stay, Painter, here a while, and I will stay,
Nor vex the future times with nice survey.   170
Seest not the monkey duchess all undressed?
Paint thou but her, and she will paint the rest.
    The sad tale found her in her outer room,
Nailing up hangings not of Persian loom,
Like chaste Penelope that ne'er did roam,   175
But made all fine against her George came home.
Upon a ladder, in her coat much shorter,
She stood with groom and porter for supporter,
And careless what they saw or what they thought,
With *Hony-pensy* honestly she wrought.   180
For in the gen'ral's breech none could, she knows,
Carry away the piece with eyes or nose.
One tenter drove, to lose no time nor place,
At once the ladder they remove, and grace.
While thus they her translate from north to east   185
In posture just of a four-footed beast,
She heard the news, but altered yet no more
Than that what was behind she turned before,
Nor would come down, but with a handkercher
(Which pocket foul did to her neck prefer)   190
She dried no tears, for she was too viraginous,
But only snuffling her trunk cartilaginous,
From scaling ladder she began a story
Worthy to be had *in memento mori,*
Arraigning past, and present, and *futuri,*   195
With a prophetic (if not spirit) fury.
Her hair began to creep, her belly sound,
Her eyes to startle, and her udder bound.
Half witch, half prophet, thus she-Albemarle,
Like Presbyterian sibyl, out did snarl: 200
    "Traitors both to my lord, and to the king!
Nay, now it grows beyond all suffering!
One valiant man on land, and he must be
Commanded out to stop their leaks at sea.

171. *all undressed: en déshabillé.*
180. *Hony-pensy:* Albemarle was a member of the Order of the Garter, whose motto is *Honi soit qui mal y pense.*
183. *tenter:* tenter-hook, for fastening the hangings.

Yet send him Rupert as a helper meet,   205
First the command dividing ere the fleet!
One may, if they be beat, or both, be hit,
Or if they overcome, yet honor's split,
But reck'ning George already knocked o' th' head,
They cut him out like beef ere he be dead.   210
Each for a quarter hopes: the first does skip,
But shall snap short, though at the gen'ralship;
Next, they for Master of the Horse agree;
A third the cockpit begs, not any me.
But they shall know, ay, marry, shall they do,   215
That who the cockpit has shall have me too.
    "I told George first, as Calamy did me,
If the king these brought over, how 'twould be:
Men that there picked his pocket to his face
To sell intelligence or buy a place,   220
That their religion pawned for clothes, nor care
('T has run so long) now to redeem 't, nor dare.
O what egregious loyalty to cheat!
O what fidelity it was to eat!
While Langdales, Hoptons, Glenhams starved abroad,   225
And here true roy'lists sunk beneath the load,
Men that did there affront, defame, betray
The king, and do so here, now who but they?
What, say I men? nay, rather monsters! men
Only in bed, nor to my knowledge then.   230
See how they home return in revel rout
With the same measures that they first went out:
Nor better grown, nor wiser all this while,
Renew the causes of their first exile,
As if (to show you fools what 'tis I mean)   235
I chose a foul smock when I might have clean.
    "First, they for fear disband the army tame,
And leave good George a general's empty name:
Then bishops must revive and all unfix

213. Albemarle had been Master of the Horse to the king since 1660.
214. *cockpit:* Albemarle's lodgings in the palace at Whitehall.
217. *Calamy:* Edmund Calamy, celebrated Puritan divine, had been appointed one of Charles II's chaplains in 1660, a post which he quickly resigned.
225. *Langdales, Hoptons, Glenhams:* devoted royalists.
237–38. Most of the army was disbanded after the Restoration.
239–42. Bishops again sat in the House of Lords after the Restoration. In 1660 a bill to modify the rigid Anglican service and extend indulgences to Nonconformists was defeated in the Commons by 26 votes.

With discontents to content twenty-six.   240
The Lords' House drains the houses of the Lord,
For bishops' voices silencing the Word.
O Barthol'mew, saint of their calendar!
What's worse, thy ejection or thy massacre?
Then Culp'per, Gloucester, ere the princess, died: 245
Nothing can live that interrupts an Hyde.
O more than human Gloucester! Fate did shew
Thee but to earth, and back again withdrew.
Then the fat scriv'ner durst begin to think
'Twas time to mix the royal blood with ink.   250
Berkeley, that swore as oft as she had toes,
Does kneeling now her chastity depose,
Just as the first French card'nal could restore
Maidenhead to his widow-niece and whore.
For portion, if she should prove light when weighed,   255
Four millions shall within three years be paid.
To raise it, we must have a naval war,
As if 'twere nothing but tara-tan-tar!
Abroad, all princes disobliging first,
At home, all parties but the very worst.   260
To tell of Ireland, Scotland, Dunkirk's sad,
Or the king's marriage, but he thinks I'm mad,
And sweeter creature never saw the sun,
If we the king wished monk, or queen a nun.
But a Dutch war shall all these rumors still,   265
Bleed out those humors, and our purses spill.

243–44. The Act of Uniformity under which Nonconformist ministers were expelled from their churches took effect on 24 August 1662, the anniversary of the St. Bartholomew's Day massacre (1572).

245. *Culp'per:* Sir John Culpeper, who helped bring about the king's restoration, died in the summer of 1660. *Gloucester:* Henry, duke of Gloucester, and Princess Mary, brother and sister to Charles II, both died the same year.

246. *an Hyde:* a punning reference to the duchess of York, insinuating that she tried to ensure her husband's succession to the throne by eliminating the immediate heirs.

249–52. An allusion to the alleged dynastic ambitions of Anne's father, the earl of Clarendon. Sir Charles Berkeley, later Lord Falmouth, who had repeatedly sworn that Anne was an immoral woman, subsequently denied these oaths. He was a close friend of the king and the duke and was killed in the Battle of Lowestoft. Cf. *Second Advice,* 181–88.

253–54. Possibly a covert allusion to the representation of clerics' mistresses as nieces.

261. See *Second Advice,* 145–50. The reference to Ireland has to do with the release of restrictions on the Irish Catholics.

262. *the king's marriage:* to the barren Catherine de Braganza. *but he thinks I'm mad:* The poet has momentarily forgotten that not Denham but the duchess of Albemarle is speaking. See headnote.

Yet after one day's trembling fight they saw
'Twas too much danger for a son-in-law;
Hire him to leave with six-score thousand pound,
As with the king's drums men for sleep compound.   270
Then modest Sandwich thought it might agree
With the state prudence to do less than he,
And to excuse their tim'rousness and sloth,
They've found how George might now do less than both.
   "First, Smith must for Leghorn, with force enough   275
To venture back again, but not go through.
Beaufort is there, and to their dazzling eyes
The distance more the object magnifies.
Yet this they gain, that Smith his time shall lose,
And for my duke, too, cannot interpose,   280
But fearing that our navy, George to break,
Might yet not be sufficiently weak,
The secretary, that had never yet
Intelligence but from his own *Gazette,*
Discovers a great secret, fit to sell,   285
And pays himself for't ere he would it tell:
Beaufort is in the Channel! Hixy, here!
Doxy, Toulon! Beaufort is ev'rywhere!
Herewith assembles the Supreme Divan,
Where enters none but Devil, Ned, and Nan,   290
And upon this pretence they straight designed
The fleet to sep'rate and the world to blind:
Monck to the Dutch, and Rupert (here the wench
Could not but smile) is destined to the French.
To write the order, Bristol's clerk they chose   295
(One slit in's pen, another in his nose)
For he first brought the news, and 'tis his place;

267–70. After Lowestoft, Parliament voted James £120,000 "in token of the great sense they had of his conduct and bravery in the late engagement." They followed this up with a humble address to the king asking him not to allow James to risk his life again. Charles readily acceded to this appeal.

275–80. Sir Jeremy Smith was dispatched to the Strait of Gibraltar to protect the Levant trade and then recalled too late to help Albemarle.

281–88. The intelligence service was operated by Arlington, the secretary of state. The only licensed newspaper, the *London Gazette,* drew its news from this source and reported in May that Beaufort was in the Channel. *Hixy* and *Doxy:* juggler's patter. The whole passage sees the division of the fleet as a plot by the duchess of York, Clarendon, and Arlington to destroy Albemarle.

295–300. Arlington had been secretary to the earl of Bristol. In the civil war he had suffered a cut on the nose, which he accentuated with a strip of black plaster. *The Dutch chink* refers to his wife.

He'll see the fleet divided like his face,
And through that cranny in his gristly part
To the Dutch chink intell'gence may start.   300
    "The plot succeeds; the Dutch in haste prepare,
And poor pilgarlic George's arse they share,
And now presuming of his certain wrack,
To help him late they write for Rupert back.
Officious Will seemed fittest, as afraid   305
Lest George should look too far into his trade.
On the first draught they pause with statesmen's care;
They write it fair, then copy 't out as fair,
Then they compare them, when at last 'tis signed.
Will soon his purse-strings but no seal could find.   310
At night he sends it by the common post,
To save the king of an express the cost.
Lord, what ado to pack one letter hence!
Some patents pass with less circumference.
    "Well, George, in spite of them thou safe dost ride,   315
Lessened, I hope, in nought but thy backside,
For as to reputation, this retreat
Of thine exceeds their victories so great.
Nor shalt thou stir from thence by my consent,
Till thou hast made the Dutch and them repent.   320
'Tis true, I want so long the nuptial gift,
But (as I oft have done) I'll make a shift,
Nor with vain pomp will I accost the shore,
To try thy valor at the Buoy of th' Nore.
Fall to thy work there, George, as I do here: 325
Cherish the valiant up, cowards cashier,
See that the men have pay and beef and beer,
Find out the cheats of the four millioneer.
Out of the very beer they steal the malt,
Powder of powder, from powdered beef the salt.   330
Put thy hand to the tub; instead of ox,
They victual with French pork that has the pox:
Never such cotqueans by small arts to wring,
Ne'er such ill housewives in the managing.
Pursers at sea know fewer cheats than they;   335
Mar'ners on shore less madly spend their pay.

302. *pilgarlic:* an expression of mock pity.
305. *Officious Will:* the venal Sir William Coventry. See *Second Advice,* 25–40.
322. A pun on Lady Albemarle's former occupation as seamstress.

See that thou hast new sails thyself and spoil
All their sea market and their cable-coil.
Tell the king all, how him they countermine;
Trust not, till done, him with thy own design.   340
Look that good chaplains on each ship do wait,
Nor the sea diocese be impropriate.
Look to the pris'ners, sick, and wounded: all
Is prize; they rob even the hospital.
Recover back the prizes, too: in vain   345
We fight, if all be taken that is ta'en.
    "Now by our coast the Dutchmen, like a flight
Of feeding ducks, morning and evening light.
How our land-Hectors tremble, void of sense,
As if they came straight to transport them hence!   350
Some sheep are stol'n, the kingdom's all arrayed,
And even Presbyt'ry's now called out for aid.
They wish e'en George divided to command,
One half of him the sea and one the land.
    "What's that I see? Ha, 'tis my George again!   355
It seems they in sev'n weeks have rigged him then.
The curious Heav'n with lightning him surrounds
To view him, and his name in thunder sounds,
But with the same shaft gores their navy near
(As, ere we hunt, the keeper shoots the deer).   360
Stay, Heav'n, a while, and thou shalt see him sail
And how George, too, can lighten, thunder, hail!
Happy the time that I thee wedded George,
The sword of England and of Holland scourge!
Avaunt, Rotterdam dog! Ruyter avaunt!   365
Thou water rat, thou shark, thou cormorant!
I'll teach thee to shoot scissors! I'll repair
Each rope thou losest, George, out of this hair.
Ere thou shalt lack a sail and lie adrift
('Tis strong and coarse enough) I'll cut this shift.   370
Bring home the old ones; I again will sew
And darn them up to be as good as new.
What, twice disabled? Never such a thing!

342. *impropriate*: annexed; used particularly of ecclesiastical benefices.
367. *scissors*: chain-shot, used against rigging.
373–76. The *Gazette* for 4–7 June 1666 reported with rare humor: "The duke had all his
tackle taken off by chain-shot, and his breeches to the skin were shot off, but he rigged them
again with jury masts, and fell into the body of the Dutch fleet, where he attacked de Ruyter."

Now, sov'reign, help him that brought in the king.
Guard thy posterior left, lest all be gone: 375
Though jury-masts, th' hast jury-buttocks none.
Courage! How bravely, whet with this disgrace,
He turns, and bullets spits in Ruyter's face!
They fly, they fly! Their fleet does now divide!
But they discard their Tromp; our trump is Hyde. 380
   "Where are you now, De Ruyter, with your bears?
See how your merchants burn about your ears.
Fire out the wasps, George, from their hollow trees,
Crammed with the honey of our English bees.
Ay, now they're paid for Guinea: ere they steer 385
To the Gold Coast, they'll find it hotter here.
Turn their ships all to stoves ere they set forth,
To warm their traffic in the frozen north.
Ah, Sandwich! had thy conduct been the same,
Bergen had seen a less but richer flame, 390
Nor Ruyter lived new battle to repeat
And oft'ner beaten be than we can beat.
   "Scarce has George leisure, after all this pain,
To tie his breeches: Ruyter's out again.
Thrice in one year! Why sure the man is wood: 395
Beat him like stockfish, or he'll ne'er be good.
I see them both prepared again to try:
They first shoot through each other with the eye,
Then—but that ruling Providence that must
With human projects play, as winds with dust, 400
Raises a storm (so constables a fray
Knock down) and sends them both well-cuffed away.
Plant now Virginian firs in English oak;
Build your ship-ribs proof to the cannon's stroke;
To get a fleet to sea exhaust the land; 405
Let longing princes pine for the command.
Strong marchpanes! Wafers light! So thin a puff
Of angry air can ruin all that huff.
So champions, having shared the lists and sun,

380. Admiral Tromp was drawn off in a separate action from the main engagement. The poet makes the far-fetched suggestion that the English follow the Dutch example by discarding Clarendon.
385. De Ruyter's fleet had returned the year before from harassing English settlements in Guinea. Cf. *Second Advice*. 259–70 and *n.*
396. *stockfish:* dried salted fish that must be pounded before cooking.
407. *marchpanes:* marzipan, a light confectionery.

The judge throws down his warder, and they've done.   410
For shame, come home, George! 'Tis for thee too much
To fight at once with Heaven and the Dutch.
   "Woe's me! what see I next? Alas, the fate
I see of England and its utmost date!
Those flames of theirs at which we fondly smile,   415
Kindled like torches our sepulchral pile.
War, fire, and plague against us all conspire;
We the war, God the plague, who raised the fire?
See how men all like ghosts, while London burns,
Wander and each over his ashes mourns!   420
Dear George, sad fate, vain mind, that me didst please
To meet thine with far other flames than these!
Cursed be the man that first begot this war,
In an ill hour, under a blazing star.
For others' sport two nations fight a prize;   425
Between them both religion wounded lies.
So of first Troy the angry gods unpaid
Razed the foundations which themselves had laid.
   "Welcome, though late, dear George! Here hadst
      thou been,
We'd 'scap'd. Let Rupert bring the navy in.   430
Thou still must help them out when in the mire,
Gen'ral at land, at sea, at plague, at fire.
Now thou art gone, see, Beaufort dares approach,
And our whole fleet angling has catched a roach."
   Gibson, farewell, till next we put to sea: 435
Faith thou hast drawn her in effigie.

To the King

   Great prince, and so much greater as more wise,
Sweet as our life, and dearer than our eyes,
What servants will conceal and couns'lers spare
To tell, the painter and the poet dare;   440
And the assistance of a heav'nly Muse
And pencil represents the crimes abstruse.
Here needs no sword, no fleet, no foreign foe:
Only let vice be damn'd and justice flow.
Shake but like Jove thy locks divine and frown—   445
Thy sceptre will suffice to guard thy crown.
Hark to Cassandra's song ere Fate destroy,
By thy own navy's wooden horse, thy Troy.

Us our Apollo from the tumult's wave
And gentle gales, though but in oars, will save.   450
     So Philomel her sad embroid'ry strung,
And vocal silks tuned with her needle's tongue.
The picture dumb in colors loud revealed
The tragedies of court so long concealed
But when restored to voice, increased with wings,   455
To woods and groves, what once she painted, sings.

449–50. Apollo was a patron deity of Troy. According to legend, England was Troynovant.
Here *oars* are small boats as opposed to men-of-war.

The Answer of Mr. Waller's Painter to
His Many New Advisers
(1667)

The series of mock *Advices* and *Instructions* provoked some loyal soul to assume the role of the harassed painter in this witty rejoinder published as a pamphlet in 1667. His protest against satirical painter poems was vain, however, for the convention continued in popularity well into the following century (see Mary Tom Osborne's *Advice-to-a-Painter Poems, 1949*).

The Answer of Mr. Waller's Painter to His Many New Advisers

Good sirs, be civil, can one man, d'ye think,
As fast lay colors as you all spill ink?
At what a pass am I! A thousand hands
I need, if I must be at all commands.
Thy sparkling fancy, Waller, first designed   5
A stately piece, true picture of thy mind.
But (how conceits engender!) on thy wit
Each scribbler new *Advices* doth beget;
And so the breed's embased, that now 'tis grown
Like royal blood when mixed with the clown.   10
'Twas racy wine ran from thy loyal quill,
But these their brandy from its dregs distill,
Or, like false vintners, they adulterate
Thy nectar with a poisonous sublimate.
Without thy muse thy fancy they purloin,   15
And bastard scions to thy stock they join.
Thus in dead bodies Satan acts a soul,
And Virgil's self's travestied to a droll.

9. *embased*: debased, obs.
18. Several burlesques of various books of the *Aeneid*, entitled *Scarronides*, appeared in 1664 and 1665. One was written by R. Monsey and others by Charles Cotton.

I shall forswear my art if I must be
Thus schooled by bunglers, whilst I paint for thee;   20
Or if I must each new adviser please,
Jumble our world with the Antipodes,
And mix the firmament and Stygian lake,
A chaos, not a picture, I shall make.
And then (as he that marred a noble draught   25
By alt'ring it as each spectator taught)
I shall forswear the piece, too, and write by:
This monster my advisers made, not I.
      However, sirs, my colors will not do,
And therefore I must be supplied by you.   30
I have no mixtures to paint Treason's face
So fair, for Loyalty to make it pass,
None that will blemish princes on report,
Which none dares own, to make the rabble sport.
Besides, Slander's a fading color: though   35
It stick a while, it will not long do so.
If I make use of that, this I shall have,
When it decays, my work will prove me knave.
      Yea princes, sirs, are gods, as they're above,
Though as men in a mortal sphere they move.   40
As gods, 'tis sacrilegious to present
Them in such shapes as may bespeak contempt,
And who allows 'em men does therewithal
Allow 'em possibility to fall.
Yet paint not their infirmities. Would you   45
In each foul posture be exposed to view?
Baulk not the noble rule and let them have
The charity, at least, that you would crave.
      My colors will not alter forms of state
After the whimsies of each crowing pate.   50
What paint will draw utopias, or where
Shall the groundwork be for castles in the air?
What colors wears the man i' the moon? Who can
Limn an *Oceana* or *Leviathan?*
Rob the chameleon, sirs, or polypus   55
For colors, if you mean t'employ me thus.
      Fie, at the old play still! What have we got

54. *Oceana:* the model commonwealth described by the Republican political theorist James Harrington in *The Commonwealth of Oceana* (1656). *Leviathan* refers, of course, to Thomas Hobbes's famous anatomy of political power published in 1651.

By Rotas, ballots, and I know not what?
Who cheats me once, he fools me, but 'tis plain
I fool myself to deal with him again.   60
Bought wit is best, 'tis said, but who buys oft
Shall never sell it at the rates he bought.
Cast up your books, sirs, and I dare engage
Creditor's falls short of the debtor's page.
Unhinge not governments except you could   65
Supply us better ere you change the old.
You would have all amended. So would I,
Yet not deface each piece where faults I spy.
'Tis true I could find colors to expose
Faulty grandees and over-paint a rose,   70
But this checks me, that whatsoe'er is aimed,
Few such are mended by being proclaimed.
Public disgrace oft smaller sinners scares,
But vice with greatness armed no colors fears.
Besides, the rout grows insolent hereby,   75
And slights the once disgraced authority,
Whence, to paint all our betters' faults would be
To hang up order in effigie.
Leave such, then, to their masters and the laws;
Who play with lions at last feel their paws.   80
    But one word more, sirs: grant I yield to you,
Am I secure I have no more to do?
If thus *Advices* spawn, your three or four
May shortly propagate to half a score,
And those, by hundreds multiplied, may make   85
A task Briareus would not undertake,
Besides the clash—"Dash out that line!" says one;
Another, "Alter this, let that alone!"
So Babel's builders marred their tow'r and made
An heap unlike the project that they laid.   90
    Pray leave advising then, for (never crave it)
No art can paint a world as all would have it,
Or, if you're set upon't, to fit your mind,

58. The Rota was a club formed by Harrington just before the Restoration to discuss his political schemes, which included elaborate systems for balloting and for rotating representatives.

61. See Aphra Behn, *Sir Patient Fancy* (1678), II.i.38; " 'Twas a saying of my grandmother's . . . that **bought** wit was best" (quoted in Tilley, *Dictionary of the Proverbs in England*).

78. *effigie:* pronounced as four syllables.

86. *Briareus:* one of three Hecatoncheires (hundred-handed giants).

I'll tell you where a painter you may find.
Look out some canvas-stainer, whose cheap skill   95
With rhythms and stories alehouse-walls doth fill.
Such men will do your work best—sorry elves—
They paint all kings and princes like themselves.
So, with jack-wheels upon their heads, they slander
Arthur and Godfrey and great Alexander.   100
Here David stands with's harp of whipcord-strings,
And Solomon's wives who, sure, loved no such things,
Yea, Ahab and Queen Jezebel, who ne'er
Painted herself as she is painted there.
Thus th' Royal Oak in country signs is found   105
In a park copied from the neighbor pound,
And royal Charles's head looks peeping through,
Much in the posture that's the dauber's due.
Employ these, then, not me, except you please
To use my art on your own visages.   110
Those I know who would thank me for 't, and then
Your faces might be famous as your pen.
And, lastly, that done, three large dashes by
I doubt would serve to paint your destiny.

95–96. Cf. *Last Instructions*, 7–11.
99. *jack-wheels:* wheels from roasting-spits.
105. *Royal Oak:* the tree at Boscobel in which Charles II was concealed after the Battle of
Worcester.
106. *neighbor:* neighboring.

The Downfall of the Chancellor
(1667)

As the preceding painter poems show, opposition to Clarendon increased steadily from the time of the Uniformity Act (1662). Nonconformists held him responsible for the hated Conventicle Act (1664) and the Five Mile Act (1665). Old Cavaliers blamed him for the government's failure to reward them with places in the new administration. He was condemned, unjustifiably, for promulgating the king's marriage to a barren and Catholic queen and for contriving the Dutch war, which ended in the humiliating defeats of the summer of 1667. While Parliament bitterly resented his efforts to curb its increasing encroachments on the royal prerogative, the king grew steadily more restive under the chancellor's uncompromising disapproval of his personal conduct. When a rumor sprang up after the prorogation of 9 July 1667 that Clarendon was urging the king to rule without Parliament by means of a standing army, Charles refused to clear his minister of a charge he privately conceded was groundless.

For personal reasons, and as a gesture of appeasement to the House of Commons, Charles removed Clarendon from office on August 30. When Parliament met in October, the chancellor's enemies, still unsatisfied, trumped up several charges against him, including the accusation that Clarendon had treasonously betrayed the king's counsels to his enemies. When Clarendon finally realized that the king would do nothing in his defense, but was indeed through intermediaries urging him to flee, he left England on November 29 for exile in France.

The *Downfall of the Chancellor* sums up most of the allegations against Clarendon and gives voice to the widespread hatred that he incurred.

Edward Earle of CLARENDON, *Lord High* CHANCELLOR *of England and Chancellor of the University of Oxford. An:° D͠ni 1667.*

Edward Hyde, earl of Clarendon. From an engraving by R. White after the portrait by Lely.

Pride, lust, ambition, and the people's hate,
The kingdom's broker, ruin of the state,
Dunkirk's sad loss, divider of the fleet,
Tangier's compounder for a barren sheet,
This shrub of gentry, married to the crown   5
(His daughter to the heir), is tumbled down.
The grand affronter of the nobles lies,
Grov'ling in dust, as a just sacrifice
T' appease the injured king and abused nation.
Who could expect this sudden alteration?   10
God is revenged too for the stones he took
From aged Paul's to make a nest for th' rook.
More cormorants of state as well as he
We shortly hope in the same plight to see.
Go on, great prince! the people to rejoice: 15
Methinks I hear the nation's total voice
Applauding this day's action to be such
As roasting Rump or beating of the Dutch.
Now look upon the withered Cavaliers,
Who for reward have nothing had but tears,   20
Thanks to this Wiltshire hog, son of the spittle—
Had they been looked on, he had had but little.
Break up the coffers of this hoarding thief:
There millions will be found for their relief.
I've said enough of linsey-woolsey Hyde—   25
His sacrilege, ambition, lust, and pride.

3. For Clarendon's reluctant part in the sale of Dunkirk see *Second Advice*, 149–50 *n*. For the disastrous division of the fleet in May 1666 see *Third Advice*, 21–28 and *n*.
4. *Tangier* was part of the queen's dowry.
5. *shrub:* a mean, inferior, insignificant person, obs.
11–12. When old St. Paul's was demolished Clarendon bought the stones to finish his house.
12. *rook:* cheat.
21. Hyde was born in Dinton, Wiltshire. *spittle:* a house for the indigent or diseased.
25. *linsey-woolsey:* Being neither one thing nor the other, also with an allusion, perhaps, to Hyde's allegedly humble origins.

ANDREW MARVELL

The Last Instructions to a Painter
(1667)

The Last Instructions to a Painter is concerned with parliamentary, court, administrative, and naval affairs between September 1666 and the downfall of Clarendon in the following autumn. The opening couplet links the poem explicitly to the two earlier *Advices,* and there are throughout numerous allusions to those satires and to Waller's encomiastic *Instructions,* which serves them ironically as a model. This sequence of three satirical painter poems thus provides a complete and continuous record of England's part in the second Dutch war. Although it amounts to a massive indictment of Clarendon's administration and the court party in the House of Commons, the record is in the main remarkably faithful to the facts insofar as they can be determined from other sources.

No other Restoration poem is more comprehensive or specific in its treatment of public affairs. Not even the ubiquitous and omniscient Pepys is so accurate in recording the events of this crucial last year of the war. After a preliminary sketch of England's besotted pro-French envoy, the earl of St. Albans, who was trying to procure Louis XIV's intervention as a peacemaker with the Low Countries, the satirist proceeds to attack with unrivaled bitterness that most unpopular member of Charles II's petticoat government, the Catholic countess of Castlemaine. The poem is studded with vivid portraits of important public figures—with hated ones like Clarendon, Sir William Coventry and his brother Henry, York and his duchess, the earl of Arlington, and so forth—and with a smaller group of patriots ("the race of English gentry nobly born") like Strangeways, Tomkins, and the heroic warrior Douglas.

These portraits are, however, subordinate in interest to two long narrative sections: the first (lines 105–334) dealing principally with the momentous session of the House of Commons in 1666; the second (523–760) recounting the Dutch attack on the unprepared British ships in the Thames and the Medway the following summer. As in the two earlier *Advices,* the chief naval action of the summer (here, the most disgraceful maritime defeat in England's history) is the climactic action of the poem, while the narrative of parliamentary issues not only provides the background for this event but provides a record of the partisan struggle over finances in the fall of 1666 unequaled in other sources. The main work of that session was to devise means to raise the royal supply of £1,800,000. The court party favored a general excise on domestic goods, which the country party and some independent M.P.s regarded as tyrannous and inquisitional. This issue of the general excise (not to be confused with the foreign excise) is scarcely mentioned in standard parliamentary records. The only adequate record outside this poem is found in Milward's *Diary* edited by Caroline Robbins, who cites *Last Instructions* to corroborate her author's account. The excise was defeated 8 November 1666 and the supply was raised by a hearth tax, a land tax (favored by the country party), and a foreign excise. But though the general excise was defeated and might therefore be well forgotten, it seems from the accounts of *Last Instructions* and Milward to have been the most important issue in crystallizing the antagonists into political parties.

Last Instructions culminates brilliantly in the night scene where the king is visited by a visionary nude figure ("England or the Peace") who tries to warn him about his evil counselors and favorites. The warning is vain, however, for the merry monarch, failing to recognize the lady's allegorical status, responds to her appeals with misdirected but characteristic gallantry (see lines 899–904). The poem abounds in mixtures of the grave and the absurd. It displays a remarkably wide range of tones from the scurrilities on Birch and the excise (142–46), which gain force from the echoes of *Paradise Lost* (published a few months before *Last Instructions* was composed), to the pastoral beauty of De Ruyter's passage up the Thames (522–50) or the metaphysical fervor of the elegy on Douglas (649–96, which forms the nucleus of another poem, *The Loyal Scot*), with their overtones of Spenser, Shakespeare, and Marvell himself. Despite the exhaustive factual information that *Last Instructions* requires, it transmutes its facts into an outstanding satirical poem of great historical interest and considerable poetic force.

Possibly because of the government's strenuous efforts to apprehend the author and the printer of the second and third *Advices*, *Last Instructions* was not published until 1689. There is a manuscript in the Osborn collection and the poem is also included in a Marvell manuscript, Bod. MS Eng. poet. d. 49, the version printed here. As to authorship, I agree with Margoliouth's statement that "of all the satires attributed to Marvell there is none of which one can feel less doubt." Only an active M.P. versed in maritime affairs and a patriot of Marvell's political complexion possessing Marvell's poetic power could have written it.

THE LAST INSTRUCTIONS TO A PAINTER

London, September 4th, 1667

After two sittings, now, our Lady State,
To end her picture, does the third time wait.
But ere thou fall'st to work, first, Painter, see
It be'nt too slight grown or too hard for thee.
Canst thou paint without colors? Then 'tis right: 5
For so we too without a fleet can fight.
Or canst thou daub a sign-post, and that ill?
'Twill suit our great debauch and little skill.
Or hast thou marked how antic masters limn
The aly-roof with snuff of candle dim,   10
Sketching in shady smoke prodigious tools?
'Twill serve this race of drunkards, pimps, and fools.
But if to match our crimes thy skill presumes,
As th' Indians, draw our luxury in plumes.
Or if to score out our compendious fame,   15
With Hooke, then, through the microscope take aim,
Where, like the new comptroller, all men laugh
To see a tall louse brandish the white staff.
Else shalt thou oft thy guiltless pencil curse,
Stamp on thy palette, nor perhaps the worse.   20
The painter so, long having vexed his cloth,
Of his hound's mouth to feign the raging froth,
His desp'rate pencil at the work did dart:
His anger reached that rage which passed his art;
Chance finished that which art could but begin,   25
And he sat smiling how his dog did grin.
So may'st thou perfect by a lucky blow

1–2. Three sittings was the usual number for "limning" a portrait. The first two, of course, were described in the *Second Advice* and *Third Advice*.

6. *without a fleet:* The fleet was laid up in May 1667.

9. *antic masters:* masters of grotesque painting.

10. *aly-roof:* ceiling of an alehouse or tavern.

14. The Indians of Florida and the Caribbean developed the art of "painting" by arranging various colors and sizes of feathers and gluing them together. Such paintings were necessarily on a large scale. *Plumes* would also represent fittingly the luxury of the court.

15. *score out:* sketch in outline. *compendious:* minute.

16–18. Robert Hooke (1635–1703) was an experimental philosopher and fellow of the Royal Society. In his *Micrographia* (1665) he depicted various objects seen under the microscope, among which was a louse climbing a human hair, which Marvell here compares to the new comptroller of the household, Lord Clifford of Chudleigh, who took office in November 1660. The comptroller carried a white staff as the emblem of his office (Margoliouth).

What all thy softest touches cannot do.
   Paint then St. Albans full of soup and gold,
The new court's pattern, stallion of the old.   30
Him neither wit nor courage did exalt,
But Fortune chose him for her pleasure salt.
Paint him with drayman's shoulders, butcher's mien,
Membered like mules, with elephantine chine.
Well he the title of St. Albans bore,   35
For Bacon never studied nature more.
But age, allaying now that youthful heat,
Fits him in France to play at cards and treat.
Draw no commission, lest the court should lie,
That, disavowing treaty, asks supply;   40
He needs no seal but to St. James's lease,
Whose breeches were the instrument of peace;
Who, if the French dispute his pow'r, from thence
Can straight produce them a plenipotence.
Nor fears he the most Christian should trepan   45
Two saints at once, St. Germain, St. Alban,
But thought the Golden Age was now restored,
When men and women took each other's word.

29. *St. Albans:* Henry Jermyn, earl of St. Albans (d. 1684), was ambassador at the French court at the beginning of Charles II's reign. He was sent to France in January 1667 to negotiate a treaty with Louis XIV. In his youth he acquired the reputation of a rake and was once banished from court for seducing Eleanor Villiers, a Lady of Honor. He was rumored to have married Queen Henrietta Maria and devoted his old age to the pleasures of the table and to cards.

35–36. In this couplet Marvell wryly compares the lecherous earl of St. Albans with the great exponent of the inductive approach to nature, Francis Bacon, first Baron Verulam and Viscount St. Albans (1561–1626).

38. *treat:* (1) to entertain, (2) to negotiate a treaty.

39. The negotiations undertaken by St. Albans were at first informal and unofficial, and Marvell attributes this failure to send a duly authorized ambassador with commission and seal to the court's desire for a large grant from Parliament. Parliament did in fact vote £1,800,000, but there was much resentment about alleged waste in the expenditure of earlier grants.

41. *St. James's lease:* St. Albans obtained a large grant of land in Pall Mall and planned St. James's Square.

42. This line seems to refer somewhat obscurely to St. Albans's widely rumored affair with Henrietta Maria. Whether or not such an affair took place, his influence with the Queen Mother was great, and it was through her that Louis XIV was persuaded to consider negotiations for peace between Holland and Britain.

43–44. These lines carry on the suggestion of line 42 about the source of St. Albans's authority to negotiate. "St. Albans's instructions, drafted by Clarendon, did not empower him even to sign preliminaries" (Feiling, *Foreign Policy*).

45. *the most Christian:* Louis XIV. *trepan:* entrap.

46. *St. Germain, St. Alban;* a play on the ambassador's name and title and on the quarter of Paris in which he resided.

Paint then again Her Highness to the life,
Philosopher beyond Newcastle's wife.   50
She naked can Arch'medes' self put down,
For an experiment upon the crown.
She perfected that engine, oft assayed,
How after childbirth to renew a maid,
And found how royal heirs might be matured   55
In fewer months than mothers once endured.
Hence Crowther made the rare inventress free
Of's Highness's Royal Society—
Happiest of women, if she were but able
To make her glassen dukes once malleable!   60
Paint her with oyster lip and breath of fame,
Wide mouth that 'sparagus may well proclaim;
With chanc'llor's belly and so large a rump,
There (not behind the coach) her pages jump.
Express her studying now if china clay   65

49–78. These lines contain much popular gossip about Anne Hyde, duchess of York. (See *Second Advice*, 69 n.) Lines 49–58 refer to the allegations against her chastity made by two of the duke's friends, Sir Charles Berkeley and Henry Jermyn (St. Albans's nephew), who wished to prevent the recognition of the marriage. For further details see *Third Advice*, 251–54 and n.
  Margaret Brooke, Lady Denham, became York's mistress in 1665, and Sir John Denham's madness was widely attributed to grief at this development. She is the "Madam Édificatresse" referred to in *Second Advice*, 340, and is mentioned in the opening line of *Third Advice*. Her sudden death on 6 January 1667 was thought, without evidence, to be from poison introduced into her cocoa, and Denham and the countess of Rochester were both blamed. Marvell, however, introduces the suggestion that the duchess of York was the culprit, an idea that agrees with the attack on her in *Third Advice*, 245–46.
  50–54. The satirical pretense that the duchess had discovered *how after childbirth to renew a maid* appears also in *Third Advice*, 253–54, where the renewal of lost virginity is attributed jointly to Berkeley's recantation and, ironically, to the intervention of Cardinal Mazarin, who prevailed on Queen Henrietta Maria to drop her opposition to the marriage. Here Anne is presented as a *philosopher* (natural philosopher or scientist) and inventress whose *engine* (device) for restoring virginity makes her superior to her friend the famed bluestocking, Margaret, duchess of *Newcastle*, and even to *Archimedes*. Archimedes founded the science of hydrostatics, as the well-known legend has it, by discovering the principle of displacement while taking a bath. He applied this principle in answering a question from a prince named Hiero, who feared that his gold crown might be alloyed with silver. In the same manner, Marvell suggests, the duchess has devised some way of demonstrating that she is not a light woman and thereby could make *an experiment upon the crown*, that is, an attempt upon it, either for herself (as future queen) or through her children. A similar ambitiousness in the Hyde family is attributed to her father in *Second Advice*, 153–54, and to Anne in *Third Advice*, 245–46.
  58. The duke of York was a charter member of the Royal Society.
  60. *glassen dukes:* a reference to the other short-lived children of this marriage: James, duke of Cambridge (born 12 July, 1663 and died 22 May, 1667) and Charles, duke of Kendal (born 4 July, 1666 and died 22 May, 1667).
  65–68. Margoliouth cites Browne, *Pseudodooxia Epidemica* (1646): "Surely the properties must be verified which by Scaliger and others are ascribed to china dishes, that they admit no poison, that they strike fire . . . for such as pass amongst us . . . will only strike fire, but not discover aconite, mercury, nor arsenic" (2, 5, sec. 7).

Can, without breaking, venomed juice convey,
Or how a mortal poison she may draw
Out of the cordial meal of the cacao.
Witness, ye stars of night, and thou the pale
Moon, that o'ercome with the sick steam did'st fail;   70
Ye neighb'ring elms, that your green leaves did shed,
And fauns, that from the womb abortive fled!
Not unprovoked, she tries forbidden arts,
But in her soft breast love's hid cancer smarts,
While she revolves at once Sidney's disgrace,   75
And her self scorned for emulous Denham's face,
And nightly hears the hated guards away
Galloping with the duke to other prey.
   Paint Castlemaine in colors that will hold
(Her, not her picture, for she now grows old):   80
She through her lackey's drawers, as he ran,
Discerned love's cause and a new flame began.
Her wonted joys thenceforth and court she shuns,
And still within her mind the footman runs:
His brazen calves, his brawny thighs (the face   85
She slights), his feet shaped for a smoother race.
Poring within her glass she readjusts
Her looks and oft-tried beauty now distrusts;
Fears lest he scorn a woman once assayed,
And now first wished she e'er had been a maid.   90
Great Love, how dost thou triumph and how reign,
That to a groom could'st humble her disdain!
Stripped to her skin, see how she stooping stands,
Nor scorns to rub him down with those fair hands,
And washing (lest the scent her crime disclose)   95
His sweaty hooves, tickles him 'twixt the toes.
But envious Fame, too soon, began to note
More gold in's fob, more lace upon his coat,
And he, unwary and of tongue too fleet,
No longer could conceal his fortune sweet.   100
Justly the rogue was whipped in porter's den,
And Jermyn straight has leave to come again.

69–74. This description of the duchess's black arts seems indebted in a general way to
Ovid's account of Medea's trafficking in sorcery (Ovid, *Metamorphoses*, 7).

75. Henry Sidney (1641-1704) Groom of the Bedchamber to the duke and Master of the
Horse to the duchess, was dismissed as a result of the duke's jealousy.

79–104. Although most of Lady Castlemaine's many love affairs seem to be minutely and
extensively recorded, this seems to be the only account of her alliance with the lackey.

Ah, Painter, now could Alexander live,
And this Campaspe thee, Apelles, give!
　　Draw next a pair of tables op'ning, then　　　　　　　　　105
The House of Commons clatt'ring like the men.
Describe the court and country, both set right
On opposite points, the black against the white.
Those having lost the nation at trick-track,
These now advent'ring how to win it back.　　　　　　　　110
The dice betwixt them must the fate divide
(As chance doth still in multitudes decide).
But here the court does its advantage know,
For the cheat Turnor for them both must throw.　　　　　　115
As some from boxes, he so from the chair
Can strike the die and still with them goes share.
　　Here, Painter, rest a little, and survey
With what small arts the public game they play.
For so, too, Rubens, with affairs of state,
His lab'ring pencil oft would recreate.　　　　　　　　　　120
　　The close cabal marked how the navy eats,
And thought all lost that goes not to the cheats;
So therefore secretly for peace decrees,
Yet as for war the Parliament would squeeze,
And fix to the revenue such a sum　　　　　　　　　　　　125
Should Goodrick silence and strike Paston dumb,
Should pay land armies, should dissolve the vain
Commons, and ever such a court maintain;

104. Apelles was court painter to Alexander of Macedonia, and fell in love with Alexander's mistress, Campaspe.

105–10. *trick-track*: a kind of backgammon on *tables*. The players (*men*) represent the two parliamentary parties: the court party, whose chiefs are enumerated in lines 113–238, and the country party, whose chiefs appear in lines 239–306. The battle, which is won by the country party with which Marvell's sympathies obviously lie, is fought on the issue of a general excise which the court party wished to impose in order to raise the £1,800,000 (line 332) voted late in 1666. The general excise was defeated on 8 November 1666.

114. *Turnor*: Sir Edward Turnor (1617–76), speaker of the House of Commons, 1661–73. *Cheat* may refer simply to several large gifts bestowed on him from the treasury through royal favor, though he was later removed as solicitor-general, according to Roger North, for having received a trifling gratuity from the East India Company.

116. *strike the die*: throw in some particularly fraudulent manner.

120. *recreate*: refresh (by change of occupation). Rubens was occasionally sent on diplomatic missions.

121. *cabal*: a committee for foreign affairs drawn from the Privy Council.

126. *Goodrick*: Sir John Goodrick, M.P. for the county of York, who sometimes acted as teller for the court party during this session (Margoliouth). Paston first moved the huge appropriation of £2,500,000 for the war. See *Second Advice*, 109–16.

Hyde's avarice, Bennet's luxury should suffice,
And what can these defray but the excise?   130
Excise, a monster worse than e'er before
Frighted the midwife and the mother tore.
A thousand hands she has and thousand eyes,
Breaks into shops and into cellars pries,
With hundred rows of teeth the shark exceeds,   135
And on all trade like cassowar she feeds:
Chops off the piece where'er she close the jaw,
Else swallows all down her indented maw.
She stalks all day in streets concealed from sight
And flies, like bats with leathern wings, by night;   140
She wastes the country and on cities preys.
Her, of a female harpy, in dog days,
Black Birch, of all the earth-born race most hot
And most rapacious, like himself, begot;
And, of his brat enamoured, as't increased,   145
Buggered in incest with the mongrel beast.
    Say, Muse, for nothing can escape thy sight
(And, Painter, wanting other, draw this fight),
Who, in an English senate, fierce debate
Could raise so long for this new whore of state.   150
    Of early wittals first the troop marched in,
For diligence renowned and discipline;
In royal haste they left young wives in bed,
And Denham these by one consent did head.
Of the old courtiers next a squadron came,   155
That sold their master, led by Ashburnham.
To them succeeds a despicable rout,
But know the word and well could face about;
Expectants pale, with hopes of spoil allured,
Though yet but pioneers, and led by Stew'rd.   160

136. *cassowar*: the omnivorous cassowary.

142–46. In matter and manner this passage seems to be a mock-epic imitation of the incestuous relationship of Satan to his daughter Sin, which produced Death. See *Paradise Lost*, 2:746–85. Milton's epic was first published in 1667.

143. *Birch*: John Birch (1616–91), excise official under the Protectorate and auditor after the Restoration.

151. *wittals*: cuckolds.

156. *Ashburnham*: John Ashburnham (1603–71) who, with Sir John Berkeley, arranged King Charles I's flight to the Isle of Wight. For a long time he was suspected of having betrayed the king to the governor of the island.

160. *Stew'rd*: Sir Nicholas Steward (1616–1710), M.P. for Lymington Borough.

The damning cowards ranged the vocal plain,
Wood these commands, Knight of the Horn and Cane.
Still his hook-shoulder seems the blow to dread,
And under's armpit he defends his head.
The posture strange men laughed at, of his poll,   165
Hid with his elbow like the spice he stole.
Headless St. Dennis so his head does bear,
And both of them alike French martyrs were.
And followed Fox, but with disdainful look.   170
His birth, his youth, his brokage all dispraise,
In vain, for always he commands that pays.
Then the procurers under Progers filed,
Gentlest of men, and his lieutenant mild,
Brouncker, Love's squire: through all the field arrayed,   175
No troop was better clad nor so well paid.
Then marched the troop of Clarendon, all full,
Haters of fowl, to teal preferring bull:
Gross bodies, grosser minds, and grossest cheats,
And bloated Wren conducts them to their seats.   180
Charlton advances next, whose coif does awe
The Mitre troop, and with his looks gives law.
He marched with beaver cocked of bishop's brim,
And hid much fraud under an aspect grim.
Next the lawyers' mercenary band appear: 185
Finch in the front and Thurland in the rear.

162. *Wood:* Sir Henry Wood (1597–1671), Clerk of the Spicery to Charles I, M.P. for Hythe, a clerk comptroller of the Board of Green Cloth, in which capacity he was responsible for maintaining order in the palace and for examining the accounts.

170. *Fox:* Sir Stephen Fox (1627–1716), M.P. for Salisbury and paymaster-general. He came from a modest Wiltshire family and after an early training in bookkeeping was employed by the Percys. In 1654 he took charge of Charles II's household.

171. *brokage:* the premium or commission of a broker. Fox made a profit on money advanced to pay the soldiers.

173. *Progers:* Edward Progers, M.P. for Brecon and one of the king's procurers.

175. *Brouncker:* cf *Second Advice*, 239–42 n.

178. A play on the name of John Bulteel, M.P. for Lostwithiel and secretary to the earl of Clarendon.

180. *Wren:* Matthew Wren (1629–72), original member of the Royal Society and cousin of Christopher Wren, M.P. for St. Michael, secretary to Clarendon, 1660–67, and to York, 1667–72.

181–82. *Charlton:* Sir Job Charlton (1614–97), M.P. for Ludlow and chief justice of Chester. *The Mitre troop* presumably refers to a group of lawyers associated with Mitre Court, one of the Inns of Court since demolished. Charlton later became speaker. Roger North described him as "an old Cavalier, loyal, learned, grave, and wise."

186. *Finch:* Heneage Finch (1621–82). Solicitor-general and member for Oxford University, who supported oppressive measures against Dissenters. Compare note to line 256. *Thurland:* Sir Edward Thurland (1624–85), M.P. for Reigate and solicitor to the duke of York.

The troop of privilege, a rabble bare
Of debtors deep, fell to Trelawny's care.
Their fortune's error they supplied in rage,
Nor any further would than these engage.   190
Then marched the troop, whose valiant acts before
(Their public acts) obliged them still to more.
For chimney's sake they all Sir Pool obeyed,
Or, in his absence, him that first it laid,
Then comes the thrifty troop of privateers,   195
Whose horses each with other interferes.
Before them Higgons rides with brow compact,
Mourning his countess, anxious for his act.
Sir Fred'rick and Sir Salomon draw lots
For the command of politics or sots,   200
Thence fell to words, but, quarrel to adjourn,
Their friends agreed they should command by turn.
Cart'ret the rich did the accountants guide
And in ill English all the world defied.
The Papists—but of these the House had none;   205
Else Talbot offered to have led them on.
Bold Duncombe next, of the projectors chief,

187. *The troop of privilege:* those who relied on the immunity of parliamentary privilege to avoid arrest for debt.

188. *Trelawny:* Sir Jonathan Trelawny (1624–85) was ruined by sequestration but, according to *Flagellum Parliamentarium* (1677), later made a fortune as an informer.

193. Sir Courtenay Pool, M.P. for Honiton, proposed the hated hearth tax (chimney money) of two shillings on every hearth in 1662.

195. *thrifty troop of privateers:* those who, like Higgons (see below, line 197) sought to enrich themselves by the passage of private bills, and whose horses are therefore represented as overriding each other.

197. *Higgons:* Sir Thomas Higgons (1624–91), court party M.P. for New Windsor, who introduced a bill in the session of 1666–67 for the recovery of £4,500. Marvell reports the defeat of this bill on 12 January 1667. Higgons married the widow of the earl of Essex and published an oration delivered at her funeral in 1656.

199. *Sir Fred'rick and Sir Salomon:* Sir Frederick Hyde (court party M.P. for Haverfordwest) and Sir Salomon Swale (court party M.P. for Aldborough). Swale was a Roman Catholic and opposed the bill against recusants at this session.

200. *politics:* politicians.

203. *Cart'ret:* Sir George Cartaret (d. 1680), a treasurer of the navy after the Restoration. He served in the navy from childhood (see Pepys, 4 July 1663, on his lack of education) and resigned his post while the Dutch were in the Medway.

206. There were three Talbots in the Commons at this time, and two of them appear in *Flagellum Parliamentarium:* Sir Gilbert Talbot, "the king's jeweller, a great cheat at bowls and cards, not born to a shilling," and Sir John Talbot, "commissioner of prizes and a great cheater therein." The Talbots were an Irish Roman Catholic family.

207. *Duncombe:* Sir John Duncombe, a privy councillor, once commissioner of the ordinance, now of the treasury, and Baptist May's brother-in-law. *projectors:* schemers, speculators, cheats.

And old Fitzhardinge of the Eaters Beef.
Late and disordered, out the drinkers drew;
Scarce them their leaders, they their leaders knew.   210
Before them entered, equal in command,
Apsley and Brod'rick, marching hand in hand.
Last then but one, Powell, that could not ride,
Led the French standard, welt'ring in his stride.
He, to excuse his slowness, truth confessed   215
That 'twas so long before he could be dressed.
The lords' sons, last, all these did reinforce:
Cornb'ry before them managed hobby-horse.
    Never before, nor since, an host so steeled
Trooped on to muster in the Tothill Field: 220
Not the first cock-horse, that with cork were shod
To rescue Albemarle from the sea-cod,
Nor the late feather-men, whom Tomkins fierce
Shall with one breath like thistledown disperse.
All the two Coventrys their gen'rals choose,   225
For one had much, the other nought to lose;
Nor better choice all accidents could hit,
While Hector Harry steers by Will the Wit.
They both accept the charge with merry glee,
To fight a battle from all gunshot free.   230

208. *Fitzhardinge:* Sir Charles Berkeley (1600–68), second Viscount Fitzhardinge in the Irish peerage and treasurer of the household, in which capacity he was in charge of the yeomen of the guard. This is the first known instance of their being called beefeaters.

212. *Apsley:* Sir Allen Apsley (1616–83), treasurer of the duke of York's household. *Brod'-rick:* Sir Allen Broderick, M.P. for both Orford and Calington (Cornwall).

213–14. *Powell:* Sir Richard Powell, Gentleman of the Horse to the duchess of York. *French standard* is an allusion to the pox, which caused him to *welter in his stride.*

218. *Cornb'ry:* Henry Hyde, Lord Cornbury (1638–1709), Clarendon's eldest son, chamberlain to the queen. *hobby-horse:* perhaps an allusion to his youth.

220. *Tothill Field:* Tothill Fields, Westminster, used for drilling troops.

221–22. This obscure couplet alludes to the rescue of Albemarle by Rupert in the Four Days' Fight (1–4 June 1666). *Sea-cod* represents De Ruyter, who was prevented from destroying Albemarle's ship by Rupert's intervention. Compare the sea dragon in *Third Advice,* 135–42. *Cock-horse* shod with cork may refer obscurely to Rupert's career as a famous cavalry leader in the civil wars.

223–24. The *feather-men* are probably the standing army raised by the government in the spring of 1667 ostensibly to prevent an invasion, which Sir Thomas Tomkins spoke against in the abortive parliamentary session of 25–29 July 1667.

225–34. The *two Coventrys* are Henry *(*1619–86*)* and Sir William (1628?–86), who "practically led the House" *(DNB).* Henry had "nought to lose," because, having concluded an embassy to Sweden, he was now without an appointment from the government, and Sir William much to lose, because he was commissioner of the treasury and of the navy and could protect the large profits allegedly made from these posts by active leadership of the court party.

Pleased with their numbers, yet in valor wise,
They feign a parley, better to surprise:
They that ere long shall the rude Dutch upbraid,
Who in a time of treaty durst invade.
   Thick was the morning, and the House was thin,   235
The speaker early, when they all fell in.
Propitious heavens, had not you them crossed,
Excise had got the day and all been lost!
For th' other side all in loose quarters lay,
Without intelligence, command, or pay: 240
A scattered body, which the foe ne'er tried,
But oft'ner did among themselves divide.
And some ran o'er each night, while others sleep,
And undescried returned ere morning peep.
But Strangeways, that all night still walked the round   245
(For vigilance and courage both renowned)
First spied the enemy and gave th' alarm,
Fighting it single till the rest might arm.
Such Roman Cocles strid before the foe,
The falling bridge behind, the stream below.   250
Each ran, as chance him guides, to sev'ral post,
And all to pattern his example boast.
Their former trophies they recall to mind
And to new edge their angry courage grind.
First entered forward Temple, conqueror   255
Or Irish cattle and solicitor;
Then daring Seymour, that with spear and shield,

233–34. Henry Coventry was one of the ambassadors who negotiated the Dutch peace, and his brother is held chiefly responsible for having failed to prepare the fleet on the grounds that peace was expected.

235–36. The court party M.P.s proposed the grant of £1,800,000 for the king before all the country party M.P.s had assembled. On October 12, "The court party moved for a general excise of all things, which was no way pleasing" (Milward). *speaker:* Turnor.

239. *loose quarters:* indefensible positions; opposite of close quarters.

245. *Strangeways:* Sir John Strangeways, who acted as teller against the government in several divisions on finance during this session.

249. *Cocles:* Publius Horatius Cocles (Macaulay's "Horatius at the Bridge"), who defended single-handedly a bridge leading into Rome against the army of Porsena, king of Etruria.

255. *Temple:* Sir Richard Temple, a leader of the country party who supported the act against the importation of Irish cattle, a major issue in this session. The act passed in January 1667.

256. *solicitor:* Sir Heneage Finch (1621–82), solicitor-general who spoke against the Irish Cattle Bill.

257. *Seymour:* Sir Edward Seymour (1633–1708), later speaker of the House, who attacked the Canary Patent, a charter for merchants trading with the Canary Islands, as an "illegal patent, a monopoly, and a grievance to the subject."

Had stretched the monster Patent on the field;
Keen Whorwood next, in aid of damsel frail
That pierced the giant Mordaunt through his mail,   260
And surly Williams, the accountants' bane,
And Lovelace young, of chimney-men the cane.
Old Waller, trumpet-gen'ral, swore he'd write
This combat truer than the naval fight.
Of birth, state, wit, strength, courage, How'rd presumes   265
And in his breast wears many Montezumes.
These and some more, with single valor, stay
The adverse troops and hold them all at bay.
Each thinks his person represents the whole
And with that thought does multiply his soul,   270
Believes himself an army, theirs one man
As eas'ly conquered; and, believing, can;
With heart of bees so full, and head of mites,
That each, though dueling, a battle fights.
Such once Orlando, famous in romance,   275
Broached whole brigades like larks upon his lance.
    But strength at last still under number bows,
And the faint sweat trickled down Temple's brows.
E'en iron Strangeways, chafing, yet gave back,
Spent with fatigue, to breathe a while toback,   280
When, marching in, a seas'nable recruit
Of citizens and merchants held dispute;
And, charging all their pikes, a sullen band

259–60. *Whorwood:* Brome Whorwood, M.P. for the city of Oxford, who helped draw up an impeachment against John, Viscount *Mordaunt* (1627–75), constable of Windsor Castle, who had allegedly imprisoned one William Tayleur because his daughter would not yield herself to him. On 8 July the King granted Mordaunt a pardon.

261. *Williams:* A committee to investigate public accounts was appointed 26 September 1666. Caroline Robbins identifies Williams as Col. Henry Williams (alias Cromwell), member for Huntingdon.

262. *Lovelace:* John Lovelace (1638?–93), an opponent of the widely hated hearth tax.

263–64. *Waller:* Waller was widely criticized as a political turncoat. "As far as his public utterances went," however, "the second half of his parliamentary career was in every way creditable to him. He spoke with great courage against the dangers of a military despotism, and his voice was constantly raised in appeals for toleration for Dissenters" *(DNB)*. Compare these lines with the opening couplet of *Second Advice. Trumpet-gen'ral* may allude to Waller's position as the poet who celebrates battles but does not participate in them.

265–66. *How'rd:* Sir Robert Howard (1626–98), M.P. for Stockbridge and collaborator and brother-in-law of Dryden with whom he wrote *The Indian Queen* (1665), a drama whose hero is Montezuma. He was prominent in the proceedings against Clarendon.

275–76. The hero of *Orlando Furioso* spitted six enemies at once on his lance.

280. *toback:* tobacco.

281. *recruit:* reinforcements.

Of Presbyterian Switzers made a stand.
Nor could all these the field have long maintained   285
But for th' unknown reserve that still remained,
A gross of English gentry, nobly born,
Of clear estates, and to no faction sworn;
Dear lovers of their king, and death to meet,
For country's cause, that glorious think and sweet;   290
To speak not forward, but in action brave,
In giving gen'rous, but in counsel grave;
Candidly credulous for once, nay twice,
But sure the devil cannot cheat them thrice.
The van and battle, though retiring, falls   295
Without disorder in their intervals,
Then closing, all in equal front, fall on,
Led by great Garr'way and great Littleton.
Lee, ready to obey or to command,
Adjutant-general, was still at hand.   300
The martial standard, Sandys displaying, shows
St. Dunstan in it, tweaking Satan's nose.
See sudden chance of war! To paint or write
Is longer work and harder than to fight.
At the first charge the enemy give out,   305
And the excise receives a total rout.
Broken in courage, yet the men the same,
Resolve henceforth upon their other game:
Where force had failed with stratagem to play
And what haste lost recover by delay.   310

284. *Presbyterian Switzers:* presumably a faction of Presbyterian members who joined the opposition.

298. *Garr'way:* William Garraway (Garway or Garroway), M.P. for Chichester, who examined Pepys's accounts 3 October 1666. According to Pepys, Sir William Coventry spoke of him as ill-used by the court but staunchly loyal to the king (6 October 1666). He seconded Tomkins's motion against the standing army. *Littleton:* Sir Thomas Littleton (d. 1681), 2d baronet, member for Great Wenlock, mentioned by Pepys as "one of the greatest speakers in the House" (18 July 1666).

299. *Lee:* Sir Thomas Lee, member for Aylesbury. Pepys mentions him and Littleton as "professed enemies to us and everybody else," when he was examined by the House, 5 March 1668.

301. *Sandys:* Col. Samuel Sandys, M.P. for Worcestershire.

302–03. "In art St. Dunstan is chiefly honored by a foolish representation of the devil caught by the nose by a pair of blacksmith's pincers. The legend relates that Satan tempted him as he was at work in his forge, by assuming the form of a beautiful girl. Dunstan at once attacked him with his pincers and put him to flight" (S. Baring-Gould, *The Lives of the Saints* [Edinburgh: J. Grant, 1914]). Dunstan (924–88) was bishop of Worcester, hence the connection with Sandys.

St. Albans straight is sent to forbear,
Lest the sure peace, forsooth, too soon appear.
The seamen's clamor to three ends they use:
To cheat their pay, feign want, the House accuse.
Each day they bring the tale, and that too true,   315
How strong the Dutch their equipage renew.
Meantime through all the yards their orders run
To lay the ships up, cease the keels begun.
The timber rots, and useless axe doth rust,
Th' unpracticed saw lies buried in its dust,   320
The busy hammer sleeps, the ropes untwine,
The stores and wages all are mine and thine.
Along the coast and harbors they take care
That money lack, nor forts be in repair.
Long thus they could against the House conspire,   325
Load them with envy, and with sitting tire,
And the loved king, and never yet denied,
Is brought to beg in public and to chide;
But when this failed, and months enough were spent,
They with the first day's proffer seem content,   330
And to land tax from the excise turn round,
Bought off with eighteen-hundred-thousand pound.
Thus, like fair thieves, the Commons' purse they share,
But all the members' lives, consulting, spare.
       Blither than hare that hath escaped the hounds,   335
The House prorogued, the chancellor rebounds.
Not so decrepit Aeson, hashed and stewed,
With bitter herbs, rose from the pot renewed,
And with fresh age felt his glad limbs unite;
His gout (yet still he cursed) had left him quite.   340
What frosts to fruit, what ars'nic to the rat,
What to fair Denham mortal chocolate,
What an account to Cart'ret, that, and more,
A Parliament is to the chancellor.
So the sad tree shrinks from the morning's eye,   345

313–14. *seamen's clamor:* As Pepys reports (19 December 1660), the seamen were beginning
to riot because they had not been paid for so long, and because the tickets they received in
lieu of cash were not being redeemed by the government.
   328. The king addressed an urgent demand for supply to the House on 18 January 1667.
   331. The land tax, which was supported by the country party against the general excise of
the court party, was passed on 8 November 1666.
   336. *prorogued:* on 8 February 1667 when the land tax bill received the royal assent.
   337–39. See Ovid, *Metamorphoses*, 7.
   345–46. *sad tree: Nyctanthes Arbor-tristis*, night-jasmine of India. During the day it loses its
brightness (Margoliouth).

But blooms all night and shoots its branches high.
So, at the sun's recess, again returns
The comet dread and earth and heaven burns.
    Now Mordaunt may, within his castle tow'r,
Imprison parents and the child deflow'r.   350
The Irish herd is now let loose and comes
By millions over, not by hecatombs;
And now, now, the Canary Patent may
Be broached again for the great holiday.
    See how he reigns in his new palace culminant   355
And sits in state divine like Jove the fulminant!
First Buckingham, that durst 'gainst him rebel,
Blasted with lightning, struck with thunder, fell.
Next the twelve Commons are condemned to groan
And roll in vain at Sisyphus's stone.   360
But still he cared, while in revenge he braved,
That peace secured and money might be saved:
Gain and revenge, revenge and gain are sweet,
United most, else when by turns they meet.
France had St. Albans promised (so they sing),   365
St. Albans promised him, and he the king:
The count forthwith is ordered all to close,
To play for Flanders and the stake to lose,
While, chained together, two ambassadors
Like slaves shall beg for peace at Holland's doors.   370
This done, among his Cyclops he retires
To forge new thunder and inspect their fires.
    The court as once of war, now fond of peace,
All to new sports their wanton fears release.
From Greenwich (where intelligence they hold)   375
Comes news of pastime martial and old,

349. See 259–60 n.

351. See 255 n.

357–58. Buckingham had been one of the chief supporters of the Irish Cattle Bill in the House of Lords, 1666–67, Clarendon opposing. His arrest was ordered 25 February 1667 for treasonable practices, one charge being that he obtained a cast of the king's horoscope. After some months he gave himself up and was sent to the Tower.

359–60. Twelve of the eighteen commissioners for the public accounts, appointed 21 March 1667, were members of the House of Commons.

367. *count:* that is, the earl of St. Albans; perhaps with a glance at his "Frenchiness."

368. The French aimed at peace with England in order to be free to carry out their designs on Flanders.

369. See 233–34 n.

375–96. These lines refer to the "Skimmington Ride," in which aggressive wives and timid husbands were ridiculed by their neighbors. Here France and Flanders are the neighbors while Holland is the masterful wife and England the beaten husband (Margoliouth).

A punishment invented first to awe
Masculine wives transgressing Nature's law,
Where, when the brawny female disobeys
And beats the husband till for peace he prays,   380
No concerned jury for him damage finds,
Nor partial justice her behavior binds,
But the just street does the next house invade,
Mounting the neighbor couple on lean jade,
The distaff knocks, the grains from kettle fly,   385
And boys and girls in troops run hooting by:
Prudent antiquity, that knew by shame
Better than law domestic crimes to tame,
And taught youth by spectacle innocent!
So thou and I, dear Painter, represent   390
In quick effigie, others' faults and feign,
By making them ridiculous, to restrain.
With homely sight they chose thus to relax
The joys of state for the new peace and tax.
So Holland with us had the mast'ry tried,   395
And our next neighbors, France and Flanders, ride.
   But a fresh news the great designment nips—
Off at the Isle of Candy Dutch and ships!
Bab May and Arlington did wisely scoff
And thought all safe, if they were so far off.   400
Modern geographers, 'twas there, they thought,
Where Venice twenty years the Turk had fought,
While the first year our navy is but shown,
The next divided, and the third we've none.
They by the name mistook it for that isle   405
Where Pilgrim Palmer traveled in exile
With the bull's horn to measure his own head
And on Pasiphäe's tomb to drop a bead.

391. *effigie:* pronounced as four syllables in the seventeenth century. Compare *Third Advice*, 436.
398. *Candy:* (1) Candia Island, off the Essex coast; (2) an old name for Crete. Marvell was probably also referring to the occasion for Busenello's "Prospective of the Naval Triumph" (trans. Thomas Higgons, 1658) achieved by the Venetian navy over the Turks near Crete. This poem was Waller's model.
399. *Bab May:* Baptist May, Keeper of the Privy Purse.
406. *Pilgrim Palmer*: a punning reference to Roger Palmer, earl of Castlemaine, a Roman Catholic. When his wife left him for Charles II he traveled to the Levant in 1664 with the Venetian admiral Andrea Conaro.
408: *Pasiphäe:* Wife of Minos, king of Crete, fell in love with a bull. The product of their union was the Minotaur, which Minos caused Daedalus to imprison in a labyrinth. See Ovid, *Metamorphoses*, especially Books 8 and 9, and reference to the myth in *Second Advice*, 345–54.

But Morice learned demonstrates, by the post,
This Isle of Candy was on Essex coast.   410
    Fresh messengers still the sad news assure;
More tim'rous now we are than first secure.
False terrors our believing fears devise,
And the French army one from Calais spies.
Bennet and May and those of shorter reach   415
Change all for guineas and a crown for each,
But wiser men and well foreseen in chance
In Holland theirs had lodged before, and France.
Whitehall's unsafe; the court all meditates
To fly to Windsor and mure up the gates.   420
Each does the other blame and all distrust,
But Mordaunt, new obliged, would sure be just.
Not such a fatal stupefaction reigned
At London's flame, nor so the court complained.
The Bloodworth-chanc'lor gives, then does recall,   425
Orders; amazed at last gives none at all.
    St. Alban's writ to, that he may bewail
To master Louis and tell coward tale,
How yet the Hollanders do make a noise,
Threaten to beat us, and are naughty boys.   430
Now Dolman's disobedient and they still
Uncivil; his unkindness would us kill.
Tell him our ships unrigged, our forts unmanned,
Our money spent; else 'twere at his command.
Summon him therefore of his word and prove   435
To move him out of pity, if not love;
Pray him to make De Witt and Ruyter cease
And whip the Dutch, unless they'll hold their peace.
But Louis was of memory but dull

---

409. *Morice:* Sir William Morice (1602–76), joint secretary of state with Arlington. *by the post:* from his knowledge of postal matters he demonstrates to Arlington, the postmaster-general, that this Candy is in Essex.

419–20. "The gates of the court were shut up upon the first coming of the Dutch to us" (Pepys, 17 June 1667).

422. See 259–60 *n.*

425. *Bloodworth:* Sir Thomas Bloodworth was mayor of London during the great fire and was noted for his fecklessness.

427–28. An express with appeals for peace went to St. Albans on 15 June.

431. *Dolman's disobedient:* Col. Thomas Dolman, an English officer, commanded the Dutch troops in the invading fleet. An act was passed in October 1665, attainting him if he and others did not surrender by a certain day.

435. *prove:* attempt.

And to St. Albans too undutiful;   440
Nor word, nor near relation, did revere,
But asked him bluntly for his character.
The graveled count did with the answer faint
(His character was that which thou didst paint)
And so enforced, like enemy or spy,   445
Trusses his baggage and the camp does fly,
Yet Louis writes and, lest our hearts should break,
Consoles us morally out of Seneque.
   Two letters next unto Breda are sent:
In cipher one to Harry Excellent;   450
The first instructs our (verse the name abhors)
Plenipotentiary ambassadors
To prove by scripture treaty does imply
Cessation, as the look adultery,
And that by law of arms, in martial strife,   455
Who yields his sword has title to his life.
Presbyter Holles the first point should clear,
The second Coventry the Cavalier;
But, would they not be argued back from sea,
Then to return home straight, *infectâ re.*   460
But Harry's ordered, if they won't recall
Their fleet, to threaten we will grant them all.
The Dutch are then in proclamation shent
For sin against th' eleventh commandment.
Hyde's flippant style there pleasantly curvets,   465
Still his sharp wit on states and princes whets
(So Spain could not escape his laughter's spleen:
None but himself must choose the king a queen),
But when he come the odious clause to pen

440. If, as Marvell assumes, St. Albans was secretly married to Henrietta Maria, he would have been Louis XIV's uncle (Margoliouth).

442. *character:* official rank or status.

447–48. This consolatory letter from Louis XIV to Charles is undoubtedly a figment of the poet's imagination. Seneca was one of the classical writers whom Louis, as a young man, was made to read.

451–56. " 'I look upon the peace as made' was the cue taken from St. Albans, and as May passed into June our blind dependence grew more marked" (Feiling, *Foreign Policy*, p. 218).

452. Coventry and Holles.

454. Compare Matt. 5:27–28. "Whosoever looketh on a woman to lust after her hath committed adultery with her already in his heart."

459. *they:* the Dutch fleet.

460. *infectâ re:* without having accomplished anything.

463–66. Clarendon's attitude toward Holland during preliminary negotiations was unyielding and contemptuous. See Feiling, *Foreign Policy*, p. 216.

That summons up the Parliament again, 470
His writing master many a time he banned
And wished himself the gout to seize his hand.
Never old lecher more repugnance felt,
Consenting, for his rupture, to be gelt;
But still in hope he solaced, ere they come, 475
To work the peace and so to send them home,
Or in their hasty call to find a flaw,
Their acts to vitiate and them overawe;
But most relied upon this Dutch pretense
To raise a two-edged army for's defense. 480
    First then he marched our whole militia's force
(As if, indeed, we ships or Dutch had horse);
Then, from the usual commonplace, he blames
These, and in standing army's praise declaims;
And the wise court, that always loved it dear, 485
Now thinks all but too little for their fear.
Hyde stamps, and straight upon the ground the swarms
Of current Myrmidons appear in arms,
And for their pay he writes as from the king
With that cursed quill plucked from a vulture's wing 490
Of the whole nation now to ask a loan
(The eighteen-hundred-thousand pound was gone).
This done, he pens a proclamation stout,
In rescue of the *banquiers banquerouts*,
His minion imps that in his secret part 495
Lie nuzzling at the sacramental wart,
Horse-leeches circling at the hem'rrhoid vein:
He sucks the king, they him, he them again.
The kingdom's farm he lets to them bid least
(Greater the bribe, and that's at interest). 500
Here men induced by safety, gain, and ease,

471. *banned:* cursed.
477–78. After the naval disgrace an army of twelve new regiments under the command of old parliamentarians was raised "to conciliate popular opinion. . . . But this was only adding fuel to the fire, since it raised the suspicion that a standing army was intended" (Ogg, *Charles II*, p. 218).
484. *These:* the Dutch.
494. *banquiers banquerouts:* bankrupt bankers, who had lent the king money.
495–98. Cf. Cleveland, *Rebel Scot*, 83–85: "Sure, England hath the hemorrhoids, and these / On the north postern of the patient seize / Like leeches. . . ."
496. *wart:* nipple.
499. *kingdom's farm:* the farming of taxes.
500. *that's:* refers to *farm*.

Their money lodge, confiscate when he please.
These can at need, at instant, with a scrip
(This liked him best) his cash beyond sea whip.
When Dutch invade, when Parliament prepare,   505
How can he engines so convenient spare?
Let no man touch them or demand his own,
Pain of displeasure of great Clarendon.
   The state affairs thus marshaled, for the rest,
Monck in his shirt against the Dutch is pressed.   510
Often, dear Painter, have I sat and mused
Why he should still b'on all adventures used:
If they for nothing ill, like ashen-wood,
Or think him, like herb john, for nothing good?
Whether his valor they so much admire,   515
Or that for cowardice they all retire,
As Heav'n in storms, they call, in gusts of state,
On Monck and Parliament yet both do hate.
All causes sure concur, but most they think
Under Herculean labors he may sink.   520
Soon then the independent troops would close,
And Hyde's last project would his place dispose.
   Ruyter the while, that had our ocean curbed,
Sailed now among our rivers undisturbed,
Surveyed their crystal streams and banks so green   525
And beauties ere this never naked seen.
Through the vain sedge the bashful nymphs he eyed:
Bosoms and all which from themselves they hide.
The sun much brighter, and the skies more clear,
He finds the air and all things sweeter here.   530
The sudden change and such a tempting sight
Swells his old veins with fresh blood, fresh delight.
Like am'rous victors he begins to shave,
And his new face looks in the English wave.

502. *confiscate:* an adjective.
503. *scrip:* receipt for a portion of a loan subscribed.
513. *ashen-wood:* The ash is a tree second in value only to the oak, and its wood has a thousand uses.
514. *herb john:* properly St. John's wort applied, in proverbial phrases, to something inert or indifferent.
521–22. I agree with Margoliouth's suggestion that *independent troops* refers to the projected standing army: "The point may be that, with Monck's death, the obstacles to the consolidation of a standing army under Clarendon's control would disappear."
533–40. This passage seems to show a general indebtedness to Enobarbus's account of the first meeting between Antony and Cleopatra in Shakespeare's play (II.2. 193–228).

His sporting navy all about him swim   535
And witness their complacence in their trim.
Their streaming silks play through the weather fair
And with inveigling colors court the air,
While the red flags breathe on their top-masts high
Terror and war but want an enemy.   540
Among the shrouds the seamen sit and sing,
And wanton boys on every rope do cling.
Old Neptune springs the tides and water lent
(The gods themselves do help the provident),
And, where the deep keel on the shallow cleaves,   545
With trident's lever and great shoulder heaves.
Aeolus their sails inspires with eastern wind,
Puffs them along, and breathes upon them kind.
With pearly shell the Tritons all the while
Sound the sea-march and guide to Sheppey Isle.   550
So have I seen in April's bud arise
A fleet of clouds, sailing along the skies;
The liquid region with their squadrons filled,
Their airy sterns the sun behind does gild,
And gentle gales them steer, and Heaven drives,   555
When, all on sudden, their calm bosom rives
With thunder and lightning from each armed cloud;
Shepherds themselves in vain in bushes shroud.
Such up the stream the Belgic navy glides
And at Sheerness unloads its stormy sides.   560
    Spragge there, though practiced in the sea command,
With panting heart lay like a fish on land
And quickly judged the fort was not tenable,
Which, if a house, yet were not tenantable.
No man can sit there safe: the cannon pours   565
Thorough the walls untight and bullets show'rs,
The neighb'rhood ill and an unwholesome seat,
So at the first salute resolves retreat
And swore that he would never more dwell there
Until the City put it in repair;   570
So he in front, his garrison in rear,
March straight to Chatham to increase the fear.

543. Pepys notes (14 June) that the easterly winds and spring tides helped the Dutch to go up the Thames and the Medway and to break the chain at Chatham.
561. *Spragge*: Sir Edward Spragge (d. 1673), vice-admiral of the Blue, then commanding at Sheerness.

There our sick ships unrigged in summer lay
Like molting fowl, a weak and easy prey,
For whose strong bulk earth scarce could timber find,   575
The ocean water, or the heavens wind—
Those oaken giants of the ancient race,
That ruled all seas and did our Channel grace.
The conscious stag, so, once the forest's dread,
Flies to the wood and hides his armless head.   580
Ruyter forthwith a squadron does untack;
They sail securely through the river's track.
An English pilot too (O shame, O sin!)
Cheated of pay, was he that showed them in.
Our wretched ships, within, their fate attend,   585
And all our hopes now on frail chain depend:
Engine so slight to guard us from the sea,
It fitter seemed to captivate a flea.
A skipper rude shocks it without respect,
Filling his sails, more force to recollect.   590
Th' 'English from shore the iron deaf invoke
For its last aid: "Hold chain, or we are broke!"
But with her sailing weight the Holland keel,
Snapping the brittle links, does thorough reel
And to the rest the opened passage shew;   595
Monck from the bank the dismal sight does view.
Our feathered gallants, which came down that day
To be spectators safe of the new play,
Leave him alone when first they hear the gun
(Cornb'ry the fleetest) and to London run.   600
Our seamen, whom no danger's shape could fright,
Unpaid refuse to mount our ships for spite,
Or to their fellows swim on board the Dutch,
Which show the tempting metal in their clutch.
Oft had he sent of Duncombe and of Legge   605
Cannon and powder, but in vain, to beg;
And Upnor Castle's ill-defended wall,
Now needful, does for ammunition call.
He finds, wheres'e'er he succor might expect,
Confusion, folly, treach'ry, fear, neglect.   610
But when the *Royal Charles* (what rage, what grief!)
He saw seized and could give her no relief—

605. *Legge:* William Legge, lieutenant-general of the ordinance.
611–12. The *Royal Charles*, formerly the *Naseby*, brought the king to Dover in 1660.

That sacred keel which had, as he, restored
His exiled sov'reign on its happy board,
And thence the British admiral became, 615
Crowned, for that merit, with their master's name;
That pleasure-boat of war, in whose dear side
Secure so oft he had this foe defied,
Now a cheap spoil and the mean victor's slave,
Taught the Dutch colors from its top to wave— 620
Of former glories the reproachful thought,
With present shame compared, his mind distraught.
Such, from Euphrates' bank, a tigress fell
After the robber for her whelps doth yell;
But sees enraged the river flow between, 625
Frustrate revenge, and love, by loss more keen;
At her own breast her useless claws does arm:
She tears herself, since him she cannot harm.
    The guards, placed for the chain's and fleet's defense,
Long since were fled on many a feigned pretense. 630
Daniel had there adventured, man of might;
Sweet Painter, draw his picture while I write.
Paint him of person tall and big of bone,
Large limbs, like ox, not to be killed but shown.
Scarce can burnt iv'ry feign a hair so black; 635
Or face so red, thine ochre and thy lac.
Mix a vain terror in his martial look,
And all those lines by which men are mistook;
But when, by shame constrained to go on board,
He heard how the wild cannon nearer roared 640
And saw himself confined like sheep in pen,
Daniel then thought he was in lion's den.
And when the frightful fireships he saw,
Pregnant with sulphur, to him nearer draw,
Captain, lieutenant, ensign, all make haste 645
Ere in the fi'ry furnace they be cast.
Three children tall, unsinged, away they row,
Like Shadrack, Meshack, and Abednego.
    Not so brave Douglas, on whose lovely chin

631. *Daniel:* probably Sir Thomas Daniel, who commanded a company of foot guards, who were supposed to defend the *Loyal London* or the *Royal James.*
  634. *shown:* like a prize ox.
  636. *lac:* a crimson pigment.
  648. Compare Daniel 3.
  649. *Douglas:* Archibald Douglas, who commanded a company of Scottish troops, died in

The early down but newly did begin,   650
And modest beauty yet his sex did veil,
While envious virgins hope he is a male.
His yellow locks curl back themselves to seek,
Nor other courtship knew but to his cheek.
Oft as he in chill Esk or Seine by night   655
Hardened and cooled his limbs, so soft, so white,
Among the reeds, to be espied by him,
The nymphs would rustle; he would forward swim.
They sighed and said, "Fond boy, why so untame,
That fli'st love's fires, reserved for other flame?"   660
Fixed on his ship, he faced that horrid day
And wondered much at those that run away.
Nor other fear himself could comprehend
Than lest Heav'n fall ere thither he ascend,
But entertains the while his time too short   665
With birding at the Dutch, as if in sport,
Or waves his sword, and could he them conjure
Within its circle, knows himself secure.
The fatal bark him boards with grappling fire,
And safely through its port the Dutch retire.   670
That precious life he yet disdains to save
Or with known art to try the gentle wave.
Much him the honors of his ancient race
Inspire, nor would he his own deeds deface,
And secret joy in his calm soul does rise   675
That Monck looks on to see how Douglas dies.
Like a glad lover the fierce flames he meets
And tries his first embraces in their sheets.
His shape exact, which the bright flames enfold,
Like the sun's statue stands of burnished gold.   680
Round the transparent fire about him glows,
As the clear amber on the bee does close,
And, as on angels' heads their glories shine,
His burning locks adorn his face divine.
But when in his immortal mind he felt   685
His alt'ring form and soldered limbs to melt,
Down on the deck he laid himself and died,
With his dear sword reposing by his side

---

defending the *Royal Oak*, which was fired by the Dutch.
   678. Actually, Douglas left a widow, Frances, who petitioned for a prize ship as compensation.

And on the flaming plank so rests his head
As one that's warmed himself and gone to bed.   690
His ship burns down and with his relics sinks,
And the sad stream beneath his ashes drinks.
Fortunate boy! If either pencil's fame,
Or if my verse can propagate thy name,
When Oeta and Alcides are forgot,   695
Our English youth shall sing the valiant Scot.
    Each doleful day still with fresh loss returns:
The *Loyal London* now a third time burns,
And the true *Royal Oak* and *Royal James*,
Allied in fate, increase with theirs her flames.   700
Of all our navy none should now survive,
But that the ships themselves were taught to dive,
And the kind river in its creek them hides,
Fraughting their pierced keels with oozy tides.
    Up to the bridge contagious terror strook: 705
The Tow'r itself with the near danger shook,
And, were not Ruyter's maw with ravage cloyed,
E'en London's ashes had been then destroyed.
Officious fear, however, to prevent
Our loss does so much more our loss augment: 710
The Dutch had robbed those jewels of the crown;
Our merchantmen, lest they be burned, we drown.
So when the fire did not enough devour,
The houses were demolished near the Tow'r.
Those ships that yearly from their teeming hole   715
Unloaded here the birth of either pole—
Furs from the north and silver from the west,
Wines from the south, and spices from the east;
From Gambo gold, and from the Ganges gems—
Take a short voyage underneath the Thames,   720
Once a deep river, now with timber floored,
And shrunk, least navigable, to a ford.
    Now (nothing more at Chatham left to burn),

695. Hercules (Alcides) was burned to death on Mt. Oeta.
    698. The *London* was blown up in March 1665. Then the *Loyal City of London* was burned by the great fire. Here the *Loyal London* (cf. *Second Advice*, 13–24) is burned.
    702. Some ships were sunk to keep them from being burned.
    712. Some merchantmen newly laden with valuable cargo and newly commissioned fire ships were sunk in a panic below Woolwich to stop the Dutch.
    715. *hole:* hold.
    722. *least navigable:* at its least navigable point.

The Holland squadron leisurely return,
And, spite of Ruperts and of Albemarles,   725
To Ruyter's triumph lead the captive *Charles.*
The pleasing sight he often does prolong:
Her masts erect, tough cordage, timbers strong,
Her moving shapes, all these he does survey,
And all admires, but most his easy prey.   730
The seamen search her all, within, without:
Viewing her strength, they yet their conquest doubt;
Then with rude shouts, secure, the air they vex,
With gamesome joy insulting on her decks.
Such the feared Hebrew, captive, blinded, shorn,   735
Was led about in sport, the public scorn.
    Black day accursed! on thee let no man hail
Out of the port, or dare to hoist a sail,
Nor row a boat in thy unlucky hour.
Thee, the year's monster, let thy dam devour,   740
And constant Time, to keep his course yet right,
Fill up thy space with a redoubled night.
When aged Thames was bound with fetters base,
And Medway chaste ravished before his face,
And their dear offspring murdered in their sight,   745
Thou and thy fellows held'st the odious light.
Sad change since first that happy pair was wed,
When all the rivers graced their nuptial bed,
And father Neptune promised to resign
His empire old to their immortal line!   750
Now with vain grief their vainer hopes they rue,
Themselves dishonored, and the gods untrue,
And to each other, helpless couple, moan,
As the sad tortoise for the sea does groan.
But most they for their darling *Charles* complain,   755
And, were it burnt, yet less would be their pain.
To see that fatal pledge of sea command
Now in the ravisher De Ruyter's hand,
The Thames roared, swooning Medway turned her tide,
And, were they mortal, both for grief had died.   760
    The court in farthing yet itself does please,
And female Stuart there rules the four seas,

735–36. *the feared Hebrew:* Samson. See Judges 16.
762. Frances Stuart, on whom Charles had set his eye, married the duke of Richmond in
1667. She was the model for Britannia on medals and coins. The farthings of Charles II bore

But Fate does still accumulate our woes,
And Richmond her commands, as Ruyter those.
    After this loss, to relish discontent,   765
Someone must be accused by punishment.
All our miscarriages on Pett must fall:
His name alone seems fit to answer all.
Whose counsel first did this mad war beget?
Who all commands sold through the navy? *Pett.*   770
Who would not follow when the Dutch were beat?
Who treated out the time at Bergen? *Pett.*
Who the Dutch fleet with storms disabled met,
And, rifling prizes, them neglected? *Pett.*
Who with false news prevented the *Gazette,*   775
The fleet divided, writ for Rupert? *Pett.*
Who all our seamen cheated of their debt,
And all our prizes who did swallow? *Pett.*
Who did advise no navy out to set,
And who the forts left unrepairéd? *Pett.*   780
Who to supply with powder did forget
Landguard, Sheerness, Gravesend and Upnor? *Pett.*
Who all our ships exposed in Chatham's net?
Who should it be but the fanatic *Pett?*
Pett, the sea-architect, in making ships,   785
Was the first cause of all these naval slips:
Had he not built, none of these faults had been;
If no creation, there had been no sin.

---

the legend *Quatuor maria vindico* (I claim the four seas).
    765. *relish:* make pleasant to the taste.
    767. *Pett:* Peter Pett (1610–70?) superintended the dockyard at Chatham. Margoliouth quotes a letter from Henry Savile to his brother, George (18 June): "Commissioner Pett was sent for from Chatham and sent the last night to the Tower. He is most undoubtedly to be sacrificed; all that are greater lay the fault upon him in hopes that he is to bear all the blame; the town has no mind to be so satisfied." Pett was arraigned 31 October and set free on bail of £5,000. Marvell spoke that day against sending him to the Tower (Milward). Impeachment proceedings were begun 19 December but the matter was dropped.
    771. On 3 June 1665. It was the duke of York's flagship that *would not follow.* Cf. *Second Advice,* 233–42. *Beat* was pronounced *bet.*
    772. Cf. *Second Advice,* 269–92.
    773–74. Cf. *Second Advice,* 293–308.
    775–76. Cf. *Third Advice,* 283–88, 291–94.
    779–80. Sir William Coventry seems to have been most culpable for the failure to set out a fleet in 1667. "It is well known who of the commissioners of the treasury gave advice that the charge of setting forth a fleet this year might be spared, Sir W. C. by name" (Evelyn, 29 July 1667).
    782. *Landguard:* a fort at Harwich attacked by the Dutch in June 1667.

But, his great crime, one boat away he sent,
That lost our fleet and did our flight prevent.   790
    Then (that reward might in its turn take place,
And march with punishment in equal pace),
Southampton dead, much of the treasure's care
And place in council fell to Duncombe's share.
All men admired he to that pitch could fly: 795
Powder ne'er blew man up so soon so high,
But sure his late good husbandry in petre
Showed him to manage the Exchequer meeter;
And who the forts would not vouchsafe a corn,
To lavish the king's money more would scorn.   800
Who hath no chimneys, to give all is best,
And ablest speaker, who of law has least;
Who less estate, for treasurer most fit,
And for a couns'lor, he that has least wit.
But the true cause was that, in's brother May,   805
Th' Exchequer might the Privy Purse obey.
    But now draws near the Parliament's return;
Hyde and the court again begin to mourn:
Frequent in council, earnest in debate,
All arts they try how to prolong its date.   810
Grave primate Sheldon (much in preaching there)
Blames the last session and this more does fear:
With Boynton or with Middleton 'twere sweet,
But with a Parliament abhors to meet
And thinks 'twill ne'er be well within this nation,   815
Till it be governed by a convocation.

789. The chief charges against Pett were "the not carrying up of the great ships and the using of the boats in carrying away his goods" (Pepys, 19 June 1667).

793. *Southampton:* Thomas Wriothesley, 4th earl of Southampton (1607–67), lord high treasurer, had died in the spring, and the treasury was put in charge of a commission consisting of Albemarle, Ashley, Sir W. Coventry, Sir John Duncombe, and Sir Thomas Clifford. Duncombe was actually appointed to the commission three weeks before the Dutch attack.

795. Pepys (31 May 1667): "I saw Duncombe look as big and take as much state on him as if he had been born a lord."

797. *petre:* saltpeter, an ingredient in gunpowder. Duncombe had been Master of the Ordnance, in which capacity he could have made illicit profits.

799. *corn:* a grain of gunpowder.

805. *brother May:* Baptist May was Duncombe's brother-in-law.

811. *Sheldon:* Gilbert Sheldon (1598–1677) archbishop of Canterbury, according to Pepys was "as very a wencher as can be" (29 July 1667).

813. *Boynton and Middleton:* Katherine Boynton and Mrs. Charles Middleton were court beauties.

816. *convocation:* i.e., bishops. The convocation of Canterbury also had a lower house of elected clergy. (Sheldon in fact abandoned the practice of voting separate clerical subsidies in convocation.)

But in the Thames' mouth still De Ruyter laid;
The peace not sure, new army must be paid.
Hyde saith he hourly waits for a dispatch;
Harry came post just as he showed his watch,   820
All to agree the articles were clear,
The Holland fleet and Parliament so near;
Yet Harry must job back and all mature,
Binding, ere th' Houses meet, the treaty sure,
And 'twixt necessity and spite, till then,   825
Let them come up so to go down again.
   Up ambles country justice on his pad
And vest bespeaks to be more seemly clad.
Plain gentlemen in stagecoach are o'erthrown
And deputy-lieutenants in their own.   830
The portly burgess through the weather hot
Does for his corporation sweat and trot;
And all with sun and choler come adust
And threaten Hyde to raise a greater dust.
But, fresh as from the mint, the courtiers fine   835
Salute them, smiling at their vain design,
And Turnor gay up to his perch does march
With face new bleached, smoothened and stiff with starch;
Tells them he at Whitehall had took a turn
And for three days thence moves them to adjourn.   840
"Not so!" quoth Tomkins, and straight drew his tongue,
Trusty as steel, that always ready hung;
And so, proceeding in his motion warm,
Th' army soon raised he doth as soon disarm.
True Trojan! While this town can girls afford,   845

---

820. *Harry:* Henry Coventry. On 8 July Pepys wrote: "Mr. Coventry is come from Breda, as was expected, but, contrary to expectation, brings with him two or three articles which do not please the king."

821–26. The idea here seems to be that Ambassador Coventry was eager to believe that the articles implied an early settlement because he was confronted by the double threat of the Dutch fleet and the approaching session of Parliament in which the war with Holland would be attacked as a grievance.

826. The House met 25 July and was dismissed 29 July.

828. *vest:* a garment designed by Charles II to make English fashions independent of France.

833. *adust:* dried up with heat.

841–44. "But before they could come to the question whether they would adjourn, Sir Thomas Tomkins steps up and tells them that all the country is grieved at the new-raised standing army; and that they thought themselves safe enough in their train-bands; and that therefore he desired the king might be moved to disband them" (Pepys, 25 July 1667).

And long as cider lasts in Hereford,
The girls shall always kiss thee, though grown old,
And in eternal healths thy name be trolled.
    Meanwhile the certain news of peace arrives
At court and so reprieves their guilty lives.   850
Hyde orders Turnor that he should come late,
Lest some new Tomkins spring a fresh debate.
The king that day raised early from his rest,
Expects (as at a play) till Turnor's dressed.
At last together Eaton come and he: 855
No dial more could with the sun agree.
The speaker, summoned, to the Lords repairs,
Nor gave the Commons leave to say their pray'rs,
But like his pris'ners to the bar them led,
Where mute they stand to hear their sentence read.   860
Trembling with joy and fear, Hyde them prorogues,
And had almost mistook and called them rogues.
    Dear Painter, draw this speaker to the foot;
Where pencil cannot, there my pen shall do't:
That may his body, this his mind explain.   865
Paint him in golden gown, with mace's brain,
Bright hair, fair face, obscure and dull of head,
Like knife with iv'ry haft and edge of lead.
At pray'rs his eyes turn up the pious white,
But all the while his private bill's in sight.   870
In chair he smoking sits like master cook,
And a poll-bill does like his apron look.
Well was he skilled to season any question
And make a sauce fit for Whitehall's digestion,
Whence ev'ry day, the palate more to tickle,   875
Court-mushrumps ready are sent in in pickle.
When grievance urged, he swells like squatted toad,
Frisks like a frog to croak a tax's load;
His patient piss he could hold longer than
An urinal and sit like any hen;   880
At table jolly as a country host

846. *Hereford:* Tomkins's county.
855. *Eaton:* Sir John Eaton or Ayton, Usher of the Black Rod.
870–72. The speaker received large fees from the passage of private bills. Turnor sweats
like a cook while the bill is being voted on, and a poll-bill such as that by which part of the
supply was raised in 1666–67 might resemble his spotted apron because of various amend-
ments attached to it.

And soaks his sack with Norfolk like a toast;
At night than Chanticleer more brisk and hot,
And sergeant's wife serves him for Pertelotte.
Paint last the king and a dead shade of night,   885
Only dispersed by a weak taper's light,
And those bright gleams that dart along and glare
From his clear eyes (yet these too dark with care).
There, as in th' calm horror all alone
He wakes and muses of th' uneasy throne,   890
Raise up a sudden shape with virgin's face,
(Though ill agree her posture, hour, or place),
Naked as born, and her round arms behind
With her own tresses interwove and twined;
Her mouth locked up, a blind before her eyes,   895
Yet from beneath the veil her blushes rise,
And silent tears her secret anguish speak;
Her heart throbs and with very shame would break.
The object strange in him no terror moved:
He wondered first, then pitied, then he loved   900
And with kind hand does the coy vision press
(Whose beauty greater seemed by her distress),
But soon shrunk back, chilled with her touch so cold,
And th' airy picture vanished from his hold.
In his deep thoughts the wonder did increase,   905
And he divined 'twas England or the Peace.
Express him startling next with list'ning ear,
As one that some unusual noise does hear.
With cannon, trumpets, drums, his door surround,
But let some other painter draw the sound.   910
Thrice did he rise, thrice the vain tumult fled,
But again thunders when he lies in bed.
His mind secure does the known stroke repeat
And finds the drums Louis's march did beat.
Shake then the room and all his curtains tear   915
And with blue streaks infect the taper clear,
While the pale ghosts his eye does fixed admire
Of grandsire Harry and of Charles his sire.

882. *Norfolk*: James Norfolk, sergeant-at-arms.
907. *startling*: starting.
913. *secure*: careless, overconfident, now arch.
918. *grandsire Harry*: Henry IV of France, father of Henrietta Maria. He was assassinated by Ravaillac in 1610.

Harry sits down, and in his open side
The grisly wound reveals of which he died,   920
And ghastly Charles, turning his collar low,
The purple thread about his neck does show,
Then, whisp'ring to his son in words unheard,
Through the locked door both of them disappeared.
The wondrous night the pensive king revolves,   925
And rising straight on Hyde's disgrace resolves.
At his first step he Castlemaine does find,
Bennet, and Coventry, as 't were designed;
And they, not knowing, the same thing propose
Which his hid mind did in its depths enclose.   930
Through their feigned speech their secret hearts he knew:
To her own husband, Castlemaine untrue;
False to his master Bristol, Arlington;
And Coventry, falser than anyone,
Who to the brother, brother would betray,   935
Nor therefore trusts himself to such as they.
His father's ghost too whispered him one note,
That who does cut his purse will cut his throat,
But in wise anger he their crimes forbears,
As thieves reprieved for executioners;   940
While Hyde, provoked, his foaming tusk does whet,
To prove them traitors and himself the Pett.
    Painter, adieu! How well our arts agree,
Poetic picture, painted poetry;
But this great work is for our monarch fit,   945
And henceforth Charles only to Charles shall sit.
His master-hand the ancients shall outdo,
Himself the painter and the poet too.

To the King

    So his bold tube man to the sun applied
And spots unknown to the bright star descried,   950
Showed they obscure him while too near they prease,
And seem his courtiers, are but his disease.
Through optic trunk the planets seemed to hear,

937. 927–28. Lady Castlemaine, Bennet, and Sir William Coventry were Clarendon's worst
enemies at court.
    934–36. Presumably an allusion to Coventry's position as the duke of York's secretary, in
which capacity, Marvell implies, he acted against the king's interests.
    951. *prease:* press.

And hurls them off e'er since in his career.
    And you, great sir, that with him empire share, 955
Sun of our world, as he the Charles is there,
Blame not the Muse that brought those spots to sight,
Which, in your splendor hid, corrode your light:
Kings in the country oft have gone astray
Nor of a peasant scorned to learn the way. 960
Would she the unattended throne reduce,
Banishing love, trust, ornament, and use,
Better it were to live in cloister's lock,
Or in fair fields to rule the easy flock.
She blames them only who the court restrain 965
And, where all England serves, themselves would reign.
    Bold and accursed are they that all this while
Have strove to isle our monarch from his isle,
And to improve themselves, on false pretense,
About the common prince have raised a fence; 970
The kingdom from the crown distinct would see
And peel the bark to burn at last the tree.
But Ceres corn, and Flora is the spring,
Bacchus is wine, the country is the king.
Not so does rust insinuating wear, 975
Nor powder so the vaulted bastion tear,
Nor earthquakes so an hollow isle o'erwhelm,
As scratching courtiers undermine a realm
And through the palace's foundations bore,
Burr'wing themselves to hoard their guilty store. 980
The smallest vermin make the greatest waste,
And a poor warren once a city razed.
But they whom, born to virtue and to wealth,
Nor guilt to flatt'ry binds, nor want to stealth;
Whose gen'rous conscience and whose courage high 985
Does with clear counsels their large souls supply;
That serve the king with their estates and care,
And as in love on parliaments can stare,
Where few the number, choice is there less hard:
Give us this court and rule without a guard. 990

A Ballad Called the Haymarket Hectors
(1671)

On 21 December 1670, when Sir John Coventry proposed a tax on theaters in the House of Commons, Sir John Birkenhead objected that the players were the king's servants and a part of his pleasure. Thinking of Nell Gwynne and Moll Davis, each of whom had recently borne the king a bastard, Coventry recklessly asked whether His Majesty's pleasure lay among the men or women players?

That night twenty Life Guards, under the command of Sir Thomas Sandys and Captain O'Brien, lay in wait for Coventry, who had been visiting a tavern in Suffolk Street, near the Haymarket. Although he defended himself vigorously, Coventry's nose was slit to the bone. Though Monmouth took no hand in the assault, as captain of the king's Life Guard of Horse he was responsible for giving the orders.

When Parliament reassembled on 10 January, many members expressed indignation and horror at the act. Sandys and O'Brien were banished, and a special "Act to Prevent Malicious Mischief and Maiming" was passed before the debate on supply was resumed. Edmund Waller remarked: "When the Greeks and Romans had slaves disfigured and marked, it was a dishonor to the master, but that a free man, an ambassador of the people, should be thus marked is much more horrible" (Grey, *1*, 338–39).

A BALLAD CALLED THE HAYMARKET HECTORS

1.

I sing a woeful ditty
Of a wound that long will smart-a,
   Giv'n, the more's the pity,
In the realm of Magna Charta.
Youth, youth, should'st better be slain by thy foes   5
Than live to be hanged for cutting a nose.

5. This line mimics the words of a well-known song, "Youth, youth, thou hadst better been starved at nurse."

Nell Gywnne. From a painting by Simon Verelst.

2.

Our good King Charles the Second,
Too flippant of treasure and moisture,
    Stooped from the queen infecund
To a wench of orange and oyster.   10
Consulting his cazzo, he found it expedient
To engender Don Johns on Nell the comedian.

3.

The lecherous vainglory
Of being limed with majesty
    Mounts up to such a story   15
This Bitchington travesty,
That to equal her lover, the baggage must dare
To be Helen the Second and cause of a war.

4.

And he, our amorous Jove,
Whilst she lay dry-bobbed under,   20
    To repair the defects of his love,
Must lend her his lightning and thunder;
And for one night prostitutes to her commands
Monmouth, his Life Guards, O'Brien, and Sandys.

5.

And now all the fears of the French   25
And pressing need of navy
    Are dwindled into a salt wench
And *amo, amas, amavi.*
Nay he'll venture his subsidy so she cloven may see,
In female revenge, the nostrils of Coventry.   30

6.

O ye Haymarket Hectors,
How came ye thus charmed
    To be the dissectors

11. *cazzo:* It., penis.
14. *limed:* coupled.
16. *Bitchington travesty:* Nell Gwynne.
20. *dry-bobbed:* coition without emission.
29. As was later proved by the suspension of work on supply until the Coventry Act was
passed, this form of revenge did venture Charles's subsidy.

Of one poor nose unarmed,
Unfit to wear sword or follow a trumpet,   35
That would brandish your knives at the word of a strumpet?

7.

But was it not ungrateful
In Monmouth, ap Sidney, ap Carlo,
    To contrive an act so hateful,
O prince of Wales by Barlow?   40
Since the kind world had dispensed with his mother,
Might not he well have spared the nose of John Brother?

8.

Beware, all ye parliamenteers,
How each of his voice disposes;
    Bab May in the Commons, C. Rex in the Peers,   45
Sit telling your fates on your noses,
And decree, at the mention of every slut,
Whose nose shall continue and whose shall be cut.

9.

If the sister of Rose
Be a whore so anointed   50
    That the Parliament's nose
Must for her be disjointed,
Should you but name the prerogative whore,
How the bullets would whistle, the cannon would roar!

38. *Monmouth, ap Sidney, ap Carlo:* There was some question as to Monmouth's parentage, and Col. Robert Sidney was reputed to be his father. *Ap* is a Welsh form of *of*, and there is a play on the Welsh associations of the duke's title.

40. *Barlow:* Lucy Walters, Monmouth's mother, adopted the name of Barlow.

42. *John Brother:* facetious reference to Sir John Coventry.

45. May's "duties as chief bribery agent of the court had long previously familiarized him with the usages of the House of Commons" *(DNB)*. Charles made a practice of attending debates in the House of Lords on the bill for Lord Roos's divorce in 1670. At first this embarrassed and angered some of the peers, but the king behaved discreetly and found this spectacle "better than going to a play" (Marvell to Popple, 14 April 1670, in Margoliouth).

49. Nell Gwynne had an elder sister named Rose.

53. *the prerogative whore:* The duchess of Cleveland.

On the Prorogation
(1671)

During the evolution of Charles's grand design for a French alliance and
war with the Dutch, Parliament was not permitted to meet. On 22 April
1671 it was prorogued to 16 April 1672, then to 30 October 1672, and finally
to 4 February 1673. This poem refers to the second of these prorogations,
which was proclaimed in September 1671, seven months before the expira-
tion of the first (see lines 94–95). A generous grant of £1,200,000 in the last
session together with grants to Charles from Louis made the king financially
independent of Parliament, and the government could thus silence parlia-
mentary critics of its policy by a succession of prorogations.

ON THE PROROGATION

Prorogued on prorogation—damned rogues and whores!
Our pockets picked and we turned out of doors!
Have we our country plagued, our trust betrayed,
Giv'n polls, loans, subsidies, and royal aid,
Hearth money, imposts, and the lawyers' fees,   5
Ruined all trades, tormented all degrees,
Crush'd poor fanatics and broke through all laws
Of Magna Charta and the Good Old Cause,
                              to be thus fobbed at last?
Have we more millions giv'n in ten years' space   10
Than Norman bastard had and all his race,
Hurried up money bills 'gainst Dutch and French,
But see all spent upon a dunghill wench?
Were we content the kingdom to undo
T' enrich an overridden whore or two,   15
                              and all for this?

11. *Norman bastard:* William the Conqueror was the natural son of Robert II, duke of
Normandy, by Arlette, daughter of a Falaise tanner named Fulbert.
   13. *dunghill wench:* Nell Gwynne.

With plague, war, fire was the kingdom cursed,
But of all plagues were we ourselves the worst,
Who just elections nulled and took much pain
To make the Parliament a rogue in grain;   20
Had Coventry's nose slit, and, through our fears,
Stood to be pissed on by the House of Peers;
Unworthy gentlemen, like servants base,
Run to our master's cellar to fox our mace,
And hundred yet more humble acts than these,   25
That we might not His Majesty displease,
                                        to be thus served?
Welfare! true Vaughan, Howard, Osborne, Carr,
Littleton, Seymour, and our great man of war,
Will Garraway, the Hector of the House,   30
Who always fetched his blow to kill a louse.
These patriots malcontent did plot

19. *just elections nulled:* A few of the returns were disputed in the session of 1670–71.

20. *rogue in grain:* thorough rogue.

21. See *The Haymarket Hectors.*

22. On 10 January 1671 the Commons voted to suspend all debate on supply until a bill to banish Coventry's attackers had been passed. Dering observed in his diary that many considered this "as great a breach of privilege upon the Lords as this affront done to Sir John Coventry was of ours" (pp. 46–47).

24. *fox:* to intoxicate, befuddle. *Mace* here refers to the speaker of the House, Sir Edward Turnor (1617–76). The mace which lies on the table in the House of Commons when the speaker is in the chair is viewed as a symbol of the authority of the House.

In a letter to William Popple (21 March 1670) Marvell writes: "the king sent for us alone, and recommended a rasure of all proceedings. . . . The same thing you know that we proposed at first. We presently ordered it, and went to tell him so the same day, and to thank him. At coming down (a pretty ridiculous thing!), Sir Thomas Clifford carried the speaker, and mace, and all members there, into the king's cellar, to drink to his health" (Margoliouth, p. 301).

28. *Welfare:* obsolete verbal phrase here employed ironically: "good luck to."

28–35. Roger Vaughan, Sir Robert Howard, Sir Thomas Osborne, Robert Carr, Sir Thomas Littleton, Sir Edward Seymour, and William Garraway had all been members of the opposition, but they appear in the court party lists printed by Browning (*Danby, 3,* 37–43) for the sessions of 1669–71. When Buckingham's group threw in its lot with the court in the autumn of 1670, "Seymour, Howard, and others among Buckingham's satellites became extremely active on behalf of the government" (Browning, *Danby, 1,* 83). Marvell comments on these and other defections in a letter to William Popple (28 November 1670): "The House was thin and obsequious. They voted at first they would supply him [the king] according to his occasions, *nemine,* as it was remarked, *contradicente;* but few affirmatives, rather a silence as of men ashamed and unwilling. Sir R. Howard, Seymour, Temple, Carr, and Hollis openly took leave of their former party to head the king's business" (Margoliouth, p. 305). Seymour had been for removal of evil ministers and redress of grievances before supply in 1668, but in 1670 was foremost in urging the granting of a supply before all other questions. He, Littleton, and Howard took the same position in January 1671, and Garraway spoke against a proviso specifying that any supply granted should be used to maintain the Triple League (Dering, pp. 45, 76).

Their country's good, till they had places got,
Blustered and huffed till they were officered,
But then o'th'country more the devil a word,   35
    Damned Buckingham, of a false sire the son,
Did we for this dismount old Clarendon
And set thee up, thou mighty man of state,
And in thy hands put the whole kingdom's fate?
Did we forget thy former treachery,   40
When, false, our king thou left'st in misery,
Turned kneeling renegade to what was trump,
And payed allegiance to the rotten Rump?
Did we free thee when chancellor thee mumbled
And wast by him from post to pillar tumbled?   45
Did we connive at spilling Shrewsbury's life,
That with more freedom thou might'st whore his wife?
And all for this return? Ungrateful wretch,
May pox and plague and devil hence thee fetch!
Or some prorogued, incensed Felton, rather,   50
Send this cursed son to find his guilty father!
No other way could'st find t' attain thy ends
Than by disgusting the king and his best friends,
Turn off the Parliament that ne'er king before
Had such a one, nor never will have more?   55
What gave thee cause to fear we should not do
Whate'er the king or thou commanded's to?
If standing army 'twas thou would'st been at,
As well as others we would have raised that.
We could have made, as well as any other,   60

40–43. Buckingham left the exiled king in 1657 to marry Fairfax's only daughter, regaining thereby part of his estates, and, through Fairfax's influence, obtaining the protector's pardon. He was imprisoned by Cromwell, but on the death of the lord-protector was released on his word of honor not to abet the enemies of the commonwealth.

44–45. Buckingham was sent to the Tower in June 1667 on a charge of treason. Regarding Clarendon as the author of his late eclipse, he took an energetic part in the prosecution of the chancellor.

46–47. The earl of Shrewsbury died of wounds inflicted by Buckingham in a duel fought on 16 January 1668. His wife was reported to have held Buckingham's horse during the encounter.

50. John Felton, a discharged officer, assassinated the 1st duke of Buckingham as a tyrant on 23 August 1628.

54–55. The further prolongation of Parliament's prorogation to October 1672 was attributed by the French to York and Buckingham (Feiling, *Foreign Policy*, p. 329).

60–63. There had been many rumors that the king intended to legitimize Monmouth as early as 1663 (see Pepys, 15 May). Buckingham took a leading part in getting a bill passed to permit Lord Roos to divorce his adulterous wife and remarry, hoping thereby to establish a precedent for Charles to follow in divorcing Catherine and marrying again. At the last minute

The bastard's right legitimate as brother,
Turned Kate a-grazing, the infecund queen,
And newer issue had, had the humor been.
League Tripartite we could have broke and dance
Framed to the measure and the pipe of France,   65
Looked through our fingers and laughed to behold
New London flaming, as we did the old.
We could have yielded to raise citadel
More our own city than the Dutch to quell.
We could plots make, as Oliver on Hewit,   70
And make them guilty on't that never knew it.
And must we, after all our service done
In field for father and in House for son,
Be thus cashiered to please a pocky peer
That neither Roundhead is nor Cavalier,   75
But of some medley cut, some ill-shaped brat,
Would fain be something if he knew but what?
A commonwealth's man he owns himself to be,
And, by and by, for absolute monarchy,
Then neither likes, but, some new knicknacks found,   80
Nor fish nor flesh, nor square is nor yet round.
Venetian model pleaseth him at night;
Tomorrow, France is only in the right.
Thus, like light butterflies, much flutter makes,
Sleeps of one judgment, and of another wakes.   85
Zealous in morn, he doth a bishop make,
Yet before night all bishops down he'd take.
He all things is, but unto nothing true,
All old things hates, but can abide no new.
But please your pocky Grace to give me leave   90
To ask why thus you do our prince deceive?
Your first prorogue might sure have stood, for then
'Twas time enough for to prorogue again,

---

however, the king refused to allow a motion for the dissolution of his marriage to be in-
troduced. There is no evidence that Buckingham was championing Monmouth as heir to the
throne as early as 1670, when the Roos bill came up.

64–65. Buckingham, of course, was a leader in establishing a pro-French policy.

70. Dr. John Hewit, Anglican priest and ardent loyalist, was executed on charges provided
by Cromwell's *agents provocateurs* in 1658.

74–89. This "character" of the whimsical Buckingham may have served Dryden as a model
for his famous portrait of Zimri in *Absalom and Achitophel*.

76. *brat*: a cloth used as an overgarment, generally of a makeshift character.

82. *Venetian model*: a republic like Venice.

And not all in a hurry, sev'n months before
Our former was expired, to add six more.   95
                              Was fob so full?
Nell's in again, we hear, though we are out.
Methinks we might have met to give a clout
And then prorogue again: our wont hath been
Never to miss a session 'gainst lying in.   100
For always 'gainst the time, the French invades,
'Gainst when we money raise to keep the jades,
And twenty to one, before next spring is over,
Marched must our horse again be unto Dover
To guard the shore against the Dutch and French,   105
When all this means but new supply for wench.
The cursed Cabal saw 'twas in vain to move
For dissolution (we had too much love
To be dissolved), which put thee to find out
This damned side wind to bring thy ends about.   110
For now the sacred codpiece must keep Lent,
Unless some kind supplies from France be sent.
Our first prorogue had many an ostent plain,
Enough to show we ne'er should sit again,
Had we but hearkened and the foregame played,   115
We had prevented our being thus betrayed.
For had we observation made, we might
'Fore morn have known the fate we found at night.
For Caesar more presages never had
Of falling greatness than to us were made.   120
Though Heav'n for us no comets kindly showed,
Yet we had portents which were all as good:
A crow crossed speaker's coach, as to th' House he came;
On crutches that day went the cripple lame;
The Thames at our proroguing backward run;   125
Moon shone at midnight and at noon the sun;
A hollow, earthy voice in the House was heard,
Which made the speaker of Guy Fawkes afeared;

94–95. The proclamation further proroguing Parliament was issued 22 September 1671.
96. *fob*: fob-pocket, the treasury.
98. Nell Gwynne's second son, James, was born on Christmas Day 1671. This line face-tiously suggests that Parliament should have been permitted to meet in order to vote the new baby a diaper (*clout*).
108–09. *we had too much love | To be dissolved*: We were too obliging to deserve dissolution. The government felt with some reason that a new Parliament would be less cooperative than the old.

Owen's pease pottage unkindly boiled that day;
Foul handkerchief in pocket had Bab May;   130
That day our clock, too, was upon his tricks:
'Twould not go right, struck five when 'twas near six.
But since there's no resisting of our fate,
We hope we may have leave to invocate:
Oh sweet Revenge! let us but live to see   135
Such rogues to be prorogued as well as we;
Indulge our envy but to see the day,
Though we be ruined all, as well as they.
We tyrants love, if we can tyrants be;
If not, next wish is we may all be free.   140

The Dream of the Cabal
(1672)

The poem describes an imaginary meeting of the Cabal, Charles's informal cabinet, in 1672. The king himself is present, as is the duke of Ormonde, who alone attempts to defend the liberties of the subject against the tyrannous incitations of the other ministers. Although the episode is fictitious, it succeeds in capturing the political attitudes and manners of the various speakers. Parliament had been prorogued since April 1671 and was not to meet until February 1673 (see *On the Prorogation*). In this long interval Charles planned to execute the great stroke of making war against Holland in alliance with France and declaring his adherence to Roman Catholicism. The Cabal met regularly with Charles to take measures for carrying out the French treaty. Parliament and people were largely opposed to an alliance with France, and Louis's military preparations in the beginning of the year made, in the words of the Puritan divine Richard Baxter, "the Protestant hearts to tremble."

The members of the Cabal were all "agreed in wishing to strengthen the royal prerogative by moderating the uniformity laws, with the help of France, and during the excitement caused by a foreign war" (Ranke, *3*, 520), but only two of them, Clifford and Arlington, knew of the secret Treaty of Dover and of its provision that Charles should proclaim himself a Catholic in return for an additional subsidy from Louis. The debate that the poem pretends to report centers mainly on ways and means for Charles to extend his prerogative and govern without Parliament.

No attributions are made in any of the texts I have seen. In subject matter, ideas, and the convention of the dream or vision, this poem resembles two satires ascribed to John Ayloffe, *Britannia and Raleigh* and *Marvell's Ghost*. For a detailed discussion of the evidence, see George deF. Lord, "Satire and Sedition: The Life and Work of John Ayloffe," *Huntington Library Quarterly* 29 (1966): 255–73.

The Dream of the Cabal: A Prophetical Satire

Anno 1672

As t'other night in bed I thinking lay
How I my rent should to my landlord pay,
Since corn, nor wool, nor beast would money make,
Tumbling perplexed, these thoughts kept me awake:
"What will become of this mad world?" quoth I.   5
What's its disease? What is its remedy?
Where will it issue? Whereto does it tend?
Some ease to misery 'tis to know its end."
Till servants dreaming, as they used to do,
Snored me asleep. I fell a-dreaming too.   10
     Methought there met the grand Cabal of seven
(Odd numbers, some men say, do best please Heaven).
When sat they were and doors were all fast shut,
I secret was behind the hangings put.
Both hear and see I could, but he that there   15
Had placed me bade me have as great a care
Of stirring as my life, and, ere that out
From thence I came, resolved should be my doubt:
What would become of this mad world, unless
Present designs were crossed with ill success?   20
     An awful silence there was held some space,
Till, trembling, thus began one called His Grace:
"Great sir, your government for first twelve years
Has spoiled the monarchy and made our fears
So potent on us that we must change quite   25
The old foundations and make new, wrong or right.
For too great mixture of democracy
Within this government allayed must be,
And no allay like nulling parliaments,
O'th' people's pride and arrogance the vents,   30
Factious and saucy, disputing royal pleasure,
Who your commands by their own humors measure.
For king in barnacles and to th'rack-staves tied

---

11. *grand Cabal of seven:* Clifford, Ashley, Buckingham, Arlington, Lauderdale, plus Ormonde and King Charles.
22. *his grace:* Buckingham.
33. *barnacles:* instruments of torture. *rack-staves:* the upright arms of a rack.

You must remain, if these you will abide."
    So spake the long blue ribbon; then a second,   35
Though not so tall, yet quite as wise is reckoned,
Did thus begin: "Great sir, you are now on
A tender point much to be thought upon,
And thought on only, for by ancient law
'Tis death to mention what my lord foresaw.   40
His trembling showed it, wherefore I'm so bold
To advise its standing, lest it should be told
We did attempt to change it; for so much
Our ancestors secured it, that to touch,
Like sacred Mount, 'tis death, and such a trick   45
I no ways like to make tongue break my neck."
    Thus said, he sat. Then lord of northern tone,
In gall and guile a second unto none,
Enraged rose, and, chol'ric, thus began:
"Dread Majesty, male beam of fame, a son   50
Of th' hundred-and-tenth monarch of the nore,
De'il split the weam of th'lowne that spoke afore!
Shame faw the crag of that ill-mannered lord
That 'nent his king durst speak so faw a word!
And aw my saul right weel the first man meant,   55
De'il hoop his lugs that loves a parliament!
Twa houses aw my saul are twa too mickle.
They'll gar the laird shall ne'er have more a prickle,
Na siller get to gie the bonny lass:
But full as good be born without a tarse.   60
Ten thousand plagues light on his crag that 'gin
To make you be but third part of a king.
De'il take my saul, I'll ne'er the matter mince,

35. *long blue ribbon:* Buckingham received the Garter in 1649. *a second:* the duke of Ormonde.
   39. *ancient law:* presumably the Magna Charta. I cannot, however, find any reference there to capital punishment for those who advocate the nullification of parliaments.
   45. *sacred Mount:* Sinai. See Exod. 19:12: "whosoever toucheth the Mount shall be surely put to death."
   47. *lord of northern tone:* Lauderdale.
   51. *nore:* the north, i.e., Scotland.
   52. *weam:* belly. *lowne:* rogue.
   53. *faw:* fall upon. *crag:* neck.
   54. *'nent:* anent or against. *faw:* false dialect for "foul."
   56. *hoop his lugs:* box his ears.
   58. *gar:* cause. *laird:* a landed proprietor in Scotland, but here referring to Charles II. *prickle:* penis.
   59. *gie:* give.
   60. *tarse:* penis.

I'd rather subject be than sike a prince.
To hang and burn and slay and draw and kill   65
And measure aw things by my own guid will
Is gay dominion; a checkmate I hate
Of men or laws, it looks so like a state."
    This eager, well-meant zeal some laughter stirred,
Till, nose half-plush, half-flesh, the inkhorn lord   70
Craved audience thus: "Grave Majesty divine
(Pardon that Cambridge title I make mine),
We now are entered on the great'st debate
That can concern your throne and royal state.
His Grace hath so spoke all, that we who next   75
Speak after can but comment on his text.
Only 'tis wonder at this sacred board
Should sit 'mongst us a Magna Charta lord,
A peer of old rebellious barons' breed,
Worst and great'st enemies to royal seed.   80
But to proceed: well was it urged by's Grace
Such' liberty was giv'n for twelve years' space
That are by passed; there's now necessity
Of new foundations, if safe you'll be.
What travail, charge, and art (before was set   85
This Parliament) we had, you can't forget;
How forced to court, cajole, and bribe, for fear
They wrong should run, e'er since they have been here;
What diligence, what study day and night,
Was on us, and what care to keep them right!   90
Wherefore, if good you can't make Parliament,
On whom such costs, such art and pains were spent,
And moneys, all we had for them to do,
Since we miss that, 'tis best dismiss them too.
'Tis true, this House the best is you can call,   95
But, in my judgment, best is none at all."

65–68. In 1673 Lauderdale offered to overawe Parliament with Scottish forces (Burnet, 2, 11).
    68. *state:* non-monarchical commonwealth.
    70. *inkhorn lord:* Arlington, who had been the earl of Bristol's clerk.
    72. An allusion, no doubt, to the formal oratory with which Charles would have been greeted on visits to Cambridge University. On such occasions Charles desired that speeches might be "few and short, or none" (Bryant, p. 219).
    78. Ormonde was descended from Theobald Butler (d. 1206), who had opposed King John.
    85. *set:* sat.
    93–94. *Moneys* is appositive to *all* and antecedent to *that.*

"Well moved!" the whole Cabal cried, "Parliaments
Are clogs to princes and their brave intents."
One did object, 'twas against majesty
T'obey the people's pleasure. Another he   100
Their inconvenience argues, and that neither
Close their designs were, nor yet speedy either.
Whilst thus confused chattered the Cabal,
And many moved, none heard, but speak did all,
A little bobtailed lord, urchin of state,   105
A Praisegod-Barebones-peer whom all men hate,
Amphibious animal, half fool, half knave,
Begged silence and this purblind counsel gave:
"Blest and best monarch that e'er scepter bore,
Renowned for virtue, but for honor more,   110
That lord spake last has well and wisely shown
That parliaments, nor new, nor old, nor none,
Can well be trusted longer, for the state
And glory of the crown hate all checkmate.
That monarchy may from its childhood grow   115
To man's estate, France has taught us how.
Monarchy's divine: divinity it shows
That he goes backward that not forward goes.
Therefore go on, let other kingdoms see
Your will's your law: that's absolute monarchy.   120
A mixed hodge-podge will now no longer do;
Caesar or nothing you are brought unto.
Strike then, great sir, 'fore these debates take wind;
Remember that Occasions's bald behind.
Our game is sure in this, if wisely played,   125
And sacred votes to the vulgar not betrayed.
But if the rumor should once get on wing
That we consult to make you abs'lute king,
The plebeians' head, the gentry forsooth,
They straight would snort and have an aching tooth.   130
Lest they, I say, should your great secrets scent,
And you oppose in nulling Parliament,

105. *A little bobtailed lord:* Shaftesbury.
106. Shaftesbury was one of the few gentlemen in the Barebones Parliament (4 July–12
December 1653). This Parliament was named for Praisegod Barebones, a London leather-
seller who took a prominent part in it.
115–16. Some of Charles's close advisers at this time were urging him to extend his pre-
rogative after the pattern of Louis XIV.
124. *Occasion:* traditionally personified as a woman bald except for a forelock.

I think it safer and a greater skill
To obviate than to o'ercome an ill.
For those that head the herd are full as rude,   135
When th' humor takes, as the following multitude.
Therefore be quick in your resolves, and when
Resolved you have, execute quicker then.
Remember your great father lost the game
By slow proceedings. Mayn't you do the same?   140
An unexpected, unregarded blow
Wounds more than ten made by an open foe.
Delays do dangers breed; the sword is yours,
By law declared, what need of other pow'rs?
We may unpolitic be judged, or worse,   145
If we can't make the sword command the purse.
No art or courtship can the rule so shape
Without a force: it must be done by rape,
And when 'tis done, to say you cannot help
Will satisfy enough the gentle whelp.   150
Fanatics they'll to Providence impute
Their thraldom and immediately grow mute,
For they, poor pious fools, think the decree
Of Heav'n falls on them, though from Hell it be;
And when their reason is abased to it,   155
They forthwith think't religion to submit,
And vainly glorying in a passive shame,
They'll put off man to wear the Christian name.
Wherefore to lull 'em, do their hopes fulfill
With liberty; they're haltered at your will.   160
Give them but conventicle-room, and they
Will let you steal the Englishman away,
And heedless be, till you your nets have spread,
And pulled down conventicles on their head.
Militia, then, and parliaments, cashier;   165
A formidable standing army rear;
They'll mount you up, and up you soon will be.
They'll fear, who ne'er did love, your monarchy,
And if they fear, no matter for their hate:
To rule by law becomes a sneaking state.   170

159–64. These lines refer to Charles's Declaration of Indulgence, which suspended the
penal laws against Nonconformists in 1672. Under pressure from Parliament it was with-
drawn in 1673.

161. The assemblies of Nonconformists were known as *conventicles*.

Lay by all fear, care not what people say,
Regard to them will your designs betray.
When bite they can't, what hurt can barking do?
And sir, in time we'll spoil their barking too,
Make coffee-clubs talk of more humble things   175
Than state affairs and interest of kings."
   Thus spake the rigling peer, when one more grave,
That had much less of fool but more of knave,
Began: "Great sir, it gives no small content
To hear such zeal for you 'gainst Parliament;   180
Wherefore, though I an enemy no less
To parliaments than you yourselves profess,
Yet I must also enter my protest
'Gainst these rude rumbling counsels indigest,
And, great sir, tell you, 'tis an harder thing   185
Than they suggest to make you abs'lute king.
Old buildings to pull down, believe it true,
More danger in it hath than building new,
And what shall prop your superstructure till
Another you have built that suits your will?   190
An army shall, say they. Content. But stay,
From whence shall this new army have its pay?
For easy, gentle, government a while
Appear must to this kingdom, to beguile
The people's minds and make them cry up you,   195
For rasing old and making better new.
For taxes with new government all will blame
And put the kingdom soon into a flame,
For tyranny has no such lovely look
To catch men with unless you hide the hook,   200
And no bait hides it more than present ease.
Ease but their taxes, then do what you please.
Wherefore, all wild debates laid by, from whence
Shall money rise to bear this vast expense?
For our first thoughts thus well resolved, we   205
In other things much sooner shall agree.
Join then with Mother Church, whose bosom stands
Ope to receive us, stretching forth her hands.
Close but this breach, and she will let you see

---

177. *rigling:* northern dialectal variant of "ridgeling," a male animal with only one testicle.
one more grave: Clifford.
  207. Clifford was the soul of the Catholic project in the secret Treaty of Dover.

Her purse as open as her arms shall be;   210
For, sacred sir (by guess I do not speak),
Of poor she'll make you rich, and strong of weak.
At home, abroad, no money, no, nor men
She'll let you lack; turn but to her again."
    The Scot could here no longer hold, but cried: 215
"De'il take the pape and all that's on his side,
The whore of Rome, that mickle man of sin,
Plague take the mother, bairns, and aw the kin!
What racks my saul? Must we the holy rood
Place in God's kirk again? Troth, 'tis not guid.   220
I defy the lowne, the de'il, and aw his work!
The pape shall lig no mare in God's guid kirk."
    The Scot with laughter checked, they all agreed
The lord spake last should in his speech proceed,
Which thus he did: "Great sir, you know 'tis season   225
Salts all the motions that we make with reason,
And now a season is afforded us,
The best e'er came, and most propitious.
Besides the sum the Cath'lics will advance,
You know the offers we are made from France,   230
And to have money and no Parliament
Must fully answer your designed intent.
And thus without tumultuous noise or huff
Of parliaments, you may have money enough,
Which, if neglected now, there's none knows when   235
Like opportunities may be had again;
For all t'extirpate now combined be
Both civil and religious liberty.
Thus money you'll have to exalt the crown,
Without stooping majesty to country clown.   240
The Triple League, I know, will be objected,
As if that ought by us to be respected!
But who to heretics or rebel pay'th
The truth engaged to by solemn faith
Debaucheth virtue: by those very things,   245
The church profaneth and debaseth kings,

---

230. The secret treaty provided a grant of two million livres to aid Charles in suppressing any insurrection that might arise from his public conversion to Catholicism and further annual grants of three million livres to support the naval war against the Dutch (John Lingard, *The History of England from the First Invasion by the Romans to the Accession of William and Mary in 1688* [Edinburgh, 1902], 183).

As you yourself have admirably shown
By burning Solemn Cov'nant, though your own.
Faith, justice, truth, plebeian virtues be,
Look well in them but not in majesty.   250
For public faith is but a public thief,
The greatest cheat in Nature's vain belief."
    The second lord, though checked, yet did not fear,
Impatient grew and could no longer bear,
But rose in heat, and that a little rude;   255
The lord's voice interrupts and for audience sued:
"Great Majesty, authentic authors say,
When hand was lifted up Croesus to slay,
The father's danger on the dumb son did make
Such deep impressions that he forthwith spake.   260
Pardon, great sir, if I, in imitation,
Seeing the danger to yourself and nation,
Do my resolved-on silence also break,
Although I see the matter I shall speak
Under such disadvantages will lie,   265
It shall exploded be as well as I.
But vainly do they boast they loyal are
That can't for princes' good reflections bear,
Nor will I call compurgators to prove
What honor to the crown I've borne with love.   270
My acts have spoken and sufficient are
Above whate'er detractors did or dare.
Wherefore, great sir, 'tis ignorance or hate
Dictates these counsels you to precipitate.
For say 't again I will, not eat my word,   275
No council's power, no nor yet the sword
Can old foundations alter or make new:
Let time interpret who hath spoken true.
Those country gentry with their beef and bacon
Will show how much you courtiers are mistaken.   280
For parliaments are not of that cheap rate
That they will down without a broken pate.
And then I doubt you'll find those worthy lords

248. The Solemn League and Covenant was burned by order of Parliament on 29 May
1661, the king's birthday.
    253. *The second lord:* Ormonde.
    258. *Croesus:* See Herodotus, *History* 1.85.
    269–70. In the court of Charles II Ormonde "was almost the sole representative of the
high-toned virtues of a nobler generation" (*DNB*).   *compurgators:* character witnesses.

More braves and champions with their tongue than swords.
Wherefore, dread sir, incline not royal ear   285
To their advice, but safer counsels hear.
Stay till these lords have got a crown to lose.
And then consult with them which way they'll choose.
Will you all hazard for their humor's sake,
Who nothing have to lose, nothing at stake,   290
And at one game your royal crown expose
To gratify the foolish lusts of those
Who hardly have subsistence how to live
But what your crown and grace to them does give?
And one of those bagpudding gentlemen   295
(Except their places) would buy nine or ten.
Then why they should thus slight the gentleman,
I see no reason, nor think how they can.
For had not gentleman done more than lord
(I'll boldly say 't) you ne'er had been restored.   300
But why of armies now, great sir, must we
So fond just now all on the sudden be?
What faithful guardians have they been to pow'rs
That have employed them that you'd make 'em yours?
Enough our age, we need not seek the glory   305
Of armies' faith in old or doubtful story.
Your father 'gainst the Scots an army reared,
But soon that army more than Scot he feared.
He was in haste to raise them, as we are,
But to disband them was far more his care.   310
How Scottish army after did betray
His trust and person both, I need not say.
Rump Parliament an army reared, and they
The Parliament that raised them did betray.
The lord protector they set up one hour,   315

295. *bagpudding:* clownish.
296. *Except their places:* except for what the noble members of the Cabal make from their offices at court.
305–06. I.e., we are old enough to have seen for ourselves how unfaithful armies can be.
307–12. In 1639 Charles I attempted with soldiers to enforce the use of the Anglican prayer book in Scotland. His troops were undisciplined, however, and he was obliged to suspend the attempt, fearing they might revolt for want of pay. In 1648 a secret treaty was signed between Charles and the Scots by which they engaged to restore him with an army in return for concessions to Presbyterianism. This army was defeated by parliamentary forces under Cromwell and Fairfax.
313–314. The parliamentary army under Monck forced the Rump to dissolve itself in 1660.
315–16. I.e., in deposing Richard Cromwell.

The next pulled down the protectorian pow'r.
Your father's block and judges the same troops
Did guard; same tongues at death of both made whoops.
And will you suffer armies to beguile
And give your crown and you to cross and pile?   320
What if a Monck should both swear, lie, and feign,
Till he does both your trust and army gain,
And you believe his oath and faith is true,
But serves himself instead of serving you?
Pardon, great sir, if zeal transports my tongue   325
T'express what e'en your greatness don't become.
Expose I can't your crown and sacred throat
To the false faith of a common redcoat.
Your law your all does fence secure from fears:
That kept, what trouble needs of bandoleers?   330
Consider, sir, 'tis law that makes you king.
The sword another to the crown may bring,
For force knows no distinction: longest sword
Makes peasant prince, lackey above his lord.
If that be all that we must have for laws,   335
Your will inferior may be to Jack Straw's,
If greater force him follow: there's no right
Where law is failing and for will men fight.
Best man is he alone whose steel's most strong;
Where no law is, there's neither right nor wrong.   340
That fence broke down and all in common laid,
Subjects may prince and prince may them invade.
See, greatest sir, how these your throne lay down
Instead of making great your royal crown,
How they divest you of your majesty,   345
For, law destroyed, you are no more than we.
And very vain would be the plea of crown,
When statute laws and parliaments are down."
    This peer proceeded on to show how vain
An holy league would be with Rome again,   350
And what dishonor 'twould be to our crowns

---

320. *cross and pile*: the toss of a coin, Cf. *Hudibras,* pt. 3, canto 3, 689: "cross, I win, and pile,
you lose." If Charles tried to secure his power with an army he would lose his crown, whatever
happened.
    330. *bandoleers*: boxes containing charges for muskets. The sense seems to be that the king
need not use force to keep his subjects in order if he is faithful to law.
    336. *Jack Straw*: a leader in the Peasant's Revolt, 1381.

If we to France give cautionary towns.
He's interrupted and bid speak no more
By's enraged Majesty, who deeply swore
His tongue had so run o'er that he'd take   355
Such vengeance on him and example make
To after ages, all which heard should fear
To speak what would displease the royal ear,
And bid the lord that spoke before go on,
And silence all should keep till he had done;   360
Who thus his speech resumed: "If lord spake last
To interrupt me had not made such haste,
I soon had done, for I was come, great sir,
T'advise your sending Dutch ambassador;
But much it does concern you whom to trust   365
With this embassy, for none true nor just,
Wise, stout, or honorable, nor a friend
Should you in any wise resolve to send,
Lest any unseen or unlucky chance
Should in this war befall to us or France.   370
We may that loathéd wretch give to the hate
Of the people's fury, them to satiate.
And when all's done that can be done by man,
Much must be left to chance, do what you can.
And if you'll make all Christendom your friend,   375
And put to Dutch Land League an utter end,
Then surely you may have of men and treasure
Enough of both to execute your pleasure."
    This speech being ended, six of seven agree
France shall be loved and Holland hated be.   380
All gone, I waked and wondered what should mean
All I had heard; methought 'twas more than dream.
And if Cabal thus serve us Englishmen,
'Tis ten to one but I shall dream again.

352. *cautionary towns:* towns given as pledges for performance of a treaty. There was no such provision in the secret Treaty of Dover, although Charles was to be granted Walcheren, Sluys, and the island of Cadsand out of the anticipated conquests.

363–70. Sir George Downing was sent as ambassador to The Hague in December 1627 to provoke a rupture with the Dutch. He was well endowed for the task, for his impertinence so incensed the Dutch that he fled before his mission was completed and was sent to the Tower on his return to England (Feiling, *Foreign Policy,* p. 112).

376. *Dutch Land League:* presumably the Triple Alliance.

JOHN AYLOFFE

Britannia and Raleigh
(1674–75)

Britannia and Raleigh is one of several saturnine "visions" or "prophecies" exposing the popish and authoritarian leanings of Charles II and his court. These poems, such as *The Dream of the Cabal, Nostradamus's Prophecy, Oceana and Britannia,* and *Marvell's Ghost,* were written in the 1670s and early 1680s. They are characterized by a grim, humorless tone, employ analogies from Roman history to underscore the decadence and tyranny of the Stuarts, and uphold republican ideals. *Britannia and Raleigh* is ascribed to "Mr. Ayloff" in Bod. MS Eng. poet. d. 49 by Captain Thompson, who edited Marvell in 1776.

I follow Margoliouth in dating *Britannia and Raleigh* after Henriette de Kéroualle married Philip Herbert, earl of Pembroke, on 17 December 1674 (see line 170). It probably was written during the long period of prorogation between February 1674 and April 1675, as "long-scorned Parliament" suggests (line 135).

BRITANNIA AND RALEIGH

Britannia

Ah, Raleigh, when thy breath thou didst resign
To trembling James, would I had yielded mine!
Cubs didst thou call 'em? Hadst thou seen this brood
Of earls, of dukes, and princes of the blood,
No more of Scottish race thou wouldst complain;   5
Those would be blessings in this spurious reign.

3. Raleigh appears as an opponent of the succession of James I. He was condemned in 1603 for complicity in a plot to kill "the old fox and his cubs" and to put Arabella Stuart on the throne (Margoliouth).
4. Charles II's bastard princes in 1675 included James, duke of Monmouth, son of Lucy Walters of Barlow; Charles Fitzroy, earl of Southampton, and Henry Fitzroy, earl of Euston, both sons of the duchess of Cleveland; and Charles Lennox, duke of Richmond, son of the duchess of Portsmouth.

Awake, arise from thy long-blessed repose!
Once more with me partake of mortal woes.

Raleigh

What mighty power has forced me from my rest?
Ah, mighty queen, why so unseemly dressed?   10

Britannia

Favored by night, concealed by this disguise,
Whilst the lewd court in drunken slumber lies,
I stole away and never will return,
Till England knows who did her city burn,
Till Cavaliers shall favorites be deemed   15
And loyal sufferings by the court esteemed,
Till Howard and Garr'way shall a bribe reject,
Till golden Osborne cheating shall detect,
Till atheist Lauderdale shall leave this land,
Till Commons' votes shall cut-nose guards disband,   20
Till Kate a happy mother shall become,
Till Charles loves parliaments, till James hates Rome.

Raleigh

What fatal crimes make you forever fly
Your own loved court and martyr's progeny?

17. Robert Howard, according to a letter from Marvell to William Popple (28 November 1670), was one of five members of the country party who deserted to the king's side. Howard's dishonesty is indicated by the following account (Browning, *Danby*, *1*, 245–46): "In September 1677 Danby revived the scheme he had first mentioned nearly three years earlier and delivered his long-expected attack upon Sir Robert Howard, formally accusing him in council of conniving at the misuse of government funds by the tellers of the Exchequer, employing his knowledge of their irregularities to compel them to lend him money, and trying to defeat an investigation by exhibiting false bags, in which were lead blanks or pieces of iron with only a little silver on top. The charge appears to have been substantially true, and the best Howard could do in his defense was to interpose one delay after another." See *On the Prorogation*, 28–35 *n*.

Some versions read *Leigh* (or *Lee*) and *Garraway*. As leaders of the opposition, Garraway and Lee were to name £600,000, which would procure peace but not prolong the war. Garraway, however, named twice that amount, and was seconded by Lee. In this manner they both obtained enough money to enable the court to carry on the war. (Burnet, *2*, 15–16 and 92 describes how Lee was bribed with £6,000.)

18. As the first minister to practice systematic bribery in Parliament, Osborne (the earl of Danby) would have been the last person to expose venality.

19. *atheist:* Lauderdale, originally a Covenanter, turned his coat at the Restoration. In 1663 he declared himself ready to take a cart-load of oaths and to turn Turk to keep his place (Margoliouth).

20. Another allusion to the maiming of Sir John Coventry. See *The Haymarket Hectors*.

21. *Kate:* Queen Catherine.

Britannia

A colony of French possess the court;   25
Pimps, priests, buffoons i'th' privy-chamber sport.
Such slimy monsters ne'er approached a throne
Since Pharaoh's reign, nor so defiled a crown.
I'th' sacred ear tyrannic arts they croak,
Pervert his mind, his good intentions choke,   30
Tell him of golden Indies, fairy lands,
Leviathans, and absolute commands.
Thus fairy-like the king they steal away,
And in his place a Louis changeling lay.
How oft have I him to himself restored,   35
In's left the scales, in's right hand placed the sword?
Taught him their use, what dangers would ensue
To those that tried to separate these two?
The bloody Scottish chronicle turned o'er,
Showed him how many kings in purple gore   40
Were hurled to hell by learning tyrants' lore.
    The other day famed Spenser I did bring,
In lofty notes Tudor's blessed reign to sing:
How Spain's proud pow'r her virgin arms controlled
And golden days in peaceful order rolled,   45
How like ripe fruit she dropped from off the throne,
Full of grey hairs, good deeds, endless renown.

25. Louise de Kéroualle, the king's mistress, was then at the height of her power.
27–28. See Exod. 8:4 "Their land brought froth frogs: yea, even in the king's chambers."
32. *Leviathans:* Charles II had been a pupil of Hobbes in Paris in 1646. *Leviathan* was
first published in 1651. Ogg comments as follows on the relevance of Hobbs to the policies of
Charles II: "In mentality the philosopher of Malmesbury was un-English; but his theories
were to find their most complete vindication in Restoration England; and if he was not the
inspiration of later Stuart absolutism, he was its prophet. Charles was restored without con-
dition; he was protected against seditious talk by a special treason act; he was given absolute
control over all the armed forces; his judges often considered themselves merely the mouth-
pieces of the royal will; he was empowered by statute to remodel corporations, and so was
enabled to destroy those 'worms' which, according to Hobbes, consumed the entrails of the
body politic. Each of these things had been advocated as a principle in the *Leviathan*. Still
more, the Test Act of 1673 and the Act of 1678 imposed a state religion, for a political purpose
and by secular penalties: with this cement Charles established an impregnable power,
whereas James transferred his foundations to the shifting sands of compromise and toleration"
(*Charles II*, 2, 745–46).
39–41. The first four Jameses all died violent deaths, James I and James III at the hands of
rebellious subjects (Margoliouth).
42–43. These lines allude to Spenser's praise of "great Gloriana" (Queen Elizabeth) in
the *Faerie Queene*. Ayloffe apparently did not know the poem, since Spenser died before the
queen.

As the Jessean hero did appease
Saul's stormy rage and checked his black disease,
So the learned bard with artful songs suppressed   50
The swelling passions of his cankered breast
And in his heart kind influences shed
Of country's love, by truth and justice bred.
Then to confirm the cure so well begun,
To him I showed this glorious setting sun: 55
How by her people's looks pursued from far,
She mounted up on a triumphal car,
Outshining Virgo and the Julian star.
Whilst in Truth's mirror this glad scene he spied,
Entered a dame bedecked with spotted pride,   60
Fair flower-de-luces within an azure field;
Her left arm bears the ancient Gallic shield,
By her usurped, her right a bloody sword,
Inscribed *Leviathan the Sov'reign Lord.*
Her tow'ry front a fiery meteor bears,   65
From exhalation bred of blood and tears.
Around her Jove's loud rav'nous curs complain.
Pale Death, Lusts, Horror, fill her pompous train.
From th'easy king she Truth's bright mirror took,
And on the ground in spiteful rage it broke,   70
And frowning, thus, with proud disdain, she spoke:
    "Are threadbare virtues ornaments for kings?
Such poor pedantic toys teach underlings!
Do monarchs rise by virtue or the sword?
Whoe'er grew great by keeping of his word?   75

48. *Jessean:* "And it came to pass, when the evil spirit from God was upon Saul, that David
[the son of Jesse] took an harp, and played with his hand: so Saul was refreshed, and was well,
and the evil spirit departed from him" (1 Sam. 16:23).

58. *Julian star:* the comet that appeared at the time of Caesar's assassination.

60. This figure represents the regime of Louis XIV.

63. *usurped:* The king of England was still *Rex Angliae et Franciae* and quartered the lilies
with the leopards (Margoliouth).

67. *Jove's . . . curs:* Cerberus and the hounds that girdled Scylla, with perhaps an allusion
to Milton's Sin, who "seemed woman to the waist, and fair," but

> about her middle round
> A cry of hell hounds never ceasing barked
> With wide Cerberean mouths full loud, and rung
> A hideous peal: yet, when they list, would creep,
> If aught disturbed their noise, into her womb,
> And kennel there, yet there still barked and howled
> Within unseen.
>
> (*Paradise Lost,* II.652–58)

Virtue's a faint greensickness of the souls;
Dastards the hearts and active heat controls.
The rival gods, monarchs of th' other world,
This mortal poison amongst princes hurled,
Fearing the mighty projects of the great   80
Should drive them from their proud celestial seat
If not o'er-awed by new found holy cheat.
These pious frauds, too slight t' ensnare the brave,
Are proper arts the long-eared rout t' enslave.
Bribe hungry priests to deify your might,   85
To teach your will's the only rule of right,
And sound damnation to those dare deny't.
Thus Heaven's designs against Heaven's self you'll turn,
And they will fear those powers they once did scorn.
When all their goblin interest in mankind,   90
By hirelings sold, to you shall be resigned,
And by impostors God and man betrayed,
The church and state you safely may invade.
So boundless Louis in full glory shines,
Whilst your starved pow'r in legal fetters pines.   95
Shake off those baby-bonds from your strong arms;
Henceforth be deaf to that old witch's charms.
Taste the delicious sweets of sov'reign power;
'Tis royal game whole kingdoms to deflower.
Three spotless virgins to your bed I bring,   100
A sacrifice to you, their god and king:
As these grow stale we'll harass humankind,
Rack nature, till new pleasures she shall find,
Strong as your reign, and beauteous as your mind."
    When she had spoke a confused murmur rose   105
Of French, Scotch, Irish, all my mortal foes;
Some English too, disguised (oh shame!) I spied,
Led up by the wise son-in-law of Hyde.
With fury drunk, like Bacchanals, they roar,
"Down with that common Magna Charta whore!"   110
With joint consent on helpless me they flew,
And from my Charles to a base jail me drew,
My rev'rend head exposed to scorn and shame,

84. *long-eared rout:* the stupid mob.
90. *their:* the priests'.
100. *Three spotless virgins:* England, Scotland, Ireland.
108. *son-in-law of Hyde:* the duke of York.

To boys, bawds, whores, and made a public game.
Frequent addresses to my Charles I send,   115
And to his care did my sad state commend,
But his fair soul, transformed by that French dame,
Had lost all sense of honor, justice, fame.
Like a tame spinster in's seragl' he sits,
Besieged by whores, buffoons, and bastard chits;   120
Lulled in security, rolling in lust,
Resigns his crown to angel Carwell's trust.
Her creature Osborne the revenue steals,
False Finch, knave Anglesey misguide the seals,
Mac James the Irish pagod does adore: 125
His French and Teagues command on sea and shore.
The Scotch scabbado of one court, two isles,
Fiend Lauderdale, with ordure all defiles.
Thus the state's nightmared by this hellish rout,
And none are left these furies to cast out.   130
Ah, Vindex, come, and purge the poisoned state!
Descend, descend, ere the cure's desperate.

Raleigh

Once more, great queen, thy darling try to save,
Rescue him again from scandal and the grave.

115–22. Britannia is here associated with Parliament, and she accuses Charles of abandoning her for a pro-French policy.

122. *Carwell:* the common Anglicized version of Kéroualle.

123. Osborne stabilized his high position by forming an alliance with the duchess of Portsmouth in 1674 (Browning, *Danby, 1,* 129).

124. *Finch:* Heneage Finch (1621–82) became lord keeper, 9 November 1673. *Anglesey:* Arthur Annesley, 1st earl of Anglesey (1614–86), became lord privy seal, 22 April 1673.

125. *Mac James:* An allusion to James's suspected reliance upon Irish soldiers to carry out his authoritarian and pro-Catholic policies. *pagod:* idol, i.e., Roman Catholicism.

126. *His French and Teagues:* Margoliouth quotes Marvell's *Growth of Popery and Arbitrary Government:* "Monsieur Schomberg, a French Protestant, had been made general and Colonel Fitzgerald, an Irish Papist, major-general, as more proper for the secret; the first advancing the French government, the second of promoting the Irish religion. And therefore the dark hovering of that army so long at Blackheath might not improbably seem the gatherings of a storm to fall upon London; but the ill successes which our fleet met withal this year [1673], also at sea, were sufficient, had there been any such design at home, to have quashed it: for such gallantries are not to be attempted but in the highest raptures of fortune." At sea Rupert had succeeded James as admiral on his refusal to take the test, but as Burnet observes: "The captains were the duke's creatures, so they crossed him all they could and complained of everything he did" (2, 17).

127. *scabbado:* the pox.

131. *Vindex:* the governor of Gaul who started the revolt against Nero but failed and committed suicide. See the references to Nero in line 172. Vindex here may only stand for the avenger in general (Margoliouth).

Present to his thought his long-scorned Parliament,   135
The basis of his throne and government.
In his deaf ear sound his dead father's name;
Perhaps that spell may's erring soul reclaim.
Who knows what good effects from thence may spring?
'Tis godlike good to save a falling king.   140

Britannia

Raleigh, no more; too long in vain I've tried
The Stuart from the tyrant to divde.
As easily learned virtuosos may
With the dog's blood his gentle kind convey
Into the wolf and make him guardian turn   145
To th' bleating flock, by him so lately torn.
If this imperial oil once taint the blood,
It's by no potent antidote withstood.
Tyrants, like lep'rous kings, for public weal
Must be immured, lest their contagion steal   150
Over the whole. Th' elect of Jessean line
To this firm law their scepter did resign.
And shall this stinking Scottish brood evade
Eternal laws, by God for mankind made?
No!   155
To the serene Venetian state I'll go,
From her sage mouth famed principles to know;
With her the prudence of the ancients read,
To teach my people in their steps to tread.
By those great patterns such a state I'll frame   160
Shall darken story, engross loud-mouthed Fame.
Till then, my Raleigh, teach our noble youth
To love sobriety and holy truth.
Watch and preside over their tender age,
Lest court corruptions should their souls engage.   165
Tell 'em how arts and arms in thy young days
Employed the youth, not taverns, stews and plays.
Tell 'em the gen'rous scorn their rise to owe
To flatt'ry, pimping, and a gaudy show.
Teach 'em to scorn the Carwells, Pembrokes, Nells,   170

149–52. See 2 Chron. 26:21 for an account of the quarantining of the leperous King Uzziah.

162–63. An allusion to Raleigh's *Instructions to His Son and to Posterity,* of which a new edition appeared in 1656.

170. *Pembrokes:* This appears in *State Poems* 1689 as P——s and in some copies has been

The Clevelands, Osbornes, Berties, Lauderdales:
Poppea, Messaline, and Acte's name
Yield to all those in lewdness, lust, and shame.
Make 'em admire the Sidneys, Talbots, Veres,
Blake, Cav'ndish, Drake, men void of slavish fears,   175
True sons of glory, pillars of the state,
On whose famed deeds all tongues, all writers, wait.
When with fierce ardor their brave souls do burn,
Back to my dearest country I'll return.
Tarquin's just judge and Caesar's equal peers   180
With me I'll bring to dry my people's tears.
Publicola with healing hands shall pour
Balm in their wounds, will fleeting life restore:
Greek arts and Roman arms, in her conjoined,
Shall England raise, relieve oppressed mankind.   185
As Jove's great son th' infested globe did free
From noxious monsters, hell-born tyranny,
So shall my England, by a holy war,
In triumph lead chained tyrants from afar.
Her true crusado shall at last pull down   190

completed in pen as "Portsmouths." Since Portsmouth and Carwell are the same person, this is clearly wrong, and the reference is to the duchess of Portsmouth's sister, Henriette de Kéroualle, who married the earl of Pembroke on 17 December 1647, is clearly right. Philip Herbert, 7th earl of Pembroke (1653–83), was a brutal profligate, who is thought by some historians to have murdered Sir Edmund Berry Godfrey by stomping him to death.

171. This line continues the list of promiscuous or politically powerful court ladies. *Osbornes* refers to Bridget Bertie, Osborne's wife, and *Berties* to her influential sisters. Bridget Osborne was reputed to exercise great influence upon her husband's policies and to have received many bribes. *Lauderdales* alludes to Elizabeth, countess of Dysart and afterwards duchess of Lauderdale (d. 1697), whose liason with Lauderdale, while her first husband was still alive "scandalized even the court of Charles II" *(DNB)*. She was rumored to have been the mistress of Oliver Cromwell and to have thereby secured immunity from the protector's exactions for herself and her family. She was immensely powerful and controlled a great deal of patronage.

172. *Poppea:* Mistress and afterwards wife of Nero. *Messaline:* This reading is supplied from Bod. MS Don. b.8. Most other visions have *Tegoline* or *Tegeline*, which Margoliouth supposes to be meant for Tigellinus, commander of Nero's praetorian guard, but since all the other names in this and the preceding lines are those of women, Messaline seems more appropriate. She was the third wife of the emperor Claudius, well known for her profligacy and avarice. *Acte:* one of Nero's mistresses.

174. *Talbots:* The earls of Shrewsbury, many of whom had distinguished themselves by military service to the crown. *Veres:* Sir Francis and Sir Howard Vere, who distinguished themselves in Queen Elizabeth's wars in the Low Countries.

175. *Cav'ndish:* Sir Thomas Cavendish, who circumnavigated the globe.

178. *their:* our youths'. See line 162.

180. *Tarquin's just judge:* Lucius Junius Brutus. *Caesar's equal peers:* Brutus, Cassius, and the others who killed Caesar.

182. *Publicola:* Publius Valerius, consul in the first year of the Republic, who earned this cognomen through his respect for the people (Margoliouth).

The Turkish crescent and the Persian sun.
Freed by thy labors, fortunate, blessed isle,
The earth shall rest, the heaven shall on thee smile,
And this kind secret for reward shall give:
No pois'nous tyrant on thy ground shall live.   195

ANDREW MARVELL

Upon His Majesty's Being Made Free of the City
(1674)

On 29 October 1674 Charles II attended the installation of Sir Robert Viner as lord mayor of London. In token of their gratitude for this favor, the lord mayor and aldermen presented a gold box containing the freedom of the City to the king in a ceremony at the Banqueting House on 18 December.

Marvell's poem, as Margoliouth notes, parodies the doggerel stanza used in songs for the lord mayor's show.

UPON HIS MAJESTY'S BEING MADE FREE OF THE CITY

1.

The Londoners gent
To the king do present
In a box the City maggot:
'Tis a thing sure of weight,
That requires the might   5
Of the whole Guildhall team to drag it.

2.

Whilst the churches unbuilt
And the houses undwelt
And the orphans want bread to feed 'em,
In a golden box   10
Set with stones of both rocks
You in chains offer your freedom.

---

1. *gent:* well-bred, polite.
1–6. Cf. Freke, *History of Inspids,* 115–18.
3. *maggot:* whimsy.
11. *both rocks:* two qualities of precious stones (Margoliouth).
12. *chains:* The lord mayor and those aldermen who had been lord mayors wore gold chains with their ceremonial robes.

3.

Oh you addle-brained cits,
Who henceforth in their wits
Would entrust their youth to your heeding? 15
When in diamonds and gold
You have him thus enrolled,
Yet know both his friends and his breeding.

4.

Beyond sea he began,
Where such riot he ran, 20
That all the world there did leave him;
And now he's come o'er,
Much worse than before,
Oh what fools were you to receive him!

5.

He ne'er knew, not he, 25
How to serve or be free,
Though he's passed through so many adventures;
But e'er since he was bound
('Tis the same to be crowned)
Has ev'ry day broke his indentures, 30

6.

He spends all his days
In running to plays,
When in his shop he should be poring;
And wastes all his nights
In his constant delights
Of reveling, drinking, and whoring. 35

7.

When his masters too rash
Entrusted him with cash,
He used as his own to spend on't;
And amongst his wild crew 40
The money he threw,
As if he should ne'er see an end on't.

25–30. The institution of apprenticeship was an essential feature of the City's business life, and Marvell compares Charles at length to an unruly apprentice.

8.

Throughout Lombard Street
Each one he could meet
He would run on the score and borrow;   45
But when they asked for their own,
He was broken and gone
And his creditors all left to sorrow.

9.

Though oft bound to the peace,
He never would cease,   50
But molested the neighbors with quarrels;
And when he was beat,
He still made a retreat
To his Clevelands, his Nells, and his Carwells.

10.

Nay, his company lewd   55
Were thrice grown so rude,
But he chanced to have more sobriety,
And the house was well barred,
Else with guard upon guard
He had burglared all your propriety.   60

11.

The plot was so laid,
Had it not been betrayed,
As had cancelled all former disasters:
All your wives had been strumpets
To His Highness's trumpets,   65
And the soldiers had all been your masters.

46–48. An allusion to the stop of the Exchequer of January 1672, which suspended payments on government loans and caused financial distress among the bankers of the City.

49. *bound to the peace*: probably an allusion to the Triple Alliance and the treaties that ended the two Dutch wars (Margoliouth).

55–60. An allusion to three main attempts of Charles's counselors to extend the royal prerogative: the Treaty of Dover, 1670; the Declaration of Indulgence, 1672; and the suspected plot to establish a military dictatorship with the Blackheath army, 1673 (Margoliouth).

60. *propriety*: property.

62. Shaftesbury refused to support the king's policy and was dismissed 9 November 1673. He was reported to have said that it was only laying down his gown and girding on his sword (Brown, *Shaftesbury*, p. 216).

65. *trumpets*: trumpeters.

12.

So many are the debts
And the bastards he gets,
Which must all be defrayed by London,
That notwithstanding the care   70
Of Sir Thomas Player,
Your chamber must needs be undone.

13.

His word nor his oath
Cannot bind him to troth,
He values not credit nor history;   75
And though he has served now
Two 'prenticeships through,
He knows not his trade nor mystery.

14.

Then, O London, rejoice
In thy fortunate choice   80
To have made this freeman of spices;
Yet I do not distrust
But he may prove more just,
For his virtues exceed all his vices.

15.

But what little thing   85
Is that which you bring
To the duke, the kingdom's darling?
How you hug it and draw,
Like ants at a straw,
Though too small for the carriage of Starling!   90

16.

If a box of pills
To cure the duke's ills,

71. *Sir Thomas Player*: chamberlain of the City, who presented the freedom to Charles II.
He was in charge of the chamber, the corporation treasury.
77. *Two 'prenticeships*: i.e., twice seven years, 1660–74 (Margoliouth).
81. *spices*: Charles was an honorary member of the Company of Grocers.
87. The duke of York also received the freedom of the City, and, according to a letter of
Marvell's, would later receive a proportionately smaller gold box (Margoliouth).
90. *Starling*: probably a reference to Sir Samuel Starling, lord mayor 1669–70, who en-
forced the penalties of the Conventicle Act very severely.
92. The duke was rumored to have syphilis.

He is too far gone to begin it;
Or does Your Grace trow
A-processioning go   95
With the pyx and the host within it?

17.

You durst not, I find,
Leave this freedom behind,
And in this box you have sent it;
But if ever he get   100
For himself up to set,
The whole nation may chance to repent it.

18.

And yet if your toy
You would wisely employ,
It might deserve a box, and a gold one;   105
In balloting it use
A new duke to choose,
For we've had too much of the old one.

19.

The very first head
Of the oath to him read   110
Shows how fit he is to govern
When in heart you all knew
He could never be true
To Charles, our king and sov'reign.

20.

And how could he swear   115
That he would forbear
To color the goods of an alien,
Who still doth advance
The government of France
With a wife and religion Italian?   120

110. *oath*: that prescribed by the Test Act of 1673. The duke would not take this oath and was obliged under the Act to surrender the office of lord high admiral.
117. To color a stranger's goods was to enter them at the customhouse under a citizen's name (Margoliouth).
120. The duke took Maria d'Este as his second wife in 1673.

21.

But all ye blind apes,
Bred in Hell by the papes,
Never think in England to swagger;
He will find who unlocks
The bottom of the box   125
London bears the cross with the dagger.

22.

And now, worshipful sirs,
Go and fold up your furs:
Turn again, Viner, turn again.
I see, whoe'er's freed,   130
You for slaves are decreed,
Until you all burn again, burn again.

126. *cross with the dagger:* the arms of the City of London.

JOHN FREKE

The History of Insipids
(1674)

The History of Insipids (insipids are persons deficient in sense, spirit, or taste) recapitulates many of the events that grieved King Charles's subjects: the Declaration of Indulgence, Blood's favor at court after his attempt to steal the crown, the establishment of systematic bribery in Parliament, naval disasters in the two wars with Holland, the stop of the Exchequer, and the king's receiving the freedom of the City in December 1674.

Although the poem was for a long time ascribed to Rochester, Frank H. Ellis has uncovered two independent sources that cite John Freke of Strictland as author (see *Philological Quarterly* 44, [October 1965]: 472–83). According to Anthony à Wood, Freke was imprisoned for high treason in the Tower in 1676 for "the insipides." A warrant issued to the earl of Northampton demanded the custody of "John Freke of the Middle Temple, esq. for dispersing a seditious libel called the chronicle from Ra: Gregge jun^r 8 March 17/8." As Mr. Ellis has noted, the poem is entitled *The Chronicle* in an Osborn MS at Yale. That Freke was acquitted on 11 September 1675 because of lack of witnesses certainly does not declare him innocent of the charge. A letter to Dr. Henry Fowler notes that Charles himself took an interest in this infamous libel. Had not the efforts of Shaftesbury and Buckingham to dissolve the Cavalier Parliament distracted the king, prosecution against Freke probably would have been pursued.

THE HISTORY OF INSIPIDS

1.

Chaste, pious, prudent Charles the Second,
   The miracle of thy restoration
May like to that of quails be reckoned,
   Rained on the Israelitish nation;
The wished-for blessing which Heaven sent   5
Became their curse and punishment.

3–6. See Exodus 16.

2.

The virtues in thee, Charles, inherent
  (Although thy countenance be an odd piece)
Prove thee as true a God's vicegerent
  As e'er was Harry with the codpiece;   10
For chastity and pious deeds,
His grandsire Harry Charles exceeds.

3.

Our Romish bondage-breaker Harry
  Espoused half a dozen wives;
Charles only one resolves to marry,   15
  And other men's he never swives.
Yet hath he sons and daughters more
Than e'er had Harry by threescore.

4.

Never was such a Faith's Defender:
  He, like a politic prince and pious,   20
Gives liberty to conscience tender
  And doth to no religion tie us:
Jews, Christians, Turks, Papists, he'll please us,
With Moses, Mahomet, Pope, and Jesus.

5.

In all affairs of church and state   25
  He very zealous is and able,
Devout at prayer and sits up late
  At the Cabal and council-table;
His very dogs at council-board
Sit grave and wise like any lord.   30

8. "The prince . . . was no beauty. Unlike his parents he was swarthy and big—a reversion to some far Provençal or Medici ancestor. 'He is so ugly,' wrote his mother, 'that I am ashamed of him' " (Bryant, pp. 4–5).

10. *Harry:* Henry VIII.

12. *grandsire Harry:* Henri IV, the most notorious womanizer of his day. The point is that he was neither chaste nor pious—"Paris is worth a mass."

21. Charles published a Declaration of Indulgence to Tender Consciences at Christmas 1662 and another in 1672.

29. "He took delight to have a number of little spaniels follow him and lie in his bedchamber, where often times he suffered the bitches to puppy and give suck, which rendered it very offensive and, indeed, made the whole court nasty and stinking" (Evelyn, 6 February 1685).

6.

Let Charles's policy no man flout—
   The wisest kings have all some folly—
Nor let his piety any doubt;
   Charles, like a sovereign wise and holy,
Makes young men judges of the bench   35
And bishops those that love a wench.

7.

His father's foes he doth reward,
   Preferring those cut off his head;
Old Cavaliers, the crown's best guard,
   He leaves to starve for want of bread.   40
Never was any prince endued
With so much grace and gratitude.

8.

Blood that wears treason in his face,
   Villain complete, in parson's gown,
How much is he at court in grace   45
   For stealing Ormonde and the crown?
Since loyalty doth no man good,
Let's seize the king and outdo Blood.

9.

A Parliament of knaves and sots
   (Members by name we must not mention)   50
He keeps in pay and buys their votes,
   Here with a place, there with a pension.
When to give money he can't collogue them
He doth with scorn prorogue, prorogue them.

35. Though I can find no trace of Charles's appointing young men to the bench, the king was guilty of selecting judges of inferior ability who would bend their consciences to fit his policies.

36. Pepys's cousin Roger told him that Gilbert Sheldon, archbishop of Canterbury, "do keep a wench, and that he is as very a wencher as can be" (29 July 1667).

43. The notorious Col. Thomas Blood (1618?–80) attempted, one night in November 1670, to waylay the duke of Ormonde in St. James's Street and hang him at Tyburn. The duke fought his way clear, and his son, Lord Ossory, charged Blood's protector, Buckingham, in the king's presence with instigating the attack. Six months later Blood attempted to steal the crown jewels from the Tower. Charles himself questioned Blood but did not punish him, and the ruffian was often seen in the presence-chamber thereafter.

49–54. Under the administration of Danby (1673–79) opposition members of Parliament were systematically bribed into compliance with court policy.

53. *collogue:* to prevail upon or influence by blandishment, obs.

10.

But they long since, by too much giving,   55
    Undid, betrayed, and sold the nation,
Making their memberships a living
    Better than e'er was sequestration.
God give thee, Charles, a resolution
To damn them all by dissolution.   60

11.

Fame is not founded on success:
    Though victories were Caesar's glory,
Lost battles made not Pompey less,
    But left him styled great in story.
Malicious Fate doth oft devise   65
To beat the brave and fool the wise.

12.

Charles in the first Dutch war stood fair
    To have been master of the deep,
When Opdam blew up in the air,
    Had not His Highness gone to sleep.   70
Our fleet slacked sails, fearing his waking;
The Dutch else had been in sad taking.

13.

The Bergen business was well laid,
    Though we paid dear for that design,
Had we not three days parling stayed,   75
    The Dutch fleet there, Charles, had been thine:
Though the false Dane agreed to sell 'um,
He cheated us and saved Skellum.

14.

Had not Charles sweetly choused the states,
    By Bergen baffle grown more wise,   80
And made them shit as small as rats,
    By their rich Smyrna fleet's surprise,

57. The Cavalier Parliament lasted 18 years.
58. *sequestration:* Under the commonwealth the livings of royalist ministers were sequestrated on various grounds and bestowed on pro-government clerics.
78. *Skellum:* cant term here used for the Dutch East Indies fleet: a thief, rogue.
79. *choused:* tricked.
82. Several Dutch merchantmen were surprised and captured by Sandwich after the

Had haughty Holmes but called in Spragge,
Hans had been put into a bag.

15.

Mists, storms, short victuals, adverse winds,   85
    And once the navy's wise division,
Defeated Charles's best designs,
    Till he became the foe's derision.
But he had swinged the Dutch at Chatham,
Had he had ships but to come at 'em.   90

16.

Our Blackheath host without dispute
    (Raised, put on board, why, no man knows)
Must Charles have rendered absolute
    Over his subjects or his foes;
Had not the French king made us fools   95
By taking Maastricht with our tools.

17.

But Charles, what could thy policy be,
    To run so many sad disasters,
Joining thy fleet with false d'Estrées,
    To make the French of Holland masters?   100

Bergen fiasco.
  83–84. When England had determined on another war with Holland in 1672, a squadron under the command of Sir Robert Holmes (1622–92) was sent out to surprise the Dutch Smyrna fleet in the channel. Holmes, not wishing to share the glory, failed to signal a passing squadron (under the command of Sir Edward Spragge) for help, and his ships were severely mauled by the Dutch. Marvell described Holmes in *A Seasonable Argument* (1677) as "first an Irish livery boy, then a highwayman (a pirate would be nearer the mark), now Bashaw of the Isle of Wight, the cursed beginner of the two Dutch wars" (quoted in Eva Scott, *Rupert, Prince Palatine* [London, 1904], p. 323).
  84. *Hans:* the Dutch.
  86. For the disastrous division of the English fleet in 1666 see *Third Advice,* 292 ff.
  89. For the Dutch attack on English ships and shore stations at Chatham in 1667 see *Last Instructions,* passim.
  91. *Blackheath host:* In 1673 "the army, assembled on Blackheath, and later at Yarmouth, for the invasion of Holland—so frequently inspected by the king—was said to be full of Papists, hired for the overthrow of English liberties" (Bryant, p. 228.)
  96. English troops under the duke of Monmouth played a crucial part in the seizure of Maastricht by the French army on 2 July 1673.
  99. *false d'Estrées:* A squadron under Vice-Admiral d'Estrées was to cooperate with the English fleet but failed to participate actively in the various encounters of the war. In a naval battle off Scheveningen on 10 August 1673 Prince Rupert charged d'Estrées with deliberately ignoring his signals to engage the enemy: "It was the plainest and greatest opportunity ever lost at sea" (Ogg, *Charles II, 1,* 376).

Was't Carwell, brother James, or Teague
That made thee break the Triple League?

18.

Could Robin Viner have foreseen
  The glorious triumphs of his master,
The Woolchurch statue gold had been,   105
  Which now is only alabaster:
But wise men think, had it been wood,
'Twere for a bankrupt king too good.

19.

Those that the fabric well consider,
  Do of it diversely discourse;   110
Some pass their censure on the rider,
  Others their judgments on the horse.
Most say the steed's a goodly thing,
But all agree 'tis a lewd king.

20.

By the lord mayor and his wise coxcombs,   115
  Freeman of London Charles is made;
Then to Whitehall a rich gold box comes,
  Which is bestowed on the French jade.
But wonder not it should be so, sirs,
When monarchs rank themselves with grocers.   120

21.

Cringe, scrape no more, you City fops,
  Leave off your feasting and fine speeches,

101–02. The duchess of Portsmouth (*Carwell*) was instrumental in persuading Charles to form an Anglo-French alliance. *Teague*, a cant term for an Irish Roman Catholic, does not here specify a particular person.

102. *the Triple League:* a defensive alliance formed in 1667 with Holland and Sweden, which was highly popular in England, especially with Nonconformists who saw in Louis XIV's growing might a threat to religious and civil liberties. It was broken by the alliance with France.

103. *Robin Viner:* Sir Robert Viner (1631–88), a goldsmith who was elected lord mayor of London in 1674, set up an equestrian statue of Charles II in the Stocks Market. It was the object of other lampoons.

108. *bankrupt king:* In order to finance naval preparations the administration announced in January 1672 that the principle of loans made to the government by City merchants would not be repaid. Many merchants went bankrupt, and Viner was ruined.

115–18. See headnote to Marvell, *Upon His Majesty's Being Made Free of the City.*

118. *the French jade:* the duchess of Portsmouth.

120. Charles was an honorary Grocer.

Beat up your drums, shut up your shops,
   The courtiers then may kiss your breeches.
Arm, tell that Romish duke that rules,   125
You're free-born subjects, no French mules.

22.

New upstarts, pimps, bastards, whores,
   That locust-like devour the land,
By shutting up th' Exchequer doors
   When thither our money was trepanned,   130
Have rendered, Charles, thy restoration
A curse and plague unto the nation.

23.

Then, Charles, beware thy brother York,
   Who to thy government gives law;
If once we fall to the old work,   135
   You must again both to Breda,
Where, spite of all that would restore you,
Turned commonwealth, we will abhor you.

24.

If of all Christian blood the guilt
   Cry loud for vengeance unto Heaven,   140
That sea by Charles and·Louis spilt
   Can never be by God forgiven:
Worse scourges to their subjects, lord,
Than pestilence, famine, fire, and sword.

25.

The wolf of France and British goat,   145
   One Europe's scorn, t'other her curse
(This fool, that knave, by public vote,
   Yet hard to say which is the worse),
To think such kings, lord, reign by thee
Were most prodigious blasphemy.   150

26.

They know no law but their own lust:
   Their subjects' substance and their blood

---

129. Clifford was chiefly responsible for the stop of the Exchequer. See line 108 n.

They count a tribute due and just,
  Still spent and spilt for public good.
If such kings be by God appointed,   155
The devil is then the Lord's anointed.

27.

Of kings cursed be the power and name,
  Let all the earth henceforth abhor 'em;
Monsters which knaves sacred proclaim
  And then like slaves fall down before 'em.   160
What can there be in kings divine?
The most are wolves, goats, sheep, or swine.

28.

Then farewell, sacred Majesty,
  Let's pull all brutish tyrants down!
Where men are born and still live free,   165
  There ev'ry head doth wear a crown.
Mankind, like miserable frogs,
Is wretched, kinged by storks or logs.

168. In Aesop's fable, the frogs, "living an easy, free life everywhere among the lakes and ponds," petitioned Jupiter for a king. Jupiter threw a log into their pool. Terrified by the splash, the frogs treated their king with fear and respect, but after a while they grew tired of the log through familiarity with it and wished a substitute. Jupiter obliged by sending a stork, who devoured them all.

JOHN AYLOFFE

Marvell's Ghost
(1678)

From 1665 to his death in 1678 Marvell had defended English liberties in Parliament, in his political verse and pamphlets, and, it now appears, as a member of an anti-French, anti-Catholic organization aimed at alerting the House of Commons to the dangers of Charles's policy. This organization, described by Haley in *William of Orange and the English Opposition, 1672–74* (Oxford, 1953), was directed by William's secretary, Peter du Moulin. While some of the members seem to have been mere adventurers, Marvell and his friend John Ayloffe were clearly involved in this dangerous enterprise from the highest patriotic motives.

Ayloffe's career is marked by daring gestures and actions in support of freedom. During the crucial debates on foreign policy in 1673 he placed a wooden shoe (for Englishmen an emblem of slavery) beside the chair of Speaker Edward Seymour, who was subservient to the court. The shoe bore the arms of England and France and the motto, *Utrum horum mavis accipe* ("Choose whichever of these you prefer"). He was also charged with printing antigovernment literature, including *England's Appeal from the Private Cabal at Whitehall . . . to the Great Council of the Nation* (1673) and was exiled for two years. He was outlawed for involvement in the Rye House Plot (1683) and fled to Scotland with the earl of Argyle, where he was seized. He was executed before the gate of the Inner Temple on 30 October 1685. Ayloffe was a member of the Green Ribbon Club, and Macaulay describes him as belonging to "that section of Whigs which sought for models rather among the patriots of Greece and Rome than among the prophets and judges of Israel" (p. 560). Grosart, with some exaggeration, calls *Marvell's Ghost* "one of the most drastic and powerful satires against the Stuarts, as burning and passionate in its invective as any of Marvell's own."

Marvell's Ghost

From the dark Stygian banks I come
T' acquaint poor England with her doom,
Which, as th' infernal Sisters sate,
I copied from the Book of Fate;
And though the sense may seem disguised,   5
'Tis in these following lines comprised:
   When England does forsake the broom,
And takes a thistle in its room,
A wanton fiddler shall be led
By Fate to stain his master's bed,   10
From whence a spurious race shall grow
Designed for Britain's overthrow.
These, while they do possess her throne,
Shall serve all int'rests but their own;
And shall be, both in peace and war,   15
Scourges unto themselves and her.
   A brace of exiled youths, whose fates
Shall pull down vengeance on those states
That harbored them abroad, must come
Well-skilled in foreign vices home,   20
And shall (their dark designs to hide)
With two contesting churches side,
Till, with cross-persecuting zeal,
They have laid waste the commonweal.
Then incest, murder, perjury   25
Shall fashionable virtues be,
And villainies infest this isle
Would make the son of Claudius smile;

---

7. *broom:* the emblem of the Plantagenets, the great house that occupied the English throne from 1154 to 1485. The name Plantagenet (originally Plante-geneste) was a personal nickname of Geoffrey, count of Anjou, father of Henry II, and it is traditionally derived from Geoffrey's habit of adorning his cap with a sprig of broom or *planta genista* (*DNB*, s.v. "Plantagenet, family of").

8. *thistle:* the heraldic emblem of Scotland, standing for the Stuarts.

9. *a wanton fiddler:* David Riccio or Rizzio (1533?–66), a musician born in Turin, who became the chief couselor and, perhaps, lover of Mary Queen of Scots. Rizzio was rumored to be the father of James VI and I. When James's advisors compared him with Solomon, his detractors said that the only similarity was that his father was called David and played a harp.

17. *A brace of exiled youths:* Charles II and James, duke of York.

28. *son of Claudius:* Nero, stepson of Claudius and son of his fourth wife, Aggripina.

No oaths, no sacraments hold good
But what are sealed with lust or blood—   30
Lusts that cold exile could not tame,
Nor plague, nor fire at home reclaim.
For this she shall in ashes mourn,
From Europe's envy turned her scorn,
And curse the days that first gave birth   35
To a Cecil or a Monck on earth.
   But as I onwards strove to look,
The angry Sister shut the book
And said, "No more! That fickle state
Shall know no further of her fate;   40
Her future fortunes must lie hid
Till her known ills be remedied,
And she to those resentments come
That drove the Tarquins out of Rome,
Or such as did in fury turn   45
Th' Assyrian's palace to his urn."

36. *Cecil:* Robert Cecil, 1st earl of Salisbury (1563?–1612), who was instrumental in bring-
ing James I to the throne of England. *Monck:* George Monck, 1st duke of Albemarle (1608–
70), who played a major role in the restoration of Charles II.

44. *Tarquins:* Tarquinius Superbus, a king of Rome noted for his arrogance and tyranny,
and his son, Tarquinius Sextus, who raped the virtuous Lucretia. They were expelled from
Rome in a popular uprising.

46. *Th' Assyrian:* "Sardanapalus, the last king of the Assyrian monarchy, so excessively ef-
feminate and luxurious that his captains conspired to kill him, but he made a pile of all his
precious things and burned himself in his palace" (Shadwell's note to his *Tenth Satire of
Juvenal*).

Church Affairs, 1662-1665

ROBERT WILD

A Poem upon the Imprisonment of Mr. Calamy in Newgate
(1662)

Edmund Calamy (1600–66), Nonconformist divine, a coauthor of *Smectym-nuus,* and member of the Savoy Conference for the composition of religious differences, was widely admired for his piety and moderation. After the Restoration he was appointed one of Charles II's chaplains. He was a noted preacher and was offered the bishopric of Coventry and Lichfield, which he refused. Calamy was one of some 2,000 Nonconformist ministers ejected from their churches on St. Bartholomew's Day (17 August 1662) under the provisions of the Act of Uniformity. This act required all the clergy to sign a declaration repudiating the Solemn League and Covenant, denying the right to take up arms against the king, undertaking to adopt the liturgy of the Church of England, and prescribing episcopal ordination. The great majority of Nonconformist ministers felt they could not subscribe to all these provisions, especially since the newly authorized Book of Common Prayer was not printed and distributed in time for most of them to familiarize themselves with provisions which they were nevertheless required to accept. After being ejected from St. Mary Aldermanbury in London, Calamy continued to attend this church. On 28 December 1662, when the regular minister failed to appear for the service, Calamy was prevailed upon to enter the pulpit and preached a fervent sermon. For this he was sent to Newgate on 6 January 1663, but was released soon after through the king's intervention.

A Poem upon the Imprisonment of Mr. Calamy in Newgate

This page I send you, sir, your Newgate fate
Not to condole but to congratulate.
I envy not our mitered men their places,
Their rich preferments, nor their richer faces:

147

To see them steeple upon steeple set,   5
As if they meant that way to Heaven to get.
I can behold them take into their gills
A dose of churches, as men swallow pills,
And never grieve at it: let them swim in wine
While others drown in tears, I'll not repine!   10
But my heart truly grudges, I confess,
That you thus loaded are with happiness;
For so it is, and you more blesséd are
In Peter's chain than if you sat in's chair.
One sermon hath preferred you so much honor   15
A man could scarce have had from Bishop Bonner.
Whilst we, your brethren, poor erratics be,
You are a glorious fixed star we see.
Hundreds of us turn out of house and home;
To a safe habitation you are come.   20
What though it be a jail? Shame and disgrace
Rise only from the crime, not from the place.
Who thinks reproach or injury is done
By an eclipse to the unspotted sun?
He only by that black upon his brow   25
Allures spectators more, and so do you.
Let me find honey though upon a rod
And prize the prison where my keeper's God.
Newgate or Hell were Heav'n if Christ were there;
He made the stable so and sepulcher.   30
Indeed the place did for your presence call;
Prisons do want perfuming most of all.
Thanks to the bishop and his good lord mayor,
Who turned the den of thieves into a house of prayer:

5–9. A reference to the pluralism practiced by many Anglican bishops.

14. *Peter's chain:* St. Peter was imprisoned under heavy guard by Herod after the crucifixion and, as an extra precaution, was chained to his two cellmates. See Acts 12:1–6.

15. *One sermon:* Calamy preached on Eli's concern for the Ark of God. See *A Sermon Preached at Aldermanbury Church*, 28 December 1662, Oxford, 1663.

16. *Bishop Bonner:* Edmund Bonner or Boner (1500?–69), bishop of London, an arch-persecutor of Puritans under Henry VIII.

17. *erratics:* erratic stars or planets, obs.

27. By dipping up some honey with his staff and licking it, Jonathan unwittingly violated an edict of his father Saul that no Israelite should partake of food during an engagement with the Philistines. The food strengthened him after his long fast and he won a great victory. After the battle his violation of the edict was reported to Saul, who was prevented from carrying out the sentence of death by the Israelites. See 1 Sam. 14:24–46. Wild seems to have distorted the meaning of the episode in his application of it.

33. Calamy was imprisoned under the lord mayor's warrant or *mittimus* (see line 37).

And may some thief by you converted be,   35
Like him who suffered in Christ's company.
   Now would I had sight of your *mittimus;*
Fain would I know why you are dealt with thus.
Jailer, set forth your prisoner at the bar:
Sir, you shall hear what your offenses are.   40
   First, it is proved that you being dead in law,
As if you cared not for that death a straw,
Did walk and haunt your church, as if you'd scare
Away the reader and his Common Prayer.
Nay, 'twill be proved you did not only walk,   45
But like a Puritan your ghost did talk.
Dead, and yet preach! these Presbyterian slaves
Will not give over preaching in their graves.
   Item, you played the thief, and if 't be so,
Good reason, sir, to Newgate you should go: 50
And now you're there, some dare to swear you are
The greatest pickpocket that e'er came there.
Your wife, too, little better than yourself you make:
She is the receiver of each purse you take.
But your great theft you act it in your church   55
(I do not mean you did your sermon lurch;
That's crime canonical) but you did pray
And preach, so that you stole men's hearts away;
So that good man to whom your place doth fall
Will find they have no heart for him at all.   60
This felony deserved imprisonment.
What, can't you Nonconformists be content
Sermons to make, except you preach them too?
They that your places have this work can do.
   Thirdly, 'tis proved when you pray most devout   65
For all good men, you leave the bishops out.
This makes seer Sheldon by his powerful spell
Conjure and lay you safe in Newgate-hell.
Would I were there too, I should like it well.
I would you durst swap punishment with me.   70

44. The *reader* is the Anglican minister. The Presbyterians and other sects, because they disliked set forms of worship, objected to the Book of Common Prayer.

56. *lurch:* pilfer.

62. *Nonconformists.* Note the very early use of this term.

65–66. Most Nonconformists objected to the Anglican institution of bishops because they felt that episcopal ordination and the doctrine of apostolic succession were papistical superstitions that gave the bishops unwarranted authority.

Pain makes me fitter for the company
Of roaring boys, and you may lie a-bed.
Now your name's up, pray do it in my stead,
And if it be denied us to change places,
Let us for sympathy compare our cases,   75
For if in suffering we both agree,
Sir, I may challenge you to pity me.
I am the older jail-bird; my hard fate
Hath kept me twenty years in Cripplegate.
Old Bishop Gout, that lordly proud disease,   80
Took my fat body for his diocese,
Where he keeps court, there visits every limb,
And makes them (Levite-like) conform to him.
Severely he doth article each joint,
And makes enquiry into every point.   85
A bitter enemy to preaching, he
Hath half a year sometimes suspended me,
And if he find me painful in my station,
Down I am sure to go next visitation.
He binds up, looseth, sets up and pulls down;   90
Pretends he draws ill humors from the crown.
But I am sure he maketh such ado,
His humors trouble head and members too.
He hath me now in hand and ere he goes,
I fear for heretics he'll burn my toes.   95
Oh! I would give all I am worth, a fee,
That from his jurisdiction I were free.
    Now, sir, you find our sufferings do agree;
One bishop clapped up you, another me.
But oh! the difference, too, is very great;   100
You are allowed to walk, to drink and eat:
I want them all and never a penny get,
And though you be debarred your liberty,
Yet all your visitors, I hope, are free.

72. *roaring boys:* riotous fellows.
79. *Cripplegate:* one of the posterns in the old City wall.
83. Wild's limbs, like parish priests (Levites), are compelled to conform to Bishop Gout.
84. *article:* indict.
104. *all your visitors:* "Newgate Street was blocked by the coaches of his visitors. 'A certain popish lady' (apparently the king's mistress), detained on her way through the city, represented to the king the disturbed state of popular feeling. Calamy was set free by the king's express order, but it was stated that the act had not provided for his longer restraint. The Commons on 19 February referred it to a committee to inquire into this defeat, and addressed the king against toleration" (*DNB*, s.v. "Wild, Robert").

Good men, good women, and good angels come 105
And makes your prison better than your home.
Now may it be so till your foes repent
They gave you such a rich imprisonment.
May, for the greater comfort of your lives,
Your lying in be better than your wive's. 110
May you a thousand friendly papers see,
And none prove empty except this from me.
And if you stay, may I come keep your door;
Then farewell parsonage! I shall ne'er be poor.

113–14. It was customary for visitors to tip doorkeepers.

"HUDIBRAS"

On Calamy's Imprisonment and Wild's Poetry
(1663)

Wild's poem on the imprisonment of Calamy brought a flood of rebuttals and counter-rebuttals, most of them devoid of substance and wit. The following attack is attributed to George Sacheverell by the *DNB* in its article on Calamy, presumably because it is found in Sacheverell's commonplace book (BM Add. MS 28758). The poem is attributed to Butler in MS Rawlinson poet. 173 and in Buckingham's *Works* (1704), and to "Hudibras" in the broadside version (1663), which is the text followed here.

As René Lamar points out, the attribution to Butler is denied in a broadside attacking this poem (*On the Answer to Dr. Wild's Poem* . . . 1663):

> But oh! bold bard with brazen front,
> That durst put Hudibras upon't.
> And filch away that author's fame
> By counterfeiting of his name,
> Not as Bathillus did, who put
> His name to Virgil's verses, but,
> With far more impudence and shame,
> Thou hast to thine put Virgil's name.

(See Samuel Butler, *Satires and Miscellaneous Poetry and Prose,* [Cambridge, 1928], pp. xiv–xv.) The contradictory evidence leaves the authorship of the poem in doubt.

The satirist adopts an extreme attitude toward Nonconformists as seditious and unjustly accuses Wild of having helped to instigate the execution of Charles I. He also fails to recognize, behind Wild's bantering tone, the deep admiration Wild felt for Calamy.

On Calamy's Imprisonment and Wild's Poetry

To the Bishops:

Most reverend lords, the church's joy and wonder,
Whose lives are lightning, and whose doctrine thunder,
The rare effects of both in this are found:
Ye break men's hearts, yet leave their bodies sound,
And from the court (as David did, they say)   5
Do with your organs fright the devil away.
Awake! for though you think the day's your own,
The cage is open, and the bird is flown,
That bird (whom though your lordships do despise)
May shit in Paul's and pick out Sheldon's eyes.   10
'Tis he who taught the pulpit and the press
To mask rebellion in a Gospel dress;
He who blew up the coals of England's wrath,
And picked men's pockets by the public faith;
He who the melting sister's bounty tried,   15
And preached their bodkins into Caesar's side;
That crocodile of state, who wept a flood
When he was maudlin drunk with Charles's blood,
Is by the sisters' gold and brethren's prayer
Become a tenant to the open air,   20
For some were grieved to see that light expire
That lately helped to set the church on fire,
And when their ghostly father was perplexed,

5–6. The Nonconformists had banned organs from the churches, but they were introduced again with the return of the Anglican clergy.

8. Calamy was released from Newgate at the king's order early in 1663.

10. There seems to be a reference here to the desecration of St. Paul's by commonwealth soldiers, who stabled their horses there. Calamy was not involved. *Sheldon:* Gilbert Sheldon (1598–1671), archbishop of Canterbury.

11–18. "Though he was a 'bitter enemy to all mobs' and a resolute opponent of the rising sectaries, his expressions on public affairs were quoted as countenancing 'incendiary' measures. The trial and execution of Charles he did what he could to oppose: his name is attached to the 'Vindication' of the London ministers' conduct in this affair drawn up by Christopher Burges" (*DNB*).

14. *the public faith:* "Jokes about the public faith were frequent in the civil war. Parliament constantly borrowed money 'on the public faith' which meant that there was no guarantee at all of repayment" (C. V. Wedgwood, *Poetry and Politics under the Stuarts* [Cambridge University Press, 1960], p. 84).

23. *perplexed:* entangled.

Could wrest an act, as he had done a text.
   Now enter Wild, who merrily lets fly   25
The fragments of his pulpit drollery.
Though his seditious ballad pleased the rout,
The verses, like the author, had the gout.
Yet he proclaims the show, invites the crew
(The Presbyters have their Jack-puddings too).   30
He tells you of a beast had lately been
Within the walls of Newgate to be seen,
That with a throat wide as the way to Hell
Could swallows oaths would choke the idol Bel
And burst the dragon, yet he could not swear   35
Obedience to the king and house of pray'r.
   Ingenious Wild, 'tis thy unhappy fate
That *Iter Boreale*'s out of date;
Love's Tragedy's forgot, for (oh, disgrace!)
Peters succeeds him in his martyr's place.   40
Publish the legend of that reverend brother,
And act the one, as thou hast writ the other;
For when St. Hugh did mount the fatal tree,
He left his coat a legacy to thee.
Oh, may the gout no more disturb thy ease,   45
But Bishop Halter take his diocese,
And now th'art dead in law, though zealots laugh,
Impartial truth shall write this epitaph:
   This Presbyterian brat was born and cried,
Spat in his mother's face, and so he died.   50
He died, yet lives, and the unhappy elf
Divides Beelzebub against himself,

24. The poet charges Calamy's supporters with dishonesty in evading penalties of the Act of Uniformity, but Calamy was released, according to the *DNB*, at the instigation of the king.
  30. *Jack-puddings*: buffoons in street shows.
  34–35. *oaths*: probably a reference to the Solemn League and Covenant. *Bel and . . . the dragon*: Babylonian idols in the apocryphal book of that name who devoured huge sacrifices. The inclusion of this book in the Bible was insisted upon by the Anglicans and opposed by the Nonconformists. The idea is that Calamy would strain at a gnat but swallow a camel.
  38. *Iter Boreale*: Wild's popular poem celebrating Monck's march from Scotland to London.
  39–44. Wild's *Tragedy of Christopher Love* (1660) celebrates the martyrdom of a fiery Puritan minister executed in 1651 for plotting the restoration of Charles II. Hugh *Peters* (1598–1660), an independent chaplain in the parliamentary army, was executed 16 October 1660 for his alleged part in the death of Charles I, "which he denied himself in his post-Restoration apologies; but his sermons during the trial, as was proved by several witnesses, justified the sentence of the court" (*DNB*).
  52–54. Wild's poem, strangely enough, is mistaken as an attack on Calamy, and hence Beelzebub is divided against himself when Presbyterians fall out. Calamy is derided as the

Abuses Calamy, that tail of Smec,
And shoots the prelates through his brother's neck.
   Bishops awake! and see a holy cheat: 55
The enemy sows tares among your wheat.
Do ye not hear the sons of Edom cry,
"Down with the Act of Uniformity!
We will compound and worship God by th' halves:
Take you the temples and give us the calves?"   60
Thus you behold the schismatic bravadoes—
Wild speaks in squibs, but Calamy granadoes.
Kirk, still these bairns, lest under Tyburn hedge,
The squire of Newgate rock them on a sledge.

---

tail of another devil, Smec, his initials forming the last two letters of this abbreviation for *Smectymnuus.*

56. See Matt. 13:24: "The kingdom of Heaven is likened unto a man which sowed good seed in his field: But while men slept, his enemy came and sowed tares among the wheat and went his way."

57. *sons of Edom:* the descendants of Esau or Edom, who lived by the sword and slaughtered the Israelites in a long succession of battles. Here, the Nonconformists.

59. *compound:* to come to terms and pay for an offense or injury with special reference to the "compounding" of Cavaliers and malignants with the government during the interregnum.

60. The ejected ministers are shown slyly bargaining with the Anglicans for the calves (tithes?). In fact, the terms under which they were ejected were more severe than those inflicted earlier on the Anglican ministers, who had been permitted a small share in tithes to help support themselves.

A Pulpit to Be Let
(1665)

A Pulpit to Be Let attacks the Anglican ministers who fled London after the plague broke out in 1665. According to Neal, "some few of the established clergy, with a commendable zeal, ventured to continue in their stations and preach to their parishioners throughout the course of the plague . . . , but most of them fled and deserted their parishes at a time when their assistance was most wanted" (*4*, 398). Many Nonconformist clergy, who had been ejected under the Act of Uniformity in 1662, ventured to fill these places in violation of the Act. As a result, according to Neal, they incurred the wrath of Clarendon, who maintained that the Nonconformists "were ready, if any misfortune had befallen the king's fleet, to have brought the war into our fields and houses" (*4*, 399).

A Pulpit to Be Let

Woe to the idle shepherd that leaveth his flock.
Zech. 11:7. With a just applause of those worthy
divines that stay with us, 1665.

Beloved, and he sweetly thus goes on;	
Now, where's Beloved? Why, Beloved's gone?	
No morning matins now, nor evening song;	
Alas! The parson cannot stay so long.	
With Clerkenwell it fares as most in town,	5
The light-heeled Levite's broke and the spark flown.	
Broke did I say? They ne'er had quit the place	
Had they but set up with a spark of grace!	
They did the pulpit as a coffin greet	
And took the surplice for a winding-sheet.	10

1. *Beloved:* The satirist wryly refers to the unfaithful minister by the term he used in addressing his congregation.
5. *Clerkenwell:* at the time a northern suburb of London.
6. *Levite:* a minister.

Had that so scared them? At the bells' sad tolls
They might have laid them by and learned of Paul's.
But for their parts, who will come in their rooms?
They are not mad to live among the tombs.
See how they choose three months to fly the rod   15
And dare not fall into the hands of God.
For God of persons no respecter is,
Then to respect themselves (pray) is't amiss?
They that should stay and teach us to reform
Gird up their loins and run to 'scape the storm,   20
And winged with fear, they flee to save their lives
Like Lot, from Sodom, with their brats and wives.
This is a tribe that for His punishments
Fear God, but keep not His commandments.
They dread the plague and dare not stand its shock,   25
Let wolves or lions feed the fainting flock;
They made the sheep the subject now, men say,
Not so much of their prayer, as their prey.
But they are gone to have (it now appears)
The country hear them with their harvest-ears,   30
Whilst here at home we find Christ's saying true,
The harvest great is, but the lab'rers few.
Yet, like enough, the heat o'th' day being o'er,
You'll have them here again at the 'leventh hour.
Think you these men believe with holy Paul   35
For them to be dissolved is best of all?
Then, their own bodies they would never mind
More than the souls of those they left behind.
Who now, those sons of Aaron being fled,
Shall stand between the living and the dead?   40
We have at home the plague, abroad the sword,
And will they add the famine of the word?
But 'tis no matter, let what will befall,
A recantation sermon pays for all.
                              Ne saevi, magne Sacerdos!   45

22. See Gen. 19:1–29.
32. "The harvest truly is plenteous, but the laborers are few" (Luke 10:2).
33–34. An allusion to the parable of the laborers in the vineyard in Matt. 20.
35–36. An allusion, perhaps, to Rom. 6:4: "Therefore we are buried with him by baptism into death: that like as Christ was raised up from the dead by the glory of the Father, even so we also should walk in newness of life."
39. *sons of Aaron:* ministers.
45. *Ne saevi, magne Sacerdos!*: Do not be angry, great priest! Aeneas's words to the Sibyl in Book VI of the *Aeneid.*

For you that stay, I have another sense;
These I revile, but you I reverence.
You have stood firm and God of mercy craved,
And holding out unto the end are saved.
You the true shepherds are, that would not keep   50
Your lives a minute, would they save the sheep.
Not hirelings, that away in peril sneak,
And leave the stones out of the wall to speak.
Whose heinous guilt is of a dye so deep,
It makes the dead even through the marble weep.   55
You, you have stood to't, as unmoved as rocks,
And proved yourselves the only orthodox.
You have at Christ's command handed your lives
Without excuse of oxen, farms, or wives.
To your shall therefore glorious crowns be given,   60
And you shall shine bright as the stars in heaven.
Of life and death before you, well you choose,
For who will lose shall save, will save shall lose.
With reverence to the sacred word I shall
My theme an emblem of the Bible call: 65
For the canonical are those that stay,
They that obscure are the Apocrypha,
Of whom a man shall make (nay e'en St. John)
No revelation till the plague be gone.
Well, let them march; we have the better bread: 70
The wheat's the purer, now the chaff is fled.
Farewell wild grapes! For my part let 'em pass:
The gleanings better than the vintage was,
And let apostates ramble where they will,
The church reserves her better angels still   75
Which she embraces, for in vain she cares
For wand'ring planets that has fixed stars.

                                        Praelucendo pereo.

51–52. Cf. John 10:11–15.
63. Cf. Matt. 10:39: "He that findeth his life shall lose it: and he that loseth his life for my sake shall find it."
72. The rebellious people of Israel are compared to wild grapes in Isa. 5:1–7.
78. *Praelucendo pereo:* Though I bear a great light I perish.

The War of Words, 1675-1679

SIR GEORGE ETHEREGE

Ephelia to Bajazet
(1675)

Bajazet, the great Turkish emperor defeated by Tamerlaine, was degraded by Marlowe into an arrogant, self-indulgent brute. Bajazet was to suffer an even greater degradation, however, in being identified with the earl of Mulgrave in this poem and the one that follows it. Ephelia, who does not appear either in historical accounts of Bajazet or in Marlowe's play, is probably a fiction fashioned by the satirist to reflect Mulgrave's complacent view of himself as the irresistible lover. This view Mulgrave reveals in *An Essay upon Satire.*

Ephelia to Bajazet is attributed to Sir George Etherege in the following lines from *A Familiar Epistle to Mr. Julian:* "Poor George grows old, his muse worn out of fashion:/Hoarsely she sung Ephelia's lamentation."

Rochester's satirical sequel, *A Very Heroical Epistle in Answer to Ephelia,* alludes (line 53) to a duel between Mulgrave and Percy Kirke on 4 July 1675, which was occasioned by Mulgrave's affair with Percy's sister Mall. Both poems were probably written later that summer.

EPHELIA TO BAJAZET

How far are they deceived who hope in vain
A lasting lease of joys from love t'obtain!
All the dear sweets we promise or expect,
After enjoyment, turn to cold neglect.
Could love a constant happiness have known,   5
The mighty wonder had in me been shown.
Our passions were so favoréd by Fate,
As if she meant 'em an eternal date;
So kind he looked, such tender words he spoke,
'Twas past belief such vows should e'er be broke.   10

Fixed on my eyes, how often would he say
He could with pleasure gaze an age away!
When thoughts too great for words had made him mute,
In kisses he would tell my hand his suit.
So great his passion was, so far above   15
The common gallantries that pass for love,
At worst I thought if he unkind should prove,
His ebbing passion would be kinder far
Than the first transports of all others are.
Nor was my love or fondness less than his: 20
In him I centered all my hopes of bliss!
For him my duty to my friends forgot,
For him I lost . . . alas! What lost I not?
Fame, all the valuable things of life,
To meet his love by a less name than wife.   25
How happy was I then, how dearly blessed,
When this great man lay panting on my breast,
Looking such things as ne'er can be expressed!
Thousand fresh looks he gave me ev'ry hour,
Whilst greedily I did his looks devour,   30
Till quite o'ercome with charms I trembling lay,
At ev'ry look he gave, melted away!
I was so highly happy in his love,
Methought I pitied them that dwelt above!
Think then, thou greatest, loveliest, falsest man,   35
How you have vowed, how I have loved, and then,
My faithless dear, be cruel if you can!
How I have loved, I cannot, need not, tell;
No, ev'ry act has shown I loved too well.
Since first I saw you I ne'er had a thought   40
Was not entirely yours. To you I brought
My virgin innocence and freely made
My love an off'ring to your noble bed;
Since when you've been the star by which I steered,
And nothing else but you I loved or feared.   45
Your smiles I only live by, and I must,
Whene'er you frown, be shattered into dust.
Oh! can the coldness that you show me now
Suit with the gen'rous heat you once did show?
I cannot live on pity or respect: 50
A thought so mean would my whole love infect.
Less than your love I scorn, sir, to expect.

Let me not live in dull indiff'rency,
But give me rage enough to make me die,
For if from you I needs must meet my fate,   55
Before your pity I would choose your hate.

JOHN WILMOT, EARL OF ROCHESTER

A Very Heroical Epistle in Answer to Ephelia
(1676)

In this "heroical epistle" (in imitation of Ovid's *Heroides*) Rochester employs the oblique device of the candid declaration to satirize the complacency and arrogance of the earl of Mulgrave (Bajazet in the preceding epistle). The satire is heroical in another sense, too, for it upholds ironically as an heroic standard a besotted and inhuman self-centeredness:

> In my dear self I center ev'rything—
> My servants, friends, my mistress, and my king;
> Nay, heav'n and earth to that one point I bring.

The irony has for some reason eluded most of Rochester's critics, and even the knowledgeable V. de Sola Pinto declares that here the poet's "complete egoism . . . is stated frankly and with a boldness that must have shocked many who practised it in their lives, but who never had the courage to admit such principles openly" (*Enthusiast in Wit,* p. 148). Nor have the critics detected a second object of Rochester's satire in John Dryden, who, in the preface to *Aureng-Zebe* (1676), served up to his patron the adulatory concept of heroic greatness the *Epistle* parodies: "True greatness, if it be anywhere on earth, is in a private virtue removed from the notion of pomp and vanity, confined to a contemplation of itself, and centering on itself." After misquoting lines from Lucretius, Dryden goes on to say, "If this be not the life of a deity, because it cannot consist with Providence, it is, at least, a god-like life." It is hard to tell where the laureate's tongue was when he composed this tribute, but there is no doubt that his noble patron's boundless complacency would have accepted any such gift horses without inspecting their mouths.

A Very Heroical Epistle was published with *My Lord All-Pride,* another of Rochester's anti-Mulgrave pieces, in 1679.

Madam,
   If you're deceived, it is not by my cheat,
For all disguises are below the great.
What man or woman upon earth can say
I ever used 'em well above a day?
How is it, then, that I inconstant am?   5
He changes not who always is the same.
In my dear self I center ev'rything—
My servants, friends, my mistress, and my king;
Nay, heav'n and earth to that one point I bring.
Well-mannered, honest, generous, and stout   10
(Names by dull fools, to plague mankind, found out)
Should I regard, I must myself constrain,
And 'tis my maxim to avoid all pain.
You fondly look for what none e'er could find,
Deceive yourself, and then call me unkind,   15
And by false reasons would my falsehood prove,
For 'tis as natural to change as love.
You may as justly at the sun repine,
Because alike it does not always shine.
No glorious thing was ever made to stay: 20
My blazing star but visits and away.
As fatal, too, it shines as those i'th' skies:
'Tis never seen but some great lady dies.
The boasted favor you so precious hold
To me's no more than changing of my gold.   25
Whate'er you gave I paid you back in bliss;
Then where's the obligation, pray, of this?
If, heretofore, you found grace in my eyes,
Be thankful for it and let that suffice.
But women, beggar-like, still haunt the door   30
Where they've received a charity before.
Oh happy sultan, whom we barb'rous call,
How much refined art thou above us all!
Who envies not the joys of thy serail?
Thee, like some god, the trembling crowd adore: 35
Each man's thy slave and womankind thy whore.
Methinks I see thee underneath the shade

Of golden canopy, supinely laid,
Thy crowding slaves all silent as the night,
But, at thy nod, all active as the light.   40
Secure in solid sloth thou there dost reign,
And feel'st the joys of love without the pain.
Each female courts thee with a wishing eye,
While thou with awful pride walk'st careless by,
Till thy kind pledge, at last, marks out the dame   45
Thou fanci'st most, to quench thy present flame.
Then from thy bed submissive she retires,
And thankful for the grace no more requires.
No loud reproach nor fond unwelcome sound
Of women's tongues thy sacred ear dares wound.   50
If any do, a nimble mute straight ties
The true-love's-knot and stops her foolish cries.
Thou fear'st no injured kinsman's threat'ning blade,
Nor midnight ambushes by rivals laid,
While here with aching hearts our joys we taste,   55
Disturbed by swords, like Damocles's feast.

JOHN WILMOT, EARL OF ROCHESTER

An Epistolary Essay from M.G. to O.B.
upon Their Mutual Poems
(1676)

In his study, *Attribution in Restoration Poetry,* David Vieth shows that the *Epistolary Essay* purports to be written by the earl of Mulgrave to his poetic collaborator, Dryden (Old Bays). The identification had eluded previous critics of Rochester, and the *Essay,* like the *Very Heroical Epistle in Answer to Ephelia,* had been regarded as Rochester's personal declaration. Like the *Heroical Epistle,* however, this satire employs a satirical persona to castigate Mulgrave for his arrogant disregard of rational human standards. The earlier poem devotes itself to Mulgrave's moral egotism, and this one exposes the false literary standards that grow out of such moral egotism:

> Which way soe'er desire and fancy lead,
> Contemning fame, that path I boldly tread,
> And, if exposing what I take for wit,
> To my dear self a pleasure I beget,
> No matter though the cens'ring critics fret.

Like its companion piece, the *Epistolary Essay* also attacks Dryden with a pervasive parody of his preface to *Aureng-Zebe (1676),* which, incidentally, had struck a glancing blow at Rochester's *Satire against Mankind.* What Rochester chiefly attacks here is Mulgrave's complacent disregard for critical standards other than his own, which Dryden describes in the following flattering terms: "How much more great and manly than Cicero is your lordship in your contempt of popular applause and your retired virtue, which shines only to a few."

The only known "mutual poem" of Mulgrave and Dryden is *An Essay upon Satire.* I assume that a draft of this poem was known by Rochester to be in existence as early as 1675 (see headnote), although the version we know, with its violent attack on Rochester, was not circulating until late 1679.

165

An Epistolary Essay from M.G. to O.B. upon Their Mutual Poems

Dear Friend,
I hear this town does so abound
With saucy censurers that faults are found
With what of late we in poetic rage
Bestowing threw away on the dull age.
But howsoe'er envy their spleens may raise   5
To rob my brows of the deserved bays,
Their thanks at least I merit, since through me
They are partakers of your poetry;
And this is all I'll say in my defense:
T' obtain one line of your well-worded sense   10
I'd be content t' have writ the *British Prince*.
I'm none of those who think themselves inspired
Nor write with the vain hope to be admired,
But from a rule I have upon long trial
T' avoid with care all sort of self-denial.   15
Which way soe'er desire and fancy lead,
Contemning fame, that path I boldly tread,
And, if exposing what I take for wit,
To my dear self a pleasure I beget,
No matter though the cens'ring critics fret.   20
These whom my muse displeases are at strife
With equal spleen against my course of life,
The least delight of which I'll not forego
For all the flatt'ring praise man can bestow.
If I designed to please, the way were then   25
To mend my manners rather than my pen:
The first's unnatural, therefore unfit,
And for the second I despair of it.
Since grace is not so hard to get as wit,
Perhaps ill verses ought to be confined   30
(In mere good breeding) like unsav'ry wind.
Were reading forced, I should be apt to think
Men might no more write scurvily than stink,
But 'tis your choice whether you'll read or no.
If likewise of your smelling it were so,   35
I'd fart just as I write for my own ease,
Nor should you be concerned unless you please.

I'll own that you write better than I do,
But I have as much need to write as you.
What though the excrement of my dull brain   40
Flows in a harsh, insipid strain,
Whilst your rich head eases itself of wit?
Must none but civet cats have leave to shit?
In all I write should sense and wit and rhyme
Fail me at once, yet something so sublime   45
Shall stamp my poem that the world may see
It could have been produced by none but me;
And that's my end, for man can wish no more
Than so to write as none e'er writ before.
Yet why am I no poet of the times?   50
I have allusions, similes, and rhymes
And wit, or else 'tis hard that I alone
Of the whole race of mankind should have none.
Unequally the partial hand of Heav'n
Has all but this one only blessing giv'n.   55
The world appears like a great family
Whose lord, oppressed with pride and poverty,
That to a few great bounty he may show,
Is fain to starve the num'rous train below.
Just so seems Providence, as poor and vain,   60
Keeping more creatures than it can maintain.
Here 'tis profuse, and there it meanly saves,
And for one prince it makes ten thousand slaves.
In wit alone 't has been magnificent,
Of which so just a share to each is sent   65
That the most avaricious is content;
For none e'er thought the due divisions such,
His own too little or his friend's too much.
Yet most men show or find great want of wit,
Writing themselves or judging what is writ,   70
But I, who am of spritely vigor full,
Look on mankind as envious and dull.
Born to my self, my self I like alone
And must conclude my judgment good or none.
For could my sense be naught, how should I know   75
Whether another man's were good or no?
Thus I resolve of my own poetry
That 'tis the best, and there's a fame for me.
If then I'm happy, what does it advance

Whether to merit due or arrogance?   80
Oh, but the world will take offence hereby!
Why then, the world shall suffer for 't, not I.
Did e'er this saucy world and I agree
To let it have its beastly will on me?
Why should my prostituted sense be drawn   85
To ev'ry rule their musty customs spawn?
But men will censure, yet 'tis ten to one
Whene'er they censure they'll be in the wrong.
There's not a thing on earth that I can name
So foolish and so false as common fame.   90
It calls the courtier knave, the plain man rude,
Haughty the grave, and the delightful lewd,
Impertinent the brisk, morose the sad,
Mean the familiar, the reserved one mad.
Poor, helpless woman is not favored more: 95
She's a sly hypocrite or public whore.
Then who the devil would give this—to be free
From th' innocent reproach of infamy?
These things considered make me, in despite
Of idle rumor, keep at home and write.   100

JOHN WILMOT, EARL OF ROCHESTER

An Allusion to Horace
(1675)

Rochester's *Allusion* follows its Horatian model quite closely, as a comparison with the opening lines of Creech's version (1684) indicates:

> Well, sir, I granted I said Lucilius' muse
> Is incorrect, his way of writing loose,
> And who admires him so, what friend of his
> So blindly partial to deny me this?

For Lucilius Rochester substitutes Dryden; for the farces of Laberius, the plays of John Crowne; for Horace's approving friends, Shadwell, Sheppard, Wycherley, and the rest. Although, from the allusions to contemporary events, Rochester probably wrote the satire late in 1675, Dryden did not reply until 1678, in his preface to *All for Love*. There he excoriated the "ignorant little zanies . . . , persecutors even of Horace himself . . . by their ignorant and vile imitations of him," who make "an unjust use of his authority" and turn "his artillery against his friends." Pretending ignorance of Rochester's authorship, Dryden went on to invite "this rhyming judge of the twelvepenny gallery, this legitimate son of Sternhold" to "subscribe his name to his censure, or (not to tax him beyond his learning) set his mark" and finished with detailed criticisms of the *Allusion* as untrue to its original and inaccurate in its judgment of contemporary poets.

Rochester's brief attack on his former friend, Sir Carr Scroope, immediately touched off a bitter feud recorded in the three satires that follow this one and in *On Poet Ninny*, but there is at present no trace of the censures with which Rochester charges Scroope (lines 115 ff.). Although Rochester seems to have fired the last shot (in *On Poet Ninny*), victory, perhaps, ultimately belongs to Scroope for his penetrating attack on his adversary's character in *In Defense of Satire*. In his final salvo of abuse, Rochester seems to have violated the principle here enunciated that "A jest in scorn points out and hits the thing / More home than the morosest satire's sting."

An Allusion to Horace

The 10th Satyr of the 1st Book
Nempe incomposito dixi pede, etc.

Well, sir, 'tis granted I said Dryden's rhymes
Were stol'n, unequal, nay dull, many times.
What foolish patron is there found of his
So blindly partial to deny me this?
But that his plays, embroidered up and down,   5
With wit and learning justly pleased the town,
In the same paper I as freely own.
Yet having this allowed, the heavy mass
That stuffs up his loose volumes must not pass.
For by that rule I might as well admit   10
Crowne's tedious scenes for poetry and wit.
   'Tis therefore not enough when your false sense
Hits the false judgment of an audience
Of clapping fools, assembling a vast crowd,
Till the thronged playhouse crack with the dull load.   15
Though e'en that talent merits in some sort
That can divert the rabble and the court,
Which blund'ring Settle never could attain,
And puzzling Otway labors at in vain.
But within due proportion circumscribe   20
Whate'er you write, that with a flowing tide
The style may rise, yet in its rise forbear

11. *Crowne:* John Crowne (d. 1703?), a playwright who dedicated his *History of Charles VIII* (1672), a rhyming tragedy, to Rochester. Rochester contrived to have Crowne commissioned in Dryden's place to write a court masque, *Calisto, or the Chaste Nymph* (1675). According to St. Evremond, Rochester withdrew his patronage out of envy for Crowne's success as a writer of heroic dramas and afterward lampooned him in this poem and in *The Session of Poets* (1676).

18. *Settle:* Elkanah Settle (1648–1724), the "City Poet," for a time surpassed Dryden in popularity as a writer of heroic tragedies. Until Rochester transferred his patronage to Crowne, Settle had enjoyed the earl's favor. Dryden, Crowne, and Shadwell attacked Settle in *Notes and Observations on the Empress of Morocco*, and Settle appeared as Doeg in *Absalom and Achitophel II:* "Free from all meaning, whether good or bad,/ And, in one word, heroically mad."

19. *Otway:* Thomas Otway (1652–85), produced his first heroic tragedy, *Alcibiades,* in 1675. Rochester commended the piece and drew the attention of the duke of York to the author. The female lead in this and in Otway's subsequent plays was taken by Mrs. Barry, who, about this time, became the mistress of Rochester, to whom she bore a son in December 1677. Otway for years was passionately in love with her, but she spurned his passion (*DNB:* Wilson, *All the King's Ladies,* p. 111). His *Titus and Berenice* (1677) is dedicated to Rochester. *Puzzling Otway,* Hayward suggests, refers to Otway's inability to write successful comedies.

With useless words t' oppress the wearied ear.
Here be your language lofty, there more light;
Your rhetoric with your poetry unite.   25
For elegance' sake sometimes allay the force
Of epithets: 'twill soften the discourse.
A jest in scorn points out and hits the thing
More home than the morosest satire's sting.
Shakespeare and Jonson did herein excell   30
And might in this be imitated well,
Whom refined Eth'rege copies not at all,
But is himself a sheer original,
Nor that slow drudge in swift Pindaric strains,
Flatman, who Cowley imitates with pains,   35
And rides a jaded Muse, whipped with loose reins.
When Lee makes temp'rate Scipio fret and rave,
And Hannibal a whining, am'rous slave,
I laugh and wish the hot-brained fustian fool
In Busby's hands, to be well lashed at school.   40
     Of all our modern wits none seems to me
Once to have touched upon true comedy
But hasty Shadwell and slow Wycherley.

32. *Eth'rege:* Sir George Etherege (1635?–91), one of the best Restoration comic dramatists. He was a close friend of Rochester and took part with him in the notorious Epsom brawl of 1676. Etherege modeled his nonchalant and witty Dorimant in *The Man of Mode, or Sir Fopling Flutter* (1676), on Rochester.

35. *Flatman:* Thomas Flatman (1637–88), poet and miniature painter. His Pindarics, according to the *DNB*, deserved the derision of Rochester. *Cowley:* Abraham Cowley (1618–67). His reputation with Dryden and other contemporary critics rested largely on his Pindaric odes.

37–40. *Lee:* Nathaniel Lee (1635?–92), son of Richard Lee, D.D. (cf. Wild's *Recantation of a Penitent Proteus,* 1664). He was patronized spasmodically by Buckingham and Rochester and "lost no time in imitating their vices, to the permanent injury of his health" (*DNB*). Lee had dedicated his heroic tragedy, *Nero* (1674), to Rochester. In April 1675 his second play, *Sophonisba,* was produced, in which the *temp'rate Scipio* raved and Hannibal became the infatuated slave of Rosalinda.

40. Lee had attended Westminster School, the stern headmaster of which was the famous Richard Busby (1606–95).

43. *Shadwell:* Thomas Shadwell (1642?–92), dramatist and, after the revolution, poet laureate. Dryden attacked him for his bad poetry and Whiggish views in *The Medal* (1682) and made him the butt of *Mac Flecknoe,* in which Shadwell is tasked inter alia with being a slow writer. Shadwell wrote *The Libertine* in five weeks, however, and often boasted of his speed in composition. *Wycherley:* William Wycherley (1640?–1716), one of the greatest Restoration dramatists, wrote only four plays, his last, *The Plain Dealer,* appearing in 1677. Dryden later attacked Rochester in the preface to *All for Love* (1678) and alluded to this line as follows: "If he have a friend whose hastiness in writing is his greatest fault, Horace would have taught him to have minced the matter, and to have called it readiness of thought and a flowing fancy . . . , but he would never have allowed him to have called a slow man hasty, or a hasty writer a slow drudge." Pope, according to Spence, said that Wycherley was far

Shadwell's unfinished works do yet impart
Great proofs of force of nature, none of art.   45
With just, bold strokes he dashes here and there,
Showing great mastery with little care,
And scorns to varnish his good touches o'er
To make the fools and women praise 'em more.
But Wycherley earns hard whate'er he gains.   50
He wants no judgment nor he spares no pains.
He frequently excels, and at the least
Makes fewer faults than any of the best.
   Waller, by nature for the bays designed,
With force and fire and fancy unconfined,   55
In panegyrics does excel mankind.
He best can turn, enforce, and soften things
To praise great conquerors or to flatter kings.
   For pointed satires I would Buckhurst choose,
The best good man with the worst-natured muse,   60
For songs and verses mannerly obscene
That can stir nature up by springs unseen
And without forcing blushes warm the queen.
   Sedley has that prevailing gentle art
That can with a resistless charm impart   65
The loosest wishes to the chastest heart,
Raise such a conflict, kindle such a fire,
Betwixt declining virtue and desire,
Till the poor vanquished maid dissolves away
In dreams all night, in sighs and tears all day.   70
   Dryden in vain tried this nice way of wit,

---

from being slow and that he wrote *The Plain Dealer* in three weeks.

54–58. *Waller:* Edmund Waller (1606–87), a poet admired by Rochester (Etherege's Dorimant, modeled on Rochester, quotes Waller continually). Rochester alludes very tactfully ("To praise great conquerors, or to flatter kings") to Waller's change of political sympathies as reflected in the famous *Panegyric to My Lord Protector* (1655); *Three Poems upon the Death of the Late Usurper, Oliver Cromwell; To the King upon His Majesty's Happy Return;* and *Instructions to a Painter.*

59–63. *Buckhurst:* Charles Sackville, Lord Buckhurst, later sixth earl of Dorset and earl of Middlesex (1638–1706), one of the court wits and a rake. He was involved with Sedley and Sir Thomas Ogle in a notorious brawl at the Cock Tavern in Bow Street (see Wilson, *The Court Wits,* p. 40). A generous patron of letters, he gave material assistance to Dryden, Butler, and Wycherley. According to Walpole, Buckhurst was the finest gentleman of Charles II's court: "he had as much wit as his master or his contemporaries, Buckingham and Rochester, without the royal want of feeling, the duke's want of principle, or the earl's want of thought" (*Noble Authors, 2,* 96).

64–70. *Sedley:* Sir Charles Sedley (1639?–1701), minor poet, wit, and rake. His literary output consists mainly of a few plays, some translations, and some commonplace love poems.

For he to be a tearing blade thought fit,
But when he would be sharp he still was blunt,
To frisk his frolic fancy he'd cry "c——!"
Would give the ladies a dry, bawdy bob, 75
And thus he got the name of Poet Squab.
But to be just, 'twill to his praise be found,
His excellencies more than faults abound,
Nor dare I from his sacred temples tear
That laurel which he best deserves to wear. 80
But does not Dryden find e'en Jonson dull,
Fletcher and Beaumont incorrect and full
Of lewd lines (as he call them); Shakespeare's style
Stiff and affected, to his own the while
Allowing all the justness that his pride 85
So arrogantly had to these denied?
And may not I have leave impartially
To search and censure Dryden's works and try
If those gross faults his choice pen does commit
Proceed from want of judgment or of wit; 90
Or if his lumpish fancy does refuse
Spirit and grace to his loose slattern muse?
Five hundred verses every morning writ
Prove you no more a poet than a wit.

75–76. *dry . . . bob:* coition without emission. *Squab,* next to *Bays,* was Dryden's most popular nickname. It referred usually to his short, fat stature, but here the primary reference is to callow inexperience.

81–86. This arraignment of Dryden's critical opinions seems largely impressionistic; at any rate not many of the judgments Rochester attributes to him are to be found in Ker's edition of the essays. Dryden does express strong dislike for Jonson's clenches, "the lowest and most grovelling kind of wit" (*Defense of the Epilogue,* Ker, *1,* 173), and mentions the irregularity of structure in certain plays of Beaumont and Fletcher (*Essay of Dramatic Poesy,* Ker, *1,* 79). I have not been able to find references in Dryden's critical writing to Shakespeare's stiffness nor to Beaumont and Fletcher's "lewd lines." Dryden's long quarrel with Shadwell on whether Jonson had "wit" culminated in his writing *Mac Flecknoe,* where Dryden also takes the opportunity of retorting to Rochester's praise of Shadwell in lines 44–47 of this poem. Shadwell had repeatedly upheld the Jonsonian "humors" against Dryden's emphasis on wit. In the *Defense of the Epilogue* Dryden observed:

> In these low characters of vice and folly lay the excellency of that inimitable writer who, when at any time he aimed at wit in the stricter sense (that is, sharpness of conceit) was forced to either borrow from the ancients . . . , or, when he trusted himself alone, often fell into meanness of expression. Nay, he was not free from the lowest and most grovelling kind of wit, which we call clenches.

Dryden goes on to make a good deal of "the last and greatest advantage of our writing, which proceeds from *conversation,*" and which makes the wit of his age "much more courtly" than that of Jonson's. Needless to say, in his next play, *The Virtuoso,* Shadwell wrote a dedication that jibed vigorously at Dryden.

Such scribbling authors have been seen before: 95
Mustapha, *The English Princes,* forty more,
Were things perhaps composed in half an hour.
   To write what may securely stand the test
Of being well read over, thrice at least
Compare each phrase, examine ev'ry line,.   100
Weigh ev'ry word, and ev'ry thought refine.
Scorn all applause the vile rout can bestow
And be content to please those few who know.
Canst thou be such a vain, mistaken thing
To wish thy works might make a playhouse ring   105
With the unthinking laughter and poor praise
Of fops and ladies, factious for thy plays?
Then send a cunning friend to learn thy doom
From the shrewd judges in the drawing room.
   I've no ambition on that idle score,   110
But say with Betty Morrice, heretofore,
When a court lady called her Bulkeley's whore,
"I please one man of wit, am proud on 't, too!
Let all the coxcombs dance to bed to you."
Should I be troubled when the purblind knight,   115
Who squints more in his judgment than his sight,
Picks silly faults and censures what I write?
Or when the poor-fed poets of the town,
For scraps and coachroom cry my verses down?
I loathe the rabble: 'tis enough for me   120
If Sedley, Shadwell, Sheppard, Wycherley,
Godolphin, Butler, Buckhurst, Buckingham,
And some few more, whom I omit to name,
Approve my sense. I count their censure fame.

96. *Mustapha:* a heroic play written in 1665 by Roger Boyle, Baron Broghill and 1st earl of Orrery (1621–79). *The English Princes, or the Death of Richard III* (acted 1667) is a tragedy by John Caryll (1625–1711).

111–12. *Betty Morrice* is probably Buckhurst's "black Bess" celebrated in "Methinks the poor town has been troubled too long." *Bulkeley* is probably Henry Bulkeley, master of the household to Charles II and James II.

121. *Sheppard:* Sir Fleetwood Sheppard (1634–98), a fashionable rake and wit who, according to Wood, after the Restoration "retired to London, hanged on the court, became a debauchée and an atheist, a grand companion with Lord Buckhurst, Henry Savile, and others" (quoted in *DNB*). Sheppard was a patron of poets, among them Prior, whom he discovered, and he himself wrote fugitive verse and lampoons.

122. *Godolphin:* Sidney Godolphin, earl of Godolphin (1645–1712), Page of Honor, Groom of the Bedchamber, and Master of the Robes. He became one of the Chits, the group that formed an administration after the fall of Danby in 1679. *Butler:* probably Lord John Butler, a son of the duke of Ormonde, who had been one of the several unsuccessful contenders for the hand of Elizabeth Mallet, countess of Rochester. See Pepys, 4 February 1667.

SIR CARR SCROOPE

In Defense of Satire
(1677)

Scroope's *In Defense of Satire,* like its precursor, has a Horatian model, the
fourth satire of the first book, but it is a much freer imitation than Roches-
ter's. It was written after the death of Captain Downs, Rochester's "brave
companion" identified in most of the manuscripts, who was wounded in a
"midnight frolic" at Epsom (see lines 53–55) and died at the end of June
1676.

In Defense of Satire

When Shakespeare, Jonson, Fletcher ruled the stage,
They took so bold a freedom with the age
That there was scarce a knave or fool in town
Of any note but had his picture shown.
And without doubt, though some it may offend, 5
Nothing helps more than satire to amend
Ill manners, or is trulier virtue's friend.
Princes may laws ordain, priests gravely preach,
But poets most successfully will teach.
For as a passing bell frights from his meat 10
The greedy sick man that too much would eat,
So when a vice ridiculous is made,
Our neighbor's shame keeps us from growing bad.
But wholesome remedies few palates please:
Men rather love what flatters their disease. 15
Pimps, parasites, buffoons, and all the crew
That under friendship's name weak man undo,
Find their false service kindlier understood
Than such as tell's bold truths to do us good.
    Look where you will and you shall hardly find 20
A man without some sickness of the mind.
In vain we wise would seem, while ev'ry lust

175

Whisks us about, as whirlwind doth the dust.
Here for some needless gain a wretch is hurled
From pole to pole and slaved about the world,   25
While the reward of all his pains and care
Ends in that despicable thing, his heir.
There a vain fop mortgages all his land
To buy that gaudy plaything, a command,
To ride on cockhorse, wear a scarf at's arse,   30
And play Jack-pudding in a May-day farce.
Here one whom God to make a fool thought fit,
In spite of Providence will be a wit,
But wanting strength t'uphold his ill-made choice,
Sets up with lewdness, blasphemy, and noise.   35
There at his mistress' feet a lover lies,
And for a tawdry painted baby dies,
Falls on his knees, adores, and is afraid
Of the vain idol he himself has made.
These and a thousand fools unmentioned here   40
Hate poets all because they poets fear.
"Take heed!" they cry. "Yonder mad dog will bite.
He cares not whom he falls on in his fit.
Come but in's way, and straight a new lampoon
Shall spread your mangled fame about the town."   45
    But why am I this bugbear to you all?
My pen is dipped in no such bitter gall.
He that can rail at one he calls his friend,

---

28. An Osborn MS (chest II, no. 14) at Yale supplies the marginal note, *Capt. Aston*. Probably the Edmund Aston or Ashton who bought a captaincy in Sir Allen Apsley's regiment in 1667. Maurice Irvine ("Identification of Characters in Mulgrave's 'Essay upon Satyr,' " *Studies in Philology* 34 [1937]: 533–51) says he was "popular in the satires of the day whenever his puny size or his vanity suggested him for comparison with the typical Restoration fops, Sir George Hewitt or Sir Carr Scroope." He fought a duel with Etherege, and the prologue, "Gentle reproofs have long been tried in vain," was credited to him as well as to Rochester. See his satire on Edward Howard ("As when a bully draws his sword").

29. Osborn MS: *Sir Edward Bash*. I have not found any significant information on this note.

35. Osborn MS: *Philip E. Pembroke*. Philip Herbert, seventh earl of Pembroke (1653–83) was notorious for his coarseness and brutality. He fought several duels, including one with Sir George Hewitt in 1676, and he killed a good many men, either in duels or in drunken brawls. He was tried by a jury of his peers in the House of Lords in 1678 for killing a Mr. Carey, but he was not convicted.

37. Osborn MS: *Charles Ld Cornwallis*. The 3d Baron Cornwallis (bap. 1655), a fortune hunter who married Elizabeth, daughter of Sir Stephen Fox. He was tried for murder in 1673 and acquitted.

38–39. Osborn MS: *Sir George Hewitt and Mrs. Marshall*. Sir George Hewitt was a coxcomb and reputedly the model for Etherege's Sir Fopling Flutter.

48–59. This portrait, the most specific in the poem, is unquestionably a sketch of Rochester

Or hear him absent wronged, and not defend,
Who for the sake of some ill-natured jest   50
Tells what he should conceal, invents the rest,
To fatal midnight frolics can betray
His brave companion and then run away,
Leaving him to be murdered in the street,
Then put it off with some buffoon conceit,   55
This, this is he you should beware of all,
Yet him a witty, pleasant man you call.
To whet your dull debauches up and down,
You seek him as top fiddler of the town.
But if I laugh, when the court coxcombs show,   60
To see that booby Sotus dance provoe,
Or chatt'ring Porus from the side box grin,
Tricked like a lady's monkey new made clean,
To me the name of railer straight you give,
Call me a man that knows not how to live.   65
But wenches to their keepers true shall turn,
Stale maids of honor proffered husbands scorn,
Great statesmen flattery and clinches hate,
And, long in office, die without estate,
Against a bribe court-judges shall decide,   70

---

and is identified as such in the marginal notes of three MSS. The incident referred to in lines 52–54 is described by Christopher Hatton on 29 June 1676 as follows:

Mr. Downs is dead. The Lord Rochester doth abscond, and so doth Etherege and Capt. Bridges, who occasioned the riot Sunday sennight. They were tossing some fiddlers in a blanket for refusing to play, and a barber, upon the noise, going to see what the matter, they seized upon him, and, to free himself from them, he offered to carry them to the handsomest woman in Epsom, and directed them to the constable's house, who demanding what they came for, they told him a whore, and, he refusing to let them in, they broke open his doors and broke his head and beat him very severely. At last he made his escape, called his watch, and Etherege made a submissive oration to them and so far appeased them that the constable dismissed his watch. But presently after, the Lord Rochester drew upon the constable. Mr. Downs, to prevent his pass, seized on him, the constable cried out, "murther!" and the watch, returning, one came behind Mr. Downs and with a sprittle staff cleft his skull. The Lord Rochester and the rest run away, and Downs, having no sword, snatched up a stick and striking at them, they run into the side with a half pike, and so bruised his arm that he was never able to stir it after.

(*Hatton Correspondence, 1,* 133–34).

61. *Sotus:* probably pseudo-Latin for *sot.* Two MSS identify him as "Mr. Griffin," probably Edward Griffin, a Groom of the Bedchamber to the duke of York and a familiar of Charles II. *Provoe* or *provost* is an assistant fencing-master.

62. *Porus:* The Latin *porus* means a passage of the body and the English noun *pore* is derived from it. The name seems to suggest a sort of spongelike creature. Osborne MS glosses Porus as Henry Jermyn, earl of St. Albans (d. 1684), a famous courtier of whom Marvell draws a satiric portrait in *Last Instructions.*

The City knavery want, the clergy pride,
E'er that black malice in my rhymes you find
That wrongs a worthy man or hurts his friend.
But then perhaps you'll say, "Why do you write?
What you call harmless mirth the world calls spite.   75
Why should your fingers itch to have a lash
At Simius the buffoon, or Cully bash?
What is't to you if Alidore's fine whore
F—— with some fop while he's shut out of door?
Consider, pray, that dang'rous weapon, wit,   80
Frightens a million where a few you hit.
Whip but a cur as you ride through a town,
And straight his fellow curs his quarrel own.
Each knave or fool that's conscious of a crime,
Though he 'scapes now, looks for't another time."   85
    "Sir, I confess all you have said is true,
But who has not some folly to pursue?
Milo turned Quixote fancied battles fights,
When the fifth bottle has increased the heights.
Warlike, dirt pies our hero Paris forms,   90
Which desp'rate Bessus without armor storms.
Cornus, the kindest husband e'er was born,

77. *Simius:* ape (L.), glossed in Osborn MS as Frank Newport, Francis Viscount Newport of Bradford (1619–1708), treasurer of the household and Privy Councillor. *Cully:* dupe.

78. *Alidore's:* Osborn MS reads *Abdy's* and supplies in the margin *Sir John Abdy: Mrs. Michell Michell.* All other texts read *Alidore's,* which satisfies the metrical requirements of this line. I suspect the scribe of Osborn MS unintentionally substituted *Abdy's* from his gloss. There seems to be a cryptic allusion to this triangle in a letter from Margaret Bedingfield to Lady Paston (25 July 1675): "Mrs. Michell is in the height of her progress at the two Sir Johns' houses (*HMC, 7,* 532a).

79. Osborn MS supplies in the margin *Ld Cornw: Ld Culpepr's issue: Willis Churchill Brouncker.* Presumably this identifies Mrs. Michell's other lovers: Lord Cornwallis (cf. line 37), the son of John Lord Colepeper (d. 1660); John Churchill, 1st duke of Marlborough (1650–1722); and Henry Brouncker (d. 1688), cofferer to Charles II and Gentleman of the Bedchamber to the duke of York. Willis is probably the noted prostitute, Sue Willis: "My Lord Culpeper is also returned from Paris with Mrs. Willis, whom he carried thither to buy whatsoever pleased her there and this nation could afford" (H. J. Wilson, ed., *The Rochester-Savile Letters, 1671–1680* [Columbus: Ohio State University Press, 1941], p. 62).

88. *Milo:* a celebrated athlete killed by wild beasts while attempting to tear down a tree.

90. *Paris:* James Scott, duke of Monmouth and Buccleuch (1649–85). One August night in 1674 he fought the battle of Maastricht over again in the meadows below Windsor Castle. See D'Oyley, p. 97.

91. *Bessus:* a cowardly braggart in Beaumont and Fletcher's *A King and No King.* A marginal note in Osborn MS identifies him as Sir Thomas Armstrong (1624?–84), an intimate friend of Monmouth executed for complicity in the Rye House Plot. According to Sprat, Armstrong was "a debauched atheistical bravo," and Scroope may have attacked him here because Armstrong had killed his brother in a playhouse brawl in 1675.

92. *Cornus:* another pseudo-Latin name—the horned one. Osborn MS identifies him as

Still courts the spark that does his brows adorn,
Invites him home to dine and fills his veins
With the hot blood which his dear doxy drains.   95
Grandio thinks himself a beau garçon,
Goggles his eyes, writes letters up and down,
And with his saucy love plagues all the town,
Whilst pleased to have his vanity thus fed,
He's caught with Gosnell, that old hag, abed.   100
But why should I the crying follies tell
That rouse the sleeping satyr from his cell,
I to my reader should as tedious prove
As that old spark Albanus making love,
Or florid Roscius, when with some smooth flam   105
He gravely on the public tries to sham.
Hold then, my Muse, 'tis time to make an end,
Lest taxing others thou thyself offend.
The world's a wood in which all lose their way,
Though by a diff'rent path each goes astray."   110

Lord Grey [of Werk]. In January 1680, according to the Dowager Lady Sunderland, Monmouth's attentions to Lady Grey caused her husband to remove her from London to Northumberland. If the report was true, "it made no difference to her husband's friendship with Monmouth" (D'Oyley, p. 162), hence Dryden represents him as "cold Caleb" in *Absalom and Achitophel*, 574.

96. *Grandio*: Osborn MS identifies this haughty, amorous fop as *Mulgrave* (John Sheffield, third earl of Mulgrave and afterwards 1st duke of Buckingham and Normanby [1648–1721]), the author of *An Essay upon Satire* (1679), which attacked Scroope, possibly in revenge for these lines.

100. *Gosnell*: Winifred Gosnell, an actress in the Duke's Company. She was at one time Mrs. Pepys's lady's-maid and Pepys thought highly of her singing and dancing, but when he saw her in Stapylton's *The Slighted Maid* in 1668 he wrote that she "is become very homely, and sings meanly, I think, to what I thought she did" (Wilson, *All the King's Ladies*, pp. 145–46).

104. *Albanus*: Osborn MS identifies him as *Col. Russell*, probably John Russell, third son of Francis, 4th earl of Bedford. He was colonel of the first regiment of foot guards and died in 1681. He was one of Miss Hamilton's suitors, and Gramont ridicules him for "a certain mixture of avarice and liberality, constantly at war with each other, ever since he had entered the lists with love" (*Memoirs*, p. 143). Harvard MS 623F identifies him as the earl of St. Albans, the aging and lecherous courtier whom Marvell satirizes in *Last Instructions*.

105. *Roscius*: Quintus Roscius Gallus (d. 62 B.C.), the most celebrated of Roman comic actors. Here Osborn MS identifies him as Heneage Finch, Baron Finch of Daventry (1621–82), appointed lord chancellor in 1674. Finch was noted for his eloquence as "the English Roscius and the English Cicero." Roger North wrote that his love of "a handsome turn of expression gave him a character of a trifler which he did not so much deserve" (*DNB*). *flam*: a sham story, a fabrication.

JOHN WILMOT, EARL OF ROCHESTER

On the Supposed Author of a Late Poem
"In Defense of Satire"
(1677)

To rack and torture thy unmeaning brain
In satire's praise to a low untuned strain
In thee was most impertinent and vain,
When in thy person we more clearly see
That satire's of divine authority,   5
For God made one on man when he made thee,
To show there are some men as there are apes,
Framed for mere sport, who differ but in shapes.
In thee are all those contradictions joined
That make an ass prodigious and refined.   10
A lump deformed and shapeless wert thou born,
Begot in love's despite and nature's scorn,
And art grown up the most ungraceful wight,
Harsh to the ear and hideous to the sight;
Yet love's thy business, beauty thy delight.   15
Curse on that silly hour that first inspired
Thy madness to pretend to be admired,
To paint thy grisly face, to dance, to dress,
And all those awkward follies that express
Thy loathsome love and filthy daintiness;   20
Who needs will be an ugly *beau garçon*,
Spit at and shunned by ev'ry girl in town,
Where dreadfully love's scarecrow thou art placed
To fright the tender flock that long to taste;
While ev'ry coming maid, when you appear,   25
Starts back for shame and straight turns chaste for fear,
For none so poor or prostitute have proved,
Where you made love, t'endure to be beloved.
'Twere labor lost, or else I would advise,
But thy half wit will ne'er let thee be wise.   30
Half witty and half mad and scarce half brave,
Half honest (which is very much a knave)—
Made up of all these halves, thou canst not pass
For anything entirely but an ass!

180

SIR CARR SCROOPE

The Author's Reply
(1677)

Rail on, poor feeble scribbler, speak of me
In as ill terms as the world speaks of thee.
Sit swelling in thy hole like a vexed toad,
And all thy pox and malice spit abroad.
Thou canst blast no man's name by thy ill word: 5
Thy pen is full as harmless as thy sword.

6. An allusion to the abortive duel between Rochester and Mulgrave (November 1669), in which Rochester reportedly demanded an unfair advantage over his opponent because of his allegedly weak condition.

JOHN WILMOT, EARL OF ROCHESTER

On Poet Ninny
(1677)

On Poet Ninny appears without ascription in the Yale Rochester *MS.* David Vieth regards it as probably Rochester's (see "Order of Contents as Evidence of Authorship: Rochester's *Poems* of 1680," *Publications of the Bibliographical Society of America,* 53 [1959]: 293–308). Poet Ninny's ugliness, foppishness, melancholy, and "head romancy" all accord in detail with Rochester's other attacks on Scroope and leave little doubt of the author's identity or that of his victim.

As Pinto notes, Ninny, a character in Shadwell's comedy, *The Sullen Lovers,* is "a conceited poet always troubling men with impertinent discourses of poetry and the repetition of his own verses."

On Poet Ninny

Crushed by that just contempt his follies bring
On his crazed head, the vermin fain would sting.
But never satire did so softly bite,
Or gentle George himself more gently write.
Born to no other but thy own disgrace,   5
Thou art a thing so wretched and so base,
Thou canst not e'en offend but with thy face,
And dost at once a sad example prove
Of harmless malice and of hopeless love,
All pride and ugliness—O how we loathe   10
A nauseous creature so composed of both!
How oft have we thy cap'ring person seen
With dismal look and melancholy mien,
The just reverse of Nokes when he would be
Some mighty hero and makes love like thee.   15

3. Cf. the last line of Buckhurst's satire on Edward Howard ("Come on, ye critics, find one fault who dare"): "Did ever libel yet so sharply bite?"
14. *Nokes:* James Nokes, a well-known comic actor.

Thou art below being laughed at out of spite:
Men gaze upon thee as a hideous sight
And cry, "There goes the melancholy knight!"
There are some modish fools we daily see,
Modest and dull; why they are wits to thee!   20
For of all folly sure the very top
Is a conceited ninny and a fop.
With face of farce joined to a head romancy
There's no such coxcomb as your fool of fancy.
But 'tis too much on so despised a theme: 25
No man would dabble in a dirty stream.
The worst that I could write would be no more
Than what thy very friends have said before.

JOHN SHEFFIELD, EARL OF MULGRAVE, AND JOHN DRYDEN

An Essay upon Satire
(1679)

This is the famous "Rose Alley satire" written by Mulgrave and circulated in manuscript in 1679. It was attributed at the time, however, chiefly to Dryden, and has long been thought to have provoked the beating he suffered at the hands of three ruffians in Rose Street, Covent Garden, on the night of 18 December 1679, as he was returning home from Will's coffeehouse. Certainly no omnibus satire of the period could have been more offensive to more powerful people, all of whom were in a position to retaliate forcefully, the king, the duchess of Portsmouth, Rochester, Shaftesbury, and the brutal Philip, earl of Pembroke being chief among them.

If we assume that *An Essay upon Satire* was the cause of the laureate's beating, the duchess of Portsmouth and Rochester are the leading suspects. Portsmouth had been very roughly handled, and there was a precedent for this kind of retaliation against those who reflected on the king's mistresses in the maiming of Sir John Coventry nine years earlier (see *The Haymarket Hectors*).

In Wood's life of George Villiers, second duke of Buckingham (*Athenae Oxonienses, 4,* 210), cited by Wilson, we have a roughly contemporary account of the incident, which distributes the blame rather vaguely between the duchess and Rochester:

> In Nov. (or before) an. 1679, there being *An Essay upon Satire* spread about the city in MS wherein many gross reflections were made on Ludovisa duchess of Portsmouth and John Wilmot earl of Rochester, they therefore took it for a truth that Dryden was the author; whereupon one or both hiring three men to cudgel him, they effected their business in the said coffeehouse at 8 of the clock at night on the 16th of Dec. 1679.

Wood, as J. H. Wilson points out, gets time and place wrong, and is apparently relying on hearsay, for in another entry (*Athenae, 1,* lxxxvii) he notes that Dryden was cudgeled "because he had reflected on certain persons in *Absalom and Achitophel.*"

Aside from such vague contemporary accounts of the affair, the case for Rochester's instigation of the attack has rested on a letter to Savile long thought to have been written shortly before, but which Wilson has incontrovertibly dated in the spring or summer of 1676. The following section of the letter clearly pertains to Dryden's reported reaction to Rochester's criticism in *An Allusion to Horace,* written earlier in the year:

> You write me word that I'm out of favor with a certain poet, whom I have ever admired for the disproportion of him and his attributes, He is a rarity which I cannot but be fond of, as one would be of a hog that could fiddle or a singing owl. If he fall upon me at the blunt, which is his very good weapon in wit, I will forgive him, if you please, and leave the repartee to Black Will, with a cudgel.

As Wilson argues, "we cannot accept as evidence of guilt a vague and careless threat uttered nearly four years before the crime was committed. Rochester failed to carry out his threat in the spring of 1677/8 when Dryden did indeed fall upon him 'at the blunt' in his preface to *All for Love.*"

However, when the two men with whom Rochester had been at odds for years on literary and personal grounds joined forces to make a violent invective deriding his wit and aspersing his honor, he may have been sufficiently exasperated to let Black Will deal with one of them. In his relations with Dryden, Rochester's gentle reproofs had long been tried in vain. His censures of Dryden's excessive concern with audience reaction and "boffo" wit in *An Allusion to Horace* (1675–76) had been more than balanced by a generous tribute to his "excellencies." *Advice to Apollo* (1677) had been both temperate and tactful. Between these Rochesterian pieces Dryden had ridiculed Shadwell and, by implication, the earl's praise of Shadwell's "nature" and "wit" in *Mac Flecknoe* and had collaborated with Rochester's loathed enemy, Mulgrave, on *An Essay upon Satire.* Then, in 1678, the laureate had compounded his offense and rejected the proffered olive branch by an unjust and insolent attack on Rochester as man and poet in the preface to *All for Love.* Thus the available evidence still leaves Rochester very much in the running as instigator of the famous Rose Alley ambuscade, although the mad earl of Pembroke or Shaftesbury have also been advanced as candidates.

How dull and how insensible a beast
Is man, who yet would lord it o'er the rest!
Philosophers and poets vainly strove
In ev'ry age the lumpish mass to move,
But those were pedants when compared with these   5
Who knew not only to instruct but please.
Poets alone found that delightful way
Mysterious morals gently to convey
In charming numbers, so that as men grew
Pleased with their poems, they grew wiser too.   10
Satire has always shined amongst the rest,
And is the boldest way, if not the best,
To tell men freely of their foulest faults,
To laugh at their vain deeds and vainer thoughts.
In satire too the wise took diff'rent ways,   15
Though each deserving its peculiar praise:
Some did all follies with just sharpness blame,
While others laughed and scorned them into shame;
But of these two the last succeeded best,
As men aim rightest when they shoot in jest.   20
Yet if we may presume to blame our guides
And censure those who censured all besides,
In other things they justly are preferred;
In this alone methinks the ancients erred.
Against the grossest follies they declaim;   25
Hard they pursue, but hunt ignoble game.

1–2. Cf. the opening of Rochester's *Satire against Mankind*:

> Were I (who to my cost already am
> One of those strange prodigious creatures man)
> A spirit free, to choose for my own share,
> What case of flesh and blood I pleased to wear,
> I'd be a dog, a monkey, or a bear;
> Or anything but that vain animal
> Who is so proud of being rational.

6. *not only to instruct but please*: a critical commonplace of the time, Horace's *aut prodesse,
. . . aut delectare*. In his *Essay on Satire* Dryden speaks of "profit and delight, which are the
two ends of poetry in general."

19–20,.Dryden makes the same observation in the *Discourse Concerning the Original and Progress
of Satire* (1692): "the best and finest manner of satire . . . is that sharp, well-mannered way
of laughing a folly out of countenance." Mulgrave expressed the same thought in his *Essay
on Poetry* (1682): "A satire's smile is sharper than his frown."

Nothing is easier than such blots to hit,
And 'tis the talent of each vulgar wit;
Besides, 'tis labor lost, for who would preach
Morals to Armstrong, or dull Aston teach?   30
'Tis being devout at play, wise at a ball,
Or bringing wit and friendship to Whitehall.
But with sharp eyes those nicer faults to find
Which lie obscurely in the wisest mind,
That little speck which all the rest does spoil,   35
To wash off that would be a noble toil
Beyond the loose-writ libels of the age,
Or the forced scenes of our declining stage.
Above all censure too, each little wit
Will be so glad to see the greater hit,   40
Who judging better, though concerned the most,
Of such correction will have cause to boast.
In such a satire all would seek a share,
And ev'ry fool will fancy he is there.
Old storytellers, too, must pine and die   45
To see their antiquated wit laid by,
Like her who missed her name in a lampoon
And grieved to see herself decayed so soon.
No common coxcomb must be mentioned here,
Nor the dull trains of dancing sparks appear,   50
Nor flutt'ring officers who never fight,
Of such a wretched rabble who would write?
Much less half-wits, that's more against our rules;
For they are fops, the others are but fools.

30. *Armstrong:* Sir Thomas Armstrong (1624?–84), who was executed for his share in the Rye House Plot. He was an intimate of the duke of Monmouth and led a "very vicious life" (Gilbert Burnet, *The Lives of Sir Matthew Hale and John Earl of Rochester,* 1820). Cf. *In Defense of Satire,* 91 *n. Ashton:* probably the Colonel Edmund Ashton or Aston, who was Mulgrave's second in the abortive duel with Rochester (see lines 248–49). He (or another of that name) is mentioned in *A Familiar Epistle, to Mr. Julian, Secretary of the Muses:* "Bow-bending Cupid doth with ballads come, / And little Aston offers to the bum." Cf. *In Defense of Satire,* 28 *n.* He was the Edmund Aston or Ashton who bought a captaincy in Sir Allen Apsley's regiment in 1667 and of whom Sir Carr Scroope wrote in his *Defense of Satire:* "There a vain fop mort- gages all his land / To buy that gaudy plaything, a command." Ashton was Mulgrave's contemporary almost to the year and he later rose to be a major and colonel in the King's Own Troop of Guards and the Horse Guards. He fought a duel with Etherege and wrote scraps of verse. The Prologue, "Gentle reproofs have long been tried in vain," was credited to him as well as to Rochester, and in Etherege's letter-book are some lines on the joys of retirement described as 'Colonel Ashton's.' " I am indebted to David Vieth for the further information that Armstrong and Ashton received their commissions in the Life Guards the same day.

Who would not be as silly as Dunbar,   55
Or dull as Monmouth, rather than Sir Carr?
The cunning courtier should be slighted, too,
Who with dull knav'ry makes so much ado,
Till the shrewd fool, by thriving so too fast,
Like Aesop's fox, becomes a prey at last,   60
Nor shall the royal mistresses be named,
Too ugly and too easy to be blamed;
With whom each rhyming fool keeps such a pother,
They are as common that way as the other.
Yet saunt'ring Charles, between his beastly brace,   65
Meets with dissembling still in either place,
Affected humor or a painted face.
In loyal libels we have often told him
How one has jilted him, the other sold him;
How that affects to laugh and this to weep;   70
But who can rail so long as he can keep?
Was ever prince by two at once misled,
False, foolish, old, ill natured and ill-bred?
Earnely and Ailesbury with all that race
Of busy blockheads shall have here no place;   75
At council set as foils on Danby's score

55. *Dunbar:* The Scott-Saintsbury edition identifies him as Robert Constable, third vis-
count of Dunbar. On 25 March 1673 a duel between Rochester and Lord Dunbar, who was
a notorious bully, was narrowly averted by the earl-marshall's intervention (Pinto, *Poems by
Rochester,* p. xxiii).

56. *Or dull as Monmouth:* à frequently repeated charge in the lampoons of the day. *Sir Carr:*
Scroope.

60. See Aesop's fables "The Ass, the Fox, and the Lion" and "The Dog, the Cock, and the
Fox."

65. In *A Character of King Charles II*, printed in Mulgrave's works, 1723, there is the follow-
ing observation: "I am of the opinion also, that in his [Charles's] latter times there was as
much of laziness, as of love, in all those hours he passed among his mistresses; who after
all, served only to fill up his seraglio; while a bewitching kind of pleasure called saunt'ring,
and talking without any constraint, was the true sultana queen he delighted in."

74. *Earnely:* Sir John Earnely was bred to the law, but became distinguished as a second-
rate statesman. He was made chancellor of the Exchequer in 1686 and was made one of the com-
missioners of treasury, in the room of the earl of Rochester (Scott-Saintsbury). *Ailesbury:*
Robert Bruce, 2d earl of Elgin, in Scotland, created after the Restoration an English peer,
by the titles of baron and viscount Bruce, earl of Ailesbury. In 1678 he was of the Privy
Council to His Majesty and Gentleman of the Bedchamber. In the reign of James II the earl
of Ailesbury succeeded to the office of lord chamberlain upon the death of the earl of Arling-
ton in July 1685, an office which he held only two months, as he died in the following Octo-
ber (Scott-Saintsbury). Irvine adds the following details: "Ailesbury and Earnely had been
appointed to the council in 1678 and 1679 respectively and continued to support Danby,
their benefactor, even after he was, in March 1679, indicted for high treason and had lost
the favor of both political parties" (*Studies in Philology* 34 [1937]: 542).

To make that great false jewel shine the more,
Who all the while was thought exceeding wise
Only for taking pains and telling lies.
But there's no meddling with such nauseous men,   80
Their very names have tired my lazy pen;
'Tis time to quit their company and choose
Some fitter subject for a sharper muse.
    First, let's behold the merriest man alive
Against his careless genius vainly strive;   85
Quit his dear ease some deep design to lay
'Gainst a set time, and then forget the day.
Yet he will laugh at his best friends and be
Just as good company as Nokes or Lee.
But when he aims at reason or at rule   90
He turns himself the best in ridicule;
Let him at business ne'er so earnest sit,
Show him but mirth, and bait that mirth with wit,
That shadow of a jest shall be enjoyed
Though he left all mankind to be destroyed: 95
So cat transformed sat gravely and demure
Till mouse appeared and thought himself secure;
But soon the lady had him in her eye
And from her friends did just as oddly fly.
Reaching above our nature does no good,   100
We must fall back to our own flesh and blood.
As by our little Machiavel we find
(That nimblest creature of the busy kind)
His limbs are crippled and his body shakes,
Yet his hard mind, which all this bustle makes,   105

84. *the merriest man alive:* the duke of Buckingham. Cf. Dryden's characterization of him as Zimri in *Absalom and Achitophel.*

89. *Nokes or Lee:* James Nokes and Anthony Lee (or Leigh) were the most noted comic actors of the day.

96. *cat transformed:* Derrick, in his edition of Dryden published in 1757 by Tonson, explained that the "cat transformed" was a cat turned into a grave and demure lady but still in her nature a cat. At dinner she was unable to resist the lure of a passing mouse, and, when she pounced upon it, she regained her old form (Irvine, p. 544). Mulgrave may have had in mind Aesop's fable of the young man and his cat. A certain youth fell in love with his cat whereupon he prayed to Venus to relieve him of his pain. The goddess accordingly changed the cat into a beautiful young girl whom the youth immediately married. On their wedding night the bride, hearing a mouse behind a hanging, sprang from her husband's arms to pursue it. Venus, enraged at having her rites thus profaned, and seeing that the bride though a woman in appearance was a cat at heart, changed her back to her original form.

102. *our little Machiavel:* Anthony Ashley Cooper, 1st earl of Shaftesbury. Cf. this porttrait with Dryden's Achitophel.

No pity of his poor companion takes.
What gravity can hold from laughing out
To see that drag his feeble legs about
Like hounds ill coupled; Jowler lugs him still
Through hedges, ditches, and through all that's ill.   110
'Twere crime in any man but him alone
To use his body so, though 'tis his own;
Yet this false comfort never gives him o'er,
That whilst he creeps his vig'rous thoughts can soar.
Alas! that soaring to those few that know   115
Is but a busy grov'ling here below.
So men in raptures think they mount the sky,
Whilst on the ground th' entranced wretches lie;
So modern fops have fancied they should fly,
Whilst 'tis their heads alone are in the air,   120
And for the most part building castles there
As the new earl, with parts deserving praise
And wit enough to laugh at his own ways,
Yet loses all soft days and sensual nights,
Kind nature checks, and kinder fortune slights;   125
Striving against his quiet all he can,
For the fine notion of a busy man;
And what is that at best but one whose mind
Is made to tire himself and all mankind?
To Ireland he would go—faith, let him reign,   130
For if some odd fantastic lord would fain
Carry my trunks and all my drudg'ry do,
I'll not pay only, I'll admire him too.
But is there any other beast that lives
Who his own harm so wittily contrives?   135
Will any dog that hath his teeth and stones

109. *Jowler:* a heavy-jawed dog. Used also as quasi-proper name for a dog of this kind.
122. *the new earl:* George Savile, created earl of Halifax in July 1679.
130. In April 1679 a successor to the duke of Ormonde was being considered and Essex, Robertes (earl of Falmouth and Radnor), and Halifax were frequently mentioned for his post. Algernon Sydney wrote at this time: "But if a lieutenant be sent, I believe it will be Essex or Halifax." Burnet states that Halifax was suspected of aspiring to the post: "Some gave it out that he had pretended to be lord lieutenant of Ireland, and was uneasy when that was denied him: but he said to me that it was offered him and he had refused it" (Irvine, p. 548).
136–39. Taking this as a libel on the countess of Halifax, Irvine (p. 549) quotes a passage from the reply to this satire, called *The Cabal or In Opposition to Mr. Dryden's Essay on Satire:*

> Halifax for empire has as great an itch
> As ever dog had for his salt swol'n bitch

Refinedly leave his bitches and his bones
To turn a wheel and bark to be employed
While Venus is by rival dogs enjoyed?
Yet this fond man, to get a statesman's name,   140
Forfeits his friends, his freedom, and his fame.
    Though satire nicely writ no humor stings
But theirs who merit praise in other things,
Yet we must needs this one exception make,
And break one rule for Polytropos' sake,   145
Who was too much despised to be accused,
And therefore scarce deserves to be abused;
Raised only by his mercenary tongue
For railing smoothly and for reas'ning wrong:
As boys on holidays let loose to play   150
Lay waggish traps for girls who pass that way,
Then shout to see in dirt and deep distress
Some silly chit in her flow'red foolish dress;
So have I mighty satisfaction found
To see his tinseled reasons on the ground;   155
To see the florid fool despised (and know it)
By some who scarce have words enough to show it
(For sense sits silent and condemns for weaker
The finer, nay sometimes the wittier, speaker).
But 'tis prodigious so much eloquence   160
Should be acquired by such a little sense;
For words and wit did anciently agree,
And Tully was no fool though this man be.

His plumes imped with ambition, up he flies,
And, to be something melts e'en in the skies:
While th' humble wretch at home lies prostrate down
To all the barking beagles of the town.

138. *to turn a wheel:* to be a turnspit, a dog kept to turn the roasting-spit by running within a kind of tread-wheel connected with it.

145. *Polytropos:* This is Heneage Finch, lord chancellor. Polytropos is the epithet of Ulysses in the *Odyssey:* turning many ways, versatile, etc. *(OED).* There is undoubtedly an added hint to be found in another sense of the term: Finch, in his florid orations, used many tropes or figures of speech.

146. This probably refers to the matter of Danby's impeachment in March 1679. Charles, to the great anger of the Commons, had given Danby a pardon in bar of impeachment.

148. *his mercenary tongue:* Finch's forensic eloquence is testified to on all hands; though Burnet says he was too eloquent on the bench, in the Lords, and in the Commons, and calls his speaking labored and affected. Roger North in his autobiography confirms this view, saying that his love of "a handsome turn of expression gave him a character of a trifler which he did not so much deserve" *(DNB).*

163. *Tully:* Finch was called the English Cicero by his contemporaries.

At bar abusive, at the bench unable,
Knave on the woolsack, fop at council table,   165
These are the grievances: such fools as would
Be rather wise than honest, great than good.
    Another kind of wits must be made known,
Whose harmless errors hurt themselves alone:
Excess of luxury they think can please,   170
And laziness call loving of their ease.
To live dissolved in pleasure still they feign,
Though their whole life's but intermitting pain;
So much of surfeit, headache, claps are seen,
We scarce perceive the little time between.   175
Well-meaning men who make this gross mistake,
And pleasure lose only for pleasure's sake;
Each pleasure hath its price, and when we pay
So much of pain we squander life away.
Thus Dorset, purring like a thoughtful cat,   180
Married (but wiser Puss ne'er thought of that)
And first he worried her with railing rhyme,
Like Pembroke's mastiff at his kindest time;
Then, for one night, sold all his slavish life
T' a teeming widow but a barren wife.   185
Swelled by contact of such a fulsome toad,
He lugged about the matrimonial load,
Till fortune, blindly kind as well as he,
Hath ill restored him to his liberty,
Which he will use in his old sneaking way,   190
Drinking all night and dozing all the day;
Dull as Ned Howard, whom his brisker time
Had famed for dulness in malicious rhyme.
    Mulgrave had much ado to 'scape the snare,

164–65. The author of *Advice to the Satirical Poets* ("Satire's despotic, now none can with-
stand") quotes this couplet as proof of the writer's wit: "Save but his bones, he's well secured
of fame, / The chancellor's epitaph must preserve his name."
    180. *Dorset:* Charles Sackville, 6th earl of Dorset and earl of Middlesex. His first wife,
Mary Bagot, widow of Charles Berkeley, earl of Falmouth (line 185, "A teeming widow"),
died 12 September 1679 without issue, and Dorset did not remarry until 1685.
    183. *Pembroke's mastiff:* "This present earl of Pembroke [Philip Herbert, 1653–83, seventh
earl of Pembroke] has at Wilton 52 mastiffs and 30 greyhounds, some bears, and a lion, and a
matter of 60 fellows more bestial than they" (Aubrey, *1*, 317, under William Herbert, 1st
earl of Pembroke).
    192–93. This is an allusion to Dorset's verses to the Honorable Edward Howard, *To a
Person of Honor, upon his Incomparable, Incomprehensible Poem called "The British Princes."*
    194–209. This passage on himself, in which the notoriously vain Mulgrave is represented

Though learned in those ill arts that cheat the fair: 195
For, after all his vulgar marriage mocks,
With beauty dazzled, Numps was in the stocks.
Deluded parents dried their weeping eyes
To see him catch his Tartar for his prize;
Th' impatient town waited the wished-for change,   200
And cuckolds smiled in hopes of a revenge;
Till Petworth plot made us with sorrow see
As his estate his person too was free.
Him no soft thoughts, no gratitude could move;
To gold he fled from beauty and from love,   205
Yet failing there he keeps his freedom still,
Forced to live happily against his will.
'Tis not his fault if too much wealth and pow'r
Break not his boasted quiet ev'ry hour.
    And little Sid, for simile renowned,   210
Pleasure hath always sought but never found:
Though all his thoughts on wine and woman fall,
His are so bad, sure, he ne'er thinks at all.
The flesh he lives upon is rank and strong,
His meat and mistresses are kept too long;   215
But sure we all mistake this pious man,
Who mortifies his person all he can:
What we uncharitably take for sin,

---

as *l'homme fatale*, was a clue to his authorship as can be seen in a letter from Colonel Edward Cooke to the Duke of Ormonde (quoted by Irvine, p. 534):

> 22 November 1679. If I may be permitted to play at small game I shall repeat a particular that I was informed part [*sic*] this week at the duchess of Portsmouth's, where just before the king came a most scurrilous, libellous copy of verse was read, severe upon almost all the courtiers save my Lord Mulgrave, whose sole accusation was that he was a cuckold-maker. This brought him under suspicion to be (if not guilty of the making, yet) guilty of being privy to the making of them, who just coming in with the king, Mrs. Buckley saluted him (in raillery) by the name of cuckold-maker, who taking it in earnest replied she knew one cuckold he never made, which she took for so great an affront that it seems her husband was entitled to the revenge. But the king, it seems, came to the knowledge of it, and interfered his authority to antidote bloodshed.

Mulgrave's first marriage took place in March 1686. I have not found any other mention of the Petworth plot.

197. J. H. Wilson quotes Etherege on the occasion of Mulgrave's marriage: "Numps [a silly or stupid person, the nickname given him by the wits] is now in the stocks in earnest" (*Court Wits*, p. 77).

210. Sir Charles Sedley or Sidley. In the 1723 edition of Sheffield's works there is a note on this line: "Remarkable for making pleasant and proper similes on all occasions." In a draft of a satire on Sedley, there is the following line: "And pretty similes sprinkled here and there" (Pinto, *Sedley*, p. 313).

Are only rules of this odd Capuchin;
For never hermit under grave pretense   220
Has lived more contrary to common sense,
And 'tis a miracle, we may suppose,
No nastiness offends his skillful nose
Which from all stinks can with peculiar art
Extract perfume, and essence from a fart.   225
Expecting supper is his great delight,
He toils all day but to be drunk at night;
Then o'er his cups this chirping nightbird sits
Till he takes Hewitt and Jack Howe for wits.

Rochester I despise for his mere want of wit   230
(Though thought to have a tail and cloven feet)
For while he mischief means to all mankind,
Himself alone the ill effect does find,
And so like witches justly suffers shame,
Whose harmless malice is so much the same.   235
False are his words, affected as his wit,
So often he does aim, so seldom hit;
To ev'ry face he cringes whilst he speaks,
But when the back is turned the head he breaks.
Mean in each motion, lewd in ev'ry limb,   240
Manners themselves are mischievous in him;
A proof that chance alone makes ev'ry creature,
A very Killigrew without good nature.
For what a Bessus hath he always lived,
And his own kicking notably contrived?   245
For there's the folly that's still mixed with fear:
Cowards more blows than any hero bear,
Of fighting sparks some may their pleasure say,

229. *Hewitt:* Sir George Hewitt was a coxcomb of the period, after whom Etherege is said to have modeled Sir Fopling Flutter's character. *Jack Howe:* One MS supports Noyes's conjecture that the usual reading, *Jack Hall,* is an error for Jack Howe, "a dissolute scribbler and politician" (p. 1042).

243. *Killigrew:* Either Thomas Killigrew the elder, dramatist, whom Oldys called the king's jester and Pepys "a merry droll" *(DNB)*, or, more probably, Henry Killigrew, son of the former by his first wife, a wild wit whom Henry Savile in a letter addressed as "sweet namesake of mine, happy-humored Killigrew, soul of mirth and all delight" (Wilson, *Court Wits,* p. 84).

244. *Bessus:* A cowardly braggadocio character in Beaumont and Fletcher's *King and No King.*

248–49. Mulgrave and Rochester had been good friends until November 1669 when Mulgrave heard that Rochester had said something malicious of him. Mulgrave felt obliged to challenge Rochester but the latter, pleading illness, failed to appear on the field of honor. According to Mulgrave in his *Memoirs,* Colonel Ashton, Mulgrave's second, "thought him-

But 'tis a bolder thing to run away.
The world may well forgive him all his ill,   250
For ev'ry fault does prove his penance still;
Falsely he falls into some dang'rous noose,
And then as meanly labors to get loose;
A life so infamous it's better quitting,
Spent in base injuring and low submitting.   255
I'd like to have left out his poetry,
Forgot almost by all as well as me:
Sometimes he hath some humor, never wit,
And if it ever (very rarely) hit,
'Tis under so much nasty rubbish laid,   260
To find it out's the cinder-woman's trade,
Who for the wretched remnants of a fire,
Must toil all day in ashes and in mire.
So lewdly dull his idle works appear,
The wretched text deserves no comment here,   265
Where one poor thought's sometimes left all alone
For a whole page of dulness to atone.
'Mongst forty bad's one tolerable line,
Without expression, fancy, or design.
    How vain a thing is man and how unwise   270
E'en he who would himself the most despise!
I, who so wise and humble seem to be,
Now my own vanity and pride can see.
Whilst the world's nonsense is so sharply shown,
We pull down others but to raise our own: 275
That we may angels seem we paint them elves,
And are but satyrs to set up ourselves.
I, who have all this while been finding fault
E'en with my masters who first satire taught,
And did by that describe the task so hard   280

---

self obliged to write down every word and circumstance of this whole matter, in order to spread
everywhere the true reason of our returning without having fought; which being never in the
least either contradicted or resented by the Lord Rochester, entirely ruined his reputation as
to courage (of which I was really sorry to be the occasion), though nobody had still greater
as to wit." Wilson, however, cites the report in *LJ* for 23 November 1669 and comments:
"Evidently Rochester had been so eager to keep his appointment with Mulgrave that he had
broken his parole to an officer of the House rather than risk losing his honor as a duelist"
(*Court Wits*, p. 234).

   277. *satyrs*: A satyr or satire in Mulgrave's time could mean a satirist. The confusion be-
tween the words "satiric" and "satyric" gave rise to the notion that the satyrs who formed the
chorus of Greek satyric drama had to deliver "satirical" speeches. Hence in the 16th and 17th
centuries satyrs were thought censorious *(OED)*.

It seems stupendous and above reward,
Now labor with unequal force so climb
That lofty hill unreached by former time.
'Tis just that I should to the bottom fall:
Learn to write well, or not to write at all.   285

The Popish Plot and the Exclusion
Crisis, 1677-1681

On the Murder of Sir Edmund Berry Godfrey
(1678)

Sir Edmund Berry Godfrey (1621–78) was a well-known justice of the peace in London. Although a zealous Protestant, he did not strictly enforce the penal laws against either the Nonconformists or the Catholics. "Few men," says Burnet, "lived on better terms with the Papists than he did." On 6 September 1678 Titus Oates brought his narrative of the Popish Plot to Godfrey and made his first depositions on oath in support of his charges. Three weeks later he signed further depositions in Godfrey's presence, and on 28 September testified before the Privy Council. Oates swore that Godfrey complained to him on 30 September of affronts offered him by both parties in the council—some condemning his officiousness and others his laxity in not disclosing his interviews with Oates earlier. Threats, added Oates, were held out that his conduct would form a subject for inquiry when Parliament met on 21 October. As the panic occasioned by Oates's revelations increased, Godfrey, according to Burnet, became "apprehensive and reserved." He believed he himself would be "knocked on the head" (2, 163). But he declined the advice of his friends to go about with a servant.

On Saturday morning, 12 October 1678, Godfrey left home at nine o'clock, and did not return that night. On the following Thursday evening (17 October) his body was found in a ditch on the south side of Primrose Hill, near Hampstead. He lay face downward, transfixed by his own sword. Much money and jewelry were found untouched in his pockets; only his pocketbook and a lace cravat were missing. Next day an inquest was held at the White House, Primrose Hill. Two surgeons, of questionable competence, swore that there were marks about the neck which showed that Godfrey died of suffocation, and was stabbed after death. An open verdict of willful murder was returned. The funeral was delayed till 31 October. On that day the body was borne to Old Bridewell, where it publicly lay in state. A solemn procession afterward accompanied it to a burial at the church of St. Martin's-in-the-Fields. Two proclamations, offering a reward of £500 for the discovery of the murderers, were issued respectively on 20 and 24 October.

The public, panic-stricken by Oates's allegations, promptly laid the crime at the door of Roman Catholic priests, and indignation against the Papists reached the pitch of hysteria. Medal-portraits of Godfrey were struck, in which the pope was represented as directing the murder. Sober persons who mistrusted Oates from the first, and were convinced of the aimlessness from a Catholic point of view of Godfrey's murder, suggested that, being of a melancholy and hypochondriacal disposition, Godfrey might have committed suicide. It was also rumored that he was pursuing some secret amours, and was in heavy debt to the parish of St. Martin's-in-the-Fields.

On 21 December 1678, Miles Prance, a Roman Catholic silversmith who sometimes worked in the Queen's Chapel at Somerset House, was arrested, on the false testimony of a defaulting debtor, as a Catholic conspirator. Much torture and repeated cross-examinations elicited from him a confession of complicity in Godfrey's murder. Certain Catholic priests, according to Prance, decided on Godfrey's murder because he was a zealous Protestant and a powerful abettor of Oates, and they and their associates dogged his steps for many days. On 12 October he was enticed into the courtyard of Somerset House, where the queen lived, on the pretext that two of her servants were fighting there. The murderers were waiting for him. He was immediately strangled, in the presence of three priests, by Robert Green, cushionman in the Queen's Chapel, Lawrence Hill, servant to Dr. Thomas Godden, treasurer of the chapel, and Henry Berry, porter of Somerset House. Meanwhile Prance watched one of the gates to prevent interruption. The body was kept at Somerset House till the following Wednesday night, when it was carried by easy stages in a sedan chair to Primrose Hill, and left as it was found. Prance said that he afterward attended a meeting of Jesuits and priests at Bow to celebrate the deed. Green, Hill, and Berry were arrested. Before the trial Prance recanted his story, but a few days later reasserted its truth. On 5 February 1679 he swore in court to his original declaration. William Bedloe, after Oates the most notorious "discoverer" of the Popish Plot, appeared to corroborate it, but his allegation did not agree in detail with Prance's statement. One of Godfrey's servants swore that Hill and Green had called with messages at her master's house on or before the fatal Saturday. The prisoners strenuously denied their guilt, and called witnesses to prove an alibi. They were, however, convicted and executed.

The people were satisfied. Primrose Hill, which had been known formerly as Greenberry Hill, was rechristened the latter name in reference to the three alleged murderers. Somerset House was nicknamed Godfrey Hall. But Prance was at once suspected by sober critics of having concocted the whole story, which Bedloe alone had ventured to corroborate. He was soon engaged in a paper warfare with Sir Roger L'Estrange and other pamphleteers who doubted his evidence. *A Letter to Miles Prance*, signed Trueman (1680), was answered by Prance in *Sir E. B. G.'s Ghost*. Prance's story was finally de-

molished when on 15 June 1686 he pleaded guilty to perjury in having con-
cocted all his evidence. He was fined £100, and was ordered to stand in the
pillory, and to be whipped from Newgate to Tyburn.

The mystery remains unsolved. According to the *DNB*, the most probable
theory is that "Oates and his desperate associates caused Godfrey to be
murdered to give color to their false allegations, and to excite popular
opinion in favor of their agitation."

ON THE MURDER OF SIR EDMUND BERRY GODFREY

Are these the pope's grand tools?
Worshipful noddies! Who but blund'ring fools
   Would ever have forgot
To burn those letters that revealed their plot?
Or in an alehouse told that Godfrey's dead   5
Three days before he was discovered;
Leaving the silly world to call to mind
That common logic, *They that hide can find?*
   But see their master policy
     On Primrose Hill,   10
   Where their great enemy
Like Saul upon Mount Gilboa doth lie,
Fall'n on his sword, as if he himself did kill.
   But oh, the infelicity!
That blood was fresh, and gushed out of the wound,   15
This so congealed that not one spot was found;

2. *noddies*: fools.

2–4. A reference to the trial of Edward Coleman, secretary to the duchess of York. Bedloe
was examined concerning packets of letters written in 1675 by Coleman to Père La Chaise,
the confessor of Louis XIV. Bedloe had carried the warrant to apprehend Coleman and
search for his papers. The finding of papers having been certified, and the handwriting,
identified as Coleman's, they were put in evidence, "as good as a hundred witnesses to con-
demn him," the attorney general said.

5–6. Roger L'Estrange was at pains to show that the fact of Godfrey's disappearance was
never concealed at all; on the contrary, the news was bruited about the town as early as the
afternoon of the day on which Sir Edmund left his house, in order to raise a cry that he had
been murdered by the Roman Catholics. Bishop Burnet, on the other hand, is positive that
the news of Godfrey's absence was not published before Tuesday, 15 October (Pollock, pp.
93–94 n.).

12. *Like . . . Gilboa*: Saul, having seen his three sons and his men slain by the Philistines
on Mount Gilboa, requested his armor-bearer to slay him. When his request was refused
"Saul took a sword, and fell upon it" (1 Sam. 31). L'Estrange suggested that Godfrey com-
mitted suicide by resting his sword on the edge of the bank beyond the ditch and falling
forward on it (Pollock, p. 100).

16–20. "The point which deservedly attracted most attention at the inquest was the strik-
ing absence of blood from the clothes of the dead man and the place where his corpse had

No, not upon his sword, as if it would
Tell us 'twas guiltless of its master's blood.
Some carcasses by bleeding do declare;
This by not bleeding shows the murderer.   20
   But to its broken neck I pray
   What can our politicians say?
He hanged, then stabbed himself, for a sure way;
Or first he stabbed himself, then wrung about
His head for madness that advised him to't.   25
Well, Primrose, may our Godfrey's name on thee
   (Like Hyacinth) inscribed be:
On thee his memory shall flourish still
(Sweet as thy flower, and lasting as thy hill)
   Whilst blushing Somerset to her   30
Eternal shame shall this inscription bear:
The devil's an ass, for Jesuits on this spot
Broke both the neck of Godfrey and their Plot.

---

been found. . . . There can be no substantial doubt that the wounds found on Godfrey's body were not the cause of his death, but were inflicted at some time after the event" (Pollock, pp. 99, 101).

21. *its broken neck:* "The neck was dislocated and showed signs of strangulation. The clerk proved that when his master went out on the morning of 12 October, 'he had then a laced band about his neck.' When the body was found, this had disappeared. Presumably it was with this that the act had been accomplished" (Pollock, p. 101).

27. *Hyacinth:* Hyacinthus, a young prince of Sparta, beloved by Apollo and Zephyrus. He returned the love of the former, and Zephyrus resolved to punish him. As Apollo was playing at quoits with Hyacinthus, Zephyrus blew the quoit thrown by Apollo so that it struck the boy and killed him. Apollo changed his blood into the flower that bears his name. The ancients thought they could decipher on the petals the letters AI, or AIAI, an exclamation of grief (Ovid, *Metamorphoses* 10. 211).

STEPHEN COLLEGE

Truth Brought to Light, or Murder Will Out
(1679)

Stephen College (1635?–81), popularly called the Protestant joiner, worked at the trade of carpentry and became known as a political speaker, denouncing what he called the superstitions of popery. He had been a Presbyterian for twenty years, until the Restoration, when he conformed to the Church of England. He made himself notorious by his declamations against the Papists, by writing and singing political ballads, and by inventing a weapon called "the Protestant flail."

TRUTH BROUGHT TO LIGHT, OR MURDER WILL OUT

Would the world know how Godfrey lost his breath?
This tells the tragic story of his death:
Not borrowed from the feigned ghost appearing
Unto us mortals, so the story clearing;
Or taken from the *Narrative* of Prance,   5
Where he too modest does on persons glance;
Though there's enough for all with half an eye
To scan some villains in this tragedy;
And Oedipus there needs not to explain
The wretched Norfolk's house in Clement's Dane;   10
Or how the owner Godfrey did persuade
To eat his last and basely him betrayed.
Hear but the villain how he did ensnare
This gen'rous soul into his bloody fare.

5. *the . . . Prance:* Following the example of Oates, while in Newgate Miles Prance, dictated to his keeper, Boyce, *A True Narrative and Discovery* of Godfrey's murder, which appeared early in 1679.

10. Arundel House in the Strand (parish of St. Clement Danes). The owner at this time was Henry Howard, 6th duke of Norfolk (1628–84). He was a Roman Catholic, but according to Evelyn he entertained the idea of becoming a Protestant in 1671 in order to recover his title of earl-marshal of England. After his disappearance and before the discovery of his body, there were rumors that Godfrey had been seen at Arundel House.

"Pray, good Sir Edmund, stay, I beg the boon   15
Of some discourse with you this afternoon,
In a rehearsal of this hellish Plot
Which you by Oates's depositions got.
You shall oblige me ever, and you will
Preserve our king and kingdom from their ill.   20
Though of the Church of Rome you know I am,
I would be thought a loyal Englishman;
For if their damned Plot be as I hear,
I'll curse the pope, and leave their church I swear!
And as to what you plead as your excuse,   25
You have some friends at home you shall abuse
By your long stay, I will a footman send
That shall acquaint your servants and your friend
You have some bus'ness that detains you here,
And therefore they must not expect you there."   30
        Thus by a siren's tongue and popish guile,
He did persuade his stay, and sent meanwhile
Unto his bandogs that they might waylay him
As home he went and barbarously slay him.
Lo! here's the project of a popish peer,   35
To murder men in love by lordly cheer:
From which, till known, the wise have no defense,
Nor can escape Rome's treacherous pretense.
The best of men by wretched means they kill,
To serve their church and gain their cursed will.   40
Say but Rome's vicar, "Such a man must die,"
That's crime enough, no matter how or why.
His hounds of blood and cruel beasts of prey
Who call it merit to deceive, betray,
Murder whole nations standing in their way.   45
So fell the noble Godfrey by the hand
Of dukes, earls, lords, and queens of royal band,
Whose direful dirge they sung in northern tone,
Where York and Norfolk kept the time as one;

33. *bandogs:* mastiffs.
44. *merit:* in theology, the quality, in actions or persons, of being entitled to reward from God.
49. Cf. Bedloe's coupling of York and Norfolk: "On 28 November [1678] Bedloe was called in and the door of the House locked. Having been given a full pardon in advance Bedloe proceeded to relate how a Jesuit consultation was held at Somerset House on 11 May. The result of the conclave was that the queen, though with tears, at last consented to 'taking off' the king. Bedloe thought that the persons of quality who stood with their backs to him might be the dukes of York and Norfolk (Ogg, *Charles II, 2,* 567–75).

Protestant flails.

And treach'rous Tom made England's treasure pay 50
Rewards to those that did his life betray,
That Osborne villain, raised by his skill
Of pimping and procuring to our will;
The worst of slaves, that so he might be great,
Expos'd his wife and daughters to our heat. 55
Ah! blessed tool at our most gracious need,
That never failed us so to do the deed!
   Next sailed the Portsmouth frigate with the elves.
And as is said, is steeréd by ourselves;
Blown by the blast of Belasyse' cursed spleen, 60
And yet it seems was music for a queen;
And so delighted England's harmless chip
That made her dance and 'bout the dead to skip
In masquerade, by Fawkes's lantern dressed,
Where her dear priests the holy murder blessed. 65
Prejudged by them they this conclusion draw:
A ducal dinner's death by martial law.
By these Rome's vassals did in order get
That Godfrey's life might have a Somerset,
And die for daring to inspect the things 70
Of Mother Church, of holy pope and kings;
And the retinue banditti of Hell,
Welsh Powis, Petre, Stafford, Arundell,
And thousands more of that accurséd brood

50. *Tom:* Danby, who discredited the testimony of Oates and his gang, was himself charged, in a paper that was signed "J.B." and sent to members of Parliament, with being privy to a plot to take Godfrey's life. Danby's secretary, Edward Christian, rebutted the charge, which was repeated by Fitzharris in 1680.

53. *our will:* Presumably this is the king speaking, using the royal plural (as in *our heat,* line 55).

58. *Portsmouth frigate:* There was a ship called the *Portsmouth,* but the reference here may be to the duchess of Portsmouth, who was commonly considered the agent of Louis XIV in England. The implication seems to be that the duchess had persuaded Charles to give his consent to the invasion ("steeréd by ourselves"). John Belasyse (1614–89) was, according to the false information of Oates *(A True Narrative of the Horrid Plot),* intended as the leader of a Catholic army to be raised in England.

62. *chip:* a type of anything worthless.

63. Queen Catherine was passionately addicted to dancing.

64. Guy Fawkes (1570–1606), the Catholic conspirator of Gunpowder Plot fame. On his person were discovered a watch, slow matches, and touchwood, while a dark lantern with a light in it was found near the cellar door.

67. Dinner with the duke of Norfolk that night was fatal to Godfrey.

69. *Somerset:* somersault, with a pun on Somerset House.

73. *Powis . . . Arundell:* along with Belasyse, the five popish lords sent to the Tower in October 1678.

Who would convert us by a sea of blood,   75
And turn the laws of England out of doors
By standing army, pensioners and whores,
Bastards sans number at the nation's charge
For whom we have been taxéd oft at large;
And made to buy our ruin with our coin,   80
Which went for votes and plots and countermine.
    Alas! poor nation, how art thou undone
By a bad father, and now a worse, his son!
What have these cubs of Scotland brought upon us?
There's nothing left but *Lord, have mercy on us!*   85

81. *votes:* possibly an allusion to Danby's policy of buying off M.P.s.

JOHN CARYLL

Naboth's Vineyard
(1679)

John Caryll, titular Lord Caryll (1625–1711), diplomatist and poet, came of an ancient Roman Catholic family and was partly educated at St. Omer. As a Roman Catholic, and probably also on account of his connection with the duke of York, he fell under suspicion in the panic of the Popish Plot and was committed to the Tower in 1679.

Luttrell's copy in the C. H. Wilkinson collection bears the following inscription: "By Mr. John Caryll in the Tower. This is a popish libel designed agt. the Judge [Scroggs], and the witnesses in the late plot." Macdonald comments: "The piece is a protest against the treatment of Catholics during the Popish Plot and was one of the earliest poetical "libels" in which biblical names were used for English politicians. It probably gave more than a hint to Dryden."

Only three identifications are certain: Malchus is Oates, Python is Bedloe, and Arod is Scroggs. Caryll could not make a one-to-one correspondence between the biblical account and the contemporary situation (Ahab is not Charles II nor is Jezebel Portsmouth or the docile and devout queen). For Caryll's purpose it is enough that the story of Naboth affords him an instance of a plot put upon an innocent man in order to rob him legally. Naboth then would seem to represent the English Catholics accused of complicity in the Popish Plot by leaders such as Shaftesbury (a closer equivalent to Ahab than Charles II) as a means to power. However, Caryll may well have intended Naboth to stand for the duke of York, in danger of losing his legal right to the crown. The poem adheres closely to the story of Naboth in 1 Kings 20–21.

NABOTH'S VINEYARD

Si fractus illabitur orbis,
Impavidum ferient ruinae.
Hor.

Fly hence those siren charms of Wealth and Pow'r,
Strong to undo, unable to restore;
At first they tickle, but at last they smart,
They please the palate, and corrode the heart.
To those gay idols, which fond men adore,　　　　　　5
Our Christian Muse all incense does abhor:
Idols! (like hungry Moloch) whose dire food
Too often is supplied by human blood!
　　That precious juice which can, with sov'reign balm,
The war and ferment of our nature calm;　　　　　　10
That can the anguish of our minds allay,
Heal wounds of grief and storms of passion sway;
That gen'rous offspring of the healing vine
I'th' Muses' temple may deserve a shrine.
　　But, hold! 'tis not the wine of common draught,　　15
Which Palma sends or greedy merchants waft
From Rhenish banks or from the Gascon shore
T' enrich themselves and make the drinkers poor;
Poor in their wasted 'states, poor in their mind,
Who in a brutish club with swine are joined,　　　　20
And greatest joy in stupefaction find:
No, our exalted taste disdains to feast
On that dull liquor which turns man to beast,
It must be nourished with some spritely juice
Which does our mortal frame immortalize:　　　　　25
Defies the arrows of malicious fate,
The people's fury, and the tricks of state.
　　Quickly, ah! quickly then, my Muse, disclose
The happy place where this true nectar grows.
Is it not Naboth's vineyard? Fame speaks loud　　　30
Of thee but louder of thy master's blood;

Epigraph: Carmina, 3. 3.8–"If the cracked orbs would split and fall, / Crush him they would, but not appall" (trans. Fanshawe).
7. *hungry Moloch:* Moloch, a Canaanite idol to whom children were sacrificed as burnt offerings.
16. *Palma:* San Miguel de la Palma, a Spanish island in the Atlantic Ocean, forming part of the Canary Islands. The reference is to Canary wine.

That hero's blood, fed by thy vital juice,
Which did, when flowing in his veins, despise
The woman's craft, the tyrant's avarice;
The bloody oaths of perjured assassins;   35
The frowns of biased Justice, which inclines
The giddy rabble to their natural bent,
With tongues and hands to tear the innocent.
    Ahab had conquered Aram, but, alas!   [1 Kings 20:29]
His very conquest his undoing was: 40
He soon forgot the Hand which did bestow   [20:42]
Edge on his sword, and laurel on his brow
Proud with the spoils of the slain Aramites,
The Pow'r which gave him victory he slights.   [13:28]
He treats, and bargains with his enemies,   [13:34] 45
And all the cov'nants of his Lord defies.
Ahab, distressed, bowed to his Lord, and prayed;
Ahab, victorious, proudly disobeyed.
Ungrateful mortals! whose corrupted will
Turns grace to poison and makes blessings kill.   50
In vain poor subjects in the justice trust
Of kings that to their Maker are unjust;
The heart once tainted with a master sin
All lesser crimes does easily let in.
    Poor Naboth's vineyard next lies in his way,   [21:2] 55
His cov'tous eye had marked it for his prey;
He parleyed first—but what he could not worm
By treaty from him, he resolved to storm.
    "How, sir! can you think worthy your large soul
To crave my spot of land, my sleeping-hole?"   60
(Says Naboth) "I myself should prize it not,
Were it not sacred made by age and lot;
By lot consigned to my forefather's hand
Who first with Joshua seized this holy land.
'Twere sacrilege in me to give or sell   65
What to my name by Heav'n's appointment fell.
May Ahab his large kingdoms long possess;
Let Naboth his small vineyard hold in peace."
    Ahab was silent, but not satisfied;   [21:4]
The cov'tous poison through his veins did glide,   70
And what his greedy eye and heart devour

69. ff. Cf. 1 Kings 21.

He will extort by an usurping pow'r.
　So have I seen the tow'ring falcon rise,
And next to nothing lessen to our eye,
Beyond the call of any game or lure;   75
The tim'rous fowl such distance can endure,
But ill they measure by their own the sight
And sharpness of their tyrant's appetite;
She sports and plies her wings i'th' liquid air
As if she minded pleasure and not war.   80
But when the fowl, betrayed by flatt'ring hopes,
Takes wing, the watchful foe as lightning stoops;
What her eye marked her talons make her own,
As thunderstruck the quarry tumbles down.
　But ill did Ahab's eyes, with all their art,   85
Cover the secret rancor of his heart;
The wound did fester that his passion made,
Which soon his face unwillingly betrayed.
First Jezebel described his secret pain: [21:5]
"My lord (she said) can your breast entertain   90
A grief or joy but what I must partake?
O do not this unkind distinction make."
Shame to reveal, and greater shame to hide
His soul from her, his troubled thoughts divide.
At last he poured his grief into the ear   95
Of his too kind and fatal counsellor:
　"In vain, my dear, our scepter does command
From the North Sea to the Arabian sand;
In vain the kings of Aram are my slaves;
In vain my justice kills, my mercy saves,   100
If stubborn Naboth must his vineyard hold   [21:6]
In spite of all entreaty, pow'r, and gold;
If a poor worm of Israel proudly dares
Resist, not my commands, my very pray'rs."   [21:6]
　"Tread on that rebel worm," says Jezebel,   105
"The weight of a king's anger let him feel;   [21:7]
Crush him to nothing that your subjects may
Be taught by his example to obey."
　Then Ahab sighed, and said, "That must not be—
People and priests would rise in mutiny.   110
Too much we hazard for a thing so small;
The tyrant law, which monarchs does enthrall,
Controls the execution of my will

And makes the slave bold to resist me still."
   At this unmovable stood Jezebel,
Like one fast bound by an enchanter's spell;   115
Her flaming cheeks had choler's deepest dye,
And like struck flints sparkled her furious eye;
Such heaving and such panting shook her breast,
As if some spirit had the place possessed.   120
Then suddenly she starts with a loud cry:
   "If law must do the work, Naboth shall die.
Let not the Sanhedrim a monarch awe;   [21:7]
He that commands the judge commands the law.
Law is a poor dumb thing, which none can hear,   125
But by the mouth of an interpreter;
And in the people's mouth 'tis the old plea
For rebels, when their prince they disobey.
Fear not the law, but by the judge be feared;
Else, as the pedants gravely wag their beard,   130
Kings must of their prerogatives be stripped
As children are for breach of grammar whipped.
Then trust my skill—I'll bring you quick relief
To heal the wounds of your unseemly grief;
Both you and Naboth your just rights shall have: 235
You shall possess his vineyard, he his grave."   [21:7]
   Thus with her oily words she skins his sore,
But adds new poison to the ulc'rous core;
And that false comfort leaves in Ahab's mind
Which villains in their thriving mischiefs find.   140
She summons then her chosen instruments,   [21:8]
Always prepared to serve her black intents.
The chief was Arod, whose corrupted youth
Had made his soul an enemy to truth;
But nature furnished him with parts and wit,   145
For bold attempts and deep intriguing fit.
Small was his learning, and his eloquence
Did please the rabble, nauseate men of sense.
Bold was his spirit, nimble and loud his tongue,
Which more than law, or reason, takes the throng.   150
Him, part by money, partly by her grace,
The cov'tous queen raised to a judge's place;

143. *Arod:* Sir William Scroggs (1623?–83), lord chief justice. He was a great voluptuary
and companion of the high court rakes. Scroggs was a notorious prosecutor of those accused
of complicity in the Popish Plot until his volte-face in the trial of Wakeman in July 1679.

And, as he bought his place, he justice sold,
Weighing his causes not by law, but gold.
He made the justice seat a common mart;   155
Well skilled he was in the mysterious art
Of finding varnish for an unsound cause,
And for the sound, imaginary flaws.
    With him fierce Jezebel consults the way
How she for harmless Naboth snares may lay.   160
"Madam," says he, "you rightly judge the course
Unsafe, to run him down by open force.
In great designs it is the greatest art
To make the common people take your part.
Some words there are which have a special charm   165
To wind their fancies up to an alarm:
Treason, religion, liberty are such;
Like clocks they strike when on those points you touch.
If some of these unto his charge you lay,
You hit the vein of their tarantula.   170
For, to say truth, the trick did never fail;
Loud calumny with them does still prevail.
I, madam, of these means no scruple make;
Means from their end their good or badness take.
Naboth, a rebel to his sov'reign's will,   175
By any ways we lawfully may kill."
Whilst thus he poured his venom in her ear,
A spiteful joy did in her face appear:
She said, "Your faithful counsel I approve—
You have chalked out the way we are to move;   180
But still you leave untouched the hardest part,
Which most requires your industry and art:
Where is the crime? where are the witnesses?"
    "It is my province, madam, to find these
(Replied the judge) and that our project may   185
Take faster hold, let there a solemn day
To seek the Lord by fasting and by pray'r
Be set apart. This will exactly square
With the whole model of our work designed.
This will the people draw body and mind   190
To act their parts in Naboth's tragedy.
This builds the stage on which the wretch shall die.

170. *tarantula:* Between 1400 and 1700, tarantism was an hysterical malady popularly
attributed to the bite of the tarantula and was characterized by an extreme impulse to dance.

As glasses, by the sun's reflected ray,
The silly lark into the net betray,
So will the people, by the dazzling thought   195
Of godliness, religiously be caught."
   When the queen saw that her design would take,
She with impatient haste the conf'rence brake;
Of av'rice and revenge such is the thirst
That with the least delay the patient's burst.   200
"Lose no more time (she cried)—with speedy care
Letters and orders for our seal prepare,   [21:8]
Such as the work requires. For till I gain
This point, each moment is an age of pain."
   Since first for acting God proud angels fell,   205
Still to ape Heav'n has been the pride of Hell.
As the bright spirits always attend His throne,
And what He wills they execute as soon,
Our fury so could not conceive the fact
More nimbly than her agent-fiend did act.   210
   Stay, hell hounds, stay! why with such rav'nous speed
Must the dear blood of innocence be shed?
Blind is your haste, and blinder is your rage;
Hell no successful war 'gainst Heav'n can wage.
You shoot at Naboth, but yourselves you wound   215
With poisoned darts, for which no cure is found;
The poison drawn from a remorseless heart
Baffles divine, much more all human art.
What will your rage effect, but lasting shame
In this, in the next world eternal flame?   220
With all your subtle arts of perjury,
And all the varnish of your bloody lie
To make him guilty, and you rightful seem,
Hell for yourselves you build, and Heav'n for him.
   Arod had always tools at his command   225
Of a fit temper for his work in hand;
But here no villains of a common size
In wickedness, or cunning would suffice.
Yet two he found, which did as much exceed
All common rogues as common facts this deed: 230
Malchus, a puny Levite, void of sense
And grace, but stuffed with noise and impudence,

230. *facts*: crimes.
231. *Malchus*: Titus Oates.

Was his prime tool—so venomous a brute
That every place he lived in spewed him out.
Lies in his mouth and malice in his heart   235
By nature grew, and were improved by art.
Mischief his pleasure was, and all his joy
To see his thriving calumny destroy
Those whom his double heart and forked tongue,
Surer than viper's teeth, to death had stung.   240
Python his second was, and his alone;
For he in ills no other first would own.
A braver impudence did arm this wight—
He was a ruffian, and no hypocrite;
And with audacious and loud villainy   245
He did at once virtue and fame defy.
These two, though Malchus wore the longer cloak,
Were e'enly paired, and drew in the same yoke.
No foresters with keener appetite
In running down their hunted game delight   250
Than these the slaughter of the guiltless view,
Whom their malicious calumny pursue.
This goodly pair were, by their teacher's art,   [21:10]
Fully prepared and tuned to play their part.
     A fast is then proclaimed—this serves as leav'n   255
To raise the people's lump with news from Heav'n.
They in the dark, when bid to seek the Lord,
Are sure for His to take the preacher's word;
These, when they toll their great Diana bell,
Look up to Heav'n and do the works of Hell.   260
Always state-fasts some strange events portend,
And often in a godly mischief end.
The fair pretense is that the Lord may weed
Treason and blasphemy from Abr'ham's seed.   [21:10]
     Great and just God! will it be always so?   265
When thy rebellious creatures here below
Their black designs of deepest mischief frame,
Shall they still stamp on them Thy holy name?
Make Thee, all good, a party in their ill?

233–34. Oates was expelled from the navy in 1675, and his scandalous behavior at the Jesuit College in Valladolid led to expulsion in 1677. He next went to the English seminary at St. Omer, where he remained until his expulsion in June 1678.

241. *Python:* William Bedloe. He declared that Oates had anticipated and outstripped him in making revelations of the Popish Plot.

259. *Diana:* object of veneration.

Thy very Word abuse to break Thy will?   270
By which their leaders draw the vulgar in,
With harmless minds, to perpetrate their sin;
By which the just are by the impious slain,
And Abel still is sacrificed by Cain.
How can Thy justice and Thy thunder sleep,   275
When such affronts on Thee and Thine they heap?
How can the earth forbear with open jaws
To swallow these condemners of Thy laws?
   Hold, Muse! thy zeal now grows to mutiny;
Thou dost ignobly from thy colors fly.   280
Under the standard of the cross we serve,
And from our Leader's ways we must not swerve.
By form of law He did submit to die,
Accused of treason and of blasphemy;
All-pow'rful He, without revenge or strife,   285
Endur'd the loss of honor and of life.
This is the way which He his foll'wers taught,
Which Him to triumph, us to safety brought.
Then in this way let us march bravely on,
Which will our innocence with glory crown;   290
And let us pity those whom prosp'rous sin
Hardens, and does on earth their Hell begin.
   Now comes the solemn and the bloody day   [21:12]
In which all Israel meets to fast and pray;
But impious is that fast and pray'r which parts   295
From lips polluted and from hardened hearts.
   In the first rank of Levites Arod stood,
Court favor placed him there, not worth or blood.
Naboth amongst the tribes the foremost place   [21:12]
Did with his riches, birth, and virtue grace: 300
A man whose wealth was the poor's common stock;
The hungry found their market in his flock;
His justice made all law contentions cease;
He was his neighbors' safeguard and their peace.
The rich by him were in due bounds contained;   305
The poor, if strong, employed; if weak, maintained.
Well had he served his country and his king,
And the best troops in all their wars did bring;
Nor with less brav'ry did he lead them on,
Warding his country's danger with his own.   310
   Scarce were the rites and ceremonies past

Which by the law attend their public fast,
When Malchus, raising up his hands and eyes,   [21:13]
With bended knees, thus to the judges cries:
"Hear me, great seed of Levi, hear me all,   315
Israel's ten tribes, I for your mercy call.
Seal me a pardon who too long have been
A dark concealer of a crying sin!
Heav'n does this day my wounded conscience heal,
And bids me the hid blasphemy reveal.   320
Naboth, stand forth! 'Tis thee of impious breach   [21:13]
Of God's and the king's laws whom I impeach."
At this the tribes a various murmur raise;
His boldness some abhorred, and some did praise.
Some would have Naboth by a public vote,   325
Without more form, found guilty of the Plot.
Others the law allege that no offense
Can be judged so on single evidence.
While thus they waver, Arod takes his cue:
"Our thanks to Heav'n in the first place are due   330
(He said) which with such gracious speed prevents
Our pray'rs, and all false traitors cursed intents.
Speak, Malchus, then, and this assembly give
Of the whole Plot a perfect narrative;
And whilst this service you to Israel do,   335
Know that we hear you, and believe you too."
    Malchus, applauded thus in public view,
Did now almost believe that he spoke true.
This armed his face with brass, his heart with steel,
That he no shame and no remorse could feel.   340
Then he the story of his Plot at large
Unfolds, and lays to guiltless Naboth's charge.
How with the Aramites he did conspire
His country to invade, the city fire,
The temple to destroy, the king to kill,   [21:13] 345
And the whole realm with desolation fill.
He told how he himself the agent was

327–29. According to Luttrell (*1*, 45), Caryll himself was brought from the Tower on 22
May 1680 to the King's Bench Bar on his writ of habeas corpus, and there being but a single
witness against him as to the Plot, he was bailed.
    331. *prevents:* to meet beforehand or to anticipate.
    343. *Aramites:* Probably both the Jesuits and the French (see "Aram's king," line 437).
    347–48. No doubt a reference to the "general consult" that Oates swore was held by the
Jesuits to discuss the Plot on 24 April 1678, at the White Horse Tavern on Fleet Street. Oates

In close consults to bring these things to pass;
Nor did he fail with proper circumstance
Of time and place to garnish his romance.   350
The priests astonished are, the people gaze,
And the dumb judges horror does amaze.
Then out steps Python, and with dext'rous art
Weaving his story, seals a counterpart
To all that Malchus had before deposed;   355
And with deep oaths the accusation closed.
   Now on poor Naboth all their eyes were set,
Some red with anger, some with pity wet;
But the fierce rabble gladly would prevent
His trial by an instant punishment.   360
   Whence this unnat'ral pleasure to destroy?
From what ill root grows this malignant joy?
Beasts worry beasts but when their hunger calls,
But man on man with a full stomach falls.
'Tis not our wants of nature to redress   365
That we this rage to our own kind express,
But for the mischief's sake we pleasure find;
It lies not in our body, but our mind.
Our seed receives a double taint and stain:
From rebel Adam, and from murd'ring Cain.   370
   Naboth, thus charged, had need for his defense
Of all his courage and his innocence.
It was a trial of no vulgar kind
To show th' heroic temper of his mind.
But the transparent brightness of his soul,   375
E'en through his eyes, their malice did control.
For his accusers, when he sternly viewed,
Their tortured looks their rack of conscience shewed.
But to his judges with a manly grace
He lowly bowed, and pleaded thus his case: 380
   "My lords, by these false oaths, this bloody lie,
God and the king are more abused than I;
For I, poor worm, weigh nothing in the scale
When their high wrongs for reparation call.

---

stated that he had received a patent from the general of the order to be of the "consult." It was true that the usual triennial congregation of the Society of Jesus was held in London on that day, but it was not held at the White Horse, and it was impossible that Oates, not being a member of the order, could have been admitted to it.

   363–64. Cf. Rochester, *A Satyr against Mankind*, 129–30: "Birds feed on birds, beasts on each other prey, / But savage man alone does man betray."

When God's dread Name, when His and the king's laws   385
Are thus blasphemed, 'tis their, and not my cause.
Pharaoh, Goliath, and that heathen brood
Less impiously blasphemed our Sov'reign Good;
They believed not His Being nor His might,
And blindly what they nothing thought did slight.   390
These know Him, and Him knowingly defy,
And signing with His awful Name their lie,
Make him a party to their perjury.
Nay, in this horrid enterprise they do
Their cursed endeavor to destroy Him too;   395
For Truth and He in essence so partake
That when you make Him false, you Him unmake.
    "These vipers in the bosom of our law
Will eat it through, its very heartstrings gnaw;
For when with artificial perjury   400
They make God's sacred Name espouse their lie,
Forthwith that lie omnipotent becomes
And governs all below—it saves or dooms;
Disposes of our honor, life, and state,
Gives rule to law, and arbitrates our fate.   405
No rage of famine, pestilence, or war
Can with this legal massacre compare.
If perjured villains may a shelter find
To make their inroads thus on human kind,
Laws, for chastisement of the guilty meant,   410
Will turn their points against the innocent
(*As cannons of a newly entered town   [*Poet speaks]
From their own walls the houses batter down).
My lords, if you this villainy endure,
Judges themselves will not be long secure.   415
And so I leave my cause in your wise breast,
The temple where Truth's oracle should rest."
    Thus Naboth spoke, with that undaunted mien
Which only in bold innocence is seen;
But lest the people's fury should relent,   420
Arod their calmer thoughts did thus prevent:
    "Naboth, what you have said in your defense
Adds to your guilt, clears not your innocence;
When the king's evidence you perjured call,
Know that your very plea is criminal.   425
Shall malefactors with reproaches tear

Their fame who for their king and country swear?
What thief, what felon may not do the same,
To purge themselves the witnesses defame?
Against two oaths, so positive and plain,   430
All your haranguing rhetoric is vain.
Should stout denying pass for innocence,
The court must be as weak as your defense.
Less confidence your bloody crimes behoved,
So weakly answered and so strongly proved.   435
Is it not doubly sworn that you conspired
With Aram's king this city to have fired,
And in that hurry to destroy the king,   [21:13]
And into Israel bondage and idols bring?"
    Strung with these dire reproaches, Nab'th again   440
Offer'd to speak, but offered still in vain;
For when the bench did thus his guilt proclaim,
Their words, like oil, enraged the people's flame;
Who hardly staying till the sentence passed,
Like hungry wolves they rush with furious haste,   445
Hurrying poor Naboth to a planted stake,
Where in his death their cruel joy they take.
Their hands and tongues they equally employ,
And him with stones and calumnies destroy.
Some gather flints, and some the victim tied   450
Ready for sacrifice. He loudly cried,
"Heav'n bless the king! And I forgive ye all.
O! may this inn'cent blood no vengeance call
On you my brethren"—off'ring more to say,
A murd'ring show'r of stones took voice and life away.   [21:13] 455
    Thus Naboth fell—Kind Heav'n! so may I fall
Rather than stand so high, and criminal,
As cov'tous Ahab and his bloody queen;
Or serve the malice of such lust and spleen;
Or judge with Arod, or with Malchus swear;   460
Or with the rabble oppressed virtue tear.
Naboth! though cast thou art by human laws,
Heav'n's writ of error has removed thy cause
    And judged it so that it shall stand from hence

441. *Offered:* attempted.
462. *cast:* condemned.
463. *writ of error:* a writ to procure the reversal of a judgment, on the ground of error. *cause:*
the matter about which a person goes to law; the case of one party in a suit.

A lasting record of wronged innocence.   465
All to thy ashes shall their duty pay;
Friends shall their tears, foes weep their blood away.   [21:19]
For lo! the great Elijah, Heav'n's envoy,
Has now surprised them in their guilty joy,
Caught in the very fact and place where they   [21:18]   470
Rejoice, pluming and hov'ring o'er the prey:
"What? have I found you in this field of blood   [21:20]
(For so thy title to 't shall be made good
More by thine own than Naboth's) graceless king!   [21:19]
I from thy dreadful Judge thy sentence bring"   475
(Says Heav'n's bold herald). Ahab heartless grew,
And the queen's fears did all her pride subdue
At this loud thunderstroke. "Know, wretched pair,"
Continues he, "the vultures in the air,   [21:24]
Wolves in the field shall be the living tomb   480
Of all that's born from Jezebel's cursed womb;
And Ahab's seed shall be the worthy food
Of birds and beasts that live by prey and blood.
Thy race no more shall mix with human kind,
But nourish beasts, and so with them be joined.   485
Thou, Ahab, here in this ill-purchased ground,
Shalt bleed thy last from a fresh mortal wound;
Mastiffs shall lick thy blood, and it shall be   [21:19]
As sweet to them as Naboth's blood to thee.
And thou, cursed woman, Eve and serpent too,   490
Cause of thine own, and of thy husband's woe,
Thy broken limbs, and into pieces rent,
Shall be of dogs the food and excrement.   [21:23]
Low falls thy body, low'r thy soul will sink;   [2 Kings 9:33]
Thy mem'ry ever shall remain and stink."   495
And so he left them thunderstruck and dumb,
Stung with their present guilt, and fate to come.

JOHN CARYLL

The Hypocrite
(1678)

This satire on Shaftesbury is dated 1678 in the fourth part of Dryden's *Miscellany*. Part III of Butler's *Hudibras* appeared in the same year, and in Canto 2 there is a long satiric portrait of Shaftesbury. Line 27 of *The Hypocrite*, "And pop'ry's growth he sounds in ev'ry ear," suggests that it was probably written late in 1678, after Oates's depositions and Godfrey's murder in October.

Anthony Ashley Cooper, first earl of Shaftesbury (1621–83), is not accused of starting the Popish Plot, but rather of nourishing the agitation (North, p. 95). He was from the first foremost in his zeal for the Plot. The temptation to use this means of avenging himself upon his enemies was probably irresistible; that he could have believed in the Plot is improbable.

THE HYPOCRITE

Written upon the Lord Shaftesbury in the Year 1678
by Mr. Caryll

> Thou'rt more inconstant than the wind or sea,
> Or that still-veering sex, out-done by thee;
> Reeling from vice to vice, thou hast run through
> Legions of sins, more than the casuists know;
> Of whom thy friends were wont to say, "Poor devil,   5
> At least he was not constant to his evil."
> Dealing so long in sins of pomp and glory,
> Who would have thought (to make up Guzman's story)
> Hypocrisy at last should enter in

8. *to . . . story*: probably a reference to *Guzman de Alfarche*, a Spanish picaresque romance by Mateo Aleman. It was translated into English as *The Rogue* in 1622 and published with an introductory poem by Ben Jonson. Guzman is by turns scullion, thief, gentleman, beggar, soldier, and page both to a cardinal and to a French ambassador. Line 6 suggests a variety of vice: hypocrisy is all that is needed to "make up" or complete this protean character.

9. *Hypocrisy*: 'Little Sincerity" was the cant name for Shaftesbury, used between the king and the duke of York.

And fix this floating mercury of sin?   10
All his old sins, like misses out of date,
Turn pensioners to this new miss of state;
His actions, looks, and garb take a new frame,
And wear the liv'ry of this sullen dame:
Plain band and hair and clothes disguise the man;   15
All but his dealing and his heart is plain.
Not Ovid's stories, nor the wife of Lot
Can boast a change beyond our state bigot:
All on the sudden, in one fatal morn,
Our courtier did to a stark Quaker turn.   20
Some think
He does, as criminals who would defeat
The course of justice, madness counterfeit.
No, godliness, that once much pitied thing,
Of his new fiddle is the only string.   25
For the poor church is all his tender care,
And pop'ry's growth he sounds in ev'ry ear;
At which the dirty rout run grunting in,
As when the old wife's kettle rings the swine.
    So the court dame, who in her youthful pride   30
No pleasure to her craving sense denied,
But, unreserved, with ev'ry fresh delight,
Did prodigally feast her appetite,
Age drawing on, when through her youth's decay
Her servants with her beauty drop away,   35
For winter quarters she religion takes,
And of necessity a virtue makes.
And when the wrinkles of her face no cure
Will longer from the help of art endure,
Cov'ring the worn-out sinner with the saint,   40
As once her face, she now her soul does paint.

11. *misses:* kept mistresses.

12. *pensioners:* hirelings. Used in the 17th and 18th centuries often with the implication of base motives: a hireling, tool, creature.

15. *Plain band:* a reference to the austere dress of the Quakers (line 20). *Band* is either a hatband or a collar.

20. *Quaker:* That Shaftesbury had never entirely severed his connections with the Presbyterian party seems certain, though the direct evidence is slight, and the extension of his connection to other forms of dissent, even to the Quakers, he advertised by spending the night at the house of a well-known Quaker. He had numerous Quaker connections in the City and elsewhere (Brown, *Shaftesbury*, pp. 224, 323 *n.*).

29. The wife brings the swine in by beating on a kettle.

30. *pride:* sexual desire, heat, especially in female animals.

Since churches are not, must religion be
Of guilty persons still the sanctuary?
When great men fall, or pop'lar men would rise,
Both from religion borrow their disguise: 45
Then, like Achilles in his fate-proof arms,
They boldly march, guided with holy charms,
And brow-beat Caesar, and defy his laws—
Who dare resist the champion of God's cause?
But when the place or pension is your own,   50
When the opposing party is run down,
Religion and God's cause aside are cast,
Like actor's habit when the play is past.
    This Dame Hypocrisy, with a sour face,
Does fit supply old Mother Mosely's place: 55
She for his body did provision find,
This caters for the lech'ry of his mind,
And for his vast ambition, and his pride,
And his insatiate av'rice does provide.
His body thus and soul together vie   60
In vice's empire for the sov'reignty;
In ulcers that, this does abound in sin,
Lazar without, and Lucifer within.
The silver pipe is no sufficient drain
For the corruption of this little man,   65
Who, though he ulcers have in ev'ry part,
Is nowhere so corrupt as in his heart.

55. *Mother Mosely:* Contemporary references suggest that Mistress Mosely, whose name is sometimes linked with Shaftesbury's, operated a house of prostitution (Vieth, p. 275 *n.*).

64. *silver pipe:* In 1668 Shaftesbury fell dangerously ill. John Locke, who combined secretarial duties with those of medical adviser to his employer, recorded the symptoms and progress of the disease so carefully that a modern physician has been able to diagnose it as a case of suppurating hydatid cyst of the liver. Ashley's condition became so serious that Locke dicided to operate. Although the operation was successful, the wound continued to discharge, and the question arose whether it would be safe to allow it to close. In the end it was decided that it should be left open, and that a silver tube, for which a gold one was later substituted, be inserted for drainage. From then until his death Shaftesbury endured the disability of a constantly suppurating wound (Brown, *Shaftesbury,* p. 185). The pipe was the source of the nickname "Tapski," which often occurs in anti-Shaftesbury literature.

A Ballad Called Perkin's Figary
(1679)

This is a Tory attack on the duke of Monmouth. When in August 1679 Charles II fell dangerously ill and it was considered urgent that the duke of York be recalled from his exile in Brussels, Monmouth requested that York be prohibited from returning. The king, however, sent for his brother. The warm reception of York by Charles was, on the recovery of the latter (15 September), followed by Monmouth's being deprived of his commission as general and ordered to absent himself for some time from the kingdom. He left reluctantly for Holland at the end of September.

The satire makes the typical Tory charges against Monmouth: his illegitimacy, his brainless buffoonery, his rowdy companions. Nell Gwynne, in or about 1679, is said to have dubbed Monmouth Prince Perkin. Perkin Warbeck (1474–99) claimed to be Richard, duke of York, son of Edward IV. He was hanged by Henry VII. The analogy proved to be strikingly exact. Perkin Warbeck, like Monmouth, had been a handsome young claimant to the crown. He hailed, as did Monmouth by birth, from the Low Countries. Finally, both pretenders waged their disastrous campaigns in the west of England (Bryan Little, *The Monmouth Episode* [London, 1956], p. 29). "Figary" is a variant form of "fegary," vagary, prank, whim.

James Scott, duke of Monmouth and Buccleuch, ca. 1680. After William Wissing.

A Ballad Called Perkin's Figary

or,

A Ballad New Which Doth Most Plainly Show
How Seventy-Nine Would Fain Be Forty-Two

Come listen, good people, to what I shall say
Concerning the blessing of this happy day;
The downfall of Perkin and joyful return
Of a prince that will make his electorate mourn.
    Though Shaftesbury plotted   5
    And Grey was besotted,
Though Armstrong to ground of artillery trotted—
Yet His Highness, God bless him, is safely come back
To the shame and confusion of Perkin Warbeck.

This Perkin's a prince whose excellency lies   10
In cutting of capers and storming dirt pies;
He aims at a crown for his noddle unfit
As Howe for a duchess, or he for a wit.
    He danceth, he skippeth,
    He frisketh, he leapeth,   15

Title. How . . . *Forty-Two:* a popular Tory motto. The Whigs are bringing on another civil war.

4. *his electorate:* Electorate here means either the state or dignity of a German elector or the dominions of an elector (with a possible play on the more familiar sense of "electorate," Monmouth's backer's). Cf. a similar term for Monmouth—the prince of Whigland.

6. *Grey:* Forde Grey, 3d Baron Grey of Werk, later earl of Tankerville (d. 1701). He was an intimate friend of Monmouth and later encouraged him to invade England.

7. *Armstrong:* Sir Thomas Armstrong (1624–84), another intimate of Monmouth's and M.P. for Stafford in 1679. He left England for a time during that year along with Monmouth to join some English regiments in Flanders.

8. "The 2d [September 1679] His Royal Highness the duke of York arrived at Windsor from Flanders, who came to wait on His Majesty, hearing of his indisposition" (Luttrell *1*, 20).

11. *In* . . . *capers:* a reference to Monmouth's love of dancing and running races. Cf. lines 14–15. *storming dirt pies:* An Osborn MS at Yale (chest 2, no. 14) glosses "the mock siege of Maastricht." Monmouth had played a distinguished role in the taking of Maastricht over again one August night in 1674, in the meadows below Windsor Castle. A rough representation of the town had been constructed, complete with fortifications. By the light of the moon Monmouth and York led their forces to the attack, dug trenches, and raised batteries. The besieged put up a stout defense, but counterscarp and ravelin were captured, Monmouth leaping the trenches with his handful of guards, and capturing his half-moon as he had when Louis XIV watched from his hillock (D'Oyley, p. 97).

13. *As* . . . *duchess:* Jon Grubham Howe or How (1657–1722), commonly known as "Jack Howe," a politician. In 1679 he brought an accusation against the duchess of Richmond, which on investigation proved to be false, and he was forbidden to attend the court.

To trumpet and drums he manfully trippeth—
But His Highness, God bless him, is safely come back
To the shame and confusion of Perkin Warbeck.

His council consists of Vernon and Rowe,
Two pages apostate, and Armstrong the beau,   20
Who lately rebuked for services done,
Is returned in his dumps from the court to the town,
    Where he may contrive
    How Perkin may swive
Since in's empty noddle no politics thrive—   25
For His Highness, God bless him, is safely come back
To the shame and confusion of Perkin Warbeck.

If pocky Sir Player with Peyton and Jenks

19. *Vernon:* Osborn MS glosses: "Vernon is Monmouth's secretary and so creature, and chosen a burgess for the University of Cambridge for this ensuing Parliament by the Lord Chancellor Monmouth's interest." This is James Vernon (1646–1727). Around 1672 he became secretary to the duke of Monmouth. In his *Journal* Edmund Warcup records on 4 July 1681: "with D. Monmouth, by appointment of Vernon his secretary." On the same day he reports: "At Man's coffeehouse Vernon wished M[onmouth] would leave the party and return to K[ing]." *Rowe:* Osborn MS glosses: "Anthony Rowe, a gentleman of low fortune, went with Monmouth to the siege of Maestricht, when His Grace took a liking to him."

20. *Two pages apostate:* All Souls College MS Codrington 116 glosses: "Two pages that were the duke of York's but now live with Monmouth."

24. *swive:* copulate.

28. *pocky . . . Peyton:* Osborn MS glosses: "Sir Thomas Player and Sir Robert Peyton, two violent persons against His Royal Highness." Sir Thomas Player (d. 1686) succeeded to the post of chamberlain of London in 1672. He was one of the City members, both in the Westminster and in the Oxford parliaments (1678, 1679, and 1681), and helped to inflame public opinion respecting the Popish Plot in the autumn of 1678 by stating in the House that Protestant citizens might expect to wake up one morning with their throats cut. When on the alarm of the king's illness, the duke of York unexpectedly returned from Brussels in August 1679, Player led a deputation to the lord mayor to express fear of the Papists and to ask that the City guards be doubled. The allusion to Player's sensual indulgence in "pocky" is borne out in the portrait in the second part of *Absalom and Achitophel:*

> Next him, let railing Rabshakeh have place,
> So full of zeal he hath no need of grace;
> A saint that can both flesh and spirit use,
> Alike haunt conventicles and the stews.

Sir Robert Peyton (1633?–89), a member of the Green Ribbon Club, was accused of deserting the Whig party when it was thought he reversed his position on the Exclusion Bill in 1679. Peyton, who had been so violent against York, probably feared retaliation upon his person and estate with the ascendancy of the Catholics after the dissolution of Palriament. In 1680 Gadbury and Cellier testified that by deserting the Whigs, Peyton had informed them that he also deserted an interest that had twice compassed his election to Parliament and that, in case the king had died at Windsor in the summer of 1679, had been ready to seize the Tower, Dover Castle, and Portsmouth, and to execute anyone who proclaimed York king. This information was enough to imprison Peyton temporarily in the Tower for high treason. The violence with which he had previously abused York was so extreme, however, that it aroused

Could pass on the City their traitorous stinks,
If Presbyter John and his fanatic crew   30
Can speed but as well in Commons' House new,
   Then Perkin might hope
   To be Presbyter pope
And serve, as Madge Howlett, to dance on a rope—
But His Highness, God bless him, is safely come back   35
To the shame and confusion of Perkin Warbeck.

Buckingham, Winchester, Shaftesbury, Grey
Would set up this fop, old England to sway;
Macclesfield's now taking wind from their tail,
While the iron's hot, cries, Let's drive the nail!   40
   But Perkin be free,
   And prithee tell me
What in the end wilt thou be better than we—
For His Highness, God bless him, is safely come back
To the shame and confusion of Perkin Warbeck.   45
Then with thy ten bullies go Hamborough view,
And there with more safety converse with a Jew;
We English will ever be just to the crown,
No bastard succession with us shall go down.
   Though plot upon plot   50
   Has kept our brains hot,

---

suspicions, and most people thought that Peyton was probably a Catholic spy. *Jenks:* Probably the Jenks (or Jinks, Jynks) mentioned in Marvell's letter to Sir Edward Harley dated 1 July 1676: "On the Wednesday [Francis] Jenks appeared before the council on summons. Sir Robert Peyton, several Templars and citizens countenanced him thither. His crime, the Saturday before at the Common Hall for elections (where the Knights of the Stocking and the Urinal, Clarges and Rich, were chosen shrives) he had moved for a new Parliament as the right remedy of the nation. There was a great well moved and afterwards a hum, and the mayor gave an insignificant plausible answer. He was committed to the gatehouse for that mutinous and seditious motion and for his arrogant defending it before the council. He is frequently visited" (Margoliouth, *2*, 322).

   30. *Presbyter John:* i.e., Presbyterians in the House of Commons.

   34. *Madge Howlett:* unidentified.

   37. *Winchester:* Charles Paulet or Powlett (1625?–99) succeeded his father as marquis of Winchester in 1675, and was put on the Privy Council in 1679. At this crisis of Charles II's reign he sided rather strongly with the Whigs.

   39. *Macclesfield:* Charles Gerard, 1st Baron Gerard of Brandon in Suffolk, Viscount Brandon. On 23 July 1679 he was created earl of Macclesfield. He was one of the band of conspirators of which Monmouth was the tool. His name appears in *LJ* with that of Shaftesbury as one of the protesters aginst the rejection of the Exclusion Bill on 15 November 1680. Lord Grey of Werk in his *Confession* (p. 61) asserts that Gerard suggested to Monmouth the expediency of murdering the duke of York by way of terrorizing Charles.

   46–47. Hamburg was a hotbed of sectarian extremism and the haven of many English exiles. In the 16th century large numbers of Jews immigrated there from Spain and Portugal.

Yet the cheat's now discovered, 'twill serve thy turn not—
For His Highness, God bless him, is safely come back
To the shame and confusion of Perkin Warbeck.

God bless our good king, and long may he reign,   55
But let not his brother leave England again;
Rebellious and factious heads let them knock off,
Some to the gallows, and some to the scaff—
   Old England till then
   Cannot hope that their men   60
Of Shaftesbury e'er will be quiet again—
Though His Highness, God bless him, is safely come back
To the shame and confusion of Perkin Warbeck.

Satire on Old Rowley
(1680)

The name of Rowley, a famous stallion of the royal stud, was often used as a sobriquet for Charles.

SATIRE ON OLD ROWLEY

1.

How our good king does Papists hate
    At ev'ry coming sessions!
Then of his laws he'll nothing bate,
    But make perhaps some fresh ones.
At other times he's ruled by's brother,   5
As was his father by his mother.

2.

Silly and sauntering he goes
    From French whore to Italian;
Unlucky in whate'er he does,
    An old ill-favored stallion.   10
Fain the good man would live at ease,
And ev'ry punk and party please.

1–4. On 6 March 1679 the king addressed Parliament: "I shall not cease my endeavors daily to find out what more I can, both of the plot and murder of Sir Edmund Berry Godfrey; and shall desire the assistance of both my Houses in that work. I have not been wanting to give orders for putting all the present laws in execution against Papists; and I am ready to join in the making such further laws as may be necessary for securing the kingdom against popery" (*LJ*, *13*, 449). In two later speeches to Parliament (21 October and 15 December 1680) the king renewed these promises.

5. *ruled by 's brother:* It was frequently charged at this time that York had a great influence over the king.

7. *sauntering:* strolling about, trifling, dawdling.

8. Specifically, from the duchess of Portsmouth to the duchess of Mazarin.

3.

How he by Hyde, then Clifford rules,
    Osborne and upstart fellows;
When the whores want they're knaves and fools,   15
    As he himself can tell us.
Till then, though Parliament complain,
He says they're rude and hate his reign.

4.

A pretty set he has at hand
    Of slimy Portsmouth's creatures: 20
Godolphin, Lory, Sunderland,
    French gamesters and deep bettors,
Who would reform this brutal nation,
And bring French slavery in fashion.

5.

King of three mighty kingdoms he   25
    Thinks beggars only loyal
Knaves wise, French true, and popery
    Quite cleared at Wakeman's trial.
Nay, what seemed never to be done,
The Chits have made him hate his son.   30

6.

Rise, drowsy prince, like Samson shake
    These green withes from about thee;

15. Whenever his mistresses are deprived of what they fancy because of his lack of money,
the king blames his poverty on his ministers, calling them knaves and fools.

21. *Godolphin, Lory, Sunderland:* Sydney Godolphin, Laurence Hyde, and Robert Spencer,
earl of Sunderland, the reigning ministers in the first half of 1680. Hyde and Godolphin were
both young treasury commissioners, and Sunderland the new secretary of state for the
northern department. The Whigs attacked the youth and inexperience of the triumvirate by
nicknaming them the "Chits."

22. In 1671 Sunderland lost huge sums to the duchess of Portsmouth in his courtship of her
patronage. He had a "passion for cards," and apparently transacted much of his routine
business in a most haphazard way at the gaming table. "French gamesters" also suggests
that the Chits were playing games with France: Godolphin, for instance, took part in the
secret negotiations with Louis XIV carried on at this time.

28. *Wakeman's trial:* Lord Chief Justice Scroggs in his acquittal of Sir George Wakeman (18
July 1679) dealt a direct blow at the Plot and the credibility of its sponsors.

30. A reference to Monmouth's disgrace at court and the removal of his offices.

32. *green withes:* "And Samson said unto her [Delilah], If they bind me with seven green
withes that were never dried, then shall I be weak, and be as another man" [Judg. 16:7].

Banish their Delilah, and make
  Thy people no more doubt thee.
In vain they fright thee with a war;   35
Thou art not hated, though they are.

7.

Rogue, knave, and bigot all love thee,
  Because they fear thy brother;
Queen Mary's days they would not see,
  And can expect no other.   40
No misery a land can want,
Ruled by a fool, goat, tyrant, saint.

8.

Men say we act like Forty-two,
  Yet none tells thee the reason:
Yet when the same diseases grow,   45
  Like medicines come in season.
Twice we thy armies have o'erthrown,
And without blood voted them down.

9.

Dukes thou creat'st, yet want'st an heir
  Thy Portuguese is barren;   50
Marry again and ne'er despair:
  In this lewd age we are in
Some Harry Jermyn will be found
To get an heir fit to be crowned.

10.

Thy brother York would come to blows   55
  While thou art yet in being;

33. *their Delilah:* the duchess of Portsmouth, seen as an agent of Louix XIV.

43. *Forty-two:* the civil war.

47–48. Parliament disbanded the standing army in 1679.

49. *Dukes thou creat'st:* Charles made these illegitimate sons dukes: Monmouth, Grafton, Richmond, St. Albans.

50. Before he took up Monmouth's cause seriously, Shaftesbury had proposed that the king should divorce Catherine de Braganza on the grounds of barrenness in order to get an heir and thus exclude York from the succession.

53. *Harry Jermyn:* Henry Jermyn, earl of St. Albans (d. 1684). The scandalmongers of his own day affirmed that he was secretly married to Henrietta Maria, the widow of Charles I.

55. At this time James was desperate for measures to ensure his succession.

He shall not rule, as now he does,
      While thou art yet foreseeing.
But if thou'rt wise deceive his hope,
Leave him to Irish, French, and pope.   60

11.

Thou dost not use the pow'r in hand—
      Yet for the ills that are done,
When rogues pretend thy own command,
      Thou'rt ready with a pardon;
As if 'twere thy prerogative   65
That murd'rers, knaves, and traitors live.

12.

For shame give o'er—new councils choose
      If with the eyes of others
Thou needst must see thy nation's use,
      And not thy popish brother's.   70
Brother to brother should be kind,
Yet bear the Littletons in mind.

63. Probably a reference to Danby. In 1678 Danby made a corrupt proposal to Louis XIV for six million livres a year for three years for Charles, with Charles's knowledge and full consent. This line suggests Charles's blatant willingness to corrupt his administrators and government.

64. *pardon:* On 22 March 1679 the king announced to Parliament that he had granted Danby a pardon under the great seal, with a reminder that on a former occasion he had done the same thing for Buckingham and Shaftesbury (*LJ, 13,* 471). The Commons attacked the pardon, asking in what manner it had been obtained and questioning the power of the king to pardon in such a case (Browning, *Danby, 1,* 322–23).

65. *prerogative:* The definition of the royal prerogative was a main issue in the struggle between the king and Parliament. See Henry Neville's *Plato Redivivus,* London, 1681, for a contemporary Whig opinion on the exercise of the prerogative.

72. *the Littletons:* Probably the two Thomas Littletons, father and son. The father, Sir Thomas, along with Halifax and Temple, was apparently a Trimmer. Burnet knew him well and reports a conversation with him concerning the advisability of "expedients" (some sort of limitations) to be put on Yorks's succession as opposed to his exclusion (Burnet, *2,* 281–82). Sir John Reresby reports on Littleton's speech in favor of an expedient during the Oxford Parliament (pp. 220–21). Since the younger Thomas Littleton (b. 1647?) was an active Whig under William III, he probably supported his father in recommending the expedient. In these last two lines the lampoonist appears to be saying that out of fraternal feeling Charles could not be expected to approve of the Exclusion Bill, but at least he should agree to an expedient if he is at all "foreseeing" or "wise."

RICHARD DUKE

A Panegyric upon Oates
(1679)

J. W. Ebsworth assigns the following lampoon to Richard Duke (1658–1711), poet and divine, in his *DNB* article on Duke. Ebsworth reasons that it must be by Duke because in Duke's acknowledged *Epithalamium upon the Marriage of Captain William Bedloe* (acknowledged because it was included in the 1717 collection of Duke's poems, whereas the *Panegyric* was not) the poet begins "I, he who sung of humble Oates before." Ebsworth calls the *Panegyric* a companion poem to the *Epithalamium,* and certainly they appear, when read together, to have come from the same pen. If we accept Ebsworth's ascription, it was published before Christmas 1679, when Ebsworth claims the *Epithalamium* was issued (arguing on the basis of the internal evidence of line 80 of that poem, "And when, as now in Christmas . . .").

A PANEGYRIC UPON OATES

Silvestrem tenui musam meditemur avena

Of all the grain our nation yields
In orchards, gardens, or in fields,
There is a grain which, though 'tis common,
Its worth till now was known to no man.
Not Ceres' sickle e'er did crop   5
A grain with ears of greater hope;
For why? some say the earth ne'er bore
In any clime such seed before.
   Yet this grain has (as all must own)
To grooms, and ostlers well been known;   10

Motto: A modification of Virgil's line, *Silvestrem tenui Musam meditaris avena (Eclogue* 1.2.) Dryden's translation of this line is "[You, Tityrus,] entertain your sylvan muse." Duke's version might be rendered as "Let us entertain the Muse of the forest on a slender oat" [*an Oaten reed,* line 36: the shepherd's pipe].

6. The pun on ears is probably an ironic reference to Oates's remarkable capacity for hearing what was never said: his fabrication of details of the Popish Plot.

And often has, without disdain,
In musty barn and manger lain;
As if it had been only good
To be for birds and beasts the food.
But now by new inspired force   15
It keeps alive both man and horse.
   Speak then, my Muse, for now we guess
What grain it is thou wouldst express:
It is not barley, rye or wheat
That can pretend to such a feat: 20
'Tis Oates, bare Oates, which is become
The health of England, bane of Rome,
And wonder of all Christendom.
And therefore Oates has well deserved
From musty barn to be preferred,   25
And now in royal court preserved;
That, like Hesperian fruit, Oates may
Be watched and guarded night and day;
Which is but just retaliation
For having guarded a whole nation.   30
   Hence ev'ry lofty plant which stands
'Twixt Berwick walls and Dover sands,
The oak itself (which well we style
The pride and safeguard of our isle)
Must wave and strike its lofty head,   35
And now salute an Oaten reed;
For surely Oates deserves to be
Exalted far 'bove any tree.
Th' Egyptians once (though it seems odd)
Did worship onions for a god,   40
And poor peeled garlic was with them
Esteemed beyond the greatest gem.
What would they've done had they, think ye,
Had such a blade of Oates as we?
Oates of such known divinity!   45
Since then by Oates such good we find,
Let Oates at least now be enshrined;
Or, in some sacred press enclosed,
Be only kept to be exposed;
And all fond relics else shall be   50
Deemed objects of idolatry.
Popelings may tell us how they saw

Their Garnett's picture on a straw;
'Twas a great miracle, we know,
To see him drawn in little so.   55
But on an Oaten stalk there is
A greater miracle than this:
A visage which, with lively grace,
Does twenty Garnetts now outface;
And like twig of Dodona's grove   60
E'en speaks as if inspired by Jove!
Nay, to add to the wonder more,
Declares unheard-of things before;
And thousand myst'ries does unfold,
As plain as oracles of old;   65
By which we steer affairs of state,
And stave off Britain's sudden fate.
　　Let's then, in honor of the name
Of Oates, enact some solemn game
Where Oaten pipe shall us inspire   70
Beyond the charms of Orpheus' lyre;
Stones, stocks, and ev'ry senseless thing
To Oates shall dance, to Oates shall sing,
Whilst woods amazed to th' echoes ring.
And as (that heroes' names may not,   75
When they are rotten, be forgot)
We hang achievements o'er their dust
(A debt to their great merits just)
So, if deserts of Oates we prize,
Let Oates still hang before our eyes,   80
Thereby to raise our contemplation,
Oates being to this happy nation
The mystic emblem of salvation.

---

53. Henry Garnett (1555–1606), Jesuit superior of the English province, executed for complicity in the Gunpowder Plot. Many Catholics sought for relics of a man whom they regarded as a martyr, and within a year of his death wonderful accounts were circulated throughout the Christian world about a miraculous straw or "ear void of corn" on which a drop of Garnett's blood had fallen. It was said that on one of the husks a portrait of him surrounded with rays of glory had been miraculously formed. Hundreds of persons, it was alleged, were converted to Catholicism by the mere sight of "Garnett's straw." Archbishop Bancroft was commissioned by the Privy Council to call before him such persons as had been most active in propagating the story, and if possible to detect and punish the impostors.

60–61. Dodona, in Epirus, was the seat of a celebrated oracle of Zeus, the oldest in Greece. The will of the god was signified by the rustling of the wind in the oak trees.

77. *achievements*: escutcheons, granted in memory of achievements.

RICHARD DUKE

An Epithalamium upon the Marriage of Captain William Bedloe
(1679)

Sometime in 1679 the informer Bedloe married the elder of two sisters, reputed co-heirs of six hundred pounds per annum, and Richard Duke wrote the following buffooning epithalamium, issued at Christmas, on the occasion.

AN EPITHALAMIUM
UPON THE MARRIAGE OF CAPTAIN WILLIAM BEDLOE

Ille ego qui quondam gracili modulatus avena
Arma virumque cano

I, he who sung of humble Oates before,
Now sing a captain and a man of war.

Goddess of rhyme, that didst inspire
The captain with poetic fire,
Adding fresh laurels to that brow
Where those of victory did grow,
And statelier ornaments may flourish now;   5
If thou art well recovered since
The Excommunicated Prince
(For that important tragedy

Epigraph: Duke's first line is the first line of the canceled proem to the *Aeneid* (with a pun on Oates) and the second line the familiar "Arms and the man I sing," which opens the epic. Dryden gives a translation of the first line in his *Dedication of the Aeneis:* "I, who before, with shepherds in the groves, / Sung, to my oaten pipe, their rural loves."

2. *captain:* When he was in Flanders, apparently sometime during the middle seventies, Bedloe bore an alias of Captain Williams. By use of this title he cheated the prince of Orange and fraudulently obtained a captain's commission from him. But this captaincy was as apocryphal as the "invisible degree" of doctor won by Titus Oates at Salamanca.

5. The horns of a cuckold? (Cf. lines 64–77.)

7. *The Excommunicated Prince:* a folio tragedy that Bedloe had had printed and published in July 1679. *The Excommunicated Prince: or, The False Relic. A Tragedy As It Was Acted by His Holiness's Servants. Being a Popish Plot in a Play by Capt. William Bedloe.* It is believed to have been written by Thomas Walter, an Oxford scholar of Jesus College. The subtitle was added to gain a sale, and it was dedicated to the duke of Buckingham.

Would have killed any muse but thee)
Hither with speed, O! hither move,   10
Pull buskins off, and since to love
The ground is holy that you tread in,
Dance barefoot at the captain's wedding.

See where he comes, and by his side
His charming fair angelic bride: 15
Such, or less lovely, was the dame
So much renowned, Fulvia by name,
With whom of old Tully did join
Then when his art did undermine
The horrid Popish Plot of Catiline.   20
O fairest nymph of all Great Britain
(Though thee my eyes I never set on)
Blush not on thy great lord to smile,
The second savior of our isle;
What nobler captain could have led   25
Thee to thy longed-for marriage bed?
For know that thy all-daring Will is
As stout a hero as Achilles;
And as great things for thee has done
As Palmerin or th' Knight of th' Sun,   30
And is himself a whole romance alone.
Let conscious Flanders speak and be
The witness of his chivalry.
Yet that's not all, his very word

15. *bride:* According to the mocking *Life and Death of Captain William Bedloe* (1681) her name was Anna Purifoy. "The wedding he [Bedloe] kept was for the gallantry of their garbs, the concourse, persons of quality, and for the nobleness and freeness of the entertainment, such that perhaps has not been excelled by any gentleman these many years, and as for epithalamiums, few princes I believe were ever troubled with a greater number of 'em. Among the rest of his papers I found nine in manuscript, besides several in print, but they are all so insipid and dull that I will not trouble myself to transcribe, nor the reader with the perusal of 'em" (pp. 114–16).

17. *Fulvia:* Fulvia, the mistress of Curius, one of the plotters in Catiline's conspiracy, kept Cicero informed of every detail of the plotters' schemes. In Jonson's *Catiline* Fulvia warns Cicero that he is to be assassinated.

24. Oates was styled "the savior of the nation."

30. *Palmerin: Palmerin of England (Palmeirim de Inglaterra)*, a chivalric romance of uncertain authorship, attributed to the Portuguese Francisco de Moraes (ca. 1500–72) or the Spaniard, Luis Hurtado (1530–79?). *Knight of th' Sun:* Cf. Falstaff's "For we that take purses go by the moon and the seven stars, and not by Phoebus, he, 'that wandering knight so fair' " (*Henry IV, Part I*, I.ii). The Knight of the Sun (or Phoebus) is El Donzel del Febo, hero of a popular Spanish chivalric romance.

Has slain as many as his sword: 35
Though common bullies with their oaths
Hurt little till they come to blows,
Yet all his mouth-granados kill,
And save the pains of drawing steel.
This hero thy resistless charms   40
Have won to fly into thy arms;
For think not any mean design,
Or the inglorious itch of coin,
Could ever have his breast controlled,
Or make him be a slave to gold: 45
His love's as freely giv'n to thee
As to the king his loyalty.
Then, O, receive thy mighty prize
With open arms and wishing eyes,
Kiss that dear face where may be seen   50
His worth and parts that skulk within,
That face that justly styled may be
As true a discoverer as he.
Think not he ever false will prove,
His well known truth secures his love;   55
Do you a while divert his cares
From his important grand affairs:
Let him have respite now a while
From kindling the mad rabble's zeal.
Zeal that is hot as fire, yet dark and blind,   60
Shows plainly where its birthplace we may find:
In Hell, where though dire flames forever glow,
Yet 'tis the place of utter darkness too.
But to his bed be sure be true
As he to all the world and you;   65
He all your plots will else betray,
All ye she-Machiavels can lay.
He all designs you know has found,
Though hatched in Hell, or under ground;
Oft to the world such secrets shew   70
As scarce the plotters themselves knew;
Yet if by chance you hap to sin,
And love, while, honor's napping, should creep in,
Yet be discreet, and do not boast

38. *mouth-granados:* violent or explosive speech.
53. I.e., his villainous looks reveal his evil nature. Bedloe was a "discoverer," an informer.

O'th' treason by the common post.   75
So shalt thou still make him love on:
All virtue's in discretion.
So thou with him shalt shine, and be
As great a patriot as he;
And when, as now in Christmas, all   80
For a new pack of cards do call,
Another popish pack comes out
To please the cits and charm the rout,
Thou, mighty queen, shalt a whole suit command,
A crown upon thy head, and scepter in thy hand.   85

82. Writing about the Pope-burning of 17 November 1679, Anthony à Wood notes: "All things imaginably done for the putting down Papists that Presbytery may rise. Plot cards came out also for children" (*Life and Times, 2,* 468).

An Historical Poem
(1680)

Margoliouth has proved that this satire, once attributed to Marvell, was written after Marvell's death (16 August 1678) on the evidence of three lines:

> Line 152, presumably a reference to the murder of Sir Edmund Berry Godfrey in October 1678.
> Line 155, possibly inspired by the title of Harry Care's Protestant publication *The Weekly Pacquet of Advice from Rome,* the first number of which appeared 3 December 1678.
> Line 182, pointing to the Exclusion Bill (introduced in 1679).

Pierre Legouis suggests, however, that Marvell may have written the first 136 lines, with the remainder added by an inferior poet. He regards the opening lines "as the apogee of the genre, however imperfect it may be, until Dryden" *(André Marvell, poète, puritain, patriote, 1621–1678* [Paris H. Didier, 1928]). There is no real evidence for such an ascription.

An Historical Poem

Of a tall stature and of sable hue,
Much like the son of Kish, that lofty Jew,
Twelve years complete he suffered in exile
And kept his father's asses all the while.
At length, by wonderful impulse of fate,   5
The people call him home to help the state;
And, what is more, they send him money too,
And clothe him all from head to foot anew.
Nor did he such small favors then disdain,
But in his thirtieth year began to reign.   10

---

2. *son . . . Jew:* "And he [Kish] had a son, whose name was Saul, a choice young man, and a goodly: and there was not among the children of Israel a goodlier person than he: from his shoulders and upward he was higher than any of the people "(1 Sam. 9:2).

4. "And the asses of Kish, Saul's father, were lost. And Kish said to Saul his son, Take now one of the servants with thee, and arise, go seek the asses" (1 Sam. 9:3).

In a slashed doublet then he came to shore,
And dubbed poor Palmer's wife his royal whore.
Bishops and deans, peers, pimps, and knights he made,
Things highly fitting for a monarch's trade.
With women, wine, and viands of delight   15
His jolly vassals treat him day and night.
But the best times have ever some mishap;
His younger brother perished by a clap;
And his Dutch sister quickly after died,
Soft in her nature and of wanton pride.   20
Bold James survives, no dangers make him flinch,
He married Mynheer Falmouth's pregnant wench.
The pious Mother Queen, hearing her son
Was thus enamored with a buttered bun,
And that the fleet was gone in pomp and state   25
To fetch for Charles the floury Lisbon Kate,
She chants Te Deum, and so comes away
To wish her hopeful issue timely joy.
Her most uxorious mate she used of old,
Why not with easy youngsters make as bold?   30
From the French court she haughty topics brings,
Deludes their pliant nature with vain things;
Her mischief-breeding breast did so prevail
The new-got Flemish town was set to sale.
For those and Jermyn's sins she founds a church,   35

12. *poor Palmer's wife:* Barbara Villiers (1641–1709) married Roger Palmer, earl of Castlemaine. In 1670 she was created duchess of Cleveland and was the ruling mistress of Charles II until 1671.

18. *younger brother:* Henry, duke of Gloucester (b. 1639) died of smallpox 13 September 1660, "by the great negligence of the doctors," according to Pepys. The variant reading, "His younger brother died by treachery," accords with the *Third Advice,* 245–46. It is suggested here that Anne Hyde, duchess of York, made sure of her husband's succession to the throne by having possible claimants Mary and Gloucester put out of the way.

19. *Dutch sister:* Mary, princess of Orange, eldest daughter of Charles I, and mother of William III. She arrived in England 23 September 1660 and died of smallpox the following December.

22. *Falmouth:* Cf. Marvell, *Third Advice,* 251–54 *n.*

26. *floury:* florid, handsome, fair, of a good complexion. Since Catherine de Braganza was not a beauty, the adjective is heavily ironic. Possibly used to mean "of a mealy complexion."

27. *comes away:* to England. Henrietta Maria was in England from October 1660 to January 1661 and again from July 1662 to June 1665. Catherine de Braganza reached England on 13 May 1662 (Margoliouth).

34. *Flemish town:* Dunkirk was sold to France in 1662 for 500,000 pistoles (Margoliouth).

35. *Jermyn:* Henry Jermyn, Master of the Horse to Henrietta Maria in 1639 and at her request created earl of St. Albans in 1660, was ambassador at the French court at the begin-

So slips away and leaves us in the lurch.

Now the court sins did ev'ry place defile,
And plague and war fell heavy on our isle.
Pride nourished folly, folly a delight
With the Batavian commonwealth to fight.   40
But the Dutch fleet fled suddenly with fear,
Death and the duke so terrible appear.
The dreadful victor took his soft repose,
Scorning the pursuit of such recreant foes.
But now York's genitals grew over hot   45
With Denham's and Carneig's infected pot,
Which, with religion, so inflamed his ire
He sells the City where 'twas set on fire.
So Philip's son, inflamed with a miss,
Burnt down the palace of Persepolis.   50
Foiled thus by Venus, he Bellona woos,
And with the Dutch a second war renews.
But here his French-bred prowess proved in vain,
De Ruyter claps him in Sole Bay again.

---

ning of Charles II's reign. The rumor of his marriage with the Queen Mother during the
exile is unsupported (Margoliouth). There is a possible pun here: germane sins, sins closely
related or akin to the others described. *founds a church:* During the exile Henrietta Maria had
founded the Convent of the Visitation at Chaillot, where she spent much time in her declining
years. Bossuet pronounced her funeral oration in the church, 16 November 1669, and there
her heart was buried (Margoliouth).

40. *Batavian:* Dutch.

41–44. The battle of 3 June 1665. Cf. Marvell's *Second Advice,* 239–42 *n.*

46. York had affairs with the wives of Sir John Denham and Robert Carnegie (Carneig),
earl of Southesk. It was popularly believed that Southesk in 1668, to avenge himself, delib-
erately contracted "a virulent distemper" in the brothels and passed it on to James by way
of his wife. Pepys, who heard about it on 6 April, declared the deed "the most pernicious and
full piece of revenge" he had ever heard of. Gramont states that the transfer was never
actually accomplished because York had directed his affections elsewhere. Southesk was
not displeased with the story but among his friends "denied the whole [of it] very solemnly"
(Burnet, *1,* 406).

48. That is, he betrays the City of London in which his ire (and himself) was inflamed,
with a double entendre on the burning of London by the Roman Catholics (Margoliouth).

49. *miss:* concubine.

50. *Persepolis:* the capital of the Persian empire, not far from the modern Shiraz, laid in
ruins by Alexander after the conquest of Darius, some say at the instigation of the courtesan
Thaïs, after a bout of drinking.

51. *Bellona:* Roman goddess of war.

54. *Sole Bay:* The battle of Southwold Bay, 28 May 1672. James eagerly threw himself into
the war and hoped to redeem the reputation of the navy. Without the help of the French, the
duke gained a victory in Southwold Bay over De Ruyter's superior numbers. James, who had
been obliged to change his ships during the battle, next morning ordered the fleet home for
refitting. De Rutyer's attempt to renew the fight ended in his withdrawal in a fog, and the
duke's hopes of prolonging the campaign were destroyed by the revolution in Holland.

This isle was well reformed, and gained renown   55
Whilst the brave Tudors wore th' imperial crown:
But since the ill-got race of Stuarts came,
It has recoiled to popery and shame;
Misguided monarchs, rarely wise or just,
Tainted with pride or with impetuous lust.   60
Should we the Blackheath project here relate,
Or count the various blemishes of state,
Our muse would on the reader's patience grate.
  The poor Priapus king, led by the nose,
Looks as one set up for to scare the crows;   65
Yet in the mimics of the spintrian sport
Outdoes Tiberius and his goatish court.
In love's delights none did him e'er excel,
Not Tereus with his sister Philomel.
As they at Athens, we at Dover meet,   70
And gentlier far the Orleans duchess treat.
What sad event attended on the same
We leave to the report of common fame.
  The senate, which should headstrong princes stay,

55. *well reformed:* alluding to the Reformation.

61. *Blackheath project:* When Charles assembled a general review of all his forces on Black-heath in June 1673, Evelyn records that the forces were thought to be "raised to invade Holland, or as others suspected for another design" (12 June 1673). Marvell defines more clearly the second alternative in *Account of the Growth of Popery:* "The dark hovering of that army so long at Blackheath might not improbably seem the gatherings of a storm to fall upon London."

66. *spintrian:* Pertaining to those that seek out or invent new and monstrous actions of lust. Cf. *spintry:* (1) a species of male prostitute, (2) a place used for unnatural practices.

67. *Tiberius . . . court:* "On retiring to Capri he [Tiberius] made himself a private sport-ing-house, where sexual extravagances were practiced for his secret pleasure. Bevies of girls and young men, whom he had collected from all over the empire as adepts in unnatural practices, and known as *spintriae,* would perform before him in groups of three, to excite his waning passions . . . so that the island was now openly and generally called 'Caprineum,' because of his goatish antics" (Suetonius, *The Twelve Caesars,* trans. Robert Graves [New York: Penguin, 1972]).

69–73. See Ovid, *Metamorphoses* 6. Tereus ravished Philomela, his sister-in-law, and then, lest she should reveal his crime, cut out her tongue (cf. "And gentlier far the Orleans duchess treat"). Grosart quotes a note on this passage from Thomas Cooke's edition of Marvell (1726): "The king's sister, the duchess of Orleans [his beloved Minette], was a woman of great intrigue. In the year 1671 [1670] she and her brother met at Dover. When she returned into France, the duke of Orleans, who had received very strange accounts of her behavior in England, ordered a great dose of sublimate to be given her in a glass of succory water, of which she died in great torment."

74–79. The Long Parliament of Charles II was sometimes called the Pensioner Parliament: "It was a Parliament that gave those vast sums of money, and therefore called the Pensioner Parliament" (Luttrell, *1,* 3). Danby relied on bribing the members to win them over to the court interests. The *black idol* is Charles II.

Let loose the reins, and give the realm away: 75
With lavish hands they constant tributes give
And annual stipends for their guilt receive:
Corrupt with gold, they wives and daughters bring
To the black idol for an offering.
All but religious cheats might justly swear   80
He true vicegerent to old Moloch were.
　　Priests were the first deluders of mankind,
Who with vain faith made all their reason blind;
Not Lucifer himself more proud than they,
And yet persuade the world they must obey;   85
'Gainst avarice and luxury complain,
And practice all the vices they arraign.
Riches and honor they from laymen reap,
And with dull crambo feed the silly sheep.
As Killigrew buffoons his master, they   90
Droll on their God, but a much duller way:
With hocus pocus and their heav'nly sleight
They dazzle both the prince and peasant's sight.
Whoever has an over-zealous wife
Becomes the priest's Amphitrio during life.   95
Who would such men Heav'n's messengers believe
Who from the sacred pulpit dare deceive?
Baal's wretched curates legerdemained it so,
And never durst their tricks aboveboard show.
When our first parents Paradise did grace,   100
The serpent was the prelate of that place;
Fond Eve did for this subtle tempter's sake
From the forbidden tree the pippin take.
His God and Lord this preacher did betray
To have the weaker vessel made his prey.   105

89. *crambo*: crambe, cabbage; applied by Juvenal to any distasteful repetition.

90. *Killigrew*: Tom Killigrew (1612–83). See Pepys, 13 February 1668: "Tom Killigrew hath a fee out of the wardrobe for cap and bells, under the title of the king's fool or jester; and may with privilege revile or jeer anybody, the greatest person, without offense, by privilege of his place." On the death of Sir Henry Herbert in 1673, Killigrew succeeded him as Master of the Revels. He appears to have treated the king with remarkable freedom.

91. *Droll on* : to make sport or fun.

95. *Amphitrio*: Jupiter, captivated by the charms of Amphitryon's wife Alcmena, borrowed the features of Amphitryon while he was gone to war and introduced himself to her as her victorious husband. Here the implication is that the overzealous wife will yield to her priest and make a cuckold of her husband.

98. *Baal*: popery.

101. Margoliouth cites Milton, *Reason of Church Government* (*Prose Works*, ed. Bohn, 2, 450): "For Lucifer, before Adam, was the first prelate angel."

Hence death and sin did human nature blot,
The chiefest blessings Adam's chaplain got.
Thrice wretched they who nature's laws detest
To tread th' fantastic mazes of a priest;
Till native reason's basely forced to yield,   110
And hosts of upstart errors gain the field.
     My Muse presumed a little to digress
And touch the holy function with her verse:
Now to the state she tends again direct
And does on giant Lauderdale reflect.   115
This haughty monster, with his ugly claws,
First tempered poison to destroy our laws;
Declares the council edicts are beyond
The most authentic statutes of the land:
Sets up in Scotland *à la mode de France*,   120
Taxes, excise, and armies does advance.
This Saracen his country's freedom broke
To bring upon our necks the heavier yoke.
This is the savage pimp, without dispute,
First brought his mother for a prostitute.   125
Of all the miscreants ever went to Hell
This villain rampant bears away the bell.
     Now must my Muse deplore the nation's fate,
Like a true lover for a dying mate.
The royal evils so malignant grows,   130
Nothing the dire contagion can oppose.
In our weal-public scarce one thing succeeds,
For one man's weakness a whole nation bleeds,
Ill luck starts up and thrives like evil weeds.
Let Cromwell's ghost smile with contempt to see   135
Old England truckling under slavery.

115. *giant Lauderdale:* Lauderdale, a large red-headed man of violent manners, was a monster in both senses (Margoliouth).

118. *council:* the Privy Council. The Commons hated Lauderdale "because he was alleged to have said that royal edicts were equal to laws and ought to take precedence over them" (Godfrey Davies in *Huntington Library Quarterly* 9 [1945/6]: 314).

120. That is, Lauderdale's government of Scottish affairs was as arbitrary as Louis XIV's rule of France.

125. *mother:* the Covenant, from which Lauderdale was a renegade, or, perhaps, Scotland (Margoliouth).

127. *bears away the bell:* carries off the prize, a golden or silver bell sometimes given as the prize in races and other contests.

130. *The royal evil:* Cf. the king's evil, scrofula.

132. *weal-public:* the general good of the community; public welfare or interest. Hence, the state or body public.

His meager Highness now has got astride,
Does on Britannia as on Churchill ride;
White-livered Danby for his swift jackal
To hunt down 's prey, and hope to master all.   140
Clifford and Hyde before had lost the day;
One hanged himself, the other fled away:
'Twas want of wit and courage made them fail,
But Osborne and the duke must needs prevail.
The duke now vaunts with popish myrmidons: 145
Our fleets, our ports, our cities and, our towns
Are manned by him, or by his holiness.
Bold Irish ruffians to his court address:
This is the colony to plant his knaves,
From hence he picks and culls his murd'ring braves.   150
Here for an ensign's or lieutenant's place
They'll kill a judge or justice of the peace.
At his command Mac will do anything:
He'll burn a city or destroy a king.
From Tiber came th' advice boat monthly home   155
And brought new lessons to the duke from Rome.
Here with cursed practices and counsels dire,
The godly cheat king-would-be did inspire;

138. *Churchill:* Arabella Churchill (1648–1730), sister of the 1st duke of Marlborough, maid of honor to the 1st duchess of York, her brother being page to the duke. She bore four children to the duke of York, one the famous duke of Berwick (1671–1734). She subsequently married a Colonel Godfrey (Margoliouth). Sometime in the years 1678 to 1680 James severed his relations with Arabella Churchill and adopted Catherine Sedley as his mistress (Turner, p. 142).

139. *White-livered:* feeble-spirited, cowardly. *jackal:* The jackal was formerly supposed to go before the lion and hunt his prey for him, hence termed "the lion's provider."

141–42. *Clifford:* Thomas Clifford, 1st Lord Clifford of Chudleigh (1630–73). On 28 November 1672 he was made lord high treasurer, and by letters patent, treasurer of the Exchequer. As a consequence of the Test Act (1673), Clifford, a Catholic in sympathy if not in practice, gave up the treasurership at the beginning of June and left the Privy Council. E. S. de Beer states that despite the suicide rumors, Clifford's death "was almost certainly due to natural causes" (Evelyn, *4*, 21, n. 1). *Hyde:* Edward Hyde, 1st earl of Clarendon (1609–74). The chancellor, alarmed by the rumors of a design to prorogue Parliament and try him by a jury of peers, left England on the night of 29 November 1667.

144. *Osborne:* Danby. *the duke:* York.

146–47. Cf. *Britannia and Raleigh:* "Mac James the Irish pagod does adore: / His French and Teagues command on sea and shore" (125–26).

152. *justice of the peace:* probably a reference to the murder of Sir Edmund Berry Godfrey in October 1678.

153. *Mac:* Irishman.

155. Possibly inspired by the title of Henry Care's Protestant publication, *The Weekly Pacquet of Advice from Rome,* the first number of which appeared 3 December 1678 (Margoliouth).

158. *godly cheat:* The Vatican, the "Scarlet Whore" of Babylon (line 171). *king-would-be:* the duke of York.

Tells him the holy church demands his aid,
Heav'n had him chieftain of Great Britain made;   160
Bid him be bold, all dangers to defy,
His brother, sneaking heretic, shall die.
A priest shall do it, from whose sacred stroke
All England straight shall fall beneath his yoke.
God did renounce him and his cause disown,   165
And in his stead had placed him on his throne.
From Saul the land of promise thus was rent,
And Jesse's son placed in the government.
The Holy Scripture vindicates his cause,
And monarchs are above all human laws.   170
Thus said the Scarlet Whore to her gallant,
Who straight designed his brother to supplant.
Fiends of ambition here his soul possessed,
And thirst of empire calentured his breast.
Hence ruin and destruction had ensued,   175
And all the people been in blood imbrued,
Had not Almighty Providence drawn near,
And stopped his malice in its full career.
 Be wise, ye sons of men, tempt God no more
To give you kings in 's wrath to vex you sore: 180
If a king's brother can such mischief bring,
Then how much greater mischief as a king?

167–68. "And as Samuel turned to go away, he [Saul] laid hold upon the skirt of his mantle, and it rent. And Samuel said unto him, The Lord hath rent the kingdom of Israel from thee this day, and hath given it to a neighbor of thine, that is better than thou" (1 Sam. 15:27–28).

168. *Jesse's son:* David.

174. *calentured:* infected with the calenture—fired.

177–78. Probably an allusion to the discovery of the Popish Plot by Titus Oates, the "savior of the nation."

179–80. Cf. 1 Sam. 8, in which Samuel warns the Israelites what a tyrant the king they desire will prove to be, but they refuse to heed his words. See *An Allusion* in *Poems on Affairs of State, From 1640 to this Present Year 1704:*

> When Israel first provoked the living Lord,
> He scourged their sin with famine, plague and sword.
> Still they rebelled; the God in's wrath did fling
> No thunderbolt among them, but a king.
> A James-like king was Heav'n's severest rod,
> The utmost vengeance of an angry God.
> God in his wrath sent Saul to punish Jewry,
> And James to England in a greater fury:
> For Saul in sin was no more like our James,
> Than little Jordan can compare to Thames.

JOHN OLDHAM

The Careless Good Fellow
(1680)

Although the two broadside versions of the following poem are anonymous and the piece is not found in John Oldham's manuscript workbook (Bod. MS Rawl. poet. 123), it is included in his *Poems and Translations, 1683,* and it has since been ascribed to him on that evidence alone (it has also been attributed to Tom Brown, in whose *Remains,* 1720, it was printed). Harold F. Brooks, after dismissing the ascription to Brown in a convincing argument, strongly supports Oldham's claim.

Luttrell inscribed his copy of the broadside "1ᵈ 14 July 1680." There is another broadside version, which J. W. Ebsworth prints in *Roxburghe Ballads* (Hertford, 1871–99), 4, 645–47. Here Oldham's seven verses are clumsily altered in many places, and five spurious verses are added. The authentic version is printed with music (entitled "The Claret Bottle," with no author's or composer's name given) in John Playford's *Choice Airs and Songs,* Book III (1681).

As in his *Satire against Virtue, Supposed to Be Spoken by a Court-Hector* (Rochester), Oldham here adopts a persona (similar to that of the king in *A New Ballad*) and puts the traditional drinking song to highly ironic use. He must have counted on the shocking effect such libertine lines would have in that time of national emergency. For a discussion of this poem and of Oldham's attitude toward Rochester, see Vieth, pp. 184–88.

THE CARELESS GOOD FELLOW

1.

A pox of this fooling and plotting of late,
What a pother and stir has it kept in the state!
Let the rabble run mad with suspicions and fears;
Let them scuffle and jar till they go by the ears.
Their grievances never shall trouble my pate,   5
So I can enjoy my dear bottle at quiet.

4. *go by the ears:* be at variance (said of animals fighting).

2.

What coxcombs were those who would barter their ease
And their necks for a toy, a thin wafer and mass!
At old Tyburn they never had needed to swing
Had they been but true subjects to drink and their king.   10
A friend and a bottle is all my design;
He has no room for treason that's top-full of wine.

3.

I mind not the members and makers of laws,
Let them sit or prorogue as His Majesty please;
Let them damn us to woollen—I'll never repine   15
At my lodging when dead, so alive I have wine.
Yet oft in my drink I can hardly forbear
To curse them for making my claret so dear.

4.

I mind not grave asses who idly debate
About right and succession, the trifles of state;
We've got a good king already, and he deserves laughter   20
That will trouble his head with who shall come after.
Come, here's to his health, and I wish he may be
As free from all care and all trouble as we.

5.

What care I how leagues with the Hollander go,   25
Or intrigues betwixt Sidney and Monsieur d'Avaux?
What concerns it my drinking if Cassel be sold,

15. *Let . . . woollen:* To promote the use of English wool, Parliament passed acts that shrouds should be made of woollen only (Ogg, *Charles II, 1,* 72).

18. Among the sources of revenue taxed in Charles's reign were the wine licenses.

19–20. Cf. Rochester, *On the Women about Town:* "Too long the wise Commons have been in debate / 'Bout money and conscience, those trifles of state" (1–2).

25. Early in 1680 both the king and Sunderland made overtures to Holland, Spain, and the emperor.

26. *Sidney:* Henry Sidney (1641–1704). In June 1679 Sidney was appointed envoy to The Hague. *Monsieur d'Avaux:* Jean-Antoine de Mesmes, comte d'Avaux (1640–1709), French ambassador to The Hague.

27. *Cassel:* Possibly Cassel in Flanders, near St. Omer. The French had defeated William of Orange there in 1677. However, it could be Casale (Cassal) in northern Italy, which Louis XIV purchased from the duke of Mantua in 1681. In the Treaty of Nijmwegen, Spain ceded to France (17 September 1678) St. Omer and other towns near Cassel such as Ypres and Poperingen, but I have not been able to discover whether Cassel was among the ceded towns. It might have fallen under the jurisdiction of Louis XIV's Chambers of Reunion— French courts of claims, established in 1680, with power to investigate and decide what dependencies had at any time belonged to the territories and towns which had been ceded

If the conqueror take it by storming or gold?
Good Bordeaux alone is the place that I mind,
And when the fleet's coming I pray for a wind.   30

6.

The Bully of France, that aspires to renown
By dull cutting of throats and vent'ring his own,
Let him fight and be damned, and make matches and treat
To afford the newsmongers and coffeehouse chat.
He's but a brave wretch, while I am more free,   35
More safe, and a thousand times happier than he.

7.

Come he, or the pope, or the devil to boot,
Or come faggot and stake, I care not a groat;
Never think that in Smithfield I porters will heat:
No, I swear, Mr. Foxe, pray excuse me for that!   40
I'll drink in defiance of gibbet and halter,
This is the profession that never will alter.

---

to France by the last four treaties of peace. Louis XIV, following a policy of judicial aggression, executed with his troops the decisions of his tribunals.

31. *The Bully of France:* Louis XIV.

31–32. Cf. *The Earl of Rochester's Verses for Which He Was Banished:*

> Him no ambition moves to get renown
> Like the French fool who wanders up and down,
> Starving his soldiers, hazarding his crown.   [5–7]

39. *Smithfield:* An open space outside the northwest walls of the City of London where heretics were burnt in the 16th century.

40. *Mr. Foxe:* John Foxe (1516–87), martyrologist. His *Book of Martyrs* was widely read at this time.

A New Ballad
(1679)

A New Ballad, in which Charles II is made to speak like a libertine tyrant, bears a close resemblance in style and attitude to Stephen College's *A Raree Show.* The latter is to the tune of "I am a senseless thing" (the first line of *A New Ballad),* which W. Chappell (*Popular Music of the Olden Time* [London, 1859]) does not list as a tune (he does cite *A New Ballad* under the tune of *The Duke of Norfolk).* MS BM Harleian 7319 attributes *A New Ballad* to College. The copy in the Osborn collection is dated 28 February 1679.

A New Ballad, to an Old Tune, Called, I Am the Duke of Norfolk, etc.

1.

I am a senseless thing, with a hey, with a hey,
  Men call me a king, with a ho;
    To my luxury and ease
    They brought me o'er the seas,
  With a hey tronny nonny nonny no.   5

2.

I melt away their treasure, with a hey, with a hey,
  And swive at my pleasure, with a ho;
    Their women and their coin
    Are now become all mine,
  With a hey tronny nonny nonny no.   10

3.

With a court and a stage, with a hey, with a hey,
  I corrupted the age, with a ho;
    The nation once were men
    But now are slaves again,
  With a hey tronny nonny nonny no .   15

4.

Let the bankers break, with a hey, with a hey,
    And the City sneak, with a ho;
        I have got a pack of knaves
        Shall ride the dull jades,
    With a hey tronny nonny nonny no.   20

5.

Let the Commons search for plots, with a hey, with a hey,
    And the lords sit like sots, with a ho;
        If my brother and my whore
        Say the word, they're no more,
    With a hey tronny nonny nonny no.   25

6.

They pulled my army down, with a hey, with a hey,
    And so they would my crown, with a ho;
        But to prevent that chance
        I've sold it all to France,
    With a hey tronny nonny nonny no.   30

7.

And whilst they all give ear, with a hey, with a hey,
    To what Oates and Bedloe swear, with a ho;
        With mirth I burst my gall
        To see the rascals sham 'em all,
    With a hey tronny nonny nonny no.   35

8.

'Twas a blast of royal breath, with a hey, with a hey,
    Gave Godfrey his death, with a ho;
        'Twas contrived by the elf

16. *Let . . . break:* an allusion to the stop of the Exchequer. Most of the "orders of re-payment" on the Exchequer were in the hands of the bankers and goldsmiths. In January 1672 Charles issued letters patent suspending for one year all payments on assignations in the Exchequer. The stop was renewed a year later, and its real effect was to make available for government needs the proceeds of the takes as they came in, while leaving unsatisfied the claims due on the paper orders of loan issued in accordance with the scheme of 1665. The loss, amounting to just over a million pounds, fell mainly on the bankers, who in 1674 were given two years' interest on their capital; a more permanent provision was that made in 1677–79, when interest was paid to them by a scheme of annuities (Ogg, *Charles II, 2,* 448–49).

26. *They . . . down:* The variant "They would have my army down" is more accurate if the poem is dated February 1679.

My brother and myself,
With a hey tronny nonny nonny no.   40

9.

My ministers of state, with a hey, with a hey,
  Whom I damn to make great, with a ho;
    Let 'em use their wisest skill,
    I'm true Sir Martin still,
  With a hey tronny nonny nonny no.   45

10.

And now to let you see, with a hey, with a hey,
  What miracles there can be, with a ho;
    The head of the church
    Left the body in the lurch,
  With a hey tronny nonny nonny no.   50

11.

Damn the Good Old Cause, with a hey, with a hey,
  Religion and its laws, with a ho;
    I scorn to sway
    By an English way,
  With a hey tronny nonny nonny no.   55

12.

Let the gentry groan, with a hey, with a hey,
  With the weight of my throne, with a ho;
    I care not a straw
    For the old fop law,
  With a hey tronny nonny nonny no.   60

13.

While the French take towns, with a hey, with a hey.
  And the seamen get wounds, with a ho;
    I have a French arse

---

44. *Sir Martin:* a reference to Dryden's comedy *Sir Martin Mar-all,* 1668. Cibber in his *Apology* describes Sir Martin as one "who is always committing blunders to the prejudice of his own interest [cf. "I am a senseless thing"]. He vainly proceeded upon his own head and was afterwards afraid to look his governing servant and counsellor in the face."

51. *Good Old Cause:* in commonwealth times the Puritan "cause." At this time it was frequently used to designate the design of the extreme Whigs to establish a commonwealth in England.

For my unruly tarse,
With a hey tronny nonny nonny no.   65

14.

And though my father like a fool, with a hey, with a hey,
Lost his life to save his soul, with a ho;
I'll not quit my present love
For a martyr's place above,
With a hey tronny nonny nonny no.   70

A Panegyric
(1681)

The following satire on Nell Gwynne (1650–87) is dated 1681 in MS BM
Harleian 7319.

A PANEGYRIC

Of a great heroine I mean to tell,
And by what just degrees her titles swell,
To Mrs. Nelly grown from cinder Nell.
Much did she suffer first, on bulk and stage,
From the black guard and bullies of the age;   5
Much more her growing virtue did sustain
While dear Charles Hart and Buckhurst sued in vain;
In vain they sued—cursed be the envious tongue
That her undoubted chastity would wrong!
For should we Fame believe, we then might say   10
That thousands lay with her as well as they.
But, Fame, thou liest, for her prophetic mind
Foresaw her greatness fate had well designed;
And her ambition chose to be before
A virtuous countess an imperial whore.   15
E'en in her native dirt her soul was high
And did at crowns and shining monarchs fly;
E'en while she cinders raked her swelling breast

3. *cinder Nell*: Nell Gwynne was born in Coal Yard, Drury Lane, according to one account.
4. *bulk*: a framework projecting from the front of a shop, a stall.
5. *black guard*: the vagabond, loafing, or criminal class of a community, the blackguardry.
7. *Charles Hart*: the actor to whom Nell owed her theatrical training. Lord *Buckhurst* is
Charles Sackville, 6th earl of Dorset and earl of Middlesex (1638–1706). In 1667 he took Nell
Gwynne (who is said to have called him her Charles I) under his protection. He and Nell
"kept merry house at Epsom" during 1667, but about Michaelmas 1668 Nell became the
king's mistress, and Dorset was sent to France on a complimentary mission to get him out of
the way.

With thoughts of glorious whoredom was possessed;
Still did she dream (nor could her birth withstand)   20
Of dangling scepters in her dirty hand.
But first the basket her fair arm did suit,
Laden with pippins and Hesperian fruit;
This first step raised, to th' wond'ring pit she sold
The lovely fruit, smiling with streaks of gold.   25
Fate now for her did its whole force engage,
And from the pit she's mounted to the stage.
There in full luster did her glories shine
And, long eclipsed, spread forth their light divine.
There Hart's and Rowley's soul she did ensnare,   30
And made a king the rival to a play'r:
The king o'ercomes, and to the royal bed
The dunghill's offspring is in triumph led.
Nor let th' envious her first rags object
To her that's now in tawdry gayness decked: 35
Her merit does from this much greater show,
Mounting so high that took her rise so low.
Less famed that Nelly was whose cuckold's rage
In ten years' wars did half the world engage.
She's now the darling strumpet of the crowd,   40
Forgets her state, and talks to them aloud;
Lays by her greatness and descends to prate
With those 'bove whom she's raised by wond'rous fate.
True to th' Protestant interest and cause,
True to th' established government and laws;   45
The choice delight of the whole mobile,
Scarce Monmouth's self is more beloved than she.
Was this the cause that did their quarrel move,
That both are rivals in the people's love?

22. *But first the basket:* Nell's first public occupation was that of a vendor of oranges in the
Theatre Royal.
24. *pit:* the place assigned during the Restoration to the orange-women.
27. A certain Robert Duncan, Dongan, or Dungan, is said to have promoted her from the
pit to the stage.
46. A portion of her popularity while mistress to the king is attributable to the aversion
inspired by her rival, the duchess of Portsmouth. When mobbed at Oxford in mistake for
Portsmouth, Nell put her head out of the window and said: "Pray, good people, be civil;
I am the Protestant whore." *mobile:* Mob (shortened form of *mobile vulgus*, the movable or
excitable crowd).
48. *their quarrel:* I can find no evidence of a quarrel between Monmouth and Nell. In
December of 1679, when Monmouth returned unbidden from his exile, Nell pleaded with
the king to grant him an audience, "saying he had grown pale, wan, lean and long-visaged,
merely because he was in disfavor" (D'Oyley, p. 149).

No, 'twas her matchless loyalty alone   50
That bid Prince Perkin pack up and be gone:
"Ill-bred thou art," says prince. Nell does reply,
"Was Mrs. Barlow better bred than I?"
Thus sneaked away the nephew overcome,
By's aunt-in-law's severer wit struck dumb.   55
   Her virtue, loy'lty, wit, and noble mind
In the foregoing dogg'rel you may find;
Now for her piety one touch, and then
To rhymer I'll resign my Muse and pen.
'Twas this that raised her charity so high   60
To visit those that did in durance lie.
From Oxford prisons many did she free,
There died her father and there gloried she
In giving others life and liberty;
So pious a remembrance still she bore   65
E'en to the fetters that her father wore.
Nor was her mother's funeral less her care,
No cost, no velvet did the daughter spare.
Fine gilded scutcheons did the hearse enrich
To celebrate this martyr of the ditch.   70
Burnt brandy did in flaming brimmers flow,
Drunk at her funeral, while her well-pleased shade
Rejoiced e'en in the sober fields below
At all the drunkenness her death had made.
Was ever child with such a mother blessed?   75
Or ever mother such a child possessed?
Nor must her cousin be forgot, preferred
From many years' command in the black guard
To be an ensign—
Whose tattered colors well do represent   80
His first estate i'th' ragged regiment.

53. *Mrs. Barlow:* alias Lucy Walter, Monmouth's mother.

55. *his aunt-in-law:* "Aunt" can mean prostitute or procuress.

63. *her father:* Nell's father, said to have been called James, was a dilapidated soldier or fruiterer in Drury Lane. Among her requests to her son in her will (1687) was one "that he would lay out twenty pounds yearly for the releasing of poor debtors out of prison." A. I. Besant mentions the popular belief that her father died in an Oxford prison (*Nell Gwynne* [London, 1924], p. 277).

67–70. Luttrell notes in July 1679: "About this time Mrs. Gwynne, mother to madam Ellen Gwynne, being in drink, was drowned in a ditch near Westminster" (*1,* 18). Evelyn says she was an "applewoman" (*4,* 392).

77. *her cousin:* unidentified.

78. *black guard:* here probably the servants and camp-followers of an army; the rabble of irregular hangers-on and followers.

Thus we in short have all the virtues seen
Of the incomparable Madam Gwynne,
Nor wonder others are not with her shown:
She who no equal has must be alone.   85

The Obscured Prince, or
The Black Box Boxed
(1680)

Luttrell writes in April 1680: "There has been for some time a flying rumor spread abroad of a black box found, wherein was contained a writing importing a marriage or contract of marriage between His Majesty and the duke of Monmouth's mother; which His Majesty hath been pleased to take notice of, and sent for Sir Gilbert Gerard to the council, who was examined about the same (being the person who was reported to have the same), but he denied on oath his having any such thing, or having ever seen it; and there is strict inquiry made to find out who was the first broacher of this scandalous lie: 'tis thought to be a popish story raised to scandalize His Majesty and the duke. And since there came out a pamphlet entitled *A Letter to a Person of Quality Concerning the Black Box*, which endeavors maliciously to prove the said marriage" (*1*, 42–43).

"In a fugitive duodecimo tract, which appears to have come from the same press [of Robert Ferguson] entitled *The Perplexed Prince* [1682?], the marriage between Charles and Lucy Walter is distinctly asserted under the thin disguise of assumed names and a romantic narrative" (*Somers' Tracts, 8,* 188). The poem is dated 19 August 1680 in BM Sloane 655.

THE OBSCURED PRINCE, OR
THE BLACK BOX BOXED

Oh, heavens! the weakness of my unkind father!
Better some peasant had begot me rather:
He would not black himself, his wife defame,
And after marriage bastard me proclaim;
Through panic fear thus in Perillus roar   5

1. *unkind:* unnatural.
4. "The 8th [June 1680] came out His Majesty's declaration touching the duke of Monmouth, whereby His Majesty does declare he never was married nor gave any contract to any woman whatsoever but to his now wife, Queen Catherine" (Luttrell, *1*, 46).
5. *Perillus roar:* Perillus made for Phalaris, tyrant of Agrigentum, a brazen bull in which

To gratify a brother or a whore;
Honor disclaim, by fools and knaves beguiled,
Nay, would it pass, deny me for his child;
Destroy my right 'gainst God and nature's laws
To prop the falling of their tott'ring cause;   10
Pursue a chase more of the goose than fox
Called the shammed story of the blackened box;
Deny the truth long in the ashes hid,
Disowning now what Bishop Fuller did;
How he performed the marriage office ere   15
You could enjoy my wrongéd mother dear.
All other terms she scornéd with her soul,
Though means were used with her both fair and foul:
Witness yourself what Mother Queen did do
Besides the offers that were made by you.   20
When mighty passions brought you down so ill,
Your grief befooled the French physician's skill,
And at grim death's approaches out did cry,
"Oh! let me marry with her, or I die."
'Twas then she yielded and became your wife: 25
Sir, this is truth! I'll prove it with my life.
But you may save the trouble, if you please:
Speak like yourself, and all the kingdom ease.
You are my father, sir; I'll duty pay
Unto yourself until your dying day.   30
But when that falls (which God foreslow), sir, I
Will take the name of royal majesty,

---

criminals were put to death by a fire lit under the beast's belly, so that their cries were like the bellowing of a bull. Phalaris made the first experiment of it on its inventor.

5–6. Robert Ferguson in *A Letter to a Person of Honor Concerning the King's Disavowing His Having Been Married to the Duke of Monmouth's Mother* (*Somers Tracts, 8*, 203), states that the king "may have been influenced and over-awed [by York] to make the late appeal and protestation . . . no less than a dread of losing his life, as well as three kingdoms, hath necessitated him to this which he hath now done." By declaring Monmouth illegitimate, Charles might have gratified the duchess of Portsmouth, who perhaps had hopes that her son by the king, the duke of Richmond, might become heir to the throne.

14. "And it is not more surprising, if there had been no such marriage, that Dr. Fuller, late bishop of Lincoln should so often, and in *verbo sacerdotis*, declare to diverse worthy persons that he married them" (*A Letter to a Person of Honor* . . ., in *Somers' Tracts, 8*, 200).

19–24. "So some of us can remember, how, through immoderate love to her, being reduced to a condition that his life was despaired of, and the late queen his mother receiving intelligence of his disease and the cause of it, she consented to his espousing of her, rather than that he should consume and perish in his otherwise unquenchable flames" (*A Letter to a Person of Honor* . . ., in *Somers' Tracts, 8*, 200).

31. *foreslow:* forestall

Without offense to any, as my due,
Giv'n me by God, by nature, sir, and you.
Then (if I live) the wrongéd world shall know   35
In wedlock I was got, and born in't too;
That I am heir undoubted to the crown,
And will enjoy it when you lay it down,
In spite of Papists, mauger all their hate;
Their hope shall find I am legitimate.   40
England, stand by me with your utmost breaths:
I'll ruin Rome, or die ten thousand deaths,
And make France tremble also, ere I've done;
Destroy those plagues that murder Christendom
That true religion in the land may flow,   45
Not forms and int'rest which are called so;
And should I ever alter what I say,
Let God forsake me on my dying day.

   Enough, brave prince we'll take your royal word,
And will defend you by the dint of sword   50
'Gainst all opposers, whosoe'er they are.
We'll stand or fall, and in your fortunes share;
And after Charles, who wrongs you of your crown,
Shall cut a million of true English down.

     Honi soit qui mal y pense.

CHARLES SACKVILLE, EARL OF DORSET

On the Young Statesmen
(1680)

For a discussion of the date and authorship of this poem see the article by Brice Harris in *Times Literary Supplement*, 4 April 1935, pp. 227–28.

ON THE YOUNG STATESMEN

1.

Clarendon had law and sense,
  Clifford was fierce and brave,
Bennet's grave look was a pretense,
And Danby's matchless impudence
  Helped to support the knave.   5

2.

But Sunderland, Godolphin, Lory
  Turn politics to jests
And will appear such chits in story
To be repeated like John Dory,
  When fiddlers sing at feasts.   10

1. *Clarendon:* Edward Hyde, 1st earl of Clarendon (1609–74). As a statesman, Clarendon's consistency and integrity were conspicuous through many vicissitudes and much corruption. Cf. *Third Advice,* 249–52 n.

2. *Clifford:* Thomas Clifford, 1st Lord Clifford of Chudleigh (1630–73). Pepys writes of him on 17 September 1666: "a very fine gentleman, and much set by at court for his activity in going to sea, and stoutness everywhere, and stirring up and down." On 6 March 1669 Pepys refers to "the rudeness of his tongue and passions when angry." Cf. *An Historical Poem,* 141–42 n.

3. *Bennet:* Henry Bennet, earl of Arlington (1618–85). In 1658 Bennet was sent as Charles II's agent to Madrid where he gained a formality of manner that was a common subject of ridicule.

4. *Danby:* For the five years between 1673 and 1678, during which Danby remained lord treasurer, the government lay mainly in his hands. Cf. *Satire on Old Rowley,* 63 n.

9. *John Dory:* An old popular song (printed 1609) about John Dory, captain of a French privateer.

3.

Protect us, mighty Providence,
   What would these madmen have?
First, they would bribe us without pence,
Deceive us without common sense,
   And without pow'r enslave.   15

4.

Shall freeborn men in humble awe
   Submit to servile shame;
Who from consent and custom draw
The same right to be ruled by law
   Which kings pretend to reign?   20

5.

The duke shall wield his conqu'ring sword,
   The chanc'llor make a speech,
The king shall pass his honest word,
The pawned revenue sums afford—
   And then come kiss my breech!   25

6.

So have I seen a king at chess
   (His rooks and knights withdrawn,
His queen and·bishops in distress)
Shifting about, grow less and less,
   With here and there a pawn.   30

21. An allusion to the duke of York's reputation for valor, gained in the Dutch wars.

22. *chanc'llor:* Heneage Finch, 1st earl of Nottingham (1621–82). He was noted for his florid speeches. Cf. the epithet "Polytropos" in *An Essay upon Satire,* 145.

26–30. "Thomas Bruce draws a striking picture of the change which for the time had come over the court, of its comparative melancholy and solitude. He was, he says, put in mind of some manuscript verses that were going about then [quotes this stanza]" (Osmund Airy, *Charles II* [London, 1904], p. 370).

A Ballad, November 1680.
Made upon Casting the Bill against the Duke of York
out of the House of Lords
(1680)

"The second Exclusion Bill passed the Commons on 11 November 1680 and was taken to the Lords on 15 November by Lord Russell, accompanied by a procession composed of M.P.s, with the lord mayor and aldermen of the City of London. Essex and Shaftesbury spoke vehemently for the bill, and the debate was prolonged late into the night, the king and members of the Commons attending as spectators. For seven hours a forensic duel was maintained between Shaftesbury and Halifax, the latter answering his opponents sixteen times, and eventually winning the day by his persistence and eloquence. In these speeches he cited the duke of York's credit in Ireland and with the fleet; he emphasized the danger of civil war and the efficacy of limitations [see note on line 53]. As the night wore on, the tension became more extreme; when at last it was clear that Halifax had won over the waverers, several peers drew their swords, while others clustered round the orator to preserve him from violence. The Lords rejected the bill by 63 to 30" (Ogg, *Charles, II 2*, 603).

"On the day the Commons were discussing the king's address and voting for exclusion he [Monmouth] and other lords were entertained by fifty military officers belonging to the hamlets beyond the Tower. After a very 'noble entertainment' a well-dressed person was brought in who sang a new ballad about 'the bishops who threw out the bill' [perhaps the following ballad]. It was the vote of the bishops that had sealed the fate of the Exclusion Bill in the Lords, and the affair was not at all relished at court" (Brown, *Shaftesbury*, p. 276).

A Ballad, November 1680.
Made upon Casting the Bill against the Duke of York out of the House of Lords

1.

The grave House of Commons, by hook or by crook,
Resolved to root out both the pope and the duke;
But let 'em move, let 'em vote, let 'em pass what they will,
The bishops, the bishops will throw out the bill.

2.

There were Harbord and Winnington, Hampden and Birch   5
Did verily think to establish the church;
But now they have found it is past all their skill,
For the bishops, the bishops have thrown out the bill.

3.

Sir William endeavored as much as he could
To show that the bill was for the duke's good,   10

5. *Harbord:* William Harbord (1635?–92) sat in the Parliaments of 1680 and 1681 as member for Launceston (Cornwall) and was violently against popery, against the succession of the duke of York, and against Tory abhorrers. He attacked Halifax as responsible for the dissolution of the Parliament of 1679 and urged his removal from the king's councils. He promoted the scheme for a Protestant association, rejected all compromises, and persisted in demanding the acceptance of the Exclusion Bill. *Winnington:* Sir Francis Winnington (1634–1700), lawyer. By the king's command he was returned to Parliament for the borough of Windsor on 19 February 1677. He supported the Exclusion Bill in 1678, and for this vote was deprived in January 1679 of the office of solicitor general, and at the dissolution in that month lost his seat at Windsor. He represented the city of Worcester in the last three Parliaments of Charles II. He was one of the committee who drew up the Exclusion Bill in 1679. *Hampden:* Richard Hampden (1631–95), second son of John Hampden. He first became prominent in politics by his zealous advocacy of the Exclusion Bill and a full investigation into the Popish Plot. On 11 May 1679 he moved for a bill to exclude the duke of York by name from the crown. "To tie a popish successor with laws for the preservation of the Protestant religion was," he said, "binding Samson with withes." He declared the securities offered by the king to be entirely illusory, and refused to the last to accept any compromises (Grey, 7, 150–51, 243–44, 421). Hampden was one of the committee who drew up the bill and was teller for the yeas in the division. *Birch:* John Birch (1616–19), Presbyterian colonel during the civil war. He was one of the committee who drew up the bill.

9. *Sir William:* Sir William Jones, as written in eight of the MSS and in a marginal note in the copy text. Sir William (1631–82) was a pronounced enemy of the court. He was returned to the House of Commons as member for Plymouth on 3 November 1680 and entered Parliament with "the fame of being the greatest lawyer in England and a very wise man." The passage of the Exclusion Bill through the Commons was generally ascribed to his strenuous efforts.

For that but disinherits the man we would kill,
Yet the bishops, the bishops have thrown out the bill.

4.

Tom Wharton, who stood behind Sir Nicholas Carew
To confront, as he thought, the plenipotentiary,
Little dreamt that when rudely he had rail'd out his fill   15
The bishops, the bishops would have thrown out the bill.

5.

There is little reason that dull six and twenty
Should oppose the whole *nemine contradicente,*
And whate'er they bring forth in its infancy kill,
Whilst the bishops, the bishops shall throw out the bill.   20

6.

The wise earl of Shaftesbury, Monmouth and Grey,

13. *Tom Wharton:* Thomas Wharton, 1st marquis of Wharton (1648–1715). In 1679 Wharton was returned for Buckinghamshire along with Richard Hampden. His interest in politics is not marked until this time, when he joined his friends Lords Russell, Cavendish, and Colchester in backing the Exclusion Bill. He voted for the bill in 1680 and was one of the members who carried it up to the House of Lords on 15 November. In 1679 he did not speak in the Commons against the succession of the duke of York, and it was commonly supposed that, his father being a Presbyterian, he was afraid of incurring the reproach of fanaticism. To judge from Grey, apparently he refrained from speaking during the 1680 debate as well. A Mr. Goodwin Wharton did speak for the Exclusion Bill on 11 November. A footnote identifies him as "a younger son of Lord Wharton, and uncle to the late duke" (Grey, 7, 448). *Carew:* Sir Nicholas sat for Gatton (Surrey) in the 1679 Parliament. He was one of the committee who drew up the bill (*CJ, 9,* 620)·. For his speeches favoring exclusion in 1680 see Grey, *7,* 396, 427.

14. *plenipotentiary:* The copy text alone glosses "Jenkins." This is Sir Leoline Jenkins (1623–85). He was sworn of the Privy Council on 11 February 1680 and succeeded Henry Coventry as secretary of state on 26 April. In this capacity he led the opposition to the bills for excluding the duke of York from the succession. For his speeches against the bill in 1680 see Grey, *7,* 403, 418–20, 425–26, 446–48. The following note from Burnet is found on page 418 of Grey: "Jenkins . . . was the chief manager for the court [cf. *plenipotentiary*]. He was suspected of leaning to popery, though very unjustly; but he was set on every punctilio of the Church of England to superstition and was a great asserter of the divine right of monarchy and was for carrying the prerogative high. All his speeches and arguments against the Exclusion were heard with indignation."

17. *six and twenty:* There were two archbishops and twenty-four bishops in England (Chamberlayne, *Angliae Notitia,* 1679, p. 215). However, only fourteen of the bishops were present at this session, all of whom voted against the bill.

18. *nemine contradicente:* with no one contradicting.

21–23. Among the lords who protested against the rejection of the bill were the following prominent Whigs: Shaftesbury, Monmouth, Grey of Werk, Essex (Arthur Capel, earl of Essex), Howard (William Howard, 3d Baron Howard of Escrick). There were twenty more lords who entered their dissents, including the lord privy seal, Anglesey (Arthur Annesley,

Lord Essex, Lord Howard, Lords *et cetera,*
Though they had drawn in too the lord privy seal,
Yet the bishops, the bishops would throw out the bill.

7.

Old Rowley was there to solicit the cause   25
Against his own life, the church and the laws;
Yet he might have lived safely against his own will,
Had the bishops, the bishops not thrown out the bill.

8.

His Highness for fear to Scotland was gone
The Cov'nant to take and be crown'd at Scone;   30
But now he may e'en return home if he will,
For the bishops, the bishops have thrown out the bill.

9.

Had he known this before, or some of his gang,
He had saved his guineas to Sir John Wetwang,
And might at St. James's have plotted his fill,   35
Since the bishops, the bishops have thrown out the bill.

10.

Had not the bishops been suffered in House for to sit,
He had been like his grandfather Jemmy besh—;
But now he is as safe as a thief in a mill,
For the bishops, the bishops have thrown out the bill.   40

1st earl of Anglesey). Anglesey had interceded for the earl of Stafford, though convinced of
his guilt, and this line of action brought upon him, on 20 October 1680, an accusation by
Dangerfield, and he was attacked by Sir William Jones in the House of Commons. Lingard
suggests that Anglesey followed the Whig leaders in protesting the rejection of the bill partly
because he was "intimidated by the evidence of Dangerfield" (*History of England, 9,* 480).
For the list of dissenting lords see *LJ, 13,* 666.

25. *Rowley:* Charles II.

29. When in August 1680 the king gave way to the cry for a Parliament, James was obliged
again to withdraw to Scotland (21 October), having in vain sought to obtain from the king a
pardon safeguarding him against the consequences of impeachment.

30. *cov'nant to take:* Catholic James will turn Presbyterian. *Scone:* Charles II was crowned
there in 1651.

34. Sir John Wetwang (d. 1684) was, perhaps, as the line suggests, captain of the ship in
which James sailed to Scotland in October.

37–38. Mr. Smith: "After he [College] came up again [from the Oxford Parliament],
I met him another time, and he told me he went down in expectation of some sport; but Old
Rowley was afraid, like his grandfather Jamy, and so ran away like to beshit himself" (*Trial
of Stephen College,* 1681, p. 27).

39. *safe . . . mill:* very safe.

11.

Father Patrick, who has a long banishment suffered,
I wish he were now made abbot of Rufford;
And sure the Lord Halifax can't take it ill,
Since he joined with the bishops to throw out the bill.

12.

In the days of Queen Bess the bishops did own   45
The truths of the gospel and rights of the crown;
But now they and the pope do piss in a quill,
And to bring in the mass have thrown out the bill.

13.

Fat Dolben loves Sodom for fear of a clap,
As Sancroft loves Rome in hopes of a cap;   50
But ere it be long, I hope on Tower Hill
To see their jolt-heads left in pawn for the bill.

14.

Now the best of expedients the lords can propose

41. *Father Patrick:* a Roman Catholic priest and member of the queen's court who appears frequently in anti-Catholic lampoons. See *A Dialogue between the Two Horses* in *POAS,* Yale, *1,* 281: "Father Patrick's disciple [the duke of York] will make England smart" (146). In his *Marvell* (*1,* 323) Margoliouth notes that Father Patrick was "named in the House of Commons 15 March 1673, with Lord Arundell of Wardour and Colonel Richard Talbot, as particularly active on behalf of Roman Catholics in Ireland, and unfit to be near the king. He was ordered to leave England and was gone by 3 October 1673 but had returned before August 1674; he was abroad in 1679."

42. *Rufford:* Rufford Abbey, the old seat of the Savile (Halifax) family in Sherwood Forest. About Christmas 1680 Lord Halifax went down to Rufford and vainly sought peace of mind "in philosophic gardening."

47. *piss in a quill:* agree. The *OED* cites North's *Examen:* "So strangely did Papist and fanatic, or the anticourt party, piss in a quill; agreeing in all things that tended to create troubles and disturbances."

49. John Dolben (1625–86), bishop of Rochester (1666) and dean of Westminster; later archbishop of York (1683–86). In an unpublished lampoon Dolben is accused of sodomy with Lord Mohun. Dolben and Sancroft were among the fourteen bishops present in the House of Lords on 15 November.

50. William Sancroft (1617–93), archbishop of Canterbury (1678). Gossip said that he was "set up by the duke of York against London [Henry Compton, bishop of London], and York put on by the Papists" (Wood, *Life and Times, 2,* 397).

52. *jolt-heads:* blockheads.

53. *expedients:* an allusion to the policy of expedients, or limitations to be put on a Catholic successor, as a substitute for total exclusion.

Our church to preserve and ruin our foes,
Is not to let lawn-sleeves our Parliaments fill,   55
But to throw out the bishops who threw out the bill.

55. *lawn-sleeves:* bishops.

JOHN AYLOFFE

Oceana and Britannia
(1681)

There are three literary antecedents for this poem. In its title and use of allegory it resembles Ayloffe's earlier verse satire, *Britannia and Raleigh*. Evidence for his authorship of this poem is presented in my article "Satire and Sedition: The Life and Work of John Ayloffe," *Huntington Library Quarterly* 29 (1966): 255–73. The second source is James Harrington's *Oceana* (1656), which Hume called the "only valuable model of a commonwealth" extant. The third literary connection is a political treatise by a friend of Harrington's: Henry Neville's *Plato Redivivus, or A Dialogue Concerning Government* (1680), an unplatonic dialogue developing a scheme for the exercise of the royal prerogative through councils of state responsible to Parliament and of which a third part should retire every year.

Plato Redivivus and the *Oceana* are both founded on the same political maxim, that of empire's always following the balance of property. But the author of the 1763 account points out that "there is this considerable difference in those works, *viz.* that the *Oceana* is only an imaginary scheme for a commonwealth; whereas *Plato Redivivus* contains in it the method of rendering a monarchy, and particularly the monarchy of Great Britain, both happy at home and powerful abroad." This account also notes the fact that Neville wrote "diverse copies of verses, which are printed in several books, and was esteemed a good poet."

Oceana and Britannia was probably written sometime between this date and 21 March, when the king's last Parliament met at Oxford. H. F. Russell Smith in *Harrington and His Oceana* (Cambridge University Press, 1914), pp. 137–38, says of the poem: "It was written to celebrate the salvation of the country from the popish terror, and the happy certainty of the Protestant succession, brought about by the efforts of Shaftesbury."

In *Oceana and Britannia* Ayloffe shows himself to be an advocate of the Good Old Cause of republicanism. The rather clumsy and opaque allegory of mother, daughter, and grandchild does not obscure the point the poem is making: Parliament (more precisely, the House of Commons) when it meets at Oxford will effect a revolution that will destroy the monarchy and make England once more a Protestant republic. This time, after two failures, the Exclusion Bill will pass, and Monmouth will head the government, presumably another Cromwell. It is surprising that Ayloffe alludes to *Plato Redivivus*, since Neville' does not advocate the overthrow of the monarchy. Moreover, far from thinking Monmouth the nation's savior, as the poet describes him here, Neville examines and then dismisses as invalid Monmouth's claim to the throne.

OCEANA AND BRITANNIA

Non ego sum vates, sed prisci conscius aevi.

Oceana

Whither, O whither wander I forlorn?
Fatal to friends, and to my foes a scorn.
My pregnant womb is lab'ring to bring forth
Thy offspring, Archon, heir to thy just worth.
Archon, O Archon, hear my groaning cries;   5
Lucina, help, assuage my miseries!
Saturnian spite pursues me through the earth,
No corner's left to hide my long-wished birth.
Great Queen o'th' Isles, yield me a safe retreat
From the crowned gods that would my infant eat.   10
To me a Delos, on my childbed smile;

Epigraph: The first line of a three-line motto on the title page of Neville's *Plato Redivivus.* The remaining two lines read: "Pluribus exemplis haec tibi mysta [*sic*] cano. / Res nolunt male administrari." I have not been able to discover the source. The former (and better) times of this first line might be read as a reference to the commonwealth. Neville, then a strong doctrinaire republican, rendered himself so obnoxious to Cromwell, after he had been made lord protector, as to be banished from London in 1654.

2. *Fatal to friends:* The extremists among the Whigs, those who supported the Good Old Cause, or republicanism, subjected themselves to the charge of treason.

4. *Archon:* In *Oceana* the Archon is the chief (Cromwell, under the name Olphaus Megaletor) who founds a new constitution.

6. *Lucina:* the Roman goddess who presided over childbirth.

7. *Saturnian spite:* Taken in connection with line 10 this phrase becomes clear: the Romans identified their god Saturn with the Greek Kronos, whose mother Gaea prophesied that one of his children would overthrow him. Kronos accordingly swallowed them all except Zeus, whom Rhea, the wife of Kronos, saved by a stratagem. Like Kronos, all monarchs are fearful of revolution on the part of their subjects and the consequent establishment of a republic.

9. *Queen o'th' Isles:* England, regarded as first among the island nations.

11. *Delos:* Delos is an island in the Aegean supposed to have been raised from the sea by Poseidon and anchored to the bottom of the sea by Zeus, to be a resting place for Latona (Leto). Zeus had impregnated Latona, and Hera, jealous of her, sent the serpent Python to persecute her during her pregnancy. Latona wandered about the earth, unable to find a retreat, until Zeus fixed the floating isle upon which she gave birth to Apollo and Artemis.

My happy seed shall fix thy floating isle.
I feel fierce pangs assault my teeming womb,
Lucina, O Britannia, Mother, come!

Britannia

What doleful shrieks pierce my affrighted ear!   15
Shall I ne'er rest for this lewd ravisher?
Rapes, burnings, murders are his royal sport;
These modish monsters haunt his perjured court.
No tumbling play'r so oft e'er changed his shape
As this goat, fox, wolf, timorous French ape.   20
True Protestants in Roman habits dressed
With Scroggs he baits, that rav'nous butcher's beast.
Tresilian Jones, that fair-faced crocodile,
Tearing their hearts, at once does weep and smile.
Neronian flames at London do him please;   25
At Oxford plots to act Agathocles.
His plot's revealed, his muck is at an end.
And's fatal hour shall know no foe nor friend.
Last Martyr's Day I saw a cherub stand
Across my seas, one foot upon my land,   30
The other on th' enthralled Gallic shore,

17. *burnings:* Cf. line 25. Like Nero, Charles plays while London burns. It was popularly thought that the great fire of 1666 and subsequent fires in London were set by Catholics, and the implication here is that Charles was privy to their designs. *murders:* perhaps a reference to the murder of Sir Edmund Berry Gòdfrey.

20. *French ape:* That is, Charles apes the French fashions, but more important, he is the ape who performs at the command of his master, Louis XIV.

21–22. Line 21 is probably a reference to Oates and Thomas Dangerfield, the false witness of the Meal Tub Plot. Following the example of Oates, Dangerfield pretended to be a Catholic convert to "discover" more of the Popish Plot and thus reap the rewards of an informer. *Scroggs:* Lord Chief Justice William Scroggs.

23. *Tresilian Jones:* Sir Thomas Jones (d. 1692). He became a judge of the King's Bench in 1676. As a judge he seems to have been subservient to the crown and to have shown considerable harshness and illiberality in presiding at political trial. *Tresilian:* Sir Robert Tresilian, lord chief justice during the reign of Richard II, hanged in 1388 for the extraordinary cruelty with which he tried the insurgents of the Wat Tyler Rebellion.

26. *Agathocles* (361–289 B.C.): a potter by trade who became tyrant of Syracuse. If I am correct in identifying Charles II as "this lewd ravisher," the reference to Agathocles points to the king's tyrannical position in attempting to rule without Parliament, although Ayloffe could not know that Charles, practically assured of his subsidy from Louis XIV, was plotting to dissolve the Oxford Parliament. "Plots" suggests that the poem was written before the Oxford Parliament on 21 March 1681.

27. *muck:* Cf. the phrase "to run amuck."

29. *Last Martyr's Day:* 30 January 1681, the anniversary of the execution of Charles I.

Aloud proclaim their time should be no more.
This mighty pow'r Heav'n's equal balance swayed,
And in one scale crowns, crosiers, scepters laid;
I'th' other a sweet smiling babe did lie,   35
Circled with glory, decked with majesty.
With steady hand he poised the golden pair:
The gilded gewgaws mounted in the air,
The pond'rous babe, descending in its scale,
Leapt on my shore—   40
Nature triumphed, joy echoed through the earth,
The heav'ns bowed down to view the blessed birth.
      What's that I hear? a newborn babe's soft cries,
And joyful mother's tender lullabies!
'Tis so, behold my daughter past all harms,   45
Cradling an infant in her fruitful arms,
The very same th' angelic vision showed—
In mien, in majesty, how like a god!
What a firm health doth on her visage dwell,
Her sparkling eyes immortal youth foretell.   50
Rome, Sparta, Venice never could bring forth
So strong, so temperate, such lasting worth.
Marpesia from the north with speed advance:
Thy sister's birth brings thy deliverance.
Fergusian founders this just babe exceeds   55
I'th' arts of peace and mighty martial deeds.
Ye Panopeians, kneel to your equal queen,
Safe from the foreign sword, and barb'rous skene.
Transports of joy divert my yearning heart
From my dear child, my soul, my better part.   60
Heav'n show'r her choicest blessings on thy womb,
Our present help, our hopes in time to come.

32. *time . . . more:* That is, Charles II and Louis XIV will go the way of Charles I.
33. *equal:* in the Latin sense, *aequus,* "just, impartial" (as in line 57).
51. *Rome, Sparta, Venice:* the Rome of Brutus, the Sparta of Lycurgus (see line 98). Lycurgus was the prototype for the Archon in *Oceana.* In planning the commonwealth, Harrington used Machiavelli as his authority (see line 104) and Venice as his model.
53. *Marpesia:* in *Oceana* the name for Scotland (literally, "the enthralled one"—Grosart).
55. *Fergusian founders:* Fergus was the first king of Scotland.
57. *Panopeians:* in *Oceana* the name for the Irish.
58. *skene:* a form of knife or dagger, in former times one of the chief weapons of the Irish kerns.

Thou best of daughters, mothers, matrons, say
What forced thy birth, and got this glorious day?

Oceana

'Scaped the slow jaws of grinding pensioners,   65
I fell i'th' trap of Rome's dire murderers;
Twice rescued by my loyal senate's pow'r,

Twice I expected my babe's happy hour.
Malignant force twice checked their pious aid,
And to my foes as oft my state betrayed.   70
Great, full of pains, in a dark winter's night,
Threaten'd, pursued, I 'scaped by sudden flight.
Pale fear gave speed to my weak trembling feet,
And far I fled ere day our world could greet.
That dear loved light which the whole globe doth cheer   75
Spurred on my flight, and added to my fear;
Whilst black conspiracy, that child of night,
In royal purple clad-outdared the light.
By day herself the Faith's Defender styles,
By night digs pits, and spreads her papal wiles.   80
By day with Laud to th' fiddling chapel goes,
By night with York adores Rome's idol shows.
Witness the stars and silent pow'rs of night
Her treacheries, my innocent forced flight.
With the broad day my danger too drew near,   85
Of help and counsel void, how should I steer?
I'th' pulpit damned, strumpet at court proclaimed,

65. *grinding pensioners:* the Pension or Pensioner Parliament, name of the Long Parliament of Charles II.

66. *trap . . . murderers:* the Popish Plot.

67. *my loyal senate:* the House of Commons, dominated by the Whigs.

68. I assume that lines 67–69 all refer to the same parliamentary business: the first two Exclusion Bills. On 15 May 1679 the first of the bills for disabling the duke of York from inheriting the crown was read in the Commons; on its second reading it passed by 207 to 128. Before the bill could be taken to the Lords, however, Parliament was prorogued (27 May) and then dissolved by proclamation. The second Exclusion Bill passed the Commons on 11 November 1680 and was taken to the Lords where, due to the eloquence of Halifax (see line 159, "the Halifax design"), it was rejected 63 to 30 (Ogg, *Charles II, 2,* 589, 603).

79. *the Faith's Defender:* Charles II.

80. *pits:* Cf. line 66.

81. *Laud:* William Laud (1573–1645), archbishop of Canterbury, executed for "bringing in Popery." *fiddling chapel:* Probably "fiddling" here means "petty, trifling, contemptible," although it is possible that the literal meaning of the word is played on as well in order to suggest the liturgical nature of the Anglican ceremony (cf. variant "pompous").

84. *Her:* refers to "black conspiracy" (line 77).

87. *I'th pulpit damned:* in the Anglican church.

Where should I hide, where should I rest defamed?
  Tortured with thought, I raised my weeping eyes
And sobbing voice to the all-helping skies;   90
As by Heav'n sent a rev'rend sire appears,
Charming my grief, stopping my flood of tears:
His busy circling orbs (two restless spies)
Glanced to and fro, outranging Argus' eyes.
Like flitting time, on's front one lock did grow,   95
From his glib tongue torrents of words did flow:
Propose, resolve, agrarian, Forty-one,
Lycurgus, Brutus, Solon, Harrington.
He said he knew me in my swaddling bands,
And often danced me in his careful hands.   100
He knew Lord Archon too, then wept and swore
Enshrined in me his fame he did adore.
His name I asked—he said, Politico,
Descended from the divine Niccolò.
My state he knew, my danger seemed to dread,   105
And to my safety vowed his hand, heart, head.
Grateful returns I up to Heaven send
That in distress had raised me such a friend.
  I asked him where I was? Pointing he showed
Oxford's old tow'rs, once the learned arts' abode   110
(Once great in fame, now a piratic port
Where hireling priests and elfish monks resort).
He added, near a new-built college stood,
Endowed by Plato for the public good.
Thither allured by learned honest men,   115
Plato vouchsafed once more to live again.
Securely there I might myself repose
From my fierce griefs, and my more cruel foes.
Tired with long flight, e'en hunted down with fear,
The welcome news my drooping soul did cheer.   120
His pleasing words shortened the time and way,

91. *a rev'rend sire:* probably Neville. He would be about sixty years old at this time.
95. An allusion to the phrase, "to take time by the forelock."
97. In Harrington's republic the higher chamber "proposes.' and the lower "resolves."
The last two terms refer to Harrington's agrarian law and to the eve of the civil war.
  104. *Niccolo:* Neville published a translation of Machiavelli's works (London, 1675).
113–14. *new-built college:* Since no college at Oxford could be called "new-built" in 1681,
I take this and the following line to be figurative. Ayloffe seems to be making a distinction
between the orthodox, conservative element at Oxford (line 113) and the unorthodox, liberal
element that is working "for the public good."
116. An allusion to *Plato Redivivus*.

And beguiled me at Plato's house to stay.
When we came in, he told me after rest
He'd show me Plato and 's Venetian guest,
I scarce replied, with weariness oppressed: 125
To my desired apartment I repaired,
Invoking sleep and Heav'n's almighty guard.
My waking cares and stabbing frights recede,
And nodding sleep dropped on my drowsy head.
    At last the summons of a busy bell   130
And glimm'ring light did sleep's kind mists dispel.
From bed I stole, and creeping by the wall,
Through a small chink I spied a spacious hall.
Tapers as thick as stars did shed their light
Around the place, and made a day of night.   135
The curious art of some great master's hand
Adorned the room—Hyde, Clifford, Danby stand
In one large piece; next them the two Dutch wars
In bloody colors paint our fatal jars;
Here London flames in clouds of smoke aspire,   140
Done so to th' life I'd almost cried out "Fire!"
But living figures did my eyes divert
From those, and many more of wondrous art:
There entered in three mercenary bands
(They diff'rent captains had, distinct commands).   145
The beggars' desp'rate troop did first appear,
Littleton led, proud Seymour had the rear.

124. *Venetian guest:* In *Plato Redivivus* one of the three characters of the dialogue is a Venetian nobleman. In the argument he is described as "not one of the young fry, but a grave sober person who had borne office and magistracy." He had spent some years in France "with a near relation of his who was ambassador at that court." I have not been able to identity him. The other two characters of the dialogue, the English gentleman and the doctor, are Neville himself and a friend, the celebrated Dr. Richard Lower (1631–91).

137. *Hyde, Clifford, Danby:* Cf. nn. 1, 2, and 4. Along with the two Dutch wars (line 138) and the great fire of London (line 140), these figures recapitulate the reign of Charles II.

144. *mercenary bands:* "mercenary" because they had been bribed by the court. All the names in the following lines are prominent members of the House of Commons and, with the exception of Garroway and Lee, they all voted against the Exclusion Bill.

147. *Littleton:* Sir Thomas Littleton, (1624–81). Pepys (18 July 1666) was told that Littleton, who was returned for Much Wenlock (Salop) in 1661, was "one of the greatest speakers in the House of Commons." Littleton made an impressive speech against the Exclusion Bill on 11 May 1679 (given in Grey, *7*, 253). He was a trimmer like Halifax and Temple (Ogg, *Charles II, 2,* 107). *proud Seymour:* Edward Seymour (1633–1708) was elected speaker of the House of Commons in 1679 but reduced to a private member by court pressure. Pepys, who met him in 1665, found him "very high," "proud and saucy." As an m.p. for Devonshire he voted against the Exclusion Bill on May 1679. In March 1681 he seems to have originated a proposal that the crown should descend to James, but that the prince of Orange should act as his regent. This expedient was endorsed by Halifax.

The disguised Papists under Garroway,
Talbot lieutenant (none had better pay).
Next greedy Lee leads party-colored slaves;   150
Deaf fools i'th' right, i'th' wrong sagacious knaves,
Brought up by Musgrave. Then a nobler train
(In malice mighty, impotent in brain)
The pope's solicitor brought into th' hall
(Not guilty lay, much guilty spiritual).   155
   I also spied behind a private screen
Colbert and Portsmouth, York and Mazarin.
Immediately in close cabal they join,
And all applaud the Halifax design.
'Gainst me and my loved senate's freeborn breath   160
Dire threats I heard, the hall did echo death.
A curtain drawn, another scene appeared,
A tinkling bell, a mumbling priest I heard.
At elevation ev'ry knee adored
The baker's craft, th' Infallible's vain lord.   165
When Catiline with vipers did conspire
To murder Rome and bury it in fire,

148. *Garroway:* Sir William Garroway. Cf. *Last Instructions to a Painter* 298 *n.* He was absent during the vote on the Exclusion Bill in 1679. Both Garroway and Lee are designated as supporters of Shaftesbury in his list prepared against the meeting of the new Parliament of 1679 (Jones, "Shaftesbury's 'Worthy Men': A Whig View of Parliament of 1679" in *Bulletin of the Institute of Historical Research 30*, [1957]: 236, 240). Lee voted for Exclusion, but Garroway apparently was one of a considerable number who deliberately abstained.

149. Sir John Talbot (c. 1630–1714). Cf. *Last Instructions,* 206 *n.* M.P. for Knaresborough 1661; Chippenham 1679; Ludgershall 1681. He voted against the Exclusion Bill in 1679.

150. *greedy Lee:* Sir Thomas Lee (d. 1691), M.P. for Aylesbury, Bucks, from 1661 to 1681. Cf. *Last Instructions,* 299 *n.* He was a well-known parliamentary debater, and, although often voting with the opposition, was credited with taking bribes from the court.

152. *Musgrave:* Sir Christopher Musgrave (1632?–1704), M.P. for Carlisle, 1661–90. He was a staunch supporter of the crown, and in the "List of Court Pensioners in Parliament," published in 1677 (said to be by Marvell), he appears as receiving £200 a year. He strongly opposed the Exclusion Bill. *a nobler train:* Line 155 seems to point to the bishops who absented themselves from the trial of Lord Stafford in 1680. Burnet states that "the whole bench of the bishops was against it" (*2,* 259 and *n.* 3).

155. *spiritual:* The bishops are the lords spiritual of the House.

157. *Colbert:* Charles Colbert, marquis de Croissy (1625–96), French ambassador in England from 1668 to 1674 when he was recalled, partly upon his own suggestion, since he found himself suspected as an agent of popery (Burnet, *2,* 11, *n.* 5; 45, *n.* 2).

159. *the Halifax design:* After Halifax had, in Dryden's words, "turned the balance" in the vote on the second Exclusion Bill (November 1680) and after he had opposed the execution of Stafford (December 1680), the furious House of Commons was determined to destroy him. They particularly resented his late advice (July 1679) to the king to dissolve Parliament. The phrase might refer, on the other hand, to the Seymour-Littleton expedient of line 146, which Halifax supported.

166–69. Jonson's *Catiline,* I. 483–85:

A sacramental bowl of human gore
Each villain took, and as he drank he swore.
The cup denied, to make their plot complete,   170
These Catilines their conjured gods did eat.
Whilst to their breaden whimsies they did kneel,
I crept away, and to the door did steal.
As I got out, by Providence I flew
To this close wood; too late they did pursue.   175
That dreadful night my childbed throes brought on;
My cries moved yours and Heav'n's compassion.

Britannia

Oh happy day! A jubilee proclaim!
Daughter, adore th' unutterable name!
With grateful heart breathe out thy soul in pray'r.   180
In the meantime thy babe shall be my care.
There is a man, my island's hope and grace,
The joy and chief delight of human race.
Exposed to fortune in his tender age,
By fate protected from usurping rage;   185
In Pharaoh's court brought up till's riper years
And full-blown virtue waked the tyrant's fears.
By's sire rejected, but by Heaven called
To break my yoke and rescue the enthralled.
This, this is he who with a stretched-out hand   190
And matchless might shall free my groaning land.
On earth's proud basilisks he'll justly fall

Catiline. I've killed a slave,
And of his blood caused to be mixed with wine.
Fill every man his bowl.

171. *gods did eat:* Cf. Scrogg's famous verdict: "This is a religion that quite unhinges all piety, all morality. . . . They eat their God, they kill their king, and saint the murderer."

179. *th' unutterable Name:* Give thanks to God for bringing about the birth of the commonwealth. The "unutterable Name" is a reference to the sacred tetragrammaton, the Hebrew word *YHWH* or *JHVH* (vocalized as Yahweh, Jahveh, or Jehovah). This four-letter word came to be considered by the Jews too sacred for utterance, and "Adonai" was substituted in reading.

182. *There is a man:* Grosart identifies him as the prince of Orange. *grace:* a reference to Monmouth's attractive person and bearing as well as to his ducal rank.

183. *delight . . . race:* an allusion to Suetonius's description of the Emperor Titus: *amor et deliciae generis humani.*

186. *Pharaoh's court:* that of Charles II? Monmouth had left the court in disgrace, November 1679, and by now was even further from the king's favor. But perhaps Pharaoh is Louis XIV, as in *Absalom and Achitophel.*

192. *basilisk:* a fabulous reptile, also called a cockatrice. Ancient authors stated that its

Like Moses' rod, and prey upon them all.
He'll guide my people through the raging seas
To holy wars and certain victories. 195
His spotless fame and his immense desert
Shall plead love's cause, and storm this virgin's heart.
She, like Egeria, shall his breast inspire
With justice, wisdom, and celestial fire.
Like Numa, he her dictates shall obey, 200
And by her oracles the world shall sway.

---

hissing drove away all other serpents, and that its breath, and even its look, was fatal. Since it literally means "kinglet" or "little king" in Greek, the word does double duty in this line.

193. See Exod. 7:8–12, especially verse 12: "For they cast down every man his rod, and they became serpents: but Aaron's rod swallowed up their rods."

195. *To holy wars:* perhaps a reference to Harrington's belief that, once the commonwealth is established, it is the duty of its citizens to wage holy wars to bring the blessing of good government to other nations.

197. *this virgin:* presumably Oceana's newborn child, the commonwealth.

198–201. *Egeria:* a nymph of Aricia, in Italy, a seat of the worship of Diana. According to Roman legend she was the counsellor and wife of King Numa (the successor of Romulus), who, in order that he might commend his laws to the people, declared that they were previously sanctified and approved by her. Ovid says that Egeria was disconsolate at the death of Numa, that she melted into tears, and was changed into a fountain by Diana.

The Parliament Dissolved at Oxford
(1681)

The Tune to the Devonshire Cant
(1681)

"March 28, Monday, the king having had notice how vigorously the Parliament proceeded on Friday and Saturday (directly opposite to what he desired in his speech) did about ten of the clock in the morning send for his robes and crown privately, the former they say in a sedan, the other under a cloak. Half an hour after, sending for the speaker and Commons, dissolved (without ceremony of attendance, as heralds, etc.) the Parliament, to the amazement of all" (Wood, *Life and Times, 2,* 532).

On his copy of the broadside Luttrell has written, "A libel on that Parliament 3 May 1681," and on his copy of the answering broadside, "In defense of the Parliament, 4 May 1681."

THE PARLIAMENT DISSOLVED AT OXFORD

Under 500 kings three kingdoms groan:
Go Finch, dissolve them, Charles is in the throne
And by the grace of God will reign alone.
  What would the Commons have? The royal line
Heav'n does dispose of: 'Tis not theirs nor mine,   5

1. *500 kings:* The approximate number of members in the House of Commons. Charles is speaking from the throne.
2. *Finch:* Heneage Finch, 1st earl of Nottingham (1621–82), lord chancellor.
    His Majesty, sitting in his royal throne, adorned with his crown and other regal ornaments (the peers sitting without their robes), commanded the Gentleman Usher of the Black Rod to signify His Majesty's pleasure to the House of Commons, "That they presently attend His Majesty."
    Who being come, His Majesty made a short speech to this effect:
    "My lords and gentlemen, that all the world may see to what point we are come, that we are not like to have a good end when the divisions at the beginning are such: Therefore, my lord chancellor, do as I have commanded you."
    Then the lord chancellor said:
    "My lords and gentlemen, His Majesty has commanded me to say that it is His Majesty's royal pleasure and will that this Parliament be dissolved:
    And this Parliament is dissolved."

[*LJ, 13,* 757]

But His by whom kings rule and are divine.
    I represent the King of Kings, who gave
The crown, the sword, the scepter, what I have;
I am God's servant, not the people's slave.
    Their frantic votes and mad resolves I hate;   10
I know a better way to heal a state
Than to sin rashly and repent too late.
    Bid them be gone, Finch! They are damned uncivil
To oblige me to follow them to the devil;
To save three kingdoms I will not do evil.   15
    The Presbyterians, sick of too much freedom,
Are ripe for Bethle'm. It's high time to bleed'em:
The second Charles does neither fear nor need'em.
    I'll have the world know that I can dissipate
Those impolitic mushrooms of our state;   20
'Tis easier to dissolve than to create.
    They shan't cramp justice with their feigned flaws;
For, since I govern only by the laws,
Why they should be exempt I see no cause.
    To the laws they must submit. 'Tis in vain   25
E'er to attempt to shake off those again;
For where Charles commands there must justice reign.
    When the people's father does espouse the law,
All those subjects from their duty draw
Do viper-like through parent's bosom gnaw.   30
    When they attend me next, Finch, bid them bring
Calmer thoughts. Bid them propose legal things,
Such as may both become themselves and kings.
    This will the joys of our little world complete,
And all attempts of foreign foes defeat,   35
Making the people happy, monarch great.

20. *mushrooms:* mushroom in the figurative sense of a person who has suddenly sprung into notice; an upstart.

22. *feigned flaws:* invalidating faults they pretend to find in the legal procedure against them.

23. Throughout the struggle with Parliament Charles II "had rested his policy on an unswerving respect for the forms and processes of law—he would leave, he constantly declared, all to the laws" (Bryant, p. 303). Cf. the end of the king's speech at the opening of the Oxford Parliament, 21 March: "I conclude with this one advice to you, that the rules and measures of all your votes may be the known and established laws of the land, which neither can or ought to be departed from nor changed, but by act of Parliament; and I may the more reasonably require that you make the laws of the land your rule, because I am resolved they shall be mine" (*LJ, 13,* 746).

29. That is, all those who draw subjects from their duty.

30. An allusion to the supposition that the female viper was killed by her young eating their way out at birth.

The Tune to the Devonshire Cant,
or An Answer to the Parliament Dissolved
at Oxford

Nonne vides ut nudum remigio latus. Horat. Ode XIV, Lib.1

The safety of the king and's royal throne
Depends on those 500 kings alone,
Those under whom some say three kingdoms groan.
    The Commons no new methods will assign
Of choosing kings. They know the royal line   5
Was wont to be reputed as divine.
    Your Englishmen, who understand who gave
Their king his royal grandeur, scorn to have
His Majesty their general, their slave.
    As frantic and outrageous as were   10
Their votes, they showed their vigilance and care,
And nought like those could dissipate our fear.
    They are dissolved and with them all our hopes;
Prepare for Smithfield fires, for racks and ropes,
For that's the pleasing exercise of popes!   15
    Now to create intestine broils what need
Is there? Of those experienced things take heed;
When th' state's blood's hot 'tis dangerous to bleed.

Title: Cant probably has here, in addition to the contemptuous meaning of jargon, the obsolete meaning of *singing* and *tone,* from Latin *cantus.* Yet another sense of the word could apply here: a set form of words repeated mechanically.

Epigraph: Seest thou not how thy bulwarks are bereft of oars? (Horace, *Odes* 1.14).

11. *Their votes:* "The Commons began [on Monday, March 21] by resolving to print their votes. . . . It was next resolved to impeach Fitzharris of high treason. . . . Not till Saturday, March 26, did the Commons debate the vital point—exclusion or a regency. . . . The sense of the House was definitely against a regency, and it was then resolved to bring in the bill excluding James and all popish successors from inheriting the imperial crowns of England and Ireland. At this point a message was received from the Lords that they refused to accept the impeachment of Fitzharris, on the ground that they were not required to proceed on anyone not a member of their own body. . . . The Commons at last brought a momentous day to a close by resolving that it is the undoubted right of the Commons to impeach before the Lords any peer or commoner for treason, or any other crime; and that the Lords' denial of this principle in the case of Fitzharris was a violation of the constitution of parliaments and an obstruction to the further discovery of the Popish Plot. They resolved that for any inferior court to proceed against Fitzharris was a breach of the privilege of Parliament.

"On Monday, March 28, the Commons read their Exclusion Bill. It was while Magna Charta was being cited in support of their impeachment of Fitzharris that the Commons were startled to hear the knocking of Black Rod on the door; this time they were not prorogued, but dissolved" (Ogg, *Charles II, 2,* 617–19).

16–18. Presumably a reference to the civil war of 1642–46.

In all true hearts it would a love create
To see the supreme power dissipate   20
All pensioners, those spongers of our state.
    The Commons' aims were but to regulate
Things shuffled out of place in church and state;
Not to cramp justice, but corroborate.
    When they offend they justly feel the smart   25
Imposed on them by some ambitious heart,
Whose swollen envy breaks out like a fart.
    But here's the mischief: they espouse the law,
Hate those who subjects from allegiance draw,
And of their royal master stand in awe.   30
    We've grounds to hope when next they meet they'll bring
Wise counsels, grave proposals, ev'rything
Conducive to th' peace of people and king.
    If so, we'll sing adieu to plots—in vain
Shall rogues attempt to shake our peace again,   35
And then great Charles most happily will reign.

25–27. Cf. lines 34–35: "in vain / Shall rogues attempt to shake our peace again." The Commons are driven to "frantic and outrageous" votes by their justified fear of rogues and ambitious hearts.

STEPHEN COLLEGE

A Raree Show
(1681)

Luttrell notes on his copy of the broadside: "A most scandalous libel against the government, for which and other things College was justly executed." At the Oxford trial of Stephen College, which began 17 August 1681, Stephen Dugdale accused College of treasonable talk and of having admitted that he was the author of several libels, among which was *A Raree Show*. According to Dugdale, College sang this ballad and distributed copies of it. On the Harvard copy of the broadside there is scribbled a date, 9 April 1681, followed by this statement: "James Astwood in the parish of St. Christ[opher] did acknowledge that he printed a ream of this and delivered them to the person that brought it to print." There follows a signature, "Mr. Rich. Clarke, Warden," and under this four more names, apparently those of witnesses. L'Estrange states that the libel was published by the notorious Francis "Elephant" Smith: "The printer informs likewise that Francis Smith upon the reading of the staves to him expounded them" (*Notes upon Stephen College*, p. 13). College himself to the last denied any connection with the libel: "I was not the author of those verses called *A Raree Show*, neither do I know who was, or the printer" (*A True Copy of the Dying Words of Mr. Stephen College*, London, 1681).

A RAREE SHOW

To the Tune "I Am a Senseless Thing"

Leviathan

Come hither, Topham, come, with a hey, with a hey,
Bring a pipe and a drum, with a ho;
Where'er about I go
Attend my raree show,
With a hey, trany nony nony no.   5

Topham

That monstrous foul beast, with a hey, with a hey,
Has Houses twain in's chest, with a ho;
O Cooper, Hughs and Snow,
Stop thief with a raree show,
With a hey, trany nony nony no.   10
For if he should escape, with a hey, with a hey,
With Halifax's trap, with a ho;
He'd carry good Dom. Com.
Unto the pope of Rome,
With a hey, trany nony nony no.   15

Title: A show contained or carried about in a box, a peep show. Charles in convening Parliament at Oxford is represented as carrying it around England (now Oxford, next York, Carlisle, etc.). The *OED* quotes Dr. Johnson on *raree show*: "This word is formed in imitation of the foreign way of pronouncing rare show."

Leviathan: Cf. "that monstrous foul beast" (line 6). Also an allusion to the *Leviathan* of Hobbes (line 51). In Hobbes's political thought "the sovereign had taken upon himself the person of the state" (Ogg, *Charles II, 2*, 744). Charles is made out to be another Louis XIV, who declared himself the state.

1. *Topham*: The sergeant-at-arms or chief executive officer of the House of Commons (Luttrell, *1*, 187). Ailesbury notes Topham's ferocious reputation, which is borne out by the character of his speeches in this lampoon: "their Sergeant Topham, a good fellow and a loyal man, but ill-natured and covetous, and it became a saying, 'To him Topham,' for he was glad to get all into his net" (*1*, 47).

2. *pipe and a drum*: the music attendant on the raree show.

8. "Here's first the king to be pulled down (under the raree show) and Cooper, Hughes and Snow (being officers belonging to both Houses) are to represent the Lords and Commons in the doing it" (L'Estrange, *Notes upon Stephen College*, p. 43).

12. *Halifax's trap*: a reference to "the Expedient," or the policy of imposing limitations on a popish successor. According to the writer it was an expedient to trap the nation into accepting a Catholic king. This alternative to exclusion had been formulated by Halifax, possibly at the suggestion of Littleton (Ogg, *Charles II, 2*, 615). Cf. *Oceana and Britannia*, 147 and *n*.

13. *Dom. Com.*: Parliament.

Leviathan

Be quiet, ye dull tools, with a hey, with a hey,
As other freeborn fools, with a ho;
Do not all gaping stand,
To see my sleight of hand?
With a hey, trany nony nony no.   20
'Tis not to Rome that I, with a hey, with a hey,
Lug about my trumpery, with a ho;
But Oxford, York, Carlisle
And round about the isle,
With a hey, trany nony nony no.   25
But if they would come out, with a hey, with a hey,
Let them first make a vote, with a ho,
To yield up all they have
And Tower lords to save,
With a hey, trany nony nony no.   30

Topham

Now that is very hard, with a hey, with a hey,
Thou art worse than cutnose guard, with a ho;
And Clifford, Danby, Hyde,
Halifax does all outride,
With a hey, trany nony nony no.   35
Holy Ghost in bag of cloak, with a hey, with a hey,
Quaking king in hollow oak, with a ho,
And Rosamond in bower

22. *trumpery:* trash, rubbish. This is how Charles regards Parliament.

26–29. Charles will let Parliament out of the chest (allow it to sit) if it is willing to give him all the funds at its command, and also to order the release of the five Catholic peers in the Tower.

32. *cutnose guard:* See *A Ballad Called the Haymarket Hectors.*

34. The Commons requested the king to remove Halifax from his councils and presence as a promoter of popery and betrayer of the liberties of the people, alleging his late advice (July 1679) to the king to dissolve Parliament.

36. *Holy . . . cloak:* "That which they call the General Council of Trent now sitting, the queen [Elizabeth] is desired to send some thither: but this she thought would be to little purpose, seeing the design of that convention (as the emperor and the French king called it) was more of interest than real honesty: Besides, it had now continued about XV years, and so improbable to alter anything upon her desire. . . . Nor would they allow anything to be concluded on, but as they received instructions from the Pope; which occasioned the proverb, That *the Holy Ghost was sent from Rome to Trent in a cloak bag*" (Henry Foulis, *The History of Romish Treasons and Usurpations* [London, 1671], p. 425).

37. *Quaking . . . oak:* the hollow oak at Boscobel where Charles hid for a time after the Battle of Worcester.

38. Rosamond Clifford (d. 1176?). "Rosamond the Fair," mistress of Henry II. Probably a reference to the duchess of Portsmouth, the reigning favorite at this time.

All badges are of power,
With a hey, trany nony nony no.   40
And popularity, with a hey, with a hey,
Adds power to majesty, with a ho;
But Dom. Com. in little ease
Will all the world displease,
With a hey, trany nony nony no.   45

Leviathan

Let 'em hate so they fear, with a hey, with a hey,
Cursed fox has the best cheer, with a ho;
Two states in blind house pent
Make brave strong government,
With a hey, trany nony nony no.   50

Topham

But child of heathen Hobbes, with a hey, with a hey,
Remember old Dry Bobs, with a ho,
For fleecing England's flocks
Long fed with bits and knocks,
With a hey, trany nony nony no.   55

Leviathan

What's past is not to come, with a hey, with a hey,
Now safe is David's bum, with a ho;
Then hey for Oxford ho,
Strong government, raree show,
With a hey, trany nony nony no.   60

———

Raree show is resolved, with a hey, with a hey,
This is worse than dissolved, with a ho;
May the mighty weight at's back

47. *Cursed . . . cheer:* Even though the fox is cursed for his slyness, that very trickery wins him a better diet than that enjoyed by less crafty beasts.

48. *Two states:* The Lords and the Commons, the "estates of the realm," met to form a constitutional assembly. By shutting them up Charles can govern arbitrarily.

51. *child . . . Hobbes:* During the commonwealth, Hobbes spent some years in France and gave mathematical lectures to Charles II, with whom he shared a lively intelligence and from whom he received a small pension (Ogg, *Charles II, 2,* 741). Indeed, Charles II was thought by some to be a Deist and a follower of Hobbes (C. E. Whiting, *Studies in English Puritanism, 1660–1688* [New York, 1931], p. 3).

52. *Dry Bobs:* See *An Allusion to Horace,* 75 and *n.*

62. The calling of Parliament at Oxford is worse than an actual dissolution.

Make's lecherous loins to crack,
With a hey, trany nony nony no.   65

Methinks he seems to stagger, with a hey, with a hey,
Who but now did so swagger, with a ho;
God's fish! he's stuck i'th' mire,
And all the fat's i'th' fire,
With a hey, trany nony nony no.   70

Help Cooper, Hughs, and Snow, with a hey, with a hey,
To pull down raree show, with a ho;
So, so, the giant's down,
Let's masters out of pound,
With a hey, trany nony nony no.   75

And now you have freed the nation, with a hey, with a hey,
Cram in the Convocation, with a ho,
With pensioners all and some.
Into this chest of Rome,
With a hey, trany nony nony no.   80

And thrust in six and twenty, with a hey, with a hey,
With not guilty, good plenty, with a ho,
And hoot them hence away
To Cologne or Breda,
With a hey, trany nony nony no.   85

Haloo! the hunt's begun, with a hey, with a hey,

68. *God's fish*. one of Charles's favorite oaths.
73. *the giant's donw:* Cf. *The Trial of Stephen College*, 1681, p. 25:

Dugdale:	And in one place of the other libel *(Raree Show)* the king was termed a rogue, and they put him in by another name.
Jeffreys:	Where is it?
Dugdale:	'Tis in *Raree Show*. In the manuscript it was, "Now, now, the rogue is down."
Jeffreys:	Let me see it, I took notice of it, 'tis, "Now, now the giant is down," here.

77. *Convocation:* in the Church of England a provincial synod or assembly of the clergy, constituttd by statute and called together to deliberate on ecclesiastical matters. There is a convocation of each of the provinces, Canterbury and York. The former is the more important and is often referred to as simply "Convocation." It consists of two houses, an upper and a lower (on the model of the Houses of Parliament).

79. *chest of Rome:* As L'Estrange points out, this line makes the king, the Convocation, and "all those whom he is pleased to call pensioners . . . all to be Papists" (p. 44).

81–82. *six and twenty:* according to L'Estrange, "the not guilty lords, in the vote upon my Lord Stafford" (p. 44). They are the lords spiritual of the House of Lords, the twenty-six bishops.

84. *Cologne or Breda:* That is, send them back to where the court lived in exile before 1660.

86. ff. Cf. L'Estrange, p. 45: "I have in my hand the manuscript of College's own writing, from whence this ballad was printed; where it is to be noted, that instead of 'Halloe'

Like father, like son, with a ho;
Raree show in French lap,
Is gone to take a nap,
And successor has the clap,   90
With a hey, trany nony nony no.

London, Printed for B.T. and Sold at His Shop in Paul's Churchyard: For the Good of the Public, 1681.

[line 86] it was in the original, 'Stand to't'; but that struck out, and 'Halloe' interlined in the place of it; the other being too broad a discovery of the violence they intended. Let me further observe that this song was calculated for Oxford; that is to say, both for the time, and the place, when and where this exploit was to have been executed. And now for a close; what can be the meaning of 'Like father, like son' [line 87] but a design and encouragement (as appears from the connection) to serve them both alike; and to conclude both father and son under one and the same condemnation."

90. "He (York) is ever going on from one intrigue to another, though it is generally thought that these have been very fatal to him and that the death of so many of his children is owing to that" (H. C. Foxcroft, *A Supplement to Burnet's History of My Own Time* [Oxford, 1902], p. 51).

The Whigs' Lamentation for the Death of
Their Dear Brother College, the Protestant Joiner
(1681)

When the Parliament was removed to Oxford in March 1681, Stephen College (see headnotes to *Truth Brought to Light* and *A Raree Show*) went up on horseback, ostentatiously displaying weapons and wearing defensive armor, speaking threateningly against the king and advocating resistance. In June 1681 he was arrested, carried before Secretary Jenkins on the 29th, and committed to the Tower. On 23 June Dugdale testified that College had written and published three libels. He was indicted at the Old Bailey on 8 July for seditious words and actions but saved by the influence of the Whig sheriffs, Slingsby Bethel and Henry Cornish. The latter packed a jury who, under the guidance of their foreman, John Wilmore, threw out the bill with "ignoramus." This did not deter the government from making an example of College. His conduct at Oxford laid him open to a fresh trial there, where a jury might be readier to comply with the direction of the court lawyers. Warcup writes on 17 July [1681]: "I was heard before Halifax, Hyde, Jenkins, Seymour, and Conway: determined to proceed against College at Oxford. Had great thanks. . . . On Monday morn met Lord Halifax at Pemberton's; he settled the trial of College at Oxford." At College's trial on 17 August 1681, Dugdale, Turberville, and John "Narrative" Smith swore positively to the guilt of College; Oates, Bolron, and others contradicted their testimony and exposed the worthlessness of their personal character. At the trial of Lord Stafford, College had been the chief asserter of Dugdale's respectability. After Oates had labored to invalidate the credit of his own former supporters, but now opponents, Sergeant Jeffrey argued to the jury that "if these three witnesses were not believed, the evidence and discovery of the Popish Plot would the tripped up." The jury returned a verdict of guilty and sentence of death was pronounced against College. On 31 August he was hanged and quartered. Ogg feels that College was a "rash but harmless man" whose trial "was one of the most unfair in a period abounding in judicial murders" (*Charles II, 2*, 626–28).

The Whigs' Lamentation for the Death of Their Dear Brother College, the Protestant Joiner

Brave College is hanged, the chief of our hopes,
For pulling down bishops and making new popes;
Our dear brother property crawls on the ground,
In Poland King Anthony ne'er will be crowned.
For now they're resolved that hearts shall be trump,　　　5
And the prentices swear they will burn the old Rump.
Brave College, both champion and carver of laws,
Who died undaunted, and stuck to the cause;
What mischief might thou to the godly have done
Had thy daring soul dreaded the world to come?　　　10
And all thy dear party to danger exposed,
If thou to the world had thy secrets disclosed.
But now thou art hanged, and that fear is past;
Were all that's in question as safe in the nest,
Then we some new means might consult or contrive　　　15
To drive on our purpose, to prosper or thrive.
But the Popish Plot has now quite lost its name,
And none thy bright blunderbuss dare to maintain.

Title: A joiner is a carpenter.

2. *making new popes:* probably refers to the effigies used in the great pope-burning processions organized by the Green Ribbon Club, the first of which took place on 17 November 1679, the anniversary of Queen Elizabeth's accession. As College was a carpenter, the lampoonist plays with the fact or fancy that College carved the effigy of the pope each year and this interpretation would support the Whig contention (and his own in his trial) that he was a violent pope baiter. Also probably an allusion to the election of popes by the College of Cardinals.

3. *brother property:* "Brother" here is Presbyterian cant (cf. "brother statesman," lines 27 and 31). Property was one of the slogans of the Whigs: the safeguarding of private property against arbitrary government.

4. *King Anthony:* Shaftesbury. Rumor had it that he had presented himself as a candidate for the throne of Poland when Sobieski was elected in 1674.

5. *hearts . . . trump:* This probably means that by the Tories' reacting after the Oxford Parliament, the nation as a whole has resolved to show their hearts loyal to the king (possibly hearts as trumps rather than clubs, emblematic of rebellion).

6. *the prentices:* "About this time [March 1680] several apprentices and rascally fellows had formed a design (as they pretended) of burning the Rump on His Majesty's birthday, but the real intent was to have made a hubub and a tumult, and thereby an insurrection" (Luttrell, *1*, 38).

8. *cause:* Cf. *A New Ballad,* 51 *n.*

17. The execution of Oliver Plunket, lord primate of Ireland, on 1 July 1681 may be taken as the end of the Popish Plot: "He [Plunket] was the last victim of the Popish Plot, and died in the company of the first victim [Fitzharris] of the counter-attack" (Ogg, *Charles II, 2,* 626).

18. *blunderbuss:* See *The Trial of Stephen College,* 1681, p. 27, where a witness Smith affirms

What king but great College could e'er make a pope,
Though he was o'erruled by the end of the rope?   20
Great College was certainly *jure divino*:
When the triple crown on the pope's head did *shino*,
He burnt him to ashes for pastime like Nero,
Then straight made a new one, such pow'r had our hero.
Great College must certainly die a good martyr,   25
Being Knight of the Halter, and above the Garter;
Our dear brother statesman, though bred in a sawpit,
Had internal genius enough to o'erthrow wit.
He framed a new model to limit the king,
In hopes crown and scepter might truckle to him.   30
Great Britain ne'er bred such a brother as College,
He made seven popes in his time on our knowledge;
Our signals of crimes he put in the pope's arms,
Which prudent contrivance our function alarms.
With threats in petition king's pow'r to restrain,   35
Yet Towser and Broomstaff ride admiral again.
Great Hannibal's conquest, nor Oliver's nose,
Could with such small slaughter subdue such great foes
As he in this three years, with help of our party,
Hath checked our three kingdoms and Magna Charta.   40
The head of our church, and the head of our cause,
He would have maintained them by perjury and blows.
He now may be called a third savior o'th' nation,

"he [College] did show me his pistols, his blunderbuss, his great sword." A great point was made in the trial of College's coming to Oxford in armor, and with the weapon known as the Protestant flail. His being so heavily armed was taken as a proof of his intention to seize the king.

21. *jure divino:* a reference to the theory of the divine right of kings: that they hold their tenure from God and are therefore above all manmade law.

27. *sawpit:* an excavation in the ground, over the mouth of which a framework is erected, where timber is placed to be sawed with a long, two-handled saw by two men: the one standing in the pit, and the other on a raised platform. Not only a reference to carpenter College but also to his low origin ("bred in a sawpit" had this figurative sense).

29. *framed:* another in the series of metaphors drawn from College's trade, like "carved," "made."

33. *signals:* signs, badges. Possibly a list of crimes put in the arms of the effigy.

34. *function:* persons following a profession or trade; an order, class.

36. *Towser and Broomstaff:* Roger L'Estrange and his publisher H. Brome. The metaphor "rides admiral again" means that the Tory propagandist has survived Whig attacks and by the number and force of his counterattacks has proved the victor.

37. *Oliver's nose:* Cromwell had a "long bulbous nose which dominate[d] the face in all the portraits and was the subject of many jests" (Maurice Ashley, *Oliver Cromwell, Conservative Dictator* [London, 1937], p. 23).

43. *third:* The first two were Oates and Bedloe.

To save his dear church he renouncéd salvation;
Like famous Cargill he died for King Jesus,   45
Defying church idols enough to amaze us.
He tied up together both his and our crimes,
And died like a devil, to damp our designs.
Our case to th' character-men we must refer,
To Shadwell and Settle, to Curtis and Care,   50
To know who succeeds our late captain the joiner;
He must be an artist, some carver, or coiner,
To make our solemnity, and some new popes,
On which our dependency hangs and our hopes.
But when the time comes that the pope must be burned,   55
I fear we shall find that the tide is much turned;
For the Tory party hath got so much ground,
To head a rebellion there's none will be found.
For now they're resolved that hearts shall be trump,
And the prentices swear they'll burn the old Rump.   60
Such a confuséd monster they swear they'll compose
Of all the Dissenters that are the king's foes;
The Baptist and Biter, the Pendent and Quaker,
From which they will draw such a prodigious creature:
More diabolical invective far   65
Than all pope's solemnities at Temple Bar.
Our Common Council let's summon together;

44. College had been a Presbyterian for twenty years, until the Restoration, when he con-formed to the Church of England.

45. *Cargill:* Donald (or Daniel) Cargill (1619?–81), Covenanting preacher. He was executed for high treason 27 July 1681.

50. *Shadwell and Settle:* Thomas Shadwell and Elkanah Settle the two leading Whig poets and dramatists. Settle produced at Shaftesbury's instance his *Character of a Popish Successor* in 1681. "Character-men" in the preceding line must refer to the authors and publishers of the many pieces beginning "A Character of——." *Curtis and Care:* Langley Curtis and Henry Care (or Carr), leading Whig publishers.

51. *succeeds:* probably, along with "character" in line 49, an allusion to Settle's *Character of a Popish Successor. captain:* "Mr. Att. Gen. . . . for he [College] boasted of himself that he should be in a little time a colonel" (*Trial of Stephen College,* p. 17).

53. *solemnity:* the pope-burning procession (cf. line 66).

55. In two weeks time, if we assume that Luttrell's date of purchase is close to that of publication.

63. *Biter:* Presbyterian. *Pendent:* Independent.

66. *Temple Bar:* Luttrell writes of the pope-burning on 17 November 1679: "At night were several bonfires, and particularly a very great one at Temple gate, where was a pope burnt in *pontificalibus* that cost above £100" (*1,* 29). The burning took place near the statue of Queen Elizabeth, worshiped by the Whigs as the great defender of the Protestant faith, at Temple Bar.

67. *Our Common Council:* the administrative body of London.

To panel-packed juries let's make't our endeavor
For an habeas corpus: insist on our power
To fetch our great patriots out of the Tower.   70
And then we'll dispute the case for reformation,
And make the proud Tories resign us the nation.

68. *panel*: jury. An ironic reference to Whig-packed juries.
69. *habeas corpus*: The Habeas Corpus Act was passed in 1679.
70. Shaftesbury and Lord Howard of Esrick were both in the Tower at this time.

A Panegyric on the Author of "Absalom and Achitophel"
(1681)

Dryden's poem on Cromwell *(Heroic Stanzas to the Glorious Memory of Crom-well)* was first printed in 1659. The first reprint, put out by some antagonist to embarrass Dryden, appeared in 1681: *An Elegy on the Usurper O.C. by the Author of Absalom and Achitophel, Published to Show the Loyalty and Integrity of the Poet.* There is a postscript signed J.D.:

The printing of these rhymes afflicts me more
Than all the drubs I in Rose Alley bore.
This shows my nauseous mercenary pen
Would praise the vilest and the worst of men.
A rogue like Hodge [Roger L'Estrange] am I, the world will know it,
Hodge was his [Cromwell's] fiddler, and I John his poet.
This may prevent the pay for which I write;
For I for pay against my conscience fight.
I must confess so infamous a knave
Can do no service, though the humblest slave.
Villains I praise, and patriots accuse,
My railing and my fawning talents use;
Just as they pay I flatter or abuse.
But I to men in pow'r a turd am still
To rub on any honest face they will.
Then on I'll go, for libels I declare,
Best friends no more than worst of foes I'll spare,
And all this I can do because I dare.
He who writes on, and cudgels can defy,
And knowing he'll be beaten still writes on, am I.

A PANEGYRIC ON THE AUTHOR OF "ABSALOM AND ACHITOPHEL,"

Occasioned by His Former Writing of an
Elegy in Praise of Oliver Cromwell, Lately Reprinted

When old philosophers wrote the world's· birth
And from wild chaos brought great nature forth,
The selfsame atoms as they different ran
Clubbed to a lion, monkey, bear, or man;
From such thin sires such solid offspring grew,   5
So, divine wit, like the first matter, thou:
Thy subtle sparks do such strange products make
That thou just nothing, yet all forms canst take.
So justly thou hast deserved they long-worn bays.
That, as a trophy to thy endless praise,   10
Let that great poem its long silence break,
The worthiest of thy vast creation speak.
   Methinks I fancy how bold Mucius' dart
Was leveled at Porsena's royal heart,
And in defeated rage I see him doom   15
His erring hand t' its flaming martyrdom.
Let his poor deeds in dull oblivion die;
Thy vengeance with a surer aim lets fly:
In keen iambics 'gainst thy sov'reign lord,
Thy pen was more successful than his sword.   20
So vast a pile thy lofty numbers raise,
Those Babel-builders to great Moloch's praise,
A pile which to thy honor will surpass
E'en thy own Corah's monumental brass.

6. *wit:* Dryden.

9. *thy . . . bays:* Dryden was made poet laureate in 1670.

10–11. The "great poem" is Dryden's elegy on Cromwell. There may be in "thy endless praise" a charge of sycophancy as well as prolixity against Dryden.

13–16. Lars Porsena was a king of Etruria who attacked Rome in order to bring back Tarquinius Superbus. Gaius Mucius Scaevola was a Roman who came to Porsena's camp to kill him. Being detected and threatened with death or torture, he thrust his right hand into the fire blazing upon an altar, and held it there until it was consumed, hence the name Scaevola (left-handed). The king, deeply impressed and dreading a further attempt upon his life, ordered Mucius to be liberated, made peace with the Romans, and withdrew his forces.

19. *thy sov'reign lord:* Charles II. The next line seems to mean that Dryden benefited from his praise of Cromwell whereas Charles II was defeated by the latter in the Civil war.

22. *Moloch:* Cromwell. Moloch was a Canaanite idol to whom children were sacrificed.

24. Dryden's portrait of Titus Oates in *Absalom* begins: "Yet, Corah, thou shalt from oblivion pass: / Erect thyself, thou monumental brass" (632–33).

Thou writ'st with so much flame, flame so refined,   25
That poetry's the fever of thy mind;
And fever-like in those bleak days of yore,
When loyalty was naked left and poor,
Thy anguished veins chilled at a starving door.
But burning high thy active spirits run   30
At prosperous rebellion's warmer sun.
When Phaeton misled the day, and hurled
His scattered fires around the scorching world,
How would his glories in thy meter chime,
The groans of worlds thus softened into rhyme?   35
Or when great Nero set his Rome on fire,
And tuned its ruin to his jocund lyre,
How with his music would thy notes agree,
A song, great bard, fit to be set by thee.
Such wonders have thy pow'rful raptures shown,   40
Pythagoras' transmigration thou'st outdone.
His souls of heroes and great chiefs expired
Down into birds and noble beasts retired;
But thou to savages and monsters dire
Canst infuse sparks e'en of celestial fire;   45
Make treason glory, murd'rers heroes live,
And e'en to regicides canst godheads give.
Thus in thy songs the yet warm bloody dart,
Fresh reeking in a martyred monarch's heart,
Burnished by verse and polished by thy lines,   50
The rubies in imperial crowns outshines,
Whilst in applause to that sad day's success,
So black a theme in so divine a dress;
Thy soaring heights Prometheus' thefts excel,
Whilst thou steal'st fire from Heav'n t'enlighten Hell.   55
But stay, my Muse, here change thy gaudy strain,

28–31. That is, Dryden deserted the king for Cromwell, since he preferred to be disloyal and warm rather than loyal and cold.

32–39. Since Dryden could celebrate Cromwell's treason, he could soften even Phaeton's crime, who laid waste half the world. Dryden is as perverse as the fiddling Nero in singing the catastrophe that was Cromwell's rule.

41. *Pythagoras's transmigration:* Pythagoras, the Greek philosopher, (6th century B.C.). adopted the Orphic doctrine of metempsychosis or the transmigration of souls from man to man, or man to animal, or animal to man, in a process of purification or punishment.

54. *Prometheus's thefts:* Prometheus surpassed all mankind in cunning and deceived even Zeus, who, to avenge himself, took fire away from earth. But Prometheus outwitted him, climbed the heavens, and stole fire from the chariot of the sun.

And show a new, no less prodigious scene.
That laureled head, whose sweet melodious tongue
To *Curse ye Meroz* Io Paean sung,
A bagpipe drone to the old priestcraft cant,   60
Who once did consecrated daggers chant,
And England's great Ravaillac sung before,
Now tunes his pipe to David's righteous lore,
In Scaevola's stump the convert pen he brings,
And his burnt hand now writes the praise of kings.   65
  Thus bold, thus great, and all in the extreme,
His panegyrics are like Daniel's dream;
This tribute now to David's glory pay,
A head of gold to his old feet of clay.
Now wonder then so feelingly he tells   70
Of Corahs, Shimeis, and Achitophels.
Such characters he may well gild so fine
Who has their rich ore from his own native mine.
How vast an orb has a poetic soul!
Grasps all from east to west, and pole to pole.   75
Its warbling voice right, wrong, truth, falsehood sings,
Tuned to all states, religions, gods, or kings.
O wit, how wide, is thy circumference
Where thy attractive center's bread and pence!

59–60. *Curse ye Meroz:* "Curse ye Meroz, said the angel of the Lord, curse ye bitterly the inhabitants thereof; because they came not to the help of the Lord, to the help of the Lord against the mighty" (Judg. 5:23). On 9 May 1680 Edmund Hickeringill preached before the lord mayor, Sir Robert Clayton at the Guildhall Chapel, London, a sermon on this text (*Curse ye Meroz: or, the Fatal Doom,* 1680). Its popularity is evidenced by the fact that it went through four editions in 1680. From the context of lines 56–65, I assume that the poet has in mind Hickeringill's opening remarks about the use of this text by commonwealth preachers on the eve of the civil war: "About forty years ago this text (I have heard) was the common theme in pulpits, and ushered in (as well as promoted) the late bloody civil wars. In this text some sagacious men could find horse and arms, and hence raise and muster battalias against sovereign majesty; nay, here they could find commissions too to vouch the quarrel." Hickeringill uses the text to preach loyalty to the king rather than rebellion. The poet, however, is alluding here to the commonwealth use of the text: yet another hit at Dryden's espousal of Cromwell's cause. The "bagpipe drone" suggests the nasal twang commonly associated with Presbyterian preachers. *Io Paean:* solemn song or chant. Originally a hymn of thanksgiving for deliverance addressed to Apollo.
  62. *England's great Ravaillac:* Cromwell as the killer of Charles I is compared to François Ravaillac (ca. 1578–1610), the assassin of Henri IV of France.
  64. *convert:* politically, not religiously converted: Dryden did not become a Catholic until 1686.
  66. Cf. *Absalom and Achitophel:* "Railing and praising were his usual themes, / And both (to show his judgment) in extremes" (555–56).
  67. *Daniel's dream:* A reference to Nebuchadnezzar's dream of a great image of gold, silver, brass, iron, and clay (Dan. 2:32–33).

Pence did I say? O they have charming skill   80
To rouse the gall of an heroic quill!
Is there not mighty sound and mighty sense
In great Iscariot's thirty chinking pence!
By this Lucina hast thou borne with pain
The num'rous offspring of thy teeming brain: 85
More various issues in Nile's slimy bed
Not thy own patron Phoebus ever bred.
Thy pregnant heats, like Israel's wanton lust,
First mold thy golden calves, then pound 'em into dust.
    Write on, and more than winds or frenzy range,   90
Keep still thy old prerogative to change;
'Tis poor humanity that's kept in bound
Whilst pow'r unlimited is godlike found.
Then thy great self, thou wondrous poet, show:
Honor and principles disdain, for know   95
Thy mercury's too proud to fix so low.
All laws and bounds let thy wild Muse despise,
And reign the Prince o'th' Air in which it flies.

84. *Lucina:* Cf. *Oceana and Britannia*, 6 *n.*

87. *thy own patron Phoebus:* (1) the sun; (2) Apollo, god of poetry and thus Dryden's patron; (3) possibly an allusion to the literary and sexual activities of Dryden's patron, the earl of Mulgrave.

98. *Prince o'th' Air:* Satan.

A Hue and Cry after Blood and Murder
(1682)

On the evening of 12 February 1682, Thomas Thynne, Esq., of Longleat, was returning from a visit to the home of the duchess of Northumberland, grandmother of the young widow he had married in the summer of 1681. Thynne had made a brilliant but strange marriage with one of the wealthiest and youngest widows in England. Elizabeth Percy, daughter of the last earl of Northumberland, had married at the age of twelve the earl of Ogle, eldest son of the duke of Newcastle. Two years later, in a mysteriously surreptitious marriage, the young widow married Tom Thynne. The marriage had never been consummated, however, and Tom Thynne was now contesting the marriage jointure. The earl of Essex, according to Luttrell, claimed that the Lady Elizabeth had been betrayed into this marriage by her grandmother; such might well have been the case, for the young widow had at this time fled to Holland. In all probability, it was this situation that had taken Thynne to the countess of Northumberland's that evening.

Thynne was known as a close friend of James, duke of Monmouth. Earlier Monmouth had been with Thynne, but when a blunderbuss was fired into Thynne's coach later that evening, Thynne was alone. The three men who committed this crime were immediately apprehended, and none of them ever denied his part. But the astonishing figure who apparently stood behind them, Count Carl Johann of Königsmarck, created a scandal not equaled since Godfrey's murder. Although Königsmarck was acquitted as an accessory before the fact, the acquittal surprised everyone and angered in particular Monmouth's followers. Several connections between Thynne and Königsmarck were uncovered, but none satisfactorily explained the shooting. The reactions of the writer of this poem to this "most barbarous murder" are not difficult to find: for him, Thynne was a second Godfrey, and he attempted to evoke the fervor of the first days of the Popish Plot; moreover, "the miraculous escape" of Monmouth constituted, for him, further evidence of Heaven's protection. Divine truth will, on the one hand, have its swift vengeance by revealing the murderers and, on the other, demonstrate its approbation of the duke's claims.

The murder was committed on Sunday evening; by Monday noon all three assailants had been captured. By Wednesday the 15th—the day Luttrell obtained his copy—the poem had been "printed for Langley Curtis."

A Hue and Cry after Blood and Murder,

or

An Elegy on the Most Barbarous Murder of Thomas Thynne, Esq.

With Some Thankful Ejaculations to Heaven, for the Miraculous
Escape of His Grace the Duke of Monmouth
from the Hands of the Bloody Ruffians

Whil'st with hot scent, the Popish Tory crew
A Presbyterian sham plot do pursue,
Behold a new and true plot of their own
Against a worthy person's life made known.
Blood after blood for God's fresh vengeance calls;   5
Now Monmouth's friend a second victim falls.
The bloody villains skilled i'th murderous sin,
Sir Godfrey's murder new act o'er ag'in:
And now the shammers must together plot
To make the world think Thynne himself had shot.   10
What was his crime that thus they sought his life?
Was it because deceived by a wife?
Or was't because that he was Monmouth's friend,
He found so fatal and so sad an end?
    In former times such murders scarce were known.   15
Are we barbarians or fierce Scythians grown?
What impious acts are minted in our age?
What tragic scenes are brought upon the stage?
What e'er the heathen did we now can do

1. A gibe at Roger L'Estrange, the arch-enemy of the Whig pamphleteers, dubbed Towzer, a common name for a large dog, such as was used to bait bears or bulls. L'Estrange was, as always, quick to take this up. He discusses this poem in *Observator*, no. 101 (20 February 1682) and on this point remarks that Langley Curtis "will have it to be the act also of the Popish Tory crew, that is to say [according to his key], the court party."

10. The story that the coroner's inquest had first found that Godfrey's death was a suicide (*felo de se*) was encouraged at this time by Tory pamphleteers.

12. With the suggestion (here and in lines 41–44) that Königsmarck had had Thynne murdered at the request of Lady Elizabeth, his paramour, L'Estrange's indignation was uncontrolled: "Nay, the malice of this prostitute libeller carries the plot on (with so many defamatory lies betwixt his teeth) even to a second assassinate, i.e. upon the honor of a lady both as a——and a murderess, who is as conspicuous in the world for her generous and unspotted virtue as for her state and quality. And this from the print of a despicable scoundrel, viler than the dirt in the kennel" (*Observator*, no. 101 [20 February 1682]).

15. Though Eveline Godley (*The Trial of Count Königsmarck* [London: P. Davies, 1929]) suggests that this "matchless murder" could be matched at least by Felton's assassination of Buckingham in 1628, the use of hired killers appears to have been the really shocking element of this particular crime.

And, though we're Christians called, surpass them too.   20
In the last end o'th' Iron Age we live;
A brother won't a brother now forgive;
But for some slight affront or weak offense,
With sword or pistol he is hurried hence.
   These murderous arts by Jesuits hither brought,   25
With their religion they in secret taught:
For murders they have their commission given,
And killing is one gate that leads to heaven.
We may believe it, as we do our creed,
None but some hired Papists did this deed.   30
A deed so horrid, barbarous, and vile
That it will leave a blot upon our Isle,
Which will a spot for our whole age remain
Unless strict vengeance wipe away the stain.
Th' ambassador whom we barbarian call,   35
When to his barbarous prince return he shall,
Amongst our crimes with horror will relate
This murder acted near the palace gate
And to his prince maliciously will say,
Christians can murders act as well as they.   40
   Hard was the fate of this most worthy man,
Whom first a wicked woman did trepan;
And now more hard, if that he lost his life
By murderous means of his disloyal wife.
But God that sees and knows the hearts of all   45
Will soon on guilty heads let vengeance fall;
And those black instruments now laid in hold
Shall all the truth of this black deed unfold.
Where Justice runs down like an unstopped flood,
It soon will wash away the stains of blood.   50

21. *Iron Age:* the last and worst age, succeeding the Golden, Silver, and Bronze ages; a period of wickedness, cruelty, oppression, and debasement. There may be, considering its source, some slight suggestion of Fifth Monarchist thinking behind the use of the image here.

35. *ambassador:* Ahmed Hadu headed a small embassy from Morocco that came to make revisions of a treaty relating to Tangiers.

38. *the palace:* St. James's. Actually, the crime occurred on Pall Mall, at the lower end of St. Albans Street.

47. Sir John Reresby recounts, with pardonable pride, that "at six o'clock in the morning [of 13 February], having been in chase almost the whole night, I personally took the captain at the house of a Swedish doctor in Leicester Fields, going first into the room, followed by my Lord Mordaunt, where I found him in bed with his sword at some distance from him upon the table, which I first seized and afterward his person, committing him to two constables" (p. 250). Stern and Borosky were taken by noon.

The murdered's friends therefore on Justice cry
And to its sacred throne together fly
That vengeance may both great and small pursue,
O'ertake the hirers and the hired too—
Both those who the damned hire for blood receive,   55
And those who to be damned their money give.
For if strict vengeance on such be not ta'en,
Our laws for murder will be made in vain;
So impious and so vile now men are grown,
As never in our age before was known.   60
   Who can't but go or ride the streets in fear,
When we have *bravoes* and *banditti* here?
Tories who here have shown their murderous skill,
And know the way as well as they to kill.
Under our English cloth men must wear buff,   65
A coat of mail, or armor pistol-proof;
For fear of some revenge from jilting drabs,
Or else for friendship or religion stabs.
Poison, or bullet, fraud, or force they take,
Both for revenge and for religion's sake.   70
Justice will visit when the murder's past
And overtake the criminals at last,
And such black deeds lie open to God's sight,
Who will the murderous plots bring forth to light.

51. *friends:* Monmouth and his party. It was one of Monmouth's servants who took the disguised Königsmarck as the latter arrived by sculler at Gravesend. The count had been planning to leave England the following day aboard a Swedish ship.

65. *buff:* a stout leather of ox-hide, used especially in military coats of the period.

66. There might be a recollection here of the fear and frenzy at the height of the Popish Plot discoveries.

67. *drabs:* sluts, prostitutes, or strumpets. There is, again, the totally unwarranted attack on Lady Elizabeth.

68. *friendship:* Reresby reports that when Königsmarck was previously in England wooing Lady Elizabeth, he "resented something as done towards him as an affront from the said Mr. Thynne; and that the said captain [Vratz], out of friendship to the count (but as he then pretended not with his privity) was resolved to be revenged of him, to which intent he . . . had committed this so barbarous act" (p. 252).

69. A gallimaufry of Oates's original charges, general fears, and the specific event. *Poison:* refers to Oates's charge that Sir George Wakeman, the queen's physician, was to be offered £10,000 to poison Charles II. *bullet:* referring to the assassination of Thynne, but probably meant to recall the endless attempts of Grove and Pickering to shoot the king. *fraud:* though almost synonomous in this context with Jesuit, may allude to anything from Edward Coleman's dealings with the French to the general apprehension of York. *force:* alludes at once to the specific crime, but, in the wider sense of the Popish Plot, suggests Oates's charge of open invasion by the Spanish and French, rebellion in Ireland, and general massacre.

74, 77. *plots:* The writer leaves little doubt of his interpretation of the events. Fortunately

Then, worthy Thynne, we shall more surely know   75
Who was thy barbarous bloody secret foe
When to the bottom of this plot we see,
And if the villains only aimed at thee.
     Rest now thy soul in peace, whilst our good king
Your bloody murderers to justice bring;   80
Whilst the scared people on thy death debate,
And all thy friends bewail thy sudden fate;
Whilst the good duke bewails with tears his friend,
Afflicted to behold his sudden end.
But let all loyal hearts to Heaven pay   85
Their thanks that Monmouth did no longer stay,
That Providence who over him takes care
Had him diverted then from being there.
Who knows what bloody ruffians did intend?
They might perhaps have yet a further end;   90
Revenge might reach both to the duke and's friend.
But Heaven will hear for him the people's prayer,
And of that noble prince his life take care
That he may still secure and safely go
And all the plots of Papists overthrow.   95
     May Heav'n preserve the king that he may run
A long, long race, and for his sake his son;
May the Almighty keep the good duke's life
From hellish plots, from popish gun or knife.
And let himself, warned, now more watchful be   100
Lest that he fall into like jeopardy.
O Heaven preserve him from a bloody end,
And let him take a warning by his friend.

---

for the court, the investigation did not fall into the hands of a rabid Whig. Reresby indicates this strongly: "I was glad to find in this whole affair no English person nor interest was concerned, the fanatics having buzzed it already abroad that the design was chiefly against the duke of Monmouth. And I had the king's thanks oftener than once, my Lord Halifax's, and several others, for my diligent discovery of the true cause and occasion, as well as the authors of this matter" (pp. 252–53).

86. "The truth is," says Reresby, "the duke of Monmouth was gone out of the coach from Mr. Thynne an hour before; but I found by the confession both of Stern and Borosky that they were ordered not to shoot in case the duke were with him in the coach" (p. 253).

92–93. As in line 87, there is the strong implication of divine approval of Monmouth. The same theme—God's discovery of the truth—was at the heart of the much-touted broadsides that told of Monmouth's touching for the "king's evil" at Hinton Park on his Western Progress in August 1680.

103. *friend:* Tom Thynne.

The Trial and Death of Shaftesbury

[ELKANAH SETTLE]

The Medal Reversed
(1682)

The assertion on the title page that this poem is "by the author of *Azaria and Hushai*" introduces a typical problem of pamphlet ascription. Luttrell, who obtained his copy on 31 March 1682, wrote on it "Sam Pordage," perhaps in keeping with his earlier views of *Azaria* (an answer to Dryden's *Absalom*), which he had marked as "by S. Pordage. 17 Jan." Some additional support comes from *The Observator*, no. 119 (5 April 1682), where L'Estrange, after devoting the first column to a Tory critique of this poem, goes on to other matters and then, starting an attack on Pordage, remarks that "limping Pordage [is] . . . violently suspected for *The Medal Reversed*."

The interlocking of the two poems only serves to complicate the problem. Dobell (*Literature of the Restoration*, London, 1918, p. 54) notes a copy of *Azaria* with "For my worthy friend Mr. Pordage" inscribed in a hand that is not Settle's, though the poem was generally thought to be his when it first appeared (Wood, *Athenae Oxonienses*, 4, 687). Second thoughts by contemporaries are equally elusive. Ham's thorough analysis of the external evidence gives very strong support to Settle's exclusive authorship of both poems; and one might add that both Macdonald and Yale University have copies of *The Medal Reversed* with "E. Settle" in manuscript on the title page. The style of *The Medal Reversed* could be that of a number of accomplished writers in the Whig idiom: Settle, of course, or perhaps his friend Pordage, or even Edmund Hickeringill, whose rhetoric, vocabulary, and phrasing seem at times remarkably similar to the poem's. The tone moves effectively from moderation and generalized indignation to specific warnings that are at once startlingly frank and prophetic.

The Medal Reversed is a rejoinder to Dryden's famous satirical poem, *The Medal* (1681), which attacks Shaftesbury and the Whig supporters who had struck a medal in honor of the dismissal of charges of treason against him.

THE MEDAL REVERSED

A Satire against Persecution

How easy 'tis to sail with wind and tide!
Small force will serve upon the stronger side;
Power serves for law, the wrong too oft's made right,
And they are damned who against Power dare fight.
Wit rides triumphant, in Power's chariot borne,   5
And depressed opposites beholds with scorn.
This well the author of *The Medal* knew,
When Oliver he for an hero drew.
He then swam with the tide, appeared a saint,
Garnished the devil with poetic paint.   10
When the tide turned, then straight about he veers,
And for the stronger side he still appears,
Then in heroics courts the great and high,
And at th' oppressed he lets his satyrs fly.
But he who stems the tide, if ground he gains,   15
Each stroke he makes must be with wond'rous pains:
If he bears up against the current still,
He shows at least he has some art and skill,
When against tide, wind, billows he does strive
And comes at last unto the shore alive.   20
Huzza, my friends! let us our way pursue,
And try what our poetic arms can do.
This latter age with wonders does abound;
Our prince of poets has a medal found,
From whence his pregnant fancy rears a piece   25

8. The elegiac verses on the death of Cromwell, written between September 1658 and January 1659, were constantly mentioned by Dryden's opponents and reprinted three times in 1681–82 to embarrass the now Tory poet (Macdonald, pp. 3–6).

9. *saint:* the term used by certain puritanical sectarians for their adherents, whom they considered members of the elect under the New Covenant of the New Testament. By those outside sects, the term was used with obloquy to signify those extremist groups that had given full support to Cromwell's government.

13. The author probably has in mind such poems as *Astraea Redux* (c. 19 June 1660); *To His Sacred Majesty . . . on His Coronation* (April 1661); *To My Lord Chancellor* (1662); and *Annus Mirabilis* (January 1667).

14. *satyrs:* The original spelling has been retained since the writer is making use of the contemporary confusion between *satire* and *satyr.*

21. *Huzza:* The writer's exclamation is mildly ironic. As North explains, "at all the Tory healths . . . the cry was reared of 'Huzza!' which, at great and solemn feasts made no little noise and gave advantage to the Whigs, that liked not such music, to charge the Tories with brutality and extravagance" (p. 617),

The Shaftesbury medal by George Bowers.

Esteemed to equal those of Rome and Greece.
With piercing eyes he does the medal view,
And there he finds, as he has told to you,
The hag Sedition, to the life displayed,
Under a statesman's gown (fancied or made,   30
That is all one, he doth it so apply);
At it th' artillery of his wit lets fly,
Lets go his satyr at the medal straight,
Worries the Whigs, and doth Sedition bait.
Let him go on, the Whigs the hag forsake;   35
Her cause they never yet would undertake,
But laugh to see the poet's fond mistake.
But we will turn the medal; there we see
Another hag, I think as bad as she;
If I am not mistaken, 'tis the same,   40
Christians of old did Persecution name;
That's still her name; though now, grown old and wise,
She has new names as well as new disguise.
Let then his satyr with Sedition fight,
And ours the whilst shall Persecution bite.   45
Two hags they are, who parties seem to make;
'Tis time for satyrs them to undertake.

   See her true badge, a prison or the Tower;
For Persecution ever sides with power.
Our satyr dares not worry those he should;   50
But there are some felt, heard, and understood,
Who, substantives of power, stand alone,
And by all seeing men are too well known—
What steps they tread and whither 'tis they drive,
What measures take and by what arts they thrive.   55
But were these little tyrants underfoot,
How bravely o'er them could our satyr strut!
What characters, and justly, could he give,
Of men who scarcely do deserve to live!
Yet these are they some flatterers can court,   60
Who now are Persecution's great support.
We on the medal see the fatal Tower;
Truth must be silent, for we know their power:

29. While the subtitle of *The Medal* is "A Satire against Sedition," Dryden does not actually use the image of the hag.

Whilst they, without control, can show their hate,
And whom they please, with grinning satyrs bait.   65
This puts our satyr into fume and chafe;
He could bite sorely could he do it safe.
Since against such he dares not spend his breath,
Th'hag Persecution he will bait to death.

Old as the world almost, as old as Cain,   70
For by this hag was righteous Abel slain;
In tyrant's courts she ever doth abide,
Accompanied with Power, with Lust and Pride.
What she has done is to the world well known;
She always made the best of men to groan.   75
Her bloody arts are registered of old,
And all her cruel policies are told.
All that is past, our Muse shall let alone,
Pass foreign, and speak only of our own;
Our own a dear ugly hag, who now has power   80
To send to Tyburn, Newgate, or the Tower.

If power be in the multitude, not few,
They show that they have faith and reason too,
Leap not their bounds, nor do their power betray,
Since they to laws and government obey.   85
If other power they exercise, 'tis force,
Or rage, that seen in a wild headstrong horse,
The more he's spurred or reined, the more doth bound,
And leaves not till the rider's on the ground.
But far it seems from our almighty crowd   90
To boast their strength or be of power proud.
Their power they of old had fruitless tried
And therefore now take reason for their guide.
Nay, faith they have in their own juster cause,
In their dread sovereign, and his righteous laws;   95
This makes them thus submit, all power lay by;
For right, for law, for peace they only cry.
For this, by some, they are accounted fools;

82. See, e.g., *The Medal*, 82–83, 91–92.

87–89. The forthright development of the image probably answers Dryden's allusion to Jehu in *The Medal* (119–22), a common symbol of uncontrollable revolt.

90–91. *almighty crowd:* Cf. *The Medal*, 91, 134.

92. *of old:* The reference is to 1640–60. Cf. *The Medal*, 127–30.

93–94. Cf. *The Medal*, 93.

So generous horses are mistook for mules,
And some court jockeys mount them in their pride   100
And with a satyr's heel spur-gall their hide;
Dull asses they suppose the people are,
Made for their burdens, and not fit for war.

   All with the forewind of religious sail;
It to all parties is the common stale.   105
I know you'll grant the devil is no fool;
He can disguise in surplice, cloak, or cowl;
But still he may be known without dispute
By Persecution; 'tis his cloven foot.
Let him be Christian, Pagan, Turk, or Jew,   110
Pretends religious zeal, it can't be true
If't Persecution raises, or maintains,
Or makes a market of ungodly gains.
When Rome had power here and sat enchaired,
How cruel and how bloody she appeared!   115
Our Church Dissenters then did feel the same;
Their bodies served for fuel to the flame:
And can this church now got into the chair,
A cruel tyrant like to Rome appear?
For bare opinion do their brothers harm,   120
Plague and imprison, 'cause they can't conform!
—But stay; our church has law upon its side:
And so had Rome, that cannot be denied.
And if these Jehus, who so fiercely drive,
In their sinister arts proceed and thrive,   125
We soon shall see our church receive its doom
And feel again the tyranny of Rome.
To bar succession is th' ungodly sin,
So often broke, so often pieced ag'in:
O may it here in England never cease,   130
Could we but hope it would secure our peace!
But men with different thoughts possessèd are;

100. *jockeys:* colloquially, cheats or fraudulent bargainers.
105. *common stale:* a prostitute of the lowest class, employed as a decoy by thieves.
117. The allusion is probably to the Marian persecutions that began in 1555.
120–21. Under such laws as the Act of Uniformity, the Conventicle Act, the Five-Mile Act, and the later Test Act (1678), nonconforming sects were harassed by the government. The second Test Act was aimed at Roman Catholics; the first (1673) harassed Nonconformists too.
124. *Jehus:* 2 Kings 9:20. See 87–89 *n.*
128–31. Cf. *The Medal,* 115–16.

We dread th' effects of a new civil war.
We dread Rome's yoke, to us 'tis hateful grown,
And Rome will seem a monster in our throne.   135

How rarely will a cope the throne bedeck?
A bishop's head set on a prince's neck?
Th' inherent right lies in the sovereign's sway,
But then the monarch must Rome's laws obey.
Head of the church he must no longer be,   140
But give that place unto Rome's Holy See.
Both of the church, and him, Rome will take care;
The throne must truckle under papal chair.

Kings can't do wrong, so does the maxim say,
But ministers of state, their servants, may.   145
Though kings themselves do sit above the law,
Justice still keeps their ministers in awe;
For if they do not make the law their guide,
Great as they are, by law they may be tried;
Else we should subject be to every ill,   150
And be made slaves to arbitrary will.
O happy isle where each man justice craves!
Kings can't be tyrants, nor the subjects slaves.
The laws some great ones fear, who rule the state;
When they can't new unto their wills create,   155
They to their minds, with cunning, try to mold,
And, with new images, to stamp the old:
What 'gainst dissenting Papists first was bent,
For Protestants now proves a punishment.
Law! Law! they cry, and then their brother smite,   160
As well upon the left side as the right;
To every jail the Protestants they draw,
And Persecution still is masked with law;
We do not know but Rome may have its turn,
And then it will be also law to burn.   165

136. *cope*: a clerical, or sacerdotal, vestment; also, the special dress of a monk or friar.
143. Cf. *The Medal*, 87.
144. Cf. *The Medal*, 135.
145 ff. The classic parliamentarian attack against royal prerogative was through the king's "evil counselors." Cf. *The Medal*, 228–31.
158. Parliament enacted certain bills for religious conformity aimed primarily at Roman Catholics; the government, however, enforced them against those of the opposite extreme, the dissenting sectarians.
165. It was not until 8 March 1677 that a bill for taking away the writ *De Haeritico Comburendo* was introduced in Commons (*CJ, 9*, 394). The bill passed, of course, quite rapidly

This is not all; for some ill men there be,
Who would the laws use in a worse degree:
Treason and traitors, plots against the state,
To reach their foes, they cunningly create.
To prison then the innocent they draw,   170
And if they could, their heads would take by law;
But law is just, and Englishmen are good,
And do not love to dip their hands in blood
Of innocents. But this has raised the rage
Of some politic actors on our stage,   175
And, spite of justice, law, and reason too,
Their wicked ends by other means pursue.
Those men whom they can neither hang nor draw,
Freed by their country, justice, and the law,
They try to murder with an hireling's pen,   180
By making them the very worst of men.
They've orators and poets at their will,
Who, with their venom, strive their fames to kill.
These rack the laws and Holy Scriptures too,
And fain would make all the old treasons new.   185
They will not let the graves and tombs alone,
But conjure up the ghost of Forty-one.
With this they try the ignorant to scare,
For men are apt the worst of things to fear;
Though that ghost is no liker Eighty-two,   190
Than a good Christian like a Turk or Jew.

London, the happy bulwark of our isle,
No smooth and oily words can thee beguile;
Thou know'st thy int'rest, that will never lie;
Eternal as thyself, the men do die.   195
'Tis truth and justice do thee uphold,

(ibid., p. 419), but Whig writers alluded to it constantly at this time (cf. *Weekly Pacquet*, 10
February, 16 June 1682).

168. *Treason and traitors*: Though closely connected with the second half of the line, the
reference here would seem to be to the government's charge of high treason against the earl of
Shaftesbury. *plots against the state*: The Meal Tub Plot, according to the Whigs, was a sham
plot fabricated by the Catholics in order to incriminate the leaders of the Whig party.

182. *orators*: George Savile, marquis of Halifax, was credited with having almost single-
handedly defeated the Exclusion Bill on 15 November 1680 by out-debating Shaftesbury.

184. Cf. *The Medal*, 156–57. On the racking of Holy Scriptures, the author is very likely
referring to Dryden's use of the Bible in *Absalom and Achitophel*.

187.   *ghost of Forty-one*: Dryden, like most Tory writers, constantly connected the anti-court
party with the parliamentarians who, in 1641, had opposed Charles I.

192. For Dryden's description of London, see *The Medal*, 167–204.

And richer in religion than in gold;
Thy piety has built thy turrets higher
Than e'er, in spite of plague, of war, and fire.
Without a sigh, we can't think on the flame,   200
Nor by what hands, and from what heads, it came.
With envious eyes, they do thy riches view;
When old ways fail, to spoil thee they find new:
No art's untried which may thy coffers drain,
For which the subtle lawyer racks his brain.   205
Thy too old charters they will new arraign.
Thou must not think thou canst in safety stand
Whilst the false Canaanite swarms in the land.
Some state-physicians cry that thou art sick,
And on thee they would try some quacking trick;   210
As yet their poisonous drugs thou dost not need,
Nor does thy body want to purge or bleed.
Thy head, we hope, with loyalty is crowned,
Thy heart and entrails we do know are sound:
Thy hands are open, honest, free, and straight,   215
And all thy members pliable and neat.
All think you well in health, and sound within;
Though some few spots appear upon your skin,
They're but the purgings of the sounder part
And are at a great distance from the heart.   220
The wealthy love to thrive the surest way;
For gain perhaps they will like slaves obey,
Give up their charters, bend their necks, now free,
To servile yokes, and stoop to that degree
As to submit to Rome's cursed tyranny.   225
But sure the wise, and the religious too,
Will all the just and lawful ways pursue

200–01. In June 1681, following the feverish months of the Popish Plot, the London Common Council ordered that the monument commemorating the fire of London (1666) should be engraved with the declaration that the disaster "was begun and carried on by the treachery and malice of the popish faction" (Walter Bell, *The Great Fire of London in 1666* [London: The Bodley Head, 1951], pp. 208–09).

206. In November 1681, Charles II began the Quo Warranto proceedings to recall the London Charter. The case was finally decided in the court's favor in 1683 (Howell, *8*, 1039–1358).

208. Cf. *The Medal*, 178.

213. *Thy head:* Sir John Moore, the lord mayor, became increasingly attached to the court during his stormy term in office. Cf. *The Medal*, 181.

215. *Thy hands:* the Whig sheriffs, Thomas Pilkington and Samuel Shute. Cf. *The Medal*, 182.

To keep that freedom unto which they're born
And which so well doth Englishmen adorn;
Which our forefathers did preserve with care230
And which we, next our souls, do hold most dear.
Let the hot Tories, and their poet, curse!
They spend in vain, and you are ne'er the worse.
Alas! they seem as only made to damn,
And then curse most when they have lost their sham;235
They are true Shimeis, or the sons of Cham.
Their mouths are open sepulchers; their tongue,
With venom full, is ever speaking wrong.
With oaths and cursings, and with looking big,
They seek to fright some harmless, peaceful Whig;240
Then boast the conquest, hector, rant, and tear,
And cry, "God-damn 'em! Protestants they are!
All the fanatics are a cursed crew,
Worse than the Papists, or the Moor, or Jew!
The City is a laystall full of mire,245
And ought again to be new purged with fire!"
All honesty, all godliness they hate,
Love strife and war, contention and debate.
These are the men from whom much mischief springs,
Whilst their bad cause they falsely make the king's.250
These wrong the king, and then to make amends,
With oaths declare they are his only friends;
But these are they who Coleman would outdo,
Blow up both kings and kingly power too.

For why is all this contest and this strife,255
This struggling in the state, as 'twere for life,
When all men owned their enjoyed happiness,
And daily did their beloved monarch bless?
But these ill men all common roads forsake;

236. *Shimeis:* The Benjamite Shimei cursed David as the royal party fled from Absalom
(2 Sam. 16:5–13). Dryden, in *Absalom and Achitophel* (585–629), had represented the former
Whig sheriff, Slingsby Bethel, under this name. *sons of Cham:* i.e. descendants of Ham, the
second son of Noah. Because of his irreverence to his father, Ham and his race were cursed
(Gen. 9:22). Hamites (a term of obloquy) are connected primarily with Egypt, which in
political verse usually referred to France.
241. *hector:* to brag, bluster, domineer.
242. Cf. *The Medal*, 110.
245–46. Cf. *The Medal*, 187–88. *laystall:* a place where refuse and dung are laid.
253. *Coleman:* the Roman Catholic secretary to the duchess of York. The discovery
of his treasonous correspondence with Père La Chaise led to his execution on 3 December
1678.

O'er hedges and through standing corn they break;   260
Though ill success they have, they will not cease
Till they have spoiled the nation's happy peace.
They see none to rebellion are inclined,
Yet plots they make, where plots they cannot find.
But their designs they did so idly frame,   265
The evil on their heads returned with shame;
And though they find their evil projects cursed,
They keep the impudence they had at first;
'Gainst honesty, law, reason, then they fight,
And falsely cry, the king can have no right.   270
The people of their judgment they bereave,
No proof, no circumstance will they believe,
Rebels and traitors they will still create,
And are men-catchers of the highest rate.
With regal rights, these men keep much ado;   275
But, with that stale, their own game they pursue.
Their monarch's safety, honor, fame, renown,
The great supports and jewels of the crown;
The people's love, their freedom, liberties,
Those they neglect, and these they do despise.   280
What e'er these men pretend, the juggling feat
Is plainly seen: 'tis to grow rich and great,
To rule, to sway, to govern as they please:
The people's grievance, and the land's disease.
All men that would oppose their pow'r and sway   285
And will not them, like galley-slaves, obey,
They brand with odious names—although they spring
From fathers ever loyal to their king;
Though they themselves sons of the church are known,
Would with their blood defend their monarch's throne,   290
And ready are their lives to sacrifice
For all their king's just rights, which much they prize.
But O the change that's now in England seen!
They who are loyal, and so e'er have been,

264–66. Another allusion to the Meal Tub Plot; see 168 *n.*
270. *can have:* i.e., is able to obtain.
274. *men-catchers:* entrappers of men. Edmund Hickeringill, the Nonconformist divine and pamphleteer, was particularly fond of this term, which he devised from Jer. 5:26 and used as the basis of his highly popular sermon (three editions in 1681 and a fourth in 1682), *The Horrid Sin of Man-catching.*
287. *although they spring:* The pronoun refers to those who are unjustly vilified.

Because they will not serve sinister ends,   295
Are rebels called, at least called traitors' friends.
Thou wicked hag that now art armed with pow'r,
That wouldst men's souls and bodies both devour,
That now dost show thy bloody armed paws,
With malice armed, and with too rigid laws;   300
With what poetic curse shall I thee paint,
Who art a devil, yet appear'st a saint?
But vengeance for thee still in Heav'n there's store;
Though many bless and thee the Beast adore,
Thou'rt dyed with blood and art the Scarlet Whore.   305
O Persecution! thou'rt a goddess blind,
That never sparest any human kind;
In every country thou dost footing gain,
In all religions thou desir'st to reign,
But never wast admitted in the true.   310
Hence grow our tears, that here thou shouldst renew
Thy strength and power in this happy realm,
Our quiet and our peace to overwhelm;
When for some years thou hast been banished,
And Protestants believed thou hadst been dead;   315
Or that at least, we never more should fear
That thou shouldst live to show thy power here,
Unless (which Heav'n avert) that thou shouldst come
By force, brought in by the cursed power of Rome.
But grieved we are to see it in our age,   320
And fear it may a greater ill presage.
Prisons and fines the punishments are now,
But who knows what at last it may come to?
For this damned hag longs still for human food,
Ne'er satisfied till she is gorged with blood.   325
Well may the Papists, when they have their turn,
Rack and imprison, torture, hang, and burn;
When Protestants to Protestants do show
That, had they pow'r, themselves as much would do.
But let the busy ministers take care,   330

304. *the Beast:* Antichrist.
305. *Scarlet Whore:* the whore of Babylon, the Roman Catholic church.
322. *punishments:* i.e., for holding illegal conventicles.
330–31. *ministers:* The author seems to have in mind principally (but not exclusively) ministers of state, who (he implies, lines 375–78) will be brought to the strict justice of a parliament.

They do but vengeance for themselves prepare;
For in all ages it was ever known,
That God His vengeance on their heads poured down.

All but mere fools may easily foresee
What will the fatal end of these things be: 335
If one bigoted in the Romish way
Should once again the English scepter sway,
Then those who in the pulpit are so loud,
Preaching succession to the vulgar crowd,
Must change their croaking notes, their coats must turn;   340
Or, if prove honest, fly the land, or burn.
Whom benefit or ignorance engage
Now to the party, then shall feel the rage
Of those fierce tyrants, who now undermine
And, hidden, carry on their cursed design.   345
The proud usurping priest and popish knaves
Shall be your lords, and all the English slaves;
The nobles then must wear the Romish yoke,
Or heads submit unto the fatal stroke.
Oppression will grow bold, the tadpole priests   350
Shall lift above the lords their priestly crests.
T'attempt or struggle then will be in vain,
For Persecution will a tyrant reign;
Her fatal pow'r will then be understood,
And she will glut herself with martyr's blood.   355
The pope's supremacy shall then be shown,
No other head in England will be known.
Then shall a general curse flow through the land,
Lord against lord, friend against friend shall stand;
Till at the last, the crowd, in their defence,   360
Provoked to rage, arm 'gainst their popish prince.
With words no longer, but with arms they'll jar,
And England will be spoiled with civil war;
True peace and happiness so long shall want
Till she shall get a monarch Protestant.   365

336. *one:* i.e., the duke of York.
339. The bishops had unanimously voted against the Exclusion Bill. The author's analysis of future events culminates in a surprisingly frank statement of the threat of civil war should York succeed to the throne (lines 361–64). Cf. the prophecy in *The Medal*, 287–317.
342. *Whom:* i.e., whomsoever.
348–49. Cf. *The Medal*, 298–99.
359. Cf. *The Medal*, 309.
361–62. Cf. *The Medal*, 306–07.

Thus factious men to civil broils engage,
And with their ferment, make the crowd to rage.
Their madness they in others would increase,
Yet wipe their mouths and cry they are for peace;
For king, for regal rights, and true succession,   370
They in the people's ears still make profession;
Yet for one man, such friends they are, so civil,
They'd send almost three nations to the devil.
But there's no way these mischiefs to prevent,
Unless we have a healing parliament.   375
Of that these faulty men love not to hear;
They've much transgressed and much they have to fear.
Until that day, England will find no rest,
Though now she slumbers on her monarch's breast;
But then the nation will be truly blessed.   380

366. Cf. *The Medal*, 318, 290–92.

370t *true succession:* A highly important, though often unnoticed, distinction of the period is that between true succession (i.e., succession solely on the basis of the most immediate consanguinity) and legal succession (i.e., succession to the nearest in line who is not debarred by existing laws). The question at this time was whether York, the nearest in blood, could, as a professed member of the Roman Catholic religion, become head of the state church, which supported the exclusion of Romanism. Burnet explains that "the word *heir* . . . imported from that person who by law ought to succeed, and so it fell to any person who by law was declared next in the succession. In England, the heir of the king that reigned had been sometimes set aside, and the right of succession was transferred to another person" (*2*, 215).

372. *one man:* i.e., York.

375. *a healing parliament:* The basic error in Whig strategy during the critical struggles of 1682 was their ever more desperate dependence on what they thought would be "the aftergame in parliament" (North, p. 611). Not until far too late did they begin to discover that the real Popish Plot lay in the subsidies that Louis XIV paid to Charles and that, with increased revenues from the customs, were sufficient to make the calling of Parliament unnecessary.

379. Cf. *The Medal*, 322.

THOMAS SHADWELL

The Medal of John Bayes
(1682)

While there is very strong evidence to suggest that this poem is by Thomas Shadwell, its authorship has never been absolutely settled. Contemporary ascription by Luttrell ("By Thomas Shadwell. Agt Mr. Dryden. very severe. 15 May [1682]") and a Trinity College, Cambridge, MS ("Shadwell is run mad") militate strongly for Shadwell, but Macdonald's position (pp. 232–33) is only a more recent example of the hesitation that some scholars have felt. D. M. McKeithan's support of Shadwell ("The Authorship of *The Medal of John Bayes*," *University of Texas Studies in English, 12* [1932], pp. 92–97) on the basis of parallel passages seems definitely weakened by the number of such passages based on contemporary commonplaces; indeed, one could make at least an equal case for Settle's authorship on such internal evidence. The most conclusive evidence for Shadwell's authorship is that presented by James M. Osborn (*John Dryden: Some Biographical Facts and Problems* [New York, 1940], pp. 154–67), his careful analysis of the poem and its epistle presents as strong proof as one can expect from anonymous poems during this period.

The poem and its epistle reply to *The Medal* with a *saeva* and *sancta indignatio* that not only give us more information (true or false) on Dryden than any other contemporary work but also express the high aims of Whig parliamentarianism and its response, however weak, to divine right and "true" succession.

The Medal of John Bayes

A Satire against Folly and Knavery
—Facit indignatio versus.

How long shall I endure, without reply,
To hear this Bayes, this hackney-railer, lie?
The fool, uncudgeled, for one libel swells,
Where not his wit, but sauciness excels;
Whilst with foul words and names which he lets fly,   5
He quite defiles the satire's dignity.
For libel and true satire different be;
This must have truth, and salt, with modesty.
Sparing the persons, this does tax the crimes,
Galls not great men, but vices of the times,   10
With witty and sharp, not blunt and bitter, rhymes.
Methinks the ghost of Horace there I see,
Lashing this cherry-cheeked dunce of fifty-three;
Who, at that age, so boldly durst profane,
With base hired libel, the free satire's vein.   15
Thou styl'st it satire to call names: rogue, whore,
Traitor, and rebel, and a thousand more.
An oyster-wench is sure thy Muse of late,
And all thy Helicon's at Billingsgate.
A libeler's vile name then may'st thou gain,   20
And moderately the writing part maintain;
None can so well the beating part sustain.
Though with thy sword, thou art the last of men,
Thou art a damned Boroski with thy pen.
As far from satire does thy talent lie   25
As from being cheerful, or good company.

Title: The dropped title gives "or, A Satire upon Folly and Knavery." The epigraph comes from Juvenal, 1.79: "Indignation makes verses."

1. Juvenal 1.1: *Semper ego auditor tantum? Numquamne reponam.*

2. *Bayes:* Dryden's name in *The Rehearsal.* See also Summers's note in *The Rehearsal* (Stratford-upon-Avon: Shakespeare Head Press, 1914), 5, 441.

3. *uncudgeled:* a reference to the famous Rose Alley ambuscade of 18 December 1679. See 95–96 n.

13. Dryden, who was born about 9 August 1631, would have been close to 51 at this time.

19. *Billingsgate:* one of the London gates near which was the fish market famous for its foul vituperative language.

24. *Boroski:* George Borosky, the "Polander" who murdered Tom Thynne by discharging a blunderbuss into Thynne's coach. Cf. *The Medal Reversed.*

For thou art saturnine, thou dost confess;
A civil word thy dullness to express.
An old gelt mastiff has more mirth than thou,
When thou a kind of paltry mirth would'st show.   30
Good humor thou so awkwardly put'st on,
It sits like modish clothes upon a clown;
While that of gentlemen is brisk and high,
When wine and wit about the room does fly.
Thou never mak'st, but art, a standing jest;   35
Thy mirth by foolish bawdry is expressed,
And so debauched, so fulsome, and so odd,
As———
"Let's bugger one another now, by God!"
(When asked how they should spend the afternoon)   40
This was the smart reply of the heroic clown.
He boasts of vice (which he did ne'er commit),
Calls himself whoremaster and sodomite;
Commends Reeves' arse and says she buggers well,
And silly lies of vicious pranks does tell.   45
This is a sample of his mirth and wit,
Which he for the best company thinks fit.
In a rich soil, the sprightly horse y' have seen,
Run, leap, and wanton o'er the flow'ry green,
Prance and curvet, with pleasure to the sight;   50
But it could never any eyes delight
To see the frisking frolics of a cow;
And such another merry thing art thou.
In verse, thou hast a knack with words to chime,
And had'st a kind of excellence in rhyme: 55
With rhymes like leading-strings, thou walk'dst; but those
Laid by, at every step thou brok'st thy nose.

27. *saturnine:* See Summers (Shadwell, *Works,* 5, 441): "In his *Defense of an Essay of Dramatic Poesy,* prefixed to the second edition of *The Indian Emperor,* 1668 . . . Dryden speaking of himself says: 'My conversation is slow and dull, my humor saturnine and reserved.' "

41. *the smart reply:* 1682 note: "At Windsor, in the company of several persons of quality, Sir G[eorge] E[therege] being present." Lines 35–41, along with 52, might echo Rochester's *An Allusion to Horace* (73–74): "But when he would be sharp, he still was blunt:/To frisk his frolic fancy, he'd cry "C——!"

44. *Reeves':* Anne Reeves, a minor actress with the King's Company (1670–72), was said to have been Dryden's mistress.

54–55. In *The Second Part of Absalom and Achitophel* (412–13) Dryden says of Doeg (Settle): "Doeg, though without knowing how or why,/Made still a blund'ring kind of melody."

56. *leading-strings:* formerly used to guide and support children when they were learning to walk.

57. Cf. *The Rehearsal,* 2.5.

How low thy farce! and thy blank verse how mean!
How poor, how naked did appear each scene!
Even thou didst blush at thy insipid stuff,   60
And laid thy dullness on poor harmless snuff.
No comic scene or humor hast thou wrought;
Thou'st quibbling bawdy and ill breeding taught;
But rhyme's sad downfall has thy ruin brought.
No piece did ever from thy self begin;   65
Thou can'st no web from thine own bowels spin.
Were from thy works culled out what thou'st purloined,
Even Durfey would excel what's left behind.
Should all thy borrowed plumes we from thee tear,
How truly Poet Squab would'st thou appear!   70
Thou call'st thy self, and fools call thee, in rhyme,
The goodly Prince of Poets of thy time;
And sov'reign power thou dost usurp, John Bayes,
And from all poets thou a tax dost raise.
Thou plunder'st all t'advance thy mighty name,   75
Look'st big, and triumph'st with thy borrowed fame.
But art (while swelling thus thou think'st th' art chief)
A servile imitator and a thief.
All written wit thou seizest on as prize;
But that will not thy ravenous mind suffice;   80
Though men from thee their inward thoughts conceal,
Yet thou the words out of their mouths wilt steal.
How little owe we to your native store,
Who all you write have heard or read before?
—Except your libels; and there's something new,   85
For none were e'er so impudent as you.
Some scoundrel poetasters yet there be,
Fools that burlesque the name of loyalty,
Who, by reviling patriots, think to be
From lousiness and hunger ever free,   90
But will (for all their hopes of swelling bags)
Return to primitive nastiness and rags.
These are blind fools: thou hadst some kind of sight;
Thou sinn'st against thy conscience and the light.
After the drubs, thou didst of late compound,   95
And sold for th' weight in gold each bruise and wound;

68. *Durfey:* Tom Durfey (1653–1723), a balladeer.
70. *Poet Squab:* Cf. *An Allusion to Horace,* 75–76.
95–96. Cf. headnote to Dryden's and Mulgrave's *Essay upon Satire.*

Clear was thy sight, and none declaimed then more
'Gainst Popish Plots and arbitrary pow'r.
The ministers thou bluntly wouldst assail,
And it was dangerous to hear thee rail.   100
(Oh, may not England stupid be like thee!
Heaven grant it may not feel before it see.)
Now he recants, and on that beating thrives:
Thus poet laureates, and Russian wives,
Do strangely upon beating mend their lives.   105
But how comes Bayes to flag and grovel so?
Sure, your new lords are in their payments slow.
Thou deserv'st whipping thou'rt so dull this time;
Thou'st turned the *Observator* into rhyme.
But thou suppliest the want of wit and sense   110
With most malicious lies, and impudence.
At Cambridge first your scurrilous vein began,
When saucily you traduced a nobleman,
Who for that crime rebuked you on the head,
And you had been expelled had you not fled.   115
The next step of advancement you began
Was being clerk to Noll's lord chamberlain,
A sequestrator and committee-man.
There all your wholesome morals you sucked in
And got your genteel gaiety and mien.   120
Your loyalty you learned in Cromwell's court,
Where first your Muse did make her great effort.
On him you first showed your poetic strain,

109. Dryden's political poems followed the political line and witty tone of the most effective Tory periodical, Sir Roger L'Estrange's *Observator*.

112–15. This incident is otherwise unknown. Dryden was admitted to Trinity College on 11 May 1650 and received his bachelor's degree in January 1654. Aside from being discommuned in July 1652 for contumacy to the vice-master (Scott-Saintsbury, *1*, 24–25), there is no official record of any difficulty.

117. *Noll's lord chamberlain:* Sir Gilbert Pickering (1613–68), an ardent parliamentarian, member of Cromwell's five councils of state, lord chamberlain to the protector and, in 1659, one of the committee of safety. His exemption from the Act of Indemnity was reversed only through the influence of the earl of Sandwich, to whom Dryden was cousin-german through both his mother and father (Scott-Saintsbury, *1*, 29 *n.*).

118. Scott-Saintsbury (*1*, 31) is undoubtedly correct in suggesting that this line refers to Pickering, not to Dryden. Pickering, early in the war, was on the parliamentary committee raising troops and money in his county; he served also on the Northamptonshire Committee of Sequestration.

123–24. Dryden's elegiac *Heroic Stanzas* (47–48) on Cromwell (1659) referred to the regicide in terms his opponents never tired of quoting: "He fought to end our fighting, and essayed/ To staunch the blood by breathing of the vein." *basilic:* kingly, royal, sovereign; the basilic vein is the large vein starting at the elbow.

And praised his opening the basilic vein.
And were that possible to come again,   125
Thou on that side wouldst draw thy slavish pen.
But he being dead who should the slave prefer,
He turned a journeyman t'a bookseller,
Writ prefaces to books for meat and drink,
And as he paid, he would both write and think.   130
Then by th' assistance of a noble knight,
Th' hadst plenty, ease, and liberty to write.
First like a gentleman he made thee live,
And on his bounty thou didst amply thrive;
But soon thy native swelling venom rose,   135
And thou didst him, who gave thee bread, expose.
'Gainst him a scandalous preface didst thou write,
Which thou didst soon expunge rather than fight.
When turned away by him in some small time,
You in the people's ears began to chime,   140
And please the town with your successful rhyme.

When the best patroness of wit and stage,
The joy, the pride, the wonder of the age,
Sweet Annabel the good, great, witty, fair
(Of all this northern court, the brightest star)   145
Did on thee, Bayes, her sacred beams dispense,
Who could do ill under such influence?
She the whole court brought over to thy side,
And favor flowed upon thee like a tide.
To her thou soon prov'dst an ungrateful knave;   150
So good was she, not only she forgave,

128. *journeyman t'a bookseller:* 1682 note: "Mr. Herringman, who kept him in his house for that purpose." Henry Herringman entered in the Stationer's Register, but did not publish, Dryden's *Heroic Stanzas.* He was, however, Dryden's publisher from 1660–78.

131. *a noble knight:* Sir Robert Howard, younger son of the royalist earl of Berkshire, Dryden's patron at this time, and (as of 1 December 1663) his brother-in-law.

137–38. In his *Defense . . . of Dramatic Poesy* (see 27 n.) in answer to Howard's preface to his tragedy *The Great Favorite* (1668), Dryden stood firmly by his literary views. While "scandalous" may be a bit strong, the literary dispute was undoubtedly becoming more personal. The *Defense* was prefixed only to the second edition of *The Indian Emperor.*

142. *patroness:* Anne, duchess of Monmouth; the name of Annabel (144) was given her in *Absalom and Achitophel,* 34. *The Indian Emperor,* acted in the spring of 1665, was dedicated to her. She and Monmouth had taken parts in a court performance of the play.

150. *an ungrateful knave:* 1682 note: "When he had thrice broken his word, oath, and bargain with Sir William Davenant, he wrote a letter to this great lady to pass her word for him to Sir William, who would not take his own; which she did. In his letter, he wished God might never prosper him, his wife or children, if he did not keep his oath and bargain, which yet in two months he broke, as several of the duke's playhouse can testify."

But did oblige anew, the faithless slave.
And all the gratitude he can afford
Is basely to traduce her princely lord:
A hero worthy of a godlike race,   155
Great in his mind and charming in his face.
Who conquers hearts and unaffected grace.
His mighty virtues are too large for verse,
Gentle as billing doves, as angry lions fierce:
His strength and beauty so united are,   160
Nature designed him chief, in love and war.
All lovers' victories he did excel,
Succeeding with the beauteous Annabel.
Early in arms his glorious course began,
Which never hero yet so swiftly ran.   165
Wherever danger showed its dreadful face,
By never-dying acts h' adorned his royal race.
Sure the three Edwards' soul beheld with joy
How much thou outdidst man when little more than boy,
And all the princely heroes of thy line   170
Rejoiced to see so much of their great blood in thine.
So good and so diffusive is his mind,
So loving too, and loved by human kind,
He was for vast and general good designed.
In's height of greatness, he all eyes did glad,   175
And never man departed from him sad.
Sweet and obliging, easy of access,
Wise in his judging, courteous in address.
O'er all the passions he bears so much sway,
No Stoic taught 'em better to obey.   180
And, in his suffering part, he shines more bright
Than he appeared in all that gaudy light;
Now, now, methinks he makes the bravest show,
And ne'er was greater hero than he's now.
For public good, who wealth and power forsakes,   185

154. *princely lord:* James, duke of Monmouth; Dryden's Absalom. Throughout the following lines, the author attempts to show that Monmouth's godlike, heroic actions prove him to be the legitimate and logical successor to Charles II.

169. In 1665, Monmouth, then 16 years old, fought at the battle of Lowestoft; in 1672–73, he gained wide acclaim for his courageous action against the Dutch, particularly at the siege of Maastricht.

181. *suffering part:* In 1679 Monmouth was stripped of his offices; his closer ties with the country party in the following years put him at complete odds with the court, and shortly after the publication of this poem he was not permitted to associate with the king's servants.

Over himself a glorious conquest makes.
Religion, prince, and laws to him are dear;
And in defense of all, he dares appear.
'Tis he must stand like Scaeva in the breach,
'Gainst what ill ministers do, and furious parsons preach.   190
Were't not for him, how soon some popish knife
Might rob us of his royal father's life!
We to their fear of thee that blessing owe:
In such a son, happy, great king, art thou,
Who can defend, or can revenge thee so.   195

Next, for thy *Medal*, Bayes, which does revile
The wisest patriot of our drooping isle,
Who loyally did serve his exiled prince,
And with the ablest counsel blessed him since.
None more than he did stop tyrannic power,   200
Or, in that crisis, did contribute more
To his just rights our monarch to restore;
And still by wise advice and loyal arts
Would have secured him in his subjects' hearts.
You own the mischiefs, sprung from that intrigue,   205
Which fatally dissolved the Triple League.
Each of your idol mock-triumv'rate knows
Our patriot strongly did that breach oppose;
Nor did this lord a Dover-journey go,
"From thence our tears, the Ilium of our woe."   210

189. *Scaeva:* Cf. *A Panegyric on the Author of "Absalom and Achitophel,"* 13–16 n.

190. *ill ministers:* at this time Halifax and his adherents.

198. Shaftesbury's parliamentarianism led him into increasing opposition to the commonwealth government; by 1659 he was strongly suspected of sympathy with royalist Presbyterians, and in the following year, he "steadily pursued the design of restoring Charles" (*DNB*).

199. Shaftesbury, while holding important offices during the preceding decade, attained his highest governmental positions as a member of the Cabal in 1670 and as lord chancellor in 1672, the year he obtained his earldom. His work in this office has received almost general approbation, and Dryden's famous lines in *Absalom and Achitophel* contrast strongly with the view presented here. In November 1673 Shaftesbury was dismissed and moved into the opposition, of which he soon became head.

206. *Triple League:* the Triple Alliance of England, Holland, and Sweden (1668), meant to serve as a check to French expansion. It was broken by the Anglo-French alliance of 1670, which led to the third Dutch war (1672–78).

207. *mock-triumv'rate:* probably three of the Cabal; perhaps Clifford, Arlington, and Lauderdale, since Buckingham at this time was in opposition.

209. *Dover-journey:* The French Alliance, which replaced the Triple Alliance, served as a mask for Charles's secret Treaty of Dover. By the 1680s the treaty was an open secret but one that could only be referred to obliquely.

210. Cf. *The Medal,* 67: "From hence those tears! that Ilium of our woe!"

Had he that interest followed, how could he
By those that served it then discarded be?
The French and Papists well his merits know;
Were he a friend, they'd not pursued him so.
From both he would our beset king preserve,   215
For which he does eternal wreaths deserve.
His life they first, and now his fame, would take,
For crimes they forge, and secret plots they make.
They by hired witnesses the first pursue,
The latter by vile scribblers hired like you.   220
Thy infamy will blush at no disgrace,
(With such a hardened conscience, and a face)
Thou only want'st an evidence's place.
When th'isle was drowned in a lethargic sleep,
Our vigilant hero still a watch did keep.   225
When all our strength should have been made a prey
To the lewd Babylonish Dalilah,
Methinks I see our watchful hero stand,
Jogging the nodding genius of our land;
Which sometime struggling with sleep's heavy yoke,   230
Awaked, stared, and looked grim, and dreadfully he spoke.
The voice filled all the land, and then did fright
The Scarlet Whore from all her works of night.
But————
With unseen strengths at home and foreign aid,   235
Too soon she rallied and began t'invade,
And many nets she spread, and many toils she laid.
To lull us yet asleep, what pains she takes!
But all in vain, for still our genius wakes,
And now remembers well the dangerous Test   240
Which might have all our liberty oppressed,

212. Shaftesbury had been dismissed from office in November 1673.

214. There was talk of danger to Shaftesbury's life during the Meal Tub Plot (Brown, *Shaftesbury*, p. 265).

219. A number of Irish witnesses, who had previously sworn to the validity of the Popish Plot, now appeared against Shaftesbury, much to the chagrin of those who had formerly accepted their evidence.

227. *Babylonish Dalilah*: the French Catholic Louise de Kéroualle, duchess of Portsmouth.

233. *Scarlet Whore*: the whore of Babylon, the Roman Catholic church.

240. *the dangerous Test*: In April 1675, Shaftesbury strongly attacked Danby's Test Bill, pointing out the futility of an oath that demanded nonresistence to the king and support of established government of church and state. He recognized, as did many at the time, that such laws were more likely to be applied against the nonconforming sects than against the Roman Catholics.

Had not the covered snare our hero found
And for some time bravely maintained the ground
Till others saw the bondage was designed
And late with them their straggling forces joined.   245
A bill then drawn by Buckingham did we see,
A zealous bill against York for popery.
Then murdered Godfrey, a loved prince's blood,
Ready with precious drops to make a purple flood.
When popish tyranny shall give command   250
And spread again its darkness o'er the land,
Then bloody plots we find laid at their door,
Than whom none e'er has done or suffered more,
Or would, to save the prince they did restore.
Amidst these hellish snares, 'tis time to wake;   255
May never more a sleep our genius take.
These things did soon our glorious city warm,
And for their own and prince's safety arm.

    Thou joy of ours, terror of other lands,
With moderate head, with unpolluted hands,   260
To which the prince and people safety owe,
From which the uncorrupted streams of justice flow,
Through thickest clouds of perjury you see,
And, ne'er by hackney oaths deceived, will be
Resolved to value credibility.   265
Thou vindicat'st the justice of thy prince,
Which shines most bright by clearing innocence.
While some would subjects of their lives bereave,
By witnesses themselves could ne'er believe,
Though wrongly accused, yet at their blood they aim,   270
And, as they were their quarry, think it shame
Not to run down and seize the trembling game.
Thy justice will hereafter be renowned.
Thy lasting name for loyalty be crowned,
When 'twill be told who did our prince restore,   275
Whom thou with zeal didst ever since adore.

244. *others:* The reference may be to Buckingham, Halifax, or any of the others who opposed Danby's bill.

245. *them:* Shaftesbury's faction.

252. *their:* the Whigs'. The reference is to the attempt of the Meal Tub Plot to show that the Popish Plot was devised by the Whigs in order to seize power.

259. The apostrophe conflates London, its grand jury, and its Parliament.

265. The line is cast in the form of a parliamentary resolution.

269. *themselves:* the antecedent is *some* (268).

How oft hast thou his princely wants supplied?
And never was thy needful aid denied.
How long his kindness with thy duty strove!
Great thy obedience, and as great his love;   280
And cursed be they who would his heart remove
Thou (still the same) with equal zeal will serve;
Maintain his laws, his person wilt preserve,
But some foul monsters thy rich womb does bear,
That, like base vipers, would thy bowels tear;   285
Who would thy ancient charters give away,
And all thy stronger liberties betray:
Those elder customs our great ancestors
Have from the Saxon times conveyed to ours,
Of which no pers'nal crimes a loss can cause,   290
By Magna Charta backed, and by succeeding laws.
This is the factious brood we should pursue:
For as in schism, so in sedition too,
The many are deserted by the few.
These factious few, for bitter scourges fit,   295
(To show addressing and abhorring wit)
Set up a Jack of Lent and throw at it.
But those, alas, false silly measures take,
Who of the few an association make.
Thou need'st not doubt to triumph o'er these fools,   300
These blindly led, these Jesuited tools,
Whilst bravely thou continu'st to oppose
All would-be Papists, as all Romish foes.
In spite of lawless men and popish flames,
(Enriched by thy much loved and bounteous Thames)   305
May into the wealth of nations flow,
And to thy height all Europe's cities bow.
Thou great support of princely dignity!

284. *foul monsters:* the court party. Cf. *Paradise Lost,* 2. 795–800.

286. A reference to the court's *quo warranto* proceedings against the London charter begun in November 1681.

296. Against the country party's petitions for a parliament, the court sympathizers sent in addresses against the petitions and abhorrences of the paper of association found in Shaftesbury's study.

297. *Jack of Lent:* a figure of a man set up to be pelted; a butt for everyone to throw at.

299. MS note in quarto edition: "Their addressing is plainly making an association."

304. *popish flames:* At this time, the fire of London (1666) was considered to have been started by Roman Catholics. Heneage Finch, who was constituted lord high steward for Stafford's treason trial in December 1680, remarked in closing, "Does any man now begin to doubt how London was burnt?"

And bulwark to the people's liberty!
If a good mayor with such good shrieves appear,   310
Nor prince nor people need a danger fear:
And such we hope for each succeeding year.
Thus thou a glorious city may'st remain,
And all thy ancient liberties retain,
While Albion is surrounded with the main.   315
Go, abject Bayes! and act thy slavish part;
Fawn on those popish knaves, whose knave thou art:
'Tis not ill writing or worse policy
That can enslave a nation so long free.
Our king's too good to take that rugged course;   320
He'll win by kindness, not subdue by force.
If king of slaves and beasts, not men, he'd be,
A lion were a greater prince than he.
Approach him then let no malicious chit,
No insolent prater, nor a flashy wit;   325
Impeachments make not men for statesmen fit.
But———
Truth, judgment, firmness, and integrity,
With long experience, quick sagacity,
Swift to prevent, as ready to foresee;   330
Knowing the depths from which all action springs,
And by a chain of causes judging things:
That does all weights into the balance cast,
And wisely can foretell the future by the past.
Where'er such virtuous qualities appear,   335
They're patriots worthy of a prince's ear;
To him and subjects they'll alike be dear.
The king's and people's interest they'll make one.
What personal greatness can our monarch own,
When hearts of subjects must support the throne!   340
And ministers should strive those hearts t'unite,
Unless they had a mind to make us fight.
Who by Addresses thus the realm divide

310. A reference to the Whig municipal officers of the previous year (1681), Lord Mayor Ward and Sheriffs Bethel and Cornish, and to the incumbent Whig sheriffs, Pilkington and Shute.

326. *Impeachments*: accusations, charges; i.e. the accuser does not become a statesman by slandering others.

343. *Addresses*: A reference both to the pro-court Addresses of Abhorrence (that were meant to counterbalance the Whig petitions for a parliament in 1679–80) and to those which voiced an abhorrence of the Paper of Association that Shaftesbury was accused of having written.

(All bonds of kindred and of friends untied)
Have, in effect, in battle ranged each side.   345
But Heaven avert those plagues which we deserve:
Intestine jars but popish ends can serve.
How false and dangerous methods do they take
Who would a king but of Addressers make!
They from protection would throw all the rest   350
And poorly narrow the king's interest.
To make their little party, too, seem great,
They with false musters, like the Spaniards, cheat.
He's king of all, and would have all their hearts,
Were't not for these dividing popish arts.   355
Statesmen, who his true interest would improve,
Compute his greatness by his people's love:
That may assist our friends, and foes o'ercome;
So much he will be feared abroad as loved at home.
He at the people's head may great appear,   360
As th' Edwards, Henrys, and Eliza were.
And cursed be they who would that power divide,
Who would dissolve that sacred knot by which they're tied.
Those miscreants who hate a parliament
Would soon destroy our ancient government.   365
Those slaves would make us fit to be o'ercome,
And gladly sell the land to France or Rome.
But Heaven preserve our legal monarchy
And all those laws that keep the people free.
Of all mankind, forever cursed be they   370
Who would or king's or people's rights betray,
Or aught would change but by a legislative way.
Be damned the most abhorred and traitorous race
Who would the best of governments deface.

Now farewell, wretched mercenary Bayes,   375
Who the king libeled and did Cromwell praise.
Farewell, abandoned rascal! only fit
To be abused by thy own scurrilous wit,
Which thou wouldst do and, for a moderate sum,
Answer thy *Medal* and thy *Absalom*.   380
Thy piteous hackney pen shall never fright us;

353. *false musters:* a fraudulent inclusion in a muster roll of men who are not available for service. Here the implication is that many of the names on the Addresses are invalid.
376. *Who the king libeled:* probably a reference to Dryden's witty treatment of Charles II in *Absalom and Achitophel.* Cf. Macdonald, p. 203.

Thou'rt dwindled down to Hodge and *Heraclitus.*
Go, "Ignoramus" cry, and "Forty-one,"
And by Sam's parsons be thou praised alone.
Pied thing! half wit! half fool! and for a knave,   385
Few men, than this, a better mixture have:
But thou canst add to that, coward and slave.

382. *Hodge:* Sir Roger L'Estrange: see 109 *n. Heraclitus: Heraclitus Ridens,* the wittiest of the periodicals of this period, has been variously attributed to Edward Rawlins, Thomas Flatman, and Roger L'Estrange. Henry Care (*Weekly Pacquet,* 12 May 1682) suggests that it was the work of a group that met on Sunday at the Sun Tavern in Aldersgate Street.

383. *Forty-one:* The year in which the civil war began. Tory propagandists frequently pointed out that 82 was 41 twice over.

383. *Sam's parsons:* note in quarto edition: "a coffeehouse where the inferior crepe-gown men [i.e., clergy] meet with their guide Roger to invent lies for the farther carrying on the Popish Plot." L'Estrange answered this "asterism" in *Observator,* no. 140 (20 May 1682).

An Ironical Encomium
(1682)

In addition to its sustained irony, *An Ironical Encomium* is unified by its frequent references to the Catilinarian conspiracy, drawing specifically from the opening lines of Jonson's *Catiline* (1611). The classical analogy must have been quite attractive to the court party. In 1682, Sulla's ghost rises in odd places and evokes the ghost of the "Hotspur" of the conspiracy, Cethegus. In the following year, 1683, the Rye House Plot not only produced *Sulla's Ghost, A Satyr against Ambition and the Last Horrid Plot*, by C. C. (Caleb Calle?) but in all probability inspired at least two translations of the Catilinarian conspiracy, *The History of Catiline's Conspiracy* and *Patriae Parricida: or, the History of the Horrid Conspiracy of Catiline against the Commonwealth of Rome*, again by C. C.

An Ironical Encomium is one of many poems written about the political crisis posed by the elections of London's two sheriffs in 1682. The court party, fully aware that control of London was a great step toward control of Commons, knew well that the effective power of the Corporation was vested traditionally in the lord mayor and practically in the two sheriffs of the City of London and the County of Middlesex. The importance of the shrieval offices had been made painfully manifest to the Tories, for the sheriffs, with their power to impanel juries, virtually controlled the legal machinery, despite the fact that the appointed judges tended to side with the government. The court had received a tremendous setback from the "Ignoramus" that had freed Shaftesbury; they had been forced to move the trial of Stephen College to Oxford in order to get a sympathetic jury; indeed, so overtly prejudiced were juries that Shaftesbury, in 1682, dropped his case of *scandalum magnatum* against Craddock, and of conspiracy against Graham, when the court ruled that the trials should be held elsewhere because of the partiality of London juries.

The subjects of *An Ironical Encomium* are the Whig candidates for sheriff, John Dubois and Thomas Papillon, who were outmaneuvered by the Tory lord mayor, Sir John Moore. Of the national implications of the contest Roger North (p. 616) trenchantly observed:

Some may think that an account of these city squabbles are but low history; but if such as these are low, I am at a loss to know what is high. For was it not a *battail rangée* between the the king and council, with the ministry and loyal party on one side, and the whole antimonarchial and rebellious party on the other? And at a time when the latter were puffed up in conceit they had the advantage, and that the other was blown and must soon render or be cut off?

An Ironical Encomium

On the Unparalleled Proceedings of the Incomparable Couple
of Whiggish Walloons.

Go on, brave heroes, you whose merits claim
Eternal plaudit from the trump of Fame,
Beyond the daring hector that aspired
To leave a name, when he the temple fired,
For after ages; and let nothing pall   5
Your well-fixed resolutions; not though all
The seas were heaped on seas, and hills on hills:
Small are secured by doing greater ills.
Go on, and may your tow'ring deeds outshine
The high achievements of blessed Catiline.   10
And let the echoes of your acts by all
Be heard as loud as those were at Guildhall.
What! Shall a puny patriot balk your flight,

Title. Whiggish Walloons: The reference is to the French background of Papillon and Dubois.

4. A favorite image of the period. Herostratus is said to have burned the temple to Artemis in October 365 B.C. in order to acquire eternal fame, even if that fame was based upon a great crime.

5–10. This passage borrows heavily from the opening lines of Catiline's first speech in Jonson's *Catiline* (73–80), following the prologue of Sulla's ghost (cf. 77):

> It is decreed. Nor shall thy fate, O Rome,
> Resist my vow. Though hills were set on hills
> And seas met seas to guard thee; I would through:
> Aye, plough up rocks, steep as the Alps, in dust,
> And lave the Tyrrhene waters into clouds,
> But I would reach thy head, thy head, proud city.
> The ills that I have done cannot be safe
> But by attempting greater . . .

13. *patriot:* Sir John Moore, the lord mayor, a supporter of the court.

And formal fops your dawning days benight?
Shall laws confine, or lawyers you withstand,   15
That have both law and lawyers in your hand?
Shall gilded chains beshackle you with fears?
Tear, tear their gowns and chains from off their ears,
And hang their worships in them; let the curs
Be swinged in scarlet and go rot in furs.   20
Damn 'em for dogs to put such worthies by,
Just i'th' nick of our tranquillity;
Just as the saints with forty thousand men
Were furnished for a holy war again.
Rally once more, and cry them in the crowd,   25
The mobile's your own; give out aloud
For Reformation, and the town's your own,
Else liberty and property are gone.
Caesar's abroad; go seize the Senate, do;
And if he comes, faith, seize brave Caesar too!   30
Let nothing be too sacred for your arms
(Love and revenge are never filled by charms);
By greatest acts your greatest glory gather,
And he's no more immortal than his father.
Serve him as Brutus did, and in his room   35
Put up young Perkin, now the time is come
That ten may chase a thousand; now or never:
Lose but this time and you are lost for ever.
A deed more bold than Blood's, more brave than them
That slyly sneaked to steal a diadem: 40

14. The form referred to was probably the time-honored right of the lord mayor to select
a sheriff by drinking to him.

15. *laws:* i.e., the lord mayor's power to adjourn a common hall as well as Moore's in-
sistence that only his books could be used to take a legal poll. *lawyers:* Moore was backed up
by Sergeant Jeffreys, the attorney general, Sir Robert Sawyer, and Lord Chief Justice North,
among others. (Cf. North, pp. 607 and 610).

17. *chains:* i.e., the chains of office.

20. *swinged:* beaten. *scarlet . . . furs:* the color and trim of the robe of office. Jeffreys re-
marked, "I know Mr. Papillon's humor so well that I am confident he would much rather
have been contented to sit in his counting-house than in Guild-hall in a scarlet gown"
(*A Full Account of the Apprehending of the Lord Chancellor, in Wapping* [London, 1688], p. 30).

23. A reference to one of the many sham plots used to keep the public stirred up.

36. *young Perkin:* the duke of Monmouth. Perkin Warbeck claimed to be Richard, duke of
York, the second son of Edward IV. His intrigues, invasions, and plots for the crown of
England were finally ended by his hanging in 1499. Monmouth is said to have received the
prophetic title of Prince Perkin from Nell Gwynne in 1680 (D'Oyley, p. 155).

39. *Blood's:* Colonel Blood, the notorious adventurer, attempted, among other notable
exploits, to steal the crown, orb, and scepter from the Tower in 1671.

For sure that soul deserves much more renown
That kills a king than he that takes his crown.
The Ides of March are past, and Gadbury
Proclaims a downfall of our monarchy;
Who saw the last conjunction did portend   45
That crowns and kingdoms tumble to their end.
A commonwealth shall rise and splendid grow,
As now predicted by the wise T.O.
Who can foretell, forestall, forswear, foresee,
Through an inch-board, or through an oaken tree;   50
Whose optics o'er the mighty main have gone,
And brought destruction on the great Don John.
Titus, whose skill in swearing doth excel
The monstrous monarch Rhadamanth of Hell,
And sent more souls to their untimely grave   55
Than the destroying angels lately have:
A walking plague, a breathing pestilence,
A cockatrice that kills a mile from thence.
Go on, brave sirs, the gaping crowds attend;

43. *Gadbury:* John Gadbury (1627–1704) was, along with William Lilly and John Partridge, one of the foremost astrologers of his day. With the Restoration, Gadbury became increasingly royalist and Roman, until by 1679 he had written at least the first half of the four-part narrative *Ballad upon the Popish Plot* and probably converted to Catholicism, despite his *Magna Veritas: or John Gadbury . . . not a Papist* (1680). He was implicated with Mrs. Cellier in the Meal Tub Plot on the evidence of Thomas Dangerfield.

48. *T.O.:* Titus Oates.

49–50. These lines have multiple meanings. The "foretell" and "forestall" probably refer to Oates's confused testimony against the queen and Sir George Wakeman. Oates had claimed to be hidden behind the door of an adjoining room when he overheard the treasonous conversation. When asked how he could, then, make identification, Oates said he had looked into the room, but later claimed that the queen had given him an audience at which time he recognized her voice and saw Sir George.

52. *Don John:* Don John of Austria. When Charles II first interviewed Oates before the Privy Council on 29. September 1678, he asked but two questions, to both of which Oates gave incorrect answers. One was on the location of the Jesuits' house in Paris; the other and more famous concerned Don John, whom Oates claimed he had seen give £10,000 to some Jesuits as a bribe to Wakeman to kill Charles. "The king asked him quick 'What manner of man Don Juan was?' Oates, knowing the Spaniards are commonly reputed tall and black answered 'He was a tall, black man' at which the king fell into a laugh, for he had known Don Juan personally in Flanders, and he happened to be a low, reddish-haired man" (North, pp. 175–76).

54. *Rhadamanth:* one of the judges of the dead in the lower world.

57. So North, describing Oates "in his trine exaltation," remarks that "the very breath of him pestilential and if it brought not imprisonment or death over such on whom it fell, it surely poisoned reputation . . . " (p. 205).

58. *cockatrice:* a serpent, identified with the basilisk, fabulously said to kill by its mere glance.

59. *sirs:* i.e., Papillon and Dubois.

They watch the word, the saints their thimbles send.   60
The cushion's cuffed, the trumpet sounds to war,
Our dying hopes in you revived are;
The people's choice, with you they'll live and die,
The guardian angels of their sanctuary.
The groans are grievous, and the hawks and hums,   65
And pulpits rattle too like kettle drums.
The sisters snivel, and their bodkins melt;
They're groped in darkness, and in pleasure felt.
More than in Pharaoh's time, the souls are sick,
And cry for light. Alas, the candlestick   70
Is quite removed. Oh! they're lost, they're gone,
They see that whore, the bawd of Babylon,
Is just approaching. Oh! the popish jade
Will tear away their teachers, and their trade!
  Call a Cabal for resolution hearty,   75
The blessed brethren of the sober party.
Let Sulla's ghost inform you in the fact;
Rouse him to earth; and in this glorious act
Consult with Pluto, let Old Noll ascend.
And if't be possible the new-made friend.   80
Our much missed oracle, let Owen know
The devil's here as well as those below.
And speed for Bethel; bid him not defer;
Tell him we want an executioner:

60. *thimbles:* It was a stock charge that the appeal of the sectarian preacher was to the middle-class female, who was constantly pictured with her thimble and bodkin (line 67). The thimble, frequently of gold or silver, would be donated to the cause in much the same way that plate had been given to the royalist cause during the civil war.

61. *The cushion's cuffed:* A cushion cuffer or cushion thumper is a preacher who indulges in violent gesture.

64. I.e., the sheriffs of London.

65. Groaning, hawking (clearing the throat noisily), and humming (an inarticulate murmur in a pause of speaking) were constantly associated with sectarian preachers.

79. *Consult with Pluto:* Cf. Jonson, *Catiline,* 1. 16–18:

> Pluto be at thy councils, and into
> Thy darker bosom enter Sulla's spirit;
> All that was mine, and bad, thy breast inherit.

Old Noll: Oliver Cromwell.

81. *Owen:* John Owen (1616–83), theologian, independent controversialist, who came to the fore under Cromwell and continued as one of the most eminent of Puritan divines after the Restoration.

83. *Bethel:* Slingsby Bethel, Dryden's Shimei who "loved his wicked neighbor as himself," the Whig sheriff (with Cornish), 1680–81. Luttrell notes Bethel's undisguised eagerness for the execution of king Charles, where it is said he was an assistant at the scaffold.

> For royal blood's in chase, and none but he   85
> To act the villain in a tragedy.
> The rogue will leap for joy, such news admire;
> The son's as sweet as was his sacred sire;
> For he's a raving Nimrod will not start
> To bathe his hands in such a royal heart.   90

89. "Nimrod would suggest to a Jew or Syrian the idea of 'rebel,' *mrd* = rebel; but this is not likely to be the etymology. . . . Many later legends gathered around Nimrod; Philo, *De gigantibus*, sect. 15, allegorizes *more suo*. Nimrod stands for treachery or desertion. . . . According to Josephus, . . . Nimrod built the Tower of Babel. According to the Rabbis, . . . Nimrod cast Abraham into the fire because he refused to worship idols. God, however, delivered him" (*EB*, s.v. "Nimrod").

[NAHUM TATE]

Old England
(May 1682)

So far as is known, *Old England* first appeared in 1685 in *Miscellany, Being a Collection of Poems by Several Hands,* compiled by and featuring the work of that notable female worthy, Aphra Behn. Although the poem appeared anonymously, it seems fairly certain that its author was Nahum Tate (1652–1715), the future laureate, who at the time of this poem was beginning to identify himself closely with the court party.

Why Tate never acknowledged authorship of the poem brings us to the political position he takes in *Old England.* Basically, Tate strongly supports the court, prerogative, and succession, though he is not an extreme Yorkist. He condemns popular interference of any sort and ardently rejects the zeal of both the sectarians and the Jesuits. While Tate's respect for the established order leads him to accept York as the legitimate successor, he cannot bring himself to admit that such an event would give tremendous encouragement to those very Roman Catholic extremists he has just condemned.

OLD ENGLAND

Or New Advice to a Painter
A Poem

> *Quis iniqua*
> *Tam patiens Urbis tam ferreus ut teneat se?*

Come Painter, you and I, you know, dare do
What our licentious fancy leads us to.
Talk is but talk; let court and country see
None has such arbitrary pow'r as we.

Epigraph: Tate misquotes Juvenal's famous lines in *Satire I,* 30–31:

> difficile est saturam non scribere. Nam quis iniquae
> tam patiens urbis, tam ferreus, ut teneat se . . .

> To view so lewd a town, and to refrain,
> What hoops of iron could my spleen contain!

(Dryden's translation)

Let's club, then, for a piece to hit the times, 5
While your poetic paint sets off my rhymes.
Old England for the love of virtue draw—
Hold, not our brazen-faced Britannica!
Let Agincourt present a warlike scene,
Abbeville Ford, or the famed Crécy's plain; 10
Let the Black Prince his English flag advance,
Or let Fifth Harry march o'er conquered France;
Show me those sons of Mars, for I'm afraid
Their race is lost, their valor quite decayed.
Give the just lines and the proportion fit, 15
None but a hero for this piece can sit.

Hold, Painter, hold! thy forward hand does run
Beyond advice. What is it thou hast done?
What crowds of pimps and parasites are here!
Ha! what a politic fop drinks coffee there! 20
See how th' apostate plies his trait'rous text,
The Gospel wracked, and church-historians vexed.
Look, look, the sovereign people here dispense
The laws of empire to an absolute prince;
Their will is law divine, themselves being owned 25
To the Almighty in the spiritual fund.
Religious rogues! new light, new worship teach,
Some St. Teresa, some St. Beckman preach;
Your very prophets here hang between both,
'Twixt God and Baal, I and Astaroth; 30
Your feathered buff is valiant but to fight,

8. *brazen-faced Britannica*: i.e., on coins.

21. *th' apostate*: The reference is probably to the famous Whig attack on the popish successor, *Julian the Apostate*, written by the "political divine" Samuel Johnson (1649–1703) and published about May 1682.

25. *Their will is law divine*: Tate ironically presses the argument that underlay so much of the political agitation especially during the reign of Charles I, i.e., *vox populi vox Dei*.

25–26. *themselves . . . fund*: I.e., they are willing to acknowledge their relationship (and virtual equality) to God. As well, Tate plays with the contemporary conflation of *owe* and *own*, thus creating a picture of sectarian saints who surpass even the most ardent Catholic's view of the "treasure of the church" and indulgences.

28. *St. Teresa*: Trances, and striking visions, and angelic messages led St. Theresa (1515–82) to establish a reformed order, the Descalzas, among the Carmelites. Theresa was canonized by Gregory XV in 1622, principally for "her asceticism and mystic visions" (*EB*). *St. Beckman*: unidentified.

30. *Baal*: the chief male deity of the Phoenician and Canaanitish nations; hence, a false god. *I*: The parallel structure would suggest that this be expanded to *Iesus. Astaroth*: the principal female deity of the Phoenicians.

31. *feathered buff*: a dandified fellow, a foppish boaster.

Clodius within, or his soft Catamite;
But your promiscuous rout, at change o' th' moon,
Are Tory, Trimmer, Whig, fool, knave, buffoon.
Unhappy isle! who thus can view thy face   35
And not lament thy base degenerate race?
Those lines of majesty that Europe awed
Now show a cast-off miss, late turned to bawd.
'Twas not from hence those worthies filled their veins,
That led at once two potent kings in chains;   40
That cropped the flow'r-de-luce with greater pride
Than ever Tarquin switched a poppy's head;
Made lion rampant couch, that long did reign,
The pride o' th' wood and terror of the plain;
Brought Cyprus' king a willing captive here,   45
While Britain did another world appear;
Gave laws to all the land, and then with ease
Led their triumphant flag o'er all the seas.
Curse on that man of mode who, with his wine,
Debauched and so debased the British line.   50
Turn thy style, Painter; let one gracious blot

32. *Clodius:* Publius Clodius (c. 93–52 B.C.), surnamed Pulcher, was a Roman politician who, being bribed by Catiline to procure an acquittal for a charge of extortion, later joined Cicero in prosecuting the Catilinarian conspiracy. Cicero broke with Clodius in December 62 B.C., when the latter invaded the rites of the Bona Dea "dressed as a woman (men were not admitted to the mysteries) . . . in order to carry on an intrigue with Caesar's wife" (*EB*).

39. *from hence:* i.e., from the sovereign mob.

40. *two potent kings:* King David II of Scotland was in prison until ransomed on 3 October 1357, and King John of France, taken by the Black Prince on 19 September 1356, was in England from 3 March 1357 as a captive. Edward III feasted them both on Christmas 1358.

42. When Sextus, the son of Tarquinius Superbus, became commander of the armies of the Gabii, he "sent to consult his father as to his conduct; [Tarquin] returned no answer to the messenger, but cut off with a stick the tallest poppies in his garden. His son, taking the hint, put to death the most powerful citizens of Gabii" (*Oxford Companion to English Literature,* p. 766).

43. *lion rampant:* while a common heraldic figure, the reference here would seem to be the Scottish lion.

45. *Cyprus's king:* possibly Peter of Lusignan, who acceded to the throne of Cyprus in November 1358 and came to England in the winter of 1363 to persuade Edward III to join in a crusade on Jerusalem. During these months Edward entertained, as well, the kings of Scotland, France, and Denmark, commemorating his jubilee with great huntings and rich jousts.

49–52. Identifications here are somewhat difficult. Assuming that Tate is still referring primarily to specific persons and not to types (i.e., not to fops and Scots in general), this might be taken to allude to John of Gaunt (1340–99), who strongly opposed his brother (and Tate's hero) the Black Prince and whose third marriage eventually led to Henry VII, who defeated Richard III at Bosworth, ending the Plantagenet line and establishing the Tudors.

51. *style:* stylus: engraving tool. "To turn one's style" means "to change *to* another subject; also, to speak on the other side" (*OED*).

Hide all that's stained with zealot, villain, Scot.
Try thy skill once again. England, alas!
Draw as it is, if't can't be as it was.

First let Confusion her dear self display,   55
To whom th' unthinking crowd obedience pay;
Next Horror, who the flying standard bears,
Decked with this motto, *Jealousies and Fears;*
Here let the rabble in allegiance meet,
With lives and fortunes at their idol's feet;   60
Arm every brigadier with sacred sword,
Inscribed, *Come fight the battle of the Lord!*
Let trumpets now proclaim immortal hate
Against all order in the church and state.
Show not the victim that did lately fall   65
By fool or rogues, the sons of Belial;
But let a curtain of black murder hide,
Till time, or kinder fate, shall draw't aside.
Haste ye infernal pow'rs from your dark cell;
Pour out the vials that were filled in Hell;   70
The plagues of the black box the world invade,
Fathers by their unnatural sons betrayed.
When thus the kingdom's by confusion rent,
Let youths of Gotham steer the government
By kind address or wise petition sent.   75
Here, Painter, let the royal eagle fly
In state through her dominions of the sky;
Let all the feathered legions of her train,
March at a distance o'er th'ethereal plain.
Some few through zeal too near their sovereign press,   80

57–64. Tate rapidly reviews the civil war in phrases of the period: the "jealousies and fears" expressed by the parliamentarians of Charles I's reign; the Solemn League and Covenant; and the final call to "fight the battle of the Lord," which marked open insurrection.

65. *victim:* Charles I was beheaded on 30 January 1649, after having been condemned for treason by a high court of justice established by the purged Parliament.

71. *black box:* In early 1680, the supporters of "the Protestant duke," Monmouth, received great encouragement from the rumor that the marriage contract of Monmouth's parents, Charles II and Lucy Walter, was "contained in a black box entrusted by Cosin, afterwards bishop of Durham, to his son-in-law, Sir Gilbert Gerard" (*DNB;* also Luttrell, *1,* 42–43). Despite the king's repeated official denials of such a marriage, this Pandora's box helped to spread the discontent of exclusion and succession.

74. *Gotham:* the name of a village proverbial for the folly of its inhabitants.

75. Tate, who objects to all popular party incursions on royal prerogative, condemns both the Tories, who sent in loyal addresses supporting the court, and the Whigs, who sent in petitions for a new parliament.

Offending by a plausible address;
Others their grievances aloud declare,
Filling with cries each region of the air,
"The tyrant does her innocent subjects tear."
Let still the mighty monarch steer her way,   85
Regardless what or those or these can say;
Her divine prudence and abounded skill
Will make all happy, though against their will.

   Now let the moral to this fable say:
Let none presume to rule who should obey;   90
Yet if all err, let's err the safer way.
Indentures give no right to shake a throne,
Nor must profane hands stay a tott'ring one;
In vain does Caesar vindicate the seas,
That men may traffic to what coast they please.   95
If universal mart thus proudly brag
That the court-sails must lower to city-flag,
If large concessions from successive kings
Be such desirable, such pow'rful things,
Pity that e'er to cities they were made,   100
Whose charter dares prerogative invade.
Sure gratitude is but an empty name,
Or pow'r would guard that hand from whence it came:
The coffee-drums beat Privilege aloud,
While Duty is not heard among the crowd.   105
The law, whose influence is kind to all,

92. *Indentures:* the contracts by which apprentices are bound to masters who undertake to teach them a trade. Apprentices had constituted a major force during the disturbances just prior to the civil war; they were being wooed by both parties during 1682.

93. Cf. the fate of Uzzah (2 Sam. 6:6–7).

96–101. At the end of 1681, Charles moved against the London Charter, on the grounds that the City had gone beyond its rights and invaded the area of royal prerogative. This major legal contest was prepared by both sides throughout 1682, the court changing the specific charges from violation of its rights in the shrieval election to violation of its right to collect market money and incitement to disloyalty in the matter of a petition for a parliament that the aldermen had supported during the mayoralty of the Whig Sir Robert Clayton. The City, on the other hand, based its defense on "large concessions from successive kings," which it argued were its rights. The case was twice argued in 1683, and the court decided for the king. See Howell, *8,* 1039–1358.

104. *Privilege:* Parliamentary privilege was set against royal prerogative.

106–08. Tate's ironic comment is aimed at the Whig "Ignoramus" juries, which refused, on hairsplitting grounds, to indict members of their own party, such as Rouse, Wilmore, College, or Shaftesbury, while at the same time, attacking all royal prerogative on the grounds of Magna Charta. See Christopher Hill, "The Norman Yoke," reprinted in *Puritanism and Revolution* (London, 1958), pp. 50–122.

Admits distinctions when a saint should fall—
Then Magna Charta is apocryphal.
Poor loyal hearts, they plot no other thing
Than first to save, then make a glorious king.   110
Yet against evil counselors, I hope,
Force may be used, and so against the pope;
That was the word, when once, for public good,
Three kingdoms innocently flowed in blood;
So felons when pursued, "Stop thief!" they cry,   115
And by that stratagem they safely fly.
Read well these men, you'll find for many years,
Who Caesar's favor wants, is sure of theirs.
Who flies disgraced from court here popular grows,
And still where Caesar frowns the city bows;   120
The blackest traitors here a refuge find,
For City painters ne'er draw justice blind.

Now cross thyself, my dear, for now is come
Sir Pacolet with his *Advice from Rome.*
Saddle a broomstaff, tie it to his side,   125
For now 'tis nothing but get up and ride;
Yet if that nag don't Pacolet befit,
Paint Pegasus, for Pacolet aims at wit;
Through all the liquid plains o' th' air he flies
And dances a Coranto 'bove the skies;   130
His racer does outstrip the eastern wind

110–11. The usual tactic employed by aggressive parliaments was to attack the king through his "evil counselors" and so seek to "save" him by replacing them with persons of their own choice. The most notable case had been the trial of Thomas Wentworth, earl of Strafford, in 1641.

112. Tate satirizes the 1641 Parliament's argument that led from the specific indictment to a generalized attack.

113. Again, Tate subjects to heavy irony the claim of the rebellious Parliament of Charles I that they were acting" for public good."

118. Tate would seem to have in mind such leaders of the anti-court party as Shaftesbury, Buckingham, and Monmouth, and possibly the five M.P.s of 1642.

124. *Sir Pacolet:* Henry Care's popular Whig periodical ran from 3 December 1678 until 13 July 1683 under several titles (all containing the word "pacquet") but chiefly as the *Weekly Pacquet of Advice from Rome.* In the early French romance of *Valentine and Orson,* Pacolet is the dwarf servant of Lady Clerimond who possesses a little magic-winged horse of wood that carries him instantly wherever he wishes.

130. *Coranto:* (1) a very quick dance done to a tune in triple time; (2) a letter or paper containing public news, a gazette, newsletter, or newspaper. Care added to the *Weekly Pacquet's* news a dialogue section entitled *The Courant,* which rather successfully countered L'Estrange's Tory *Observator* and the delightful *Heraclitus Ridens.*

131. *eastern wind:* probably that which comes from Rome, the theoretical place of origin

And leaves the horses of the sun behind;
Swifter than thought, from Tiber he's at Thames;
Good Lord! what castles of the air he names,
What vast discoveries does he there descry,   135
Unseen by all but Salamanca's eye!
What lady's there distressed, what knight's in wall
Locked up, yet Pacolet still frees 'em all.
Talk not of Rome's Zamzummins; he no more
Will make of them, than Bellarmine before.   140
Windmills and castles in the air must down,
Quickset and Hudibras here meet in one.
Is one romantic hero not enough?
Join Protestanti, Cardinalo Puffe.
These lead in chains that pagan priest that first   145
Invented surplice, ever since accursed:
For pagan priest of old wore vests of white:
Ergo, the surplice is a pagan rite.
By the same logic, they might thus infer:
Pagans built temples, offered praise and pray'r;   150
Ergo, prayer, praise, and temples, pagan are.
Good God! that such unthinking things as these
Should once pretend to write, and writing please!
Some little use might of their books be made
If Smithfield fires they duly had displayed;   155
If they exposed by telling miracles
Of legendary saints in nasty cells;
Had their impartial writings rendered plain

---

of the *Weekly Pacquet.* The suggestion here and in the following line is that Care gets his news before it happens.

136. *Salamanca's:* Titus Oates, the principal discoverer of the Popish Plot, claimed a doctorate in theology from the University of Salamanca despite the fact that he had been there only briefly and that the university firmly denied his right to any degree.

139. *Zamzummins:* a name of "a people great, and many, and tall, as the Anakims" (Deut. 2:21).

140. *Bellarmine:* Robert Bellarmine (1542–1621), the Italian cardinal and theologian, was considered by advocates of Protestantism to be "the champion of the Papacy, and a vindication of Protestantism generally took the form of an answer to his works" *(EB).*

142. *Quickset:* i.e., Quixote. *Hudibras:* the Presbyterian knight who, accompanied by his independent squire Ralpho, ventures forth "a-colonelling" in Butler's fine tetrameter satire which appeared in three parts (1663, 1664, 1678) and was modeled somewhat on Cervantes' work.

155. *Smithfield fires:* Tate is referring to the burning of Protestants that took place at the London market during the persecutions of Mary Tudor.

158. *impartial:* This, like "modest," was a word much used in the titles of anti-court writings. In *Observator,* no. 162 (29 June 1682), Whig protests, "There's no harm, I hope, in

Mariana's politics, and Mary's reign;
Had they in point of doctrine errors showed,   160
Idolatry in point of worship, good!
But against Rome while they proclaim their war,
The Church of England does their fury bear;
She wears the mark o' th' beast upon her seal,
For Titus does as well as John reveal.   165
Sir Pacolet, now boast that the holy fire
In all our candlesticks does e'en expire.
Hence, thou profane, those are above thy reach!
Why should one damned to th' cart presume to preach?
Solicit on for some ignoble fee,   170
For I know Simon, Simon too knows me.
Come, Painter, to th' crowd this thingum show,
And to Saint Pacolet let London bow.
Yet let a loyal praetor sway the sword
That's never raised but to exalt its lord;   175
Happy to future ages be his name,
And may it sound from all the trumps of fame.
No popular breath can steer his prosp'rous sails,
No bribes of zealous gold does turn his scales;
He sits like Justice in his chair of state,   180
Weighing the City's, and the kingdom's fate,
So is the realm of London swol'n of late.

---

the publishing of an *Impartial Account*"; to which Tory replies, "No, none at all, Whig; but
you have no luck in the world with your *Modests* and *Impartials,* for they are commonly the
most shameless and partial of all the pamphlets we have to do withall."

159. Tate might be distinguishing here between Mary Stuart, queen of Scots, and Mary
Tudor, queen of England.

164. Protestant writers had interpreted Rev. 17:1, 3 of St. John the Divine as the Roman
Catholic Church ("the great Whore") seated upon Antichrist ("the scarlet colored beast").
The "mark of the beast" is "upon them which worshipped his image," and upon them is
poured the first vial of God's wrath (16:2). Titus Oates (and radical sectarians in general)
often used St. John's mystical language when they attacked the higher Anglican clergy for
Roman inclinations.

167. *candlestick :* See Rev., esp. 2:5 and 11:4.

169. On 2 July 1680 Henry Care was found guilty of libel for his remarks on Chief Justice
Scroggs in the *Courant* section of the *Weekly Pacquet* for 1 August 1679 (see Howell, *7,* 1111–30,
and Luttrell, *1,* 50).

171. An allusion to Simon Magus and the practice (derived from his name) of simony, or
trafficking in sacred things.

172. *thingum:* a contemptuous reference to something or someone that the speaker does not
think fit to name.

174. *a loyal praetor:* After 366 B.C., the praetor was the annually elected curule magistrate of
Rome; in the 17th century, the word was used for a mayor or chief magistrate. This reference
is to Sir John Moore, the lord mayor of London, whose increasing sympathy for the court was
an important factor in Charles's recapturing of the municipal offices.

To th' height of glory justly he aspires;
Thrice happy is the knight, not so his squires;
They with a diff'rent zeal from his do burn,   185
And to the faction would the balance turn.
No care to duty or allegiance had,
Yet one is more unfortunate than bad:
So meek his mien, so circumspectly low,
That he has taught his very horse to bow;   190
Yields to the church, conforms to all her laws,
Yet still embarks in the dissenters' cause;
To Roman idols he'll ne'er say his beads,
Yet if mistaken zeal this vot'ry leads,
He'll split upon the very rock he dreads.   195
His tongue speaks naked swords, his passion flames,
Not to be quenched by all the floods of Thames;
But yet that tongue that once had felt the smart,
Holds no great correspondence with his heart.
He from himself does strangely disagree,   200
Lives not that thing he talks himself to be;
His goodly fabric has been long possessed,
And wants the help of some kind exorcist;
Clear is his soul from all this clamorous din,
'Tis some fanatic demon raves within.   205
T'other, by Bacchus well inspired, can see
The mystic charms of lawless prophecy;
When he is warm with wine and drunk with zeal,
He'll with an *euoi* to his synagogue reel,

184. *his squires:* Thomas Pilkington and Samuel Shute were the Whig sheriffs who, as officers in charge of the election, led the struggle against the court candidates.

188. *one:* Thomas Pilkington was, in point of fact, the active leader of the Whig party during these critical months. Little is known about him, but it is reasonably clear that he acted with courage and conviction despite the legal threats that were eventually carried out. Tate, indeed, has difficulty in sustaining indignation and seems more to pity than censure.

191. In order to hold office in a municipal corporation, a candidate had to show that he had taken the oaths and communion according to the Anglican church within the previous year. This had become an issue in the case of Pilkington's predecessor, the radically sectarian Slingsby Bethel (Luttrell, *1*, 49).

194. Though Tate may mean that Pilkington's zeal to hold the shrieval post has led him to take the oath and Anglican communion (191) or that Pilkington's zeal for the rights of his office will ultimately destroy that office (202), he is more probably using the conventional Tory argument that the sectarians are merely the equal and opposite of the Catholics (217 ff.).

206. *T'other:* Samuel Shute, who was far less active, is regularly charged by Tory writers with excessive drinking.

209. *euoi:* From the Greek εὑοῖ, the Bacchanalian expression, usually written *evoe*.

And the indwellings of the spirit reveal.   210
From kings' commands, by drink and charter, free,
He can distinguish our mixed monarchy:
Ill politics that empire can decide
Between the sov'reign and the subject's side.
Nor pope, nor people do this scepter sway,   215
Whate'er the Leman Lake or Tiber say.

   Now, Painter, draw two factions both allied
In blood and ruin, though they now divide.
Those make for Rome and brisk winds fill their sails,
These for Anticyra with equal gales;   220
Both with fanatic zeal, yet here's the odds,
Those make, then worship, and then eat their gods;
These brutish bigots most unwilling come
To th' God of Heaven, because he's God of Rome;
With that devotion to their chaos bow,   225
That those to painted deities do owe.
Both parties boast a star to lead their train,
One but of late dropped out of Charles's wain.
Unhappy prince! (by Tapomursky led)
To feed on husks, before thy father's bread!   230
Fly to his arms, he like th' Almighty stands,
Inviting penitents with both his hands.
Let the True Protestant frogs croak for a king,

210. Sectarians, and particularly Quakers, emphasized the inner search for "the indwellings of the spirit."

216. *Leman Lake*: i.e., Geneva, the center of Calvinism. *Tiber*: i.e., Rome.

220. *Anticyra*: A city in Greece of considerable importance in ancient times. It was "famous for its black hellebore, a herb which was regarded as a cure for insanity" *(EB)*.

222. The comment on transubstantiation was not unusual. Lord Chief Justice Scroggs, summing up the evidence for the jury in the trial of Ireland, Pickering, and Grove, remarked of Catholics, "They eat their God, they kill their king, and saint the murderer" (Howell, *7*, 134). See also Dryden, *Absalom and Achitophel*, 119–21.

227. *a star*: There may be a dual sense of a person of brilliant reputation or talents and the insignia marking the Order of the Garter.

228. *One*: James, duke of Monmouth. *Charles his wain*: a group of seven bright stars in Ursa Major; known also as the Plough. During the closing months of 1679, Monmouth had been deprived of his chief military and civil posts; Charles's disfavor grew with Monmouth's popularity.

229. *Tapomursky*: i.e., Shaftesbury. The Tory nickname was based first on the tap that Shaftesbury had in his side for the draining of a liver cyst (cf. *The Hypocrite*, 64 *n*.) and second on the rumor that he had aspired to the elective kingship of Poland.

230–31. For the story of the prodigal son, see Luke 15–11:32, esp. 16–17, 20.

233. *True Protestant*: a phrase which, when used derisively by Tory writers, applies generally to Whig dissenters.

233–34. Cf. *The History of Insipids*, 168 *n*.

Be not that block, that despicable thing;
Disdain the sham of an utopian crown,   235
Put on those laurels you so early won;
Let Caesar's lawful line the scepter sway,
Thine is as great a glory to obey.
If, by that other star Rome's pilot steer
O'er sands and rocks, that soon will disappear,   240
And leave 'em to be swallowed in despair.
The Jesuit politics ne'er found a seat
In that brave soul, that is divinely great.
May he still next to Caesar sit at helm,
Assisting to confirm this floating realm.   245
Delos at last on a firm basis stood,
Checking the rage of an impetuous flood;
So the fair sons of Leda still dispense
A happy fate, by their joint influence.
Who knows the weight of an imperial crown   250
Would not forever bear it all alone.
When the celestial globe, from age to age,
Atlas his shoulders singly did engage,
None ever envied him a little ease,
To sit and rest, and admire Hercules;   255
Both poles, and all the gods he stoutly bore,
Ev'n those that squeezed to make his burden more.
The church on both hands threat'ning danger sees,
Like Jason's ship 'twixt the Symplegades;

235. Tate would seem to be warning Monmouth that the Whigs are only supporting his accession to the crown as a sham, since a Harringtonian utopia expressly rejects monarchy for republicanism.

239. *that other star:* James, duke of York. *Rome's pilot:* the pope.

243. *that brave soul:* i.e., York's.

245–47. Cf. *Oceana and Britannia,* 11 *n.* Tate may well be attempting a royalist explication of lines from the Harringtonian poem *Oceana and Britannia,* where Oceana begs Britannia to allow her refuge (15–16).

248. *the fair sons of Leda:* Castor and Pollux. Here, Charles and James.

249. *influence:* in astrology, the supposed flowing or streaming from the stars or heavens of an ethereal fluid acting upon the characters and destiny of men and affecting sublunary things generally. Castor and Pollux, the Gemini, form one of the twelve constellations of the zodiac.

252–57. Atlas, whose burden it was to support the tall pillars that keep heaven and earth asunder, was thought by Hesiod to stand at the western end of the earth, near the dwelling place of the Hesperides. Hercules, carrying out his eleventh labor, the search for the golden apples of the Hesperides, asked Atlas to get them from the garden for him. The Titan agreed, provided that Hercules would bear his burden in the meantime; but, having obtained the apples, Atlas refused to reassume his task and had to be tricked into doing so by Hercules.

259. *Symplegades:* "In Greek mythology, two cliffs or floating islands near the entrance of

Nor doth this panic fear less seize the state, 260
Content to perish in one common fate.
Meanwhile lock Caesar's temples fast asleep;
So slept the almighty pilot on the deep
When wind and waves the sacred vessel tossed,
When faith was sinking, the ship almost lost. 265
Sleep gently glide and calm those raging storms
That daily wrack his soul with fresh alarms;
Serene be all his dreams, happy his rest,
No politic fright disturb his thoughtful breast.
This to secure, let the Cyllenian god 270
Stroke both his temples with his charming rod;
Let Morpheus at an awful distance stand,
Observant of his mighty lord's command.

Now, Painter, if thou'rt learned, with keen effort
Give a bold dash of Pluto's dismal court; 275
Arm that black guard t'attempt great Caesar's life
With consecrated gun, devoted knife.
Let all the factious spirits i'th' Furies' train
Shake all their snakes, and all their rods in vain;
While a winged boy, with a triumphant smile, 280
The mighty genius of this British Isle,
Defend all danger, this loose sleeping while.
Let all the Titans, those bold sons of earth,
That challenge Heaven by their right of birth,
With fire and thunder their own force annoy, 285
Aegeon's hundred hands himself destroy;
Let 'em all die by one another's sword—

---

the Black Sea, which crushed all vessels that tried to pass between them. The Argonauts, with the help of Hera (or Athene) were the first to succeed in passing through; after this, the rocks became immovably fixed" (Oskar Seyffert, *A Dictionary of Classical Antiquities* [New York, 1957], p. 608).

263–65. Luke 8:22–25.

270. *Cyllenian:* of Mercury, or Hermes. The god was born upon the Arcadian mountain of Cyllene.

276. *that black guard:* those involved in the assassination attempts on Charles II, as described by Oates in his discovery of the Popish Plot.

282. *loose:* relaxed, free, untroubled, unhampered.

285. *annoy:* injure.

286. *Aegeon:* The three Hecatoncheires ("hundred-handed ones") were Briareus, Cottus, and Gyes. "Homer mentions Briareus, called by men Aegeon, as the son of Poseidon, and mightier than his father" (Seyffert, *Dictionary of Classical Antiquities*, p. 272).

287. This mutual destruction of Charles's enemies is found also in *Absalom and Achitophel*, 1016–17: "Their Belial with their Belzebub will fight; / Thus on my foes, my foes shall do me right."

So fall the enemies of my dreadful lord!
Then let the angel o'er the throne appear,
And with soft accents strike his sacred ear.   290
Here if to paint a sound be a hard thing
Give me this label, Painter—

To the King

"Awake, great sir, thy guardian prays thee wake,
Who to secure thy rest, no rest can take;
See the globe reels, the scepter's tumbling down;   295
One such another nod may lose a crown.
Awake, great care of Heav'n, rise, pay thy vows
To him that neither sleep nor slumber knows;
Yet if thy wearied head more rest must have,
Secure the crosier, so the crown you save.   300
The crowds of thy court parasites are gone
With early zeal to meet the rising sun.
That prince that shared thy banishment must now,
To yield to popular rage, an exile go,
Till kinder Providence commission me   305
To bring him safe to's country and to thee;
Then will appear the greatness of his mind,
Like gold that in the fire is thrice refined.
Some friends are left, whose importunity
Will give no rest either to Heav'n or thee;   310
See a poor few, alas, at silent prayers,
No rhetoric sure, like that of sighs and tears;
Those soft addresses they will ne'er forsake—
Nor I my just alarms. Caesar awake!
Awake great care of Heav'n, rise, pay thy vows   315
To him who neither sleep nor slumber knows."

302. *the rising sun:* either a pun on "son," with an allusion to Monmouth's growing pop-
ularity as evidenced in the crowds that met him on his "progresses," or a reference to the
famous medal that appeared at the time of the Whig celebrations over Shaftesbury's release.
Cf. Dryden, *The Medal,* 12–13: "On the reverse, a tow'r the town surveys,/O'er which our
mounting sun his beams displays."

303–04. *That prince:* York had shared his brother's exile in France during the common-
wealth period. *must now . . . an exile go:* We must conjecture that Tate believed that York's
departure for Scotland on 3 May 1682 was to be another "exile" similar to those of 4 March
1679 (when York retired to Brussels in the face of the uproar over the Popish Plot and the first
Exclusion Bill), 27 October 1679 (when he first went to Scotland as high commissioner), and
21 October 1680 (when he was once more forced to return to Scotland in the face of an
imminent parliament and a second Exclusion Bill).

308. *thrice:* possibly a reference to York's three major "exiles," in France, Brussels, and
Scotland.

316. Cf. Psalm 121: "Behold, he that keepeth Israel shall neither slumber nor sleep."

   Now, Painter, force thy art, thy utmost try;
Let day arise from Caesar's waking eye;
And while he grasps the scepter, put in's hand
The long-lost reins of sovereign command;   320
Thus let the beams of majesty outrun
The morn, and be more glorious than the sun.
Once, Painter, when the blust'ring winds grew rough
And o'er the seas did domineer and huff,
Great Neptune then, thinking himself betrayed,   325
Since his prerogative they durst invade,
Sprung from the deep and, with an awful nod,
Confined the slaves of the Aeolian god;
Straight the proud billows from their tumults cease,
And all his wat'ry subjects flow in peace.   330
Let Caesar thus arise, and thus the world,
That was to ruin and confusion hurled,
Retire to order, and allegiance pay
In the most loyal and submissive way.

   Now let the piece with thy best colors shine,   335
While every man sits under his own vine.
Ye Sisters, run this thread t' an endless date;
Now ev'ry one carves to himself his fate;
None are unhappy but who force their woe,
Make themselves wretched lest chance make 'em so,   340
As Fannius killed himself t' escape the foe.
Now justice flows to all in equal streams,
Whilst Liberty and Property, those themes
Canted by politic bigots, quit the schools,
Blushing their patrons are such bawling fools.   345
Let the two factions in one interest join,
And that fall'n star in his first glory shine.
Restore those lights to their own sphere again,
That falling Lucifer drew in his train.
Let court and country now be understood   350
One heart, one hand, one purse, one common good.
Let ev'ry faithful shepherd tune his lays

   323-30. Tate's description is based on Virgil, *Aeneid*, 1. 124-56, where Neptune finds his
realm invaded by the winds sent by Aeolus, at Juno's request, to destroy the Trojans.
   341. *Fannius:* possibly the Roman annalist, consul in 122 B.C., I have been unable to locate
the incident.
   343. *Liberty and Property:* watchwords of the Whig party.
   347. *fall'n star:* Monmouth. See lines 227-28.
   349. *Lucifer:* Tate is probably alluding to the earl of Shaftesbury.

To fold his sheep, and to recall his strays;
Let him search ev'ry down, climb ev'ry rock,
And lead his stragglers to the Cath'lic flock.   355
Let Towzer range the plains (so some of late
Have termed Il Pastor Fido's constant mate);
Staunch to his scent, no tonsure can disguise
The fox; the wolf, though clad in sheepskin, dies;
None of more service, or of better use,   360
When Tityrus thinks fit to let him loose.
Let the plains laugh and sing, the hills rejoice,
While ev'ry sheep hears her own shepherd's voice.
Religion wears her proper dress again.
Oh happy fate, that thus has changed the scene!   365
Such is the force of kings, when there's no cloud
To hide their pow'r from the tumultuous crowd.
So Julius, when his legions once rebelled,
With but a word, a look, the mutiny quelled.

  Awake my lute, of Caesar is my song.   370
Ah! Painter, why did'st let him sleep so long?
Caesar gives life to nature, fills each soul
With peace and joy, while plenty crowns each bowl.
Let great Apollo strike his Delphic lyre,
With all the well-tuned virgins of the choir;   375
Infuse ye goddesses a loyal vein
On all th' attendants of the Hippocrene;
Let not th' infection of uneasy times
Pollute the fountain with seditious rhymes;

355. *Cath'lic:* Though the epithet was claimed by Rome for that part of the Western church that remained under its obedience, Anglicans held that it was not so limited but included the Church of England as the continuation, in its proper historical sense, of the ancient and Western church.

356. *Towzer:* a common name for a large dog, such as was used to bait bears or bulls. About 1680 the name was applied to Roger L'Estrange, the most prolific and aggressive of the Tory propagandists, by his Whig opponents, who burnt him in effigy during the pope-burning procession of 17 November 1680.

357. *Il Pastor Fido:* a pastoral sobriquet for Charles, the shepherd of the country (cf. line 361).

358–59. L'Estrange insisted, as does Tate in this poem, that the sectarian zealot (the wolf) who preached republicanism was just as dangerous, though a Protestant, as the Roman Catholic priest (the fox).

361. *Tityrus:* the name of a shepherd in Virgil's *Eclogues;* Virgil himself or his *Eclogues;* a shepherd. Here it would seem to refer to the king.

368–69. The incident is recounted by Suetonius in *The Lives of the Twelve Caesars.* When soldiers at Rome revolted before Caesar and demanded discharge as well as reward for service, Caesar addressed them as "quirites" instead of "soldiers," and "by this single word so thoroughly brought them round and changed their determination, that they immediately cried out, they were his 'soldiers,' and followed him to Africa . . ."

Restrain licentious prophets, and let none   380
Come with unhallowed lays to Helicon;
May still fresh laurels round his temples spring,
That to the royal harp does sit and sing.
On wretched Oates, Doeg his lips shall wear,
And murder his ill tunes that fright the ear,   385
Beneath Apollo or the Muses' care.
When thus the poet shall his notes divide
And never play but to the juster side,
The painter shall his trembling pencil bring
To serve the most august and godlike king;   390
Yet all his colors can't set off this scene;
Art, in a piece of nature, is a stain.

Now the great month proceeds; this is that spring
The Sibyll and the Mantuan bard did sing.
Let Saturn envy Caesar's greater bliss;   395
His Golden Age was but a type of this.
Now all the spheres in peaceful measures move;
The very sectaries do order love.
Old England I no more shall long to see;
We're just as happy as we please to be.   400
No prostituted oaths our fears create,
No pilgrims' march alarms the church or state.

Asaph record these times; no more refuse
The pow'rful impulse of thy charming muse;
Those royal heroes that attend the king,   405
None but an Asaph may presume to sing.
When Hybla to the bee shall dew deny,
When suppliants in vain to Caesar fly,
Then shall this age be lost i'th' rolls of time;
Then Asaph's song shall be like Doeg's rhyme.   410

384. *Doeg:* Saul's chief herdsman, who informed on David and Ahimelech, and, when others refused, carried out Saul's orders to destroy the priests and their families (1 Sam. 21: 7; 22:9–10, 17–22). Here, Doeg stands for Elkanah Settle, at this time the principal Whig poet and organizer of the famous pope-burning procession of 1680. In 1683, Settle went over to the Tory side, exposing the perjuries of Oates and attacking the Whigs in *A Narrative of the Popish Plot. wear:* wear out.

393. An allusion to the restoration of the Golden Age prophesied in Virgil's *Fourth Eclogue.*

402. Part of the frenzy caused by the Popish Plot discoveries arose from rumors that an "army of foreigners landed in Ireland and an army of Spanish pilgrims in England" (*The Dissenter Unmasked*, London, 1683).

403. *Asaph:* one of the leaders of David's choir (1 Chron. 6:39) to whom a number of the psalms are attributed. Here Asaph represents Dryden, and Tate's tribute bears striking resemblance to that which he penned for *Absalom and Achitophel II* (1037–64).

After acquiring his copy of this poem on 16 October 1682, Luttrell wrote on it, "A libel against the Lord Shaftesbury and several of that party. A virulent, prophane thing." The form of the "last will and testament," long popular in political verse, allowed the writer to itemize his victim's alleged errors, portray him as unrepentant to the end, and show who his heirs of evil were. Generally, such a poem was an *omnium gatherum* of stock charges, spiced with a "virulent, profane" tone that produced strong invective, if not *saeva indignatio*. It is not far from the mock "last words," and indeed, it was only eight days later that Luttrell bought his copy of *The King of Poland's Last Speech to His Countrymen*.

In this attack, all the stock comments are brought together: the Tory gibe that Shaftesbury coveted the Polish throne to which Sobieski was elected in 1674; the reference to the silver tap that drained the liver cyst that had been operated on in 1668; the consequent nickname of "Potapski," which combines "*Po*, from Poland or Polish king, *tap* [because of the] . . . silver tap . . . , and *ski* . . . a form in Poland proper to the king and all the nobility thereof"; the treasonous paper of an association that was said to have been found in his study; the charge that the earl developed the Popish Plot; the assertion that he planned, through demagogues, fanatics, and republicans, to bring in a new commonwealth through civil strife. All these are bound together not only by the form of a mock testament, but, even more, by the items being disposed of: with a certain shock, one realizes the author is parceling out the mutilated remains of someone who has suffered a traitor's death. In this particular case, only the entrails may be allowed burial; and for this, the author fittingly changes to the epitaph tetrameter, which contrasts sharply with the brutality of the sense of the lines.

As the number of texts testify, the poem was quite popular, and there was the inevitable reply. The deposition of a certain Joshua Bowes (*CSPD*, 11 November 1682) furnishes a rare insight into the production and distribution of such manuscript verse:

Elkanah Settle gave him the enclosed libel, the title of which is *Mac's Triumph, in Imitation of the King of Poland's Last Will and Testament*, beginning "My game is won, then, Patrick, tell me why," and ending, "Then let my praise be tuned to Roger's fiddle." He [Bowes] was desired by Settle not to give it to any but such as he knew to be Whigs. The deponent then mentioned the earls of Essex, Anglesey, Macclesfield and Stamford, Lords Grey, Herbert and Gerard and some others, which Settle liked very well and conditioned with the deponent for half the profit.

Settle to the deponent's knowledge composed the enclosed libel, for he showed to the deponent piecemeal, now about 6 lines and afterwards 8 or 10 more, and in the deponent's presence corrected several words in the old copy and in his sight put commas to the enclosed and said that, if that took, he would make others. . . .

The deponent asked Settle who Mac was. Settle answered the duke of York and that by Carnegie was meant a countess who formerly had clapped the said duke.

THE LAST WILL AND TESTAMENT OF ANTHONY, KING OF POLAND

My tap is run; then Baxter, tell me why
Should not the good, the great Potapski die?
Grim Death, who lays us all upon our backs,
Instead of scythe doth now advance his axe;
And I, who all my life in broils have spent,   5
Intend at last to make a settlement.
    Imprimis: For my soul (though I had thought,
To 've left that thing I never minded, out)
Some do advise, for fear of doing wrong,
To give it him to whom it doth belong.   10
But I, who all mankind have cheated, now
Intend likewise to cheat the devil too:
Therefore I leave my soul unto my son,
For he, as wise men think, as yet has none.

1. *Baxter:* Richard Baxter (1615–91), probably the most famous of the Presbyterian divines, left the Anglican church a few days before the Act of Uniformity was passed (1662). An active force in the civil war, a prolific writer (the best known of his tracts being *The Saints' Everlasting Rest*), and the most popular Nonconformist preacher, Baxter embodied the highest principles of moderate dissent.
    4. *axe:* i.e., for execution (cf. line 20).
    14. Cf. Dryden's famous description in *Absalom and Achitophel,* 169–73:

        And all to leave what with his toil he won

Then for my Polish crown, that pretty thing,   15
Let Monmouth take't, who longs to be a king;
His empty head soft nature did design
For such a light and airy crown as mine.
   With my estate, I'll tell you how it stands:
Jack Ketch must have my clothes, the king my lands.   20
   Item: I leave the damned Association
To all the wise disturbers of the nation;
Not that I think they'll gain their ends thereby,
But that they may be hanged as well as I.
   Armstrong (in murders, and in whorings skilled,   25
Who twenty bastards gets for one man killed),
To thee I do bequeath my brace of whores,
Long kept to draw the humors from my sores;
For you they'll serve as well as silver tap,
For women give, and sometimes cure, a clap.   30
   Howard, my partner in captivity,

To that unfeathered, two legged thing, a son;
Got while his soul did huddled notions try,
And born a shapeless lump, like anarchy.

16. James, duke of Monmouth, was the Whigs' choice of successor to the throne in place of the Catholic duke of York.

20. By law, those convicted of treason forfeited their entire estate to the crown. By custom, the executioner (at this time, the famous Jack Ketch) received the clothes that the condemned man wore at the time of his death.

22. Luttrell's gloss reads: "to the Parliament."

24. This is not in conflict with line 4, since the punishment for treason included hanging, drawing, emasculation, disemboweling, beheading, and quartering. Most of these are referred to in the course of the poem.

25. *Armstrong:* Sir Thomas Armstrong (1624–84) had been knighted at the Restoration for his work and suffering in behalf of the royalist cause. He became an intimate of Monmouth and, according to prejudiced writers, "led a very vicious life" as a "debauched, atheistical bravo" (Burnet and Sprat, quoted in *DNB*). In 1679, he and Monmouth joined an English regiment in Flanders, Armstrong having earlier been granted a royal pardon for having killed the brother of Sir Carr Scroope at the duke's playhouse. As M.P. for Stafford in 1679 and 1681, he aligned himself with the Shaftesbury faction and was evidently in the earl's confidence at this time. He was eventually executed (20 June 1684) for complicity in the Rye House Plot.

31. *Howard:* William Howard, baron of Escrick, "had learned his preaching from the Anabaptists and his plotting from Cromwell's guards" (Ogg, *Charles II, 2,* 642). In 1681 he was sent to the Tower "on the false charge preferred by Edward Fitzharris of writing the *True Englishman*" (*DNB*). There he was joined by Shaftesbury, who had been committed on a charge of treason, and the two tried unsuccessfully to petition for trial or bail under the Habeas Corpus Act. Through the influence of Algernon Sidney, Howard was released in February 1682 and joined the anti-court forces. The writer's words (lines 35–36) were to prove all too true; Howard, when arrested for complicity in the Rye House Plot (1683), turned state's evidence and was largely responsible for the conviction of at least Sidney.

False to thy God and king, but true to me,
To the some heinous legacy I'd give,
But that I think thou hast not long to live;
Besides, thou'st wickedness enough in store   35
To serve thyself, and twenty thousand more,
　　To thee, young Grey, I'll some small toy present,
For you with any thing can be content;
Then take the knife with which I cut my corns;
'Twill serve to pare and sharp your lordship's horns,   40
That you may rampant Monmouth push and gore
'Till he shall leave your house, and change his whore.
　　On top of Monument let my head stand,
Itself a monument, where first began
The flame that has endangered all the land.   45
　　But first to Titus let my ears be thrown,
For he, 'tis thought, will shortly lose his own.
　　I leave old Baxter my envenomed teeth
To bite and poison all the bishops with.
　　Item: I leave my tongue to wise Lord North,   50
To help him bring his *What-de-call-ums forth*;

37. *Grey:* Forde, Lord Grey of Werk, was in the inner circle of Whig politics. He was, as well, constantly involved in the most sensational gossip of the time. First, there was the persistent rumor of an affair between Monmouth and his wife, Lady Mary Grey; then there was his secret, romantic, and pathetic liaison with his sister-in-law, the 18-year-old Lady Henrietta Berkeley, which culminated in her running away from home and the charge against him of debauchery. The ensuing trial proved to be one of the most dramatic courtroom scenes of the period.

43. *Monument:* The London Monument, which commemorated the fire of 1666, was erected near the spot where the conflagration began. *my head:* The heads of traitors were impaled on spikes, usually on London Bridge but occasionally at Westminster.

45. *The flame:* in this case, the anti-Catholic fervor with which Shaftesbury fired the country. The most convinced soon came to believe that the conflagration of 1666 had been caused by Jesuits, and an inscription to that effect was engraved on the Monument in June 1681, by order of the Common Council, during the mayoralty of the Whig Sir Patience Ward. For Alexander Pope, the column stood "like a tall bully [that] lifts the head, and lies."

46. *Titus:* i.e., Titus Oates, the discoverer of the Popish Plot. *my ears:* The punishment for libel included cutting off one or both of the offender's ears. The most notable sufferer had been William Prynne, who, in the 1630s and 1640s, was considered a martyr to the parliamentary cause.

50. *North:* Francis North (1637–85), chief justice of Common Pleas (1675–82) and lord chancellor (1682). In the following year he was created Baron Guilford. His inclusion here is surprising, since he was a firm adherent of the court and had advanced his brother Dudley as that party's candidate to the hotly contested shrieval post.

51. Roger North stresses Francis's extreme shyness as a youth (*The Lives of the Norths* [London, 1890], *I*, 45–47) and his extraordinary caution when older: "For, although all the company understood him perfectly well, yet his sense was so couched that, if it had been delivered in the center of his enemies, no crimination, with any force, could have been framed out of it; and this way he used with his intimate friends as with strangers" (p. 307).

'Twill make his lordship utter treason clear,
And he in time may speak like Noble Peer.
　My squinting eyes let Ignoramus wear,
That they may this way look, and that way swear.　　　55
　Let the cits take my nose, because 'tis said,
That by the nose I them have always led;
But for their wives I nothing now can spare,
For all my lifetime they have had their share.
　Let not my quarters stand on City gate,　　　　　60
Lest they new sects and factions do create;
For certainly the Presbyterian wenches,
In dirt will fall to idolize my haunches.
But that I may to my old friend be civil,
Let some witch make them mummy for the devil.　　65
　To good King Charles I leave (though, faith, 'tis pity)
A poisoned nation and deluded City,
Seditions, clamors, murmurs, jealousies,
False oaths, sham stories, and religious lies.
There's one thing still which I had quite forgot,　　70
To him I leave the carcass of my plot;
In a consumption the poor thing doth lie,
And when I'm gone 'twill pine away, and die.
　Let Jenkyns in a tub my worth declare,
And let my life be writ by Harry Care.　　　　　75
And if my bowels in the earth find room,
Then let these lines be writ upon their tomb.

Epitaph upon His Bowels.

Ye mortal Whigs, for death prepare,
For mighty Tapski's guts lie here.

53. *Noble Peer:* a stock sobriquet for Shaftesbury.
54. *Ignoramus:* the name applied to the Whig grand jury that returned the treason indictment against Shaftesbury "Ignoramus" and thus blocked the court's action.
56. *cits:* citizens.
60. *my quarters:* See 24 n.
71. *my plot:* The direction, if not the initial idea, of the Popish Plot was frequently ascribed to Shaftesbury.
74. *Jenkyns:* William Jenkyn (1613–85), the ejected minister, was a rigorous Presbyterian who continued to preach privately even after his meetinghouse in Jewin Street was disturbed. His funeral sermon on Lazarus Seaman (1675) provoked a pamphlet exchange that continued through 1681. *tub:* a term of obloquy for the pulpit of a nonconforming preacher.
75. *Harry Care:* Care was one of the principal writers for the Whigs. His most regular production at this time was *The Weekly Pacquet of Advice from Rome* which, with its appended *Courant,* was the party's answer to L'Estrange's *Observator.*
76. *boewls:* Ordinarily, the bowels of a traitor were to be taken out and burned before the victim's eyes.

Will his great name keep sweet d' y' think?   80
For certainly his entrails stink.
Alas! 'tis but a foolish pride
To outsin all mankind beside,
When such illustrious garbage must
Be mingled with the common dust.   85
False Nature! that could thus delude
The cheater of the multitude,
That put his thoughts upon the wing,
And egged him on to be a king;
See now to what an use she puts   90
His noble great and little guts.
Tapski, who was a man of wit,
Had guts for other uses fit;
Though fiddle-strings they might not be
(Because he hated harmony),   95
Yet for black puddings they were good;
Their master did delight in blood:
Of this they should have drank their fill,
(King Cyrus did not fare so ill).
Poor guts, could this have been your hap,   100
Sheriff Bethel might have got a snap;
But now at York his guts must rumble
Since you into a hole did tumble.

96. *black puddings*: sausages made of blood, meal (cf. line 97), and suet. The mixture is stuffed in animals' entrails.

101. *Sheriff*: The word might quite possibly have been pronounced monosyllabically, as in its alternate form, *shrieve*. *Bethel*: Slingsby Bethel, the leader of the extreme republican wing of the Whig party, had been sheriff in 1680–81. He fled north in early July 1682, probably recognizing by then that, without the shrieval posts, Charles's control of the municipal government was inevitable. *snap*: a slight or hasty meal, a snack; also, a scrap, fragment, or morsel.

102. *York*: By 9 September, Leoline Jenkins had heard that Bethel, a Yorkshire man, had been at Durham and later Newcastle. Eventually, Bethel managed to arrive in the free city of Hamburg, where he had been earlier in his life (1637–49). *guts must rumble*: Bethel's parsimony was a constant target for Tory gibes (see *Iter Boreale* and *Absalom and Achitophel*, 618–29).

The Great Despair of the London Whigs
(1683)

This poem was probably written shortly after the court gave its judgment against the City on 12 June 1683.

THE GREAT DESPAIR OF THE LONDON WHIGS

For the Loss of the Charter

Then is our charter, Pollexfen, quite lost?
Is there no aid from the new-sainted post?
Are our sham plots and perjuries all in vain?
If not, we'll summon Patience back again.
Saints' prayers to Heaven we've found will not prevail,　　　　5
But more propitious Hell will never fail.
　　　Then let almighty Titus—for you know
He needs must be a magic doctor too;
For how do you think at Salamanca he

1. *Pollexfen:* Henry Pollexfen (1632?–91) was best known for his work as a defense lawyer, having been counsel to College, Fitzharris, and, in the following year, Sacheverell and Sandys.

2. *Post:* perhaps the whipping post or pillory. The term "knight of the post," which is probably being alluded to here, refers to a notorious perjurer, one who gets his living by giving false evidence. The "new sainted post" would therefore be Sir Patience Ward (see 4 *n.*).

4. *Patience:* Sir Patience Ward, one of the Whig leaders in the City and lord mayor prior to Moore, had testified at the *scandalum magnatum* trial of Pilkington on 24 November 1682 that he had not heard the former sheriff say, on the particular occasion in question, that the duke of York was responsible for the burning of London and would cut the citizens' throats. On 19 May 1683, Ward was brought to trial for perjury and, after five hours of conflicting testimony skillfully maneuvered by Jeffreys (Howell, *9*, 299–350), the jury gave a private verdict of guilty, "which they affirmed the 21st in open court" (Luttrell, 1, 259). "But before the day for sentence, he thought it best to go out of the way, having had intelligence they intended to set him in the pillory" (Howell, *9*, 350). Ward may have hidden in London before fleeing to Holland; he did not regain his former rank until the accession of William III.

5. *Saints':* the appellation used by certain sectarians who considered themselves among the elect.

9. *Salamanca:* See *Old England,* 136 *n.* In October 1682, Roger L'Estrange had published the

Could take such an invisible degree,   10
Unknown to all the university—
Let him raise up the once great Tapski's ghost,
With his retinue, all that num'rous host
Of brave heroic spirits, who could die
For treason, and rebellion justify: 15
Amongst those, Stephen, condemned by wicked laws,
The proto-martyr for the last Good Cause.
Advance you brave arch-traitors from the grave,
Who made slaves princes, and your prince a slave:
Bradshaw and Cromwell, those two glorious names   20
That raise dull treason up to active flames.
Let these infernal worthies then be backed
By Zimri and the jury that he packed
With all the fiery zealots of the town,
But chiefly our great patriot of renown,   25
To whom we'll give some pretty Polish crown
(Not that we promised him, for all our zeal
Is only how to raise a commonweal).
With this cabal we'll fool all equity,
And gain what law has lost by polity.   30
Here godlike Tapski once shall speak again,
And what he speaks fates shall oppose in vain;

---

absolute denial of that ancient institution in *Observator*, nos. 225 and 227 (17 and 21 October 1682), with the attestations in no. 237 (8 November 1682). See also Lane, pp. 56–58.

10. Cf. Dryden, *Absalom and Achitophel*, 658–59: "And gave him his rabbinical degree, / Unknown to foreign university."

12. *Tapski*: a common Tory nickname for Shaftesbury, who had died 21 January 1683. For the derivation of the sobriquet, see the headnote to *The Last Will and Testament of Anthony, King of Poland*.

16. *Stephen*: Stephen College, "the Protestant joiner," had been a zealous believer in the validity of the Popish Plot. In 1681 his ballads and pamphlets led to a charge of high treason which, though thrown out by a London jury, was found against him at Oxford, where he was executed.

17. *Good Cause*: i.e., the "Good Old Cause," the commonwealth.

20. *Bradshaw*: John Bradshaw (1602–59) had been lord president of the parliamentary commission that condemned Charles I and other leading royalists. *Cromwell*: Oliver Cromwell, lord protector (1653) of the commonwealth, had been active in the prosecution of Charles I. Bradshaw and Cromwell (along with Ireton and Pride) were attainted in 1660, whereupon their bodies were exhumed, hanged, and buried beneath Tyburn.

23. *Zimri*: George Villiers (1628–87), 2d duke of Buckingham; see *Absalom and Achitophel*, 544. Though Buckingham was one of the Whig leaders in the City, there is evidently a confusion here between Zimri and Shimei, who, in Dryden's poem (585), represents Slingsby Bethel, the Whig sheriff responsible in 1680 for packing the "Ignoramus" juries.

25. *patriot*: Monmouth.

26. Cf. *The Last Will and Testament*, 15–16: "Then for my Polish crown, that pretty thing, / Let Monmouth take't who longs to be a king."

For if alive he treason taught so well,
What a vast traitor now he's schooled in Hell!
Could Cromwell once by force assume the crown,   35
And sha'n't this angry ghost relieve one town?
Sha'n't Ignoramus, who with no ado
Could save great Tapski, save our charter too?
    But what are only councils now? The course
That we would take in this distress is force;   40
But the militia now, alas, is gone;
'Tis odds to what we had in Forty-one.
The saints are all sequestered of their right,
The City governed by a Jebusite;
What then should we distresséd rebels do?   45
Is it too late? can't we for pardon sue?
Why, good King Charles's clemency may spare
Though we in two rebellions had our share,
Nor need we hang orselves like Judas for despair!
But let's, like Origen, since other hopes are past,   50
Hope the poor devil may be saved at last.

37–38: The most famous check that the Whig grand juries of London gave to the king was their refusal to consider as a true bill the treason indictment that the crown had brought against Shaftesbury on 24 November 1681.

    41. *militia:* Following the Restoration, Charles II made certain that these auxiliary forces (to be distinguished from the far more effective professional army) remained firmly under his control in order to prevent any repetition of the parliamentary dominance that had occurred in the civil war of 1641.

    44. *Jebusite:* In *Absalom and Achitophel,* 86, Dryden's term for Roman Catholics. Whig propaganda held that those sympathetic to the court were Catholic. The "Jebusite" in this instance is Sir William Prichard, the lord mayor.

    50–51. "I have not so much as an uncharitable wish against Achitophel, but am content to be accused of a good-natured error, and to hope with Origen that the devil himself may at last be saved" (*Absalom and Achitophel,* "To the Reader," ed. Kinsley, p. 216, 51–53). Origen (ca. 185–254) was one of the most distinguished, influential, and controversial theologians of the ancient church. His doctrine of the ultimate restoration of all things was part of a system that led to his degradation in his own time and to the anathematizing of his teaching in 553.

Algernon Sidney's Farewell
(1683)

Though the matter of Russell's political intentions and the legality of his trial have occasioned a great deal of partisan debate (see, for example, Harold Armitage's *Russell and Rye House* [Letchworth, 1948]), such questions are rarely evoked in the case of Algernon Sidney (1622–83). Sidney's life demonstrates his unequivocal republican principles as clearly as his execution testifies to a blatant distortion of the law. It is not unlikely, of course, that Jeffreys, now lord chief justice, felt that there was such a clear and present danger in Sidney's political theories and in his involvement in the conspiracy, that these overruled the exigencies of the treason laws. This, however, scarcely excuses his allowing, as evidence of an overt act (even under the law of 25 Edward III, where "the compassing or imagining the death of the king" was high treason), the private notes that Sidney had penned in answer to Filmer's *Patriarcha*, on the basis that "scribere est agere."

These verses reflect the somewhat ambivalent feeling of the court party toward Sidney: a grudging admiration for the integrity of the old republican and a wholehearted detestation of the principles in which he believed.

Sidney had been indicted on 7 November 1683, tried on the 21st, sentenced on the 26th, and executed on 7 December, the day on which Monmouth was forbidden the court. Of the so-called Council of Six, three were dead by the end of the year; Monmouth, shortly to go into exile, would die on the block; Howard had turned informer; only Hampden managed to survive politically. The times called for moderation, compromise, and trimming.

ALGERNON SIDNEY'S FAREWELL

Welcome, kind Death: my long tired spirit bear
From hated monarchy's detested air;
And waft me safe to th' happier Stygian land
Where my dear friends with flaming chaplets stand;
And seat me high at Shaftesbury's right hand.   5

There worshipping, my prostrate soul shall fall.
Oh! for a temple, statues, altars, all!
Volumes, and leaves of brass; whole books of fame!
For all are due to that immortal name.
For my reception then, great shades, make room,   10
For Sidney does with loads of honor come.
No braver champion, nor a bolder son
Of thunder, ever graced your burning throne.
Survey me, mighty Prince of Darkness, round:
View my hacked limbs, each honorable wound,   15
The pride and glory of my numerous scars
In Hell's best cause, the old republic wars.
Behold the rich, gray hairs your Sidney brings,
Made silver all in the pursuit of kings.
Think of the royal martyr, and behold   20
This bold right hand, this Cyclops arm of old,
That labored long, stood blood and war's rough shock,
To forge the ax and hew the fatal block.
    Nor stopped we here. Our dear revenge still kept
A spark that in the father's ashes slept,   25
To break as fiercely in a second flame
Against the son, the heir, the race, the name.
Revenge is godlike, of that deathless mold,
From generation does to generation hold.
Let dull religion and sophistic rules   30
Of Christian ignorants, conscientious fools,
With false alarms of Heaven's forbidding laws,
Blast the renown of our illustrious cause:
A cause (whate'er dull preaching dotards prate)
Whose only fault was being unfortunate.   35
Oh, the blessed structure! Oh, the charming toil!
Had not Heav'n's envy crushed the rising pile,
To what prodigious heights had we built on!
So Babel's tower had Solomon's church outshone.
    True! my unhappy blood's untimely spilt;   40
And some soft fools may tremble at the guilt,
As if the poor vicegerent of a God
Were that big name that our ambition awed!
A poor crowned head, and Heav'n's anointed! No!

27. *the son . . . name:* i.e., Charles II, James, duke of York, the Scots in general, and the Stuarts in particular.

34. *whate'er . . . prate:* probably a reference to the sermons preached on 9 September, the official day of thanksgiving for the king's "deliverence from the late conspiracy."

42. *the poor vicegerent of a God:* the king.

We stop at naught that souls resolved dare do, 45
And only curse the weak and failing blow,
Whilst like the Roman Scaevola we stand,
And burn the missing, not the acting, hand.
Nay, the great work of ruin to fulfill,
All arts, all means, all hands are sacred still. 50
No play too foul to win the glorious game:
Witness the great, immortal Teckley's fame.
In holy wars 'tis all *True Protestant*
Kings to dethrone, and empires to supplant;
Nay, and the antichristian throne to shake. 55
Curst monarchy! 'tis famous even to make
The Alcoran the Bible's cause assume,
And Mahomet the prop of Christendom.
Such aid, such helps, sublime rebellion wants:
Rebellion, the great shibboleth of saints, 60
Which current stamp to Reformation brings;
For all is *God With Us* that strikes at kings.
Now Charon, land me on th' Elysian coast,
With all the rites of a descending ghost.
A stouter, hardier murmurer ne'er fell 65
Since the old days of stiff-necked Israel;
Since the cleft earth in her expanded womb
Op'd a broad gulf for mighty Corah's tomb.
Methinks I saw him, saw the yawning deep.
Oh! 'twas a bold descent, a wondrous leap! 70
More swift the pointed lightning never fell.
One plunge at once t' his death, his grave, his Hell.

52. *Teckley:* In reaction to the rigorous religious and political persecutions of the Haps-
burgs, the Hungarian Protestants under Count Tököli (regularly anglicized to Teckley) re-
volted against Leopold I and thrice fought against him between 1678 and 1682. In that year,
they allied themselves with the Turks (or, rather, against the Holy League of Innocent XI) in
a war that culminated in the famous siege of Vienna, 1683. The Dissenters in England looked
with sympathy on Teckley and his "malcontents," and considered that his alliance with the
Mohammedan infidels was more than offset by his Protestantism and anti-Catholicism.

62. *God With Us:* the motto of the commonwealth.

68. *mighty Corah's tomb:* To punish Corah and his followers for rebelling against Moses, God
caused the earth to "open her mouth and swallow them, with all that appertain unto them,
and they [went] down quick into the pit" (Num. 16:30). Corah, along with Cain and Balaam,
typified those who "despise dominion and speak evil of dignities" (William Smith, ed., *A
Dictionary of the Bible* [Boston, 1863], *2,* 50; also Jude 11). For Dryden, Corah was Titus Oates
(*Absalom and Achitophel*).

70. Sidney's courage and resolution were with him to the end: "When he came on the scaf-
fold, instead of a speech he told them only that he had made his peace with God, that he came
not thither to talk but to die; put a paper into the sheriff's hand and another into a friend's,
said one prayer as short as a grace, laid down his neck and bid the executioner do his
office" (Evelyn, *4,* 353).

The Character of a Trimmer
(1683)

Among many clear indications of the extent of the court's victory, not the least is the significant change of personae that carried on the dialogue in L'Estrange's newssheet. "Observator" remained; but "Whig," whose blind fanaticism had evoked an equally strident conservatism, gave way to "Trimmer," a more subtle antagonist whose apparent moderation masked a character composed of compromise, pusillanimity, and specious logic. For ten successive numbers (240–49 [13–29 November 1682]), L'Estrange attempted to anatomize his opponent, but in so doing he had to develop a new vocabulary and new images. Yet, since his target was closer to his own position, he had to elevate the cannon of his rhetoric and aim his salvoes with far greater care. On the one hand, therefore, he seeks to establish all the stock images of the political Laodicean (the boat-balancer, the weathercock, the bat, and so on); while, on the other hand, he tries to distinguish between virtue, moderation, and trimming:

> Moderation . . . is that by which we govern ourselves in the use of things that a body may have too much of . . . but it is ridiculous to talk of moderation in a case that admits of no excess. Did you ever hear of any man that was too wise, too temperate, too brave, too loyal, too pious, too continent, too charitable? (no. 247, 25 November 1682).

While Observator has some difficulty maintaining this position, he has none in separating himself from Trimmer. "You are upon the point of what the government ought not to do; and I'm upon the question, on the other side, of what the subject is bound to." At best, Trimmer sins by omission:

> He that is a member of the community and withdraws his service from the public is, in my opinion, little less criminal than he that by downright treachery and corruption betrays it. And 'tis much a case whether a town is lost by confederacy or by desertion (no. 245, 22 November 1682).

But, more frequently, Trimmer's moderation "is only the cover of a vice"; desire for gain, or (as Dryden also suggested at this time in *The Vindication of "The Duke of Guise,"*) a disguise for "secret Whigs." Halifax's famous defense, which has the same title as this poem, did not appear in print until 1688.

The Character of a Trimmer

Hang out your cloth, and let the trumpet sound;
Here's such a beast as Afric never owned;
A twisted brute, the satyr in the story,
That blows up the Whig heat and cools the Tory;
A state hermaphrodite, whose doubtful lust   5
Salutes all parties with an equal gust;
Like Iceland shoughs, he seems two natures joined,
Savage before and all betrimmed behind,
And the well-tutored curs like him will strain,
Come over for the king, and back again.   10
'Tis such a sphinx, the devil can't unriddle:
A human schism upward from the middle,
And splits again below, which gives us light
To the sole point that can all sects unite.
Thus did the famed Dutch double-monster trim,   15
And that cleft soul's pythagorized in him.
    Noah (whom for the sake of wine we love)
Saved Nature's breed by mandate from above,
But all the learned sages do agree
He kept his ark from mules and leopards free: 20
All such mixed animals he scorned to float,
And would not save one trimmer in his boat.
    Beasts feed on beasts, and fishes fish devour,
And o'er weak birds the winged tyrants tower;
But this same land-fish with his feathered fins   25

1. *cloth*: the painted cloth set before a fair tent depicting the "monster" on exhibition within.

7. *Iceland shoughs*: An Iceland is a shaggy sharp-eared white dog, formerly in favor as a lap-dog in England; a shough (sometimes "shock") refers to the same species, though it was more generally applied to shaggy dogs and, more specifically, to poodles.

15. *Dutch double-monster*: perhaps an allusion to the union of the two principal political groups of the Dutch Republic under the prince of Orange in 1672.

16. *pythagorized*: passed, or changed, by transmigration.

17. Gen. 9:20–21.

20. The leopard was erroneously thought to be a hybrid resulting from the cross-breeding of a lion and a pard, or panther.

23–24. Cf. Rochester, *A Satire against Mankind* (129–30): "Birds feed on birds, beasts on each other prey, / But savage man alone does man betray."

25. Dryden, in the epilogue to *The Duke of Guise* (W. B. Gardner, *The Prologues and Epilogues of John Dryden* [New York, 1951], p. 136 and Scott-Saintsbury, 7, 133) describes trimmers as:

> Damned neuters, in their middle way of steering,
> Are neither fish, nor flesh, nor good red herring;
> Not Whigs nor Tories they; nor this, nor that;

Commits both air, and earth, and water, sins;
Complies with those that fly, and walk, and dive,
But fastens only upon those that thrive.
    In short, his only art is to inveigle,
Flatter the popular power as well as regal,   30
Like a state Janus or a church spread-eagle.

Not birds, nor beasts; but just a kind of bat,
A twilight bird, true to neither cause,
With Tory wings but Whiggish teeth and claws.
                    (39–44)

26–28. "These amphibious participators of both interests . . . join at last with them that have the better on't" (*Observator*, no. 240, 13 November 1682).

30. In *Observator*, no. 246 (23 November 1682), Trimmer concludes: "I am utterly against all reflections upon the king; but for the rest, it may do well enough to tell the people who are their friends and who are their enemies." Thus, he feels it his function to "do good offices betwixt the king and his people by making the best of what one does and the best of what the other" (*Observator*, no. 248, 27 November 1682).

31. *Church spread-eagle:* The image is based on the symbol of the Holy Roman Empire, the double-headed spread-eagle which, like Janus, looks both left and right.

Song. Old Rowley the King

Using a highly popular tune that was " 'ancient' in 1575" (Chappell, p. 792), a tune that had been given, since the late commonwealth, a series of relatively genial anti-Puritan lyrics, the writer of this particular version reviews the political situation in the last two months of 1683 with a delightful "plague on both your houses" attitude that he voices through the king himself. So far as is known, the ballad was never printed, though it circulated in manuscript. Indeed, it is not at all unlikely, as Brice Harris has suggested in his article on "Robert Julian, Secretary to the Muses" (*ELH* 10 [1943]: 294–309), that the distribution of manuscript copies of these verses led to the "captain's" indictment and later conviction, with the sentence "to pay 100 mark fine; to stand in the pillory at Westminster, at Charing Cross, and at Bow Street; and be bound for his good behavior for life." Obviously, the court was not amused; and Julian, who had already lost an ear for peddling libels, heard all the more clearly the strong voice of authority.

SONG. OLD ROWLEY THE KING

To the Tune of "Old Simon the King"

1.

"This making of bastards great,
  And duchessing every whore,
  The surplus and treasury cheat,

1–2. Charles ennobled the following: James Scott (also known as Crofts, and Fitzroy), duke of Monmouth and Buccleugh (by Lucy Walter); Charles Fitzcharles, earl of Plymouth (by Catherine Pegge); Charlotte, countess of Yarmouth (by Lady Shannon); Charles Fitzroy, duke of Southampton and Cleveland, Henry Fitzroy, duke of Grafton, George Fitzroy, duke of Northumberland, Anne, countess of Sussex, Charlotte, countess of Lichfield (by Barbara Villiers, countess of Castlemaine and duchess of Cleveland); Mary Tudor, countess of Derwentwater (by Margaret or Mary Davis); Charles Beauclerk, duke of St. Albans (by Nell Gwynne); and Charles Lennox, duke of Richmond (by Louise de Kéroualle, duchess of Portsmouth).

3. In January 1683, Halifax, probably angered by Sunderland's advancement and alliance with Rochester, made public a fraud of £40,000 in the management of the treasury, of which Rochester was principal commissioner.

Have made me damnable poor,"
 Quoth old Rowley the King,   5
 Quoth old Rowley the King,
  At council board,
  Where every lord
 Is led like a dog in a string.

2.

"And as my wants grow more,   10
 The factions likewise do;
The cudden son of a whore
 You see outreaches me too,"
 Quoth old Rowley the King,
 Quoth old Rowley the King.   15
  "Not Ketch's ax
  Nor Halifax
 You see can bring him in."

3.

Then Keeper Guilford cried,
 "Good sir, why fret you so?   20
Leave all to York and Hyde,
 And see what they can do."
  Thinks old Rowley the King,
  Thinks old Rowley the King,

5. *Rowley:* Rowley was the name of the king's stud horse.

7. *council board:* the Privy Council.

12. *cudden:* a born fool, a dolt. *son of a whore:* Monmouth, "the Protestant duke," had been quite deeply involved in the Rye House conspiracy's plans for insurrection, though he might have been unaware that the plot included attempts on the lives of Charles II and York.

16–18. Following the discovery of the plot, Monmouth went into hiding, perhaps at Toddington (D'Oyley, p. 233). During July, the month in which a number of the conspirators suffered traitors' death under the ax of Jack Ketch, the public executioner, Monmouth "received a message that if he would come in his offense would be condoned" (ibid.). Halifax might have been the messenger, then, as he was in October, when negotiations led to Monmouth's private letter of submission on 24 November (ibid., pp. 237–44). When the letter was made public (*London Gazette,* no. 1880 [22–26 November 1683]), Monmouth disowned it and then, probably under Halifax's direction, submitted anew his statement on the plot. But on the following morning, he regretted his action, and Charles, in a fury, returned the paper. Monmouth gave no further support to the court and left England at the beginning of the year.

19. *Keeper Guilford:* Francis North (1637–85), Keeper of the Great Seal.

21. Monmouth "saw now, he said, that the duke of York, his implacable enemy, had a mind to ruin him, and that he had been brought back to court 'only to do a job' " (D'Oyley, p. 247). *Hyde:* Laurence Hyde (1641–1711), earl of Rochester, worked with York against Halifax and his policy of reconciliation.

"Gud's fish these fools 25
Have been the tools
From whence all mischiefs spring."

4.

The double duke then bows
And cries, "Give ear to me:
Suppress the Whigs, and use laws 30
That knock down popery."
Quoth old Rowley the King,
Quoth old Rowley the King,
"My lord, we know
How all things go; 35
You've got our art for to trim."

5.

Then Rochester declared
Expedients might be found;
His brother and colleagues stared,
At which a loud hum went round. 40
Then thinks old Rowley the King,
Then thinks old Rowley the King,
"Expedients and shifts
Were his father's gifts
And are all the sense he left him." 45

6.

Then Holy Orders spoke,
Like oracles out of Hell,
"Let conventicles be broke
And all things will go well."

25. *Gud's fish:* God's fish, a mild oath that Charles frequently employed.

25–27. To what extent Charles was constrained by his brother's faction is difficult to determine. The Monmouth pocket-book, or diary, notes that the king stated that he had been inclined to save Lord Russell but was forced to allow the execution, "otherwise he [Charles] must have broke with [the duke of York]" (James Wellwood, *Memoirs* [London, 1700], pp. 375–76).

28. *double duke:* James, duke of York and Albany.

39. *His brother:* Henry Hyde (1638–1709), 2d earl of Clarendon.

44. *his father's:* The religious and foreign policies of Edward Hyde (1609–74), 1st earl of Clarendon, led to his impeachment and banishment in 1667.

46. *Holy Orders:* probably Henry Compton (1632–1713), lord bishop of London and a member of the Privy Council, and William Sancroft, archbishop of Canterbury (1617–93) and a rigorous persecutor of Nonconformists.

Then thought old Rowley the King,   50
Then thought old Rowley the King,
"These lawn-sleeved lords,
With lukewarm words,
Wise Heav'n may trust, not him."

7.

The council then did rise,   55
The usefuller dogs did bark;
The devil a lord more wise,
For everything's in the dark,
Says old Rowley the King,
Says old Rowley the King,   60
"To sit only and prate
Of tricks of state
Is a very insipid thing."

[Enter Old Rowley at Portsmouth's lodging.]

8.

"Sir, Monmouth is fit for a roy,   65
And Richmond for another.
Will you both your babes destroy
For one poor cully brother?"
"Soft and fair," quoth Rowley the King,
"Soft and fair," quoth Rowley the King,   70
"The fool I must please
Or not be at ease,
But I'll have a trick for him.

9.

"Though having two queens be dear,
And rarely more than one do appear,   75

53. *lukewarm:* The implied charge against the Anglican church is that of Laodiceanism in accepting the Catholic position.

56. *The usefuller dogs:* Charles "took delight to have a number of little spaniels follow him" wherever he went (Evelyn, *4*, 410).

65. *roy:* king. The use of French here not only suggests the duchess's background but also creates a pun on one of the names by which Monmouth was known, Fitzroy.

66. *Richmond:* Charles Lennox, duke of Richmond, the son of Charles and Portsmouth.

68. *cully:* a dupe, gull, or simpleton. 74–75. Portsmouth "became the queen while the queen herself, happy to be relieved of affairs of state that she had never understood, stayed in her apartments, or was rowed down the river, or listened to the counsels of her peculiar confessors" (John Lindsey [J.St. Clair Muriel], *Charles II and Madame Carwell* [London, 1937], p. 195).

I'll make two: and then 'tis clear
One has got a son and heir
  For brave old Rowley the King,
  For brave old Rowley the King;
    And when I've done,   80
    My brother and son
May end their tricks in a string."

TOM DURFEY

The Newmarket Song
(1684)

Under Charles's aegis, Newmarket and horse racing reached their glory and became almost synonymous. The town, set within the downs, had been a favorite hunting resort of James I; under Charles, its famous course—the Rowley Mile and the Ditch—became the center of court and country re-creation, of booths and gambling and holiday mood. Here at Newmarket, the king

> let himself down from majesty to the very degree of a country gentleman. He mixed himself amongst the crowd, allowed every man to speak to him that pleased; went a-hawking in the mornings, to cock matches in the afternoon (if there were no horse races) and to plays in the evenings, acted in a barn and by very ordinary Bartholomew-Fair comedians (Reresby, p. 259).

Durfey set his verses to a long-popular tune, one that had been recently revived for *Old Rowley the King,* but in Durfey's lyrics, party feeling fades. Whigs are damned more from habit than passion, and Tories are admired but not apostrophized. Fanatic sham has ended; the tone of moderation and monarchy is broken only by the healthy, masculine invective of the country squire saddling up to ride off for Newmarket's "sporting and game."

THE NEWMARKET SONG

To the Tune of "Old Simon the King"

1.

The Golden Age is come;
   The winter storms are gone;
The flowers do spread and bloom,
   And smile to see the sun,
Who daily gilds each grove   5
   And calms the angry seas.

The Last Horse Race at Dorset Ferry, 24 August 1684. Drawn by Francis Barlow, 1687.

Dame Nature seems in love,
   And all the world's at ease.

"You rogue, go saddle Ball,
   I'll to Newmarket scour.   10
You never mind when I call;
   I should have been there this hour!

"For there is all sporting and game,
   Without any plotting of state.
From Whigs, and another such sham,   15
   Deliver us, deliver us, O Fate!

"Let's be to each other a prey;
   To be cheated be ev'ryone's lot,
Or choused any sort of a way
   But by another damned plot.   20
Let cullies that lose at the race
   Go venture at hazard and win;
And he that is bubbled at dice,
   Recover't at cocking again:

"Let jades that are foundered be bought;   25
Let jockeys play crimp to make sport;
For, 'faith, it was strange, methought,
   To see vintner beat the court.

2.

"Each corner of the town
   Rings with perpetual noise: 30
The *oyster*-bawling clown
   Joins with *Hot Pudding-Pies;*
And both in consort keep
   To vend their stinking ware;

19. *choused:* duped, cheated, tricked.
21. *cullies:* dupes, gulls; simpletons.
22. *hazard:* "The most bewitching game that is played on the dice," says Charles Cotton in his *Compleat Gamester* (1674), and he remarks that it is properly named, "for it speedily makes a man or undoes him; in the twinkling of an eye either a man or a mouse" (*Games and Gamesters of the Restoration,* pp. 82–84).
25. *jades that are foundered:* worn-out horses that have an inflammation of the foot.
26. *jockeys:* anyone who manages or has to do with horses; a horse dealer; a crafty or fraudulent bargainer, a cheat. *play crimp:* "to lay or bet on one side and (by foul play) to let 'tother win, having a share in it"; "to run a crimp" is "to run a race or horse match foully or knavishly" (*A New Dictionary of the Canting Crew* [London, 1690]).
28. To see a taverner's horse beat one of the king's?

The drowsy god of sleep   35
   Hath no dominion there.

" 'Hey boys!" the jockeys roar,
   'If the mare and the gelding run,
I'll hold you five guineas to four
   He beats her, and gives half a stone."   40

" 'God d————me,' quoth Bully, ' 'tis done,
   Or else I'm a son of a whore;
And fain would I meet with the man
   Would offer it, would offer it once more.
"See, see the damned fate of the town!   45
   A fop that was starving of late,
And scarcely could borrow a crown,
   Puts in to run for the plate.
Another makes chousing a trade,
   And dreams of his projects to come,   50
And many a crimp match has made
   By bribing another man's groom.

"The townsmen are Whiggish, God rot 'em,
   Their hearts are but loyal by fits;
For, should you search to the bottom,   55
   They're as nasty as their streets.

3.

"But now all hearts beware.
   See, see on yonder downs!
Beauty now triumphs there,
   And at this distance wounds.   60
In the Amazonian wars
   Thus all the virgins shone,
And, like the glittering stars,
   Paid homage to the moon.

"Love proves a tyrant now,   65
   And there doth proudly dwell;
For each stubborn heart must bow,
   He has found a new way to kill.

"For ne'er was invented before
   Such charms of additional grace,   70

40. *gives half a stone:* gives a handicap of seven pounds.
51. *crimp:* fraudulent.

Nor has divine Beauty such pow'r
In ev'ry, in ev'ry fair face.

" 'Od's bud,' cries my countryman John,
'Was ever the like before seen?
By hats and by feathers they've on,   75
Ise took 'em e'en all for men.
Embroidered and fine as the sun,
Their horses and trappings of gold;
Such a sight I shall ne'er see again,
If I live to a hundred years old.'   80

"This, this is the country's discourse,
All wond'ring at this rare sight:
Then Roger, go saddle my horse,
For I will be there tonight."

73. *'Od's bud:* an attenuated form of the oath "God's body."

A New Ballad
(1684)

In a period when Tory writers exulted over the revelations of a plot to kill Charles on his way to Newmarket at the Rye House and the post-Shaftesbury disillusion of their opponents, the Whig press remained all but silent. One of these rare expressions of opposition can be found in this remarkable little ballad which, with finely controlled irony, begins in the manner of so many Tory songs and then, with a *Realpolitik* and with increasing sharpness, converts past Whig defeats into motives for action.

A New Ballad

To the Tune of "The Irish Jig"

1.

'Twere folly if ever
The Whigs should endeavor
Disowning their plots, when all the world knows 'em;
Did they not fix
On a Council of Six   5
Appointed to govern, though no body chose 'em?

5. *Council of Six:* In order to prevent either stagnation or precipitousness among the Whigs, according to Lord Howard's confession, "it was thought necessary that some few persons should be united into a cabal or council, which should be as a concealed spring both to give and to guide the motion of the machine" (reprinted in Howell, *9,* 434). The members, he said, were Monmouth, Essex, Russell, Sidney, Hampden, and himself.

6. During Russell's trial (Howell, *9,* 612), the following exchange occurred:

Lord Russell:	Pray, my lord [Howard], not to interrupt you, by what party (I know no party) were they chosen?
Lord Howard:	It is very true, we were not chosen by community but did erect ourselves by mutual agreement, one with another, into this society.
Lord Russell:	We were people that did meet very often. . . . He says it was a formed design, when we met about no such thing.

376

Those that bore sway
Knew not one would obey.
Did Trinculo make more ridiculous pother?
Monmouth's their head 10
To strike monarchy dead.
They chose themselves viceroys all o'er one another.

2.

Was't not a damned thing
For Russell and Hampden
To serve all the projects of hot-headed Tony? 15
But more untoward
To appoint my Lord Howard
By his own purse and credit to get men and money;
That at Knightsbridge did hide
Those brisk boys unspied 20
That at Shaftesbury's whistle were ready to follow;
When aid he should bring,
Like a true Brentford king,
Was here with a whoop, and gone with a hollow.

3.

Algernon Sidney, 25
Of commonwealth kidney,
Composed a sad libel (aye, marry, was it!),
Writ to occasion
Ill blood in a nation,
And therefore dispersed all o'er his own closet. 30

9. Possibly an allusion to Shakespeare's *Tempest*, where the jester, Trinculo, takes part in the comic homage offered by Caliban to Stephano.

19. In Act V of *The Rehearsal*, the heralds announce to the two kings of Brentford (see 23–24 *n.*) that the" army's at the door, and in disguise . . . having, from Knightsbridge, hither marched by stealth."

20–21. According to Howard, Shaftesbury asserted that "there is above ten thousand brisk boys are ready to follow me whenever I hold up my finger" (Howell, *9*, 604).

23–24. In Act V of *The Rehearsal*, the first king of Brentford sings out:

So firmly resolved is a true Brentford king
To save the distressed, and help to them bring,
That, ere a full pot of good ale you can swallow,
He's here with a whoop, and gone with a hollow.

27. *a sad libel:* Since Howard was the only witness against Sidney, the crown introduced, as the necessary second evidence, private notes answering Filmer's *Patriarchia*. See headnote to *Algernon Sidney's Farewell*.

'Tis not the writing
Was proved, nor inditing,
And though he urged statutes, what was it but fooling,
Since a new trust is
Placed in the chief justice   35
To damn law and reason by overruling?

4.

What if a traitor,
In spite of the state, sir,
Will cut his own throat, from one ear to t'other?
Why should a new freak   40
Make Braddon and Speke
To be more concerned than his wife or his brother?
A razor all bloody,
Thrown out of his study,
Is evidence strong of his desperate guilt, sir!   45

31–32. Though these notes were almost certainly Sidney's, he never admitted that he had composed them and the crown proved no more than "a similitude of hands" (see Howell, *9*, 853–67, 901).

33. Sidney, throughout his trial, argued brilliantly on the basis of the past law both as to the basis of the charge against him and the admissibility of the notes (e.g., Howell, *9*, 860–66; 876–79).

35. *chief justice:* Jeffreys had been appointed lord chief justice on 29 September 1683.

37. *a traitor:* The services of the earl to the English crown, at least until 1680, seem models of devoted and outstanding conduct. His youthful engagement in the royalist cause, his brilliant embassy to Denmark in 1670, his exemplary work as lord lieutenant of Ireland (1672–77) and as head of the Treasury Commission (1679), stand in sharp contrast to the general practices of others. In England, Essex's association with the anti-court party probably originated in his opposition to the Danby ministry, and his ever deeper involvement very likely stemmed from his feeling that a Catholic prince represented England's greatest danger. Though he differed often with Shaftesbury, he remained at the center of opposition and, after the old earl's death, was counted among the Whig leaders.

39. One of the many points that aroused Whig suspicions of foul play was the extent of the wound. At the inquest, Robert Andrews, a surgeon, testified that Essex's throat was "cut from one jugular to the other, and through the windpipe and gullet, unto the vertebrae of the neck, both jugular veins being also quite divided" *(An Account How the Earl of Essex Killed Himself)*.

40. *freak:* a capricious humor, notion, whim, or vagary.

41. *Braddon and Speke:* The attempts of Laurence Braddon and Hugh Speke to establish the Whig view of Essex's death led to their conviction for subornation of witnesses on 7 February 1684.

42. Evidently, Lady Essex believed the earl had killed himself and "therefore qesired the business might fall. . . . Brother Capel [Henry] excused himself, pretending to be indisposed, which looked very odd" (*Diary of Henry, Earl of Clarendon* [Oxford, 1763]).

43–44. The story of the bloody razor being thrown from a Tower window, then quickly picked up by a maid who ran out, with the subsequent alarm, was principally the evidence of the 13-year-old William Edwards. The boy's later testimony in court led to the conviction of Braddon and Speke for subornation.

So Godfrey, when dead,
Full of horror and dread,
Ran his sword through his body up to the hilt, sir.

5.

Can the case be thought hard
Of Sir Patience Ward,   50
Who loved his own rights more than those of His Highness?
Of disloyal ears,
As on record appears,
Nor to hear, when 'twould do the Papists a kindness!
An old doting cit,   55
With his Elizabeth wit,
Against the French mode, for freedom to hope on;
Those ears that told lies
Were less dull than his eyes,
And both of them shut when all others' were open.   60

6.

All Europe together
Can't show such a father,
So tenderly nice of a son's reputation,
As our good king is
Who labored to bring his,   65
By tricks, to subscribe to a sham declaration.
'Twas with good reason
He pardoned his treason,
To obey (not his own, but) his brother's command, sir;
To merit whose grace   70
He must in the first place
Confess he's a villain under his hand, sir.

50. *Sir Patience Ward:* In the course of the vengeance by law that the court followed, Ward, a former Whig lord mayor (1680) and sheriff (1670), was charged with having deliberately perjured himself at Pilkington's trial for *scandalum magnatum* on 24 November 1682. Ward had stated that he had not heard the sheriff say that the duke of York "hath burnt the City and is come to cut our throats"; indeed, Ward claimed that all talk about James had ended before Pilkington had entered the room. Other witnesses had sworn to the contrary; the jury had found for the duke to the full sum of £100,000; and now, on 19 May 1683, the court moved against Ward. The defense tried to show that Ward's version of the event had no greater discrepancies than those shown by the crown's own witness, but, the jury found the contrary and Ward fled to Holland before sentence was imposed.

56. *Elizabeth:* The meaning is probably loyal, honest, patriotic. Whigs generally looked on the Elizabethan period as a golden age.

57. *French mode:* the government's pro-French policies as well as the court's dependence on French fashions and manners.

7.

While fate the court blesses

With daily successes,

And giving up charters goes round like a frolic;   75

While our Duke Nero,

The church's blind hero,

By murders is planting his faith apostolic;

Some modern sages,

More wise than past ages',   80

Would ours establish by popish successors.

Queen Bess never thought it,

And Cecil forgot it—

'Twas lately found out by the prudent Addressors.

75. During the early months of 1682, a great number of towns willingly yielded their charters to the king, but when London contested the court's Quo Warranto, the resignations ceased. Once the case was lost, "all towns and corporations . . . strove to . . . outrun each other to the throne of majesty" in order to surrender.

76. *Duke Nero:* The implication of this not uncommon Whig comparison is that James was responsible for the burning of London as Nero had been for the burning of Rome.

78. *murders:* In the Whig view, these would probably include the judicial murders of at least Russell and Sidney (if not all those connected with the Whig conspiracy) and the outright murder of the earl of Essex.

83. *Cecil:* The reference would seem to be either to the famed William Cecil, Lord Burghley (1520–98), who served as a diplomat under Philip and Mary (1554–58) but who, as Elizabeth's chief minister, followed a rigorously anti-Catholic line after Elizabeth's excommunication in 1570, or to Burghley's son Robert, earl of Salisbury (1563?–1612), whose career as a statesman reached a critical point in 1601 when "Essex accused [him] of having said that the infanta of Spain was the right heir to the crown of England.'" Following the discrediting of the charge and the punishment of Essex, "Cecil allowed himself to enter into communication with James I, precisely as his father had done with Elizabeth" (*DNB*).

84. *the prudent Addressors:* Those who sent in addresses of loyalty to the crown and abhorrence of the conspiracy following the discovery of the Whig plot in mid-1683.

Sir Thomas Armstrong's Last Farewell to the World
(1684)

Thomas Armstrong, who had been knighted for his daring loyalty to the royalist cause, early attached himself to Monmouth's faction, transferring to the duke that brash loyalty that made him at once the "bully of [the Whig] cause" and that deeply involved him in the private and public life of the youthful idol. The precise extent to which he influenced the Protestant duke's actions is difficult to determine, since Monmouth's Whig followers tended to blame Armstrong for their hero's questionable private life, while the court writers sanctimoniously pointed to him as a rakehell who far outdid all that Tories were reputed to have done. For differing reasons, both parties wished to avoid direct attack on Monmouth; Armstrong, therefore, was the obvious choice for his whipping boy.

Following the discoveries of the Whig conspiracy, he fled to the Continent, and the court promptly declared him outlaw and offered a reward for his capture. In early June 1684, he was captured at Leyden and extradited to England on the 11th; by the 14th, the courts ruled for his execution, not allowing a trial since he was considered outside the law. He suffered a traitor's death on 20 June, despite his daughter's petition, his wife's appeal, and his own plea that he had been outside the kingdom at the time of the outlawry and, by statute, had a year in which to return (Howell, *10*, 105–24; Luttrell, *1*, 309–11).

Sir Thomas Armstrong's Last Farewell to the World

He Being Condemned for High Treason, and Conspiring the
Death of the King and the Duke, and Subverting the
Government of These Three Kingdoms.

A Song. To the Tune "State and Ambition"

1.

Adieu to the pleasure of murder and whoring,
  Of plotting, conspiring the death of a king:

Confound the temptation of bastard-adoring,
   For which I confess I deserve for to swing.
Poor Monmouth may curse me, 'twas I overruled   5
   In all his intrigues by Tony's black spell;
His timorous contrivance I constantly schooled,
   And told him how safe it was then to rebel.

2.

I showed him the glimpse of a crown and a scepter,
   The strength of the crowd, and applause of the town,   10
Till glory did dazzle his soul in a rapture,
   That all things inferior appeared but a crown.
Then I was in hopes to be second assistant;
   Therefore to un-king him our party would bring:
But now as the devil would have it I missed on't,   15
   For which I before the damned doctor must swing.

3.

The doctor confused three parts of the nation:
   He murdered thirty, I murdered but two.
With long sword and codpiece, I made it the fashion
   Rogues, whores to advance, and the kingdom subdue.   20
Brave Monmouth I showed him all ways of debauching,
   And ne'er let him want procurer nor whore.
Some aldermen's wives they were proud to approach him;
   I often as Grey have stood pimp at the door.

4.

Nay, many were sure that their souls would be sainted   25
   Had they but one hour his sweet grace to enjoy;
How oft in my arms they have sighed and panted,
   Until I conveyed 'em to their princely boy.
But now all those pleasures are faded with glory,
   His Grace in disgrace and Tom is condemned;   30

---

3. *bastard:* Monmouth.

10. Monmouth's second "Western Progress" in September 1682 was a bold move designed (according to some) to culminate in a popular insurrection.

12. *but:* except for.

16. *damned doctor:* Titus Oates, the chief discoverer of the Popish Plot, unjustly claimed a theological doctorate from the University of Salamanca.

18. *He murdered thirty:* i.e., those who were found guilty of the Popish Plot and executed for treason. *I murdered but two:* One of these was the brother of Sir Carr Scroope. See John Wilmot, earl of Rochester, *On Poet Ninny.*

Jack Ketch now looks sharp for to shorten my story,
    And leaves me no time to murder or mend.

5.

Yet I must confess, I was oft Monmouth's taster,
    For fear lest some fire-ship might blow up her prince,
Which caused our party to flock in much faster,   35
    All officers from the plot office advance.
Old Tony took care, too, that nothing was wanting,
    In Wapping, the Square, and Aldersgate Street;
I brought in Bess Mack'rel, to help out the tapping,
    And Tony swore damn him, there's nothing so sweet.   40

6.

Sweet Betty, farewell: 'twas for thee I abjured
    My lady and children this fourteen long years;
They always were kind, but I still was obdured,
    Seeking the destruction of king, church, and peers.
Had I Grey and Mellvin now here to condole with,   45
    And their recommendations to th' cabal below,
I might have commissions in Hell to control with,
    But sure I shall find some friends where I go.

34. *fire-ship:* a vessel freighted with combustibles and explosives, and sent adrift among ships, to destroy them; here a woman suffering from venereal disease.

38. *Wapping:* the center of Whig strength in London. *the Square:* uncertain, though the reference is probably to Soho Square, laid out in 1681, on the south side of which Monmouth had a mansion. *Aldersgate Street:* the location of Thanet House, Shaftesbury's London residence.

39. *Bess Mack'rel:* Betty Mackarel began as an orange girl at the Theatre Royal, by 1674 was acting minor parts, and at this time was well known for her connection with Armstrong (see Wilson, *All the King's Ladies,* pp. 167–68). *tapping:* The usual allusion to the silver tap to drain Shaftesbury's liver. Cf. *The Hypocrite,* 64 *n.*

45. *Mellvin:* unidentified.

A New Litany in the Year 1684

One of the most durable forms for poetry of social complaint was the litany. Each line could hammer out a grievance, and the triple rhythm, echoing the General Supplication in The Book of Common Prayer, was capped by the "Libera nos Domine." Frequently it was followed by a series of positive triplets (concluding "Quaesimus te Domine"), and on occasion it would even be sung to an old ballad such as "Cavallily Man" (Chappell, p. 440).

The *New Litany*, which gives voice to Whig helplessness in the face of Charles's judicial vengeance, was probably written about July 1684.

A NEW LITANY IN THE YEAR 1684

From Braddon's penniless subornation,
From immoderate fines and defamation,
And from a bar of assassination,

      Libera nos Domine.

From a lawyer that scolds like an oyster wench,   5
From an English body and a mind that is French,
And from the new Bonner upon the bench,

      Libera nos Domine.

1. Once the municipal offices were firmly in hand, the court effectively silenced the opposition and revenged itself upon Whig leaders through charges of *scandalum magnatum*. York had successfully prosecuted the former sheriff, Thomas Pilkington, on 24 November 1682 and Titus Oates on 18 June 1684; in each case the jury awarded "immoderate fines" to the amount of £100,000. *Braddon:* Laurence Braddon (along with Hugh Speke) had been found guilty of suborning witnesses to prove that the earl of Essex had been murdered in the Tower by his keepers. The government, however, was unable to establish that any money or reward had ever been promised or given to the children whose testimony was the basis for Braddon's action.

3. *bar:* a court of law. The allusion, at this time, would probably be to Jeffreys's "judicial murder" of Sir Thomas Armstrong, who had been executed for high treason on 20 June 1684.

5. *lawyer:* very likely Sir Robert Sawyer, the attorney general, though the description could refer to any one of the court's impressive battery of lawyers.

6. Probably Charles II.

7. *new Bonner:* Sir George Jeffreys, at this time lord chief justice of King's Bench and a zealous supporter of court policy. Edmund Bonner (1500?–1569), bishop of London, in his judicial capacity pushed forward with great severity the Marian persecutions.

From the partial preaching that is now in fashion,
From divinity to undo a nation,   10
From wooden shoes and transubstantiation,
                    Libera nos Domine.

From the nonsensical cant of a loyal Addressor,
From the impudent shams of popish professor,
And from Protestant zeal in a popish successor,   15
                    Libera nos Domine.

From all those Esau's within their nonage,
That would both our laws and liberties forage,
And sell their birthright for a mess of court pottage,
                    Libera nos Domine.   20

From juries that murder do justice call,
And undoing of men a matter but small,
And from the Star Chamber in Westminster Hall,
                    Libera nos Domine.

11. *wooden shoes:* The *sabots* of the French peasantry symbolized for the English Whigs the tyranny of a Catholic monarchy. The most notable use of the symbol occurred on 28 October 1673, when John Ayloffe placed a wooden shoe on the chair of Speaker Williams in the House of Commons (see *POAS,* Yale, *1,* 284).

13. *Addressor:* One who supported the court, as opposed to the petitioners, who called for a new parliament. Addresses of abhorrence were particularly numerous and fulsome following the discovery of the Association Paper in 1681 and the disclosure of the Whig conspiracy in 1683.

15. *successor:* James, duke of York.

17–19. Gen. 25:29–34. The writer might very well be alluding to Charles II and York in this reference to the famous incident between Esau and Jacob (i.e., James). "Jacob takes advantage of his brother's distress to rob him of that which was dear as life itself to an Eastern patriarch. The birthright not only gave him the leadership of the tribe, both spiritual and temporal, and the possession of the great bulk of the family property, but it carried with it the covenant blessing" (*A Dictionary of the Bible, 1,* 574). By this device, the writer could lay the blame for Charles's acceptance of French subsidies and for his support of the Catholic duke as successor on the trickery of James.

21. Again, the reference is most probably to the proceedings against Armstrong. The essence of these can be found in the pathetic cry of his daughter, Mrs. Matthews, who, when Jeffreys resolutely refused to allow a trial, burst out: "My lord, I hope you will not murder my father. This is murdering a man" (Howell, *10,* 113).

23. *Star Chamber:* "A court, chiefly of criminal jurisdiction, developed in the 13th century from the judicial settings of the King's Council in the Star Chamber at Westminster. . . . The abuse of it under James I and Charles I has made it a proverbial type of an arbitrary and oppressive tribunal. It was abolished by an act of the Long Parliament in 1641" *(OED).* The trial of Armstrong, among others, was held at Westminster Hall.

True and Joyful News
(1684)

When the outlawed Sir Thomas Armstrong was taken at Leyden in June 1684, found among his papers were letters reputedly written by the London merchant Joseph Hayes concerning a bill of exchange to the amount of 150 guineas to be paid Armstrong under his alias of Henry Laurence by Hayes's brother Israel in Amsterdam. Though the crown's lawyers produced a witness who swore he had seen the bill of exchange, and though they attempted to prove that the letters were in the merchant's handwriting, Hayes swore he had never known Armstrong, or ever lent him money, and, suggesting that the letters were forgeries, he made "remarks on the evidence which were very pertinent, as also he called several persons who testified as to his loyalty, credit, and behavior" (Howell, *10,* 307–20; Luttrell, *1,* 321). The jury, despite Jeffreys's summary from the bench, found the defendant not guilty. Like the Wakeman trial during the Popish Plot, this was the first clear acquittal and indicated that the strong feelings that the Whig conspiracy had engendered were beginning to decline.

Hayes, who had pleaded not guilty at his arraignment on 3 November 1684, was tried and acquitted on 21 November. Luttrell purchased his copy of the poem 26 November 1684.

True and Joyful News

or
A Word of Comfort to the
Godly Party

A Poem upon Mr. Hayes's Late Deliverance.

What! Hayes acquitted! Armstrong's magazine!
Tory turned Ignoramus, without spleen!
The Old Cause's grand Goliah's Pym is come,
Has slipped the noose, bilked Ketch, escaped his doom;
The City's hope, the charter's chief upholder,   5
Dissenters' joy, the Scriptures' best unfolder,
Is safe arrived. Proclaim a solemn day;
Let's halleluiahs to his praises pay,
For he's the hero of our state-plot-play.
The confined savior of the nation's gone,   10
His crystal plot and mighty train's undone;
Succeeding Hayes shall be his adopted son.
Can Salamanca's brood e'er want a boy
Whilst Hayes 's the acteonized fanatics' joy?

Title. Godly Party: derisively, the Whigs, among whom were many sectarians.
1. *magazine:* a place where goods are laid up; a storehouse, depot. The indictment charged
that Hayes, for Armstrong's "relief and maintenance, did pay the sum of 150 [guineas]" and
thus traitorously supplied and comforted an outlaw.
2. *Tory turned Ignoramus:* While the phrase ironically recalls the Whig grand juries of 1679–
81 that had successfully crushed certain indictments, in point of fact Hayes was acquitted by
a regular trial jury. *spleen:* The word appears to be used in the general sense of passion, anger,
spite, or irritability.
3. The line would seem to mean that Hayes is like Pym, the agent of the grand Goliath
(i.e., Parliament) of the Good Old Cause (i.e., the commonwealth). John Pym (1584–1643)
spearheaded the Commons' attack on Charles I's government, which led to the civil war.
4. *bilked:* cheated. *Ketch:* Jack Ketch, or Catch, the public executioner.
7. *solemn day:* The allusion is to the solemn days of prayer and thanksgiving proclaimed by
Parliament for their victories over Charles I during the civil war.
10. *savior of the nation:* Titus Oates had received this title from his supporters for his dis-
covery of the Popish Plot.
11. *train:* an act or scheme designed to deceive or entrap.
13. *Salamanca's brood:* Oates was regularly referred to as the doctor, or the Salamanca doc-
tor, though that ancient university had publicly denied ever having conferred any degree
upon him. His opponents used the term opprobriously and encouraged the ugly rumors of
pederasty that had long been associated with Oates.
14. *acteonized:* a nonce-word, not in *OED*, the meaning of which would seem to be "turned
into a stag," as Actaeon had been metamorphosed for offending Diana. The relationship of
the word to the charge of sodomy can be seem more closely in *The Sodomite; or the Venison
Doctor, with His Brace of Aldermen-Stags,* which Luttrell purchased on 13 September 1684.

Who brings an ordered Babel on his tongue,   15
Turning sedition to the good old song
Of *All Health to Old Noll,* in each cabal,
Whose empty words the vulgar Gospel call.
The dove (precise dissenters say) 's returned
(For whom, through fear, the City faction mourned)   20
With olive branches, since the floods decrease,
And fatal tidings of the raven's case;
Who boldly wing'd o'er th' surface of the deep,
Till boist'rous billows did imprisoned keep
The wand'ring messenger of the active side,   25
Whose vast fanatic ark does doubtful glide,
Longing for th' 'batement of a blessed state tide.
Big with ill hopes, ill-meaning zealot's crew,
Whom no religion pleases but a new,
Can bless, speak fair, with the same breath undo.   30
Geneva's Trojan horse, adored by some,
Filled with armed men, traitors supposed from Rome,
Whose out-swelled Salamanca sides contain
The numerous offspring of Augusta's train.
Whitehall made room for this outlandish beast;   35
Each did admire, and for his favor pressed,
Till sable clouds of unexpected grief
O'erveiled the state, not thinking of relief.

15. For the confusion of tongues at Babel, see Gen. 11:1–9.

17. *All Health to Old Noll:* Old Noll was the nickname of Oliver Cromwell. I have been unable to locate the song.

19–27. These lines are based on the story of Noah, especially Gen. 8:1–14.

19. *dove:* The printed gloss identifies this as Hayes. *precise:* Overexact, overnice; strict or scrupulous in religious observance; in the 16th and 17th centuries, puritanical.

22. *the raven's case:* The printed gloss, filled out by Luttrell, reads: D[r.] O[ates]. Prior to releasing the dove, Noah had sent forth a raven, which never returned. Oates had been arraigned at King's Bench on 13 November for perjury; he was allowed a delay until the following term and "any counsel in England. He then asked liberty to go to them but was told that, being prisoner in execution, that could not be granted" (Lane, p. 302). Oates's black canonical habit would have encouraged the parallel to the raven.

25. *wand'ring messenger:* probably a reference to Oates and the travels he said he had undertaken as the Jesuits' messenger for the Popish Plot (see also line 46).

31. *Geneva's Trojan horse:* The printed gloss gives "D.T.," presumably D[octor] T[itus Oates] again.

34. *Augusta's:* The printed gloss gives "London."

35. Through the entreaties of the Privy Council, Oates had assigned to him "a pension of £600 per annum, a suite of apartments in Whitehall, and a guard for his precious person." He received this at the end of September 1678; on 31 August 1681 he was asked to quit Whitehall.

36. *admire:* wonder, marvel.

The mighty monster's bowels yearned again,
And then brought forth a wondrous plot, not men;   40
Which (Hydra-like) when spoiled, another rose,
Debauched the land and its parent's heads expose;
Whose Jove-like brain a fruitful womb supplied,
Gave birth to Hayes and great Tom's princely pride.
When Hayes, their bully-cock, the party's head,   45
And Oates, the devil's mercury, are dead,
They, self-thought saints, a dissolution dread.

39. *yearned:* were deeply moved. The writer is, of course, parodying the language of sectarian preachers.

40. *plot:* very likely the Meal Tub Plot, which Tories said had been engineered by the Whigs.

41. *another:* the Whig conspiracy.

42. *its parent's heads:* the allusion is to those who were seized for complicity in the conspiracy. Their heads were, quite literally, exposed to the public following their execution for treason. While punctuation has been added here, the grammar still seems questionable.

43. *Whose:* The antecedent would appear to be the Hydra-like plot. *Jove-like brain:* The allusion is to the story of the birth of Minerva, who is said to have sprung forth full grown and fully armored from the brain of Jove when Vulcan split open the god's head with an ax.

44. *Tom:* The printed gloss reads "Armstrong." For other Tory views on him, see the poems on his execution.

45. *the party's head:* At this time the Whigs were virtually leaderless; certainly, there is no indication that Hayes could be considered their head—save by default.

46. *mercury:* a messenger, guide, dexterous thief; (generically) a news pamphlet.

47. *saints:* the term applied by certain sects to their members to indicate their election under the New Covenant.

A Trick for Tyburn
(1685)

James II and his ministers were anxious about the reception the proclamation of his accession would receive throughout the country. Fear of popery might easily prove stronger than faith in monarchy. The suddenness, the unexpectedness of Charles's death, with the inevitable rumors as to its cause, could be counted on greatly to increase the danger of reaction. Accordingly, free wine was distributed in the streets at the accession in an effort to win the masses. Along the same vein was His Majesty's free and gracious pardon for seventy-six Newgate prisoners on 21 March. This poem is one of the most popular responses to this amnesty.

A TRICK FOR TYBURN,
OR
A PRISON RANT

Being a Song of the Prisoners of Newgate at the
Jail Delivery
To the Tune of "Hark, the Thundering Cannons Roar"

> Trumpets sound and steeples ring,
> Every loyal subject sing
> With a health to James our king
>   For his pardon granted.
> Prisoners half dead that lay,   5
> Closed in stone instead of clay,
> Have their liberty today
>   Which before they wanted.
>
> Newgate lately did bring forth
> Seventy children at a birth,   10
> All in wantonness and mirth
>   At a jail delivery.
> But her keepers they lie in,

Money-sick for want of sin;
They will look both pale and thin   15
  Till a new recovery.

Now the doors are open wide
Jack may take his mare and ride
With a leg on every side,
  And the jade be flinging;   20
Take her halter, Ketch, and try
What's the nearest course to die,
And we'll write thine elegy,
  "He's hanged for want of hanging."

Henceforth we will steal no more   25
Though we should be ne'er so poor.
If by chance we take a whore
  In single fornication,
We get a soldier to the king
Or a seaman who doth bring   30
From the Indies everything:
  It doth not wrong the nation.

We were rebels more than base
To abuse an act of grace;
We'll ne'er do't in any case,   35
  We'll legal be and loyal.
If the French begin to reel
(English hearts are true as steel),
We'll make their breasts our bullets feel
  For James our king, the royal.   40

Should our case be ne'er so bad,
We will never be so mad
As to go upon the pad
  Whilst our life endureth.
This rogue that was a great trepan   45
Is two parts turned a civil man

16. *recovery:* a recovery of the prisoners, the objects of the keepers' extortion, and of the keepers' health.
18. *Jack:* a knave, obs. *mare:* horse and also gallows, the two- or three-legged mare.
19. Without leg irons.
37. *reel:* behave recklessly.
43. *to go upon the pad:* to commit robbery on the highway.
45. *trepan:* a deceiver.

And honestly drinks off his can
    And nothing deadly feareth.

We wish that those that cannot pay
Their debts may have a jubiley,   50
That poor men for the king may pray
    At his great coronation.
To see the usurers go mourn
And take with Jack a second turn,
When their bills and bonds they burn,   55
    Would overjoy the nation.

Whittington did build an house,
Enough to starve a rat or mouse,
But left allowance for a louse
    To give poor men the fever.   60
But James the Great hath found a way
To turn his scepter to a key
And give his children all the play:
    God bless him then forever.

50. *jubiley:* a time of restitution, remission, or release. The original spelling indicates the pronounciation of this rime-word in normal 17th-century usage.

54. *turn:* here also a step off the ladder at the gallows.

57–60. Richard Whittington (d. 1423), the famous "Dick," mayor of London, left legacies to rebuild Newgate prison and to establish, among other institutions, an almshouse.

The Humble Address
(May 1685)

Standing as a warning against the addresses that filled the *London Gazette* in February and March, *The Humble Address* mocks their willingness to welcome, even if only as a matter of form, a Catholic king to the throne of England. Supposedly presented by the leaders of law and religion, the address links Jeffreys with James and ironically prays for their success in subverting English law and religion. The warning was not without reason. Within ten days of his accession James had declared his own religious position by publicly attending mass in the chapel of St. James's Palace and even moderate Anglicans were ready to admit that Roman Catholics showed themselves "more boldly than ever" at court. Moreover, though a parliament had been elected, there were strong rumors and some evidence that these elections had not been free of interference from the crown and its officers.

Only one of the petitioners can be identified. He is William Sancroft (1617–93). archbishop of Canterbury, who was in James's debt. In 1677 James had been instrumental in obtaining Sancroft's appointment to the archbishopric, opposing the strong candidacy of Henry Compton, bishop of London. We may safely assume that the representative of the judiciary was equally appropriate to his role—in the satirist's mind at least. The poem is endorsed, "Address to King James, 1684," which would indicate that it was written prior to 25 March 1685, but internal evidence suggests a date after the assembly of Parliament on 19 May. The endorsement is presumably a scribal error of the kind so frequently made in the first weeks of a "new year."

THE HUMBLE ADDRESS

Of the Loyal Professors of Divinity and Law
That Want Preferment and Practice
Introduced by Their Graces of Canterbury and B[?].

Great sir, our poor hearts were ready to burst
    For the loss of your brother when we heard it at first.
But when we were told that you were to reign

We all fell a roaring out huzzas again.
With hearts full of joy, as our glasses of wine,   5
    In this loyal address both professions do join.

May Jeffreys swagger on the bench
    And James upon the throne,
Till we become slaves to the French
    And Rome's dominion own;   10
May no man sit in Parliament
    But by a false return,
Till Lords and Commons by consent
    Their Magna Charta burn.
Though Smithfield now neglected lie,   15
    Oh, may it once more shine
With Whigs in flaming heaps that fry
    Of books they call divine;
From whence may such a blaze proceed,
    So glorious and so bright,   20
That the next parish priest may read
    His mass by Bible light.
Then holy water pots shall cheer
    Our hearts like aqua-vitae
Whilst singing monks in triumph bear   25
    Their little God Almighty.
More blessings we could yet foretell
    In this most happy reign,
But hark, the king's own chapel bell
    Calls us to prayers again.   30
May trade and industry decay,
    But may the plague increase,
Till it hath swept those Whigs away
    That sign not this address.

15. *Smithfield:* made infamous in the 16th century by the burning of heretics, especially the Marian martyrs.
18. *Of books:* i.e., in a fire fed by "books they call divine."
26. The Host, or the crucifix.
29. *the king's own chapel:* the oratory connected to James's old lodgings as duke of York. Charles had closed it, fearing scandal, but James reopened it and made it virtually the Chapel Royal, hearing mass with "the doors set wide open" (Evelyn, *4,* 416).

The Trial and Punishment of Titus
Oates, May 1685

On 8–9 May at the court of King's Bench Bar, Titus Oates was tried and convicted on two counts of perjury. A week later he was sentenced. The day before Parliament assembled, he was pilloried in Palace Yard. Twice during the following week, as Parliament took up its tasks, the cries of the perjurer could be heard in the streets as he was scourged across London. Though the coincidence of the dates seems to confirm Burnet's conclusion that the whole ghastly affair was staged "as a preparation" to the sitting of Parliament (*1*, 637), in fairness to James it should be remembered that Burnet was biased and that preliminaries to Oates's trial had been going on for almost a year: Oates had been arrested on 10 May 1684 at the Amsterdam Coffeehouse in an action of *scandalum magnatum* brought by the duke of York, fined £100,000, and lodged in King's Bench Prison in default of payment. When the writs for Parliament went out late in February 1685, the date af the actual trial was still uncertain. The court could easily arrange such an intimidating display, but there was little need to do so. James was pleased with his Parliament and, indeed, few of the members themselves, as they listened to the royal address on 22 May, would have felt any sympathy for the victim. The nation had been diabolically fooled, and it would have its revenge.

The next two poems are selected from the numerous ballads hawked in the London streets throughout May. They pick up a thread that had already been spun long and coarse, a thread fretted with a hundred allusive strands from the angry days of the Plot when Oates's "very breath . . . was pestilential, and, if it brought not imprisonment or death over such on whom it fell, it surely poisoned reputation and left good Protestants arrant Papists, and something worse than that, in danger of being put in the Plot as traitors" (North, p. 205).

THE SALAMANCA DOCTOR'S FAREWELL

Or Titus's Exaltation to the Pillory
Upon his Conviction of Perjury

A Ballad, to the Tune of "Packington's Pound"

1.

Come listen, ye Whigs, to my pitiful moan,
All you that have ears when the Doctor has none.
In sackcloth and ashes let's sadly be jogging
To behold our dear savior o'th'nation a-flogging.
   The Tories to spite us,   5
   As a goblin to fright us,
With a damned wooden ruff will bedeck our friend Titus.
Then mourn all to see ungrateful behavior
From these lewd popish Tories to the dear nation-savior.

2.

From three prostrate kingdoms at once to adore me   10
And no less than three parliaments kneeling before me,
From hanging of lords with a word and a frown,
And no more than an oath to the shaking a crown;
   For all these brave pranks
   Now to have no more thanks   15
Than to look through a hole through two damned wooden planks:
Oh, mourn ye poor Whigs, with sad lamentation
To see the hard fate of the savior o'th'nation.

3.

Forever farewell, the true, Protestant, famous,
Old days of th'illustrious, great Ignoramus!   20

2. A standard joke. Oates did not have his ears "cropped" when he was pilloried. If the poem were written prior to the passing of sentence, however, the poet would have expected Oates to undergo this ferocity as punishment for perjury.

4. *savior o'th'nation:* At the height of his powers Oates "put on an episcopal garb (except the lawn sleeves), silk gown and cassock, great hat, satin hatband and rose, long scarf, and was called or most blasphemously called himself the 'savior of the nation'" (North, p. 205).

11. *three parliaments:* the three Whig or Exclusion Parliaments, 1679–81.

20. *great Ignoramus:* In July 1681 London grand juries selected by the Whig sheriffs, Slingsby Bethel and Henry Cornish, threw out the indictments for treason against Stephen College and Shaftesbury as "not true bills." College was later tried and convicted in Oxford. For Shaftesbury's release see *The Medal Reversed*.

Had the great headsman Bethel, that honest Ketch royal,
But sat at the helm still the rogues I'd defy all.
       The kind Tekelite crew,
       To the Alcoran true,
Spite of law, oaths, or gospel would save poor True Blue.   25
But the Tories are up and no quarter nor favor
To trusty old Titus, the great nation-savior.

4.

There once was a time, boys, when to the world's wonder
I could kill with a breath more than Jove with his thunder,
But, oh, my great *Narrative's* made but a fable,   30
My pilgrims and armies confounded like Babel.
       Oh, they've struck me quite dumb
       And to tickle my bum
Have my oracles turned all to a tale of Tom Thumb.
Oh, weep all to see this ungrateful behavior   35
In thus ridiculing the great nation-savior.

5.

From honor and favor and joys my full swing,
From twelve pound a week and the world in a string,
Ah, poor falling Titus, 'tis a cursed debasement
To be pelted with eggs through a lewd wooden casement.   40
       And oh, muckle Tony,
       To see thy old crony
With a face all benointed with wild locust honey,
'Twould make thy old tap weep with sad lamentation
For trusty old Titus, thy savior o'th'nation.   45

21. *great headsman Bethel*: Alludes to a boast Bethel is said to have made that had a headsman been lacking to execute Charles I he would have done it himself (Luttrell, *1*, 187).

23. *Tekelite crew*: Cf. *Algernon Sidney's Farewell*, 52 n.

25. *True Blue*: Whig.

30. *my great Narrative's*: *The True Narrative of the Horrid Plot, 1679*, was concocted by Oates and Israel Tonge, rector of St. Mary Staining and anti-Catholic pamphleteer.

31. *My pilgrims and armies*: William Bedloe, a witness in the trial of the Catholic lawyer Richard Langhorne, June 1679, deposed that Langhorne was an accomplice in a Jesuit design to land an army of cashiered Irish soliders disguised as Spanish pilgrims at Milford Haven in Wales (L'Estrange, *History of the Plot*, p. 51).

38. *twelve pound a week*: In October 1678 Oates was assigned a suite of apartments in Whitehall, a bodyguard, and a pension of £600 per annum (Lane, p. 107).

41. *muckle Tony*: Shaftesbury.

6.

See the rabble all round me in battle array,
Against my wood castle their batteries play;
With turnip-grenadoes the storm is begun,
All weapons more mortal than Pick'ring's screwed gun.
        Oh, my torture begins   50
        To punish my sins,
For peeping through key-holes to spy dukes and queens,
Which makes me to roar out with sad lamentation
For this tragical blow to the savior o'th'nation.

7.

A curse on the day, when the Papists to run down,   55
I felt buggering at Omers to swear plots at London.
And oh, my dear friends, 'tis a damnable hard case
To think how they'll pepper my sanctified carcass.
        Were my skin but as tough
        As my conscience of buff,   60
Let 'em pelt their hearts-blood I'd hold out well enough.
But oh, these sad buffets of mortification,
To maul the poor hide of the savior o'th'nation.

8.

Had the Parliament sat till they'd once more but put
Three kingdoms into the Geneva old cut,   65
With what homage and duty to Titus in glory
Had the worshipping saints turned their bums up before me:

46–49. Oates was treated unmercifully when he stood in Palace Yard. But the next day at the Royal Exchange his partisans rioted and overturned the pillory.

49. *Pick'ring's screwed gun:* Thomas Pickering and John Grove "were ordered to make an attempt upon the king's person . . . to be done with screwed pistols, shorter than some carbines; . . . they had silver bullets, which Grove would have champed [i.e., made jagged by biting] that the wound might prove incurable" (*The King's Evidence Justified; or Doctor Oates's Vindication of Himself*, etc. [1679], p. 9).

52. *peeping through key-holes:* This is an oft-prophesied parallel of this activity and the pillory.

56. *buggering:* The charge of sodomy was brought against Oates on several occasions, although only once, during his brief career as a naval chaplain, was he actually punished for his vice (Lane, pp. 30–31). *Omers:* Oates obtained admission to the English seminary at St. Omers in Flanders in December 1677 and spent the next six months there, until he was expelled, gathering ideas and "information" for the Plot.

60. *buff:* thick, tough leather.

64–65. I.e., converts of England, Ireland, and Scotland to the puritan fashions of the Genevan, John Calvin.

But oh, the poor stallion,
A la mode d' Italian.
To be futtered at last like an English rapscallion. 70
Oh mourn, all ye brethren of th'Association,
To see this sad fate to the savior o'th'nation.

9.

Could I once but get loose from these troublesome tackles,
A pocky stone doublet and plaguy steel shackles,
I'd leave the damned Tories and to do myself justice 75
I'd e'en go a mumping with my honest friend Eustace.
       Little Comins and Oates
       In two pilgrim coats,
We'd truss our black bills up and all our old plots;
We'd leave the base world all for their damned rude behaviors 80
To two such heroic true Protestant saviors.

10.

But alack-and-a-day, the worst is behind still,
Which makes me fetch groans that would e'en turn a windmill:
Were the pillory all I should never be vexed,
But oh, to my sorrow, the gallows comes next; 85
       To my doleful, sad fate
       I find though too late
To this collar of wood comes a hempen cravat;
Which makes me thus roar out with sad lamentation
To think how they'll truss up the savior o'th'nation. 90

70. *futtered:* "to coit with," derived from the French, *foutre;* according to Partridge a literary coinage of Sir Richard Burton.

71. *th'Association:* At Shaftesbury's arrest in July 1681, his papers were seized as evidence for the crown. Among them a document, not in his hand, projected an Association for the defense under Parliament of the Protestant religion and for the exclusion by force, if necessary, of the duke of York.

74. *stone doublet:* a prison.

76. *mumping:* begging. *Eustace:* Eustace Comins, one of the perjured Irish "evidences" against Dr. Oliver Plunket, the Catholic archbishop of Dublin. Plunket was tried and executed in the summer of 1681, the last victim of the Plot.

79. *black bills:* a weapon like a halberd. One of the allegations made against Coleman by Oates was that 40,000 of these weapons were to be provided for the projected rebellion in Ireland.

85. *the gallows comes next:* not part of Oates's sentence. Sir Francis Withins said, nevertheless, after passing sentence, "if it had been in my power to have carried it further, I should not have been unwilling to have given judgment of death upon you. For I am sure you deserve it" (Lane, p. 317). There can be little doubt that the judges intended Oates's punishment to be fatal.

The Tragi-Comedy of Titus Oates

Who Sometime Went under the Notion of the Salamanca Doctor;
Who Being Convicted of Perjury and Several Other Crimes at
the King's Bench Bar, Westminster, May 16, 1685, Had His
Sentence to Stand in the Pillory, to Be Whipped at the Cart's
Arse, and to Be Sent Back to Prison

Whet all your wits and antidote your eyes
Before you hazard here to play this prize,
Or gaze like eagles on a show so rare,
No time brought forth an object yet so fair.
Lo, here's the bugbear rampant of the Plot,   5
Which Whig on Tory in a sham begot,
Here *à la mode* the guardian of the land
In a new-fashioned pulpit now doth stand.
The tub's o'erwhelmed and all the hoops are flung,
And depute-Jack he peeps out through the bung.   10
Bar-Cochab's here, the star of England's sky.
Deciphered now the son of Perjury,
Th'Egyptian cow, the oaten-blasted blade,
Which hath these several years eat up our trade,
The state's anatomist, the church confusion,   15
Who dreamed a plot and swore it was a vision;
A doctor who degree did ne'er commence,
A rhetorician that spoke never sense:
Like Proteus he still changeth to the time,
His pulse and temper suits with any clime.   20

Subtitle. Convicted of Perjury and Several Other Crimes: Officially, Oates was tried and convicted on two counts of perjury: first, that he had falsely sworn to a "consult" of Jesuits held at White Horse Tavern on 24 April 1678, at which the king's death was determined; second, that he had falsely sworn to the presence in London between 8–12 August 1687 of William Ireland, whom Oates had claimed had orders to murder the king. Other crimes only came into the verdict by implication.

3. *gaze like eagles:* allusion to the old idea that the eagle could look directly at the sun with open eyes.

5. *bugbear rampant:* hobgoblin, imaginary terror. Here with a pun on heraldic forms (cf. line 36).

9. *tub:* derisively, a pulpit, especially that of a Nonconformist preacher.

10. *depute-Jack:* the imputed knave, or the appointed serving-man.

11. *Bar-Cochab:* "Barcochebas" or "Bar Kochba"—"son of a star." In Christian sources the name for Simeon, leader of the Jewish revolt against Rome during Hadrian's reign. He is called "Bar (Ben) Coziba," "son of deceit," in Rabbinic writings after the failure of the rebellion.

13–14. A reference to Genesis 41 and Pharaoh's dreams of the seven lean kine and the seven "blasted" ears which devoured the fat ones. Puns on Oates's name were numerous.

TESTIS OVAT

Behold y^e Heroe who has done all this
In a small Triumph stand, such as it is.
A kind of an Ovation only; true,
But such for Bloudlese Victories are due;
His were not such; he merrits more S_{...}fe
Let him in Tryumph swing & case his legs.

Titus Oates in the pillory.

His birth's equivocal, by generation
Sedition's by-blow, loyalty's privation,
A linsey woolsey emp'ric of the state
That hugs the church and knocks it o'er the pate.
He stands in state and well becomes his station,   25
Using a truckling-stool for recreation.
Now should he, in contempt of Peter's chair,
Leap from the pillory to the three-legged mare
And, with Empedocles, desire to be
But canonized an oaten-deity,   30
He would spring up, but that he is a sot,
A mandrake to conceive another plot.
　　His crime no man can balance with a curse,
For still the Hydra doth deserve a worse.
Then let him live a Minotaur of men,   35
Like Hircocervus couchant in his den,
The monument of mischief and of sin,
To spread no farther than the sooterkin
Of old sedition, set before our eye
As buoy and beacon unto loyalty.   40
Yet at the wheels of fortune let him dance
A jig of penance that can make him Prance,
Resenting all his errors though in vain
With fruitless wishes calling time again.
His face is brass, his breech no rod will feel,   45
And who knows but his back is made of steel.
His soul is proof, perhaps his body may
Be made of metal harder than the clay.
Then put him to the touch, make Titus roar;

23. *linsey woolsey emp'ric:* a quack, figuratively a curious medley, neither one thing nor the other.

26. *truckling-stool:* literally, a stool on truckles, or casters; here perhaps the pillory.

28. *three-legged mare:* the gallows.

29. *Empedocles:* According to tradition, the philosopher Empedocles, desiring to be a god, jumped to his death into the crater of Mt. Etna.

31–32. *sot . . . mandrake:* two noisome growths, with a pun on "sot," meaning "drunkard." The mandrake plant, its fleshlike root growing in the shape of a man's lower limbs, was highly prized as an aphrodisiac and as an aid in facilitating pregnancy.

36. *Hircocervus:* a fabulous creature, half goat, half stag.

38. *sooterkin:* a chimerical kind of afterbirth.

42. *Prance:* a pun on Miles Prance, the Catholic goldsmith, one of Oates's witnesses.

45. *His face is brass:* a humorous development from Dryden's lines, *Absalom and Achitophel,* 632–33, themselves derived from Num. 21:6–9: "Yet, Corah, thou shalt from oblivion pass; / Erect thyself, thou monumental brass. . . . "

48. *metal:* a common quibble on "metal" and "mettle." Cf. *Absalom and Achitophel,* 310.

The chase is turned now he's son of a whore.   50
Then conjure him with eggs and kennel dirt
And contradictions that his mouth did squirt.
To tell his name we'll Christian him once yet
And mold an agnoun which can with him sit.
He is no doctor, for by horrid lies   55
He cures sedition only tinker-wise.
He is no Papist, for he ne'er had merit;
Nor yet a Quaker, for he hath no spirit;
He is no Protestant, for want of grace
To keep him from a falsifying face.   60
He is no Turk for always, like a swine,
He loved to wallow in a tub of wine.
    No name can fit him, therefore, let him be
The grumbling ghost of old Presbytery.

53. *Christian:* i.e., "christen," interchangeable in the 17th century.
54. *agnoun:* variant spelling of "agname," a sobriquet.
56. *tinker:* an adjective long-popular to describe the kind of clumsy and inefficient mending, or botching, of state matters that the Whigs were so caught up in during the last years of Charles's reign.

Monmouth's Rebellion, June-July 1685

The political exiles who had sought asylum in Holland during the early 1680s were a widely diverse group, ranging from cowards and malcontents to brave and principled men driven from England by Charles II's legal vengeance. They shared the exile's tendency, however, to see the situation at home in terms of their own frustrations rather than as it really was. For a time James Scott, duke of Monmouth, remained indifferent to their schemes, content to live quietly with his mistress, Henrietta Wentworth, at Gouda. But the death of the king added point to their importunities. While Charles lived, Monmouth could convince himself that his father might have a change of heart and find a legal means of bringing him to the throne. He had been reminded on more than one occasion of "how easy 'tis for parents to forgive," most recently in November 1684, when he had returned in secret for what was to be his final interview with the king. In less than three months Charles was dead, and the unchallenged accession of James dashed whatever hopes the "son of David" had to succeed his father peacefully.

In the spring of 1685 Monmouth joined in a plan urged chiefly by Robert Ferguson, "The Plotter," and Forde, Lord Grey of Wark. There were to be two landings. In the first Archibald Campbell, earl of Argyle, would lead an attack on the west coast of Scotland. There this prominent Presbyterian, who had fled in 1681 to escape a sentence of death and forfeiture on trumped-up charges of treason, perjury, and assumption of the legislative power, could expect strong support from the members of his powerful clan. The second attack was to be led by Monmouth. It would begin in the southwest of England, where his own popularity was assured. Faulty intelligence magnified the unrest in England, claiming that the lower classes, who had suffered long under the penalties imposed on dissent, would come in, as would the Whig nobility in the south and northwest counties. London itself was thought sympathetic and might lend support. On every count the plotters had grossly miscalculated.

The carnage following defeat need not be described at any length. The slaughter of the duke's followers immediately after the battle could not compare with the rapaciousness of "Kirke's Lambs" or that of Jeffreys's own western "campaign," as James called it (Dalrymple, *1*, ii, 206). The haughty judge rode through the west with "four troops of the county horse attending him," which he commanded "as generalissimo" (*HMC, Portland, 3,* 388). As a result, the country was left a shambles; for months the air was heavy with the odor of death and decay (*Hatton Correspondence, 2,* 60). Horrible as the retribution was, however, it seems to have called forth little comment from the nation. Not only were people accustomed to brutal reprisal, but they were unsure of its extent and feared for themselves. Moreover, Monmouth and his fellows had committed high treason; punishment could not but be severe.

Grey and Monmouth were captured near Ringwood in the New Forest. The former made himself infamous in the eyes of his contemporaries by compounding for his life, forfeiting to the crown his large estates. Monmouth, after desperate pleas and groveling submission to James, resolved to die courageously and was executed on 15 July at Tower Hill.

THE WESTERN REBEL

Or the True Protestant Standard Set Up

To the Tune of "Packington's Pound"

1.

See, the visor's pulled off and the zealots are arming,
For our old Egypt-plagues the Whig locusts all swarming.
The true Protestant Perkin in lightning has spoke
And begins in a flash to vanish in smoke.
    Little Jemmy's launched o'er   5
    From the old Holland shore,
Where Shaftesbury marched to the devil before.
The old game's a-beginning, for high shoes and clowns
Are turning state tinkers for mending of crowns.

2.

Let his desperate frenzy to ruin spur on   10
The rebel too late and the madman too soon;
But politic noddles without wit or reason,
When empty of brains, have the more room for treason.
    Ambition bewitches
    Through bogs and through ditches   15

5. *Little Jemmy:* another of Monmouth's nicknames. James was known as "Old Jemmy."

7. *Where Shaftesbury marched:* Shaftesbury fled to Holland in November 1682 and died there two months later.

8. *high shoes and clowns:* Rustics, or plain men, who wore high shoes in the 17th century.

9. *state tinkers:* See *The Tragi-Comedy of Titus Oates,* 56 and n.

Like a will-with-a-wisp, for the bastard blood itches;
And the bully sets up with his high shoes and clowns,
A true Protestant tinker for mending of crowns.

3.

Let him banter religion, that old stale pretense
For traitors to mount on the neck of their prince,   20
But clamor and nonsense no longer shall fright us,
Our wits are restored by the flogging of Titus.
    Their canting delusion
    And Bills of Exclusion
No longer shall sham the mad world to confusion.   25
The old cheat's too gross, and no more boors and clowns,
For perching on thrones and profaning of crowns.

4.

So the great murdered Charles, our church, freedom, and laws
Were all martyrs of old to the sanctified cause.
Whilst Gospel and Heaven were the popular name,   30
The firebrands of Hell were all light from that flame.
    Reformation once tuned,
    Let religion but sound,
When that kirk bagpipe plays, all the devils dance round.
But the whining tub cheat shall no longer go down,   35
No more kings on scaffolds and slaves on a throne.

5.

Let his hot-brained ambition with his renegade loons
Mount the son of the people for lord of three crowns.
The impostor on one hand and traitor on t'other
Set up his false title, as cracked as his mother.   40
    But whilst peacock-proud
    He struts and talks loud,

16. *will-with-a-wisp:* an early form of will-o'-the-wisp.

17. *bully:* chiefly in the sense of a "blustering gallant."

19. *that old stale pretense:* The "Good Old Cause" of republicanism and Puritanism, constantly referred to by the Tories, who implied that the basic motive of the Whigs was the same as that of the rebels in the civil war.

34. *kirk bagpipe:* the tune is Presbyterianism, the Scottish religion. There was a widespread Tory belief that the Whigs were working for the restoration of the commonwealth.

37. *loons:* rogues or scamps; rhymes with "crowns."

40. *false title:* Though Monmouth did not allow himself to be proclaimed "king" until 20 June in Taunton, his pretensions had been clear for more than five years. *cracked:* blemished, of ill-repute.

The head of the rabble and idol o'th' crowd,
From his false, borrowed plumes and his hopes of a crown
To his black feet below, let th' aspirer look down.   45

6.

Then let him march on with his Politic Pol
To perch up his head by old Bradshaw and Nol;
Whilst the desperate Jehu is driving headlong
To visit the relics of Tommy Armstrong.
      But there's vengeance a-working   50
      To give him a jerking
And humble the pride of the poor little Perkin.
Great James his dread thunder shall th'idol pull down,
Whilst our hands, hearts, and swords are all true to the crown.

46. *Politic Pol:* perhaps Argyle, but probably Grey. The meaning of *poll,* "to cut off or cut short horns," would have an ironic bearing on the report that Monmouth had had an illicit affair with Grey's wife.

47. *Bradshaw and Nol:* the regicides John Bradshaw and Oliver Cromwell. Their bodies were exhumed in 1661 and hung on the gallows at Tyburn on January 30, the anniversary of Charles I's execution. Subsequently, their heads were displayed on poles atop Westminster Hall.

48. *Jehu:* "A fast and furious driver" in humorous allusion to 2 Kings 9:20. Orginally one of Shaftesbury's numerous epithets (cf. Dryden, *The Medal,* 119 ff.), the term here applies perhaps to Ferguson, "The Plotter," or John Wildman.

49. *Tommy Armstrong:* Cf. *Sir Thomas Armstrong's Last Farewell to the World,* 1684.

GEORGE STEPNEY

*On the University of Cambridge's Burning the Duke
of Monmouth's Picture*

George Stepney (1663–1707) was elected a scholar of Trinity College, Cambridge, in 1682, where he gained a considerable reputation for his Latin verse. He was graduated B.A. in 1685, M.A., 1689. In 1687 he was elected a major fellow of his college. Stepney praised James in an elegy on the death of Charles. In the present poem, as its epigraph indicates, he is more concerned with the foolish rout at Cambridge than with the new monarch. In time, he found himself turning to William.

ON THE UNIVERSITY OF CAMBRIDGE'S BURNING THE DUKE OF MONMOUTH'S PICTURE, 1685, WHO WAS FORMERLY THEIR CHANCELLOR

In answer to this question:

In turba semper sequitur fortunam et odit damnatos.

Yes, fickle Cambridge, Perkin's found this true,
Both from your rabble and your doctors too,
With what applause you once received His Grace
And begged a copy of his godlike face.

Title: Shortly after his appointment to the university on 14 July 1674, Monmouth sent the vice chancellor a portrait "drawn by Mr. Lely in full proportion, to be placed in the Regent House" (C. H. Cooper, *Annals of Cambridge,* [1845], *2,* 563). Monmouth was removed from the office by order of Charles II on 4 April 1684, and the portrait was taken down. On 3 July 1685 it was ordered "by a grace of the senate" to be burned by "the yeoman beadle." Eight days later Monmouth's name was struck from all catalogues of university officials. The 26th of July was proclaimed a day of thanksgiving for the suppression of the abortive western rising (ibid., pp. 611–13).
Epigraph: Juvenal, x. 73 (Dryden's translation):

> Sed quid
> turba Remi? sequitur fortunam ut semper et odit
> damnatos.
> How goes the mob . . . ?
> They follow Fortune, and the common cry
> Is still against the rogue condemned to die.

But when the sage vice-chancellor was sure   5
The original in limbo lay secure,
As greasy as himself he sends a lictor
To vent his loyal malice on the picture.
The beadle's wife endeavors all she can
To save the image of the tall young man,   10
Which she so oft when pregnant did embrace,
That with strong thoughts she might improve her race;
But all in vain since the wise House conspire
To damn the canvas traitor to the fire.
Lest it like bones of Scanderbeg incite   15
Scythemen next harvest to renew the fight.
　　Then in comes Mayor Eagle and does gravely allege
He'll subscribe if he can for a bundle of sedge.
But the man of Clare Hall that proffer refuses,
'Snigs, he'll be beholden to none but the Muses,   20
And orders ten porters to bring the dull reams
On the death of good Charles and crowning of James,
And swears he will borrow of the provost more stuff
On the marriage of Anne, if that ben't enough.
The heads, lest he get all the praise to himself—   25
Too greedy of honor, too lavish of pelf,
This motion deny and vote that Tite Tillet
Should gather from each noble doctor a billet.
The kindness was common and so they'd return it;
The gift was to all, all therefore would burn it.   30

5. *the sage vice-chancellor:* MS gloss, "Dr. Samuel Blyth, master of Clare Hall."

6. *in limbo:* See above note to title. The grace for burning the portrait passed three days before the battle of Sedgemoor and five days before Monmouth was captured.

10. *tall:* lusty, valiant.

13. *House:* i.e. the university senate.

15. *Scanderbeg:* the Turkish name for George Castriota (1403–67), who championed Albanian independence and long resisted the Ottoman forces. His body was exhumed by the Turks, and pieces of it worn to induce "fortune, felicity, and privilege" (*The History of George Castriot* [1596], p. 496). Cf. Dryden's *The Medal,* "Epistle to the Whigs:" "I believe, when he [Shaftebury] is dead, you will wear him in thumb-rings, as the Turks did Scanderbeg; as if there were virtue in his bones to preserve you against monarchy."

17. *Mayor Eagle:* Nicholas Eagle, mayor of Cambridge. According to the MS he "could neither read nor write."

19. *the man of Clare Hall:* Dr. Blyth; see 5 *n.*

20. *'Snigs:* a minced oath.

21. *dull reams:* Stepney is poking fun at the ballads, elegies, and panegyrics (his own included) written by every devotee of the Muses on any important state occasion. James's daughter Anne (see line 24) married George, Prince of Denmark, in July 1683; Stepney's Latin ode on the marriage was included in *Hymenaeus Cantabrigiensis,* 1683.

27. *Tite Tillet:* Titus Tillet, the yeoman beadle.

Thus joining their stocks for a bonfire together,
As they club for a cheese in the parish of Cheddar,
Confusedly crowd on the sophs and the doctors,
The hangman, the townsmen, their wives, and the proctors,
While the troops from each part of the country in mail   35
Come to quaff his confusion in bumpers of stale.
But Rosaline, never unkind to a duke,
Does by her absence their folly rebuke.
The tender creature could not see his fate
With whom she had danced a minuet so late.   40
The heads, who never could hope for such frames,
Out of envy condemned six score pounds to the flames;
Then his air was too proud, and his features amiss,
As if being a traitor had altered his phiz!
So the rabble of Rome, whose favor ne'er settles,   45
Melt down their Sejanus to pots and brass kettles.

32. *club for a cheese*: to combine or join together in the making of cheese. The industry dates from the 17th century.
37. *Rosaline*: According to notes in most MSS, she was "Walker's wife," but Walker's identity remains a mystery.
45–46. Cf. Juvenal, x. 61–64.

MATTHEW PRIOR

Advice to the Painter

Like George Stepney, Matthew Prior (1664–1721) was at Cambridge (St. John's College) in 1685 and was a close personal friend of Charles Montagu, with whom he later collaborated in the writing of *The Hind and Panther Transversed*. Since Prior and Stepney were men of similar political sympathies, it seems probable that their poems on Monmouth are directly related in inception as well as in subject matter. Though Prior's poem represents that genre which instructs a painter in order to build up a detailed and ironic "visual" representation of a series of events (see Osborne, *Advice-to-a-Painter Poems*), the events in this case gain in ironic complexity, as Stepney and Prior would have recognized, by the actual destruction of one image (or painting) of Monmouth and the resultant need to create another.

ADVICE TO THE PAINTER

On the Happy Defeat of the Rebels in the West
and the Execution of the Late Duke of Monmouth

*—Pictoribus atque Poetis
Quidlibet—*

Since by just flames the guilty piece is lost—
The noblest work thy fruitless art could boast—
Employ thy faithful pains a second time;
From the duke's ashes raise the king of Lyme,

Epigraph: Horace, *Ars Poetica*, 9–10.
pictoribus atque poetis
quidlibet audendi semper fuit aequa potestas.

Painters and poets, you say,
always have had an equal right in venturing anything.

1. "The duke of Monmouth's picture burnt at Cambridge" (MS gloss in Rawl. poet. 19. With slight variations this and the following glosses occur in most witnesses to the text.).
2. Sir Peter Lely (d. 1680) painted the portrait Monmouth presented to the university. Here, of course, Prior intends a fictional painter.
4. Monmouth landed at Lyme Regis in Dorsetshire.

And make thy fame eternal as his crime.   5
    The land, if such it may be counted, draw,
Where int'rest is religion, treason law;
Th'ungrateful land whose treach'rous sons are foes
To the kind monarchy by which they rose,
And by instinctive hatred dread the power   01
Joined in our king and in their conqueror.
Amidst the counsels of that close divan,
Draw the misled, aspiring, wretched man,
His sword maintaining what his fraud began;
Draw Treason, Sacrilege, and Julian nigh,   15
The cursed Achitophel's kind legacy.
And lest their horrid force too weak should prove,
Add tempting woman's more destructive love;
Give the ambitious fair———
All nature's gifts refined by subtlest art   20
Too able to betray his easy heart
And, with worse charms than Helen's, to destroy
That other hope of our mistaken Troy.
    The scene from dullness and Dutch plots bring o'er
And set the hopeful parricide ashore,   25
Fraught with the blessings of each boorish friend
And the kind helps their prayers and brandy lend,
With those few crowns———
Some English Jews and some French Christians send.

6. *The land:* "Holland" (MS Rawl.). It was thought, and is still possible, that Monmouth
sailed from Holland with the connivance of the Dutch authorities. The animosity the English
bore the Dutch throughout the reign of Charles II is very much alive in this and in the fol-
lowing lines.

11. *their conqueror:* Prior is probably thinking of James's naval successes against the Dutch
at Lowestoft and Sole Bay in the second and third Dutch wars.

12. *divan:* "An oriental council of state," here specifically alludes to the Turk and the as-
sociation of Whig sympathies with his aid of the Hungarian revolution.

15. *Julian:* The Reverend Samuel Johnson (1649–1703), a Whig divine and controversial-
ist, published in 1682 an attack on the duke of York entitled *Julian the Apostate,* for which
he was imprisoned on a conviction of seditious libel.

16. *cursed Achitophel:* Cf. Dryden's *Absalom and Achitophel,* 150–51: "Of these the false Achito-
phel was first: / A name to all succeeding ages cursed." Wright-Spears point out that Prior
employs Dryden's names throughout this poem and apparently imitates the sytle of *Absalom
and Achitophel* (*The Literary Works of Matthew Prior* [Oxford, 1959], *2,* 817).

18. *tempting woman's love:* The Lady Henrietta Wentworth had been Monmouth's mistress
since 1680 and, perhaps guided by her own ambitions, assisted him by pawning her jewels
to raise enough capital to undertake the rebellion.

25. *hopeful parricide:* The charge assumes that Monmouth hoped to kill his uncle, James II.

29. *English Jews:* Cf. *Absalom and Achitophel,* 45 ff.

Next in the blackest colors paint the town   30
For old hereditary treasons known,
Whose infant sons in early mischief bred
Swear to the Cov'nant they can hardly read,
Brought up with too much charity to hate
Aught but their prayer book and their magistrate;   35
Here let his gaudy banner be displayed,
While the kind fools invoke their neighbor's aid
T'adore the idol which themselves have made,
And peasants from neglected plows resort
To fill his army and adorn his court.   40
    Near these exalted on a drum unbraced
Let Heav'n's and James's enemy be placed,
The wretch that hates like his Argyle the crown,
The wretch that like our Oates defames the gown,
And through the speaking-trumpet of his nose   45
Blasphemously Heav'n's sacred word expose,
Bidding the long-eared rout, "With one accord
Stand up and fight the battles of the Lord."
    Then near the pageant prince, alas! too nigh,
Draw Grey with a romantic constancy,   50
"Resolved to conquer, or resolved to—fly."
And let there in his guilty face appear
The rebel's malice and the coward's fear,

30. *the town:* Taunton, which had long been the stronghold of Presbyterianism. During the civil war it was twice besieged by royalist forces under Goring, but the spirit of the towns-people and their leaders remained indomitable. Almost two centuries earlier the town had figured in the abortive invasion of the pretender Perkin Warbeck (Cf. *An Ironical Encomium*, 36 *n.*).

38. Cf. Exod. 32:1–6.

42. *enemy:* Robert Ferguson (d. 1714), "The Plotter," originally a Presbyterian minister. A strong supporter of Shaftesbury and one of the contrivers of the desperate Rye House Plot to assassinate the royal brothers, he was outlawed in 1683, but escaped to the Netherlands. The Judas in Dryden's *Absalom*, he helped goad Monmouth to rebellion, served as his expedition's chaplain, and wrote the infamous *Declaration of James, Duke of Monmouth, etc.*, issued 11 June 1685, which charged James II with numerous crimes, including the burning of London in 1666 and the poisoning of Charles II. Ferguson escaped after Sedgemoor and, at the revolution in 1688, turned Jacobite because he felt he had received insufficient recognition from William of Orange.

43. *Argyle:* Archibald Campbell, 9th earl of Argyle, the leader of the forces of rebellion in Scotland.

47. *long-eared:* Cf. *Hudibras*, I. 1.9–10: "When gospel-trumpeter, surrounded / With long eared rout, to battle sounded."

49. *pageant prince:* Monmouth, who fought his victorious battles over again at Windsor.

50. *romantic:* fantastic or extravagant.

51. *Resolved to conquer or resolved to—fly:* Cf. Waller's *Instructions to a Painter*, 18: "Resolved to conquer or resolved to die."

That future ages in thy piece may see
Not his wife falser to his bed than to his party he.   55
   Now let the cursed triumvirate prepare
For all the glorious ills of horrid war;
Let zealous lust the dreadful work begin,
Backed with a sad variety of sin;
Let vice in all its num'rous shapes be shown—   60
Crimes which to milder Brennus were unknown,
And innocent Cromwell would have blushed to own;
Their arms from pillaged temples let 'em bring
And rob the Deity to wound the king.
   Excited thus by their camp priest's long prayer,   65
Their country's curses, and their own despair,
Whilst Hell combines with its black offspring Night
To hide their treach'ry or secure their flight,
The watchful troops with cruel haste come on,
Then shout, look terrible, discharge, and run.   70
   Fall'n from his short-lived power and flattered hopes,
His friends destroyed by hunger, swords, or ropes,
To some near grove the western monarch flies
In vain. The grove her innocent shade denies.
The juster trees———   75
Which when for refuge Charles and virtue fled
By grateful instinct their glad branches spread
And round the sacred charge cast their enlarged head—
Soon as the outcast Absalom comes nigh
Drop off their trembling leaves and blasted die.   80
Not earth itself would hide her guilty son

59. Cf. Dryden, *The State of Innocence*, I.1.5–6: "In liquid burnings, or on dry to dwell, / Is all the sad variety of Hell."

61. *Brennus*: The leader of the Gauls, who defeated the Romans at the Allia in 390 B.C. He besieged Rome for six months; then quitted the city after receiving a ransom of 1000 pounds of gold. It was said he threw his sword onto the scales in which the ransom was being weighed and cried, "Vae victis."

63. *pillaged temples*: The rebels unleaded the Cathedral of Bath to make bullets. At Wells on 30 June Monmouth's forces took lead from the roof of the cathedral and desecrated the building, stealing some of its plate.

65. On the eve of the Battle of Sedgemoor, Ferguson and other Puritan ministers held a lengthy service at Bridgewater. Ferguson selected as his text Josh. 22:22: "The Lord God of gods, the Lord God of gods, He knoweth, and Israel He shall know; if it be in rebellion or if in transgression against the Lord (save us not this day)."

74. *The grove*: New Forest, where Charles II had found refuge after the Battle of Worcester (1651). The image also fits the account of the death of Absalom in 2 Sam. 18:9–14.

81. The duke of Monmouth was taken in a ditch. For an account of his capture see the *London Gazette*, 6–9 July 1685.

Though he for refuge to her bowels run.
Seditious Corah to her arms she took
When angry Heav'n his Good Old Cause forsook,
But now provoked with a more just disdain   85
She shrinks her frightened head and gives our rebel back again.
   Now, Artist, let thy juster pencil draw
The sad effects of necessary law.
In painted words and speaking colors tell
How the great, pitied, stubborn traitor fell.   90
On the sad scene the glorious rebel place,
His pride and sorrow struggling in his face;
Describe the labors of his tortured breast
(If by thy imag'ry thought can be expressed),
Show with what difference two vast passions move   95
And how the hero with the Christian strove.
   Then draw the sacred prelate by his side
To raise his sorrow and confound his pride
With the dear, dreadful thought of a God crucified.
Paint if thou canst the powerful words which hung   100
Upon the holy man's persuasive tongue,
Words sweet as Moses writ or Asaph sung,
Words whose prevailing influence might have won
All but the haughty, hardened Absalon.
   At distance round the weeping mother place   105

83. *Seditious Corah:* Though this was Dryden's name for Oates, the reference here points directly to the biblical text (Num. 16:32).

88. Cf. *Absalom and Achitophel,* 1003: "Oh cursed effects of necessary law!"

97. *the sacred prelate:* The bishop of Ely, Francis Turner, who, with Ken, bishop of Bath and Wells, Tenison, then vicar of St. Martin's, and Dr. George Hopper, rector of Lambeth, ineffectually tried to persuade Monmouth to confess the sinfulness of his affair with Lady Henrietta Wentworth and to acknowledge the doctrine of Non-Resistance.

102. *Asaph:* one of David's chief musicians; also a compliment to Dryden. Cf. Asaph in *Absalom and Achitophel,* II, 1039.

105–08. While the "Grecian artist" may be Anacreon, the probable originator of the poetic genre of "advice-to-a-painter," more likely Prior was thinking of lines 17–22 from Waller's *Of His Majesty's Receiving the News of the Duke of Buckingham's Death:*

> The famous painter could allow no place
> For private sorrow in a prince's face:
> Yet, that his piece might not exceed belief,
> He cast a veil upon a supposed grief.
> 'Twas want of such a precedent as this
> Made the old heathen frame their gods amiss.

Thorn-Drury says of these lines, "The allusion is to the picture by Timanthes of the sacrifice of Iphigenia, wherein the painter, having expressed various degrees of grief in the faces of Calchas, Odysseus, Ajax, and Menelaus, represented Agamemnon, the father of the victim, with his face buried in the folds of his drapery" (Edmund Waller's *Works,* [1893], *2,* 157).

The too unmindful father's beauteous race,
But like the Grecian artist spread a veil
O'er the sad beauties of fair Annabel;
No art, no muse those sorrows can express
Which would be rendered by description less.   110
Now close the dismal scene, conceal the rest—
That the sad orphans' eyes will teach us best—
Thy guilty art might raise our ill-placed grief too high
And make us, whilst we pity him, forget our loyalty.

108. *Annabel*. duchess of Monmouth. See *Absalom and Achitophel*, 34.
110. Macaulay, *2*, 616–20, assembles the various accounts of Monmouth's execution in a graphic description. Despite Prior's admonition, I give Burnet's admittedly partial report of the event:

> And he went to the place of execution on Tower Hill with an air of undisturbed courage that was grave and composed. He said little there, only that he was sorry for the blood that was shed; but he had ever meant well to the nation. When he saw the axe, he touched it, and said it was not sharp enough. He gave the hangman [Ketch] but half the reward he intended; and said, if he cut off his head cleverly, and not so butcherly as he did the Lord Russell's, his man would give him the rest. The executioner was in great disorder, trembling all over; so he gave him two or three strokes without being able to finish the matter, and then flung the axe out of his hand. But the sheriff forced him to take it up; and at three or four more strokes he severed his head from his body; and both were presently buried in the chapel of the Tower (*1*, 646).

Survey of Events, 1686

Quick, easy victory over Monmouth brought James to the height of his power—he had money, military strength, influence abroad, and no serious opposition at home. A politically cautious and intelligent man would have nourished these advantages with unhurried care, content to await an abundant harvest. But James was not inclined to be overly cautious, and his political shrewdness was open to question. He was gradually coming more directly under the influence of the radical and opportunistic elements led by the Jesuit Edward Petre, Jeffreys, and Sunderland, men whose husbandry knew only reaping. In allowing the advice of these men to dominate his thinking, James turned from the counsel of the moderate Catholic party led by William Herbert, marquis of Powis, and John, Lord Belasyse, and failed to act in accordance with the will of the majority even of his own faith. James's chief aims had been, from the beginning, to secure toleration for Roman Catholics under the law. The early successes of the reign and the constant prodding of the radical faction worked insidiously to reshape this policy, however, into a program aimed at no less than the reconversion of England. To the moderates, this was a dangerous plan. Although they considered James the rightful king, they could see that the succession must soon revert to the Protestant line, if there were no male heir. At that time, they could expect to pay dearly for gains too forcibly won.

Their fears at James's growing ambitions were undoubtedly increased by James's opening speech at the reassembly of Parliament (9 November 1685). He was blunt and uncompromising on his need for a strong standing army and on his right to retain the Catholic officers he had appointed during the summer emergency. Parliament had grown more certain of itself since its adjournment in July, but it was ready to grant a sizable supply and, perhaps, to concur with the king's desire for a strengthened army. It could not tolerate the employment of Roman Catholic officers in that army. Compliance on this point would subvert the laws of the realm that guaranteed the Established Church. Exasperated and fearing a possible court pronouncement on the legality of his position, James prorogued Parliament until 10 February 1686. In the interval a chastened opposition might reconsider its arguments. A flurry of civil and military dismissals followed, but as the time approached for Parliament to reconvene, James grew apprehensive. Throughout December

417

the dismissals, particularly that from the council of Henry Compton, bishop of London, occupied town and court. There were also fresh rumors about a toleration. In January the printing of letters from Charles's strongbox, which seemed to prove he died a Catholic, caused general consternation, though some had known of their existence since October. The old fears were growing. Gossip said *quo warranto* proceedings could be expected against the universities and some of the bishops. The factions at court were strong in their concern over James's renewed attentions to his mistress Catherine Sedley, The result of all this was, for Parliament, a further prorogation until August. To most it seemed an act of arbitrary power. Yet one might also argue that it was the act of a strong king faced with an ungrateful and recalcitrant people. James was not alone in seeing the situation as analogous to his father's dilemma. The author of the panegyric on *England's Happiness* emphasized the analogy in his exhortation to loyalty, developing in sombre tones the theme of the martyred king. For many the poem undoubtedly represented a reasonable appraisal of affairs, and in attacking the "self-willed man" and upholding divine Providence, it followed the orthodox Anglican position on the relationship between church and state. But against this position, like an insistent recitative, sounded fear of popery. This theme overrode all others as the year progressed and turned the *Song*, "What think you of this age now," a commemorative poem on Monmouth's rebellion, into a searing attack on every manifestation of treachery and bad faith that could be claimed against James and the Roman church. By mid-summer James's intentions seemed only too clear. Ruefully Englishmen acknowledged the aptness of the following description of the reign.

A Poem on England's Happiness

In vain did Heav'n its miracles produce
When man would put them to no pious use;
In vain the Deity our good designed
When self-willed man was otherwise inclined.
Bliss from above but to no purpose flows   5
When men will stubbornly that bliss oppose.
In vain the Heav'ns do man with good caress
When man resisteth his own happiness.
Unconstant man that for uncertain noise
Would hazard all the good he now enjoys,   10
And but to satisfy unbridled will
Would change a present good for future ill;
Who when a godlike monarch does command
In the hard rule of this unworthy land—

A godlike monarch who, beyond what we   15
Have merited from such great dignity,
His virtue in abundant measure showed
By winking at our black ingratitude,
Whilst with a bounty scarce heard of before
He offers to increase our blessings's store—   20
The brutish land so strangely does reject
The good we might from such a king expect.
In meager stubbornness they'd rather live
Than on the Canaan of his bounty thrive.
We, like the Jews when the Supreme Power   25
Did down from Heav'n his pleasant manna shower,
With envy murmur and shall murmur on
Till Heav'n its pestilential wrath send down
And by affliction teach us how to prize
The manna of our first felicities;   30
And if its goodness should at last restore
The bliss we might have well enjoyed before,
Rememb'ring th'ill we did ourselves create,
Should prudently avoid our former fate:
So an old mariner by tempest split   35
Upon a rock again remembers it
And with a dear-bought skill will turn aside
From the vast danger he before had tried.
But senseless England to itself unkind
Will thwart the happiness the Heav'ns designed,   40
Would dally with the fire and tempt the flame
That once had like to have consumed its frame;
With matchless boldness would that sea repass
In which the beauteous island shipwrecked was;
Would once more handle these injurious arms   45
By which she had received so many harms.
Self-vexing nation, when all things agree
To make thy sum up of felicity!
Thou, only thou, with a malicious hand
Against thy own advantages wilt stand!   50
Ill-natured people who, when they may taste
Of every fruit within that compass placed,
Condemn the proffer and with lustful eyes
To th'top of the forbidden tree will rise,

---

26. *manna:* The image from Exod. 16 became a commonplace in the poetry, tracts, and sermons illustrating God's Providence.

Or possess all or none of Paradise.   55
Remember, England, how thy giddy zeal
For the supporting of the commonweal
Did willfully your own enthraldom seal.
And is't so long you wore the chains you would
Again go under such a servitude?   60
Oh, rather change your purpose and consent
To the completion of thy own content;
Sincerely weigh your int'rest, and you'll find
Each honest subject of another mind
Will alter thoughts and not with stubborn pride   65
But humble loyalty be beautified.
Ah, happy island! if thou couldst it know
Or wouldst be satisfied in being so;
Oh, happy isle! in thy luxuriant land
And in great James, who does o'er that command—   70
Like the meridian sun he does dispense
O'er all the soil his fruitful influence—
Unclouded let him shine with glorious rays,
Dispel those fogs that would eclipse his face,
While strengthened with the vigor of his heat   75
We learn of him to be sincerely great
And better humors from his influence get.
So shall the land be truly blessed: he reign
For our protection; we his rights maintain.

Song

To the Tune of "A Begging We Will Go"

1.

What think you of this age now
    When popery's in request,
And he's the loyalest subject
    Slights not the laws the least?
When a-Torying they do go, do go, do go,   5
    When a-Torying they all go.

---

76. *sincerely:* completely, thoroughly, wholly. Cf. Dryden's *Absalom and Achitophel*, 43: "But life can never be sincerely blessed."

2.

What think you of a Whiggish plot
  And of their evidence,
When all the laws cannot protect
  The people's innocence?
When a-swearing they do go, do go, do go,
  When a-swearing they do go.

3.

What think you of a general
  That did betray his lord,
For which he does deserve to swing
  In Ketch's hempen cord?
Such a rogue you ne'er did know, did know, did know,
  Such a rogue you ne'er did know.

4.

What think you to be tried, sir,
  By proclamation laws,
And zealously destroy a prince
  T'advance the popish cause?
And to mass to make us go, us go, us go,
  And to mass to make us go.

5.

What think you of the chancellor,
  Be sure he'll do the work,
Establish a religion
  Although it were the Turk?
And for int'rest he'll do so, do so, do so,
  And for int'rest he'll do so.

13. *a general:* Gray.
14. *his lord:* Monmouth.
16. *Ketch:* Jack Ketch, the hangman.
20. *proclamation laws:* Monmouth was executed on 15 July 1685 without benefit of trial. His death was followed by numerous proclamations for the apprehension of suspected rebels. See Luttrell, *1,* 356–57.
21. *a prince:* Monmouth.
25. *chancellor:* Jeffreys was appointed lord chancellor on 28 September 1685.

6.

In Lime Street now we do say mass
 T'advance the popish cause
And set the mayor to guard it
 Against his oath and laws.
To the court you must bow low, bow low, bow low,   35
 To the court you must bow low.

7.

And what think you of proving
 A popish army awful
And bant'ring the church with
 Arguments unlawful?
But a-fiddling let him go, him go, him go,   40
 But a-fiddling let him go.

8.

What would you give to be, sir,
 In contrite Prance's place
And sentenced to a pillory   45
 For one small mite of grace?
When recanting he did go, did go, did go,
 When recanting he did go.

9.

What think you of our penal laws
 That made the pope to bow?   50
If damned rogues had not betrayed us
 They'd been as penal now.

31. *Lime Street:* In 1686 a Roman Catholic chapel was set up on this East London Street by the resident of the Elector Palatine. Protests from members of the corporation met with a stern rebuke from James. On Sunday, 18 April, shortly after the chapel was opened, riots broke out "so that the lord mayor and aldermen were there with the trained bands to quell the same; some of the chief ringleaders were taken and His Majesty, having had an account of it, sent for the lord mayor and told him to take care of the peace of the city, or otherwise he should be forced to send some assistance to them" (Luttrell, *1*, 375).

44. *Prance:* Miles Prance, one of the perjured witnesses of the Popish Plot, was sentenced on 15 June 1686.

49. *penal laws:* Known to those afflicted by them as the "bloody" or "sanguinary" laws, the penal laws were severe, though not always scrupulously enforced. They date from the reign of Elizabeth, and the chief elements of the laws against the Catholics have been concisely summarized by Turner (p. 116).

51. *damned rogues:* The judges who, on 16 June 1686, handed down the verdict in the test case of *Godden* v. *Hales* (see below, *To the Respective Judges*). This poem thus dates from after this verdict and perhaps as late as 15 July 1686, the anniversary of Monmouth's execution.

But their opinions were not so, not so, not so,
    Their opinions were not so.

10.

Yet fear we not that bugg'ring dog   55
    That sits in the porph'ry chair,
That swears he is infallible
    'Cause he's St. Peter's heir,.
'Tis a lie we all do know, do know, do know,
'Tis a lie we all do know.   60

Dryden's Conversion, January–April 1686

No two literary figures received more abuse during James's reign from their fellow writers than did Sir Roger L'Estrange and John Dryden. By many of their contemporaries they were regarded as political opportunists who would "with all revolutions still comply" to insure their well-being. In the case of the politico-journalist L'Estrange the charges of changeability and self-interest were recognized by attacker and attacked alike as more or less occupational. But for Dryden, the foremost poet of the age, the attacks were much more damaging. Though the charges were groundless, turning back to the poet's youth for what seemed to be evidence of his willingness to embrace with equal fervor first Cromwell and then Charles, contemporary opinion was largely set against Dryden. When he became a convert, attacks renewed and multiplied (see Macdonald, pp. 3–4). His name was linked with L'Estrange's, both because L'Estrange's staunch support of Tory policy "under pretense to serve the Church of England . . . gave suspicion of gratifying another party" (Evelyn, *4*, 439), and because Dryden apparently had lowered himself once again to the hack estate. There was money to be got—or so it seemed to many observers. Evelyn writes of the man and his conversion, "such purchases were no great loss to the church" (*4*, 497). Not all felt the loss to be so inconsiderable; the king and his religion had gained a valuable adherent.

Dryden's sincerity in becoming a convert to the Roman Catholic faith is no longer an issue. He had little to gain in material reward and much to lose as a Catholic even in James's England. Dryden described his own situation in *The Hind and the Panther*, III (374–83):

Panther: Methinks in those who firm with me remain,
           It shows a nobler principle than gain.
             Your inf'rence would be strong, the Hind replied,
           If yours were in effect the suff'ring side;
           Your clergy sons their own in peace possess,
           Nor are their prospects in reversion less.
           My proselytes are struck with awful dread,
           Your bloody comet-laws hang blazing o'er their head.
           The respite they enjoy but only lent,
           The best they have to hope, protracted punishment.

[CHARLES SACKVILLE, EARL OF DORSET]

To Mr. Bays

Thou mercenary renegade, thou slave,
Thou ever changeling, still to be a knave;
What sect, what error wilt thou next disgrace?
Thou art so lewd, so scandalously base,
That anti-Christian popery may be   5
Ashamed of such a proselyte as thee.
Not all the rancor and felonious spite
Which animates thy lumpish soul to write
Could have contrived a satire more severe,
Or more disgrace the cause thou would'st prefer.   10
Yet in thy favor this must be expressed:
It suits with thy poetic genius best.
There thou————
Thy mind disused to truth may'st entertain
With tales more monstrous, fanciful, and vain   15
Than e'en thy poetry could ever feign.
Or sing the lives of thy old fellow saints—
'Tis a large field and thy assistance wants.
There copy out new operas for the stage
And with their miracles divert the age: 20
Such is thy faith (if thou hast faith indeed,
For well we may distrust the poet's creed.)
Rebel to God, blasphemer to thy king,
Oh, tell whence could this strange compliance spring:
So may'st thou prove to thy new gods as true   25
As your old friend, th' devil, has been to you.
Still conscience and religion's the pretense,

2. *changeling*: a waverer, turncoat, or renegade.
17. Dryden translated Bouhours's *Life of St. Francis Xavier* in 1686.
19. *new operas*: See prologue and epilogue to *Albion and Albanius*.
23. Cf. Tom Brown's epigram *To Mr. Dryden, and His Conversion* (*Works* [1707], *1.* ii. 17),
which often occurs in MS following the present poem:

> Traitor to God and rebel to thy pen,
> Priest-ridden poet, perjured son of Ben,
> If ever thou prove honest, then the nation
> May modestly believe transubstantiation.

But food and drink the metalogic sense;
'Twas int'rest reconciled thee to the cheat,
And vain ambition tempted thee to eat.   30
Oh, how persuasive is the want of bread!
Not reasons from strongbox more strongly plead.
A convert thou! Why, 'tis past all believing;
'Tis a damned scandal of thy foes' contriving,
A jest of that malicious monster, Fame: 35
The honest Layman's Faith is still the same.

28. James continued Dryden's office and the pension of £100 granted by his brother, but he omitted the laureate's butt of sack. *metalogic:* i.e., after logic.

32. *strongbox:* In January 1686 the printing of letters from Charles's strongbox, which seemed to prove he died a Catholic, caused general consternation, though some had known of their existence since October. In 1686 Dryden assisted in the preparation of *A Defense of the Papers* reputed to have been written by Charles and by Anne Hyde. The latter, whose statement gave her reasons for becoming a convert, was defended by Dryden against attack from Edward Stillingfleet.

36. *Layman's Faith:* the subtitle of Dryden's *Religio Laici.*

The Trial of *Godden* v. *Hales,* June 1686

Lacking parliamentary acquiescence in his policy of appointing Catholics to military posts, James sought support from the bench for his use of the royal prerogative to dispense with the Test Act, which required public servants to receive the sacrament according to the rites of the established church and to take the oaths of allegiance and supremacy within three months of their appointment to office. If he could secure a ruling in favor of the prerogative, James reasoned that he would then be free to install Catholics in whatever posts he saw fit. He had contemplated recourse to the judiciary from the time of his return from Scottish exile in 1682, when the possibility was first put into his mind by Edward Herbert, then chief justice of Chester, and approved in principle by Chief Justice Jeffreys (Clarke, *James II,* 2, 80–81).

With the elevation of Herbert to the office of chief justice of the King's Bench (23 October 1685), the advice to seek a judicial ruling on the dispensing power was, no doubt, renewed with vigor by its chief proponent. The first step was to prepare a case that could be tested. It was arranged that Arthur Godden, coachman to Colonel Edward Hales, should bring an action against his master, a convert in November 1685, to secure the £500 due to an informer under the Act of 25 Car. 2 for preventing "dangers from popish recusants" (Howell, *2,* 1165 ff.). Tried and convicted at the assizes held at Rochester on 29 March 1686, Hales appealed on grounds that he had received "letters patent under the Great Seal" which dispensed with the oaths in his case (Howell, *2,* 1180–82).

During April James took it upon himself to sound judicial opinion through a system of personal interview, which came to be known as "closetting," in hope that he could convince or coerce the opposition to support his point of view. The upshot was that Sir Thomas Jones, chief justice of the Common Pleas, and three other refractory judges were dismissed. In reply to James's determination to have twelve judges of his own opinion, Jones had said that possibly His Majesty "might find twelve judges of his opinion, but he could scarce find twelve lawyers of that mind" (Echard, *3,* 797; Reresby, p. 422). And indeed when James sought counsel to defend the dispensing power, he met with another setback. Heneage Finch, solicitor general, refused the brief and, as a result, was turned out of office. Some thought that the refusal to comply with the king's wishes was less a result of conscientiousness than of "apprehension of being called to account for compliance by Parliament at some future time" (Ranke, *4*, 290).

James was undaunted by the resistance to his plans, however, and by mid-June he felt he could proceed in his attempts to secure judicial sanction for the dispensing power. Accordingly, he had Herbert assemble the judges beforehand to obtain their opinion on the case. Herbert said of the meeting:

> Truly, upon the argument before us, it appeared as clear a case as ever came before this court. But because men fancy I know not what difficulty, when really there is none, we were willing to give so much countenance to the question in the case, as to take the advice of all the judges in England. They were all assembled at Sergeant's Inn, and this case was put them . . . whether the dispensation . . . were legal, because upon that depended the execution of all the law of the nation. And I must tell you that there were then ten upon the place that clearly delivered their opinions that the case . . . was good law (Howell, *2*, 1302).

Justice John Powell required additional time to consider his opinion but later concurred. Only Baron Street dissented. On 21 June Herbert delivered judgment in favor of Hales, thus upholding the dispensing power as part of the royal prerogative.

James had won a major victory, though there can be little doubt that the decision was unpopular (Clarke, *James II, 2*, 82 ff.). It aggravated the danger of a Catholic and thus hostile standing army. It supplied what seemed to be a clear instance of the corruptibility of the judiciary, as well, with the resultant destruction of the legal safeguards to the church and state. Despite these aspects of the decision, however, there was apparently little actual demonstration against it during the remainder of the summer. The following two poems, for example, are the only ones so far uncovered that concern themselves with the decision, and *To the Respective Judges,* may not have been written until 1688 (see line 29 and *n.*). The paucity of satiric attack probably reflects either the populace's tendency to wait and see, secure in the knowledge that the succession was Protestant, or its fear of the power James had secured to himself during the first year of his reign.

A Stanza Put on Westminster Hall Gate

When nature's God for our offenses died
Amongst the twelve one Judas did reside.
Here's twelve assembled for the nation's peace
Amongst which twelve, eleven are Judases.
One's true to's trust, but all the rest accord   5
With Jews and pagans to betray their Lord.
What madness, slaves! What is't could ye provoke
To stoop again unto the Romish yoke?
May ye be cursed and all your hopes demolished—
And perish by those laws ye have abolished!   10

To the Respective Judges

Dignified things, may I your leaves implore
To kiss your hands and your high heads adore?
Judges you are—but you are something more.
May I draw near and with a rough-hewed pen
Give a small draft of you, the worst of men,   5
Tell of your merits and your mighty skill
And how your charms all courts of justice fill?
Your laws, far stronger than the Commons' votes,
So finely flow from your dispensing throats,
What Rome will ask, you must not her deny,   10
If Hell command you, too, you must comply!
There's none but you would in this cause combine—
Things made like men but act like brutes and swine.
Law books are trash, a student—he's a drudge;
Learn to say "yes"—he's an accomplished judge: 15
He wins the scarlet robe and wears it too,

5. *One's true to's trust:* The dissenting judge was Baron Street. Macaulay thought he was acting collusively to lend the bench an appearance of independence (*2*, 738). Turner feels that this suggestion "does not carry any conviction" (p. 320) and cites evidence from Bramston that shows that Street was "closeted" with James for a considerable time after the trial, but that he was not dismissed. Whatever the truth of the matter, this poem indicates that the popular attitude toward Street's dissension was unequivocally behind him.

Title: In the *Muses Farewell to Popery* (1689), this poem is called *To the Ten Dispensing Judges*. The present title suggests that the poem may have been circulated in MS prior to 21 June, when Herbert announced the court's decision and explained Powell's initial hesitancy in coming to an opinion in line with the majority.

Aye, and deserves it well, for more's his due—
All that completes a traitor dwells in you.
Thus you like villains to the benches get
And in defiance to the laws you sit,   20
And all base actions that will please commit.
There must you toil for Rome and also try
Your Irish sense and cobweb policy:
Complete your crimes—and then you're fit to die!
True loyal babes, pimps to the Church of Rome!   25
Tresilian's heirs, heirs to his crimes and doom!
Was e'er the hall filled up with such a brood
All dipped in treason, villainies, or blood!
Worse than fanatic priests, for they being pressed
By a wise prince preached to repeal the Test.   30
Then here's the difference 'twixt you popish tools:
Your're downright rogues, they only knaves and fools.

23. *Irish:* suggests papistical loyalty to James and his policies. *cobweb:* unsubstantial.

26. *Tresilian's heirs:* Sir Robert Tresilian, lord chief justice during the reign of Richard II, was hanged in 1388 for the extraordinary cruelty with which he tried the rebels of the Wat Tyler uprising.

29. *fanatic priests:* Presumably a general reference to those members of the Anglican church who, by pursuing the doctrine of Passive Obedience or Non-Resistance, were willing to assent to the repeal of the Test Act. The phrase may, however, allude quite specifically to those Anglican priests in 1688 willing to read the second Declaration of Toleration from their pulpits. If so, the date of the poem's publication (1688) would, of course, also be the date of its composition.

30. *wise prince:* James. The reference is ironic, but the satirist may intend further to condemn the priests' stupidity by showing James to be wise in comparison.

DR. WILD'S GHOST

On His Majesty's Gracious Declaration
for Liberty of Conscience, April 4, 1687

How! Liberty of Conscience! that's a change
Bilks the crape-gowns and mortifies L'Estrange;
Two lines of brisk *Gazette* in pieces tears
The *Observator's* pains of many years;
The clergy-guide himself is left i'th'lurch,   5
To which he quail-piped easy daughter church;
So the foul fiend at Halberstadt, they say,
In fiddler's guise so charmingly did play
That all the buxom youth of the mad town
Followed his tweedling music up and down,   10
Till the whole troop an unseen gulf did drown.

What's now become of our informing crew,
The Browns, the Hiltons? O loyal men and true!
Once pillars of our church—true church by law—
For more were bugbeared to her out of awe   15
Then all our sermon-readers e'er could draw;
Those useful sparks, implements orthodox,
Soon as they found their church was i'th'wrong box,
Fled from her faster than from whore with pox—
So rats by instinct quit a falling house,   20
So dying beggar's left by every louse.

Pinfold, that spiritual dragoon, who made

Title: Robert Wild (1609–79) was a Puritan minister with royalist views and a popular, though controversial poet. Called by Dryden "the very Wither of the City," Wild sought poetically to defend the loyalty to the crown of his Nonconformist brethren and praised Charles's Declaration of Liberty of Conscience in 1672.

2. *crape-gowns:* clerics. *L'Estrange:* Sir Roger L'Estrange, author of the Tory newssheet *The Observator.*

3. *Gazette:* The *London Gazette* published the Declaration of Indulgence on 7 April 1687.

6. *quail-piped:* to lure, as with a quail-call. L'Estrange employed the term in his attacks on Presbyterians (*State Divinity* [1661], p. 14): "to give over . . . their quail-piping in a pulpit to catch silly women."

7. *Halberstadt:* a town in Saxony. I have not been able to determine whether it has its own version of the Pied Piper legend.

13. *Browns . . . Hiltons:* "One Brown and [John] Hilton, and one Shafto, a woman, the chief informers against conventicles, having been discovered to be guilty of perjury in those matters, are prosecuted by the justices of Middlesex for the same" (Luttrell, *I*, 387 and 241).

18. *i'th'wrong box:* in the wrong position; perhaps derived from the boxes of an apothecary.

22. *Pinfold:* Dr. Thomas Pinfold, an official of Doctors' Commons for Nonconformity under

By soul-money a pretty thriving trade,
Gave to old Nick each refractory ninny
But whisked him back for a repentant guinea,   25
Is now grown bankrupt, weary of his life,
And almost wild and frantic as his wife.

    Those that erewhile no mortal sin could spy
So bad, so gross as Nonconformity
Are now become the only malcontents,   30
And each in sullen sighs his passion vents;
Passive Obedience once was all their clutter,
But soon as their own nails were pared they mutter:
"Dear Whigs! dissenting brethren! pray forbear
To meet. Indulgence is a royal snare,   35
This declaration is a Trojan horse;
The form's illegal and the matter worse;
There is a snake i'th'grass!"—That, that's their cry,
Which is in short to give their prince the lie
And charge the best of kings with treachery.   40
Is this your Church of England loyalty?

    Hark! the hunt's up, backwards they chime their bells,
And every one a frightful story tells;
The doctors stand aghast, and country vicar
Fancies there's holy water in his liquor;   45
Each pulpit echoes, Bellarmine, thou li'st,

Charles and James. In November 1692, he was arraigned before the council "about money levied on the Protestant Dissenters and not returned into the Exchequer" (Luttrell, *2*, 606, 612; *CSPD*, p. 499).

23. *soul-money:* money subscribed to pay for masses for the soul of a dead person.

32. *Passive Obedience:* The doctrine of Passive Obedience or Non-Resistance demanded respect for and compliance with the office of the lawful king. Resistance was thought both wicked and sacrilegious. The lawful demands—even the doubtful ones—of the king were to be obeyed. *clutter:* noisy turmoil or disturbance, hubbub, arch. or dial.

41. *Church of England loyalty:* In a sermon of this title preached to the Commons on 29 May 1685, Dr. William Sherlock concluded " 'tis a Church of England loyalty I persuade you to. This our king approves, commends, relies on as a tried and experienced loyalty, which has suffered with its prince but never yet rebelled against him—a loyalty upon firm and steady principles and without reserve."

42. *backwards they chime their bells:* "To give the alarm . . . [derived from] the practice of beginning with the bass when the bells were rung" (Partridge, p. 25).

46. *Bellarmine:* Roberto Bellarmino (1542–1621), the great cardinal and theologian. His *Disputationes de Controversiis Fidei adversus hujus temporis Haereticos* (1581–93) provided the finest contemporary statement of Roman Catholic doctrine. So forceful and uncompromising was it that for more than a century most Protestant attempts to vindicate their position found it necessary to begin by answering the *Disputationes*.

And Pelling swears the pope is Antichrist.
Does not the inundation make you quake:
The Roman Sea joined with the Leman Lake?
How soon will Father Peters make a hand on's,   50
When Baxter's self has seized on petty canons?
Turn out, my masters! aloft! aloft, all hands—
Religion that's our tithe-pigs and glebe lands—
The Protestant religion now will fall;
Bel and the Dragon will devour us all!   55

  O tender, zealous hearts! O sad condition!
Idolatry will eat up superstition;
The calf at Bethel fears the calf at Dan:
The English cannot Latin mass withstand;
And now the jacks have lost their wonted prey,   60
They dread the sharks will carry all away;
So conjurers grow toward their end in fear
That their familiar devil will them tear.

  But why this sudden zeal when t'other day
With popery you could so freely play?   65
Their church you then acknowledgéd was true—
A rev'rence to the western patriarch due—
And from that coast no danger you could view;
On each occasion Papists favor found,
And all your cry was knock Dissenters down!   70
Yet now you bawl Tiber the Thames will drown,

47. *Pelling:* Edward Pelling (d. 1718), vicar of St. Martin's, Ludgate, and prebendary of Westminster. An Anglican Controversialist, he attacked Roman Catholics and Dissenters both from the pulpit and through the press. His *True Mark of the Beast* was first published in 1682 and reprinted in 1685.

50. *Father Peters:* Jesuit Edward Petre (1631–99), clerk of the Royal Closet, and one of the most influential figures at court.

51. *Baxter:* Richard Baxter (1615–91), Presbyterian divine. In May 1685 he was brought to trial before Jeffreys on a charge of libeling the church in his *Paraphrase of the New Testament*, 1685, grossly insulted, fined, and imprisoned until the fine was paid. He was released on 24 November 1686, when "James had need of the Nonconformists as a make-weight (if possible) against a recalcitrant clergy." If the crown hoped to turn him to its cause, it was deceived. Even in prison he apparently worked on a "Defense of his Paraphrase" (Frederick J. Powicke, *The Reverend Richard Baxter* [1927], pp. 152, 160 ff.).

55. *Bel and the Dragon:* idols in the Apocrypha exposed by Daniel.

58. *Bethel . . . Dan:* the sites where Jeroboam set up the golden calves for his people to worship (1 Kings 12:28–33).

60. *jacks:* pike.

61. *sharks:* those who enrich themselves by taking advantage of the necessities of others.

67. *western patriarch:* the Pope.

But why, pray, must our faith be quite undone
Because your persecuting pow'r is gone?
The wise suspect religion's not your fear,
But you are vext, you cannot domineer,   75
And rail at Jesuits for cruel elves,
Because you'd have none spoil us but yourselves.

   Well, rev'rend sirs, if popery must be,
You'll find the nuns are pretty company,
And if the fiery trial should return,   80
Most of you wet yourselves too much to burn.
But though you will not hazard your dear lives,
You may be glad to part with your old wives.
At worst—
'Tis but conforming t'other step and then,   85
Jure divino, whip and spur again.

86. *Jure divino:* by divine right.

The Summer Encampment, June–July 1687

The muster of James's army on Hounslow Heath in June and July 1687 substantially defined the particular threat of popery and the temper of Englishmen in the face of that threat. This was the third time during the reign that James had put on such a military display. On 23 July 1685 "six thousand of His Majesty's forces, horse and foot" were reviewed on the Heath (Luttrell, *1*, 355). The next summer he held his first full encampment. Though always fascinated by military pomp, he sought in these musters to intimidate the city of London. Initially, the encampment of 1686 may have awed the populace, though inclement weather and illness reduced its effectiveness. But it soon became a place of diversion for most Londoners.

The third campaign encountered less fear and more familiarity. In attempting to cow his subjects by a show of force, James had as a precedent Charles's encampment on the Heath in 1678, of which he had not accurately assessed the impact. Charles's attempt to bully Parliament in 1678 had been futile, yet James may have seen that display as a moment of monarchical strength among years of complacency. He seems never to have understood the use of Passive Resistance to turn opposition back upon itself. It was a lesson Charles had early learned and effectively reaffirmed in the muster of 1678.

In addition to a jibe at Dryden and a mocking account of the reenactment of the siege and capture of the Hungarian city of Buda, wrested from the Turks in September 1686, the following satire attacks James with bitter irony. With each new phrase of acclaim, the poet manages more thoroughly to condemn the king and points to the discrepancy not only between the image and the man, but also between that man's past and his present self. As duke of York, James had been renowned for his courage and "his constant keeping of his word." Now these qualities had apparently vanished, to be replaced by an awesome, if slightly clownish, truculence that threatened havoc even while it invited ridicule.

HOUNSLOW HEATH

Upon this place are to be seen
Many rare sights: God save the queen!

Near Hampton Court there lies a common
Unknown to neither man nor woman,
The Heath of Hounslow it is styled,
Which never was with blood defiled,
Though it has been of war the seat   5
Now three campaigns almost complete.

Here you may see great James the Second
(The greatest of our kings he's reckoned),
A hero of such high renown
Whole nations tremble at his frown,   10
And when he smiles men die away
In transports of excessive joy.
A prince of admirable learning!
Quick wit! of judgment most discerning!
His knowledge in all arts is such   15
No monarch ever knew so much.
Not that old blust'ring king of Pontus,
Whom men call learned to affront us,
With all his tongues and dialects
Could equal him in all respects;   20
His two and twenty languages
Were trifles, if compared to his;
Jargons which we esteem but small:
English and French are worth 'em all.
What though he had some skill in physic,   25
Could cure the dropsy or the phthisic,
Perhaps was able to advise one

---

14. *Quick wit!*: James's slowness of wit had become almost proverbial, due both to his phlegmatic nature and to such well-known remarks as Catherine Sedley's on the reasons for the duke's passion for her: "It cannot be my beauty, for he must see I have none; and it cannot be my wit, for he has not enough to know that I have any."

17. *king of Pontus*: Mithridates VI (c. 131–63 B.C.), king of Pontus and enemy of Rome. The figure of Mithridates was elaborately glorified by ancient authorities: "His courage, his bodily strength and size, his skill in the use of weapons, in riding, and in the chase, his speed of foot, his capacity for eating and drinking, his penetrating intellect and his mastery of 22 languages are celebrated to a degree which is almost incredible" *(EB)*.

26. *phthisic*: a wasting disease of the lungs.

To 'scape the danger of rank poison,
And could prepare an antidote
Should carry't off—though down your throat!   30
These are but poor, mechanic arts,
Inferior to great James's parts.
Shall he be set in the same rank
With a pedantic mountebank?
He's master of such eloquence,   35
Well-chosen words, and weighty sense,
That he ne'er parts his lovely lips,
But out a trope or figure slips;
And, when he moves his fluent tongue,
Is sure to ravish all the throng;   40
And every mortal that can hear
Is held fast pris'ner by the ear.

   His other gifts we need but name,
They are so spread abroad by fame:
His faith, his zeal, his constancy,   45
Aversion to all bigotry!
His firm adhering to the laws,
By which he judges every cause
And deals to all impartial justice,
In which the subject's greatest trust is!   50
His constant keeping of his word
As well to peasant as to lord;
Which he no more would violate,
Than he would quit his regal state!
Who has not his least promise broke,   55
Nor contradicted what he spoke!
His governing the brutal passions
With far more rigor than his nations
Would not be swayed by's appetite
Were he to gain an empire by't!   60
From hence does flow that chastity,
Temperance, love, sincerity,
And unaffected piety,
That just abhorrence of ambition,
Idolatry, and superstition,   65
Which through his life have shined so bright

28–29. Mithridates was said to have inured himself to the effects of poisons by their constant use—hence mithridatism.

That nought could dazzle their clear light!
These qualities we'll not insist on,
Because they all are duties Christian;
But haste to celebrate his courage,   70
Which is the prodigy of our age:
A spirit which exceeds relation
And were too great for any nation
Did not those virtues named before
Confine it to its native shore,   75
Restrain it from the thirst of blood,
And only exercise't in good!

The tedious Mithridatic War—
The noise whereof is spread so far—
Was nothing to what's practiced here,   80
Though carried on for forty year
'Gainst Pompey, Sulla, and Lucullus—
High-sounding names, brought in to gull us—
In which the Romans lost more men
Than one age could repair again,   85
Who perished not by sword or bullet
But melted gold poured down the gullet.
Heroes of old were only famed
For having millions killed or maimed,
For being th'instruments of fate   90
In making nations desolate,
For wading to the chin i'th'blood
Of those that in their passage stood;
And thought the point they had not gained
While any foe alive remained.   95
Our monarch, by more gentle rules,
Has proved the ancients arrant fools:
He only studies and contrives,
Not to destroy, but save, men's lives;
Shows all the military skill,   100
Without committing ought that's ill.
He'll teach his men, in warlike sport,
How to defend or storm a fort,

81. *forty year:* Mithridates actively opposed the Romans for less than 20 years.
82. *Pompey, Sulla, and Lucullus:* L. Cornelius Sulla (138–78 B.C.). L. Lucullus (114–57 B.C.), and Pompey the Great (106–48 B.C.) successively commanded the Roman forces that waged the interminable struggle against Mithridates. Possibly more than 80,000 Roman citizens were slaughtered in Asia by the Persians.

And in heroic interlude
Will act the dreadful scene of Bude: 105
Here Lorraine storms, the vizier dies,
And Brandenburg routs the supplies;
Bavaria there blows up their train,
And all the Turks are took or slain.
All this performed with no more harm   110
Than loss of a simple gunner's arm;
And surely 'tis a greater good
To teach men war than shed their blood.

   Now pause, and view the army royal,
Composed of valiant souls and loyal;   115
Not raised (as ill men say) to hurt ye,
But to defend, or to convert ye;
For that's the method now in use,
The Faith Tridentine to diffuse.
Time was the word was powerful,   120
But now 'tis thought remiss and dull,
Has not that energy and force
Which is in well-armed foot and horse.
Thus, when the faith has had mutation,
We change its way of propagation;   125
So Mohammed with arms and terrors
Spread over half the world his errors.

   Here daily swarm prodigious wights
And strange variety of sights,
As ladies lewd and foppish knights,   130
Priests, poets, pimps, and parasites,
Which now we'll spare and only mention
The hungry bard that writes for pension:
Old Squab—who's sometimes here, I'm told—
That oft has with his prince made bold,   135
Called the late king a saunt'ring cully
To magnify the Gallic bully;

106–07. Charles, duke of Lorraine, with the aid of the electors of Brandenburg and Bavaria,
recovered Buda from the Turks in 1686.

119. *Tridentine:* The council of the Roman Catholic church sat, with considerable intervals,
from 1545–63 at Trent to organize the church in opposition to the Reformation.

120. Presumably a play on John 1:1 and on the Bible as the Word.

134. *Old Squab:* Dryden.

136. *a saunt'ring cully:* a leisurely dupe. See Mulgrave-Dryden, *An Essay upon Satire,* 65.

137. *Gallic bully:* Louis XIV.

Who lately put a senseless banter
Upon the world with *Hind and Panther,*
Making the beasts and birds o'th'wood   140
Debate what he ne'er understood,
Deep secrets in philosophy
And mysteries in theology,
All sung in wretched poetry;
Which rambling piece is as much farce all   145
As his true mirror, *The Rehearsal,*
For which he has been soundly banged
But hain't his just reward till hanged.

Now you have seen all that is here
Have patience till another year.   150

146. *The Rehearsal:* The popular farce, probably written by Buckingham in collaboration with other wits in 1671, satirizing the heroic tragedies of the time and chiefly those of Dryden, the laureate "Bayes" of the play.

147. *soundly banged:* In the Rose Alley ambuscade. Most people thought that Dryden's cudgeling in 1679 was the outcome of his quarrel with Rochester.

The Trial of the Seven Bishops, June-July 1688

No single event did more to precipitate James's fall than the imprisonment and subsequent trial of the Seven Bishops. After nearly two years of some patience and more cynical forbearance, a great many Englishmen had come to see the need for active resistance to James's policies. Indications of their willingness actively to oppose the crown were manifest in the determined stand of the fellows of Magdalen College and in the more circumspect checks from the lords-lieutenant. Had James been astute in interpreting the signs of resistance, he might have avoided the impasse with the bishops.

Early in 1688 a letter was printed, nominally by Gaspard Fagel, Grand Pensionary of Holland, which set forth "An Account of the Prince and Princess of Orange's Thoughts Concerning the Repeal of the Test and the Penal Laws." Though William and Mary concurred with the concept of toleration, the letter made it clear that they felt strongly the need to restrain Catholics (*Somers' Tracts, 9*, 183–89). The letter presented an accurate statement of William's position, long clear to James. In the summer of 1686 during several interviews at the Hague with William Penn, the prince of Orange made it clear that "no man was more for toleration in principle than he was. He thought that conscience was subject only to God. And as far as a general toleration, even of Papists would content the king, he would concur in it heartily." The real issue was the Test Act. The prince "would enter into no treaty" on this point, the Test was the only "real security" in maintaining the Protestant religion (Burnet, *1*, 693–94). The printing of Fagel's letter in 1688 made public the prince's position, clarifying any uncertainty about the differences between him and his father-in-law concerning religious toleration. James might have ignored the letter publicly while heeding it privately as in indication that restraint was required in the pursuance of his policies. Had he done so, all might still have been well. Instead, he chose—in face of the letter, as it were—to reissue the Declaration of Indulgence on 27 April 1688, explaining his actions by saying:

> Our conduct has been such in all times as ought to have persuaded the world that we are firm and constant to our resolutions. Yet, that easy people may not be abused by the malice of crafty, wicked men, we think fit to declare that our intentions are not changed since the 4th of April 1687, when we issued out our Declaration for Liberty of Conscience (reprinted in *EHD, 8*, 399–400).

The second declaration, like the first, concluded with the hope that parliamentary ratification could be obtained by autumn at the latest. Again, as in 1687, addresses poured in, filling the *London Gazette* for weeks after the event. As if in response to the general show of enthusiasm of the side of dissent, James ordered that the declaration be read on two successive Sundays from pulpits throughout the realm. (The Order in Council was issued on 4 May; the declaration was to be read in London on 20 and 27 May, elsewhere on 3 and 10 June: *London Gazette,* 7 May 1688.)

Royal declarations were often disseminated in this fashion, but the method was normally reserved for secular matters. Now, James was asking his clergy by implication to approve what, in their eyes, "would make them accomplices in the destruction of their church" (Turner, p. 396). Reaction to the order was swift. A group of the London clergy met at the suggestion of Bishop Compton, long denied the court, and sent around a letter proscribing the order. A more formidable force gathered on 12 May at Lambeth Palace, in the presence of Archbishop Sancroft, but perhaps at the instigation of Compton. The group decided to petition the king against the reading of the declaration. A second meeting was arranged to allow others to join in formulating the protest, and on the evening of 18 May the Bishops Ken (Bath and Wells), White (Peterborough), Turner (Ely), Lloyd (St. Asaph), Trelawney (Bristol), and Lake (Chichester) presented James with their petition, written out in Sancroft's hand. Startled by the rebuff from men he considered would remain loyal to their doctrine of Non-Resistance, James called the petition "a standard of rebellion." James's wrath might have been quelled but for the clandestine publication of the petition on the same evening. "In the king's closet the petition was not, as James said it was, 'a standard of rebellion,' but, dispersed in the streets, that is exactly what it became" (Turner, p. 400). James felt forced to act, forced to make an example of his antagonists. On 8 June the bishops were ordered to appear before the Privy Council and, following a tempestuous hearing, they were committed to the Tower. A week later they appeared before the four judges of the King's Bench, and after a plea of "not guilty" were released to await trial.

The date of the trial was set for the 29th of June. The prosecution was entrusted to a battery of James's minions, chief among them Sir William Williams, a renegade from the Whig cause. Attorney General Sir Robert Sawyer was chief counsel for the defense.

> The 29th being the day appointed for the trial of the seven bishops at the Court of King's Bench, it accordingly came on. The court was filled with noblemen and other persons of quality, and all the hall below and galleries as full as possible . . . the trial held till six in the evening; and the jury went away, and lay together till six the next morning, when

they agreed. . . . They would give no privy verdict, but came into court, and being called they found all the defendants not guilty, at which there was a most mighty huzzah and shouting in the hall, which was very full of people. And all the way they came down people asked their blessing on their knees. There was continued shoutings for one-half an hour, so that no business could be done; and they hissed the solicitor. And at night was mighty rejoicing, in ringing of bells, discharging of guns, lighting of candles, and bonfires in several places, though forbid, and watchmen went about to take an account of such as made them. A joyful deliverance of the Church of England. (Luttrell, *1*, 446, 448)

James heard the news of the verdict while he was visiting the encampment at Hounslow Heath. His comment, oft repeated, was "so much the worse for them." But the must have recognized that the toil of several years was culminating in frustration. The dispensing power, which at great pains had been confirmed to him in the trial of *Godden* v *Hales* in 1686, was now impugned and a major weapon successfully denied him.

The poems that follow are interesting in light of the writers' less than enthusiastic feelings toward the bishops. There were, of course, many poems of the unqualified praise of *A New Catch*, but the strongly ironic, anticlerical view taken in *The Clerical Cabal* and *The Sentiments* presents the position of men who had seen and understood the implications of shifting allegiances all too well and too often in the previous decade. *The Sentiments* is particularly noteworthy for its play on such ominous words as "principles" and "heretics"— words that would be recalled within the year as five of the seven bishops become non-jurors at the outset of William's reign. *The Paradox* presents the injustice of James's own position, which sought to uphold religious toleration by imprisoning the chief clerics of the land. *The Church of England's Glory* is, on the other hand, a strong sectarian, pro-Catholic attack on the Anglican church, issued immediately after the acquittal of the bishops. With *The Story of the Pot and the Kettle*, it indicates how strongly the Dissenters had rallied to James. It is one of the last important satiric statements directly in James's behalf.

The Dissenters' Thanksgiving for the Late Declaration

For this additional declaration,
This double grace of dispensation,
For liberty and toleration
Against anti-Christian violation:
Whatever zeal-misguided passion   5
Persuades the sons of reformation,
'Tis but a sly insinuation
To work a popish inundation.
We of the new regeneration,
The well affected of the nation   10
That will be useful in our station,
Do offer up our due oblation
And make our humble supplication:
While Test and penals are in fashion,
We be not brought in tribulation   15
By the next synod of the nation.

The Clerical Cabal

When lately King James, whom our sovereign we call,
For reasons of state and the good of the nation,
By advice of his council commanded that all
Should read in their churches his last declaration;
As soon as it was to the clergy reported,   5

Title: This mock-address parodies prayers of thanksgiving offered in church or at home. For a similar riposte, but in prose, see "The Humble Address of the Atheists, or the Sect of the Epicureans," 1688 (reprinted in *Somers' Tracts, 9,* 46–47), which observes that James's "universal indulgence hath introduced such unanswerable objections toward all religion, that many have given over the troublesome enquiry after truth and set down easy and happy inference that all religion is a cheat." It bears the following imprint: "From the Devil Tavern, the fifth of November, 1688. Presented by Justice Baldock and was graciously received." Sir Robert Baldock (d. 1691) was "one of the counsel employed by the crown in the prosecution of the seven bishops, and showed himself so thorough-paced a stickler for prerogative" that on 6 July he was named justice of the King's Bench (Edward Foss, *Biographical Dictionary of Judges* [1870], p. 51).

16. *the next synod:* The second declaration, like the first, expressed the hope that toleration would be confirmed by Parliament, which James resolved to call "in November next at furthest."

To a place in the City they in private resorted
To advise on the matter and gravely debate
Whether conscience should truckle to reasons of state;
Which though we must own was most prudently done
Yet some think they'd better have let it alone,   10
Since 'twill no small suspicion to schismatics give
That they're not quite so loyal as they'd make us believe;
For if conscience be thought a sufficient pretense,
Why should it not salve the Dissenters' offense,
When refusing to bow to their Common Prayer idol,   15
They were forced to take quarters in Newgate and Bridewell?

But the case is now altered, th'ecclesiastical club
Met with countenance solid and wond'rous meek,
Consulting like coopers to mend an old tub,
Which for want of good hooping does now spring a leak.   20
Each man in his order began to dispute:
Some few would submit, but the rest would not do't;
Some boldly alleged that the Tests were the thing
That secured them now from the lash of the king,
"And should we comply, the gentry would say   25
We had virtually given our safeguard away.
And if we displease them, whom can we expect
Should hereafter our cause and our persons protect?
Besides the great loss of our princely dominion
Might serve one would think t'enforce this opinion,   30
That should we submit to His Majesty's order,
The world would regard our church thunder no further."

"That's true," says another, "and when the king's dead

6. *a place in the City:* Prior to the meeting of the bishops at Lambeth Palace, 15 of the
London clergy assembled to consider what action, if any, should be taken on James's order.
They agreed not to read the declaration, drawing up and signing a resolution to that effect,
which was then circulated around the city and signed by 85 clerics.

14–15. This points with considerable irony to the double standard that the bishops con-
doned by raising the question of conscience. The bishops had long enforced the penal laws
with rigor against the scruple of conscience held by Dissenters.

16. *Newgate and Bridewell:* London prisons.

17. *th'ecclesiastical club:* probably the London clerics, and not the ecclesiastical commission.
The "old tub" (line 19) would then refer to the doctrine of Passive Obedience.

22. *Some few would submit:* Those bishops who either demurred or were not asked to sign
were Chester (Cartwright), St. David's (Watson), Durham (Crew), Hereford (Croft), Exeter
(Lamplugh), Coventry and Litchfield (Wood), and Lincoln (Barlow); York was vacant.

32. *thunder:* traditionally figurative for the exercise of the church's harshest powers, e.g.
excommunication.

You know that the princess of Orange comes in,
And then this denial may stand us instead   35
To purchase her favor and fix us again.
Though of Passive Obedience we talk like the best,
'Tis prudence, when interest sways, to resist.
What though Jupiter thunder, and Juno do scold,
We'll still our true int'rest and principles hold.   40
Our livings alone supply us with treasure,
When those are once gone, we may starve at our leisure.
No argument better than this can convince us
How much 'tis our duty to please the Dutch princess;
But some will now say, since the queen is with child,   45
If a male should be born, our project is spoil'd:
We've a salvo for that, too, if he lives to be man,
Like true vicars of Bray we'll retract all again."

    Their ponderous reasons when put in the scale,
With duty and manners did quickly prevail,   50
For a churchman's civility never is seen
Till preferment appears as a medium between.

    Straight orders are issued t'enjoin the young fry
That on pain of ejectment they should not comply,
Which were strictly observed, such respect do they bear   55
To the wretched allowance of ten pounds a year
That for fear of displeasing a stingless old drone
They disgrace their religion and incur the king's frown.

    What they get by the bargain will soon be made plain,
'Twill be well if their godliness turns to their gain.   60

34. *Princess of Orange:* Mary, James's eldest daughter and William of Orange's wife. She was a Protestant and next in line, if there were no male heir.

45. *the queen is with child:* The prince was born on 10 June 1688, about three weeks after this meeting took place.

47. *salvo:* a saving clause; reservation.

48. *vicars of Bray:* refers to the time-serving parson of Bray in Berkshire who, though variously identified, was probably Simon Aleyn. During the reigns of Henry VIII, Edward VI, Mary, and Elizabeth, he was twice a Papist and twice a Protestant to preserve his choice living. The well-known ballad dates from the 18th century and places the vicar's apostacies from the Restoration through the reign of George I.

56. *ten pounds a year:* The stipend which went with most minor clerical posts was notoriously small even for that time.

57. *a stingless old drone:* presumably, Archbishop William Sancroft (1617–93), characterized by Trevelyan as "by nature a shy and retiring man," belonging "to the strictest school of high churchmen, who had hitherto taught that the king's will was the guide for all true subjects and Christians." Up to the publishing of the second declaration, he "had been hesitating and backward in resistance to James, much as he regretted his policy" (*The English Revolution, 1688–1689* [1939], p. 92).

The Sentiments

To the Bishops

1.

Ye mitered fathers of the land,
Is your obedience at a stand?
   Now does your conscience boggle?
That nicety was laid aside,
Canon and common law denied,   5
   When you i'th'House did juggle?

2.

What prince could doubt you'd not go on,
Whom you had placed upon the throne,
   Whose principles you knew;
The consequence of which each man   10
That has but common sense might scan;
   There's no excuse for you!

3.

Who puts a sword in's enemy's hand
And weaponless denies command,
   May strive, but 'tis in vain;   15
Had you the first great evil waived,
You by the last had ne'er been braved,
   Nor in the Tower lain.

4.

In Holy Writ you're conversant,
In Romish maxims ignorant;   20
   Good men I mourn your case:
They'll plight their faith and give their oath,
Keep either, neither, rarely both,
   If interest does give place.

5.

To heretics no faith is due,   25

Title. Sentiments: Here presumably, "what one feels with regard to something: . . . an opinion or view as to what is right or agreeable" *(OED).*
  6. *i'th'House:* As members of the House of Lords, the bishops had supported James during the Whig attempts in 1679–81 to exclude him from the throne.

449

Would you expect it then to you,
　When you are in the role?
Promises are only words,
'Tis binding when the heart accords—
　They're licensed to cajole.　　　　　　　　　　　30

6.

Passive Obedience you did preach,
A virtue which we all must reach,
　And now you're to it brought;
For when the nail you'd no more drive,
Straight to remove you they contrive,　　　　　35
　Though they lost the point they sought.

7.

You see the judges of the land
Are listed in the Roman band,
　And what they're bid they do;
Hope of preferment does o'erawe　　　　　　　40
Both conscience, justice, and the law—
　Faith and religion, too.

8.

Sacred engagements are but vain
Your rights and properties to maintain;
　They are but words, of course,　　　　　　　45
And not obliging any more
To heretics than to a whore,
　Nor valid, nor of force.

9.

'Tis obvious now to every one,
Since Romish measures are begun,　　　　　　50
　What we must all expect;
Those sheep are in a woeful stead,
Where wolf and shepherd are agreed
　To kill without respect.

10.

Stick to your principles, howe'er,　　　　　　55

52–53. Traditionally, of course, sheep are "believers," wolves "heretics," and shepherds "priests."

> And neither ax nor faggot fear:
> That is the worst can come;
> But ere to those they shall you bring,
> Though justly we will serve our king,
> We'll try a tug with Rome.   60

The Paradox

Upon the Confinement of the Bishops and Their Bailing Out

Let Cynics bark, and the stern Stagirite,
At Epicurus' precepts vent their spite;
Let churchmen preach their threadbare paradox,
Passive Obedience, to their bleeding flocks.

Let Stoics boast of a contented mind,   5
The joy and pleasure of a life confined,
That in imprisonment the soul is free—
Grant me, ye gods, but ease and liberty!

That there is pleasure in a dirty road,
A tired horse that sinks below his load,   10
No money, and an old, inveterate pox—
This I'll believe without a paradox.

But to affirm 'twas the dispensing power
That did decree the prelates to the Tow'er,
And such confinement's for the propagation   15
O'th'faith and doctrine of the Reformation;

That to remove the candlesticks from sight
Is to enlarge the Gospel and the light;
And the seven angels under sequestration,
To guard the church from pagan innovation;   20

To say that this is keeping of our word,
The only means we have to be secured;

---

17. *candlesticks:* the seven bishops.
19. *sequestration:* The bishops are compared to the dispossessed Anglican clergy during the years of the commonwealth.
21. *our word:* From his accession James had promised to maintain the government in church and state according to the laws of the realm. From the beginning he had insisted as well that his word was all the security necessary, though he felt it conditional upon the support of the Establishment.

Supporting of the English church and cause
In all its privileges, rights, and laws:

Pardon my faith, for sooner I'll believe   25
The subtle serpent was deceived by Eve;
Rome shall with heretics her promise keep,
And wolves and bears protect the straggling sheep!

That Powis shall be mild and moderate,
Not out of mere regard to his estate;   30
And for a hopeful heir invoke the saints
Our of his tender love to Protestants.

That this young heir, great Orange to prevent,
Being assigned to the next parliament,
Shall be brought up i'th'Protestant profession   35
To ratify a Catholic succession.

That Father Petre's counsel shall prevail
To quit their guiltless lordships without bail;
And Giffard beg, i'th'name of the young prince,
Dispensing pow'r may with their crimes dispense.   40

That Condom with the Jesuits shall side
To beg their lordships never may be tried,
Chiefly old Sancroft, the dear hopes to shun
Of being England's metropolitan.

That Durham shall propitiate for His Grace,   45

29. *Powis:* William Herbert (1617–96), first marquis and titular duke of Powis, was leader of the moderate Catholic party and a member of James's Privy Council.

33. *this young heir:* prince of Wales.

35. For attempts to have the prince brought up a Protestant, see the *DNB* account of his life and Trevelyan, "The Peace," *England Under Queen Anne, 3,* 268–69.

37. *Petre:* Father Edward Petre, the Jesuit confessor of James and an influential member of the Privy Council.

39. *Giffard:* Bonaventure Giffard, bishop of Madaura. One of the four vicars-apostolic of England, he had been installed as president of Magdalen College, Oxford, by James early in 1688.

41. *Condom:* Jacques Bénigne Bossuet, bishop of Condom and Meaux (1627–1704), he sought to reconcile Prostestants with the Roman Catholic position, particularly in his *Exposition of the Doctrine of the Catholic Church,* first published in England in 1672. His hatred of the Jesuits was underlined early in the 1680s during the Gallican controversy by his *Defensio Cleri Gallicani.*

43. *Sancroft:* The point of these lines appears to be that being metropolitan, i.e. bishop of London, under the pope, is a greater honor than being primate.

45. *Durham:* Nathaniel Crew, bishop of Durham, and a staunch supporter of James's policies. Luttrell records that he "hath taken an account of his clergy that have read His Majesty's declaration and those who have not" (*1,* 449). *His Grace:* Sancroft.

And Chester shall with Chichester change place;
And Hereford, when made a cardinal,
Shall make a learned apology for all.

That for old Ely, Bristol, Bath and Wells,
The Jesuits shall pawn their beads and bells;   50
For Lloyd and Peterborough to be bail
Good Rochester will lie himself in jail.

That Mulgrave's pride and lust, in Dryden's rhymes,
Shall make atonement for their lordship's crimes;
And wife's sobriety shall recompense   55
For their apostate disobedience.

Or that the Groom o'th'Stole, since he declared,
Should from his former luxury be debarred;
Or the grave president should reinstall
The English church upon the bishop's fall.   60

That the lord chancellor should quit the purse
For their respective fines to reimburse;
Or that the judges should not all conspire
To find 'em guilty of a praemunire.

That Pemberton's sound counsel should prevail,   65

46. *Chester:* Thomas Cartwright, the sycophantic bishop of Chester, was appointed to that see by James in December 1686. *Chichester:* John Lake, bishop of Chichester.

47. *Hereford:* Herbert Croft (1603–91), bishop of Hereford. Though "generally energetic in his efforts to prevent the growth of 'popery' in his diocese" during Charles's reign *(DNB)*, in 1688 he was one of the bishops mentioned by Luttrell "for reading the king's declaration" *(1,* 440).

49. *Ely, Bristol, Bath and Wells:* Bishops Turner, Trelawney, and Ken.

52. *Rochester:* Thomas Sprat, bishop of Rochester, a member of the ecclesiastical commission that continued to function after the trial of the bishops. Sprat asked in August "that he might be dismissed that board, being unwilling to act against his brethren the clergy" (Luttrell, *1,* 455–56).

53–56. *Mulgrave:* John Sheffield, earl of Mulgrave. He was Dryden's patron and had collaborated with him in writing *An Essay upon Satire.* Notoriously vain and proud, in 1686 he had married Ursula, widow of Edward, Lord Conway, who matched her husband's reputation for vanity with her own for drunkenness.

57. *Groom o'th'Stole:* Henry Mordaunt, 2d earl of Peterborough. He became a convert in March 1687.

59. *president:* Robert Spencer, 2d earl of Sunderland and president of the Privy Council.

61. *lord chancellor:* George Jeffreys.

64. *praemunire:* the charge of calling into question the supremacy of the English crown by resorting to a foreign court or authority, e.g., that of the pope.

65. *Pemberton:* Sir Francis Pemberton (1625–97), counsel for the bishops. Luttrell notes during the trial "the dispensing power . . . was so strangely exposed and so run down, even very boldly, especially by Pemberton and Finch, that it is hardly credible" *(1,* 447).

And Allibone should sue to be their bail;
Or Halifax, that lies upon the lurch,
Who left the charters, shall restore the church.

That Melfort's Cross, erected at the Bath,
With Perth, an emblem of their new-got faith;   70
The cause o'th'queen's conception do remain,
And will produce the same effects again.
That city treats with masquerades are graced,
To keep their wives upright, their daughters chaste;
And court intrigues with balls are carried on   75
For virtue only to preserve the throne.

That she who lately took into her choice
The witty author of the brace of mice
Shall battle the old panther in her race,
And crown her husband with the laureate's bays.   80

All this I freely can believe and more,
But that the lords are bailed out of the Tow'r
With greater loads to be sent there again,
For breach of laws they endeavored to maintain.

That they have guilt of disobedience,   85
In this you must excuse my diffidence;
Who placed upon the monarch's head the crown:
Props of the church, and pillars of the throne?

A NEW CATCH IN PRAISE OF THE REVEREND BISHOPS

True Englishmen, drink a good health to the miter;
Let our church ever flourish, though her enemies spite her.
May their cunning and forces no longer prevail;

66. *Allibone:* Sir Richard Allibone (1636–88), a Papist and one of the four judges of the King's Bench.
67. *Halifax:* George Savile, marquis of Halifax. A staunch opponent in the 1680s of all attempts to exclude James, he had been out of favor since the autumn of 1685, lying "upon the lurch," i.e., lying in wait, at Rufford Abbey, the family seat in Sherwood Forest, for "the next probable revolution," which he predicted in his *Letter to a Dissenter.*
68. *the charters:* As lord privy seal, Halifax had assisted in the removal of corporation charters in the last year of Charles's reign.
69–70. *Melfort . . . Perth:* John Drummond (1649–1714), 1st earl and titular duke of Melfort, and James (1648–1716), his elder brother, the 4th earl and 1st titular duke of Perth, both converts to the Roman Catholic church. "Melfort's Cross" was a pillar erected at Bath by John Drummond in 1688 in memory of Queen Mary.

And their malice, as well as their arguments, fail.
Then remember the Seven, which supported our cause,   5
As stout as our martyrs and as just as our laws!

THE CHURCH OF ENGLAND'S GLORY

or The Vindication of Episcopacy

Now call to mind Edom, remember well
Your curséd cries against God's Israel.
Now who's disloyal, where's the obstinate
And busy fops that talk of things of state?
"A plot, a plot!" Who is't that now looks blue?   5
Now where's sedition? Where's the factious crew?
Now mock no more, go consecrate the room
Where Essex died, and think on Russell's doom.
Now who are they that cried, "ram us" and "damn us?"
Who is't that now comes off with "ignoramus"?   10
Now who's surmising fears and jealousies?
Now who's malicious, fomenting of lies?
Now whose nice conscience pleads religion?
Nay, rather they that once swore they had none!
Now let's "huzza, huzza, huzza," examine   15

1. *Edom:* Esau, from the red color of the lentil pottage for which he sold his birthright. The Edomites remained generally hostile to the Israelites, refusing them the right to cross their land during the flight from Egypt and much later joining Nebuchadnezzar in his siege of Jerusalem. This allusion to the Church of England and its "apostasy" was fairly common in controversialist tracts and sermons of the period. On 1 April 1688, Thomas Ken, bishop of Bath and Wells, preached a sermon before Princess Anne, "describing the calamity of the reformed church of Judah under the Babylonish persecution," saying "she should certainly rise again and be delivered by him who would avenge her enemies, as God did upon the Edomites her apostate brother and neighbors" (Evelyn, *4*, 577–78).

5. *Who . . . now looks blue:* a pun on the blue of "True Blue Protestantism" and on the "blue look" of disappointment.

8. *Essex:* Arthur Capel, earl of Essex. Accused of complicity in the Rye House Plot, he committed suicide in July 1683 while prisoner in the Tower. *Russell:* Lord William Russell, executed in 1683 for his part in the plot.

9. *"ram us" and "damn us":* an ironic reference to Whig outcries against the Tories during the furor of plot and counterplot in 1679–83.

10. *"ignoramus":* As in the previous reference to the Whigs' outcry during 1679–83, here the acquittal of the bishops is compared with that of Shaftesbury in 1681, when the grand jury found the evidence against him insufficient to constitute a "true bill." Shaftesbury's "escape" would have seemed to most of the Anglican clergy a miscarriage of justice. Throughout this passage the satirist deflates the present Anglican jubilation by likening it to the jubilation of their opponents of the 1680s.

15. *huzza:* The cry of Tory partisans in the 1680s.

Now for the loyalty expressed by damning,
Roaring, and whoring—that—rotting and sinking:
"Hey boys! new healths with bumpers bravely drinking."
But say these are the worst, whose words are wind;
But mark our doctrines, and the more refined.   20
Now where's the doctrine made the pulpits ring?
'Twas all divine to love and laud the king!
Where's loyal sermons now? Where are they gone?
Hark, hark a while, and you shall hear anon.
Where's Non-Resistance now? Now where's compliance?   25
Why here, in this, to bid the king defiance!
In what, an edict? No, his declaration
For conscience liberty, to free the nation
From those accursed penal laws and Test,
That tender conscience ever might have rest.   30
But now 'tis "Popery, Popery," that's the song;
'Tis coming like a flood—But, pray, how long
Has fear of popery been this dreadful tone?
Just since you let the Protestants alone.
'Tis fear of Papists—good lack!—sad's the case,   35
Since they've excelled Episcopals in grace.
No sooner Clemency doth peace propose,
But Envy cries, "Take heed of popish foes."
Was't not for fear of popery once ago
You writ and printed, preached and ragéd so?   40
"Down with Dissenters"—thus with storm and thunder;
"Magistrates, mind your duty, seize and plunder,
Fine and imprison, ruin—follow't hot!"
This was for fear of popery, was it not?
Thus persecution echoed from the pulpit;   45
But now look simply, say you cannot help it.
Law was not then so much as it is since,
But the king's pleasure, as you made pretense:
Yet though you've lost the spur, you'd hold the bridle—
With a straight rein, too. Oh! but that's as idle   50
As those that blame this Liberty of Conscience

18. A parody on the typical opening line of a broadside rehearsing a popular event.
34. I.e., just since the Anglican church turned its attention from the Dissenters to the
Catholics, considering the latter, under James, a more serious threat to the Establishment.
41–50. Dissenters and Catholics alike had long suffered under acts nominally directed
against Dissenters. A particular instance of this coincided in 1683 with the extralegal attack
on local self-government by Charles in 1683–84 in his attempts to extirpate Nonconformity.

And have the impudence to say 'tis nonsense.
Were they (which God forbid) but half so long
To feel the right that did Dissenters wrong,
They'd wiser be, kinder, and humbler, too,   55
Who're now so proud they know not what they do.
Now who are they that cannot be content
With regal right, but acts of Parliament
Of their own choosing? Yet this will not do;
But must have also Convocation, too.   60
Now who like toads spit venom, swell, and pant?
Now who are they that have the way to cant?
Now who's most busy to degrade the king?
And who knows what? With secret whispering,
And holding consults, who makes parties now?   65
For to rebel the malcontent knows how.
Fat benefits, and tithes, and bishoprics
Do not content you; O these little tricks!
For Mordecai stoops not: here's the dispute;
You want the power still to persecute.   70
Whence comes this rule to lord it o'er the rest?
From Tory-Gospel, penal laws, and Test—
Touch 'em in that, and they'll begin to wince,
And galled loyalty spurns at their prince.
But poor Dissenters, now, as heretofore,   75
Thankful for peace, rejoice, and seek no more.
But now, 'tis well, your curséd power's subdued;
Here's peace, which others like—but let's conclude:
Here's your own language and the work of late
You gloried in and still would vindicate.   80
Look in this glass and learn to blush for shame;
Be Christians once, and stain no more that name.

56. *they know not what they do*: Luke 23:34.

60. *convocation*: the general assembly of the clergy of the Church of England. Probably also a derisive allusion to the gatherings of the heads of the church both in London and at Lambeth.

65. *consults*: specifically (17th century), a secret meeting for purposes of sedition or intrigue.

69. *Mordecai stoops not*: The foster father of Esther who, when Ahasuerus made Esther his queen, sat at the palace gates and would not bow to Haman, the king's chief minister. Whatever Mordecai's motive, here the context suggests religious scruples, and Mordecai becomes a type of religious dissent. The irony of the original story lies in the execution of Haman on the scaffold he had ordered built for Mordecai (Esther 7).

70. *You*: the bishops.

74. *spurns*: Kicks.

[CHARLES MONTAGU]

THE STORY OF THE POT AND THE KETTLE

As It Was Told by Colonel Titus the Night before
He Kissed the King's Hand

As down the torrent of an angry flood
An earthen pot and a brass kettle flowed,
The heavy caldron sinking, and distressed
By its own weight, and the fierce waves oppressed,
Slyly bespoke the lighter vessel's aid,   5
And to the earthen pitcher friendly said,
"Come, brother, why should we divided lose
The strength of union and ourselves expose
To the insults of this poor, paltry stream,
Which with united forces we can stem?   10
Though different, heretofore, have been our parts,
The common danger reconciles our hearts.
Here, lend me thy kind arm to break this flood."
    The pitcher this new friendship understood
And made this answer, "Though I wish for ease   15
And safety, this alliance does not please.
Such different natures never will agree;
Your constitution is too rough for me.
If by the waves I against you am tossed,
Or you to me, I equally am lost.   20
And fear more mischief from your hardened side,
Than from the shore, the billows, or the tide.
I calmer days and ebbing waves attend,
Rather than buoy you up and serve your end
To perish by the rigor of my friend,"   25

Ascription: It is likely that Montagu was, indeed, responsible for these rhymes. The ascription comes from a gloss in *An Epistle to . . . Charles Montagu, Baron of Halifax. Writ upon Occasion of the Signal Successes of Her Majesty's Arms in the Last Summer's Campaign* [1707], p. 6. The note reads: "Your 'Fable of the Pot and Kettle' kept the most prudent Dissenters from joining with Papists against the church."

Subtitle. Colonel Titus: Col. Silius Titus (1623?–1704), a prominent Presbyterian and vigorous parliamentary opponent both of Papists and of the Catholic succession during the last years of the reign of Charles II. In July 1688 James put aside his own animosity for Titus and invited him to join the Privy Council. Titus attended the last meeting of the council but, within a few weeks, openly declared for William.

2. brass kettle: probably James himself. He was frequently fixed by his opponents with the word "brass" or "brazen," suggesting his hard-headedness.

458

Moral

Learn hence, you Whigs, and act no more like fools,
Nor trust their friendship who would make you tools;
While empty praises and smooth flatteries serve,
Pay with feigned thanks what their feigned smiles deserve,
But let not this alliance further pass;   30
For know that you are clay, and they are brass.

The Birth of James Francis Edward, Prince of Wales, 10 June 1688

Long before James came to the throne, fear of a Papist dynasty had been working in the minds of the English. It led to attempts by the parliaments of 1679 and 1680–81 at an Exclusion Bill, and the question became critical after the accession. Yet throughout most of the reign it operated not only to stir up the populace but also to pacify it. As long as a Protestant succession seemed secure in James's daughter Mary, the English were inclined to wait; without a male heir all the Papist machinations would ultimately prove ineffectual. A Catholic heir would be disastrous to English Protestantism, because he would require a nation still strong in its beliefs in obedience and in the right of kings to take drastic action to free itself from the rule of popes. But a male heir seemed a virtual impossibility, and the people could willfully indulge themselves, even during the worst moments of Papist encroachment, by rehearsing the popular tale of James and Mary's ability to produce only a "race of ninnies" whose life expectancy was very short indeed. Yet the impossible happened. On 10 June a prince was born.

Though the birth of the prince is rightly regarded by historians as the catalyst that caused the ultimate reaction to James's policies, at the historical moment the imagination of the London mob was already seething with the spectacle of the bishops leaving the barge to pass along Tower Wharf and through Traitor's Gate, which three years before had received the duke of Monmouth. As the summer progressed, however, the old fears grew in proportion, fed on the refuse of rumor and scurrility. On 10 June, Evelyn saw fit merely to remark, "a young prince born," and to follow this with a brief description of the day's celebration. The event was "very surprising, it being universally given out that Her Majesty did not look till the next month." (*4*, 586–87). Later Evelyn, perhaps in an attempt to appear a more acute judge of events, added to his entry that the birth "will cost dispute."

On 29 June the bishops were acquitted, and the people were again able to turn their full attention to the young prince. Newsletters had been, as Luttrell said, "stuffed with nothing but rejoicings" for the birth (*1*, 444), ironically providing a continual reminder of the situation. Within a fortnight of the acquittal, Luttrell put down that there was "great liberty in discoursing about

461

the young prince, with strange reflections upon him, not fit to insert here"
(*1*, 449). Over the next few months the reaction grew. Late in October James
assembled a council to hear evidence on the legitimacy of his son, once and
for all to lay the specter of popish fraud that filled the minds of nearly all his
subjects. But the absurdity of James's condescension in this matter, the
apparent collusion of the witnesses making depositions, and the anxieties
over Irish marauders, Dutch threats, and Papist pretensions nullified any
advantage James had hoped to gain. He had, however, made public record
of the facts, and in his mind that was undoubtedly a gain.

From the beginning of this sordid affair the image of James and Mary as
parents worked against acceptance of the facts of the birth. It had been five
years since Mary had given birth. Twice since, in October 1683 and in April
1684, her delicate constitution had failed her, and she had miscarried. Her
five previous children had died in infancy. The blame for these unfortunate
occurrences, however, was largely shifted to James. In 1668 it was rumored,
Lord Carnegy, earl of Southesk, had sought a desperate remedy to avenge
his wife's infidelity with James, and thus put an end to later hopes of a
Catholic line. *A Catholic Hymn* opens with a lengthy allusion to the affair
(the lampoon is in *Popery 3* [1689]: 20. Accounts of the affair are given by
Pepys and Anthony Hamilton.):

> When enraged Southesk
> In his female's womb cast
> A clap, which cost twenty guineas,
> A project he had
> Of revenge on the dad,
> And to blow up the race of the ninnies.

The "virulent distemper" James was thought thus to have contracted made
an heir improbable; for

> The poison entailed
> So far had prevailed,
> 'Twas high time to seek out a wonder;
> Our case must be sad,
> If a boy can't be had
> To keep the heretics under.

Though this scurrilous tale could be shrugged off by most, the early death
of James's children might well have been the result of the irregularities of his
sexual conduct. Beyond this, it was known that Mary Beatrice was not
robust, a weakness underlined on 2 November 1687, when Luttrell recorded
that "the queen, two months gone with child, had been let blood to prevent
miscarriage."

On 23 December 1687, James issued a proclamation appointing a time for public prayer and thanksgiving throughout the kingdom for the queen, "who (through God's great goodness) is now with child." He ordered Nathaniel Crew, Thomas Sprat, and Thomas White, bishops of Durham, Rochester, and Peterborough, "to prepare a form of prayer and religious service" to be celebrated in the London area on 15 January and elsewhere in the realm on 29 January (*A Form and Order of Thanksgiving and Prayer, 1687; London Gazette*, 5 January 1688). Abraham de la Pryme, the Yorkshire antiquarian who had noted shortly after the proclamation that "no one scarce believes that she is really with bairn," summed up one aspect of the imputation. It was a common jest "that the Virgin Mary [had] appeared to her and declared to her that the holy thing that shall be born of her shall be a son. They say likewise that the pope has sent her the Virgin Mary's smock and hallowed bairn clothes" (Charles Jackson, ed., *Diary* [Surtees Society, 1869], p. 11). Anthony Wood noted that the queen's "breeding was occasioned, as the Papists say, by the prayer of the chaplain of Our Lady of Loreto to whom the duchess of Modena, mother of the said queen, bequeathed a golden heart at her death [in July 1687], purposely to pray for her breeding a son."

After the birth formal addresses came in from all parts of the kingdom, and special envoys arrived from neighboring countries to offer their monarchs' congratulations. Londoners remained skeptical. Their doubts were increased when in August a wet nurse was brought in for the young prince, who lay ill at Richmond with "the gripes" (Luttrell, *1*, 453). Evelyn said of the illness: "After long trials of the doctors to bring up the little Prince of Wales by hand (so many of Her Majesty's children having died infants) not succeeding, a country nurse [named Cooper] (the wife of a tile-maker) is taken to give it suck" (*4*, 597). By October discontent had become so great that James felt himself compelled to answer back. He summoned an extraordinary council to give testimony on the birth. Forty-three witnesses gave evidence, but the deposition did not shake the story the mob wished to believe. They suspected collusion and, as it was pointed out in the *Answer to the Depositions*, p. 1, felt "the depositions themselves were made from inconclusive evidence." Moreover, few of the opposite party had been present to attest to the truth of the affair.

Having rehearsed the events surrounding the birth of the prince, it is difficult to avoid the conclusion drawn by G.N. Clark in his study of *The Later Stuarts* (1949). "In the seventeenth century people would believe anything. The Catholics thought the birth was a miracle, and the Protestants said it was an imposture. It was neither" (p. 121). The truth remains that most Englishmen recognized the difficulties the birth put them in. Within three weeks Admiral Edward Russell, in the guise of an ordinary seaman, had left for Holland with the invitation to William in his care.

UPON THE KING'S VOYAGE TO CHATHAM
TO MAKE BULWARKS AGAINST THE DUTCH,
AND THE QUEEN'S MISCARRIAGE THEREUPON

When James, our great monarch, so wise and discreet,
Was gone with three barges to face the Dutch fleet,
Our young prince of Wales, by inheritance stout,
Was coming to aid him and peeped his head out;
But seeing his father, without ships or men,   5
Commit the defense of us all to a chain,
Taffy was frighted and skulked in again;
Nor thought, while the Dutch domineered in our road,
It was safe to come further and venture abroad.
Not Waldegrave, or th'epistle of seigneur le duke,   10
Made Her Majesty sick, and her royal womb puke;
But the Dutchmen pickeering at Dover and Harwich,
Gave the ministers agues and the queen a miscarriage.
And to see the poor king stand in ships of such need,
Made the Catholics quake, and Her Majesty bleed.   15
I wish the sad accident don't spoil the young prince,
Take off all his manhood and make him a wench;
But the hero, his father, no courage did lack,
Who was sorry on such a pretext to come back.

6. Late in April 1688, Luttrell writes: "The king hath ordered a new platform of 50 guns at Sheerness, and a chain to be laid over to block up the mouth of the River Medway that runs to Chatham, and a fort to protect it." Another entry for this period reports that the "king is going down to Sheerness to view that place, Chatham and others" (*1*, 438; and see *London Gazette*, 10 May). Although sympathies were much different, the posture of James's naval defenses would certainly have brought to mind the great naval defeat inflicted on the English in 1667 by De Ruyter, when the Dutch broke through the chain and fell upon the unprepared ships in the Thames and the Medway (see Marvell, *Last Instructions to a Painter*, 11).

7. *Taffy*: a nickname for Welshmen, from the River Taff; the child was to be the Prince of Wales.

10. *Waldegrave*: William Waldegrave, the queen's first physician; he was knighted by James shortly after the birth of the prince. *th'epistle of seigneur le duke*: On 11 May "the queen, having received an account that the duke of Modena, her brother, was dead, fell into fits, which occasioned an express to His Majesty and brought him to town immediately" (Luttrell, *1*, 439).

12. *pickeering*: "to forage, maraud, pillage," or "to skirmish, scout, or reconnoiter" obs. or arch.

14. Feverish efforts were being made by James to get his fleet in readiness. Reports of the Dutch preparations for war had been coming in since February; late in April came word that a Dutch fleet of 25 sail had put to sea (Luttrell, *1*, 441).

19. *a pretext*: Antagonists viewed the alarm as such: " . . . the king's going to Chatham just before this pretended likelihood of a miscarriage, [was] for no real occasion known but the

He marked out his ground, and mounted a gun,   20
And, 'tis thought, without such a pretense he had run;
For his army and navy were said to increase,
As appears (when we have no occasion) in peace.
Nay, if the Dutch come, we despise 'em so much,
Our navy incognito will leave 'em i'th'lurch;   25
And, to their eternal disgrace, we are able
To beat 'em by way of a post and a cable.
Why was this, sir, left out of th' wise declaration
That flattered with hopes of more forces the nation?
'Twould have done us great good to have said you intended   30
The strength of the nation, the chain should be mended.
Though we thank you for passing so kindly your word
(Which never was broke) that you'd rule by the sword,
This promise we know you meant to fulfill,
And therefore you have reason (by Gad!) to take't ill   35
That the bishops, the bishops did throw out the bill.

An Excellent New Ballad Called the Prince of Darkness

Showing How Three Nations May
Be Set on Fire by a Warming Pan

As I went by St. James's, I heard a bird sing,
"Of certain the queen has a boy in the spring."
But one of the chairmen did laugh and did say,

---

private one of designing to have her pretend a miscarriage and so send for him" (*Answer to the Depositions, etc.* [1689], p. 5).

22–23. These lines refer to the general fears throughout the reign of James's efforts to increase the size of his standing army rather than remodel the trainbands as Parliament had suggested in November 1685.

28. *declaration:* The Declaration of Toleration had appended to it remarks concerning the army and the fleet "which with good management shall be constantly the same, and greater, if the safety or honor of the nation require it."

33. *Which never was broke:* The king's word became a standing joke during the reign.

36. *the bishops:* the Seven Bishops.

1. The present ballad reworks a scurrilous song of 1666 attacking Margaret, wife of Sir John Denham and mistress of the duke of York, which begins:

> As I went by St. James's, I heard a bird sing
> That Denham's fair wife was a miss for a king,
>
> But the king goes without her, as I have been told,
> And the duke does enjoy her, though Nan pout and scold.

"It was born overnight and brought forth the next day."
This bantling was heard at St. James's to squall,   5
Which made the queen make so much haste from Whitehall.
"Peace, peace, little master, and hold up thy head;
Here's money bid for thee," the true mother said.
But nobody knows from what parish it came,
And that is the reason it has not a name.   10
Good Catholics all were afraid it was dying,
There was such abundance of sighing and crying;
Which is a good token by which we may swear
It is the queen's own and the kingdom's right heir.
Now if we should happen to have a true lad   15
From the loins of so wholesome a mother and dad,
'Twere hard to determine which blood were the best—
That of Southesk, or the bastard of Est!
But now we have cause for thanksgiving, indeed,
There was no other way for mending the breed!   20

Tom Tiler, or The Nurse

Old stories of a Tyler sing
That did attempt to be a king.
Our age is with a tiler graced,

4. It was said that a child had been born at St. James's before the queen went there for her lying-in, and that this child was later brought in, perhaps in a warming pan, and put into the queen's bed. It was also commonly said that the prince seemed a strong, healthy child, beyond his age.

6. *so much haste from Whitehall:* Burnet records that the queen, though in haste, actually "by a sort of affectation" insisted on being "carried thither by Charing Cross through the Pall Mall," a route longer than her accustomed way through the park (*1*, 751). This, too, was viewed suspiciously in retrospect.

10. *it has not a name:* "Amongst these distractions and preparations for war, the king forgot not the ceremony of naming the Prince of Wales, which had not been done when he was christened, but on 15 October was performed in the king's chapel at St. James's with great solemnity, the pope being godfather, represented by the Nuncio, and queen dowager godmother" (Clarke, *James II, 2,* 191–92).

11–12. Charles Middleton, second earl of Middleton, and one of James's secretaries of state, deposed that he had stood near the bed's foot on the left side, from where he had heard the queen's groans and several loud shrieks. The Lady Susanna Belasyse testified that when she did not hear the infant cry she was afraid it was in a convulsive fit, its skin seeming to her unnaturally dark.

18. *Southesk:* James was supposed to have caught the pox in a liaison with the countess of Southesk. *Est:* James's second wife was Maria d'Este. Her alleged illegitimacy is unfounded.

Title: The nurse, a tile-maker's wife named Cooper, was brought in shortly after the prince's illness at Richmond. The child was supposed to have a birthmark, by which several

By more preposterous planets raised.
His cap with Jocky's matched together,   5
Turned to a beaver and a feather;
His clay transformed to yellow gilt,
And trowel to a silver hilt.

His lady from the tiles and bricks
Kidnapped to court in coach and six;   10
Her arms a sucking prince embrace,
Whate'er you think, of royal race;
A prince come in the nick of time
(Blessed d'Adda!), 'tis a venial crime
That shall repair our breach of state;
While all the world congratulate,   15
Shall, like his sire, suppress the just,
Raise knaves and fools to place of trust:
Titus and Vane, who sought his fate;
Tilers and Macs to chits of state.   20
But here, unhappy babe, alas,
I cannot but lament thy case.
That thou, fed up with Rome's strong meats,
Should long for milk of heretic teats.
Among the daughters was there none   25
Worthy to nurse a monarch's son?

---

of the deponents claimed to know him as the king's son. Marie de la Baudie remarked that
Mrs. Danvers, a former nurse to the Lady Isabella, observed the same marks upon the eye of
the prince as the queen's former children had had. Lampoonists were quick to turn the
wet-nurse's success with the baby to their own account, appropriating at the same time the
story of the birthmark. In *Father Petre's Policy Discovered* (*Popery 2* [1689]:29) the satirist writes:
"They knew sweet babe from a thousand, they cried,/ 'Twas born with the point of a tile on
his side."

1. *Tyler:* Wat Tyler, leader of the Peasants' Revolt of 1381.

5. *Jocky:* One of James's numerous nicknames.

6. *a beaver and a feather:* The beaver hat, worn chiefly by men, was looked on as expensively
stylish. The Prince of Wales's emblem is three ostrich feathers, first adopted as a crest by the
Black Prince. Also, the feather is a personal decoration and mark of honor, e.g. "to put a
feather in one's cap."

7. *yellow gilt:* gold, the metal of kings; here a play on the idea of "guilt."

8. *a silver hilt:* the scepter.

14. *d'Adda:* Count Ferdinand d'Adda, the Papal Nuncio, with a play on the baby-talk
word for "father." Both d'Adda and Petre were slandered as responsible for the child.

15. *breach of state:* an obscene pun.

19. *Titus and Vane:* Col. Silius Titus and Christopher Vane (1653–1723), sworn to the Privy
Council on 6 July (*London Gazette,* 9 July 1688). Both were Dissenters with reputations as
opponents of the crown.

20. *Macs:* Irishmen.

But if thy uncle, who before
Was always right, changed the last hour;
If thy undoubted sire, so sage,
Declar'd i'th'evening of his age;   30
Why should'st not thou, Papist so soon,
Be a staunch Protestant ere noon?
This said, the tiler laughed in's sleeve
And took his audience of leave.
The prince, who answered ne'er a word,   35
That he should travel did accord;
To Paris sent to learn grimace,
To swear and damn with a *bonne grâce*.

27–30. Charles II was said to have died a Roman Catholic (Evelyn, *4*, 407–08 and *nn*.);
James's conversion took place in 1667, when he was 34, though it was not publicly admitted
until 1676 (Turner, pp. 87, 125).

32. Ironically, attempts were made to bring the prince up in the Protestant faith, but they
failed.

34. *audience of leave:* farewell interview.

37. *To Paris sent:* Mary Beatrice fled with the prince on 10 December, arriving in Calais
the next day.

Invasion Fears
(Spring-Summer 1688)

For most Englishmen the first ten months of 1688 were a period of extraordinary tension—tension so great that the anticlimactic nature of William's November campaign was an almost inevitable result of it. From the end of February when the country received the first reports of Dutch military preparations until 5 November when William finally landed at Tor Bay, a state of near crisis prevailed. During this time Luttrell records no fewer than twenty-one separate reports of the Dutch build-up and of the imminence of invasion. At first these reports were officially denied through such "unofficial" organs as Henry Care's newssheet *Public Occurrences,* which as late as 15 May dismissed reports of the Dutch fleet putting to sea, calling the activities merely those normally connected with the spring convoys. But rumors persisted and became more welcome as the events of June and July confirmed the possibility of a Papist dynasty and gave evidence of the kind of suppression it would lead to. These fears were to some extent counterbalanced by the Englishmen's abiding animosity for the Dutch, while James's own military preparations and the hint of a few reforms in his Romanizing policy provided some further stimulation to patriotic zeal. Even these elements heightened the tension, however, and by 3 November defection had become so common that one writer remarked "for everybody that's missing but two or three days, we say here, is gone" (*HMC, Rutland,* 2, 122). When, two days later, news of the invasion reached the nation, it must have come almost as a relief, even to the king.

Throughout the months that led up to William's landing, James pursued three distinct courses of action in his attempt to maintain his position. Foremost were his military preparations. In the fall of 1687 disaffection in the army and stiffening resistance to his policies first caused him to consider recalling the English and Scottish troops serving in Holland in the pay of the States General. The queen's pregnancy made it seem even "more imperative that the dynasty should, if necessary, be preserved by military force" (Ogg, *James II,* p. 191). Not until February 1688, however, did he finally determine to recall the troops. In March a proclamation was issued, but to James's consternation the States General refused to comply with it and held the troops from him. Only a few officers reached England from the continent.

Commissions were granted for the raising of five new regiments, but these James found difficult to staff. By August he was desperate for soldiers on whose loyalty he could depend. An obvious, but unwise, solution offered itself. In August and September he ordered Irish and Scottish troops mustered in England for his defense.

Similar preparations were carried out to refit the navy. Early in January the first orders were sent down from the admiralty to the dockyards (Luttrell, *1,* 429). Throughout the spring the yards were unusually busy, and the press boats made frequent trips down the Thames seeking seamen. By June a fleet of twenty ships sailed for the Downs under Sir Roger Strickland. In August and September activities increased, leave was refused officers, the dockyards at Chatham and Portsmouth were put in a state of defense, the fleet was divided into three squadrons to patrol all waters in the Channel and to the south, and an ingenious plan was actually carried out to mislead a possible attack up the Thames by removing the buoys in the river and by replacing the lights at Harwich with a fake lighthouse.

The second step James took involved the stricter enforcement of censorship and the wider dissemination of anti-Dutch propaganda. Rumor was so strong in and around London that "each graver Sir Pol unfolded his sheet" of computations and prognostications, and little else was talked of after the beginning of August. James's counteractivities were so numerous during these months that it was said his declarations were as common as ballads.

Finally, toward the end of August James undertook a series of reforms, or concessions, to win support in his struggle to retain the throne. On August 24 the king ordered that writs be issued for the calling of Parliament for the end of November (*London Gazette,* 27 August). The writs went out in mid-September though they were recalled on the imminent threat of invasion. James began, as well, openly to court the Anglican church. In September and October he disbanded the Ecclesiastical Commission and restored the bishop of London and the fellows of Magdalen College. Early in October he ordered Jeffreys to return the corporation charters—a move met like the others with unreserved skepticism.

In general, it was thought that the "king began now to find his error, but too late" (Reresby, p. 516), and most, like Luttrell, attributed the reforms to the "rare invasion" that occasioned "so many gracious acts in restoring things to their old, legal foundation, which hath been the work of some years past to unhinge!" (*1,* 468; see also Evelyn, *4,* 599–600).

All Shams

To the Tune of "Packington's Pound"

1.

An invasion from Dutchland is all the discourse,
An incredible tale of incredible force!
While each graver Sir Pol unfolded his sheet,
An exact computation of army and fleet,
  Of their horse and their foot
  And their great guns, to boot,
Each fire-ship, each tender, and flat-bottomed boat;
The time of their landing and place can reveal,
But that, as a secret, as yet he'll conceal.

2.

While each busy-brained coxcomb, mechanic, and fool,
Each chattering barber, each apron and rule,
Let his private concern be of ne'er so much weight,
And nought but his trade, he can call his estate;
  Yet straight he declares
  It has long been his fears,
He dreaded this business for several years;
Nay, the future events he could eas'ly relate,
But 'tis dangerous, neighbors, and touches the state.

3.

Now while we are hearing and telling of lies,
A cloud from the west does quite darken the skies;
All Egypt's ten plagues do at once on us fall,
For in naming the Irish, it comprehends all.
  To what purpose they come
  Is no secret to Rome,
And to guess at the consequence we may presume:
Old England was ne'er so unhappy before,
While the scum of three nations for aid we implore.

3. Cf. *Volpone*, the character of Sir Politic Would-be.
22. *the Irish:* A few scattered incidents and many rumors gave rise to an exaggerated fear
of the Irish troops. Evelyn says, e.g., "The popish Irish soldiers commit many murders and
insolences; the whole nation disaffected and in apprehensions" (*4*, 596–97).

4.

Now lay by chimeras of fleets and armados,
And, if you can, fairly march off to Barbados,
Jamaica, Virginia, or any plantation,   30
Except that of Will Penn, the disturber o'th'nation;
   To Lapland or Greenland,
   Nay, sail into Finland,
To Presbyter John or the islands within land;
And leave both your honors' estates and your wives,   35
On condition that you may depart with your lives.

31. *Will Penn:* William Penn (1644–1718) spoke of himself on one occasion as not a Papist
but a "dissenting Protestant." He published *Advice to Freeholders and Other Electors of Members
Who Serve in Parliament in Relation to the Penal Laws and the Tests, &c.,* in 1687, the postscript of
which begged "the Church of England to yield to Christ his own throne in the kingdom of
God, and to magistrates their thrones in the kingdom of the world." Whatever side one takes,
however, there is little doubt that the majority of the opponents to James's policy saw Penn
as a despicable sycophant. "He was, in fact; a sanguine optimist, destitute of the penetration
into human nature and capacity for determining the limits of the ideal and the practical
which mark the statesman" (*DNB*).
34. *Presbyter John:* Prester John, the fabulous medieval Christian king and priest, whose
vast domains originally were placed in Asia, though from the 15th century on he was usually
identified with the king of Ethiopia. Contemporary satirists were wont to play on the mean-
ings of priest and Presbyterian suggested by his title. *the islands within land:* perhaps the fabul-
ous lands of Prester John.

In Defiance to the Dutch

The first part of this poem originally appeared in the spring of 1672, shortly after the outbreak of the third Dutch war, ascribed to "Mr. Benjamin Willy, sometime master of the Free School of Newark-upon-Trent" (*Political Recreations*, 1685). Willy was greatly indebted to Marvell's *Character of Holland* both for the particular allusions cited below and for the general tone and method employed.

On or about 13 November 1688, according to Luttrell's MS notes on the Harvard broadside, the revised version of this poem "Against the Dutch" was published with an envoy to the king. The broadside was probably circulated as a last-minute endeavor on the part of the crown to stir Englishmen to stand with their king against an old and common enemy.

In Defiance to the Dutch

Robbed of our rights, and by such water-rats?
We'll doff their heads, if they won't doff their hats.
Affront too Hogen Mogen to endure!
'Tis time to box these butter-boxes sure.
If they the flag's undoubted right deny us,   5
Who won't strike to us, must be stricken by us.
A crew of boors and sooterkins that know
Themselves they to our blood and valor owe;
Did we for this knock off their Spanish fetters,
To make 'em able to abuse their betters?   10
If at this rate they rave, I think 'tis good
Not to omit the fall, but let them blood.
    Rouse then, heroic Britains, 'tis not words
But wounds, must work with leather-apron lords.

3. *Hogen Mogen*: nickname for the Dutch, a corruption of *Hoogmogend heiden*, "High Mightinesses," the official designation of the States of the United Provinces.
6. *strike*: to lower sail, or haul down one's flag in surrender. By tradition, the English claimed that all ships salute their flag in "British seas" (see lines 20 and 70, and *nn.*).

Since they are deaf, to them your meaning break   15
With mouths of brass, that words of iron speak;
I hope we shall to purpose the next bout
Cure 'em, as we did Opdam, of the gout.
And when i'th'bottom of the sea they come,
They'll have enough of *Mare Liberum*.   20
Our brandished steel, though now they seem so tall,
Shall make 'em lower than Low Country fall.
But they'll ere long come to themselves, you'll see,
When we in earnest are at snick-a-snee;
When once the boors perceive our swords are drawn,   25
And we converting are those boors to brawn.
    Methinks the ruin of their Belgic banners,
Last fight almost as ragged as their manners,
Might have persuaded 'em to better things,
Than be so saucy to their betters, kings.   30
Is it of wealth they are so proud become? —
James has a wain, I hope, to fetch it home,
And with it pay himself his just arrears
Of fishing tribute for this hundred years,
That we may say, as all the store comes in,   35
The Dutch, alas, have but our factors been.
They fathom sea and land; we, when we please,
Have both the Indies brought to our own seas.

18. *Opdam:* Jacob Wassenaer, baron von Opdam, admiral of the Dutch fleet, killed during the second Dutch war at the Battle of Lowestoft, 3 June 1665. *gout:* Cf. Marvell's *Second Advice,* 45–46: "Then in kind visit unto Opdam's gout,/ Hedge the Dutch in only to let them out."

20. *Mare Liberum:* A short treatise by Hugo Grotius (1583–1645), Dutch publicist and statesman, in which he maintained that the seas were free to all nations. The treatise was first printed in 1609 and referred to Portuguese claims of possession of eastern waters. It did not become important until the 1630s, however, when Anglo–Dutch rivalries for the freedom of the seas, particularly in relation to fishing rights, became severely aggravated. Cf. Marvell's *Character,* 26.

24. *snick-a-snee:* obs. variant of "snick and snee," i.e., a combat with cut and thrust knives. The phrase was derived from the Dutch *steken and snijen.* Cf. Marvell's *Character,* 96.

28. *Last fight:* Originally, the second Dutch war, and, more specifically, the English victory at Lowestoft in 1665, during which the Dutch suffered heavy casualites both in ships and men.

32. *a wain:* a wagon or cart. The original version read "Charles" for "James," of course, and thus included a not particularly noteworthy pun on Charles's Wain, the Big Dipper.

34. *fishing tribute:* In March 1636 the English imposed tribute on the Dutch fishing fleet for the right to fish in British waters. To be paid yearly, it succeeded in little more than establishing a precedent productive of future irritation to Anglo–Dutch relations.

36. *factors:* commercial agents.

For rich, and proud, they bring in ships by shoals,
And then we humble 'em to save their souls.   40
   Pox of their pictures! if we had 'em here,
We'd find 'em frames at Tyburn, or elsewhere.
The next they draw, be it their admirals
Transpeciated into fins and scales;
Or, which would do as well, draw if they please,   45
Opdam, with th' seven sinking provinces;
Or draw their captains from the conquering main,
First beaten home, then beaten back again;
And after this so just, though fatal strife,
Draw their dead boors again unto the life.   50
Lastly, remember, to prevent all laughter,
Drawing goes first, but hanging follows after.
If then lampooning thus be their undoing,
Who pities them that purchase their own ruin?
Or will hereafter trust their treacheries,   55
Until they leave their heads for hostages?
For, as the proverb has of women said,
"Believe 'em not, nay, though you'd swear they're dead."
The Dutch are stubborn, and will yield not fruit,
Till, like the walnut tree, ye beat 'em to't.   60

---

41. *Pox of their pictures:* Cf. Dryden's prologue to *Amboyna* (1673):

> No map shows Holland truer than our play;
> Their pictures and inscriptions well we know;
> We may be bold one medal sure to show. (26–28)

"The war being thus resolved on, some pretenses were in the next place to be sought out to excuse it. . . . Some medals were complained of that seemed dishonorable to the king; as also some pictures. And though these were not made by public order, yet a great noise was raised about them" (Burnet, *1*, 305).

   44. *Transpeciated:* transformed.

   46. *seven sinking provinces:* The seven states of the United Provinces, with a pun on the sinking of their ships and on the failure of their political and military prowess.

   52. *Drawing goes first:* a pun on the "drawing" or dragging of a criminal "at a horse's tail, or on a hurdle or the like to the place of execution," and, of course, on the artist's "drawing," or delineation of a figure.

   59–60. Cf. Marvell's *Second Advice:*

> The Dutch armada yet had th'impudence
> To put to sea to waft their merchants hence;
> For, as if their ships of walnut were,
> The more we beat them, still the more they bear; . . . (289–92)

See the English proverb," A woman, ass, and walnut tree, the more you beat the better be."

To the King

I see an age when, after some few years,
And revolutions of the slow paced spheres;
These days shall be 'bove others far esteemed,
And like the world's great conquerors be deemed.
The names of Caesar, and feigned Paladin,   65
Grav'n in Time's surly brows, in wrinkled Time,
Shall by this prince's name be passed as far
As meteors are by the Idalian star;
For to Great Britain's Isle thou shalt restore
Her *Mare Clausum,* guard her pearly shore;   70
The lions passant of th' Dutch bands shall free,
To the true owner of the lilies three.
The seas shall shrink; shake shall the spacious earth,
And tremble in her chamber, like pale death.
Thy thund'ring cannons shall proclaim to all   75
Great Britain's glory, and proud Holland's fall.

Run on, brave prince, thy course in glory's way;
The end the life, the evening crowns the day.
Reap worth on worth, and strongly soar above
Those heights which made the world thee first to love.   80
Surmount thyself, and make thy actions past
Be but as gleams or lightnings of thy last.
Let them exceed those of thy younger time,
As far as autumn doth the flow'ry prime;
So ever gold and bays thy brow adorn,   85
So never Time may see thy race out-worn;
So of thine own still may thou be desired,
Of Holland feared, and by the world admired;
Till thy great deeds all former deeds surmount:
Thou'st quelled the Nimrods of our Hellespont.   90
So may his high exploits at last make even
With earth his honor, glory with the Heaven.

68. *the Idalian star:* Venus (as the "morning star," called Phosphorus, as the "evening star," Hesperus).

70. *Mare Clausum:* the title of a treatise by John Selden, which was written as a rejoinder to Grotius's *Mare Liberum,* line 20. Though written almost 20 years earlier, the treatise was not published until 1632.

71–72. Heraldic devices of England.

William's Campaign
(5-27 November 1688)

During October tension grew. James's show of reform, according to Evelyn, "gave no satisfaction to the nation but, increasing the universal discontent, brought people to so desperate a pass" that they seemed "to long for and desire the landing . . . praying incessantly for an easterly wind" (*4*, 600). Much of the month, however, the wind remained in the north and William's fleet was "damnified" by its harshness (*Ellis Correspondence, 2,* 237–44). On 19 October his ships had put to sea only to be scattered and driven back again by storm. The insignificant losses were apparently magnified by the time James received word of them. It was thought "that the whole armament was lost. James received the news at dinner and, with an appearance of great devotion, remarked, 'It is not to be wondered at, for the host has been exposed these several days!' " (Dalrymple, pt. 1, bk. 6 p. 192). Within two weeks, however, Orange received that "Protestant wind" for which he and his well-wishers in England had so patiently waited. He set sail on 1 November. Between his fleet and its landfall lay the English ships of the line, fifty-two strong, anchored in the Gunfleet on the northern shore of the Thames estuary, commanded by the Protestant George Legge, Lord Dartmouth, who had remained faithful to his prince even during the days of disfavor in Charles's reign. Dartmouth had replaced Sir Roger Strickland, whose open Catholicism had brought his seamen to mutiny. The fleet was now felt once again to be fit for the king's service, but as Ogg has pointed out, "other influences" undermined the morale:

> It has been said that harbors corrupt men and ships. The sailors in Dartmouth's fleet were receiving pamphlets and newsletters from ashore, and were caballing among themselves; indeed, the situation at the Gunfleet was not unlike that on Hounslow Heath (Ogg, *James II,* p. 214).

Moreover, despite Pepys's attempts to rebuild the navy, a great want of good, reliable equipment and armaments remained. After some prodding by James, Dartmouth ventured out of the Gunfleet on 30 October, only to meet an easterly wind that forced him to ride at anchor off Longsands Head for the next five days, during which time he sighted Orange's fleet passing to the south of him on its way westward. On 5 November 1688, William landed without incident at Tor Bay, near where three years earlier Monmouth had planted his Protestant standard. This time, however, James's campaign would be futile and not a little absurd.

During the week immediately following word of Orange's landing in Devon, fear and suspicion of the Catholics in general and of the Irish troops in particular produced numerous disturbances in London. When James determined to go to the west on 17 November, he was compelled to leave an entire regiment behind to guard London at night.

William had established his headquarters in Exeter, where he remained until 21 November, awaiting the gentry's support. Although several men of eminence had already determined to join Orange, the defection of Clarendon's eldest son (and James's nephew by his first marriage), Edward, Lord Cornbury, with a portion of his command, on 14 November, represented the first important loss sustained by the king's forces. When James reached Salisbury on the 19th, however, he might still have achieved a decisive victory, had he been able to summon the kind of forceful leadership for which he had been known in his youth. But in a council of war on 22 November, he allowed the dull-witted Feversham, general of the army, to prevail over the younger officers' urgings for attack. The meeting broke up determined on retreat to London even though James's forces outnumbered William's by almost two to one.

During two of the five days James spent at Salisbury, he was incapacitated by severe nosebleeds that kept him from going to Warminster to review the troops under the command of Col. Percy Kirke. Later it was rumored that Kirke and some of his officers had plotted to seize James on his tour, and the nosebleeds suddenly seemed providential. On the 23d, however, the eve of James's departure for London, Providence must have seemed more than a little indifferent to a king's plight. That night he learned that Churchill and the duke of Grafton had gone over to Orange. Upon returning three days later, he was dismayed to learn that Princess Anne had left the city for Nottingham, escorted by the bishop of London. Her husband, Prince George, had already defected at Andover during the retreat. The losses, most certainly influenced by Churchill, proved mortifying for James at this crucial time. A much-chastened king, within a few hours of his arrival back in London, met with the members of his Privy Council to reopen discussion of the petition from nineteen peers of the realm calling for a free Parliament, which had been received on the 17th with astonishment and had been given a very short answer. Now it elicited a much more conciliatory response from James.

The Advice

Would you be famous and renowned in story,
And, after having run a stage of glory,
Go straight to Heav'n, and not to purgatory?
                   This is the time.

Would you surrender your dispensing power,   5
And send the western hangman to the Tower,
From whence he'll find it difficult to scour?
                   This is the time.

Would you send Father Penn and Father Lobb,
Assisted by the Poet Laureate Squab,   10
To teach obedience passive to the mob?
                   This is the time.

Would you let Reverend Father Peters know
What thanks the Church of England to him owe
For favors past, he did on them bestow?   15
                   This is the time.

Would you with expedition send away
Those four dim lights made bishops t'other day,
To convert Indians in America?
                   This is the time.   20

4. *This is the time:* The refrain recalls a speech given in the Commons by Sir Heneage Finch, lord chancellor to Charles II, at the opening of the 3d Parliament, 6 March 1679:

> Would you secure religion at home, and strengthen it abroad, by uniting the interest of all the Protestants in Europe? This is the time. Would you let the Christian world see the King in a condition able to protect those who shall adhere to him, or depend on him? This is the time. . . . (Richard Chandler, *History and Proceedings of the House of Commons* [1742], *1*, 328–29).

5. *dispensing power:* the royal prerogative, by which a sovereign could exempt individuals from the operation of the penal laws. James had won a legal decision for his rights in the *Godden* v. *Hales* trial of 1686; the decision in the trial of the bishops was, essentially, a vote against his prerogative.

6. *western hangman:* Jeffreys, who conducted the Bloody Assizes of 1685.

7. *scour:* cant for "run away."

9. *Father Penn and Father Lobb:* William Penn, the Quaker, and Stephen Lobb, called the "Jacobite Independent," had both attempted to win Dissenters to James's cause in 1687 and had fully endorsed the Declaration of Indulgence.

10. *Poet Laureate Squab:* Rochester's nickname for Dryden.

12. *Father Peters:* Edward Petre, Jesuit confessor to the king and a member of the Privy Council.

18. *Those four dim lights:* Bonaventure Giffard (1642–1734), Philip Ellis (1652–1726), James Smith (1645–1711), and John Leyburn (1620–1702). The first three men were made bishops by James in February 1688 (Luttrell, *1*, 430); Leyburn was elected vicar-apostolic of England on 6 August 1685 and first vicar-apostolic of the London district in January 1688. All four men were Roman Catholics.

Would you the rest of that bald-pated train
No longer flatter with thin hopes of gain,
But send them to Saint Omer's back again?
             This is the time.
Would you (instead of holding birchen tool)   25
Send Pulton to be lashed at Busby's school,
That he in print no longer play the fool?
             This is the time.
Would you that Jack-of-all-religions scare,
Bid him for hanging speedily prepare,   30
That Harry Hills may visit Harry Care?
             This is the time.
Would you let Ireland no more fear Macdonell,
And all the rabble under Philem O'Neill,
And Clarendon again succeed Tyrconnel?   35
             This is the time.
Would you court-earwigs banish from your ears,
Those carpet knights and interested peers,
And rid the kingdoms from impending fears?
             This is the time.   40
Would you at once make all the Hogen Mogens yield,

23. *Saint Omer's:* the seminary for English Roman Catholics at Pas-de-Calais, France, irrevocably associated with the name of Titus Oates.

26. *Pulton:* Father Andrew Pulton, master of the Jesuit school at the Savoy and a prominent controversialist. *In Remarks of A. Pulton . . . upon Dr. Thomas Tenison's Late Narrative,* 1688, he says that "having been eighteen years out of his own country, [he] pretends not yet to any perfection of the English expression or orthography; wherefore for the future he will crave the favor of treating with the doctor in Latin or Greek, since the doctor finds fault with his English." *Busby's school:* Westminster School, of which Richard Busby, famous for his canings, was master.

29. *Jack-of-all-religions:* Henry Hills, Sr. (1641–89). He was printer to Cromwell, Charles, and James, and became a convert to Roman Catholicism. On 12 December 1688 a mob attacked his establishment in Blackfriars, "spoiled his forms, letters, etc., and burned 200 or 300 reams of paper, printed and unprinted" (*English Currant,* 12–14 December 1688; see Henry R. Plomer, *A Dictionary of the Booksellers and Printers who were at Work in England, Scotland, and Ireland from 1668–1725* [Oxford, 1922]). Hills fled to St. Omer, where he died within a few weeks.

31. *Harry Care:* Henry Care (1646–88), the much despised journalist and pamphleteer, best known for his *Weekly Pacquet of Advice from Rome,* and for *Public Occurrences.* Care died on 8 August.

33–35. *Macdonnell . . . O'Neill . . . Clarendon . . . Tyrconnel:* Alexander, or Alaster, Macdonnell and Philem O'Neill were leaders of the Irish rebellion, 1641–42. Henry Hyde, earl of Clarendon, was viceroy of Ireland under Charles and James, until replaced in February 1687 by James's tool, the Roman Catholic Richard Talbot, earl of Tyrconnel.

38. *carpet knights:* Though subservience is here implied, the term "knight of the carpet" normally distinguished knights dubbed by the king in court from those dubbed as soldiers in the field.

41. *Hogen Mogens:* the Dutch.

And be at once their terror and our shield,
And not appear by proxy in the field?
                              This is the time.
Would you no more a woman's counsel take,   45
But love your kingdoms for your kingdoms' sake,
Make subjects love, and enemies to quake?
                              This is the time.

The Plowman

As Ralph and Nick i'th'field were plowing,
One of the oxen fell a-lowing
With such a strange and uncouth voice,
As if the beast seemed to rejoice;
Which put the youths in consternation   5
To see the creature in that passion,
But, after they had gazed awhile,
The wonder turned into a smile.
Says Ralph to Nick, there's more in this
Than either thou or I can guess,   10
And was old Father Ant'ny here,
That does all dreams and riddles clear,
He could prognostic, being a scholar,
What put old Brindle in that choler;
For I have drove him fifteen year   15
And never yet so much did hear.
    But, Nick, to pass the time along,
I prithee, sing the Irish song;
The tune I like, the story's base—
And so is all that curséd race;   20
Each bears the mark of Cain in's face.

Nick

Thou bidd'st me sing, I'd more need pray
To keep our enemies away,
Who now are landed in the west—
The thing's too true to make a jest.   25

45. *a woman's counsel:* Queen Mary of Modena's, hence Roman Catholic counsel.
13. *prognostic:* obs. form of "prognosticate."
18. *the Irish song: Lilliburlero,* see p. 485.
24. *landed in the west:* William landed at Tor Bay in southeast Devon.

Ralph

Our enemies, you simple lurdan!
They're come to ease us of our burden,
To free us from the popish brood
That never did to England good.
Why prithee, I have read my book,   30
On which poor Papists never look;
Thy ignorance does move my pity—
All are not destined to be witty;
Come, come, you fool, mind you your singing,
I hope ere long to see some swinging.   35

Nick

No, I will never sing again,
Unless the meaning you explain.

Ralph

Nay, if thou wilt not sing before
Thou hear'st my tale, thou'lt ne'er sing more,
For I shall tell thee such a story   40
Will make thee laugh, and yet be sorry.
Along the road the soldiers pass
Like herds of cattle going to grass
Or droves of sheep to Smithfield fair,
In the same pickle, too, they are,   45
And with like cheerfulness each goes.
Poor men, their hearts are in their hose!
Where one is silent, ten do curse;
None goes by choice, but all perforce;
When the road's dirty, or if't rain,   50
Aloud on popery they complain,
And all declare they'll never fight
'Gainst that church they believe the right—
Rome ne'er shall bring their conscience under,
(Conscience in soldiers made me wonder!)   55
Then railed on some whom I'll not name.
But, faith, I doubt they are to blame,
Yet I have nought to do with that,
Still let the mouse beware the cat.

26. *lurdan:* "a general term of opprobrium . . . implying either dullness and incapacity, or idleness and rascality."
44. *Smithfield fair:* the cattle market.

But if you'd trust a London parson,   60
A popish priest's a very whoreson,
A wolf that's in sheep's clothing dressed,
A saint without, within a beast.
For when I thither went last week,
The people did not stick to speak   65
Such horrid stories of the Papists
That I believe 'em worse than atheists.
Nay, worse than devils, I'm afeard,
If all be true that I have heard;
They say the Jesuit priests have ordered   70
That all the Protestants must be murdered;
The faithless Irish with 'em join
As partners in their black design,
And though we now do plow and sow,
They are come o'er to reap and mow.   75

Nick

They reap and mow! They suck the sow!
Zoons, though I'm born to hold the plow
And never bred to read and write,
By the Lord Harry! I can fight;
And if the Irish are but men,   80
Why thou and I can master ten.
Ne'er fear 'em, Ralph, we country boys
Will piss on their beloved dear joys;
And if we're forced to make an head,
'Od's heart! we'll stave the vermin dead.   85
When once we're vexed they'll find us sour;
Rome and its rubbish soon will scour.

Ralph

Nay, boy, we don't the country fear,
I for poor London take such care;
There in each house they sculk and lurk,   90

---

76. *suck the sow:* to become drunk.

79. *By the Lord Harry:* Perhaps jocular, apparently derived from "old Harry," the devil (Partridge).

83. *dear joys:* cant for Irishmen.

84. *to make an head:* to make head; to advance or press forward, especially in opposition to some one or thing.

85. *'Od's heart:* God's heart—an oath.

87. *scour:* flee.

But naturally do hate to work.
Though, as that parson did declare,
They've Jacob's voice and Esau's hair,
Their conscience base, religion worse;
Their conversation is a curse;   95
'Tis more than time they were removed.
They neither love nor are beloved,
Folk shun them like infected men;
There's not a grain of sense in ten;
Yet all the while good Catholics—   100
None closer to religion sticks—
Such as their church is, such are they.
Then never 'gainst preservers pray,
But let our bullocks bellow still,
And Pro. prince act Heaven's high will.   105
If this be still the year of wonder,
Or they or we must truckle under;
Therefore unyoke, let's home to dinner,
There'll be two losses for one winner.

105. *Pro. prince:* William, the Protestant prince.
106. *the year of wonder:* Cf. *To the Prince of Orange: A Packet of Advice, etc.;* the "original" year
of wonder was, of course, 1666, proclaimed in Dryden's *Annus Mirabilis.*

THOMAS WHARTON

Lilliburlero (A New Song)
(October–December 1688)

The question of the significance of verse satire in shaping events constantly confronts the student of this period. Though many proofs of influence could be adduced, perhaps none is as convincing as the doggerel ballad *Lilliburlero* with its numerous progeny.

With the approach of William's fleet, the satirist warmed to his task knowing that the simplest ideas or the rudest jargon might excite. Into the emotionally charged atmosphere late in October the first broadside copies of *Lilliburlero* were introduced (Luttrell purchased his copy on the 25th, according to his MS note). Written in 1687 by Thomas Wharton against the then new administration in Ireland of Richard Talbot, earl of Tyrconnel, the ballad was set to a brisk march rhythm by Henry Purcell and swept the country like a tune from Tin Pan Alley. Burnet said of it, "A foolish ballad was made at the time treating the Papists and chiefly the Irish in a very ridiculous manner, which had a burden said to be Irish words 'lero lero, lilli burlero'"—words which Swift in his *Marginalia* on Burnet called "not Irish . . . but better than Scotch." Burnet went on to say that it "made an impression on the [king's] army that cannot be imagined by those who saw it not. The whole army and at last the people, both in city and country, were singing it perpetually" (*1*, 792). The tune which, as Wharton boasted, "sung a deluded prince out of three kingdoms" (*A True Relation . . . of the Intended Riot and Tumult of Queen Elizabeth's Birthday, etc.*, 1712, p. 5), became so popular that a host of new poems was set to it. Recognizing the impact of the tune, government satirists unwisely wrote their own lines to the tune and circulated them about, vainly hoping thus either to compromise the effectiveness of the original or to capture for their own cause some of its magic.

Written in an Englishman's concept of the Irish brogue, *Lilliburlero* achieved little if any popular success before October 1688, when the presence of Irish troops in England to bolster James's weakening position produced the immediate cause for its revival. Fortuitously, the poem contained a few phrases that lent themselves well to the present situation, particularly the reference to a "Protestant wind," which, while it had originally referred to the storms faced by Tyrconnel in 1687, now quite obviously stood fair for William.

The author, Thomas Wharton (1648–1715), afterward first marquis of Wharton, was one of the greatest profligates of his time. He was a staunch Whig throughout James's reign, corresponding with Orange in 1688 and joining him at Exeter. No evidence challenges Wharton's claim that he wrote this ballad. The broadside in the Firth collection bears the following MS notes in Luttrell's hand: "2d. Made upon the Irish upon Tyrconnel's going deputy thither, 25 Oct. 1688." Luttrell has also filled in the blanks within the body of the poem. The broadside is reproduced in Macaulay, p. 1075.

Almost immediately the second part of *Lilliburlero* was published (the publication may, indeed, have been simultaneous). It bears directly on the events of late October, giving the verses an immediacy lacking in the first part. Like those of part one, the new verses purport to be the conversation of two Irish soldiers in England who, having had more than enough of the English hatred for them and the Catholics, wish to go home before it is too late.

LILLIBURLERO (A NEW SONG)

Ho, brother Teague, dost hear de decree,
  Lilli burlero, bullen a-la;
Dat we shall have a new debittie,
  Lilli burlero, bullen a-la,
  Lero lero, lero lero, lilli burlero, bullen a-la;   5
  Lero lero, lero lero, lilli burlero, bullen a-la.

Ho, by my shoul, it is a Talbot,
And he will cut de Englishman's troat.

Though, by my shoul, de English do prat,
De law's on dare side, and Chreist knows what.   10

But if dispense do come from de pope,
Weel hang Magno Cart and demselves on a rope.

And the good Talbot is made a lord,
And he with brave lads is coming aboard.

1. *Teague:* cant name for an Irishman.
3. *debittie:* Opposition to the appointment of Tyrconnel in place of Clarendon was very great. James's only concession to it, however, was to call Talbot lord deputy instead of lord lieutenant. Talbot never attained the higher title.
5. *Lero, lero . . . :* None of the several suggestions concerning the meaning of the refrain is satisfactory. The phrases are proably meaningless, as the *OED* says, but see *The Historical Songs of Ireland* ed. T. Crofton Croker (The Percy Society, 1841), pp. 1–2.

Who'll all in France have taken a swear,   15
Dat day will have no Protestant heir.

Oh, but why does he stay behind,
Ho, by my shoul, 'tis a Protestant wind.

Now Tyrconnel is come a-shore,
And we shall have commissions gillore.   20

And he dat will not go to mass,
Shall turn out and look like an ass.

Now, now, de heretics all go down,
By Chreist and St. Patrick, the nation's our own!

ARTHUR MAINWARING

Tarquin and Tullia
(1689)

The story of Tullius's reign from Echard's *Roman History* is frequently alluded to in the satires of the period. It was Arthur Mainwaring's treatment, however, that first made the bloody tale a potent weapon for satirical attack on the new regime. A somewhat modified version of the story runs as follows:

Tarquin's grandson Lucius Tarquinus, a proud, tyrannical man, was married to the modest daughter of Tullius. Another of Tarquin's grandsons, but one of a mild, sweet temperament, married Tullius's other daughter, who was of a haughty and wicked disposition. Lucius was enraged that Tullius had inherited his grandfather's throne and began to plot against him. He first agreed with his brother's wicked wife, a woman of temper even more fiery than his own, that each would dispatch his consort. This done, they were married, vowing in their evil union the utter ruin of King Tullius.

But Tullius, despite their efforts, grew even more honored by both the senate and the people. The enraged Lucius resorted to more subtle methods: he feigned repentance, and did it so realistically that even Tullius himself was deceived.

One day, however, when most of the people were out of the city, Lucius went to the senate house dressed in the king's robes, and boldly took possession of his father-in-law's throne. Tullius rushed to the senate when he learned of this treasonous act, but Lucius pushed him violently aside, and the weak old man was led homeward. When Lucius's wife came to see her husband, the king, she advised him to do away with her father. In her passage homeward that day, she came suddenly upon the body, which lay barely alive in a bloody bath. Her charioteer, frozen by the inhuman spectacle, halted; in a rage she threw her footstool at him and in a barbarous manner forced him to drive over her father's body.

The story obviously offers many opportunities for a Jacobite satirist to identify William III with Lucius, and James II with Tullius. By overlooking the murder of spouses, the two daughters of Tullius might even be identified as Mary and Anne, and Aruns Tarquinus as Prince George of Denmark.

TARQUIN AND TULLIA

In times when princes canceled nature's law
And declarations (which themselves did draw),
When children used their parents to dethrone
And gnawed their way like vipers to a crown,
Tarquin, a savage, proud, ambitious prince,   5
Prompt to expel yet thoughtless of defense,
The envied scepter did from Tullius snatch,
The Roman king, and father by the match.
   To form his party (histories report)
A sanctuary was opened in his court,   10
Where glad offenders safely might resort.
Great was the crowd and wondrous the success
(For those were fruitful times of wickedness),
And all that lived obnoxious to the laws
Flocked to Prince Tarquin, and embraced his cause.   15
   'Mongst these, a pagan priest for refuge fled,
A prophet deep in godly faction read,
A sycophant that knew the modish way
To cant and plot, to flatter, and betray,
To whine and sin, to scribble, and recant,   20
A shameless author, and a lustful saint.
To serve all times, he could distinctions coin,
And with great ease flat contradictions join.
A traitor now, once loyal in extreme,
(And then obedience was his only theme)   25
He sang in temples the most passive lays
And wearied monarchs with repeated praise,

---

2. *declarations:* This is possibly a reference to the so-called Third Declaration, which William disowned. More probably, it is a Jacobite exaggeration of the claim that by "usurping" the throne, William had not lived up to his original declarations.

4. *gnawed . . . like vipers:* an allusion to the supposition that the female viper was killed by her young eating their way out at birth.

10. *court:* William's court was normally kept at The Hague, which Burnet (*1,* 691) considered to be a place safe from "the outlawed persons," i.e., the exiles who tended to gather in the great ports.

16. *pagan priest:* Burnet had made an extensive European tour before he finally settled at The Hague about May 1686. William Stanley, chaplain to Princess Mary at The Hague, wrote letters to his superior, the suspended bishop of London, which reveal how conservative Anglican opinion viewed Burnet's activities in The Hague during the latter half of 1686. He seemed to Stanley to be setting up for faction and popularity and employing "his busy flattering and insinuating carriage" for interests not consonant with those of the church.

But managed awkwardly that lawful part,
For to vent lies and treason was his art,
And pointed libels at crowned heads to dart.   30
This priest, and others learnéd to defame,
First murdered injured Tullius in his name,
With blackest calumnies their sovereign load:
A poisoned brother, and dark league abroad,
A son unjustly topped upon the throne,   35
Which yet was proved undoubtedly his own,
Though as the law was there, 'twas his behoof
Who dispossessed the heir, to bring the proof.
This hellish charge, they backed with dismal frights—
The loss of property, and sacred rights,   40
And freedom—words which all false patriots use,
The surest names the Romans to abuse,
Jealous of kings, and always malcontent,
Forward to change, yet certain to repent.
      Whilst thus the plotters needful fears create,   45
Tarquin with open force invades the state.
Lewd nobles join him with their feeble might,
And atheist fools for dear religion fight;
The priests their boasted principles disown,
And level their harangues against the throne.   50
Vain promises the people's minds allure;
Slight were their ills, but desperate the cure.
'Tis hard for kings to steer an equal course,
And they who banish one, oft get a worse;
Those heavenly bodies we admire above,   55
Do every day irregularly move.
Yet Tullius, 'tis decreed, must lose his crown
For faults that were his counsel's, not his own.
He now in vain commands even those he paid:
By darling troops deserted and betrayed   60
By creatures which his genial warmth had made.

---

30. Possibly an allusion to the celebrated letter of 29 January 1679 / 80 in which Burnet attempted to reform the moral and religious nature of Charles II.

34. *A poisoned brother:* Evelyn (*5*, 197–98) mentions a visit to the marquis of Normanby on 29 November 1694 in which they discoursed about Charles II's being poisoned. Charles II died of chronic granular kidney (a form of Bright's disease) with uremic convulsions. But one of the physicians, Thomas Short, seems to have begun the rumors that he had been poisoned. *dark league abroad:* presumably a reference to an international Catholic plot to take over Protestant England.

35. *son:* James, prince of Wales. *topped upon:* to impose (a thing) upon a person.

Of these a captain of the guards was worst,
Whose memory to this day stands accursed.
This rogue, advanced to military trust
By his own whoredom and his sister's lust,   65
Forsook his master after dreadful vows,
And plotted to betray him to his foes.
The kindest master to the vilest slave,
As free to give, as he was sure to crave,
    His haughty female, who (as books declare)   70
Did always toss wide nostrils in the air,
Was to the younger Tullia governess
And did attend her, when, in borrowed dress,
She fled by night from Tullius in distress.
This wretch by letters did invite his foes   75
And used all arts her father to depose:
A father always generously bent,
So kind that he her wishes did prevent.
    'Twas now high time for Tullius to retreat
When even his daughter hastened his defeat,   80
When faith and duty vanished, and no more
The name of father, nor of king, he bore:
A king whose right his foes could ne'er dispute.
So mild, that mercy was his attribute,
Affable, kind, and easy of access,   85
Swift to relieve, unwilling to oppress,
Rich without taxes, yet in payment just,
So honest, that he hardly could distrust.
His active soul did ne'er from labors cease,
Valiant in war, and sedulous in peace,   90
Studious with traffic to enrich the land,
Strong to protect, and skillful to command,
Liberal and splendid, not without excess,

62. *a captain of the guards*: John Churchill, later earl of Marlborough.

64. After 1674 Churchill's military promotion was certainly due mainly to his military ability, but it is quite possible that earlier commissions were the result of the duke of York's favor, which was to a certain extent influenced by Churchill's and his sister's amours at court. His sister Arabella, mistress to the duke of York, was superannuated when James took over the more serious task of filling the throne of England.

70. Churchill married Sarah Jennings in 1678.

72. *the younger Tullia*: Princess Anne. Sarah Churchill was made one of the princess's Ladise of the Bedchamber at the princess's request after her marriage to the prince of Denmark in 1683. They quickly became friends on an intimate basis typified by their frank correspondence under the names of Mrs. Freeman and Mrs. Morley.

73. *prevent*: anticipate.

Loth to revenge, and willing to caress.
In sum, how godlike must his nature be,   95
Whose only fault was too much piety.
   This king removed, the assembled states thought fit
That Tarquin in the vacant throne should sit,
Voted him regent in their senate house,
And with an empty name endowed his spouse,   100
The elder Tullia, who (some authors feign)
Drove o'er her father's corpse a trembling wain.
But she, more guilty, numerous wains did drive
To crush her father, and her king, alive;
In glad remembrance of his hastened fall   105
Resolved to institute a weekly ball;
She, jolly glutton, grew in bulk and chin,
Feasted on rapine and enjoyed her sin;
With luxury she did weak reason force,
Debauched good nature, and crammed down remorse.   110
Yet when she drunk cool tea in liberal sups
The sobbing dame was maudlin in her cups.
   But brutal Tarquin never did relent,
Too hard to melt, too wicked to repent,
Cruel in deeds, more merciless in will,   115
And blessed with natural delight in ill.
From a wise guardian he received his doom,
To walk the 'change, and not to govern Rome;
He swore his native honors to disown,
And did by perjury ascend the throne.   120
Oh! had that oath his swelling pride repressed,
Rome then had been with peace and plenty blessed;
But Tarquin, guided by destructive fate,
Wasted the country, and embroiled the state,
Transported to their foes the Roman pelf,   125

102. Cf. *HMC, Le Fleming,* p. 288, for the following superstitious incident: "Yesterday [2 September 1690] the queen dined at Kensington. Her coach and horses stood in the square at Whitehall and upon a sudden fright the horses rushed upon the late king's effigy and defaced it. The harness of the horses was so entangled about the statue that one of them was killed by struggling." *wain:* wagon; "trembling wain" is a heroic circumlocution for coach.

117. Possibly an allusion to the story of the ultimate expulsion of the Tarquins from Rome as a result of Sextus Tarquinus's rape of Lucretia; however, the parallel with the states' attempt to limit the power of the house of Orange is not very close, and the prophecy that William would be expelled from England is just as wild.

125. Luttrell (*1,* 508) reports Williams's speech to Parliament on 8 March 1688 / 89. Prominent among the recommendations he made to hasten matters of supply was "the condition of our allies, especially Holland, by whom he was enabled to undertake this expedi-

And by their ruin hoped to save himself.
Innumerable woes oppressed the land
When it submitted to his cursed command;
So just was Heaven that 'twas hard to tell,
Whether its guilt or losses did excel. 130
Men who renounced their God for dearer trade
Were then the guardians of religion made;
Rebels were sainted, foreigners did reign,
Outlaws returned, preferments to obtain,
With frogs and toads and all their croaking train. 135
No native knew their features nor their birth;
They seemed the greasy offspring of the earth.
The trade was sunk, the fleet and army spent,
Devouring taxes swallowed lesser rent,
(Taxes imposed by no authority: 140
Each lewd collection was a robbery).
Bold self-creating men did statutes draw,
Skilled to establish villainy by law,
Fanatic drivers, whose unjust careers
Produced new ills exceeding former fears. 145
    Yet authors, here, except that faithful band
Which the prevailing faction did withstand,
And some who bravely stood in the defense
Of baffled justice and their injured prince.
These shine to aftertimes; each sacred name 150
Stands still recorded in the books of fame.

tion, that the charge they have been at may be reimbursed. . . . " The House of Commons had voted a donative to the Dutch forces that were shipped back to Holland in February, ranging from 50s. for every soldier to £200 for every colonel. Eight thousand English, horse and foot, were to go to Holland pursuant to the Treaty of Nimeguen, and were to have English pay and to remain for two years. Such payments explain the resentment of Jacobites.

131. *dearer trade: commerce.*

151. Oldmixon's comment (*Life of Maynwaring*, p. 13) is "those records are unhappily kept by the officers of justice. In the records of the Old Bailey, we shall find, Sir William Parkyns, Sir John Friend, Sir John Fenwick, etc. Plotters and assassins, a faithful band, under the command of Sir George Barclay, and Mr Charnock, to stand up in defense of baffled justice at Turnham Ground, and right one injured prince, by murdering another. Thus easy it is to be merry with Mr. Maynwaring when he was Jacobite, who was himself so merry with his own party afterwards."

Burnet's Character
(1689)

For his role in the revolution, Burnet was much attacked by Jacobite satirists, and the vilification went on during the first year of the new regime. In most of the imitations of Dryden's *Absalom and Achitophel* after the revolution, Burnet usually appears in the list of heroes who still faction by his loyalty. But the attacks are far more frequent. It was probably Burnet's seeming influence on Queen Mary (who controlled ecclesiastical preferment) and seeming political intimacy with the new monarchs that caused most fear among his opponents and motivated the several verse "characters" that have survived.

Line 90 of the present poem reveals the particular source of many a satirist's fear of Burnet. The unknown author is apprehensive of the possibility that William and Mary will raise Burnet to the archbishopric of Canterbury, from which position he will be able to mend the liturgy. This fear was probably more real before Convocation than after, for events there revealed the true alignment of forces for Comprehension and marked a significant step toward the elevation of Tillotson. But Burnet was popularly considered to be a Presbyterian in bishop's guise, and therefore a more patent threat than even "Presbyter John," as Tillotson was later to be called.

BURNET'S CHARACTER

> 'Mongst all the hard names that denote reproach,
> The worst in the whole catalogue is Scotch;
> For rascal, rakehell, vagabond, vile sot,
> Are only faint synonyms to a Scot.
> To what a height then mounts that mighty he   5
> Who is whole Scotland in epitome!
> Imperious layman first, then lofty priest,
> A trimming Jew, half Mahomet, half Christ,

7. Burnet was ordained a priest in February 1665.
8. *trimming*: balancing between opinions or parties so as to remain in favor with both sides.

Rebel in heart, though loyalist in tongue
While Charles's praises he demurely sung;   10
When native loyalty was stamped on all
And just obedience epidemical
None so devoutly mourned the martyr's blood,
Nor seemingly the faction's growth withstood,
'Till daring saints a glorious turn afford   15
To brand his master and betray his lord.
Officious Shimei then withdrew his mask,
Obliged his patrons and outdid his task;
And Lauderdale a sacrifice must fall,
Abused at Glasgow, ruined at Whitehall.   20
Thus the state Proteus swallowed up the priest
Henceforth he spurned the crown and clawed the beast.
Assemblies now are only treason clubs
And sermons cant to please the gaping mob;
Cabals and mutinies all o'er the land   25
Shimei proclaims for signs of God's right hand,
And spies deliverance approach from far
As plain as e'er the Magi viewed their star.
Thus the vile wretch exalts his traitorous crest
And vents the rancour of his cankered breast,   30
'Till royal vengeance roused its awful head
And Shimei justice and his country fled.
Our laws (to traitors famously severe)
Thundered him hence and topped him on Myn Heer.

Halifax's patronage of Burnet in the late seventies and early eighties, and Burnet's own claim to be "free of party" gave rise to the charge of "trimming."

13. A reference to Burnet's *The Royal Martyr* (1675), which was maliciously reprinted in 1689.

15. *daring saints:* Presbyterians, under the leadership of William Douglas, duke of Hamilton, to whom Burnet was related by marriage.

16. John Maitland, duke of Lauderdale. Burnet probably became intimate with the Scottish member of the Cabal in 1663, when he visited London in connection with the impending execution of his uncle, Archibald Johnston, Lord Warriston, the framer of the Covenant.

22. *clawed the beast:* perhaps a reference to his attacks on Rome.

31. Burnet was dismissed by Charles II in 1683 from the Chapel of the Rolls "as a person disaffected to the government." Burnet implies that James, duke of York, was ultimately responsible for his persecution.

34. *topped him on Myn Heer:* imposed him on the Dutch. Burnet had, in his own words, "spent the greatest part of the year 1664 in Holland and France, which contributed not a little to root and fix me in those principles [of liberty and moderation]." He naturally took refuge there in 1686, but not until he had traveled extensively throughout Europe.

Scarce had the church's and the nation's plague   35
Escaped the deep and landed at The Hague,
When a new sect of jovial saints appear,
Accost the vagrant, and dispel his fear,
Crave his assistance in the godly work
To enslave this country and exalt the kirk.   40
Shimei, surprised at his successful fate
To ease his spleen and gratify his hate,
With joy concurs and ratifies assent
By speaking quick as lewdly as he meant
"Would you my friends effect what you've begun?   45
Against the father stimulate the son?
Our thoughtful enemy's most constant care
Centers on apish herd and frivolous prayer.
Heaven and such fooleries have seized his breast,
No jealous thoughts disturb his pious rest,   50
And we the glorious work may half have done
Before he'll be persuaded we've begun.
We'll whore his wife and bastardize his son;
If proof's required we'll then outface the sun,
Exalt their jealousies, foment their fears   55
Of French invisible about their ears;
Of leagues and massacres we'll coin whole shoals,
(To gull the credulous and fright the fools)
'Till startled loyalty shall cease to act,
Tamely look on while we the cause transact."   60
He spake and all the motley herd approved.
This is the spring that all their actions moved.
Success has made the counselor admired,
Since Lucifer has blessed what he desired.
Shimei no more appears in native rug,   65
Quits native bonnet too, and native shrug.
All gay, defiles the court amongst the rest,
And mounts his merits higher than the best.
When lo! beyond the brute's aspiring hopes,

37. *jovial saints:* Possibly the Remonstrant community, among whom Philip van Limborch (1633–1712) became a close friend of Burnet. This Arminian sect dated from their Remonstrance of 1610.

46. I.e., persuade William of Orange to rebel against James II. Burnet's animosity toward James is the keynote of the speech.

66. *native shrug:* The meanings given in *OED* do not seem to fit the context, but it is possible that something of the flavor of "the Neapolitan shrug, when one intends to play the villain" may be intended.

An aged pillar from poor Sion drops,   70
And Shimei's creature (who then ruled the roast)
In reverend pillar's place fixed brawny post.
Dear Mother, sure he ne'er thy good intends
Who thinks such ravening wolves can prove thy friends.
This parricide has left thee in the lurch,   75
Disgraced the order and betrayed the church.
For foppish Durham's self compared to him
Appears a bright angelic seraphim;
In vain did Rome attempt that sect to form,
For daring Shimei was a Jesuit born.   80
Mischief's his essence, tyranny his will,
Good his antipodes, his center ill.
His justice cheat, all his religion trick,
His prayers are banter, and his God Old Nick.
His noise of virtue and his prate of grace   85
Are birdlime twigs to catch the greatening mace,
And all the medley politics new stamped
Are Hobbes's and Milton's atheism new vamped.
Good Gods, what pious doctrine would come next
Could he gain Lambeth and reform the text?   90
But time is precious, though my subject's vile;
Therefore, for once, let's use laconic style
I scorn to wish him Hell; it's sad to be endured.
Howe'er, he knows how it may be procured.
He wants prayers most; may this prayer be his doom: 95
(A Scotchman's greatest plague) God send him home.

70. Seth Ward, bishop of Salisbury, died 6 January 1689.
71. *Shimei's creature:* possibly William of Orange, but more probably Henry Compton, Bishop of London, who consecrated Burnet bishop of Salisbury on 31 March 1689.
77. Nathaniel Crew, bishop of Durham, was, with Thomas Sprat, bishop of Rochester, a member of James II's ecclesiastical commission. Burnet remarked, "Durham was lifted up with it, and said, now his name would be recorded in history; and when some of his friends represented to him the danger of acting in a court so illegally constituted, he said, he could not live if he should lose the king's gracious smiles; so low, and so fawning was he."
79. *that sect:* Presumably this is a reference to James II's attempt to Romanize the Church of England through the ecclesiastical commission.
86. *greatening mace:* increasing political power.
88. Thomas Hobbes's reputation as an atheist was widespread; but in calling John Milton's Puritanism "atheism," the persona reveals Anglican bigotry. The satirist imputes Jesuitical cunning to Burnet in order to accuse him of being an atheist intent on ruining the Church of England.
90. *Lambeth:* Lambeth Palace was the London seat of the archbishop of Canterbury.

Vox Clero, Lilliburlero
(1689)

Written in January 1690, this broadside ballad was immensely popular, as its wide distribution shows. It is ascribed to Fleetwood Sheppard in a MS copy of the broadside, but this is unlikely since he is disdainfully attacked in stanza 6. The author's witty allusiveness (especially to proverbial lore) puts him a notch above the author of those pieces that have usually been attributed to Sheppard, so the poem must perforce remain anonymous. The poem is, of course, meant to be sung, and just as *Lilliburlero* itself was reputed to have sung King James out of his three kingdoms, it was hoped that conservative Anglicans could be sung out of their established position in the forthcoming Convocation.

Vox Clero, Lilliburlero, or
The Second Part of a Merry New Ballad

To Be Sung in the Jerusalem Chamber, the 24th of This Instant January.
To the Tune of "Youth, Youth, Thou Hadst, etc."

1.

Canonical black-coats, like birds of a feather,
In town and from country are flocking together;
As if our religion was never intended,
But for want of a better, to be still amended.
　　　　　Commissioners all　　　　　　　　　　　　5
　　　　　Ecclesiastical,
To make a new creed, meet at Westminster Hall.
Yet Tories had rather see Protestants burn,
Than that their old liturgy should not serve the turn.

Title: Convocation met on 24 January.
1. *black-coats:* a depreciative term for a clergyman, parson.
4. An echo of *Hudibras 1,* 1, 205–06.
8. The refrain has an interesting adumbration in an opinion expressed by the lord privy seal in a conversation with Sir John Reresby (p. 572). Speaking on 14 April 1689 about the

2.

There's no Catholic note that more does belong 10
To a fallible church than to be in the wrong.
And if the deceived may also deceive,
Then in what a condition are those that believe.
   In divinity schools
   Are forged many tools, 15
Whereby knaves get their living by working on fools.
Yet Tories had rather, etc.

3.

Whole troops of crape-gowns, with their captains in lawn,
In the pale of the church together were drawn. 20
A learned good doctor did fairly propose
To let in our friends, and shut out our foes,
   But Rochester stood by,
   And refused to comply,
For he scorned all commissions, unless they were high.
And rather the Tories would see the Inquisition, 25
Than part with one title of vain repetititon.

Church of England party, Halifax said "They hated the Dutch and had rather turn Papists than take in the Presbyterians amongst them; that the Presbyterians hated the Church of England men as much, and spoiled their own business by the ill preparing of their bill of comprehension" This was only one day after the Commons had asked William to call a convocation of the clergy.

10. *note:* one of the characteristics by which the true church may be known.

12. This is possibly a reference to Anglican equivocation over the doctrine of transubstantiation.

18. *crape-gown:* clergyman. *captains in lawn:* bishops (cf. *OED*, "lawn sleeve's"). The military image prolongs the implied comparison of black-coats and red-coats introduced in line 1.

20. John Tillotson was the power behind the "Comprehension party," but he failed in his attempt to be elected prolocutor of the Convocation. William Jane was elected 55 to 28. Compton, prolocutor of the upper house, was therefore the major speaker for Tillotson's viewpoint on the day that Jane was presented to the upper house as prolocutor (21 November). Compton may therefore be referred to here.

22. Thomas Sprat, bishop of Rochester, among others, raised doubts about the legality of the actions of the commissioners at their first meeting in the Jerusalem Chamber on 10 October. Sprat finally withdrew at the second meeting.

24. Sprat had served on James II's Commission for Ecclesiastical Affairs, until the prosecution of the Seven Bishops convinced him of its illegality and its purpose to weaken the Church of England. This commission was "high" because it was a revival of the Tudor "Court of High Commission," an ecclesiastical equivalent of the Star Chamber.

26. Joseph Boyse, in his *Vox Populi* (1690), lists various repetitions that he disapproves of: the Gloria Patri 10 times in the ordinary morning service; the Lords Prayer 5 or 6 times every Sunday morning; the "confused babbling" of the Kyrie Eleisons; the Good Lord Deliver Us 8 times in the Litany; and We Beseech Thee to Hear Us Good Lord 22 times in the Litany.

4.

This maggot o'th'mass, the prayers, ye call common,
Conceived by a boy, brought forth by a woman,
Who to cure all the sores in the souls of the nation
Have published this noble receipt for salvation: 30
      Cut in parcels it is,
      Lest the parson should miss,
Who prays all by spurt, as his tithe-pigs do piss;
Yet Tories had rather, etc.

5.

To show that our soul not likely to starve is,   35
Here's both the first course, and the second service;
'Tis served up to relish your ale and your toast well,
With a cut of the 'pistle, and a slice of the gospel.
      Then the curate so pert,
      Brings in the dessert.   40
Lord, how Robin Spencer rejoices at heart!
When man, with the Lady of Babylon's rag on,
Stands by the dark candle, and the empty flagon.

6.

Stand firm to your sins, and have a great care
That you mend not your lives, lest ye spoil all the prayer.   45
Ye must never press forward—round, round, ye must reel,
And sin, and repent, like a dog in a wheel.
      Be still the same men
      In the morning at ten,
In the evening, at three, have at it again.   50

27. *maggot:* a worm of the kind formerly supposed to be generated by corruption. See *Hudibras, 3,* 2, 1–12, and the notes in Zachary Grey's edition. The Book of Common Prayer was frequently jeered at as generated by corruption of the Catholic Mass.

28. Edward VI and Elizabeth I.

31. Presumably the rubrics cut the text into "parcels." Much of the traditional criticism of the Book of Common Prayer was directed at specific rubrics (such as the "ornaments rubric"). Most of the controversial rubrics were in fact modified or altered by the commission.

33. *by spurt:* with responses at intervals? *tithe-pig:* a pig due or taken as tithe.

41. *Robin Spencer:* Robert Spencer, earl of Sunderland, who had turned Catholic for a short time and was now (through the good offices of his wife) attempting to prove his true Anglicanism.

42. *Babylon:* applied polemically to Rome or to the papal power.

43. An allusion to the ornaments rubric. The commission recommended a new rubric commending the surplice as an ancient and decent habit. Controversy over the eucharistic vestments was of course still very strong in 1689.

But who would have thought that old Cranmer and Ridley
Should confess all the sins of Sheppard and Sedley.

7.

The Kit Wrens of our creed, those spiritual surveyors,
First found that our matrimony wanted repairs.
Grave Tenison thought things obscenely expressed   55
And fain would have left out the cream of the jest.
          But 'twould not be decreed
          To leave out the word "seed,"
For 'twould dry-bob our marriage, and mar all the breed.
So Tories had better see, etc.   60

8.

When our sacrament's old hocus-pocus is done,
One would think it is bread, or else it is none;
Though our senses say bread, as to God we must bow,
Or the church has ta'en care all our cake shall be dough.
          Should they mystery boast,   65
          And would call it the host,
In a cup of canary 'twould serve for a toast.
Yet Tories had rather, etc.

9.

From a brother o'th'mug (grown a peer with a mitre)

51. Thomas Cranmer and Nicholas Ridley were major formulators of Anglican rites and theological doctrines. They were also reformers of ecclesiastical polity and thus stand for the ritual aspects of the Church of England. Cranmer was largely responsible for the original form of Edward VI's Book of Common Prayer.

52. Fleetwood Sheppard and Sir Charles Sedley were two of the most notorious survivors of the Court Wit circle of Charles II's reign, a circle synonymous with godlessness and immorality to the Puritans of their day.

53. Sir Christopher Wren retained the office of surveyor-general throughout William and Mary's reign.

55. Thomas Tenison was renowned for his moderation toward Dissenters, many of whom still felt strongly about some aspects of the marriage service in the Book of Common Prayer. The commission recommended a canonical restraint of the abuses then connected with the special license system, the ring was rubrically defined to placate Dissenters, and the frank terms of the preface were slightly modified. Tenison was presumably one of the leaders of the discussion on the last topic.

59. *dry-bob:* to copulate without ejaculation.

67. *toast:* The primary sense is the current one (bread browned by fire); the punning sense implied here and elsewhere in the satires is of a cheat, but nothing in *OED* appears to support it. "On toast" (swindled) is a 19th-century sense.

69. *brother o'th'mug:* The earliest recorded use of *mug* (a drinking vessel with its contents) is 1664; it was quickly associated with beer drinking, so presumably "brother o'th'mug" implies that the bishop was once one of a company of beer drinkers.

They promise our souls than their lawn should be whiter,   70
Till with passive obedience the nation enslaved;
One had better be damned than so to be saved.
        Old Noll had a trick
        To keep souls from Old Nick,
Without either bishop, or a bishopric.   75
But Presbyter puppies needs the king would restore,
And by putting him in, put 'emselves out o' door.

10.

With the tail of a horse, when such gambols were played,
What might we expect from the jolly Nag's Head?
On their *jure divino*, whip, they mount in the air,   80
And run their tantivy, the devil knows whether.
        Then begin they to sing,
        No bishop, no king,
Till together, Old Nick has 'um all in a string,
And still ye might beat the lawn sleeves in a mortar,   85
Yet not find so much brain as in Oliver's porter.

75. Cromwell, by his system of "Triers," ensured that benefices could be held without an ecclesiastical hierarchy.

76. Presbyterians, supported by the army of George Monck, were largely responsible for inviting Charles II to take the English throne. The Convention Parliament called by Monck was predominantly Presbyterian, but free elections after Charles's Restoration returned a predominantly Cavalier and Anglican Parliament, which proceeded to pass laws against Nonconformists.

79. *Nag's Head:* A reference is intended to the Papist fable that in 1559 Matthew Parker was irregularly consecrated archbishop of Canterbury by Scory, bishop of Chichester, in an inn in Cheapside called the Nag's Head, thus calling into question the validity of subsequent Anglican orders.

80. *jure divino:* by divine right. Hence the "Tory" dogma, here represented as a horse.

81. *tantivy:* (1) a rapid gallop; (2) a nickname given to the post-Restoration high church-men and Tories, especially in the reigns of Charles II and James II. This nickname arose in 1680–81, when a caricature was published in which a number of high church clergymen were represented as mounted upon the Church of England and "riding tantivy" to Rome, behind the duke of York.

83. *No bishop, no king:* Monarchy is inseparable from episcopacy.

86. *Oliver's porter:* The porter of Oliver Cromwell went mad and was confined to Bedlam.

The Shash
(1690)

The incident satirically celebrated in the following poem has been dated in one MS as the Sunday after Christmas Day "when Mr. Barkely preached," that is, presumably, 29 December 1689. A newsletter of 13 January 1689/90 *(CSPD)* dated the event "ten days ago" and made the claim that "the sash fell upon his neck and held him fast till one of the lords came and lifted it up." The poem is wittily organized around the emotionally charged ideas of preservation and deliverance.

THE SHASH

A Song to the Tune of "Old Simon the King"

1.

Ye members of Parliament all
    That quarrel to settle the nation,
Prepare an address for Whitehall,
    And thank God for your king's preservation.

2.

Last Sunday to chapel he went   5
    To hear a fine nightingale sing;
God knows whether treason was meant,
    But there happened a wonderful thing.

Title. Shash: window sash.
3. *Whitehall:* the palace which, until it was burned down in 1698, was the royal residence. James II normally kept his court there, but William and Mary's frequent absences from Whitehall reduced its importance as the center of court life.
6. George Berkeley, brother of Lord Berkeley, was installed as one of the prebendaries of Westminster on 13 June 1687. Apparently none of his subsequent sermons was printed.

503

3.

To the window His Majesty came
  To show his desirable face,   10
And a lord (whom I list not to name)
  Unluckily slippéd the shash.

4.

The portcullis came rottling down
  And threatened the noddle anointed,
Lord! how the blue prelate would frown   15
  To see all his hopes disappointed!

5.

Count Lansdown, that gravely stood by
  A-snuffing up politic powder,
To his sovereign's assistance did fly—
  A pox of the loyal intruder!   20

6.

The royal snail pulled in his horns
  And thanked him for being so zealous;
'Twas enough to set Benting on thorns
  And make the he-bedfellow jealous.

7.

For had he but let him alone   25
  Our protector had safely been locked there,
And in pillory penance had done
  Like his brother deliverer the doctor.

11. Algernon Capel, earl of Essex, a young courtier of 19, was later (1691–1702) to be a Gentleman of the Bedchamber to William III, a seasoned military campaigner and a frequent target for the lampooners.

13. *rottle:* rattle.

15. *blue prelate:* Gilbert Burnet?

17. *Count Lansdown:* Charles Granville, viscount Lansdown, was son of the earl of Bath and in 1684 was made a count of the Roman Empire for valor at the siege of Breda.

23. *Benting:* Hans Willem Bentinck, earl of Portland. This is the usual homosexual charge that prompted such squibs as this one:

  If a wily Dutch boor for a rape on a girl
    Was hanged by the law's approbation,
  Then what does he merit that buggers an earl
    And ravishes the whole nation?

28. *doctor:* Titus Oates, who also claimed to be delivering England from the Catholics during the Popish Plot.

8.

Such an engine in Scotland is known
    (And thither he's going 'tis said)   30
But it's feared while he snaps at the crown
    The maiden may snap off his head.

9.

No longer let Overkirk boast
    Of saving so puny a thing;
He preserved but a burgher at most,   35
    But Lansdown delivered a king.

30. A false rumor. William did not go to Scotland but managed affairs in that kingdom through intermediaries. But the rumor was rife in early December.

32. *maiden:* the instrument, similar to the guillotine, formerly used in Edinburgh for beheading criminals.

33. *Overkirk:* Henry Nassau, count and lord of Auverquerque, saved William's life at the risk of his own at Mons, August 1678. He was captain of William's bodyguard during the revolution, and distinguished himself in William's military campaigns thereafter.

On the Late Metamorphosis
(1690)

Of many possible satirical parallels, that between William III and Oliver Cromwell was most capable of stirring prejudice against the new monarch. Firth supplies in his edition of Macaulay an example of W. Faithorne's emblematic portrait of Cromwell altered to represent William III, and it may be the one alluded to here. William's hooked nose is obvious, but many details show that it was originally intended for Cromwell. Some of these details are pointed out in the commentary.

ON THE LATE METAMORPHOSIS OF AN OLD PICTURE OF OLIVER CROMWELL'S INTO A NEW PICTURE OF KING WILLIAM: THE HEAD CHANGED, THE HIEROGLYPHICS REMAINING

Whether the graver did by this intend
Oliver's shape with William's head to mend,
Or grace King William's head with Cromwell's body,
If I can guess his meaning I'm a noddy.
Howe'er, I pity Cromwell. Thirty year 5
And more are past since he did disappear.
Now, after all this time, 'tis hard to be
Thus executed in effigie—
This is a punishment he never dreaded;
What did His Highness thus to be beheaded? 10
Perhaps the artist thinks to get a name
By showing us how two may be the same.
If so, he's gained his point, for he's a witch
That suddenly can tell one which is which!
As these two noble heroes t'other day 15
Together hung, both as they ought and may,
The staring crowd were all confounded—"See,"

1. *graver: engraver.*

The Embleme of Englands Distractions (Williamite version).

Says one, "here's the two czars of Muscovy."
"No," says another, "that can never be;
It's not their country habit. Here's no fur.   20
'Tis the two kings of Brentford; never stir."
"Hold!" says a cobbler. "You mistake the pictures:
'Tis Oliver and Richard, the protectors.
I know 'em by their wrinkled boots. 'Twas then
The only fashion with the trooping men.   25
Jack boots were then unborn, and in my thinking
The only use for jacks was then for drinking.
Many a pull and many a pleasant tug
I've had with the black jack and double jug.
Well, I may say, my masters (no dispraise   30
To any), Oliver's were blessed days:
Th' excise was small, the measure large; they'd draw
A full pot for five farthings, cobbler's law.
But now I hear, to my eternal trouble,
That all our drink (God bless us) must pay double!   35
What shall a poor man do, if they invade
Our drinking thus, to carry on his trade?"
    "You all shoot wide, my masters," says another.
"He in the wig is neither son nor brother,
But a late conqueror of different fame.   40
Sirs, pull off all your hats, and hear his name!
'Tis good King William. See Rome trampled down.
See his victorious sword thrust through the crown.
See his triumphant foot on Papists' necks.

18. Peter I (1672–1725) was "junior" czar to Ivan, the infirm and stupid half-brother of Sophia Aleksyeevna (1657–1704). She was virtually ruler of Russia from 1682 to 1689, and the "two czars," her brothers, mere figureheads.

21. These mythical personages seem to date from *The Rehearsal* by George Villiers, duke of Buckingham (1672).

23. Richard Cromwell was in fact still alive (1626–1712).

25. *trooping men:* soldiers in a troop of cavalry, horse soldiers. The term trooper was used in connection with the Covenanting army that invaded England in 1640.

26. *Jack boot:* a large strong boot the top of which came above the knee, serving as defensive armor for the leg, worn by cavalry soldiers in the 17th and 18th centuries.

27. *jacks:* black-jacks, large leather jugs for beer, etc., coated externally with tar.

33. *cobbler's law:* Cf.Tilley, "Cobbler's law, he that takes money must pay the shot."

35. Refers to an act for doubling the duty of excise upon beer, ale, and other liquors during the space of one year, passed 25 November 1690.

42. "Rome" is a woman trampled underfoot, labeled "Babilon" (Macaulay, p. 1433).

43. There are three crowns—the three kingdoms (Macaulay, p. 1433).

See *Salus Populi Suprema Lex*.   45
See Magna Charta. Can all this agree
With any man but Oliver and he?
Then talk no more of taxes and excise;
Such little thoughts true Protestants despise:
That though they come at times when money's scanty,   50
Whilst our religion's safe, it's all not tanti.
Let no free quarter grieve you or disturb you,
Nor think that Dutch or Dane came here to curb you.
What though they spoil your goods and pox your wives
So long as all our throats 'scape popish knives?   55
Pound rates or polls are nothing great or small:
Deliverance! Deliverance! is all—
Whilst you are Protestants, who can oppress you?
Go home, my friends, and so King William bless you!"
The devil mob had here no more to say,   60
But charmed at William's name marched all away.

45. This Roman law is said to be among the twelve tables drawn up by the decemviri, 451–450 B.C.: "The supreme law is the people's welfare."

51. *tanti*: of so much value, worth so much; worthwhile.

52. *free quarter*: the obligation or impost of having to provide free board and lodging for troops.

56. *Pound rate*: a rate of so much in the pound. *poll*: short for poll money—money levied, exacted, or paid at a fixed rate per head for every person.

The Embleme of Englands Distractions (Commonwealth version).

The Female Parricide
(1689)

Satires attacking Queen Mary without referring to her husband are rare after the first year of the revolution. This is strange, as she was, in effect, sole regent during William's absences on military campaigns from 1690 to 1694. She is attacked in *To the Queen on Her Proclamation Concerning Passes* for omitting to refer to her father's confirmation in 1686 of her uncle's earlier proclamation, and ironically asked whether she has forgotten the father she has cheated. Other satirists attempted to trace Mary's iniquities to her Hyde ancestry, and some extended the disapproval to her sister in such a poem as *On the Two Sisters*:

> To be but half a Hyde is a disgrace
> From which no royal seed can purge its race.
> Mixed with such mud the clearest streams must be,
> Like Jordan's sacred flood, lost in the Sodom Sea.
> Ambition, folly, insolence, and pride
> Proves it too well you're on the surer side.

Whatever the satirists say, nothing in the extant poems is quite so devastating as the duchess of Marlborough's statement in *An Account of the Conduct of the Dowager Duchess of Marlborough* (1742), p. 25: "And here I cannot forebear saying, that whatever good qualities Queen Mary had to make her popular, it is too evident by many instances *that she wanted bowels*."

THE FEMALE PARRICIDE

> Oft have we heard of impious sons before,
> Rebelled for crowns their royal parents wore;
> But of unnatural daughters rarely hear
> 'Till those of hapless James and old King Lear.
> But worse than cruel lustful Goneril, thou!　　　　　5
> She took but what her father did allow;
> But thou, more impious, robb'st thy father's brow.

509

Him both of power and glory you disarm,
Make him, by lies, the people's hate and scorn,
Then turn him forth to perish in a storm.   10
Sure after this, should his dead corpse become
Exposed like Tarquin's in the streets of Rome,
Naked and pierced with wounds on every side,
Thou wouldst, like Tullia, with triumphant pride
Thy chariot drive, winged with ambitious fire,   15
O'er the dead body of thy mangled sire.

The Impartial Inspection
(1690)

Imitations, parodies, and imitations of parodies of the popular song "Would you be a man of fashion?" were very common just before and after the revolution. Immediately preceding William's arrival came an attack on popish idolatry and—the most popular of all the parodies—advice on how to please a popish king and an account of the consequences. After the revolution came a bitter denunciation of William's usurpation and the forthcoming coronation; a blunt complaint against William's alleged neglect of honest men for preferment; a jeering and triumphant attack appropriately entitled *Popery Pickled;* and the poem here printed.

The poem is a product of the period of turmoil following William's announcement that he intended to take personal charge of the campaign in Ireland, and shortly after, that he was dissolving the Convention Parliament. Although Macaulay (p. 1958) quotes from stanzas 4 and 6 as from a Whig lampoon, the persona in this poem is a trimmer of the Halifax tradition who seems at times to be addressing William directly. His fear of factional dispute is strong, but his opposition to the ascendancy of those making up the present government is just as firm. Indeed, the satire represents a moderate royalist position.

THE IMPARTIAL INSPECTION

1.

Would you be preserved from ruin?
    Stem the tide with all your might?
Such feuds are everywhere a-brewing
    Will unhinge the nation quite.
Those who should cement our breaches,   5
    Make 'em wider every day;
And what the sober clergy preaches
    Prelates in the House gainsay.

511

2.

Sancroft unto James was loyal,
    But to William's nothing so;   10
Which shows when put unto the trial
    He's the king's and church's foe.
The public weal while you're pursuing,
    To your aims he's counter still;
Let the nation sink to ruin,   15
    He can never balk his will.

3.

London once was famed in story,
    Equal to the suffering seven;
'Till choosing members showed him Tory,
    Savoring of old James's leaven.   20
"The temple of the Lord," he cries,
    "Preserve the church from violence!"
While Rome and France in ambush lies
    To take both it and us from hence.

4.

Yorkshire Tom was raised to honor,   25
    For what cause no creature knew;
Yet he was false to the royal donor,
    And will be the same to you.
'Tis not marquisates can please him,

9. William Sancroft, archbishop of Canterbury. The first attack is therefore upon non-jurors.

16. *balk:* thwart.

17. *London:* Henry Compton, bishop of London. The second attack is upon turncoats. Compton, at first a vigorous supporter of the revolution, gradually soured into an opponent of the revolution settlement, and favored "The Church in Danger" party.

19. Compton's activities in the election campaign of 1690 are not known, but he obviously must have shown his hand as a follower of Carmarthen, his cousin.

20. *leaven:* After 1 Cor. 5: 6–7, the traces of unregenerate condition; hence often applied to prejudices of education inconsistently retained by those who have changed their religious or political opinions.

25. *Yorkshire Tom:* Thomas Osborne, earl of Danby and marquess of Carmarthen, was born in Yorkshire and was the manager of the revolution in that locality, where his local influence was far greater than that of any other nobleman. The third attack is on ambitious, all-powerful ministers.

27. This presumably implies that the duke of York was partly responsible for Osborne's succeeding Clifford as lord treasurer and for his elevation to the peerage.

29. Danby was created marquess of Carmarthen, 20 April 1689, and his presence in William's court produced a spate of satirical forebodings. His political reputation is fairly well summed up in this doggerel:

Since he aims at greater things, 30
And such impious thoughts do seize him
To give rule and law to kings.

5.

Finch's fortunes lie before him
(Sure he must not die in's bed)
Pity 'tis the beast that bore him 35
Had not then licked off his head.
Mounted contrary to merit,
He with proud disdain looks down,
And his never sated spirit
Would be equal with the crown. 40

6.

Stock the cards and lift for dealing,
Shuffle and cast knaves again:
Other salves will be more healing
Which may put us to less pain.
If a marquis needs must steer us, 45
Take a better in his stead,
Who will in your absence cheer us
And has far a wiser head.

7.

Counselors take Romish measures;
Pilots are debarred the helm 50

To a certain Dutch court
Some sparks do resort,
The first of the gang is Carmarthen
Who our senators guides
By sprinkling his bribes
And has helped us to a fine bargain.

33. Daniel Finch, earl of Nottingham, was greatly feared as a church party adviser to
William III because of his eloquence and legal training.

41. *stock:* to put playing cards together in a pack.

45. Macaulay (p. 1958) quotes these four lines and comments, "A Whig poet compares
the two marquesses, as they were often called, and gives George the preference over Tho-
mas." It is doubtful whether a "Whig" would favor the supremacy of "the White Marquess,"
George Saville, marquess of Halifax, for he was still a supporter of the royal prerogative, as
William very well knew. But early in February 1690, Halifax was to resign his office of lord
privy seal and retire from active political life. The satirist is expressing "moderate party"
fears, not Whig aspirations.

47. William's intention to go personally to Irealnd was common knowledge in the first
week of January.

50. Halifax and other trimmers (such as Shrewsbury?) are referred to.

By such as waste the nation's treasures,
    And would gladly sell the realm.
George is jostled out by Thomas
    (Two can't of a trade agree);
Nor must we peace to England promise,   55
    Whilst the Finches favorites be.

8.

The peerage every day are jarring,
    Sick of loyalty and zeal;
Factious members are preparing
    To advance a commonweal.   60
So have I seen two dogs contending
    Who should bear away the bone,
And whilst they are each other rending,
    A third steps in and leaves them none.

53. *George:* the White Marquis (Halifax): *Thomas:* the Black Marquis (Carmarthen).

[JOHN SHEFFIELD, EARL OF MULGRAVE]

The Nine
(1690)

The Nine seems to have been intended as an "advice to a painter" (see line 43), but may have been disseminated as soon as it reached the stage of being a catalogue of nine "characters," members of the cabinet established by William in 1690. The peculiar grammar is also evidence of speedy composition. Macaulay had a manuscript copy of this satire, evidently contemporary, and bearing the date 1690.

THE NINE

1.

A thin ill-natured ghost that haunts the king
Till him, and us, he does to ruin bring,
Impeached and pardoned, impudently rides
The council and the Parliament bestrides,
Where some bought members (like his serving men)   5
To all his lies devoutly say "amen."
This brazen liar, this known carted knave,
Is now the man the church and state must save.

1. Carmarthen (Thomas Osborne, successively 1st earl of Danby, marquis of Carmarthen, and duke of Leeds [1631–1712]) was now lord president and chief adviser to Queen Mary during the king's absence. Macaulay used this line as evidence of Carmarthen's physical appearance.

3. In 1681 Carmarthen had been indicted on the false witness of Edward Fitzharris of plotting Godfrey's murder. He was cleared in 1684.

5. Danby's use of treasury funds for bribing Commons members in the 1670s was not forgotten; but his genius in organizing a court party in the 1690s was severely hampered by lack of funds with which to bring in men whose family and regional interests he well knew how to manipulate for political purposes.

8. *Church and state* is presumably the object of *save.* Carmarthen sets up for leader of the church party and supporter of the royal prerogative.

515

2.

Room for the pink of starched civility!
The emptiness of old nobility!   10
The fop, without distinction, does apply
His bows, and smiles to all promiscuously
With an affected careless wave of his wand,
And tottering on, does neither go nor stand:
So humbly proud and so genteelly dull,   15
Too weak for council and too old for trull,
That to conclude with this bilk-stately thing
He's a mere costly piece of garnishing.

3.

A drowsy wittall drawn down to his last,
Dead before's time for having lived too fast,   20
Lives now upon the wit that's long since gone:
Nothing but bulk remains; the soul is flown.
The little good that's sometimes on him said
Is because men will speak well of the dead.
For when all's done this honest, worthy man   25
Has no remorse for taking what he can.

4.

A grave eye and an o'er-thinking face
Seem to distinguish him from all his race.
But Nature's proud, and scorning all restraint,
By sudden starts shows there's a mortal taint,   30
Which to a good observer makes it plain
The frenzy will ere long break out again.

9. *pink:* the "flower," or finest example of excellence.
10. William Cavendish, earl (later duke) of Devonshire was descended from the famous Elizabethan family of Cavendishes. He was now lord steward of the king's household.
13. *ward:* The lord steward carried a white staff.
16. Devonshire was 49 years old. *trull:* a low prostitute.
17. *bilk-state:* defrauder of the state?
18. Chamberlayne, *Angliae Notitia, 1,* 112, tells us that the lord steward's fee is £1,200.
19. *wittall:* a complaisant cuckold.
20. Charles Sackville, earl of Dorset, now lord chamberlain of the household, did most of his fast living in the 1660s and 1670s, when he was a prominent member of the Court Wits circle. He was now in his fifties.
28. Thomas Herbert, earl of Pembroke, now first lord of the admiralty, had already, in his early thirities, established a reputation for diplomatic gravity and thoughtfulness, having been ambassador to the States General during the first year of the revolution, although his family was otherwise infamous for violence and intemperance.

But after all, to do him right, 'tis sad
The best of all the nine should be stark mad.

5.

A good attorney was spoiled when his ill fate   35
(And ours) made him a secretary of state.
Or if his part had been to give a charge
At county sessions where he might enlarge!
He has a rare method to display a thing
(With mighty force) not worth the mentioning.   40
But the fine gilded reed is much too weak
To bear the weight he's under; he must break.

6.

Next painter, draw a jackanapes of state,
A monkey turned into a magistrate.
A saucy wight borne up with heat and noise,   45
Fit only for a ringleader of boys,
To untile neighbors' houses and to play
Such uncouth gambols on a holiday.
Strange! that so young a government should dote,
So as to let a whirlwind steer the boat.   50

34. The satirist's preference for Pembroke may be a pretense, but if one can take the statement at its face value it would seem that the persona is a Jacobite moderately inclined toward a Tory Williamite position.

35–36. Daniel Finch, earl of Nottingham, had been bred a lawyer, and while a member of the House of Commons, was a lord (eventually first lord) of the admiralty. After succeeding his father in the House of Lords, he gradually became recognized head of the church party, greatly trusted by the clergy. His interest in, and responsibility for, naval affairs continued in the new reign, but it is probable that his legal training and inflexible integrity gave him his real power. He had been secretary of state for the South since 1689, but acted for the earl of Shrewsbury as well from June 1690, when the latter resigned from the Northern Department.

37. *charge:* an official instrument or admonition given by a judge to a jury, by a bishop or archdeacon to his clergy, or by a member of a presbytery or senior minister to a young minister at his ordination. Both legal and ecclesiastical meanings may be drawn upon in this allusion, because of Nottingham's identification with the church party.

41. A sarcastic allusion to his lack of independence? Cf. Queen Mary to King William, 7 July 1690: "I believe Lord President and Lord Nott. agree very well, though I believe the first pretends to govern all; and I see the other is always ready to yield to him" (Dalrymple, 2, pt.2, 133).

43. *jackanapes:* the flamboyant Charles Mordaunt, earl of Monmouth, until recently first commissioner of the treasury.

49. Monmouth, about age 31, was the youngest member of this "government" of nine; Pembroke was a little older; Lowther and Russell were in their late thirties; Marlborough, Nottingham, and Devonshire were in their forties; only Dorset and Danby were over 50.

7.

Ungrateful toadstool! despicable thing!
Thus to betray thy master and thy king!
Nay, he was thy maker too, who, from the dust,
Raised thee—though 'twas to all mankind's disgust.
William, with all his courage, must be afraid   55
To trust the villain who has James betrayed.
For sure, nothing can e'er redeem thy crime
But the same brutal trick a second time.

8.

As rich in words as he is poor in sense,
An empty piece of misplaced eloquence,   60
With a soft voice and a moss-trooper's smile,
The widgeon fain the Commons would beguile;
But he is known, and it is hard to express
How they deride his northern genteelness
While he lets loose the dull insipid stream   65
Of his set speeches, made up of whipped cream.

9.

'Tis here alone you'll find (where'er you seek)
A profound statesman with a cherry cheek;
He has a quick eye and a sprightly glance;
His face is a map of jolly ignorance.   70
The lilies and the roses so disposed
Should not by careful thought be discomposed.
Pity the fat, round, pretty, blushing thing
Should ere be thus condemned to counseling.

51–52. John Churchill, earl of Marlborough. He may have been appointed to the Council of Nine as a military adviser. A note in MS BM Harl. 7317 slanders the of earl Marlborough by stating that although the protégé of the duke of York, the earl "conspired against James and laid with him at night at Salisbury with his army, when he deserted him and ran over to the prince of Orange and had his coach and horses ready to take up the king and carry him away to the prince, whose army and him was nigh Salisbury."

59. Sir John Lowther of Lowther, later Viscount Lonsdale, was at present vice-chamberlain of the household. His appointment to the Council of Nine may be due to Carmarthen's influence. It is strange that so many household officials were so appointed, but Lowther wielded considerable influence in the House of Commons.

61. *moss-trooper:* one of a class of marauders who infested the "mosses" of the Scottish border in the middle of the 17th century; a border freebooter. Lowther was lord lieutenant of Cumberland and Westmorland, and M.P. for Westmorland County.

62. *widgeon:* fool.

68. John Ehrman, *The Navy in the War of William III* (1953), pp. 270–73, gives an excellent account of the life and character of Edward Russell, later earl of Orford. Inset into it is a quotation from this satire that is carefully evaluated in the light of the known facts about Russell.

CHARLES SACKVILLE, EARL OF DORSET

An Excellent New Ballad Givng a true Account of the Birth and Conception of a Late Famous Poem Called the Female Nine

To the Tune of "Packington's Pound"

1690

1.

When Monmouth the chaste read those impudent lines
Which have tied her dear monkey so fast by the loins,
Showed his jackanapes tricks and his apish false smiles,
And set him a-chattering aloft on the tiles,
      She saw with a fright,   5
      Howe'er they came by't,
The rogues had described pretty Whirligig right,
And none can be certain, when scandals begin
To draw so near home, but that they shall come in.

2.

She heard that the nine ladies' turn would be next,   10
And fearing some bungler should mangle the text,
And paint her sweet person like some hagged elf,
She wisely contrived how to draw it herself,
      And luckily hit
      On a method so fit   15
At once to display both her virtue and wit,
Not doubting to have from herself a good word,
And thus she bespoke the kind help of her lord:

3.

"Methinks this same Nine which they count so well writ

---

1. Carey Fraser privately married Charles Mordaunt, then Viscount Mordaunt, about 1678. Mordaunt "owned his lady" in May 1680. The "impudent lines" are of course lines 43–40 of *The Nine*.
7. *Whirligig:* Monmouth.
12. *hagged:* bewitched, haglike.

519

Has nothing of *air, bon sens,* or *l'esprit;*   20
The numbers so rough, and so harsh the *cadence*
As e'en blister a mouth embellished in France,
   Come, *pour amusement,*
   Let us make a song
And do our selves right whome'er we do wrong.   25
We'll give a *beau tour* to the feminine nine
Among whom my prudence and virtue shall shine.

4.

You yourself shall appear the great Turk of the scene
And I'll recommend you so far to the queen
And soothe the vain humor to which you incline   30
As to make you beloved by two of the Nine;
   And that's very fair
   For a poor sickly peer,
Who to my certain knowledge has nothing to spare;
And since these lampoons are the wit of the times,   35
I'll furnish the sense if you'll tag it with rhymes."

5.

Her spouse, fired at this, screamed aloud and cried forth,
And fetching his dead-doing pen in his wrath,
He worked off his piece with such art of the pen
That he aimed at the ladies, but wounded the men,   40
   And labored so hard,
   The doors were all barred,
And none were admitted but trusty Blanchard.
'Twas writ in such haste, you're desired to dispense
With the want of true grammar, good English, or sense.   45

---

26. *beau tour:* apparently a very up-to-date Gallicism: the manner of presenting or exhibiting something.
31. I.e., Lady Pembroke and Lady Nottingham.
43. *Blanchard:* J. P. Kenyon suggests that Blanchard may possibly be Monmouth's steward or butler.

[SIR HENRY SHEERS]

A Long Prologue to a Short Play
(1690)

Luttrell reports a humiliating event in Holland: "The effigies of the earl of Torrington is made in Holland, riding on a dog with two women on his back, one hand combing his peruque, the other filling his pocket with French gold, with this motto in capital letters over his head: The Dutch got the honor, the French the advantage, and the English the shame" (2, 117). The sense of shame produced many bitter attacks by satirists on those that were thought guilty of the fiasco.

Said to have been written by Sir Henry Sheers, the satire borrows the form of a prologue spoken at Oxford; there is nothing to suggest that it was actually meant to be spoken, but the female persona provides an ironic comment on the manliness of English naval men.

A Long Prologue to a Short Play
Spoken by a Woman at Oxford
Dressed Like a Sea Officer

With Monmouth cap and cutlass by my side,
Strutting at least a yard at every stride,
I'm come to tell you (after much petition)
The admiralty has given me a commission,
And now with Tourville I'll engage,   5
And try my fortune on a floating stage.
What blustering tar at this dare take offense,
While I stand thus to prove my just pretense?
Will he pretend to fight better than I?
'S death! I'd tell him "Damn you, sir, you lie!"   10

1. *Monmouth cap*: a flat round cap worn by soldiers and sailors, after the name of the county town.
5. Anne-Hilarion de Cotentin, comte de Tourville, was commander-in-chief of the French Navy against the Confederates at this time.

And then I'd ask him how they fought at Rye.
Your Bantry business too was but a fetch
Where you call running, "battering on a stretch."
But you'll reply, your leaders were to blame,
While I'll condemn you all to bear the shame: 15
For who the devil e'er refused his meat
Because another had no mind to eat?
"The Dutch were drunk," you barbarously say,
Pray next do you be drunk too, so you'll stay,
For 'twas your sober fighting lost the day,   20
For which two millions we at least must pay.
Old Albemarle would say, that men of war
In navy stunk not half enough of tar:
Your o'ergrown pages, and attorney's clerks,
To fight and govern fleets are proper sparks.   25
Then let the spruce land pirates be content
To swagger in their native element,
And let tarpaulins rule by my consent.
For things now look as if men took commission
To damn all discipline and sow sedition,   30
And fighting were the least of their ambition!
No matter who comes home with broken bones,
So you but come to touch the patacoons:
The pitch of honor is desire of money,
That paltry coward vice has quite undone ye.   35

11. *Rye:* between Beachy Head and Dungeness, very near the latter headland. Torrington, after allowing the Dutch van to engage the French off Beachy Head, anchored his fleet to allow the French fleet to move westward with the ebb-tide, and then retreated up-channel past Hastings and Rye to safe anchorage in the mouth of the Thames.

12. *fetch:* contrivance, dodge, stratagem. The battle of Bantry Bay was a mere skirmish, very inconclusive, but sufficient to reassure Englishmen that the new regime's navy was sound and to consolidate the morale of the seamen. The satirist here jeers at Herbert's failure to engage, but the French were just as reluctant. Chateau-Renault, the French admiral, was also able to claim a "victory."

13. *battering on a stretch:* In John Knox Laughton, ed., *Memoirs Relating to Lord Torrington* (Camden Society, 1889) the phrase "continuing the fight upon a stretch" is used (p. 38) of Herbert's action at Bantry Bay in May 1689.

21. The estimates were made known on 9 October 1690 and amounted to £1,791,695.

22. *Albemarle:* George Monck, duke of Albemarle, the hero of the Dutch wars as well as architect of the Restoration. The professional contempt for "gentlemen volunteers" was a product of his experience at sea in 1666.

26. *land pirates:* The implication is that even on land the behavior of these gentlemen volunteers is piratical and that their motive for going to sea is profit, not patriotism.

28. *tarpaulins:* professional seamen.

33. *patacoons:* Portuguese and Spanish silver coins each worth about 4s. 8d. in English money.

You court preferment on no other score
But to be poorly rich, and basely poor;
For who would not propose a trip to Spain
That has in's prospect double gain,
To line his pockets, and to save his skin;   40
For none must fight with merchants' money in.
Your heads run round with Mexico and Seville;
I wish the shipping place were at the devil.
Would the good king had but a just relation,
What infamy, what sums 't has cost the nation,   45
He'd quickly damn your trade of importation,
And add it to the Act of Navigation;
"But how then shall we love," you murmurers say,
'S life! can't you be satisfied with double pay?
Show us your twofold merit, sirs, I pray.   50
Some have got two commands by land and sea,
While one might safely swear (might he be free)
They've neither flesh nor fish nor good red herring,
These are your colonels, captains, with a murrain.
Boldy to those two elements you aspire,   55
But at an awful distance then you fire.
A few there are (and they are very few)
To whom a fairer character is due:
Time was, when captains went on their own errands
And in their pockets carried their press warrants.   60
Now you employ the villains of the fleet,
While you date from the Downs in Bedford Street;
But times are altered, 'tis not now as then,
For now you press the money, spare the men.
Those plain dull fellows no such secrets found   65
To make press warrants worth a hundred pound.
'Tis our fate, our frailty, or disease,
To trust our honor in such hands as these,

38. A reference to the Mediterranean squadron, one of the duties of which was to convoy merchant ships to Cadiz.

50. This accusation that gentlemen volunteers could draw army pay or other emolument for services on land while they were actually at sea drawing naval pay is probably not quite accurate, but little is known about "half-pay" officers at this period.

54. *with a murrain*: an exclamation of anger (*murrain*: plague, pestilence).

62. *Bedford Street*: Inhabited by "eminent tradesmen" according to Strype. The satirist is contrasting trading and naval motives. The Downs was a favorite for naval rendezvous.

65–66. Possession of a press warrant enabled a man to blackmail able-bodied seamen. Thus a captain could obtain £100 from any man willing to misuse the warrant in this manner.

Raw in their trade, their principles not right,
With hearts too tender, and with heads too light,   70
Too weak for council, and too nice to fight.
Their bodies are not made of battering stuff,
Their cracknel carcasses not splinter proof,
And yet will fairly tell a sailor's tale,
But must attempt it in a coat of mail.   75
Some swaggering bully snaps me short and swears,
"Damn me, these fellows would be kicked down stairs."
Sirs, by your leaves, do but fight at sea
And then kick down the Monument for me.
The Parliament may plague us with taxation,   80
But till they cure this grievance of the nation,
Monsieur will make the Narrow Seas his station;
Then what becomes of all our ancient rule,
Our right from Edgar and command from Thule?
Believe me, sirs, it will be then confessed   85
Your flag's a dishclout, and your claim a jest.
The hardy duke we mentioned, whose great name
Stretched the blown cheeks of trumpet-sounding Fame,
Once boldly tried what Englishmen could do.
But such examples who dare now pursue?   90
A four days' fight he gloriously maintained,
And what he lost in blood, in honor gained;
To keep that spotless, he the ocean stained,
Each day he tacked, and fought from sun to sun,
Against the odds at least of two for one.   95
Had you been there, sirs, what would you have done?
He ne'er stood shilly, shally, keep aloof,
But fought as if his skin was cannon proof.
Then all that can be said to do you right,
You'll keep a wind, as long as he did fight.   100

73. *cracknel:* a light, crisp biscuit, of a curved or hollowed shape, easily broken.
79. *the Monument:* the Doric column designed by Wren, erected to commemorate the great fire of London.
84. *right from Edgar:* Edgar (944–75) was popularly held to be the unifier of England, and the originator of the English navy. *command from Thule:* Thule was the mythical land "farthest north" said to be six day's sail from Britain; the British navy thus claimed dominion from the farthest north to the "Narrow Seas."
87: *mentioned:* i.e., in line 22.
91. The Battle of Sole Bay, 1–4 June 1666.
97. *shilly, shally:* to vacillate, to be irresolute.

CHARLES BLOUNT

A Dialogue between King William and the Late King James
(1690)

The appearance of this poem in Charles Blount's *Works* (1695) has resulted in frequent MS ascriptions of the poem to that ill-fated and much maligned deist. The poem is a justification of elective monarchy and seemingly of "right by conquest," a doctrine that William III was at great pains to extirpate from consideration during the arguments about his right to the throne. As such, it could very well have been written by Blount. But there is nothing to prove his authorship except the authority of the editor of his works, Charles Gildon.

A
DIALOGUE BETWEEN
KING WILLIAM AND THE LATE KING JAMES
ON THE BANKS OF THE BOYNE
THE DAY BEFORE THE BATTLE

King James

If injured monarchs may their cause explore,
An uncle's and a father's right is more.
Nature here pleads; your blood is on my side
Each beating pulse and every vein allied.
What fever then has boiled you into arms?   5
Is it religion or a crown that charms?
If a mistaken zeal thus pushed you on,
'Twas hard to shake my glass so nearly done;
The ebbing sand had little more to run.
If from my daughter's right your claim you bring,   10

2. James was uncle to King William (whose mother was James's sister Mary) and father to Queen Mary.
10. Mary was next in the line of succession only if James III (the old Pretender) was ignored.

She's too, too, early queen, whilst I am king;
That crime Rome blushed to punish, you pursue,
Make it your glory and your conscience, too;
A pious parricide, when to your wife
You pay a victim of her father's life.   15
Your love for her appears in that to me,
You praise the fruit and yet cut down the tree.

King William

I took but up that crown you durst not wear,
And am no less your conqueror than heir.
If right divine does e'er to crowns belong,   20
They lose that right when once the kings do wrong.
Them justice sacred makes, law makes 'em strong.
The monarchy you justly once enjoyed
By the same rule as justly you destroyed.
Titles to crowns from civil contracts spring,   25
And he who breaks the law dissolves the king.
Nor can you here a parent's right pretend,
Since public safety knows no private friend,
Thus, generous Pompey for his country drew,
Forgot his Julia, and her Caesar too!   30

King James

New titles may be scaffolded with laws,
And frothy monarchs of the mob's applause
Take up a crown on terms too mean to wear,
Then boast themselves to be the People's heir.
But they who crowns from contracts do receive   35
Are kings at will, and govern but by leave:
A marble Caesar pinioned to a throne,
The People regnant, and the monarch stone.

King William

When free-born men (by Providence designed

12. *crime:* presumably parricide.

19. Right to the throne by conquest was *not* a favored concept at William's court, even
though many Englishmen were willing to accept the principle, for it would mean that anyone
who overthrew William by force would automatically have the right to the throne. The poet
is therefore not reflecting William's real opinions. Even in the matter of the rule of law, Wil-
liam's real opinions were not quite so clear-cut.

29. Pompey the Great had married Caesar's daughter but fought against Caesar in the civil
war. The parallel is not very promising, for Julia died before the civil war, and Pompey was
defeated by Caesar at Pharsalus.

Both to preserve and propagate their kind)   40
Did first their brutish appetites pursue
And force alone was all the law they knew,
When sense was guardian, and when reason young,
'Twas then the weak submitted to the strong.
Then, as the bull walks monarch of the ground,   45
So Nimrod, Cyrus, and the rest were crowned.
For he who could protect, and conquest bring,
Was from a captain ripened to a king.
Thus they the People's safety made their choice,
And Heaven confirmed it by the People's voice.   50
When you to France and priests the laws betrayed,
The injured nation called me to their aid,
And in their choice the noblest title brings,
For subjects are the surest guard of kings.

46. Legends surrounding Nimrod's name made him a symbol of rebellion, treachery, and desertion as well as a hunter and the builder of cities. Like Cyrus, the founder of the Persian empire, he is probably mentioned here as a successful conqueror. Accretions to the legends make it difficult to decide.

THE DUCHESS OF YORK'S GHOST

1691

At dead of night, after an evening ball,
In her own father's lodgings at Whitehall,
As youthful Tullia unregarded lay
By a dull lump of Netherlandish clay,
Whose frozen veins not all her charms could move   5
(The hero is uncapable of love,
Thanks to a secret gripe he got, when young;
The family had rid the states too long).
Neglected thus, the longing, wishing, queen
Contemplates on the gallant youths she'd seen,   10
Whose brisk ideas feed her warm desire,
And fancy adds more fuel to her fire:
When lo! the scene upon the sudden turns,
Her blood grows chill, the taper dimly burns;
A trembling seizes all her limbs with fear   15
At a majestic shade, which does appear,
Draws wide the curtain, and approaches near,
Then thus begins:
"Impious wretch! behold thy mother's ghost,
By fate's permission, come from Stygian coast,   20
To warn you of that vengeance Heaven provides
To punish unrepenting parricides!
Can quiet slumber ever close thy eyes?
Or is thy conscience sunk too low to rise?
From this same place was not thy aged sire   25
Compelled by midnight summons to retire?
Then, with a canting, fulsome trick of state,
The world was bantered with an 'abdicate';

1. Cf. *Tarquin and Tullia*, 106.
2. See Evelyn, 22 February 1688/89, for his rather scandalized report of Queen Mary's behavior at Whitehall after the coronation. She "went about from room to room, to see the convenience of Whitehall; lay in the same bed and apartment where the late queen lay; and within a night or two, sat down to play at basset, as the queen her predecessor used to do."
3. Mary II was nearly 29 at this time.
4. William III's reputed coldness to his queen was based on the folklore stereotype of the Dutchman.
7. *gripe*: the "clutch" or "pinch" of something painful. Presumably, the satirist is implying that someone opposed to the house of Orange deliberately maimed him when a child.
19. Anne Hyde, first wife of James, duke of York, had died in 1671.
25. James II was 55 at the time of the revolution.

Had he been murdered, it had mercy shown,
'Tis less to kill a king, than to dethrone: 30
The miserable in their graves find rest,
But his afflictions cannot be expressed.
So great a monarch to be brought so low,
And his own children strike the fatal blow,
Distracts his soul, and breaks his heart with woe; 35
Go learn of Afric monsters nature's law,
Whose sacred ties those savage brutes do awe,
A lesson yet unlearned by grand Nassau.
Where are those crimes of which he was accused?
How is the nation gulled, and he abused! 40
How boldly did some villains sell their king,
Engaging to the next Sanhedrim to bring
Substantial proof of warming-pan intrigue,
Of horrid murders, and a Gallic league!
The senate met, and time has slipped two years, 45
But no proof made, no witness yet appears.
They did pretend to know the place, when, and how;
Where are those Fergusons and Braddons now?
Those bold defamers are grown hush and still
For lack of evidence, not want of will. 50
Consider by what men this work is done,
Chief agents in the revolution,
The major part composed of such as these:
Old lechers, atheists, public debauchees,

38. William, prince of Orange, was of the house of Nassau, so many Jacobites referred to him as "Nassau" to avoid giving him higher titles (including king of England).

42. *Sanhedrim:* Parliament.

43. James II had attempted to clear away the "warming-pan" theory of the birth of the Prince of Wales by calling an Extraordinary Council. The report of this Privy Council meeting was then published.

44. Presumably a reference to the death in the Tower of Arthur Capel, earl of Essex. See line 48 *n. Gallic league:* i.e., with Louis XIV, to root out heresy.

45. The Convention Parliament sat from 22 January 1689. If "two years" is to be taken literally, this poem was written in January 1691.

48. Lawrence Braddon in Hilary Term 1683 was tried and convicted of a high misdemeanor in endeavoring to raise a belief that the earl of Essex did not kill himself in the Tower, contrary to what was found by the coroner's inquest. He was fined £2000. Not until 22 June 1691 was he discharged of the penalties. Robert Ferguson, the plotter, accompanied William of Orange to England at the revolution, but by 1693 was a suspected Jacobite. A satire purporting to be sung by a high churchman claims that, in 1690, the church Tories had taken care not only to print a book called *Brethren in Inquity* (1690) accusing Papists and Whigs of plotting against monarchy, but also to have Ferguson seized as a suspect.

Traitors proscribed, known cheats, and perjured knaves.   55
This sanctimonious crew the nation saves;
These blessed reformers have the king dethroned;
Under such Pharisees Judea groaned.
Of natives these; to them a foreign aid
Of vermin, who adore no God but trade,   60
Insects, who once a monarchy obeyed;
But by rebellion did themselves create
From a poor province to a mighty state;
Unjust and cruel to the last degree,
Griping at wealth by fraud and perfidy;   65
Barbarous, bloody, where they once trepan,
(Witness Amboyna, and the Isles Japan,
In which last place the monsters did deny
For dear commerce their Christianity).
Can any thing that's good from Holland come,   70
The very sink and plague of Christendom?
A Dutchman is a rogue; whate'er he seems,
No muddy fountain can yield crystal streams.
Awake, Britannia, guard thy sinking crown,
Which by republicans is pulling down!   75
Ambitious Orange serves but for a tool;
They set him up, that they themselves may rule.
For, one usurper's title being good,
The right of princes lies not in the blood,
Nor is confined to any certain line.   80
Possession makes all government divine:
Good pagan doctrine! broached to serve all times;
Success will sanctify the worst of crimes.

60. The trading rivalry of the English and the Dutch prompted these anti-Dutch sentiments.

61. *monarchy:* Charles I of Spain relinquished the Netherlands to his son Philip II in the early 16th century.

62. *rebellion:* William the Silent began the revolt in 1568. The northern provinces, Protestant in religion, formed a "mighty state" by the Declaration of Utrecht in 1579 and began to build the mighty commercial empire that made them the natural rivals of England in the 17th century.

66. *trepan:* to catch in a trap; to ensnare, beguile.

67. The massacre of English merchants at Amboyna was a popular subject for anti-Dutch propaganda during the Dutch wars, and English jealousy of the exclusive footing in Japan secured by Dutch merchants explains the other allusion. Japanese by custom and law treated all foreigners with cruelty if they set foot on their soil.

75. The "republicans" are presumably both English and Dutch, and are largely a figment of the monarchists' imagination. In one satire England is depicted as a horse being ridden so hard by the Dutch that his old master will scarcely recognize him.

In former days, when English kings did err,
The fault was punished in the counselor;   85
But now poor James is into exile sent,
And not one statesman brought to punishment;
For priests and advocates have wondrous skill
To qualify the same things good or ill,
And can produce, from Scripture and the laws,   90
Arguments pro and con for any cause.
Night's watchful sentinel here blew his horn,
A certain sign of the approaching morn;
Which summons wandering spirits to retire
Into their prisons of a purging fire.   95
"I must be gone," the ghost then said, "Farewell!
What you have seen and heard your sister tell:
Repent your crimes, before it be too late,
And by contrition, shun impending fate."
Thus having said, the vision disappears,   100
Leaving the trembling princess drowned in tears.

92. I.e., the cock crowed.
97. *sister*: Anne, princess of Denmark. Jacobites hated her as much as they hated Mary.

The False Favorite's Downfall
(1692)

This poem, obviously written by a Jacobite for Jacobites (see line 60), summarizes most of the vicious slanders concocted by those who thought of John Churchill, duke of Marlborough, as the archtraitor to James II. The cause of Marlborough's temporary loss of royal favor is still rather obscure, but his influence over Princess Anne seems to have annnoyed Queen Mary.

THE FALSE FAVORITE'S DOWNFALL

1.

Deserted and scorned, the proud Marlborough sate
Upbraiding himself with the turn of his fate
Till, o'ercharged with sorrow, he raiséd his head
And in praise of himself, and his family, said:
      "The staff I did wield   5
      At the court (ne'er in field)
I now to a Sooterkin Dutchman must yield.
Ah, Churchill! how much better mightst thou prevail,
Would'st thou hang up thy sword, and stick to thy tail!

2.

"Must I who in battles such wonders did do,   10
(That still my own guts and my breeches do rue)

---

1. Luttrell *2*, 342, describes how on the morning of 20 January 1692, Marlborough put on the king's shirt as usual; before noon he had received notice from the earl of Nottingham that the king had no further service for him, so that he was cut out of all his places.

5. *staff*: presumably a baton indicating his military rank.

6. Churchill had in fact taken part in several campaigns. He had fought at Sole Bay in 1672 and was wounded in the siege of Maastricht in 1673.

7. *Sooterkin*: the alleged rat-shaped afterbirth of Dutch women.

9. *tail*: perhaps an allusion to Churchill's celebrated affair with Charles II's mistress, the duchess of Cleveland, twenty years before.

Must I, who alone did a regiment maul,
By receiving their pay and carrying off all,
    (Nay stories can tell
      I fought it so well, 15
I stripped very many, though ne'er a one fell.)
Ah, Churchill! etc.

3.

"Admit that I have no desert of my own,
Yet that of our family's publicly known. 20
My mother ne'er failed to quench the chaste fire
Of every young spark who declared his desire;
    Nay, since her youth's past,
      She her time does not waste,
But procures that for others which she cannot taste. 25
Ah, Churchill! etc.

4.

"The spawn of the sexton, my sister, you'll find,
Enjoyed once by all, now scorned by mankind,
The sink of the nation, outcast of the stews, 30
As pocky as Hinton, as lewd as Peg Hughes;
    Nay, one would have swore
      That had seen this sly whore,
When she married the colonel, she'd ne'er done it more.
Ah, Churchill! etc. 35

5.

"There's the bully, my brother, the lord of the seas,

12–16. This Jacobite slander was embroidered in later years into the well-known charge that Marlborough, as paymaster-general of his forces, drew the pay of soldiers killed in battle in order to line his own pockets. Here he is apparently accused of taking the pay of non-existent soldiers, or embezzling the pay of existing soldiers.

27. Marlborough's sister, Arabella Churchill, at this time wife of Colonel Charles Godfrey, had been mistress to James II from about 1667 to 1676.

28. This calumny no doubt originated in the date of her birth, when Sir Winston was a royalist refugee in rebel territory. She was the first child of the marriage, which apparently took place in May 1644.

31. *Hinton:* Mall Hinton was a famous whore. *Peg Hughes:* Margaret Hughes had been mistress to Sir Charles Sedley, and (in the early 70s) to Prince Rupert.

34. The actual date of the marriage has not been determined.

36–37. George Churchill indeed was a gentleman commander in the navy and was eventually to become an admiral. But his courage is falsely aspersed. He commanded a brigade at Landen in 1693.

Who ne'er fired a gun but to their majesties.
My wife (the dear partner of my marriage bed)
Though disarmed of the rest, takes care of my head.
    The peer with one eye   40
    Does as oft with her lie,
As Portland with him I raised so high.
Ah, Churchill! etc.

6.

"Lest I should a line of such worthies disgrace,
Great deeds I have done to ennoble my race: 45
I pimped for my sister when first she turned whore,
And the title of lord I got on her score;
    I always took care
    That whene'er I did swear,
My oath was as false and as common as her.   50
Ah, Churchill! etc.

7.

"At last to complete my life and my glory,
And make me renowned for ever in story,
I called foreign forces our religion to aid;
And so by that cheat, king and country betrayed.   55
    My master dethroned,
    The true prince disowned,
I fall by the man I unjustly have crowned.
Then I the mark of ingratitude stand
For betraying the church and enslaving the land."   60

39. *wife:* Sarah, second daughter of Richard Jennings of Sandridge, Herts.
40. I.e., gives him the cuckold's horns.
41. Charles Talbot, earl of Shrewsbury.
42. This calumny has been given unworthy credence by Macaulay (p. 1819).
43. The accusation of homosexual relations between William III and Hans Willem Bentick, duke of Portland, is also part of the stock-in-trade of the lampooners.
48. The Duchess of Marlborough in 1744 countered this: "Now I fain would have any reasonable body tell me what the duke of Marlborough could do when a boy at school to prevent the infamy of his sister" (Winston L. S. Churchill, *Marlborough, His Life and Times* [London, 1947], *1,* 46).
57. Churchill was not one of those who signed the invitation, but he did send a letter to William by Henry Sidney in August.

CHARLES SACKVILLE, EARL OF DORSET

À Madame, Madame B, Beauté Sexagenaire
(1693)

The identity of the addressee of the poem (Madame B) and the identity of the subject (Mopsa) are closely bound with the problem of the date and the authorship. The poem's inclusion in scriptorium MSS of 1695 provides a *terminus ad quem;* the relative position in the roughly chronological sequence of poems in those MSS as well as the explicit date "1693" in one of them and in the earliest printed source helps to fix the occasion. One MS of dubious textual authority, however, suggests the date 1694. The scribe of this MS identified the addressee as Mrs. D——P, and this, in combination with the variant "Doll" in line 1, suggests that he thought the addressee was one Dorothy P——. Mopsa, according to him, was the countess of Manchester. The sexagenarian Anne Yelverton, dowager countess of Manchester, had married (shortly before 18 February 1688) the twenty-six-year-old Charles Montagu, later to be created earl of Halifax. Most texts are agreed in supporting this identification of Mopsa, so it is understandable why the scribe of the text dated 1694 should assert that the poem was "supposed to be written by her husband Mr Montagu," a tradition hardened into apparent fact by later printings. The earliest texts ascribe the poem to Charles Sackville, earl of Dorset—a much more likely attribution.

If the poem is by Dorset and is indeed an attack on Lady Manchester, his choice of an addressee may perhaps be guessed at. Not only would she be an equally aged beauty, but also, in accordance with Dorset's common satirical strategy, she would be of a very low social standing in contrast to the countess. As Dorset in earlier years frequently wrote poems in sardonic and two-edged praise of various ladies of easy virtue, one might speculate that "Moll" is perhaps the notorious Moll Howard or, less likely, Moll Hinton. If we may believe a lampoon of 1690, Moll Howard was the principal procuress of Southborough, or chief of the demimonde who frequented this village a mile or two north of Tunbridge Wells. Dorset's *Lamentation for Moll Howard's Absence,* a satire probably of the late 70s or early 80s, established Dorset's intimacy with her during one season at Tunbridge. In a Tunbridge satire of 1696, she is said to be "now decayed" and is included among contemporaries who "are all too old for new lampoons."

Moll Hinton seems a less likely candidate. Dorset's name was apparently linked with hers a decade or so earlier, when she was, as well as Moll Howard, a frequenter of the playhouse.

À Madame,
Madame B, Beauté
Sexagenaire

Courage, dear Moll! and drive away despair;
Mopsa, who in her youth was scarce thought fair,
In spite of age, experience, and decays,
Set up for charming in her fading days:
Snuffs her dim eyes to give one parting blow—   5
Have at the heart of every ogling beau!
This goodly goose, all feathered like a jay,
So gravely vain and so demurely gay,
Last night, to grace the court, did overload
Her bald buff forehead with a high commode;   10
Her steps were managed with such tender art
As if each board had been a lover's heart.
In all her air, in every glance, was seen
A mixture strange 'twixt fifty and fifteen.
Crowds of admiring fops about her press—   15
Hampden himself delivers their address,
Which she accepting, with a nice disdain,
Owned 'em her subjects and began to reign.
Fair Queen of Fopland is her royal style:
Fopland, the greater part of this great Isle,   20
Nature did ne'er more equally divide
A female heart 'twixt piety and pride.
Her watchful maids prevent the peep of day,
And all in order on her toilet lay;

5. *Snuffs*: to make clearer or brighter; to purge.
7. *jay*: a showy or flashy woman, one of light character.
10. *buff*: of the nature or appearance of buff leather. *commode*: a tall headdress fashionable at this time, consisting of a wire framework variously covered with silk or lace; sometimes with streaming lappets that hung over the shoulders.
16. Probably Richard Hampden, a leader of the "Beaux," the chancellor of the Exchequer.

Prayer book and patch box, sermon notes and paint,   25
At once t'improve the sinner and the saint.

Farewell, friend Moll, expect no more from me;
But if you would a full description see,
You'll find her somewhere in the litany
With pride, vainglory, and hypocrisy.   30

25. Pope imitated this line in *The Rape of the Lock*, I: 138: "Puffs, powders, patches bibles, billet-doux."

CHARLES SACKVILLE, EARL OF DORSET

On the Countess of Dorchester
(1694)

("Dorinda's sparkling wit and eyes" and "Tell me Dorinda, why so gay?")

A decade before the revolution, Charles Sackville, earl of Dorset, wrote a poem beginning "Sylvia methinks you are unfit" in which he attacked Catherine Sedley after she had become mistress to the duke of York. Pinto (*Sedley* p. 138) dated the first two stanzas of "Dorinda's sparkling wit and eyes" even earlier—in 1677—but there is no external evidence that supports the conjecture. Most commentators have accepted, without question, the date 1680 attached to two printed sources of "Tell me Dorinda, why so gay," but as Catherine Sedley was only twenty-two or twenty-three in 1680, it is most unlikely that a mere three years as the duke of York's mistress had resulted in "a ruined face." For both poems, the MS sources suggest a much later date.

The first of the two poems survives in a five-stanza version in four substantive texts and in a four-stanza version in two others. The first two stanzas of this poem survive as a separate poem in three substantive texts; stanzas four and five survive as a separate poem in only one substantive text. Were two poems (or even three?) combined to make one, or was a five-stanza original broken down into two? Literary taste suggests the first possibility; textual evidence rather equivocally suggests the second. It would seem that the transmitters of the text, actuated by their literary preconceptions, attempted to edit the poem into a more acceptable shape and ultimately produced two poems.

The countess is frequently castigated in the Tunbridge satires of the period. In 1690 her name is linked with that of George Howard, earl of Suffolk, but a second poem exonerates her from the implied charge of looseness of behavior. Cryptic insinuations about her reputation are also made in the winter of 1695. She was said to stand very well at court in the winter of 1692, but there are frequent stories of her brazen behavior in both Queen Mary's and Princess Anne's entourages. Her advantageous capture of Sir David Colyear was her crowning triumph, and naturally brought her to the attention of the court satirist, Lord Chamberlain Dorset.

On the Countess of Dorchester

Dorinda's sparkling wit and eyes,
    United, cast so fierce a light,
Which blazes high, but quickly dies,
    Warms not the heart but hurts the sight.

Love is a calm and tender joy,   5
    Kind are his looks and soft his pace,
Her Cupid is a blackguard boy
    That runs his link into your face.

Proud with the spoils of royal cully,
    With false pretense to wit and parts,   10
She swaggers like a battered bully
    To try the courage of men's hearts.

Though she's set out as charming fine
    As jet and gems and paint can make her,
She ne'er shall win a heart like mine—   15
    The devil or Sir Davy take her.

Her bed is like the Scripture feast
    None she invited came
So, disappointed of her guest
    She took up with the blind and lame.   20

On the Countess of Dorchester

1.

Tell me Dorinda, why so gay?
    Why such embroidery, fringe, and lace?

7. *blackguard:* a shoe-black or street Arab.

8. *link:* a torch made of tow and pitch, for lighting people's way along the streets.

9. Pinto (*Sedley*, p. 135) believes that the two previous stanzas form a poem written much earlier, possibly 1677, when Mrs. Sedley first appeared at court and before she became the duke of York's mistress. The following stanzas, however, were written late in 1694.

16. Sir David Colyear did take her, for he married her in August 1696.

17. Matt. 22.

20. Sir David (who was about the same age as his future wife) was, according to Macky, a brave and bold officer of foot, punctilious in matters of honor, "pretty well shaped, dresses clean, has but one eye." He implies that it was the countess of Dorchester's estate that overcame any scruples about marrying the cast mistress of King James. It is probable that he suffered from "lameness" due to war wounds.

Can any dresser find a way
To stop the approaches of decay,
   And mend a ruined face?   5

2.

Wilt thou still sparkle in the box
   And ogle in the Ring?
Can'st thou forget thy age and pox?
Can all that shines on shells and rocks
   Make thee a fine young thing?   10

3.

So have I seen in larder dark
   Of veal, a lucid loin,
Replete with many a heatless spark
(As wise philosophers remark)
   At once both stink and shine.   15

7. Presumably the Ring in Hyde Park.

Oxford Barber's Verses
(1695)

Anthony Wood reported on Shrove Monday, 4, February 1695, that the university verses on the death of the queen were published at Oxford. It is just possible that the following poem anticipated the publication, for academic collections of verses commemorating the birth, marriage, death, or other significant event in the royal family had long been customary in both universities. *Pietas Universitatis Oxoniensis* (1695) contained verses in Latin, Greek, Hebrew, Arabic, Persian, Turkish, Syriac, Samaritan, Ethiopic, Egyptian, Malay, Welsh, and Old English. *Lacrymae Cantabrigienses* (1695) confined itself to Latin, Hebrew, Greek, French, and English. It is therefore obvious why an Oxford barber should be chosen as the persona of a poem lampooning the pretentious academic collections.

Oxford Barber's Verses
on the Queen's Death

Soon as the dismal news came down
And spread itself about the town,
I in a trice, with heavy soul,
As snails their horns, drew in my pole;
Shut shop and, in a passion, swore   5
I'd never use my scissors more,
Since Lachesis so rash had been
To cut the thread of gracious queen.
But I, designing more
Than ever barber did before,   10
Resolved on the too sad occasion
To exercise a strange vocation—
Rhyme, the great business of the nation.

7. *Lachesis:* with Clotho and Atropos, one of the Fates of Greek myth. The barber's "learned" allusion gives the scissors to the wrong Fate.

I thought it arrant shame to fetter
Free English sense in foreign meter;   15
For none do bury, I conjecture,
Folks in outlandish manufacture.
Not but that I my grief could tell
In any other tongue as well:
Whether in Turkish or Arabic   20
In Ethiopic or Malabric
In Cambro-Britannic or Togray
Or lingo Balaam's ass did bray.
But why should I my readers vex
With those barbarian dialects?   25
In short, already I have ended
And done what I at first intended.
'Tis uncorrected, unamended;
No tutor did this work peruse,
Nor money hired a hackney muse—   30
Though that's the fashion of the town.
This, I protest, is all my own.

17. The Act that provided that all persons should be buried in woollen, which came into force in 1678, was designed not only to foster England's most important industry, but also to conserve linen rags for paper-making.

21. *Malabric:* possibly a Hudibrastic nonce-word from "Malay" by analogy with "Ethiopic."

22. *Cambro-Britannic:* The British language of Wales. *Togray:* possibly a Hudibrastic nonce-word to achieve a rhyme with "bray."

23. Num. 22: 28.

29. Oxford tutors frequently helped their students to write the verses expected of them on such occasions. For instance, Rochester's tutor, Robert Whitehall, is said by Anthony à Wood to have been the author of the verses ascribed to Rochester in *Britannia Rediviva* (1660).

30. *hackney muse:* a muse put out for hire, like a hackney coach.

A Jacobite Scot in Satire
(1695)

This poem illustrates very well how a satire directed against one object may
be twisted by context to attack another. The last two lines change the object
of the satire from William III to his enemies, the staunch Scottish Jacobites.
The apparent author of the verses ("a Jacobite Scot") may be a mere statis-
tical persona, for songs in the Scotch fashion were very popular toward the
end of the century in London.

A Jacobite Scot in Satire on England's Unparalleled Loss

Is Wolly's wife now dead and gone?
    I'se sorry for't he's left alone.
O cursed Death, I do thee ban!
    That took the wife and left the man.
Come Atropos now with thy knife   5
    And take the man to his guid wife;
And when thou hast rid us of the knave,
    A thousand thanks then thou shalt have.
        Is the opinion of a false
        Jacobite loon.   10

3. *ban:* to curse, anathemize, interdict.
5. *Atropos:* Cf. *Oxford Barber's Verses,* 7 *n.*

[HENRY HALL]

Upon the King's Return from Flanders
1695

Rejoice you sots, your idol's come again,
To pick your pockets and kidnap your men.
Give him your moneys, and his Dutch your lands.
Ring not your bells ye fools, but wring your hands.

Death and the Cobbler
(1695)

Macaulay, in dealing with the victory of Charles Montagu and Sir Stephen Fox over Sir Walter Clarges in the election (held at the end of October) for Westminster, claims that, "In the course of the night which followed the nomination [of Montagu and Fox], broadsides filled with invectives against the two courtly upstarts who had raised themselves by knavery from poverty and obscurity to opulence and power were scattered all over the capital" (Macaulay, p. 2558). Only one of these invectives in verse has survived, however, and it is directed against Clarges, not against his Whig opponents. And although Macaulay also claims that "the bishop of London canvassed openly against the government," it is the duke of Leeds whose canvassing is here ridiculed. A subtitle in a poor version of the text actually states that the poem was "supposed to be written by Mr. Montagu who stood against Sir W. Clarges for Parliament man." The poem does not show party malice so much as confident amusement at the downfall of the old Tory. Tory principles were no longer the dominant theory of government, and the fallen leaders could be treated with lofty condescension.

DEATH AND THE COBBLER

Being a Full and True Account of the Late Conference
Between a Meager Duke and Will Green, Cordwainer, of
Saint James's, Westminster.

Says His Grace to Will Green, whom he found in his stall,
"Sir, hearing you pay scot and lot for your awl,
I am come here in person and humbly entreat

1. *His Grace:* Thomas Osborne, marquis of Carmarthen, had been created duke of Leeds on 4 May 1694. As the old stateman's political influence waned, he was given compensatory honors. The number of satires that mention him steadily declined as his power declined. *Will Green:* William Green, cordwainer (a shoemaker, or one who works in cordwain or cordovan), owed his franchise to the fact that he was a householder paying scot and lot (a tax levied by a municipal corporation in proportionate shares upon its members for the defraying of municipal expenses).

You will help little Wat in the courtier's defeat.
Honest friend, here's my hand; you'll be welcome at hell   5
And shall have all my custom, who pay very well."
    The cobbler stared hard at his garter and star,
And replied, "Since Your Highness descendeth so far
(For I have not been used to see dukes at my door
Though your wife and your daughter had called here before),   10
I promise my vote, if you'll tell me the case
Wherein a poor Mouse could anger Your Grace?"
    "You must know I had taken some gold on account
Of my favor or so (as courtiers are wont)
And this rogue, among others, did make such a pother   15
In bawling for justice from one House to the other,
They fairly at last put my friend in the pound."
"That's hard." "Nay, what's worse, they made me refund."
"But you had it again?" "Not a groat, by my troth."
"Indeed? Nay then, you have cause to be wroth.   20
But yet, an 't shall please you, I wish you prevail;
These vagabonds scorn your roast beef and your ale."
"But sure, they remember what things have been done
For this nation by me, my wife, and her son!

4. *little Wat*: Sir Walter Clarges was the son of Sir Thomas, one of the "grand old men" of the Parliament. The "courtiers" were Sir Stephen Fox and Charles Montagu. Fox had been returned for Westminster in the previous Parliament, while Montagu had been member for Maldon.

5. Hell is presumably the home of the "thin ill-natured ghost" that was the nickname of the "White Marquis." (See *The Nine*, 1.)

7. Leeds had been installed Knight of the Garter in succession to the earl of Bristol as long ago as 1677.

10. Bridget, duchess of Leeds, had not been mentioned in the satires since the days of her husband's greatest power under William III.

12. *Mouse*: Charles Montagu, still known by the nickname conferred upon him in 1687.

15. The main "rogue" seems to have been Thomas Wharton, comptroller of the household and the chairman of the joint committee of the two Houses.

17. Sir Thomas Cook, unsuccessful Tory candidate for the mayoralty of London in September 1693, M.P. for Colchester, and during 1692 and 1693 governor of the East India Company. He had been deputy governor under Sir Joseph Herne in 1690 and 1691. He was ordered to be committed prisoner to the Tower of London on 26 March 1694 for refusing to divulge how he distributed a sum of £90,000 allowed to him by the East India Company for their "special service."

18. The money had apparently not left the hands of Monsieur John Robart, who after six months gave it to Bates to pay back on the morning that Sir Thomas Cook was first examined (i.e., 26 March 1694).

22. *These vagabonds*: the electors, whom it was traditional to woo with roast beef and ale.

24. Peregrine Osborne (1658–1729), son of the duke of Leeds, had made his name as a naval commander and had helped to capture the men involved in Preston's plot of 1690. The duchess of Leeds probably did nothing of particular note for the nation, but as a representative of the Bertie family, whose ramifications in Lincolnshire, Oxfordshire, the peerage, and

You know, I suppose, that I married the king?" 25
"No, indeed; though your chaplain talks much of that thing.
But, my lord, shall I tell you my mind very plain
(And they say you love truth). You tap it in vain;
The squire will out-poll us and 'peach you again."

Parliament were well known, she was a suitable butt for the satirist.

25. Browning (*Danby*, *1*, 252, *n.* 1) deals with Danby's role in bringing about the marriage of the Princess Mary to the prince of Orange in 1677.

28. *tap it:* act as tapster (presumably in the matter of ale, as mentioned in line 22).

29. Wharton had moved the impeachment in the House of Commons on 27 April and was sent to the Lords with the impeachment.

WILLIAM PITTIS

The Battle Royal between Dr. Sherlock, Dr. South, and Dr. Burnet
(1695)

The publication of William Sherlock's *A Vindication of the Doctrine of the Holy and Ever Blessed Trinity* (1690) did not attract quite as much attention as his more famous (or infamous) *Case of the Allegience Due . . .* , which appeared four months later in November 1690. But by January or February 1691, as the controversy over allegiance was beginning to simmer down, the range of attacks on Sherlock began to widen to take into account what seemed to many people to be unorthodox views of the Trinity put forward in Sherlock's *Vindication.*

THE BATTLE ROYAL
BETWEEN DR. SHERLOCK, DR. SOUTH, AND DR. BURNET

To the Tune of "A Soldier and a Sailor"

1.

A dean and prebendary
Had once a new vagary,
And were at doubtful strife, sir,
Who led the better life, sir,
And was the better man.　　　　　　　　5

2.

The dean, he said that truly
Since Bluff was so unruly,
He'd prove it to his face, sir,
That he had the most grace, sir,
And so the fight began.　　　　　　　　10

1. William Sherlock had succeeded Tillotson as dean of St. Paul's. Robert South had been prebendary of Westminister since 1663, when he was a chaplain of Charles II.
7. *Bluff:* evidently a nickname for South.
10. This is Sherlock's counterargument to the "nominal" Trinitarian's claim of orthodoxy.

3.

When preb replied like thunder,
And roared out, 'twas no wonder,
For Gods the dean had three, sir,
And more by two than he, sir,
For he had got but one.   15

4.

Now while these two were raging,
And in disputes engaging,
The master of the Charter
Said, both had caught a Tartar,
For Gods, that there were none.   20

5.

And all the books of Moses
Were nothing but supposes,
And he deserved rebuke, sir,
Who wrote the Pentateuch, sir,
'Twas nothing but a sham.   25

6.

And as for Father Adam,
With Mrs. Eve his madam,
And what the serpent spoke, sir,
Was nothing but a joke, sir,
And well-invented flam.   30

7.

Thus in this battle royal,
As none would take denial,
The dame for which they strove, sir,

15. South's charge of tritheism against Sherlock (see Headnote) is summed up in *Biographia Britannica*, 6, 3683: "He [Sherlock] thought there were three eternal minds, two of these issuing from the Father, but that these were one by a mutual consciousness in the three to every of their thoughts." Tom Brown makes merry with Sherlock by making Jo Haynes, in describing his descent into the underworld, explain that "the three-headed Geryon put me in mind of the master of the temple's three intellectual minds" (*The Works of Mr. Thomas Brown, in Prose and Verse*, 1707, 2, 2).

22. Thomas Burnet master of the Charter-House, had published in 1692 *Archaeologia philosophicae*, in which he impugned the divine authority of the Old Testament. He had not actually become involved in the Trinitarian controversy as such, but is dragged in by Pittis to make a witty point.

Could neither of 'em love, sir,
For all had given offense.   35

8.

She therefore slyly waiting,
Left all three fools a-prating,
And being in a fright, sir,
Religion took her flight, sir,
And ne'er was heard of since.   40

On Squire Neale's Projects
(1696)

Thomas Neale, groom-porter of the court from 1678, master of the Mint from 1686, incorrigible "projector" and speculator, became a national figure when in 1693 he set up a private lottery "after the Venetian manner." But Neale's greatest fame (or notoriety) came with the First Million Lottery, which was in effect the first state sweepstake. On 23 March 1694, royal assent was given to an act of Parliament which granted Their Majesties duties amounting to £140,000 to be used as a public bank to raise a million pounds for carrying on the war. The million was to be raised by shares that were to be repaid over a number of years at 10 percent interest, and 2,500 shares that would carry an extra chance of winning a prize by lot. Neale not only gained the rewards but also the penalties of the project, which included satirical attack. In one satire entitled *Upon Mr. Neale's Projecting New Taxes* (1695) "Bankrupt Neale" is accused of attempting to cheat people into poverty:

> And leave our children like his own
> To gnaw upon a naked bone;
> And we ourselves this year shall be
> Turned to a Million Lottery,
> Where for two thousand that get plumbs
> Ninety-eight thousand suck their thumbs.

On Squire Neale's Projects

Your Musgraves, Clarges, Harleys, Foleys, Lowthers,
Who in the House are wont to make great pothers
And squander taxes-time in long debates,
To save those foolish trifles our estates—
Be silent now, and for the public weal   5
Give ear to learned Barbon, prudent Neale!
Those oracles, raised by relenting fate
Both to direct and prop the puzzled state
(As once the hungry geese in Capitol
Saved Rome from the same direful foe, the Gaul),   10
And ne'er did fate or human wisdom yet
More proper tools to the employment fit.
For, who can help so well at a dead lift
As those who always live by shark and shift?
Most members in vacation take their pleasure,   15
Or waste their time upon their private treasure;
Whilst these great public souls, humbly content
With the bare privilege of being pent,
And safe ensconced within their forts at home,
Against the assaults of dun and dreadful bum,   20
Lay out their hireling thoughts how to reduce
The French by bringing us to wooden shoes.
  As the old monkey who his tail had lost
Did the convenience of bare buttocks boast;
Advise his friends to the same amputation   25
As the most useful and becoming fashion;
So Neale (who long since threw his lands away,

1. Sir Christopher Musgrave, Sir Thomas Clarges, Robert Harley, Paul Foley, and Sir John Lowther were leaders of the country party in the House of Commons. They represented in different ways the "country" interest.

3. Efforts to avoid land taxes and a general excise were strenuously made during "taxes time." Country getlemen were eager to have the wealthy merchants contribute more to the tax coffers.

6. *Barbon:* Dr. Nicholas Barbon is listed as a placeman in MS Rawl. D 846. There the comment is "his privileges are worth to him £1000 per annum". *Neale:* Thomas Neale, M.P. for Ludgershall borough, Wiltshire, is also listed in MS Rawl. D 846. The comment provided on him is "Groom-porter, master and worker of the Mint, with a reward of £10,000 lately given him."

13. *at a dead lift:* in an extremity.

14. *by shark and shift:* by practicing fraud or the arts of a "shark," parasite, or sharper.

20. *bum:* bum-bailiff.

His wife's exchequer, prince's boons, at play;
Has been his own executor and heir,
And sunk his desperate ruins past repair;   30
Whose life all parts of Fortune's wheel hath seen
And a mere bubble in all senses been)
To level the whole nation to his size
Cries up the advantages of blank and prize,
Loudly proclaims the only way to baffle   35
The French, is to put all estates in raffle.
Trust chance with what you have already got,
Draw lots whether you shall eat bread or not,
Whilst he like state groom-porter holds the stakes,
And out of all events a living makes.   40
So drunken vintner, meeting with mishap,
Shrinks into drawer and still lives by the tap.
　　The amphibious doctor (who more years hath spent
In making mortar than medicament),
Many fair palaces and fields defaced   45
And stately nothings on the same spots placed,
Has made the suburbs to outswell the town
Yet han't a hut which he dares call his own;
In new foundations has the ruins laid
Of many artists whom he never paid,   50
Stuffed the King's Bench, the Fleet, Mint, and Whitefriars

34. Neale's proposals for his first private lottery point out the superiority of his "blanks" and prizes to those provided in Venice. His later private lotteries point out the superiority of his ventures even to his own Million Lottery and (of course) to rival imitations.

39. Neale had been groom-porter (of the household) since 1678; he is wittily accused here of coveting a similar position in the state. The principal functions of the groom-porter were to regulate all matters connected with gaming within the precincts of the royal court, to furnish cards and dice, etc., and to decide disputes arising at play.

43. Nicholas Barbon was responsible for many building projects after the great fire; but presumably he also practiced as a physician, having graduated M.D. at Utrecht in 1661.

45. An allusion to Barbon's treatment of Essex House (which he bought from the executors of the duchess of Somerset) and to his treatment of Red Lion Fields.

47. The precise extent of Barbon's architectural adventures cannot be determined on available evidence, and even accounts of the rebuilding of London after the great fire do not go into details as to his particular responsibility.

50. There is no external evidence for this charge. But his will (executed by John Asgill, his successor as M.P. for Bramber) directed that none of his debts should be paid.

51. *King's Bench:* the King's Bench jail, in which debtors and criminals were kept. (The Court of King's Bench was the supreme court of the common law.) *the Fleet:* the prison near Fleet Ditch. The *Mint* was exempt from certain legal jurisdictions, so presumably it could be termed a sanctuary; but Thomas Neale's role there may account for its being listed with prisons and a sanctuary. *Whitefriars:* formerly a sanctuary for debtors and lawbreakers.

With broken building knights, Alsatia squires,
(To avoid which fate himself was forced to tamper
For a dear bargain with the men of Bramber).
He weary grown of ruining by retail,   55
Gravely prescribes destruction by wholesale;
As if the cursed spirit of your pool
Had in a double share informed this tool,
Would lay our new-erected fences waste,
And the glory of the revolution blast;   60
Revive damned chimney money, and impose
Gabels on children's warming hands and toes.
If, doctor-like, the builder would advise
Close-stools and urinals should pay excise,
Unhappy sure must be that nation's fate   65
Where quacks and cullies do direct the state.
     Britannia listened at the senate house
And, groaning, spake thus with contracted brows:
"This House, once my stout guard of property,
Now harbors sniveling pimps to beggary.   70
A pack of senseless fools (as well as knaves)
Who take a bribe, and sell themselves for slaves;
But thus it must be" (letting fall a tear)
"Whilst officers and pensioners sit here,
Whilst by self-ended knaves deluded kings   75
Make England's interest, and their own, two things."

52. *Alsatia:* cant name for the precinct of Whitefriars, and hence an asylum for criminals.

54. Barbon was elected to Parliament from Bramber, in Sussex, a "burgage borough." Lord Windsor controlled the "interest" there at the end of the century. In the previous Parliament another physician (Dr. John Radcliffe) had shared the two seats, despite the petition of William Stringer, who accused Barbon and Radcliffe of "practice" (*CJ, 10,* 361). Stringer was elected with Barbon in 1695.

57. *pool:* This proposal, seemingly put forth by Barbon in the House of Commons, has not been identified in extant proposals. The context implies that Barbon's proposals for raising money by taxes, excise, and "pooling" of money in some way had alarmed M.P.s as much as Thomas Neale's gambling projects.

61. *chimney money:* The hearth-tax had been abolished at the revolution.

62. *Gabel:* a tax, specifically the salt tax imposed in France before the revolution.

66. *cullies:* That Neale should be categorized as the fool that is cheated rather than as the cheat himself seems curious.

75. *self-ended:* selfish.

[HENRY HALL]

A Ballad on the Times
(1696)

The witty use of proverbial expression in this satire suggests an author more than usually competent. The attribution of the poem to Tom Brown by its inclusion in his *Remains* (1720) may be ignored, even though the sentiment in lines 21–22 is also to be found in one of Brown's genuine poems. The poem expresses the perennial complaint of the taxpayer, but emphasizes the multiplicity of tax measures current in 1696. Its inclusion in the Hall Fo. MS may be taken more seriously, however. Henry Hall, organist of Hereford, was perhaps capable of both the wit and the musical background.

A BALLAD ON THE TIMES

1.

Good people: What? Will you of all be bereft?
Will you never learn wit, while a penny is left?
We are all like the dog in the fable, betrayed,
To let go the substance and snap at the shade.
    Our specious pretenses   5
    And foreign expenses
To war for religion will waste all our chink.
    It's clipped, and it's snipped,
    It's lent, and it's spent,
Till 'tis gone, till 'tis gone, to the devil I think.   10

2.

We pay for our newborn, and we pay for our dead;
We pay if we're single, we pay if we wed;
Which shows that our merciful senate don't fail

---

12. The tax on bachelors over 25 and on childless widowers was to be one shilling yearly (*CJ, 11,* 232) plus "one-fourth part of the sum to be paid upon the burial of such persons."

To begin at the head, and tax down to the tail.
    We pay through the nose   15
    For subjecting of foes,
But for all our expenses, get nothing but blows.
    Abroad we're defeated;
    At home we're cheated;
And the end on it, the end on it, the Lord above knows.   20

3.

We have parted with all our old money, to show
How we foolishly hope for a plenty of new;
But might have remembered, when it came to the push,
That a bird in the hand is worth two in the bush.
    We now like poor wretches,   25
    Are kept under hatches,
At rack and at manger, like beasts in the ark.
    Since our burgesses and knights
    Make us pay for our lights,
Why should we, why should we, be kept in the dark?   30

26. The act for a duty on houses (7 & 8 Wm III c. 18) received the royal assent on 10 April 1696.

29. An allusion to the tax on windows, a substitute for the hated hearth tax abolished at the revolution. It was established by the act mentioned above and was intended to pay for the cost of the recoinage.

[HENRY HALL]

On Sir John Fenwick
(1697)

This poem, written for the anniversary of King Charles I's death (30 January 1697), is preserved in a letter now among the Trumbull MSS. The letter is in the form of a single half-sheet addressed to Mr. William Wiseman in Whittlesea by Stilton bag and was both written and postmarked on 23 February 1697. It seems reasonable to assume, then, that *On Sir John Fenwick* was written soon after Fenwick's execution on 28 January.

ON SIR JOHN FENWICK

1.

Here lie the relics of a martyred knight,
Whose loyalty, unspotted as the light,
Sealed with his blood his injured sovereign's right.

2.

The state his head did from his body sever
Because, when living, 'twas his chief endeavor   5
To set the nation and its head together.

3.

He boldly fell, girt round with weeping soldiers,
Imploring Heaven (for the good of the beholders)
So to cut Holland's head from England's shoulders.

1. In one satire Fenwick is coupled with the royalist martyr James Graham, marquess of Montrose. He is thus being mythologized as one more "royalist" martyr.
4. The same satire also attacks William for giving the royal assent to the bill of attainder: "The king, consenting to his enemy's fall,/ With Nero, wished that neck contained them all." It bitterly attacks Parliament ("The state") for bypassing the courts after Cardell Goodman had removed all certainty of conviction by fleeing the country. Many men were horrified that Parliament could so palpably negate the spirit of their act for regulating trials for treason by passing a bill of attainder against Fenwick.
7. Macaulay (p. 2687) is very careful to deny that any sympathy was shown for Fenwick by the spectators at his execution. The Jacobite's report (as might be expected in a satire) is less accurate than Macaulay, for Fenwick is said to have uttered only one public utterance, "Lord Jesus, receive my soul."

[HENRY HALL]
[JOHN GRUBHAM HOWE]

A Panegyric
(1697)

A Panegyric is included in Hall's "Remains," the less authoritative of two dubious MSS, and might conceivably belong in the canon of the organist of Hereford. But the ascription in Buckingham's *Works*, vol. 1 (1704) to "J. H. Esq." makes it possible that it was written by one of William's non-Jacobite opponents—Jack Howe. As Macaulay (p. 1336) says of Howe:

> All his great contemporaries felt his sting in their turns. Once it inflicted a wound which deranged even the stern composure of William, and constrained him to utter a wish that he were a private gentleman, and could invite Mr. Howe to a short interview behind Montague House.

Perhaps, then, Howe is a better candidate for the authorship of the poem then the musical Mr. Hall.

A PANEGYRIC

1697

Hail happy William, thou art strangely great,
What is the cause, thy virtue or thy fate?
For thee the child the parent's heart will sting;
For thee the favorite will desert his king;
For thee the patriot will subvert the laws;   5
For thee the judge will still decide the cause;
For thee the prelate will his church betray;
For thee the soldier fights without his pay;
For thee the freeman mortgages his hold;
For thee the miser lavishes his gold;   10

4. John Churchill, earl of Marlborough, was the prototype.
7. John Tillotson was possibly the archvillain, because of his "usurpation" of Sancroft's position as archbishop of Canterbury. But several of the Williamite prelates are probably alluded to.

For thee the merchant loses all his store;
For thee the tradesman is content and poor;
For thee the sailor's pressed and starves on shore;
For thee the senate our best laws suspend,
And will make any new to serve thy end.   15
The chief design of all their loyal votes
Is to invent new ways, new means, and plots.
No credit in the land but thine will pass,
Nor ready money if it want thy face.
Thy loyal slaves love thy oppression more   20
Than all their wealth and liberty before.
For thee, and tyranny, they all declare—
And beg the blessing of eternal war.
And that this wonder may more wondrous seem,
Thou never yet didst one kind thing for them.   25
Rebels, like witches, having signed the rolls
Must serve their masters, though they damn their souls.

13. *pressed:* forced to serve in the navy by press gangs.
14. Possibly an allusion to the suspension of Habeas Corpus in 1689 and 1696.
15. The bill providing that Parliament would not be dissolved by the death of William (introduced in the Commons on 24 February 1696) was the first of many that helped to ensure the stability of William's government and reign after the death of Mary.
17. Allusions to the financial ingenuities of the 1695–97 period, and to the discoveries of Jacobite plotting of 1696.
19. Old silver coins were demonetized from 4 May 1696 as part of the great recoinage plan.

Farewell to England
(1697)

The persona of this satire is apparently a tired Tory, weary of war and wartime privations. Shocked by the legal murder of Sir John Fenwick, and contemptuous of those who brook the humiliations of the time, he is apparently departing for St. Germains.

The poem must have been written after the names of the nine lord justices became known on 22 April 1697; the imaginary departing Jacobite would no doubt be making his gesture well before the Treaty of Ryswick was concluded in September.

FAREWELL TO ENGLAND

Farewell false friends, farewell ill wine,
Farewell all women with design,
Farewell all pretty cheating pranks,
Farewell lotteries, farewell banks;
And England, I in leaving thee   5
May say farewell to poverty.
      Adieu! where'er I go, I'm sure to find
      Nothing so ill as that I leave behind.

Farewell a nation without sense,
Farewell Exchequer without pence,   10
Farewell army with bare feet,
Farewell navy without meat,
Farewell writing, fighting, beaus,
And farewell useless Plenipo's.
      Adieu! etc.   15

Farewell you Good Old Cause promoters,

14. *Plenipo:* Luttrell (*4,* 153) reports that on the night of 11 December 1696 Pembroke, Villiers, and Sir Joseph Williamson were named plenipotentiaries at the treaty of the general peace.

Farewell bribed military voters,
Farewell to all attainting bills,
And record which for witness kills;
Farewell to laymen's villainy,   20
And farewell churchmen's perjury.
          Adieu! etc.

Instead of one king, farewell nine,
And all who Association sign;
Farewell you gulled unthinking fops,   25
Poor broken merchants, empty shops,
Farewell packed juries, culled for blood,
With eight years' war for England's good.
          Adieu! etc.

Farewell you judges, who dispense   30
With perjured cutthroat evidence;
Farewell thou haughty little Mouse,
With those that chose thee for the House;
Farewell long nose and spiteful looks
With Reverend Oates and all his books.   35
          Adieu! etc.

Adieu once more Britannia! fare thee well.
          And if all this won't mend thee,
May the Dutch triumph in your spoil,
May beggary run throughout your isle,   40
And no one think it worth his while
          To take up to defend thee.

18. *attainting bills:* Two acts of attainder received royal assent 11 January 1696/97; Fenwick's bill of attainder had been introduced 9 November 1696 and passed after a stormy debate. The word as used here has been strongly influenced by false etymological association with "attaint."

19. *record:* perhaps the vote of the House of Commons, which was substituted for the witness required by law.

23. *nine:* William's cabinet.

24. The list may be consulted in Browning, *Danby, 3,* 187–213.

32. *Mouse:* Charles "Mouse" Montagu had been successful in the 1695 elections and was chosen (with Sir Stephen Fox) for Westminster against the Tory candidate Sir Walter Clarges Those who chose him were "a court for that liberty . . . consisting of the principal inhabitants" (Luttrell *3,* 533). It was also rumored that Sir Benjamin Bathurst had been ordered by Princess Anne to instruct her servants to vote for Montagu and Fox (Luttrell *3,* 537).

34. Possibly an allusion to William III, whose hooked nose was often referred to by satirists. But aristocratic hauteur is obviously implied, so any one of a number of high-born Whigs may be intended.

35. Probably prompted by Titus Oates's εἴκων βασιλική: *or the Picture of the Late King James,* Part I (1696). This scurrilous compilation was the climax of a series of calumnies, some of which had determined Queen Mary to cancel the annuity that had been paid Oates after the revolution as compensation for his having suffered at the hands of James II's judges.

THOMAS BROWN

A Satire upon the French King
(28 October 1697)

The night of 14 September 1697, when Matthew Prior brought to London the news of the signing of the Treaty of Ryswick, the guns at the Tower were discharged, the flag displayed, bells rung, and bonfires lit. But joy in London was by no means unconfined. Neither this poem nor the next one are celebratory; both in fact are almost desperate.

The present poem is a soliloquy. It begins in incredulity and ends in an obscene curse. The imagined speaker is a nonjuring Anglican parson, one of an estimated 400 who lost their livings in 1689 when they refused to take the oath of allegiance to William and Mary. Thus the speaker is also a man of principle, albeit a quixotic principle: he refused "to admit that an absurd doctrine had been discredited by events" (Ogg, *James II*, *3*, 234). The absurd doctrine was the Anglican doctrine of nonresistance, the belief that the authority of a *jure divino* king could not be resisted under any circumstances. What this principle had cost the speaker is set forth in lines 34–40, which constitute the emotional center of the poem: two rural benefices worth £160 a year, yielding a fat sufficiency for the parson, his wife, and daughter. In his impassioned recollection of this life, the tithe eggs were not collected; they flew in of their own accord.

Since 1689 the speaker has lived in London on pawn-tickets, credit, and the hope of a second Stuart restoration. One of the favorite toasts at Sam's coffeehouse, which the speaker frequents, was "to the king's fast friend," meaning Louis XIV. For after James had fled Ireland in 1690, it was obvious that he could not be restored without Louis and it was widely believed that Louis had engaged his word of honor as a king not to make peace with the Confederates until he had restored James to the throne of England. And it cannot be denied that Louis tried. But Louis's interests were never so simple, or so single-minded, as James's, and when the two came into conflict, James's, of course had to be sacrificed.

This occurred in December 1696 and became public knowledge in February 1697 when Louis ordered his plenipotentiaries to proceed to Ryswick to negotiate a treaty of peace with the Confederates. All of Europe was astonished at the concessions Louis was willing to make at the conference table that summer. Now Louis pledged "not to assist directly or indirectly any of the enemies of William III." Yet even while the French plenipotentiaries at

Ryswick were demanding the highest price for Louis's abandonment of James, "the court of France did, to the last minute, assure King James, that they would never abandon his interests."

Thomas Brown must have begun to write this poem very soon after the news of the peace reached London. It was published in a folio half-sheet on 28 October. Two days later Brown was arrested along with Abel Roper, the publisher, for having violated "the new-made treaty, between the two crowns of England and France" (Oldmixon, p. 167). Brown and Roper were released on bail, and six months later, after serving a short sentence in Newgate, Brown was finally discharged.

During Brown's lifetime all sorts crowded round him to hear his conversation. His writing also is best when it most closely approximates the vocabulary and rhythms of the literary Alsatia in which he lived. He was, we are told by James Drake (Thomas Brown, *Works* [1707], *1*, sig. A7v), "unambitious of a reputation" as a poet, but his best poetry is like brilliant conversation, alternately witty, learned, obscene, inconsecutive, larded with Latin tags, underworld slang, and even, as in the present poem, the refrain of a current popular song.

A Satire upon the French King

Written by a Non-Swearing Parson, and Dropped Out of His Pocket
at Sam's Coffeehouse.

Facit indignatio versum.

And hast thou left old Jemmy in the lurch?
A plague confound the doctors of thy church!
Then to abandon poor Italian Molly—
Would I'd the firking of thy bum with holly!
Next to discard the virtuous prince of Wales,   5
How suits this with the honor of Versailles?
Fourthly, and lastly, to renounce the Turks,

Epigraph: Juvenal, Sat. *1,* 79.

3. *Italian Molly:* Maria d'Este (1658–1718), called Mary of Modena in England. When she became James's second wife in 1673, Louis XIV underwrote her dowry of 300,000 crowns.

4. *firking:* whipping.

5. *prince of Wales:* James Francis Edward (1688–1766), the only son of James II.

7. *renounce the Turks:* His most Christian Majesty's subvention of the infidel was frequently noticed in England (Luttrell, *3,* 44, 387–88, 433, 450). In 1697, however, while peace negotiations were under way at Ryswick, Louis's failure to create a diversion on the Rhine exposed the Turks to two crushing defeats—one at Azov in the Crimea and another at Zenta in Hungary—which afforded them "but too much reason to repent, when they [saw] themselves

Why, this is the devil, the devil, and all his works!
Were I thy confessor, who am thy martyr,
Dost think that I'd allow thee any quarter?   10
No—thou shouldst find what 'tis to be a starter.
Lord! with what monstrous lies, and senseless shams,
Have we been cullied all along at Sam's.
Who could have e'er believed, unless in spite,
Lewis le Grand would turn rank Williamite?   15
Thou, that hast looked so fierce, and talked so big,
In thy old age to dwindle to a Whig!
By Heaven, I see thou 'rt in thy heart a prig.
I'd not be for a million in thy jerkin,
'Fore George thy soul's no bigger than a gherkin.   20
Hast thou for this spent so much ready rhino?
Now, what the plague will become of *jure divino*?
A change so monstrous I could ne'er have thought,
Though Partridge all his stars to vouch it, brought.
S'life, I'll not take thy honor for a groat,   25
Ev'n oaths, with thee, are only things of course.
Thou, Zoons, thou art a monarch for a horse.
Of kings distressed thou art a fine securer;
Thou make'st me swear, that am a known non-juror.
But though I swear thus, as I said before,   30
Know, king, I'll place it all upon thy score.
    Were Job alive, and bantered by such shufflers,
He'd out-rail Oates, and curse both thee and Boufflers.
For thee I've lost, if I can rightly scan 'em,

---

left in the lurch" (Edward D'Auvergne, *The History of the Campagne in Flanders, for the Year 1697* [1698], p. 159).

8. *the devil, the devil, and all his works:* the last line of a catch by Henry Purcell, "Let's live good honest lives," of which the music is recorded.

11. *starter:* a deserter from a principle or cause.

13. *Sam's:* Sam's coffeehouse in Ludgate Street near St. Paul's was known to be a center for the dissemination of Jacobite literature.

18. *prig:* a precisian in religion.

22. *jure divino:* Cf. *Dr. Wild's Ghost,* 86 n.; *jure* is monosyllabic.

24. *Partridge:* John Partridge (1644–1715), the famous Whig astrologer and almanac maker.

33. *Oates:* The railings of Titus Oates (1649–1705) in 1697 were indeed epical. He complained to the king that "he had run into debt £1600 . . . [that] he had afterwards incurred further debt, for which he was arrested, and must inevitably perish . . . [and] that he had a poor aged mother to maintain, and his wife and family likely to be turned out of doors" (*CTP,* 2, 116). *Boufflers:* Louis François, duc de Boufflers (1644–1711), a marshal of France in command of one of Louis's armies in Flanders, played an important part in the peace negotiations in July 1697. In five conversations with the earl of Portland the crucial phrase by which Louis agreed to recognize William as king of England was worked out.

Two livings worth full eightscore pounds per annum,   35
Bonae & *legalis Angliae monetae;*
But now I'm clearly routed by the treaty.
Then geese and pigs my table ne'er did fail,
And tithe-eggs merrily flew in like hail;
My barns with corn, my cellars crammed with ale.   40
The dice are changed, for now, as I'm a sinner,
The devil, for me, knows where to buy a dinner.
I might as soon, though I were ne'er so willing,
Raise a whole troop of horse, as one poor shilling.

    My spouse, alas, must flaunt in silks no more;   45
Pray Heaven, for sustenance, she turn not whore;
And daughter Peggy too, in time, I fear,
Will learn to take a stone up in her ear.
My friends have basely left me with my place,
What's worse, my very pimples bilk my face.   50
And frankly my condition to disclose,
I most resent th' ungratitude of my nose,
On which though I have spent of wine such store,
It now looks paler than my tavern score.
My double chin's dismantled, and my coat is   55
Past its best days, in *verbo sacerdotis.*
My breeches too this morning, to my wonder
I found grown schismatics, and fallen asunder.

    When first I came to town with household clog,
Rings, watch, and so forth, fairly went for prog.   60
The ancient fathers next, in whom I boasted,
Were soon exchanged for primitive boiled and roasted.
Since 'tis no sin of books to be a glutton,
I trucked St. Austin for a leg of mutton.
Old Jerome's volumes next I made a rape on,   65
And melted down that father for a capon.
When these were gone, my bowels not to balk,
I trespassed most enormously in chalk.
But long I had not quartered upon tick,
E'er Christian faith, I found, grew monstrous sick: 70
And now, alas! when my starved entrails croak,

48. *to take . . . ear:* to play the whore (Partridge, p. 834).
58. *schismatics:* accented on the first syllable.
60. *prog:* food.
64. *trucked:* exchanged.
68. *chalk:* credit; referring to the custom in alehouses and inns of "ticking" or writing up
with chalk a "score" or account of credit given.

At Partner How's I dine and sup on smoke.
In fine, the government may do its will,
But I'm afraid my guts will grumble still.
    Dennis of Sicily, as books relate, sir,   75
When he was tumbled from the regal state, sir,
(Which, by the by, I hope will be your fate, sir,)
And his good subjects left him in the lurch,
Turned pedagogue, and tyrannized in birch:
Though thus the spark was taken a peg lower,   80
Some feeble signs of his old state he bore,
And reigned o'er boys, that governed men before.
For thee I wish some punishment that worse is;
Since thou has spoiled my prayers, now hear my curses.
May thy affairs (for so I wish by Heavens)   85
All the world o'er, at sixes lie and sevens.
May Conti be imposed on by the primate,
And forced, in haste, to leave the northern climate:
May he rely upon their faith, and try it,
And have his bellyful of the Polish Diet.   90
May Maintenon, though thou so long hast kept her,
With brand-venereal singe thy royal scepter.
May all the poets, that thy fame have scattered,
Un-god thee now, and damn what once they flattered.
The pope, and thou, be never cater cousins,   95

---

72. *Partner How's:* presumably a coffeehouse. Brown himself is consigned to "dine on smoke at How's again" in *To the Quibbling, Dribbling, Scribbling Poetaster, who has let himself out for Scandal to the Wits at Will's Coffeehouse, Discommendatory Verses,* 1700, p. 13.

75–82. *Dennis of Sicily:* Dionysus II (?395–after 343 B.C.), the pupil of Plato and tyrant of Syracuse. There is a tradition that after his second deposition, in 343 B.C., he was allowed to retire to Corinth. "Here looking upon the humblest station to be safest, he stooped to the meanest things imaginable" and "turned a pedagogue in his own defense" (*Justin's History of the World . . . Made English by Mr. T. Brown. The Fifth Edition* [Dublin, 1724], pp. 180–81).

80. *spark:* an easily angered bully.

87–90. *Conti:* François-Louis de Bourbon, prince de Conti (1664–1709), was the candidate of Louis XIV for the throne of Poland left vacant by the death of Jan Sobieski in June 1696. Large bribes, administered by Louis's ambassador to Poland, Abbé Melchior de Polignac, secured Conti's election by the Polish Diet in June 1697. This election was challenged by the elector of Saxony who, after illegal coronation by a bishop, was accepted by the Polish Diet.

91. *Maintenon:* Françoise d'Aubigné, marquise de Maintenon (1635–1719), began her long career at the French court in 1669 as governess to Louis's bastards and ended it as governess to Louis himself.

93. *poets:* "The French king had taken Namur in the campaign of '92, in sight of the army of the allies, who were unable to raise the siege. This was extolled by the flatterers of that prince, as a most inimitable action; and the celebrated Boileau . . . composed an ode on this occasion in imitation of Pindar" (Matthew Prior, *Miscellaneous Works,* ed. John Banks, 2 vols. [1740], *1,* 17).

95. *pope:* After having broken diplomatic relations with the Vatican in 1688 and imprison-

And fistulas thy arse-hole seize by dozens.

Thus far in jest; but now, to pin the basket,
Mayst thou to England come, of Jove I ask it,
Thy wretched fortune, Lewis, there to prop,
I hope thou'lt in the Friars take a shop.   100
Turn puny-barber there, bleed lousy Carmen,
Cut corns for chimney-sweepers, and such vermin,
Be forced to trim (for such I'm sure thy fate is),
Thy own Huguenots and us nonjurors gratis.
May Savoy likewise with thee hither pack,   105
And carry a raree-show upon his back.
May all this happen, as I've put my pen to 't,
And may all Christian people say amen to 't.

---

ing the papal nuncio, Louis effected a reconciliation with Innocent XII (1615–1700) in
November 1693 (Luttrell, *3*, 219).

97. *to pin the basket:* to settle the matter.

100. *Friars:* Blackfriars, a precinct in the ward of Farringdon Within, between St. Paul's
and Fleet Ditch, well inhabited by tradesmen.

101. *Carmen:* carters, carriers, traditionally rude, exacting and quarrelsome.

104. *Huguenot:* Pronounce disyllabically, with accent on second syllable.

105. *Savoy:* Victor Amadeo II, duke of Savoy (1666–1732), whose wife was a granddaughter
of Charles I, as well as a niece of Louis XIV, had been a hero in England when he recognized
William as king. He joined the league of Augsburg and fought five campaigns against the
French. In 1696, however, he capitulated to French pressure, accepted bribes to make a
separate peace, and married his daughter to Louis's eldest grandson, Louis, duc de Bourgogne

106. *raree-show:* Cf. Stephen College, *A Raree Show*. The early exhibitors of peep-shows seem
to have been Savoyards.

Advice to a Painter
(December 1697)

Among the "other demonstrations of joy" that succeeded upon the signing of
the Treaty of Ryswick in September 1697 were "the columns, the triumphal
arches, and the obelisks" that were ordered to be made ready to welcome the
king back to London. These were never to be completed, however, for when
William returned to England in November he put a stop to it. He seemed, as
Burnet goes on to say, "to have contracted an antipathy to all vain shows"
(Burnet, *2*, 205).

These maimed rites reflect perfectly the Tory patriot's feeling that there
was really very little to celebrate in the fall of 1697. "Disgraced and discon-
tent," his mood, as reflected in this anonymous *Advice to a Painter,* was that of
an almost existentialist despair. This poem is not a mere bill of complaints
or list of grievances to be patched up or put right. It implies an intrinsic
rottenness in the human condition. The end of the poem does not envisage a
reform, but rather "knaves in embryo, and rogues to come," who will "sell
their country in a closer way." The methods of corruption and betrayal will
be refined, not eliminated.

Within the convention of the advice-to-a-painter genre, the poem com-
mands a series of tableaux. This series begins at the top, with the king on the
throne, flanked by the two main supports of the crown, the church and the
law, the archbishop of Canterbury and the lord chancellor of England. Then
it works its way through the king's favorites, the king's ministers, who were
still legally *partes regis corporis,* and the king's loyal House of Commons. The
series ends in a subhuman swarm of "nameless somethings," "Of yelping yeas
and no's, who poll by rote, / And multiply the units of a vote."

More particularly, the poem attacks placemen, the holders of lucrative
offices in the gift of the crown. These ranged from sinecures such as secretary
to the lord chief justice in eyre of all His Majesty's forests on the south side of
the Trent, who was James Sloan (line 108), to the chief executive officers of
the state, such as the chancellor of the Exchequer, Charles Montagu (line
81).

What hand, what skill can form the artful piece,
To paint our ruins in a proper dress?
Inspire us, Denham's Genius, while w' indite,
Urged by true zeal to do our country right;
As when the daring artist, taught by you,   5
With master strokes the first bold landskip drew.

    Here, Painter, here employ thy utmost skill;
With war and slav'ry the vast canvas fill:
And that the lines be easier understood,
Paint not with fading colors, but with blood;   10
Blood of our bravest youth in battle slain,
At Steenkirk and at Landen's fatal plain;
Or that which flowed, and does just Heaven invoke,
When Fenwick yielded to the cruel stroke.

    First draw the hero seated on the throne,   15
Spite of all laws, himself observing none;
Let English rights all gasping round him lie,
And native freedom thrown neglected by:
On either hand the priest and lawyer set,
Two fit supporters of the monarch's seat.   20
There in a greasy rochet clothed, describe
The bulky oracle of the preaching tribe;
That solid necessary tool of state,
Profoundly dull, divinely obstinate.

---

  3. *Denham:* Sir John Denham (1615–69) is invoked as the supposed author of *The Second Advice to a Painter* (April 1666), the first satirical use of this genre.

  6. *the first bold landskip:* the scene depicted in *Second Advice.* The wording may reflect the opening lines of that poem: "Nay, Painter, if thou dar'st design that fight / Which Waller only courage had to write."

  12. *Steenkirk:* Steenkirke, a village 20 miles southwest of Brussels, was the scene of the Confederates' worst defeats in the war of 1689–97. *Landen:* a village in the province of Liège near which William's army was deployed when it sustained a massive onslaught by the French.

  14. *Fenwick:* Sir John Fenwick (1645?–97), the Jacobite conspirator, was beheaded on Tower Hill on 28 January 1697 for complicity in a plot to assassinate William III. This conviction by a Whig act of attainder made Fenwick a martyr to the Tories.

  15. *the hero:* William III (1650–1702).

  21. *rochet:* surplice

  22. *The bulky oracle:* Thomas Tenison (1636–1715), archbishop of Canterbury. His "moderation with dissenters" made him particularly unpopular with Tories. He voted for the attainder of Fenwick.

  24. *dull:* "James II spoke of [Tenison] as 'that dull man,' and the epithet stuck" (*DNB,* *19,* 540).

Here in polluted robes just reeking, draw　　　　　　　　25
Th'adulterous moderator of the law;
Whose wrinkled cheeks and sallow looks proclaim,
The ill effects of his distempered flame.
If more you'd know, consult his friend Tom Hobbes
Who vamps him up with his mercurial jobs.　　　　　　30
　　　Next cringing Benting place, whose earth-born race
The coronet and garter does disgrace;
Of undescended parentage, made great
By chance, his virtues not discovered yet.
Patron o'th'noblest order, O be just　　　　　　　　35
To thy heroic founder's injured dust!
From his ignoble neck thy collar tear,
Let not his breast thy rays of honor wear;
To black designs and lust let him remain
A servile favorite, and grants obtain:　　　　　　　40
While ancient honors sacred to the crown
Are lavished to support the minion.
Pale envy rages in his cankered breast,
And to the British name a foe professed.
　　　Artist, retire, 'twere insolence too great　　　　45
T'expose the secrets of the cabinet;
Or tell how they their looser moments spend;
That hellish scene would all chaste ears offend.
For should you pry into the close alcove,
And draw the exercise of royal love,　　　　　　　50
Keppel and he are Ganymede and Jove.

26. *Th'adulterous moderator:* John Somers (1651–1716), created Baron Somers of Evesham in 1697, was lord chancellor of England. He was unmarried but the name of his mistress was said to be "Madam Blount."

29. *Tom Hobbes:* Thomas Hobbes (d. 1698), (the famous London surgeon, figures in *The Dispensary* under the name of Guaiacum, a favorite specific for syphilis.

31. *Benting:* Hans William Bentinck (1649–1709) was the younger son of a petty Dutch nobleman whose service to William of Orange began in childhood when he was appointed a page at the court of the stadholder. At the revolution he marched with William from Tor Bay to London at the head of his regiment of horse guards in the Dutch army. In 1689 he was raised to the peerage as earl of Portland and installed Knight of the Garter in 1697.

35. *Patron o'th noblest order:* The patron of the Order of the Garter is St. George, "and none of those fabulous St. Georges as some have vainly fancied; but that famous saint and soldier of Christ, St. George of Cappadocia" (Chamberlayne, *Angliae Notitia*, 1692, p. 1253).

36. *founder:* The Order of the Garter was founded by Edward III in 1350.

40. *grants:* Since 1690 the Tories in the House of Commons had been trying to divert the income from the forfeited estates of English and Irish Jacobites from the Privy Purse of the king into the public revenue to help defray the costs of the war. As a result of William's benefactions, Portland was supposed to be the richest subject in Europe.

51. *Keppel:* Arnold Joost van Keppel (1670–1718) was the eldest son of Oswald, heer van

Avert the omen, Heaven! O may I ne'er
Purchase a title at a rate so dear:
In some mean cottage let me die unknown,
Rather than thus be darling of a throne. 55
    Now, Painter, even art is at a stand,
For who can draw the Proteus Sunderland?
The deep reserves of whose apostate mind,
No skill can reach, no principles can bind;
Whose working brain does more disguises bear 60
Than ever yet in vision did appear.
A supple whispering minister, ne'er just,
Trusted, yet always forfeiting his trust,
And only constant to unnat'ral lust.
For prostituted faith alone made great, 65
And this is he who must support the weight,
And prop the ruins of a sinking state.
    Artist proceed, next the bribed senate draw,
That arbitrary body above the law;
Place noise and faction and disorder there, 70
And formal Paul set mumping in the chair;
Once the chief bulwark of the church and state,
Their darling once, but now their fear and hate:
So a rich cordial, when its virtue's spent,
Contributes to the death it should prevent; 75
Of public treasure lavishly profuse,
Large sums diverted to their private use;
By places and by bounty largely paid,
For rights given up, and liberty betrayed.
    Expose the mercenary herd to view, 80
And in the front imperious Montagu:

Keppel in Guelderland. He accompanied William to England in 1688 as a page of honor and served successively as Groom of the Bedchamber and Master of the Robes. William made him grants of forfeited estates in Ireland that amounted to 108,634 acres, although he was then but a handsome young man "who had rendered no service whatever to his adopted country" (GEC, *1*, 92).

57. *Sunderland:* Robert Spencer (1640–1702), 2d earl of Sunderland. Princess Anne told her sister in March 1688 that "everybody knows how often this man turned backwards and forwards" (*DNB, 18*, 781).

81. When the Tories learned that a Mr. Railton, to whom a grant had been passed of some £10,000 in recognizances forfeited in Ireland, was really a nominee of Montagu, they leaped to the attack, Montagu "being the person they have the greatest mind to lower, as one that stands in their way" (*CJ, 12*, 116; Vernon, *1*, 461). Seeing which way the wind was blowing, Montagu installed his brother in the profitable post of auditor of the Exchequer when it fell vacant in September 1698 (Vernon, *2*, 165–67) and subsequently retired to it himself in November 1699.

With venal Wit, and prostituted sense,
With matchless pride and monstrous impudence;
To whose successful villainies we owe
All his own ills, and all that others do.   85
Slavish excises are his darling sin,
And 'Chequer bills the product of his brain;
No public profit but conduces most
To raise his fortune at the public cost.
Orders and precedents are things of course,   90
Too weak to interrupt his rapid force;
Till wiser Commons shall in time to come
Their ancient English principles resume,
And give their base corrupter his just doom.
Thus have I seen a whelp of lion's brood   95
Couch, fawn and lick his keeper's hand for food,
Till in some lucky hour the generous beast,
By an insulting lash, or some gross fraud oppressed,
His just resentment terribly declares,
Disdains the marks of slavery he wears,   100
And his weak feeder into pieces tears.
     Let Gaffney's noble hangman next advance,
And tell his fears of popery and France;
And for the blust'ring pedant leave a space,

86. *excises:* The mounting costs of the war with France had required substantial increases in excise taxes.

87. *'Chequer bills:* In April 1696 Montagu tacked to Harley's Land Bank Bill clauses empowering the treasury to issue negotiable paper payable to bearer (7 & 8 William III, c. 31). These were the first Exchequer bills. Upon issue, they yielded no interest, but after they had been tendered in payment of any tax obligation and reissued by the Exchequer, they bore interest at 3d. per cent per day. Consequently a number of customs, excise, and treasury officials maintained a dangerous trade in forging endorsements.

94. I.e., impeach Montagu for procuring grants to himself of forfeited Irish estates.

95–96. *whelp . . . keeper:* In the somewhat strained terms of this metaphor, the "whelp of lion's brood" is the House of Commons and its "keeper" is Montagu.

102. *Gaffney's noble hangman:* Thomas Coningsby (1656?–1729) was successively paymaster-general of William's forces in Ireland, one of the lord justices, and vice-treasurer of Ireland. He was created Baron Coningsby of Clanbrassil in the Irish peerage in April 1692 and a year later was sworn as Privy Councillor. In December 1693 Richard Coote, earl of Bellamont, moved his impeachment in the House of Commons for crimes committed during his term as lord justice, 1690–92. The 4th article claimed that he ordered one Gaffney, a witness in a pending murder case, to be hanged without even a written order for his execution. Coningsby was saved from replying to the articles by a pardon under the king's hand.

104. *pedant:* Marginalia in various MSS identify the "pedant" as "Norris" presumably William Norris (1657–1702), of Speke, in Lancashire. He succeeded his elder brother Thomas as Whig member for Liverpool in October 1695. He signed the Association in 1696, was active in the prosecution of Fenwick, and in April 1697 he was mentioned for a post in the admiralty. He was said to be "a violent man, but speaks well" (HMC, Kenyon MSS., p. 400).

Who wears Corinthian metal in his face: 105
See where the florid warlike Cutts appears,
As brave and senseless as the sword he wears.
Here Sloan baits Seymour, Littleton, Jack How,
And all the while old Bowman cries bow-wow.
To Palmes and Strickland, and the Yorkshire crew   110

105. *wears . . . face:* looks like a shameless debauchee.

106. *Cutts:* John Cutts (1661–1707), created Baron Cutts of Gowran in the Irish peerage (December 1690), was one of England's few authentic military heroes in the period between the crossing of the Boyne in July 1690 and Blenheim in August 1704. He secured election to Parliament by 13 votes in a disputed election for Cambridgeshire that was almost overturned in the House (*CJ, 11,* 91–93). Thereafter he sat for Cambridgeshire until July 1702 and for Newport, Isle of Wight, until his death.

108. *Sloan:* James Sloan (d.1704), "blustr'ing Sloan," as he is called in *A Description of the Chancellor of Ireland,* was elected in the rotten borough of Thetford, Norfolk, where the 32 burgesses demanded "fifty guineas for a vote" (Robert Walcott, *English Politics in the Early Eighteenth Century* [Cambridge: Harvard University Press, 1956], p. 16)in January 1696. He so distinguished himself in his first session that he "had like to have been called to the barr" for defending the king's veto of the Members Property Qualification Bill. In February 1697 he was elected one of the commissioners of the public accounts in the room of Lord William Paulet (line 125 *n.*) and in the following April he was made secretary to Thomas, Lord Wharton, chief justice in eyre south of Trent and one of the leading Whig magnates. He voted against disbanding the army in January 1699. *Seymour:* Sir Edward Seymour (1633–1708) of Berry Pomeroy, Devonshire, explained to the Prince of Orange in November 1688 that "the proud duke" of Somerset represented a younger branch of *his* family. He was speaker of the House of Commons in the 2d Parliament of Charles II and survived to sit in the 3d Parliament of Queen Anne. Seymour refused to join the Association in 1696 and spoke in defense of Sir John Fenwick. Burnet called him "the ablest man of his party" (Burnet, *1,* 382). *Littleton:* Sir Thomas Littleton (1647?–1710), of Stoke St. Milborough, Shropshire, was the Whig member for New Woodstock, Oxfordshire (1689–1702), and a close associate of Montagu. He was appointed a lord of the treasury in May 1696, and supported the attainder of Fenwick. In the next parliament (December 1698) he was elected speaker. Burnet called him "the vehementest arguer of them all" (Burnet, *1,* 389). Cf. *Oceana and Britannia,* 147 *n. Jack How:* John Grubham Howe (1657–1722), a younger brother of Sir Scrope Howe of Nottinghamshire, was from 1689 to 1698 a member for Cirencester and subsequently served for Gloucestershire (1698–1705). He began his career as a staunch Whig, like his brother, but soon became a violent Tory and partisan of Sir Edward Seymour. He refused to sign the Association in 1696, opposed the attainder of Fenwick, and with "a boldness of speech, which, till *then,* had never been heard in Parliament . . . contributed more than any other man in the kingdom to embarrass the measures of the government" (*Gentleman's Magazine* 19 [August 1749]: 364–65]. Cf. *A Ballad Called Perkin's Figary,* 13 *n.*

109. *Bowman:* identified by a marginal note in one MS as "Boscowen," presumably Hugh Boscawen (1625–1701), the member for Cornwall who distinguished himself in the Parliament of 1685 by his opposition to James II. A Privy Councillor under William, he controlled Tregoney, of which he was lord of the manor, in the interest of his brother-in-law, Sidney Godolphin. The joke may depend upon the fact that one "Bowman . . . kept the Dog Tavern in Drury Lane," which was a Jacobite center (Thomas Brown, *A Continuation or Second Part of the Letters from the Dead to the Living* [1703], p. 273; Luttrell, *3,* 484).

110. *Palmes:* William Palmes (1668–1713), the member for Malton, Yorkshire, was a friend and partisan of the Whig magnate, Thomas Wharton, Lord Wharton. He controlled the borough of Malton and secured the second seat for his son-in-law, Sir William Strickland. In 1694 he had been mentioned for a commissionership of the treasury, but the post went instead

By Smith directed, the next station's due.
Smith while he seems good-natured, frank and kind,
Betrays th'inveterate rancor of his mind.
    To the chit Spencer, Painter, next be just,
That roiling withered offspring of forced lust,   115
Which his unnatural father grudged to spare
From his Italian joys, and spoiled his heir;
From hence the awkward politician came,
To commonwealths, which he admires, a shame,
And slave to kings, though he abhors the name.   120
He votes for armies, talks for liberty,
In th' House for millions, out, for property;
Thus father-like, with flattery betrays
The government which he pretends to raise.
Near him Lord William draw, whose well-stocked brain   125

---

to John Smith (line 111 *n*.). He signed the Association in 1696 and voted for the army in 1699. *Strickland*: Sir William Strickland (1665–1724) of Boynton, Yorks., was a Whig member for Malton, Yorks.

111. *Smith*: John Smith (1655–1723) had been a stauch Whig since 1678 when he was first elected for Ludgershall, in Wiltshire. Subsequently he represented Beeralston, Devonshire, and Andover, Hants. (1695–1713). In 1694 he was appointed lord of the treasury and sworn of the Privy Council in May 1695. Later he served twice as chancellor of the Exchequer and once as speaker of the House of Commons. James Vernon, who refers to him as "a leading man" in February 1698, also provides an example of his "inveterate rancor." He was unalterably opposed to restoring Sunderland to the ministry after his resignation in December 1697 and told Montagu that "others might be as good-natured as they please, and forget all that was passed; but for his part, he would never trust those who were capable of such practices, and he must leave those who would enter into such engagements" (Vernon, *1*, 484).

114. *chit*: the young of a wild animal, and a long-established derogatory term for the triumvirate. *Spencer*: Charles Spencer (1674–1722), 2d son of Robert Spencer, 2d earl of Sunderland, became Lord Spencer in 1688 upon the death of his older brother. In October 1695 he was elected a Whig member for Tiverton, Devonshire, a small borough in which his father "had a great deal of influence" (Walcott, *English Politics*, p. 20). He was an enthusiastic partisan of Montagu and during the debate on Fenwick boldly proposed that bishops be excluded from voting (Vernon, *1*, 69).

117. *Italian joys*: buggery; Thomas Brown called it "cathedral exercise, or bestial backslidings."

119. *commonwealths . . . admires*: In 1712 Jonathan Swift found that Spencer "hath much fallen from the height of those republican principles with which he began: for, in his father's lifetime, while he was a member of the House of Commons, he would often among his familiar friends refuse the title of lord; (as he hath done to myself) swear that he would never be called otherwise than Charles Spencer; and hoped to see the day, when there should not be a peer in England" (Swift, *Prose*, *7*, 9).

121. *votes for armies*: On considering the king's speech at the opening of the 1st session of Parliament after "the happy conclusion" of the war, the first resolution, proposed by Robert Harley, was to disband all land forces raised since 1680. Lord Spencer must have opposed this measure in a division of 11 December 1697. His name also appears in a list of court Whigs who voted for the army in a division of January 1699.

125. *Lord William*: Identified by marginal notes in some copies as William Paulet, second

Outweighs his index-learning half a grain.

Next, Painter, draw our politician Boyle,

That fawning arse-worm with his cringing smile;

Relations, country, court do all despise him,

He's grown so low ev'n buggery can't raise him.   130

With these as fellow empirics in design,

Let Wharton, Rich, Young, Clark, and Hobart join;

And let not Hawles pass unregarded by.

---

son of Charles Paulet, 1st duke of Bolton, who was one of the prime movers of the revolution. Lord William, as he was styled by his courtesy title, became a personal friend of the junto lords and of their leading henchmen in the House of Commons, where he sat for Southampton County and then for Winchester. He was another one of the king's friends who "voted for the army" in 1699.

126. *his:* Lord Spencer's; Evelyn had remarked in 1688 that he was "a youth of extraordinary hopes, very learned for his age and ingenious" (*4,* 595).

127. *Boyle:* Henry Boyle (d. 1725), a representative in the House of Commons where he sat for Tanworth, Staffs., Cambridge University, and Westminster. He was a lord of the treasury, Privy Councillor, and chancellor of the Exchequer. Macky's prediction that he "obliges everybody in the Exchequer; and in time may prove a great man," was subsequently fulfilled when Boyle was appointed lord treasurer of Ireland, lord lieutenant of the West Riding of Yorkshire, secretary of state, and elevated to the peerage as Baron Carleton of Carleton. Although said to be "agreeable amongst the ladies," he died unmarried (Spring Macky, ed., *Memoirs of the Secret Services of John Macky* [2d edition, 1733], p. 126).

128. *arse-worm:* "a little diminutive fellow" (*A New Dictionary* [1699]).

132. *Wharton:* Goodwin Wharton (1653–1704) was the second son of Philip, 4th Baron Wharton, of Wharton in Westmorland, and the brother of "honest Tom Wharton," the Whig magnate who became the first marquis. He was a wayward genius whose eccentricities included spiritualism, underwater salvage, and a two-volume autobiography preserved in BM Add. MSS 20006 and 20007. His parliamentary career began in 1679 as an exclusionist member for East Grinstead, Sussex. In 1696 he signed the Association twice, for Cockermouth and Malmesbury, both of which had returned him, and in 1699 he voted for the army. *Rich:* Presumably Sir Robert Rich (1648–1699), of Rous Hall, in Beccles, Co. Suffolk, and Whig M.P. for the neighboring borough of Dunwich. He was a member of the Puritan family headed by the earls of Warwick and also a grandson of John Hampden. He served as lord of the admiralty (1691–99), signed the Association, and voted for the army in 1699 (Browning, *Danby, 3,* 208, 216). *Young:* Sir Walter Yonge (1653–1731), of Colyton, Co. Devon, represented the neighboring boroughs of Honiton and Ashburton in Parliament and long served as a commissioner of customs. He began his career as one of Shaftesbury's lieutenants, signed the Association in 1696 and on 18 January 1699 upon the third reading of Harley's bill for disbanding the army, he was a teller for the noes, along with Lord William Paulet (line 125 n.). *Clark:* Edward Clarke (?1649–1710) of Chipley; the lifelong friend of John Locke, represented Taunton, Somerset, as a nominee and partisan of Somers. He was chosen one of the 24 original directors of the Bank of England in July 1694, but "desired to be excused." He was auditor of the queen's household and served as a commissioner of the excise. He signed the Association in 1696 and voted for the army in 1699. *Hobart:* Sir Henry Hobart (?1658–98) of Blickling, Co. Norfolk, began his parliamentary career in 1681 as a member for king's Lynn, Norfolk. He was prominent in the opposition to James II, served as Gentleman of the Horse to William at the Boyne, and signed the Association in 1696 as a member for Norfok. In August 1698 he was killed in a duel with Oliver Le Neve.

133. *Hawles:* Sir John Hawles (1645–1716), of Salisbury and Lincoln's Inn, began his parliamentary career in the Convention Parliament as a member for Old Sarum. Anthony à Wood called him "a great Williamite . . . but ill-natured, turbulent and inclining to a

'Twere endless to recount the meaner fry
Of yelping yeas and no's, who poll by rote,   135
And multiply the units of a vote;
Oppressed with clamor, truth and justice flies,
And thus pursued, down-hunted reason lies.
    Some few untainted patriots still remain,
Who native zeal and probity retain;   140
These sullen draw, disgraced and discontent,
Mourning the ruin which they can't prevent.
    But, Painter, hold—reserve the vacant room
For knaves in embryo, and rogues to come;
Who undiscovered, yet will us betray,   145
And sell their country in a closer way.

---

republic" (*Athenae Oxonienses, 4,* 527 *n.*). Knighted in November 1695, he served as solicitor-general (1695–1702), signed the Association, and voted for the army.

135. *poll by rote:* vote at the poll as they have been instructed or bribed.

136. *multiply:* Multiple voting was a frequent cause of contested parliamentary elections.

JOSEPH ADDISON

The Play-House
(December 1698–April 1699)

Although it is called *The Play-House. A Satire* in most copies, Addison's poem is a satire in which a fascination for the stage in "all its pomp and pageantry" is revealed in every paragraph. *The Play-House,* written only a year after Jeremy Collier had published *A Short View of the Immorality and Profaneness of the English Stage,* attacks neither the immorality nor the profaneness of the stage. It takes it for granted that when an actress plays a whore she is not playing a part and that when an actor works for "thrifty Rich" he may literally "stink" in his own clothes. Nowhere is it suggested that these conditions should be changed.

The occasion for the present poem is probably the production of Peter Motteux's opera, *The Island Princess,* at the Theatre Royal in 1698. This play, based on John Fletcher's tragicomedy, meets all the requirements of *The Play-House:* it has two kings, each attended "with a numerous train," a "stern exasperated tyrant," a princess in constant jeopardy, clowns, "dull cits," and even an allusion to Amphion.

THE PLAY-HOUSE

Near to the Rose where punks in numbers flock
To pick up cullies, to increase their stock;
A lofty fabric does the sight invade,
And stretches round the place a pompous shade;
Where sudden shouts the neighborhood surprise,   5
And thund'ring claps, and dreadful hissings rise.
   Here thrifty Rich hires heroes by the day,
And keeps his mercenary kings in pay;
With deep-mouthed actors fills the vacant scenes,
And drains the town for goddesses and queens: 10

1. *the Rose:* the Rose Tavern, on the corner of Bridges and Russell streets, adjacent to the Theatre Royal, was a great resort for loose women and minor poets.
3. *A lofty fabric:* the Theatre Royal.
7. *Rich:* Christopher Rich (d. 1714), theatrical manager, noted for his greed and cunning.

Here the lewd punk, with crowns and scepters graced,
Teaches her eyes a more majestic cast;
And hungry monarchs with a numerous train
Of suppliant slaves, like Sancho starve and reign.
  But enter in, my Muse, the stage survey,   15
And all its pomp and pageantry display;
Trap-doors and pit-falls, from th' unfaithful ground,
And magic walls, encompass it around:
On either side maimed temples fill our eyes,
And intermixed with brothel-houses rise;   20
Disjointed palaces in order stand,
And groves obedient to the mover's hand
O'er-shade the stage, and flourish at command.
A stamp makes broken towns and trees entire:
So when Amphion struck the vocal lyre,   25
He saw the spacious circuit all around,
With crowding woods, and rising cities crowned.
  But next survey the tyring-room and see
False titles, and promiscuous quality
Confusedly swarm, from heroes and from queens   30
To those that swing in clouds and fill machines;
Their various characters they choose with art,
The frowning bully fits the tyrant's part:
Swol'n cheeks and swagging belly make a host;
Pale meager looks, and hollow voice, a ghost;   35
From careful brows, and heavy downcast eyes,
Dull cits, and thick-skulled aldermen arise:
The comic tone, inspired by Farquhar, draws
At every word, loud laughter and applause:
The mincing dame continues as before,   40
Her character unchanged, and acts a whore.
  Above the rest, the prince with haughty stalks,
Magnificent in purple buskins walks:
The royal robes his awful shoulders grace,
Profuse of spangles and of copper-lace: 45
Officious vassals, to his mighty thigh,
Guiltless of blood, th' unpointed weapon tie:
Then the gay glittering diadem put on,

19–20. Cf. *Mac Flecknoe*, 70: "From its own ruins brothel-houses rise."
24. On cue—a stamp of the foot (?)—the scenes are changed.
34. *swagging*: swaying heavily to and fro.

Pondrous with brass, and starred with Bristol stone.
His royal consort next consults her glass   50
And out of twenty boxes culls a face;
The whit'ning first her sallow looks besmears,
All pale and wan th' unfinished form appears;
'Till on her cheeks the blushing purple glows,
And a false virgin modesty bestows.   55
Her ruddy lips the deep vermillion dyes;
Length to her brows the pencil's touch supplies,
And with black bending arches shades her eyes.
Well pleased at last the picture she beholds,
And spots it o'er with artificial moles: 60
Her countenance complete, the beaux she warms
With looks not hers, and spite of nature, charms.
    Thus artfully their persons they disguise,
'Till the last flourish bids the curtain rise.
The prince then enters on the stage in state;   65
Behind, a guard of candle-snuffers wait:
There, swol'n with empire, terrible and fierce,
He shakes the dome, and tears his lungs with verse:
His subjects tremble, the submissive pit,
Wrapped up in silence and attention, sit;   70
Till freed at length, he lays aside the weight
Of public business, and affairs of state:
Forgets his pomp, dead to ambitious fires,
And to some peaceful brandy-shop retires;
Where in full gills his anxious thoughts he drowns,   75
And quaffs away the cares that wait on crowns.
    The princess next her painted charms displays,
Where every look the pencil's art betrays.
The callow 'squire at distance feeds his eyes,
And silently for paint and patches dies: 80
But if the youth behind the scenes retreat,
He sees the blended colors melt with heat,
And all the trickling beauties run in sweat.
The borrowed visage he admires no more,
And nauseates every charm he loved before: 85
So the same spear, for double force renowned,
Applied the remedy, that gave the wound.

49. *Bristol stone:* rock crystals cut to imitate diamonds.
  86. *spear:* The spear was Achilles' and the victim was Telephos. The Delphic oracle, "He that wounded shall also heal," was correctly interpreted by Odysseus to mean the spear

In tedious lists 'twere endless to engage,
And draw at length the rabble of the stage,
Where one for twenty years has given alarms,   90
And called contending monarchs to their arms;
Another fills a more important post,
And rises every other night a ghost,
Through the cleft stage, his mealy face he rears,
Then stalks along, groans thrice, and disappears;   95
Others with swords and shields, the soldiers pride,
More than a thousand times have changed their side,
And in a thousand fatal battles died.
    Thus several persons, several parts perform;
Pale lovers whine, and blust'ring heroes storm.   100
The stern exasperated tyrants rage,
Till the kind bowl of poison clears the stage.
Then honors vanish, and distinctions cease;
Then with reluctance, haughty queens undress.
Heroes no more their fading laurels boast,   105
And mighty kings, in private men are lost.
He, whom such titles swelled, such power made proud,
To whom whole realms and vanquished nations bowed,
Throws off the gaudy plume, the purple train,
And in his own vile tatters stinks again.   110

---

itself that had given the wound. When scrapings from the spear were applied, therefore, the wound healed.

[ARTHUR MAINWARING]

The Brawny Bishop's Complaint
(January-February 1699)

Gilbert Burnet (1643–1715), cashiered chaplain of Charles II, *éminence grise* of the revolution, and William's latitudinarian bishop of Salisbury, was a frequent target for Tory satirists in four reigns. *The Brawny Bishop's Complaint* simply takes up and expands an insinuation in Dryden's characterization of Burnet as the noble buzzard in the "Fable of the Swallows" from *The Hind and the Panther, 3*, 1145–46: "Broad-backed and brawny, built for loves delight, / A prophet formed, to make a female proselyte." In 1698 Burnet had been much in the news. In June his second wife had died, leaving him with five children under the age of ten. Burnet commented on this event with typical bluntness: "At that time I saw it was convenient for me to marry again." In the same month the king had appointed him preceptor to Prince William, duke of Gloucester, the nine-year old heir apparent to the Princess Anne. On 30 January 1699 Burnet had preached an eloquent sermon before the House of Lords in the Abbey church.

During this period of his life Burnet lived in a rented house in Windsor, which was within his diocese, but during sessions of Parliament, when he stayed in town, "he failed not of preaching every Sunday morning, in some church or other in London" (Burnet, *2*, 721). Presumably, as the poem implies, he was also in the habit of preaching before the fashionable and influential congregation of St. James, Piccadilly.

The church itself, which Sir Christopher Wren called "the most capacious" of those he had designed, had been consecrated only in 1684. It had been built to accommodate the court *faubourg* that was growing up around St. James's Square. The interior of the church was richly furnished, with an excellent organ that had been donated by Queen Mary, "a curious font, and the galleries well set off with tapestries and Persian carpets" (Strype, *2*, 381). The same wealthy parishioners who provided this luxury "also altered the pews to suit their convenience and sent carpenters to put up benches, and rails on the seats" (Charles Ashbee et al., *The Survey of London*, 32 vols. [London City Council, 1900–], *29*, 36), and this fact must have provided the occasion for the present poem.

An Excellent New Ballad,
Called
The Brawny Bishop's Complaint.

To the Tune of "Packington's Pound"

1.

When Burnet perceived that the beautiful dames,
Who flock to the chapel of holy St. James,
On their lovers above their kind looks did bestow,
And smiled not at him when he bellowed below,
  To the princess he went   5
  With a pious intent,
This dangerous ill in the church to prevent:
O Madam! said he, our religion's quite lost,
If the ladies thus ogle the Knights of the Toast.

2.

Your Highness observes how I labor and sweat,   10
Their affections to raise, and new flames to beget;
And sure when I preach, all the world will agree,
That their ears and their eyes should be pointed at me:
  But now I can find
  No beauty so kind,   15
My parts to regard, or my person to mind:

 2. *the chapel of holy St. James:* correctly identified in Dryden's letter of 23 February 1699 as "St. James's church" and not the Chapel Royal in the palace of St. James, as Edmund Malone supposed (Dryden, *Prose, 1,* ii, [1]109). Evelyn (*6,* 373) explains that the Chapel Royal was "not always distinguishable from the chapel of ease of St. James, Piccadilly," but Dryden was describing events that took place in the adjoining parish, barely a quarter mile from his house on Gerrard Street.
 4. *bellowed:* Malone cites William Shippen, *Faction Displayed,* 96, where Burnet boasts of his "thund'ring voice."
 5. Burnet's favor with Anne, princess of Denmark, began with his appointment in June 1698 as preceptor to William, duke of Gloucester (1689–1700), Anne's sole surviving child and heir apparent to the throne of England. Burnet filled this post so capably that "the princess of Denmark ever after retained a peculiar regard for him" (Burnet, *2,* 718).
 9. *Knights of the Toast:* a festive society, whose ritual included drinking toasts in succession to the reigning beauties (W.J. Cameron, "John Dryden and Henry Heveningham," *Notes and Queries* 202 [May 1957]: 199–203).
 12. *preach:* John Evelyn heard Burnet preach on 15 November 1674 "with such a flood of eloquence, and fullness of matter as showed him to be a person of extraordinary parts" (*4,* 47–48).

Nay, I scarce have a sight of one feminine face,
But those of old Oxford, and ugly Arglass.

3.

These sorrowful matrons with hearts full of truth
Repent for the manifold sins of their youth: 20
The rest with their tattle my harmony spoil;
And Burlington, Anglesey, Kingston, and Boyle
   Their minds entertain
    With thoughts so profane,
'Tis a mercy to find that at church they contain;   25
Ev'n Heveningham's shape their weak fancies entice,
And rather than me they will ogle the Vice.

18. *old Oxford:* Diana Kirke (d. 1719), of whom H. B. Wheatley claimed that "nothing more need be said than that she bore an inappropriate Christian name" (Pepys, *2,* 224 *n.*), became the second wife of Aubrey de Vere, 20th earl of Oxford, shortly before 12 April 1673 (GEC, *10,* 260–61). *ugly Arglass:* Honora Boyle (d. 1710), daughter of Michael Boyle, archbishop of Armagh and chancellor of Ireland, married first Thomas Cromwell, earl of Ardglass in Ireland and Baron Cromwell in England (1653–82), then Francis Cuffe (1656–94), and finally Thomas Burdett (d.1727) (GEC, *1,* 193).

22. *Burlington:* Juliana (1672–1750), daughter of Henry Noel, wife of Charles Boyle, 2d earl of Burlington and Cork (Dryden, *Prose,* ed. Malone, *1,* ii, ¹116, 6 *n.;* "What Beauties *Burl——n* pursues," *POAS,* 1703, *2,* 256). *Anglesey:* Malone identifies her as Lady Catharine Darnley (1683–1743), natural daughter of James II by Catharine Sedley. Since she married James Annesley, 5th earl of Anglesey, on 28 October 1699 (Collins, 1741, *2,* 344), the attribution is probably correct (Dryden, *Prose,* ed. Malone, *1,* ii, ¹116, 7 *n.).* *Kingston:* Malone (Dryden, *Prose, 1,* ii, ¹116, 8 *n.)* identifies her as Mary, daughter of William Fielding, 3d earl of Denbigh, and first wife of Evelyn Pierrepoint, 5th earl of Kingston, but since she died in 1697 (GEC, *7,* 307), the reference must be to Anne, the dowager countess of Kingston (d. 1702), whose amorous inclinations are recorded in Holkham MS 686, p. 266. *Boyle:* Perhaps Arethusa, daughter of Charles Boyle, Baron Clifford of Lanesborough, by his second wife, and half-sister to Charles Boyle, 2d earl of Burlington and Cork, and therefore, as Malone suggests, "likely to have been grouped with his lady" (Dryden, *Prose, 1,* ii, ¹116, 9 *n.).*

25. *contain:* refrain from expressing or yielding to passion. "But if they cannot contain, let them marry" (1 *Cor.* 7:9).

26. Henry Heveningham (c. 1651–1700), was M.P. for Dunwich, in Suffolk, and held a minor post at court, where he was lieutenant of the band of gentlemen pensioners, the king's House Guards. He was also, apparently, an occasional or renegade Knight of the Toast, for he is charged with profaning its mysteries and exposing its president "in rude rhyme." These rhymes have never been published, although the reply to them is printed in *POAS,* 1703, *2,* 255. In those lines Heveningham is represented as an aging and impotent roué. *shape:* The best MSS read "shape," but the grammar requires "shapes." *OED* cites B. E., *A New Dictionary* [1699], "shapes, said (often) to an ill-made man," and T. Dyche and W. Pardon, *A New General English Dictionary,* 1735, "shapes, a cant name for . . . an ill-made, irregular lump of flesh, etc." Heveningham was "a tall thin-gutted mortal" (Thomas Brown, *Works* [1707], *2,* 10–11).

27. *the Vice:* Peregrine Bertie, second son of Robert Bertie, 3d earl of Lindsey, was vicechamberlain of the royal household, a Privy Councillor, and knight of the Toast. His feat of running the mall in St. James's Park eleven times in less than an hour to win a wager, is recorded in Luttrell, *2,* 98.

4.

These practices, Madam, my preaching disgrace;
Shall laymen enjoy the just rights of my place?
Then all may lament my condition so hard,   30
Who thresh in the pulpit without a reward.
    Therefore pray condescend
    Such disorders to end,
And from the ripe vineyard those laborers send;
Or build up the seats that the beauties may see 35
The face of no brawny pretender but me.

5.

The princess by rude importunity pressed,
Though she laughed at his reasons, allowed his request:
And now Britain's nymphs in this Protestant reign
Are locked up at pray'rs like the virgins in Spain; 40
    So they are all undone,
    For as sure as a gun,
Whenever a woman is kept like a nun,
If any kind man from her bondage will save her,
The lady in gratitude grants him the favor. 45

 34. *the ripe vineyard:* apparently an allusion to the parable of the wicked husbandmen (Mark 12:1–12), with the Knights of the Toast cast in the role of the usurping husbandmen and Burnet in the role of the excluded heir.

 40. *virgins in Spain:* Sympathy for the Spanish was widespread. It was explained to Joseph Spence that "Spanish ladies are of a constitution particularly apt to take fire. As they are more confined they are fuller of passion than other women are" (Spence, *2,* 536).

DANIEL DEFOE

An Encomium upon a Parliament
(1699)

The Parliament in the title is the fourth of William III, which a recent historian has called "a Parliament more xenophobic and obstructive, more essentially 'country,' than any since the revolution" (Kenyon, p. 307). "Country," of course, means anti-court, and the intensity of hatred generated during this session would be difficult to exaggerate. William came to believe that it was he himself who was aimed at, but it is more likely that power, rather than principle or personality, was the matter at issue.

The quality of the fourth Parliament of William III had been determined in the General Election of July–August 1698. The "new country party," as the Whigs called it, campaigned everywhere against such perennially reliable bogies as standing armies, corruption, and high taxes. One of their most successful election pamphlets, by "Mr. Harley's creature," John Toland, was entitled *The Danger of Mercenary Parliaments*. The new country party was at first only a shaky coalition of "old Whigs" (as they preferred to be called), like the Harleys and the Foleys and their followers, and Tory high churchmen like Sir Edward Seymour and John Granville, together with a fringe of unrepentant Jacobites like Sir Christopher Musgrave. What success they met with in the election was not immediately known. James Vernon, secretary of state, thought that the Whigs might retain "a considerable majority," but Somers, the lord chancellor, feared that the new Parliament would be "somewhat difficult to be dealt with" (Vernon, 2, 149; William Coxe, ed., *Private and Original Correspondence of Charles Talbot, Duke of Shrewsbury* [1681], p. 554).

The precise moment when the new country party seized the initiative in the House of Commons can be stated with certainty. It occurred on 14 December 1698 when they stopped the motion for a supply, until a committee considered the army both in England and Ireland. "The business of the standing army," as Toland observed, "finished all" (*A Collection of Several Pieces*, 2 vols. [1726], 2, 341). On 16 December the earl of Ranelagh laid before the House the estimates that showed that even after the cutback to the level of 1680, 14,834 troops remained on the English establishment. The next day the House "acted as in a fury"; without even a division they cut that figure in half, and Robert Harley, who had made the motion, was instructed to bring in a bill to disband all forces exceeding 7000 officers and men. John Grubham Howe's amendment that none but natural-born subjects of England be included was also accepted without a division. This meant dismissal of the Dutch guards, which included the famous Blue Guards regiment, Portland's regiment of Horse Guards, and a troop of Life Guards, some 2500 men.

William thought this was not only "ruinous" in face of the *cauchemar perpetuel* of the Spanish succession and a claimant to the English throne at the French court, but also a personal affront to him. On 29 December 1698 Somers reported to Shrewsbury the shocking news that William was planning to give up the throne. He had in fact retired to Windsor to write his speech of abdication. "It was one of Somers's most notable achievements," according to David Ogg, "that he induced the king to give up his intention of returning to Holland" (Ogg, *James II, 3,* 450).

Meanwhile the triumph of the new country party was complete. The disbanding bill passed by a large majority, 221 to 154, and by February 1699 James Vernon had to confess that "we are a dispersed routed party, [and] our opposers bear hard upon us" (Vernon, *2,* 262). Vernon also acknowledged that what was going on had no ideological basis but was simply a struggle for power. "The public has no place in our thoughts," he said, "but we are pushing at each other as fast as we can" (Vernon, *2,* 245, 265–66). This explains why the present poem is neither Whig nor Tory, or, more exactly, why it is anti-Whig and anti-Tory.

"This miserable session of Parliament," as the king called it, finally drew to an end on 4 May 1699, and William could look forward to a summer in Holland. "God knows how I long for that moment," he added.

An Encomium upon a Parliament

Ye worthy patriots go on
    To heal the nation's sores,
Find all men's faults out but your own.
Begin good laws, but finish none,
    And then shut up your doors.   5

4. Among half a dozen "reform" bills dropped during the session was one that may have particularly interested Defoe. It was a bill for suppressing the ill practices of pawnbrokers, ordered to be brought in on 2 March 1699 but never mentioned again. Another was a bill ordered to be brought in on 4 May, the day Parliament was prorogued, by a committee appointed to inquire into the ill practices and abuses of the prisons of the King's Bench and the fleet (*CJ, 12,* 687), of which Defoe said later, "I had the honor to be one of the first complainers, and . . . to have had some hand in the dissolution of their monstrous privileges" (*Review* 4 [8 April 1707]: 100). White Kennett mentions another bill that was "unhappily

Fail not our freedom to secure,
　　And all our friends disband,
And send those fools to t'other shore
Who knew no better than to come o'er
　　To help this grateful land.   10
And may the next that hear us pray,
　　And in distress relieve us,
Go home like those without their pay,
And with contempt be sent away
　　For having once believed us.   15

And if the French should e'er attempt
　　This nation to invade,
May they be damned that 'list again,
But lead your famed militia on,
　　To be like us betrayed.   20

As for the crown you have bestowed
　　With all its limitations,

---

dropped" (*3*, 766). This was a bill for the conveying of lands, tenements, rents, tithes, and hereditaments to any college or school for the education of poor scholars or advancement of learning.

6. *freedom to secure:* The Tories represented the advantages of disbanding the army to be ideological as well as economic. A French intelligence report of December 1698 explained that "the hope of the restoration of King James being entirely lost," the Tories "may speak and act more boldly for liberty" (Paul E. Grimblot, ed., *Letters of William III and Louis XIV . . . 1697–1700* [1848], *2*, 193). Accordingly, in the next month, Robert Harley maintained that the only alternative to disbanding the army was "keeping it up, shutting up the Exchequer, governing by sword and edicts" (HMC, *Portland*, *3*, 601).

7. *friends disband:* By the terms of John Grubham Howe's amendment to the disbanding bill, excluding all but "natural-born subjects of England" from the armed forces, William had to order the famous Dutch guards regiments to return to Holland.

10. *this grateful land:* The five so-called French regiments, made up entirely of Huguenot refugees and now stationed in Ireland, had also to be disbanded.

13. *without their pay:* The situation of the foreign mercenary in the army on 25 March 1699, the day set by Parliament for the disbanding, may be judged by the petition of three troopers in the earl of Macclesfield's regiment, two German and one Scottish, who claimed that they were "now disbanded, and barbarously used by their officers, having their horses and accoutrements taken from them, which was given them by the king, and themselves stripped from the waist upwards: that being aliens, and forced to leave this kingdom; and having not one penny to buy them bread withal," they prayed some relief might be afforded them (*CJ*, *12*, 650).

19. *famed militia:* The legendary ineffectiveness of the militia was a constant source of amusement and the importance assigned to it as a consequence of disbanding the army had already been noticed in verse: "Then will our prince, like Mars in warlike guise, / Encamp at Hounslow, to shoot butterflies" (*Aesop in Select Fables*, 1698, sig. Elr).

22. *limitations:* William of Orange was offered "the crown and royal dignity of the kingdoms of England, France, and Ireland," not unconditionally, but "according to the resolution and desire of the . . . Lords and Commons" contained in the Bill of Rights (1 W. & M.,

The meanest prince in Christendom
Would never stir a mile from home
   To govern three such nations.   25

The king himself, whom ye have called
   Your savior in distress,
You have his first request denied,
And then his royal patience tried
   With a canting sham address.   30

Ye are the men that to be chose
   Would be at no expenses,
Who love no friends, nor fear no foes,
And have ways and means that no man knows
   To mortify our senses.   35

Ye are the men that can condemn
   By laws made ex post facto,
Who can make knaves of honest men,
And married women turn again
   To be virgo et intacta.   40

Go on to purify the court,

---

sess. 2, cap. ii). The main limitation was the abrogation of the dispensing power, the power that James II had claimed of suspending the execution of the laws by regal authority.

26–27. *called . . . savior:* In the Bill of Rights (February 1689) William is called "the Prince of Orange (whom it hath pleased Almightly God to make the glorious instrument of delivering this kingdom from popery and arbitrary power)." Exactly ten years later, the 4th Parliament addressed the king in similar terms, referring to "the labors you have sustained, and the hazards you have run, in rescuing us from popery and arbitrary power, restoring our liberties, and giving peace and quiet to all Christendom" (*CJ, 12,* 481).

28. *first request:* Even after the date for their departure had been set, William made a final attempt to keep the Dutch guards in England.

29. *patience tried:* "On all sides," the king wrote to Heinsius in May 1699, "my patience is put to the trial" (Grimblot, *Letters of William III, 2,* 334). The fact of his resentment was public knowledge. Richard Lucas, the blind rector of St. Stephens's in Coleman Street, said in a sermon preached on 5 April 1699 that the king "was born to have his person exposed to his enemies abroad, and his patience tried by his subjects at home" (Luttrell, *4,* 502).

30. *address:* William told Heinsius that his attempt to keep the Dutch guards had produced only "a very impertinent address on the subject" (Grimblot, *Letters of William III 2,* 310).

36–37. *condemn . . . ex post facto:* The "honest men" who were condemned ex post facto may be Defoe's friend Dalby Thomas and the projector, Thomas Neale, both of whom were accused in 1698(?) of embezzlement arising out of their management of a state lottery that had raised £1,000,000 for the government.

39–40. *married women . . . intacta:* This may be a reference to the divorce case of Charles Gerard, 2d earl of Macclesfield, against his wife, Anne, the alleged mother of Richard Savage. It caused considerable stir in the last session of the preceding Parliament because it was the first divorce bill to pass without a prior decree from a spiritual court. The bill, while it could not restore the countess's virginity, did restore her fortune.

And damn the men of places,
Till decently you send them home,
And get your selves put in their room,
And then you'll change your faces.   45

Go on to reestablish trade,
And mend our navigation,
Let India India invade,
And borrow on funds that will ne'er be paid,
And bankrupt all the nation.   50

'Tis you that calculate our gold,
And with a senseless tone
Vote what you never understood,
That we might take them if we would
Or let them all alone.   55

Your missives you send round about
With Mr. Speaker's letter,
To fetch folks in, and find folks out,

42–43. *men of places:* It was evident early in the session that "those . . . who are in the possession of offices are to be tossed up and down" (Vernon, *2,* 241). Finally on 10 February, the storm broke. "The Commons . . . are in a rage," Tallard reported. "Instead of proceeding with the affair of the fleet, they attacked, by virtue of an act of Parliament, which, to this hour, had never been [enforced], all those who were receivers of the king's money, saying that they cannot be chosen members of Parliament" (Grimblot, *Letters of William III, 2,* 277). Within the next ten days, five members were expelled and new elections ordered. The reason for this, as Tallard explained, was simply "to diminish the court party" (ibid., p. 289).

48. *India India invade:* In 1698 the East India Company offered the government a loan of £700,000 at 4 per cent to maintain the trading monopoly it had enjoyed for 40 years. It was outbid, however, by a syndicate of bankers and merchants headed by Samuel Shepherd, who offered a loan of £2,000,000 at 8 percent. In May 1698 Charles Montagu, chancellor of the Exchequer, introduced a bill creating a new East India Company and allowing the old one three years to wind up its affairs. When this bill, tacked to a money bill, reached the House of Lords it was debated with such acrimony that Montagu himself regretted that he had proposed it.

49. *funds that will ne'er be paid:* As David Ogg explains, "what we now call the national debt was then thought of, not as an aggregate, but as a series of deficiencies, of greatly varying amounts, in the funds—deficiencies which, it was thought, could eventually be made good by taxation" (*James II, 3,* 413). Defoe is expressing his doubt that these deficiencies, which Montagu estimated to amount to more than £10,000,000 would ever be made good.

51. *calculate our gold:* On 14 February 1699 Commons read a report from the commission of trade, of which John Locke was a member, which pointed out that "over-valuing [gold] in the currency of guineas at 22s. is a prejudice to this kingdom in our trade" and recommended a devaluation to 21s. 6d. (*CJ, 12,* 511).

54. *them:* gold guineas.

56–57. On 6 April 1699 complaint was made on the floor of the House of Commons "of several letters, sent into the country by Henry Chivers," the Tory member for Calne, Wiltshire, "wherein several of the members of this House are not only reflected on, but misrepresented as to their votes in this House" (*CJ, 12,* 632).

Which fools believe without dispute,
   Because they know no better.   60

You borrowed ships and hired men
   The Irish to reduce,
Who will be paid the Lord knows when;
'Tis hoped whene'er you want again,
   You'll think of that abuse.   65

Ye laid sham taxes on our malt,
   On salt, and glass, and leather,
To wheedle coxcombs in to lend;
Then like true cheats you drop the fund,
   And sink them all together.   70

And now y'are piously inclined
   The needy to employ;
You'd better much your time bestow
To pay the neglected debts you owe,
   Which make them multiply.   75

Against profaneness you declared,
   And then the bill rejected;
And when your arguments appeared,
They were the worst that e'er were heard,
   And the best that we expected.   80

'Twas voted once, that for the sin

61. *ships:* Owners of ships which had been chartered for transport during the Irish campaigns of 1689–91 were issued debentures in 1695 which were still unpaid in July 1703.

69. *drop the fund:* While no funds had actually defaulted, on 4 March 1699 there was a deficit of £2,759,854 "for which no provision (for refunding) is made" (*CJ, 12,* 548–49). Consequently, there must have been many anxious creditors in the City.

72. *The needy:* In his address at the opening of the session, the king urged that "some effectual expedient . . . be found for employing the poor," but a bill to this effect, was allowed to die in committee after a second reading.

74. *neglected debts:* The arrears due the army and navy were estimated to be nearly £3,000,-000.

75. *them:* the needy. As in line 54 the syntax is telegraphic, but it is "the neglected debts" which make "the needy" multiply.

76. *Against profaneness:* In his address at the opening of the session, the king hoped that the Parliament would employ its "thoughts about some good bills for . . . the further discouraging of vice and profaneness" (*LJ, 16,* 352). Accordingly, on 2 January 1699, Sir John Philipps brought in a bill for more effectual discouragement and suppression of profaneness and all manner of vice and immorality. The bill narrowly survived its second reading, 134 to 124 and then was allowed to die quietly in committee (*CJ, 12,* 368, 387, 401–02).

78. *arguments:* The only argument against the bill was said to be that it would profit the Whig justices of the peace "who live by their commission."

81–82. *for . . . die:* In the last session of the preceding Parliament Sir John Philipps and

Of whoring men should die all;
But then 'twas wisely thought again,
The House would quickly grow so thin,
    They durst not stand the trial.   85

King Charles the Second knew your aim,
    And places gave and pensions;
And had King William's money flown,
His Majesty would soon have known
    Your consciences' dimensions.   90

But he has wisely given you up
    To work your own desires,
And, laying arguments aside
As things that have in vain been tried,
    To fasting, calls, and prayers.   95

Chorus

Your hours are choicely employed,
Your petitions lie all on the table,
    With funds insufficient,
    And taxes deficient,
And debts which are innumerable.   100

For shame leave this wicked employment,
Reform both your manners and lives;
    You were never sent out
    To make such a rout,
Go home and look after your wives.   105

Edward Harley had been ordered to bring in "a bill for suppressing all sorts of debauchery; but the bill was clogged by a clause of one of these two members, which made not only houses of ill fame, but even hackney-coaches, where suspicion might be had of unlawful commerce between men and women, liable to the law; adultery was proposed to be punished with death" (Oldmixon, p. 175; *CJ*, *12*, 132, 147, 155, 160).

97. *petitions . . . table:* All the petitions of the unemployed leather workers mentioned were, in the parliamentary formula, ordered to "lie upon the table, to be perused by the members of the House." Instead of providing some "relief in the premises," the Commons simply made it easier for the excise men to collect the tax.

99. *taxes deficient:* The king told Heinsius on 28 April 1699: "They have not even voted the wherewithal to supply the taxes that were granted, nor a single farthing to discharge any kind of debt; so that credit is gone" (Grimblot, *Letters of William III, 2,* 324).

102. *Reform:* "It would be better, indeed, that Parliament reformed themselves, and save that trouble to others; but corruption and partialities have taken fast hold of us" (Vernon, *2,* 264).

SIR RICHARD BLACKMORE

A Satire against Wit
(23 November 1699)

By an instructive coincidence Blackmore's *Satire against Wit* was published in
the same month as Peter Motteux's translation of *The History of the Renowned
Don Quixote*. Before Blackmore began to practice medicine in the 1680s he
had sought advice from Thomas Sydenham, who was then the most successful
practitioner in London. Sydenham advised him to read Cervantes and it is
not difficult to imagine Sir Richard Blackmore of Cheapside as the Don
Quixote de la Mancha of English literature. Even by his admirers he was
"looked upon as a sort of madman" (Hearne, *8*, 101).

No less than four windmills are tilted at in *A Satire against Wit*: wit, of
course; obscenity; "science"; and *The Dispensary*. It was the last of these that
actually precipitated *A Satire against Wit*, accurately described on the title
page of a pirated Dublin edition as *"Designed an Answer to a Poem Stiled the
Dispensary."* Blackmore had been the leader of the "Apothecaries Physicians"
in the College of Physicians who for ten years had prevented the opening of a
free out-patient clinic in the college. In *The Dispensary*, however, it is not
Blackmore's obstructionist tactics, but his verses that Garth "most wittily
ridicules." As a consequence, Blackmore saw no need to defend his medical
politics, although the last dozen lines of *A Satire against Wit* refer unmistakably
to the dispensary. What he did find it necessary to defend was his literary
practice. And here he decided, quite rightly, that the best defense is a good
offense. So he runs down *The Dispensary* as a satire "with little in't but praise"
(line 181), and as contraband goods stolen in France and illegally vended in
England. And he rejects Dryden, whose "vigorous turns" Garth had urged
Blackmore to "consider" as a model, on account of the "lewd allay" (line
208) in his verses.

The year before *A Satire against Wit* appeared, Jeremy Collier, a nonjuring
clergyman under a sentence of outlawry, published *A Short View of the Im-
morality, and Profaneness of the English Stage,* and then, as the story is commonly
told, "The pulpit [got] the better of the stage." But as J. E. Spingarn has
pointed out, "the victory had been achieved before Collier wrote; and in the
year before the revolution Sedley compared the change of public taste to
the sudden whims of the English weather" (*Critical Essays of the Seventeenth*

Century, 3 vols. [Oxford: Clarendon, 1908], *1,* lxxxv). Sedley was "very unhappy that the ice that has borne so many coaches and carts should break with my wheelbarrow," but there was no doubt in his mind that the ice was breaking. "This sudden change," as he called it, was nothing less than a major shift in the sensibility of the English people, and Blackmore was one of the first to register and define it. In 1695, in his preface to *Prince Arthur. An Heroic Poem,* he discovered that wit is "either immodest or irreligious," and in the same year Colley Cibber tacked a sentimental ending onto his first play, *Love's Last Shift; or, The Fool in Fashion.* In *A Satire against Wit* (lines 289–90) we are witnesses, delighted or horrified, according to our predilection, to the emergence of bourgeois morality: "Therefore some just and wholesome laws ordain, / That may this wild licentiousness restrain." These words, with their inevitable corollary, "Therefore let satire writers be suppressed," (352) are merely a restatement of current government policy. In December 1698, in his speech at the opening of his fourth Parliament, William had urged that "you will employ your thoughts about some good bills . . . for the further discouraging of vice and profaneness."

As William's words imply, morality had been an affair of state for some time. John Evelyn, in fact, had noticed a change in the moral climate as soon as Charles II was buried, and James II "spoke openly against lewdness, and expressed a detestation of drunkenness" (Burnet, *1,* 624). The Society for the Reformation of Manners was founded in 1690 and its informers began operations against "loose persons" soon after.

William III turned to public morality as soon as he had brought the war to a conclusion. "I esteem it one of the greatest advantages of the peace," he said in December 1697, "that I shall now have leisure . . . effectually to discourage profaneness and immorality" (*CJ, 12,* 1). Parliament responded with an act for the more effectual suppression of blasphemy and profaneness (9 & 10 William III c. 32), which was disappointing to the king because it simply established penalties for those who denied the doctrine of the Trinity. On his own side, the king kept up a steady barrage of proclamations and orders, "to prevent the profaneness and immorality of the stage," "not to act anything contrary to religion and good manners," and the like.

With all this encouragement, whole "troops of informers" sprang up to "serve God for gain" and "pick harmless words out of plays to indite the players and squeeze twenty pound a week out of them." Sir Harry Ashurst's coachman was fined for swearing at the chocolate house door and "a few poor whores" were forced to shift their quarters. Otherwise, it was the theatre that was hardest hit. Both playhouses were presented as public nuisances by the grand jury of Middlesex county; actors were fined £10 for using indecent language on the stage, and Vanbrugh's new comedy, *The Provoked Wife,* which had opened without incident in 1697, was presented as obscene only two years later. Vanbrugh was forced into the duller but safer work of adapting Beaumont and Fletcher and eventually into the peaceful province of architecture.

In a poem entitled *A Satire against Wit,* it is obviously relevant to determine what the poet meant by "wit." During most of the poem the term is synonymous with obscenity and blasphemy. There are some contexts, however, where this equation does not hold (for example, lines 97, 225, 315–16). Considering it simply as a literary commodity, Blackmore thinks of "wit" as "intellectual enameling," as he described it in his *Essay upon Wit* in 1716, or "a rich embroidery of flowers and figures," something delightful but useless and unnecessary. Blackmore's stated literary ideals are by no means despicable. There is no reason why comedy, as Blackmore demanded, could not at the same time be "delightful and promote prudence and sobriety of manners" (*Essays upon Several Subjects* [1716], pp. 192, 219), but the truth seems to be that Blackmore himself remained inaccessible to "delight" and responded only to didacticism. His values are not literary or aesthetic at all, but utilitarian: "The labors of the meanest persons," he said in *Essay upon Wit,* "are more valuable, because more useful, than . . . those, who apply themselves only, or principally, to divert and entertain the fancy." Blackmore was aware that "wit" is not merely "intellectual enameling; besides this," he said, "it animates and warms a cold sentiment, and makes it glow with life and vigor." Blackmore simply preferred "cold sentiment."

Just beneath the surface of the dispensary quarrel there may lurk a more important difference of opinion between Garth and Blackmore on the subject of medical education and practice. Blackmore observed that logic and metaphysics had become "the subject of much raillery, and the great abomination of the wits." For himself, on the contrary, he found that "Logic and metaphysics, wherein I was carefully instructed in the university . . . fit a man for any kind of business or profession, [better] than . . . all the searches which I have made after the reasons and causes of natural phenomena" (King Arthur [1697], pp. 10–11). This depreciation of basic research contrasts sharply with the opinions of at least two of the dispensary physicians whom Blackmore opposed. Garth insisted that the study of medicine be based on "wondrous searches" into the "wondrous cause" of physiological phenomena just as Daniel Coxe demanded "a mass of experiments" to establish the "unquestionable verities." Whereas Blackmore demanded that medical practice should be totally empirical, undertaken without preconceptions or hypotheses, Garth insisted that it should be accompanied by the constant testing of hypotheses in laboratory research. "Hypothesis" in science takes the place of "wit" in literature as Blackmore's antithesis to "sense" or common sense.

Ever since Sydenham advised Blackmore to read *Don Quixote,* there has been speculation as to what he meant. Samuel Johnson, who deplored "this foolish apophthegm," supposed that Sydenham meant that whether Blackmore read "Cervantes or Hippocrates he would be equally unqualified for practice" (G. B. Hill, ed., *The Lives of the English Poets*, 3 vols. [Oxford: Clarendon, 1905], *2*, 236 *n*.). A better guess, however, is that Sydenham was warning Blackmore against what John Locke called "the romance way of physic." What Sydenham hated most in the practice of medicine was the intrusion of theories. John Locke was delighted with all this, but it seems obvious that without hypotheses, and without imagination and "fancies," medicine as a science would have been stillborn.

A Satire against Wit, as Samuel Johnson has said, was "a proclamation of defiance," and it builds up in the last lines to an impressive climax of scorn for the witless subscribers to the dispensary: "Let 'em pound drugs; they have no brains to beat." And since it was "a proclamation of defiance," there can be no doubt that the poem "made a great noise" when it was published on 23 November 1699. More copies were needed even before the type for the first edition could be distributed, and a so-called third edition was advertised in *The Post Man*, no. 740, 18–20 April 1700.

A SATIRE AGAINST WIT

Who can forbear, and tamely silent sit,
And see his native land undone by wit?
Boast not, Britannia, of thy happy peace,
What if campaigns and sea-engagements cease?
Wit, a worse plague, does mightily increase.   5
Some monstrous crimes to ages past unknown,
Have surely pulled this heavy judgment down.
Fierce insect-wits draw out their noisy swarms,
And threaten ruin more than foreign arms.
O'er all the land the hungry locusts spread,   10
Gnaw every plant, taint every flowery bed,
And crop each budding virtue's tender head.
    How happy were the old unpolished times,
As free from wit as other modern crimes?
As our forefathers vig'rous were and brave;   15

8–9. Cf. Swift, *Prose, 1,* 24: "The wits of the present age being so very numerous and penetrating, it seems, the grandees of church and state begin to fall under horrible apprehensions, lest these gentlemen, during the intervals of a long peace, should find leisure to pick holes in the weak sides of religion and government."

So they were virtuous, wise, discreet and grave,
Detesting both alike the wit and knave.
They justly wits and fools believed the same,
And jester was for both the common name.
Their minds for empire formed would never quit   20
Their noble roughness, and dissolve in wit.
For business born and bred to martial toil,
They raised the glory of Britannia's isle.
Then she her dreadful ensigns did advance,
To curb Iberia, and to conquer France.   25
But this degenerate, loose and foolish race
Are all turned wits, and their great stock debase.
Our learning daily sinks, and wit is grown
The senseless conversation of the town.
Enervated with this our youth have lost   30
That stubborn virtue, which we once could boast.
The plague of wit prevails; I fear 'tis vain
Now to attempt its fury to restrain.
It takes men in the head, and in the fit
They lose their senses, and are gone in wit.   35
By various ways their frenzy they express,
Some with loose lines run haring to the press,
In lewdness some are wits, some only wits in dress.
Some seized like Gravar with convulsions, strain
Always to say fine things, but strive in vain,   40
Urged with a dry tenesmus of the brain.
   Had but the people scared with danger run
To shut up Wills, where first this plague begun:
Had they the first infected men conveyed
Straight to Moorfields, the pest-house for the head;   45
The wild contagion might have been suppressed,
Some few had fal'n but we had saved the rest.
An act like this had been a good defense

37. *haring*: very fast *(OED)*.
39. *Gravar*: unidentified.
41. *Tenesmus*: a continual inclination to void the contents of the bowels or bladder, accompanied by straining, but with little or no discharge.
43. *Wills*: It was here, at the northwest corner of Russell and Bow streets, that Alexander Pope thrust himself in to see "the most celebrated wits of that time" presided over by "Mr. Dryden" (Spence, *1*, 29, 274). These included "Mr. Wicherley, Dr. Garth, Mr. Congreve, the Honorable Mr. Boyle, Colonel Stanhope, Mr. Vanbruk, Mr. Cheek, Mr. Walsh, Mr. Burnaby, Mr. Rowe, and some few others" (*Letters of Wit, Politics, and Morality*, p. 216).
45. *Moorfields*: the site of Bethlehem hospital for the insane, known as Bedlam.

Against our great mortality of sense.
But now th'infection spreads, the bills run high,   50
At the last gasp of sense ten thousand lie.
We meet fine youth in every house and street,
With all the deadly tokens out, of wit.

    Vannine that looked on all the danger past,
Because he scaped so long, is seized at last.   55
By pox and hunger and by Dryden bit
He grins and snarls, and in his dogged fit
Froths at the mouth, a certain sign of wit.

    Craper runs madly midst the sickest crowd,
And fain would be infected, if he could.   60
Under the means he lies, frequents the stage,
Is very lewd, and does at learning rage.
Pity that so much labor should be lost
By such a healthful constitution crossed.
Against th'assaults of wit his make is proof,   65
Still his strong nature works the poison off.
He still escapes, but yet is wondrous pleased,
Wit to recite, and to be thought diseased.
So hypocrites in vice in this vile town
To wickedness pretend, that's not their own.   70

    A bant'ring spirit has our men possessed,
And wisdom is become a standing jest.
Wit does of virtue sure destruction make;
Who can produce a wit and not a rake?
Wise magistrates lewd wit do therefore hate,   75
The bane of virtue's treason to the state.
While honor fails and honesty decays,
In vain we beat our heads for means and ways.

50. *bills:* weekly bills of mortality.

54. *Vannine:* identified by one reader as Charles Gildon and by another as Samuel Garth.

59. *Craper:* One reader identified Craper as Thomas Cheek (d. 1713?), "a gentleman of above £2000 per annum" who enjoyed drinking with the Covent Garden wits and writing songs and prologues for his friends' works, including *The Dispensary*. This identification cannot be certain, however, for another reader identified Craper as "Drake." Besides being a distinguished candidate of the College of Physicians and subscriber to the dispensary, James Drake (1667–1707) was also an enthusiastic littérateur. In 1699 he published a remarkable 367-page attack on Jeremy Collier entitled *The Ancient and Modern Stage Surveyed,* which may be the subject of the reference in line 62.

61: *Under the means:* a theological phrase applied here to a medical metaphor. "To live under the means of grace" is to live in such a manner that divine grace is imparted to the soul. Craper lives in a manner to invite the disease of wit.

65. *make:* kind, sort, species.

What well-formed government or state can last,
When wit has laid the people's virtue waste?   80
   The mob of wits is up to storm the town,
To pull all virtue and right reason down.
Quite to subvert religion's sacred fence,
To set up wit, and pull down common sense.
Our libraries they gut, and shouting bear   85
The spoils of ruined churches in the air.
Their Captain Tom does at their head appear,
And Smalwood in his gown brings up the rear.
Aloud the church and clergy they condemn,
Curse all their order, and their God blaspheme.   90
Against all springs of learning they declare,
Against religion's nurseries, and swear
They will no Alldridge, Mill, or Charlett spare:
But the lewd crew affirm by all that's good,
They'll ne'er disperse unless they've Bentley's blood.   95
For that ill-natured critic has undone
The rarest piece of wit that e'er was shown.
Till his rude strokes had thresh'd the empty sheaf,
We thought there had been something else than chaff.
Crowned with applause, this master critic sits,   100
And round him lie the spoils of ruined wits.

87. *Captain Tom:* a generic term for leader of a mob.
88. *Smalwood: James* Smalwood (d. 1719), the "Epigrammatic Parson." He responded to the attack here and in line 160 below with *To Sir R——Bl———upon his Unhappy Talent at Praising and Railing (Commendatory Verses* [1700], p. 19).
93. *Alldridge:* Henry Aldrich (1647–1710) was dean of Christ Church, Oxford. Blackmore may not have known of his inadvertent part in precipitating the attack on Bentley. It was Aldrich's practice each year to assign one of his students to edit a classical text, a copy of which was then presented to every member of the college on New Year's Day. In 1693 he assigned Charles Boyle, the eldest son of the 3d earl of Orrery, to edit the epistles of Phalaris. *Mill:* John Mill (1645–1707) was a biblical scholar and principal of St. Edmund Hall, Oxford, where Blackmore passed 13 years as student and tutor. Bentley's first publication, which established his reputation, was a letter to John Mill, published as an appendix to Mill's edition of the *Chronicle of Malelas* (June 1691). *Charlett:* Arthur Charlett (1655–1722) was a classics scholar and master of University College, Oxford.
95. *Bentley:* Richard Bentley (1662–1742), the great classics scholar and butt of the Tory satirists, was the protégé of one Whig bishop and had been appointed keeper of the library in St. James's Palace in December 1693 by another.
96–97. *undone . . . wit: Dr. Bentley's Dissertations . . . Examined* was published in March 1698 under the name of Charles Boyle. It was celebrated as a "very ingenious and learned book, penned in an elegant clean style" (Hearne, *11*, 364). But Bentley's reply, *A Dissertation upon the Epistles of Phalaris: With an Answer to the Objections of the Hon. Charles Boyle,* published in March 1699, effected "the most crushing blow that was ever dealt to insolent and aggressive sciolism" (*DNB, 2*, 310).

How great a man! What rev'rence were his due,
Could he suppress the critic's Fastus too?
As certain words will lunatics enrage,
Who just before appeared sedate and sage.   105
So do but Locke or books or Bentley name,
The wit's in clammy sweats, or in a flame.
   Horror and shame! What would the madmen have?
They dig up learnéd Bernard's peaceful grave.
The sacred urn of famous Stillingfleet,   110
We see profaned by the lewd sons of wit.
The skillful Tyson's name they dare invade,
And yet they are undone without his aid.
Tyson with base reproaches they pursue,
Just as his Moorfields patients use to do.   115
For next to virtue, learning they abhor,
Laugh at discretion, but at business more.
A wit's an idle, wretched fool of parts,
That hates all liberal and mechanic arts.
   Wit does enfeeble and debauch the mind,   120
Before to business or to arts inclined.
How useless is a saunt'ring empty wit,
Only to please with jests at dinner fit?
What hopeful youths for bar and bench designed,
Seduced by wit, have learnéd Coke declined?   125
For what has wit to do with sense or law?
Can that in titles find or mend a flaw?
Can wit supply great Treby's nervous sense?
Or Somers' more than Roman eloquence?
Which way has Holt gained universal fame?   130
What makes the world thy praises, Finch, proclaim?
And charming Powys, what advanced thy name?
'Twas application, knowledge of the laws,
And your vast fund of sense, gained you applause.

103. *Fastus:* pride, arrogance.
104. *certain words:* Cf. "These two words ["presbytery" and "commonwealth"], as if they
carried some potent charm, like some notes of music, that strangely affect particular persons,
and as certain accents vehemently disturb and enrage lunatics, had an unaccountable in-
fluence upon many, who scared themselves with imaginary and fantastic terrors" (Black-
more, *A True and Impartial History of the Conspiracy against the Person and Government of King
William III* [1723], p. 18).
106. *Locke:* John Locke "used to compliment Blackmore highly for his skill in poetry"
(Hearne, *11,* 395).
109. *Bernard:* Francis Bernard, physician to St. Bartholomew's Hospital, justice in eyre
south of the Trent.

The law will ne'er support the bant'ring breed, 135
A Sloan may sometimes there, but wits can ne'er succeed.
   Radcliffe has wit, and lavishes away
More in his conversation every day,
Than would supply a modern writer's play.
But 'tis not that, but the great master's skill, 140
Who with more ease can cure, than Colbatch kill,
That does the grateful realm with his applauses fill.
   Thy learning, Gibbons, and thy judgment, How,
Make you in envied reputation grow.
This drew invectives on you, all agree, 145
From the lean small craft of your faculty.
Had you been wits you had been both secure
From business, and for satire too obscure,
Ill-natured, arrogant, and very poor.
But let invectives still your names assail, 150
Your business is to cure, and theirs to rail.
Let 'em proceed and make your names a sport
In lewd lampoons, they've time and leisure for't.
Despise their spite; the thousands whom you raise
From threatened death will bless you all their days, 155
And spend the breath you saved, in just and lasting praise.
But wit as now 'tis managed would undo
The skill and virtues we admire in you.
In Garth the wit the doctor has undone,
In Smalwood the divine: Heav'ns guard poor Addison. 160

137. *Radcliffe:* John Radcliffe (1650–1714) graduated B.A. from University College, Oxford, in 1669. He was then elected a fellow of Lincoln College and proceeded M.D. in 1682. Two years later he settled in Bow Street, Covent Garden, and soon became the most eminent general practitioner in London. "His conversation at this time was held in as much repute as his advice; and what with his pleasantry of discourse, and readiness of wit in making replies to any sort of questions, he was a diverting companion to the last degree. Insomuch that he was very often sent for, and presented with fees for pretended ailments, only for the gratification to hear him talk" (*Biographia Britannica,* 5, 3453).

141. *Colbatch:* Sir John Colbatch (d. 1729) started out as an apothecary but became a physician. According to MS key to Garth's *Dispensary* he "wrote several ridiculous treatises in physics and chirurgery."

143. *Gibbons:* William Gibbons (1649–1728), a physician who opposed the dispensary but was nevertheless accused of malpractice by an apothecary. In *King Arthur* Blackmore called him "one with Aesculapian skill inspired." *How:* George How (c. 1655–1710), licensed physician, also opposed the dispensary and was often at odds with his colleagues. He appears in Garth's *Dispensary* as Querpo.

159. *Garth:* The success of *The Dispensary* encouraged detractors to belittle Garth's medical skill: "tho poetry is a very pretty accomplishment, yet a poet and a physician are vastly different" (*Bellum Medicinale, or the Present State of Doctors and Apothecaries in London* [1701], p. 9).

160. *Addison:* Joseph Addison (1672–1719), at this time still a student at Magdalen College,

An able senator is lost in Moyle,
And a fine scholar sunk by wit in Boyle.
After his foolish rhymes both friends and foes
Conclude they know who did not write his prose.
Wit does our schools and colleges invade,   165
And has of letters vast destruction made.
Has laid the Muses' choicest gardens waste,
Broke their enclosures and their groves defaced.
We strive in jests each other to exceed,
And shall e'er long forget to write or read.   170
Unless a fund were settled once that could
Make our deficient sense and learning good,
Nothing can be expected, for the debt
By this loose age contracted, is so great,
To set the Muses' mortgaged acres free,   175
Our bankrupt sons must sell outright the fee.
The present age has all their treasure spent,
They can't the int'rest paÿ at five percent.
What to discharge it can we hope to raise
From Durfey's, or from poet Dennis' plays,   180
Or Garth's lampoon with little in't but praise?
O Somers, Talbot, Dorset, Montagu,

Oxford, had published only half a dozen poems. But Dryden had singled him out for praise in the postscript to this translation of Virgil.

161. *Moyle:* Walter Moyle (1672–1721) left Exeter College, Oxford, without taking a degree. He took up residence in the Middle Temple to read law, but soon moved to Covent Garden, loitered at Will's, and was praised by Dryden.

180. *Durfey:* Thomas D'Urfey (1653–1723) was called "sing-song Durfey," but he stuttered —although he could speak plain "when he swears 'G—Damn Me' "—and he made up for his diminutive size by an enormous output of verse: "Some 7953 songs, 2250 ballads, and 1956 catches, besides madrigals, odes, and other lyric copies of verses"—not to mention 25 comedies that he wrote or adapted for the London stage. *Dennis:* By 1699 John Dennis (1657–1734) had written only three plays, but the prologue to the first one, *A Plot, and No Plot, a Comedy* (1697), claimed that it had been written "in some coffeehouse in Exchange Alley," in ridicule of Blackmore's claim that "the greatest part" of *Prince Arthur* had been "written in coffeehouses, and in passing up and down the streets." In June 1696 Dennis published his *Remarks on a Book Entitled, Prince Arthur, an Heroic Poem* in which he complained that "the action is nothing but an empty fiction, of no manner of concern to us, without any kind of instruction, and without any reasonable meaning" (*Critical Works, 1,* 61).

182. *Talbot:* Charles Talbot, 12th earl and 1st duke of Shrewsbury (1660–1718), was the namesake and godson of Charles II but deserted James II, mortgaged his estates for £40,000, and joined William of Orange in The Hague, landing with him at Tor Bay in November 1688. William, who called him "the King of Hearts," made him his secretary of state (1689–90, 1694–December 1698), Privy Councillor, and lord chamberlain (October 1699–June 1700). "Whigs and Tories both spoke well" of him, but in William's reign he assumed leadership of the Whig junto. His effectiveness was severely limited, however, by real or feigned ill health and (unproved) accusations of treasonable correspondence with James II. He was "a

Grey, Sheffield, Cavendish, Pembroke, Vernon, you
Who in Parnassus have imperial sway,
Whom all the Muses subjects here obey,   185
Are in your service and receive your pay;
Exert your sovereign power, in judgment sit
To regulate the nation's grievance, wit.
Pity the cheated folks that every day
For copper wit good sterling silver pay.   190
If once the Muses' chequer would deny
To take false wit, 'twould lose its currency.
Not a base piece would pass, that passed before
Just washed with sense, or thinly plated o'er.
   Set forth your edict, let it be enjoined   195
That all defective species be recoined,
St. Evremont and Rymer both are fit

---

great man," but with "nothing of the stiffness of a statesman," and "generally beloved by the ladies" (Spring Macky, ed., *Memoirs of the Secret Services of John Macky* [2d ed., 1733], pp. 13, 15). *Dorset:* Charles Sackville, 6th earl of Dorset (1635–1706) was "the finest gentleman in the voluptuous court of Charles II and in the gloomy one of King William" (Horace Walpole, *Noble Authors, 2,* 96). One of Milton's "sons of Belial, flown with insolence and wine," he was the author of ribald minor verse and became the patron of Dryden, Wycherley, and Prior as well as of the dunces, Thomas Shadwell, John Dennis, and Susanna Centlivre. *Montagu:* Charles Montagu (1661–1715), a protégé of Dorset's, collaborated with Matthew Prior on *The Hind and the Panther Transversed* (1687). His main interests were, however, political.

183. *Grey:* Presumably Thomas Grey, 2d earl of Stamford (1654–1720), "a very honest man himself" (Macky, *Memoirs of John Macky,* p. 72), whose only claim to dominion on Parnassus is that he was once the patron of Thomas Rymer (Curt A. Zimansky, *The Critical Works of Thomas Rymer* [New Haven, 1956], p. xvi). A violent Whig who raised 400 horse and joined William of Orange in December 1688, he was rewarded by being appointed Privy Councillor (1694), one of the commissioners of trade and plantations (1695), and chancellor of the duchy of Lancaster (1697). In 1708 he was elected a fellow of the Royal Society. *Sheffield:* John Sheffield (1648–1721), 3d earl of Mulgrave, marquis of Normanby, and, in Queen Anne's reign, duke of Buckingham, was another of the noble literary rakes who frequented the court of Charles II. A two-volume folio of his works, "overlooked" and corrected for the press by Alexander Pope, appeared in 1723. *Cavendish:* William Cavendish, 4th earl and 1st duke of Devonshire (1641–1707). *Pembroke:* Thomas Herbert, 8th earl of Pembroke (1656?–1733) was much admired both for his simple, unostentatious way of life, and for his virtuoso learning. *Vernon:* James Vernon (1646–1727), Whig M.P. and Sir William Trumbull's successor as secretary of state.

196. *species be recoined:* Cf. "After the debates on this subject, the House came to a resolution, to recoin the money according to the old standard, both as to weight and fineness" (Blackmore, *A Short History of the Last Parliament* [1699], p. 30).

197. *St. Evremont:* Charles Marguetel de St. Denis de St. Évremond (1613?–1703), after a brilliant career as soldier, diplomat, and littérateur, fell into disfavor at court and fled France in 1661. In England he was welcomed by Charles II, who granted him a pension of £300 a year. He became the friend, not only of the rakes and royal mistresses, but of the poets Cowley and Waller, and of the philosophers Hobbes and—during visits to Holland—Spinoza. With his "satirical" smile and leather skullcap, he survived into the reign of William III—who remembered him only as "a major-general in the French service"—as an *arbiter elegantiarum*

To oversee the coining of our wit.
Let these be made the masters of essay,
They'll every piece of metal touch and weigh,   200
And tell which is too light, which has too much allay.
'Tis true, that when the coarse and worthless dross
Is purged away, there will be mighty loss.
Even Congreve, Southerne, manly Wycherly,
When thus refined will grievous suff'rers be.   205
Into the melting pot when Dryden comes,
What horrid stench will rise, what noisome fumes?
How will he shrink, when all his lewd allay,
And wicked mixture shall be purged away?
When once his boasted heaps are melted down,   210

---

and memento of a more brilliant epoch. *Rymer:* Thomas Rymer (1643?–1713), the dramatic critic and antiquarian, left Sidney Sussex College, Cambridge, without taking a degree and then read law at Gray's Inn. Rymer's most important critical work, *A Short View of Tragedy,* appeared in 1692, the same year in which he was appointed Historiographer Royal and began to compile the collection of treaties which became the *Foedera.* Blackmore, who also admired rules and unities, praised "our own excellent . . . Mr. Rymer" for having "seen farther into them, than any of the English nation" (*Prince Arthur,* 1695, sig. clr.).

203. *mighty loss:* Cf. "the farmer and common tradesman . . . abounded with guineas which they received at thirty shillings . . . [But] whatever losses and inconveniences the people might suffer by the reducing of guineas, yet the mischiefs that arose . . . from not doing it, did infinitely over-balance those on the other side. Upon this the House resolved to lower the price of guineas . . . [to] twenty-two shillings" (Blackmore, *A Short History of the Last Parliament* [1699], pp. 33–34).

204. *Congreve:* William Congreve (1670–1729), comic dramatist, was a habitual offender in this respect. Alexander Pope, for example, told Spence that he "never knew anybody that had so much wit as Congreve "(Spence, *1,* 304). *Southerne:* Thomas Southerne (1659–1746) graduated from Trinity College, Dublin, in 1680 and had written seven plays by 1699, of which the most successful was *Oroonoko* (1696). His wit is attested by Dryden: "Yet those who blame thy tale, commend thy wit; / So Terence plotted; but so Terence writ" (*Poems, 2,* 581). *Wycherly:* William Wycherley (1640–1716), comic dramatist. As George Granville said, "He is not only the greatest wit," but "by the unanimous assent of the world, is called, the manly Wycherley" (*Letters of Wit, Politicks, and Morality,* pp. 254–56). *Manly* is the misanthropic hero in *The Plain Dealer* (1677).

206. *Dryden:* Cf. Henry Hall, *To Mr. Charles Hopkins upon My Lending Him Mr. Waller's Poems* (Leeds University MS, Brotherton Collection Lt.q.5, p. 51): "He [Dryden] first our native language did refine, / Rugged and rough, like metal in the mine, / He purged the dross and stamped it into coin."

207. *noisome fumes:* Cf. Dryden, *To the Pious Memory of the Accomplished Young Lady Mrs. Anne Killigrew:*

> . . . why were we hurried down
> This lubrique and adult'rate age. . . .
> T'increase the steaming ordures of the stage?

> (*Poems, 1,* 461)

210–11. Cf. Dryden, Preface to *Troilus and Cressida* (1679): If [Shakespeare's] embroideries were burned down, there would still be silver at the bottom of the melting-pot" (*Prose, 1,* 295).

A chest-full scarce will yield one sterling crown.
Those who will Dennis melt and think to find
A goodly mass of bullion left behind,
Do, as th'Hibernian wit, who as 'tis told,
Burnt his gilt leather to collect the gold.   215
    But what remains will be so pure, 'twill bear
Th'examination of the most severe.
'Twill Somers's scales and Talbot's test abide,
And with their mark please all the world beside.
    But when our wit's called in, what will remain   220
The Muses' learnéd commerce to maintain?
How pensive will our beaus and ladies sit?
They'll mutiny for want of ready wit.
That such a failure no man may incense,
Let us erect a bank for wit and sense.   225
A bank whose current bills may payment make,
Till new milled wit shall from the mint come back.
    Let Somers, Dorset, Sheffield, Montagu,
Lend but their names, the project then will do.
The bank is fixed if these will underwrite;   230
They pay the vastest sums of wit at sight.
These are good men, in whom we all agree,
Their notes for wit are good security.
Duncombs and Claytons in Parnassus all,

213. *bullion:* Cf. Wentworth Dillon, earl of Roscommon, *An Essay on Translated Verse* (1684), 53: "The weighty bullion of one sterling line."

216–19. When he revised the poem in 1718 Blackmore deleted these lines, which Samuel Johnson called "an abatement of the censure" of Dryden and Dennis.

221. *commerce to maintain:* Cf. "'Twas plain, England could not subsist unless some expedient was found out to support its trade, till the new money returned from the mint" (Blackmore, *A Short History of the Last Parliament,* p. 31).

226. *current bills may payment make:* Cf. "Parliament agreed to augment and enlarge the common capital stock of the bank of England by admitting new subscriptions . . . in tallies and bank notes. . . . [Whereupon] the credit of the bank began to recover apace, till in a short time their notes were all equal with, and their bills that bore interest, better than money" (ibid., pp. 50–51).

234. *Duncomb:* After serving as an apprentice to Edward Blackwell, the leading goldsmith in London, Charles Duncombe set up in business for himself about 1675 "at the Grasshopper in Lombard Street." He soon became "immensely rich," a fact that was advertised in 1696 when, during the recoinage that made it difficult for most people to find "current money to carry on . . . the smallest concerns" (Evelyn, *5,* 245), Duncombe bought Helmsley Castle, the estate of the late duke of Buckingham, for £95,000 cash (Ralph, *2,* 778). He was knighted in October 1699 (Le Neve, p. 468). *Clayton:* Sir Robert Clayton (1629–1707), another "poor boy," was apprenticed to his uncle, Robert Abbot, a London scrivener, and came to be "vastly rich" (Le Neve, p. 270), a director of the Bank of England, lord mayor (1679–80), and Whig M.P. for London, or for the rotten borough of Bletchingley, in Surrey, which he owned.

Who cannot sink unless the hill should fall.   235
Their bills, though ne'er supported by trustees,
Will through Parnassus circulate with ease.
If these come in, the bank will quickly fill,
All will be scrambling up Parnassus hill.
They'll crowd the Muses' hall and throng to write   240
Great sums of wit, and will be gainers by't.
    Vanbrugh and Congreve both are wealthy, they
Have funds of standard sense, need no allay,
And yet mixed metal oft they pass away.
The bank may safely their subscriptions take,   245
But let 'em for their reputation's sake,
Take care their payments they in sterling make.
    Codron will underwrite his Indian wit,
Far-fetched indeed, so 'twill the ladies fit.
By hearsay he's a scholar, and they say   250
The man's a sort of wit too in his way.
    Let 'em receive whatever Prior brings,
In nobler strains no happy genius sings.
'Tis complaisance when to divert his friends,
He to facetious fancies condescends.   255
    Tate will subscribe, but set no payment day,

236. *supported by trustees:* Cf, "Parliament created money . . . by authorizing the lords of His Majesty's treasury to issue out bills from the Exchequer . . . to supply the place of our silver coin, which was called in to be new made. . . . By this means the credit of the aforesaid notes . . . daily arose nearer to par . . . and whereas the trustees contracted with to exchange them for money, were before as a premium allowed ten percent, they have been since contented to do it for four" (Blackmore, *A Short History of the Last Parliament,* pp. 53–54). As Samuel Johnson observed, Blackmore "had lived in the City till he had learned its note" (*Lives,* 2, 328).

242. *Vanbrugh:* In 1699 Captain John Vanbrugh (1664–1726), as he was then known, was enjoying the success of his first plays, *The Relapse: Or Virtue in Danger* (1696) and *The Provoked Wife* (1697), and of his witty rejoinder to Collier's *Short View of the Immorality, and Profaneness of the English Stage,* which had attacked them both.

248. *Codron:* Christopher Codrington (1668–1710) was born in Barbados, educated at Christ Church, Oxford, "made all the campaigns during the war" as a captain in His Majesty's foot guards (Luttrell, *4,* 430), and succeeded his father in May 1699 as governor general of the Leeward Islands. Before leaving to assume this post in August 1700, Codrington enjoyed a brief career in London as poet and wit, and even fought a duel about the etymology of a Greek word (*The Post Boy,* no. 840, 24–27 August 1700; BM Add. MS 4245, f. 74). He contributed a set of commendatory verses to *The Dispensary,* which ridiculed Blackmore as "the City-bard," and mobilized the Covent Garden wits to an effort of mock-commendation of *A Satire against Wit.* In this work, *Commendatory Verses on the Author of the Two Arthurs and the Satire against Wit* (28 February 1700), Codrington's contribution appears first, in the place of honor. It is entitled *A Short and True History of the Author of the Satire against Wit.*

255. *facetious fancies:* The phrase is quoted from the first edition of *The Dispensary.*

256. *Tate:* Nahum Tate (1652–1715) graduated B.A. from Trinity College, Dublin, in

For his slow Muse you must with patience stay,
He's honest, and as wit comes in, will pay
    But how would all this new contrivance prize,
How high in value would their actions rise?   260
Would Freke engraft his solid, manly sense,
His learning Locke, Fleetwood his eloquence?
The bank when thus established will supply
Small places, for the little, loit'ring fry
That follow Garth, or at Will Urwin's ply.   265
Their station will be low, but ne'ertheless
For this provision they should thanks express:
'Tis sad to be a wit and dinnerless.
    Tonson the great wit-jobber of the age,
And all the Muses' brokers will engage   270
Their several friends to cry the action up,
And all the railing mouths of envy stop.
    Ye lords who o'er the Muses' realm preside,
Their int'rests manage and their empire guide;
Regard your care, regard the sacred state,   275
Laid by invaders waste and desolate.

1672 and published his first volume of poems in London five years later. His version of Shakespeare's *King Lear*, with its happy ending, was first acted in 1681, and the next year he collaborated with Dryden to produce *The Second Part of Absalom and Achitophel* (*POAS*, Yale, *3*, 278). He succeeded Thomas Shadwell as poet laureate in November 1692 and his latest work, published only a few weeks before *A Satire against Wit*, was "a curious ode" celebrating William's forty-ninth birthday (Luttrell; *4*, 579).

260. *actions*: shares in the bank for wit and sense, imagined to be a joint stock company.

261. *Freke*: John Freke left Oxford without taking a degree, studied law at the Middle Temple, and was one of the first supporters of Shaftesbury. In May 1676 he was committed to the Tower on charges of high treason for having written *The History of Insipids*. He became a close friend and collaborator of John Locke in the 1690s and remained active in Whig propaganda at least until 1704.

262. *Fleetwood*: William Fleetwood (1657?–1723) first achieved fame as a preacher by a sermon delivered in the chapel of King's College, Cambridge, whence he had graduated B.A. in 1679 and M.A. 1689. He was a staunch Whig, one of the king's chaplains-in-ordinary, rector of St. Augustine's in Watling Street, and a lecturer at St. Dunstan's in the West. Evelyn heard him preach at the latter church and pronounced it "a most excellent discourse" (Evelyn, *5*, 222).

264. *the little, loit'ring fry*: Cf. *The Dunciad* (1742), 337–39: "a lazy lolling sort . . . Of ever-listless loit'rers."

265. *Will Urwin*: proprietor of Will's coffeehouse, Bow Street.

269. *Tonson*: By engaging Dryden to translate Virgil, the bookseller Jacob Tonson (1656?–1736) became in effect the first modern publisher. In May 1698 he was presented for printing two obscene plays, Congreve's *The Double Dealer*, and D'Urfey's *The Comical History of Don Quixote* (Luttrell, *4*, 379). For Blackmore he published *King Arthur* (1697) with A. & J. Churchill, and *A Short History of the last Parliament* (1699), but not *Prince Arthur* (1695) or *A Satire against Wit*.

Tartars and Scythians have in barb'rous bands
Riffled the Muses and o'er-run their lands.
The native subjects, who in peace enjoyed
The happy seat, are by the sword destroyed.   280
Gardens and groves Parnassus did adorn,
Condemned to thistles now, and cursed with thorn.
Instead of flowers and herbs of wholesome use,
It does rank weeds and pois'nous plants produce,
Fitter to be for witches a retreat,   285
Owls, satyrs, monkeys, than the Muses' seat.
Ev'n these debauched by Dryden and his crew,
Turn bawds to vice and wicked aims pursue.
Therefore some just and wholesome laws ordain,
That may this wild licentiousness restrain.   290
To virtue and to merit have regard,
To punish learn, you know how to reward.
Let those corrections have, and not applause,
That Heav'n affront and ridicule its laws.
No sober judge will atheism e'er permit   295
To pass for sense, or blasphemy for wit.
Declare that what's obscene shall give offense,
Let want of decency be want of sense.
   Send out your guards to scour the ways and seize
The footpads, outlaws, rogues, and rapparees,   300
That in the Muses' country rob and kill,
And make Parnassus worse than Shooter's Hill.
Poetic justice should on these be shown,
Or soon, the Muses' state must be undone.
For now an honest man can't peep abroad,   305
And all chaste Muses dread the dangerous road.
If in Parnassus any needy wit
Should filch and petty larceny commit,
If he should riffle books, and pilferer turn,
An inch beside his nose the felon burn.   310

287. *these:* the Muses.
298. *sense:* "Immodest words admit of no defense, / For want of decency is want of sense" (Roscommon, *An Essay on Translated Verse* [1684], pp. 113–14).
302. *Shooter's Hill:* In Blackheath, a place of notorious danger to travelers on the Dover road. The bodies of executed criminals were left hanging there.
303. *Poetic justice:* J. E. Spingarn said that Jeremy Collier, *A Short View of the Immorality and Profaneness of the English Stage* (1698), "follows the arguments of Blackmore pretty closely" and that " 'Poetical justice' is the basis of his [Collier's] theory" (Spingarn, *1*, lxxxvi; *3*, 335).
310. *burn:* In the quarter-sessions at Old Bailey in the month before *A Satire against Wit* was published, "six were burnt in the left cheek" (Luttrell, *4*, 572).

Let him distinguished by this mark appear,
And in his cheek a plain signetur wear.
   Chastise the poets who our laws invade,
And hold with France for wit an owling trade.
Felonious Garth pursuing this design,   315
Smuggles French wit, as others silks and wine.
But let his suff'rings doubly be severe,
For he both steals it there, and runs it here.
Condemn all those who 'gainst the Muses' laws
Solicit votes, and canvass for applause.   320
When Torman writes he rattles up and down,
And makes what friends he can, to make the town.
By noise and violence they force a name,
For this lewd town has setters too for fame:
It is not merit now that recommends,   325
But he's allowed most sense, that makes most friends.
   In panegyric let it be a rule,
That for his sense none praise a wealthy fool.
Dryden condemn, who taught men how to make
Of dunces wits, an angel of a rake.   330
By treats and gifts our youth may now commence
Wits without brains, and scholars without sense.
They cry up Darfel for a wit; to treat
Let him forbear, and they their words will eat.
Great Atticus himself these men would curse,   335
Should Atticus appear without his purse.
Of any price you may bespeak a name,
For characters they cut, and retail fame.

312. *signetur*: A statute adopted by the College of Physicians in 1687 required that directions for taking medicines be signed (signetur) by the attending physician and sent to the patient rather than to the apothecary. The purpose of the "signetur statute" was to prevent apothecaries from learning the purpose of the prescription.

314. *owling*: smuggling; cf. "many ill men continued to export English wool . . . to foreign parts, to the unspeakable detriment of the nation, notwithstanding the severe laws that were in force against such offenders" (Blackmore, *A Short History of the Last Parliament*, p. 61).

316. *silks*: Cf. "The Parliament likewise this session [the 3d session of the 3d Parliament of William III, 1697–98], applied themselves with great diligence to discover such offenders, who by fraudulent and surreptitious ways had carried on a secret commerce with France; and to the great damage of this kingdom, had brought in for diverse years past, great quantities of alamodes and lutestrings [kinds of silk]" (Blackmore, *A Short History of the Last Parliament*, p. 61).

318. *runs*: imports illegally, smuggles. Earliest use cited by *OED*, s.v. "run", 45c, is 1706.

321. *Torman*: To one reader, Torman suggested Dr. Edward Baynard, but see line 384 *n*.

333. *Darfel*: unidentified.

335. *Atticus*: John Somers; see line 129.

338. *cut*: a pun on "cut" meaning "slandered, injured by gossip" and "cut" meaning

Bounty's the measure of a patron's mind,
For they still have most sense, that prove most kind.   340
Fame on great men's a charge that still goes on,
For wits, like scriv'ners, take for pro and con.
Without his gold what generous Oran writ,
Had ne'er been standard, sheer Athenian wit.
   Those who by satire would reform the town,   345
Should have some little merit of their own,
And not be rakes themselves below lampoon.
For all their libels panegyrics are,
They're still read backward like a witch's prayer.
Elliot's reproofs who does not make his sport?   350
Who'll e'er repent that Smalwood does exhort?
Therefore let satire writers be suppressed,
Or be reformed by cautious Dorset's test.
'Tis only Dorset's judgment can command
Wit, the worst weapon in a madman's hand.   355
The biting things by thăt great master said,
Flow from rich sense, but theirs from want of bread.
Whatever is by them in satire writ
Is malice all, but his, excess of wit.
To lash our faults and follies is his aim;   360
Theirs is good sense and merit to defame.

"divided into small quantities and sold at higher unit price" (cf. French *tailler*).

343. *Oran:* Richard Norton, "a person of quality" and author of *Pausanias, The Betrayer of His Country* (1696), was recommended to Blackmore as a model of "Athenian wit" in *The Dispensary,* 4, 224–25.

345. *reform the town:* In the preface to the second edition, Garth recounted that he had undertaken *The Dispensary* in an "endeavour to rally some of our disaffected members (like Blackmore) into a sense of their duty."

348. Cf. "The slanders therefore and invectives of these men who heartily wished the ruin of our establishment, is an honorable and lasting encomium on the proceedings of this assembly [the 3d Parliament of William III]" (Blackmore, *A Short History of the Last Parliament,* p. 64).

349. *read backward like a witch's prayer:* Cf. Charles Sackville, earl of Dorset, *On Mr. Edward Howard upon his British Princes,* 2–3: " . . . read it backward like a witch's prayer, / 'Twill do as well" (*POAS,* Yale, *1,* 338).

350. *Elliot:* Presumably the "John Elliot of New Coll. LL.D." (Wood, *Athenae Oxonienses,* *4,* ²279) whose sermon, *The Grace of God Asserted,* was published in 1695. Another possibility, however, is the infamous Robert Elliot, who graduated M. A. from the University of Edinburgh in 1668. This Elliot was deposed as minister of Lessuden, or St. Boswell's in Roxburghshire, in 1690, for refusing to take the oaths to William and Mary. When hired by Lord William Paulet to transcribe Burnet's *History of His Own Time,* he illicitly made extracts available to the nonjuror Charles Leslie.

353. *Dorset's test:* "Those dangerous weapons [pen and ink] should be kept from fools" (Charles Sackville, earl of Dorset, *On the Same Auther upon His New Utopia,* 29; *POAS,* Yale *1,* 341).

In Dorset wit (and therefore still 'twill please)
Is constitution, but in them disease.
   Care should be taken of the impotent,
That in your service have their vigor spent.   365
They should have pensions from the Muses' state,
Too old to write, too feeble to translate.
But let the lusty beggar-wits that lurk
About the hill, be seized and set to work.
Besides, some youths debauches will commit,   370
And surfeit by their undigested wit.
Th'intoxicating draught they cannot bear,
It takes their heads before they are aware.
Weak brothers by excesses it appears
Have oft been laid up months, and some whole years.   375
By one debauch a tender wit was tried,
And he 'tis known was likely to have died.
That neither sick nor poor you may neglect,
For all the Muses' invalids erect
An hospital upon Parnassus hill,   380
And settle doctors there of worth and skill.
This town can numbers for your service spare,
That live obscure and of success despair.
Fracar has many sour invectives said,
And jests upon his own profession spread,   385
And with good reason, 'twill not find him bread.
And some such doctors, sure you may persuade
To labour at th'apothecary's trade.
They'll med'cines make, and at the mortar sweat,
Let 'em pound drugs, they have no brains to beat.   390

384. *Fracar:* One reader identified Fracar as "Baynard," presumably Dr. Edward Baynard (b. 1641?) and lines 385–86 seem to be reflected in Baynard's contribution to *Commendatory Verses,* entitled *Melancholy Reflections on the Deficiency of Useful Learning.* Blackmore's quarrel with Baynard must have been based on personal grounds, for professionally the two were equally intransigent. Baynard called one president of the College of Physicians "the son of a whore" and refused to extend his support to another. He walked out of the meeting convened to promulgate the new statutes and repeatedly refused to subscribe to the dispensary.

387. *some such doctors:* Blackmore alludes to what the subscribers called "the vilest objection" to the dispensary, namely, that with the exception of the president, Sir Thomas Millington, the members of the College of Physicians who subscribed to the dispensary were neither so distinguished nor so successful as some of those who refused to subscribe, namely, Dr. Edward Tyson, Fellow of the Royal Society and a distinguished anatomist; Dr. John Radcliffe, the most successful practitioner of the age; Dr. Hugh Chamberlen, the fashionable "man midwife"; and Sir Richard Blackmore himself, physician-in-ordinary to William III.

SIR CHARLES SEDLEY

Upon the Author of the "Satire against Wit"
(27 February 1700)

Since Blackmore had scattered his shot so widely in *A Satire against Wit,* it is appropriate that the wits should reply individually and collectively in *Commendatory Verses on the Author of the Two Arthurs and the Satire against Wit; By Some of His Particular Friends.* The pity is that so little wit could be mustered in defense of wit. Nor was the idea of an anthology of mock-panegyrics original with the "Covent Garden wits"; it repeats an earlier joke on Sir William Davenant entitled *Certain Verses Written by Several of the Author's Friends; to Be Re-printed with the Second Edition of Gondibert* (1653). The title of *Commendatory Verses,* however, is both original and witty, but it requires a little explanation.

Blackmore had published *Prince Arthur: An Heroic Poem* in 1695 and *King Arthur: An Heroic Poem* in March 1697, but Henry and John Arthur were heroes of quite a different breed. They robbed the western mail in September 1698 and their subsequent fate was eagerly followed in the news sheets:

> *1 December 1698.* The two Arthurs, who robbed the mails, are broke out of Newgate. . . .
> *13 December 1698.* The two Arthurs are taken and committed to Salisbury gaol [this was a false report].
> *31 December 1698.* The two Arthurs . . . were on Thursday night taken at a tavern by Doctors Commons, being discovered by one Bellenger, a companion of theirs.
>
> (Luttrell, 4, 457, 461, 466)

Inchabod Dawks's account (*Dawk's News Letter,* no. 298 [Jan. 1699], p. 3) in the best journalistic tradition, is rich in circumstantial detail:

> The two Arthurs . . . during the time of their escape out of Newgate, lodged in Black-friars, and went frequently about the town in Grecians habit . . . particularly the day before they were taken they went through Newgate in a coach, with the glasses down; they have discovered the person who helped them to the springs of watches notched, fastened to a bow, to file off the iron bars, to facilitate their escape, he being one Mr. E[llis], a tobacconist, who is since taken and committed to Newgate, where he is double fettered.

Public interest in the two Arthurs, which had subsided in March 1699 when John was found guilty and hanged but Henry acquitted, flared up again most conveniently just two weeks before publication of *A Satire against Wit*: "*14 November 1699*. Saturday night last one Henry Arthur a noted highway man . . . quarrelling with one Parry about paying the reckoning in a tavern, fought in Covent Garden, and was killed" (Luttrell, *4*, 582).

The preface to *Commendatory Verses* is written in the person of Owen Swan, whom Thomas Brown called "the most sincere and honest man / That e'er drew wine in quart or can." Swan was the proprietor of the Black Swan Tavern, in Bartholomew Lane, near the Royal Exchange and the Bank of England in the heart of the City. This fact made it possible to add a topographic dimension to the battle of "The men of sense against the men of wit," for Blackmore had localized the wits at Will's coffeehouse, well outside Temple Bar.

Swan first directs the attention of "all . . . honorable citizens"—and the word "citizen" itself was a term of opprobrium in 1700—to the existence of "a certain author" who "has writ twenty thousand verses and upwards without one grain of wit in them; nay, he has declared open war against it." Then he goes on to draw invidious comparisons between "those flashy fellows, your Covent Garden poets," who "write for fame and immortality," and Blackmore, who "writes for the good of trade. . . . His main design in writing the two Arthurs, whatever he pretended in his preface, was only to help the poor trunk-makers at a pinch, when Quarles and Ogilby were all spent." Swan, in effect, recommends Blackmore to succeed Elkanah Settle as the City poet of London and to write a "panegyric upon custard."

Not all the authors of the forty *Commendatory Verses* have been finally identified, but there is enough evidence to say that they include few figures of any literary importance: Richard Steele, certainly, and possibly John Dennis and William Walsh. It has been suggested that part of the strategy was to recruit authors who had been praised in *A Satire against Wit*. While it is true that there is a squib by John Sheffield, earl of Mulgrave and marquis of Normanby, and possibly another by Vanbrugh (who is praised with reservations), in general such figures are more conspicuous by their absence: they include Charles Sackville, earl of Dorset, William Congreve, Matthew Prior, William Wycherley, and Thomas Southerne.

It has also been suggested that Sir Charles Sedley "may have been stirred to action because he was ignored in the *Satire against Wit*" (Richard C. Boys, *Sir Richard Blackmore and the Wits*, University of Michigan Contributions in Modern Philology, no. 13 [Ann Arbor, 1949], pp. 51, 142). But there is no evidence for this surmise and it seems unlikely that Sir Charles Sedley of Southfleet, the fifth baronet, "whom Nature had furnished for the conversation of princes," could be offended by the City bard. He was, as he told his friend Dorset, "neither ambitious nor covetous" (Pinto, *Sedley*, p. 207).

If an alternate speculation may be entertained, Sir Charles Sedley might be imagined at this time as *The Maimed Debauchee,* his skull fractured and his "famous" pox now hopefully only a taunt, but still content to say, "Past joys have more than paid what I endure," and

> Thus statesman-like I'll saucily impose,
>   And, safe from danger, valiantly advise;
> Sheltered in impotence, urge you to blows,
>   And, being good for nothing else, be wise.

For the truth of the matter is that after Charles's death, Sedley "seemed to dislike the town" and settled down to a useful career in the House of Commons as a member for New Romney, Kent, one of the Cinque Ports. Sedley had been one of Shaftesbury's "worthy" supporters in the first Whig Parliament but was absent on 21 May 1679 when the Exclusion Bill was defeated. He was an early supporter of William of Orange, and lent him £4600 before Parliament was convened to vote a supply. But he almost invariably opposed the court during William's reign. He once complained that William kept "out of the reach of all whose places do not afford them six horses to follow him with."

Upon the Author of the "Satire Against Wit"

> A grave physician, used to write for fees,
> And spoil no paper, but with recipes,
> Is now turned poet, rails against all wit,
> Except that little found among the great;
> As if he thought true wit and sense were tied   5
> To men in place, like avarice, or pride.
> But in their praise, so like a quack he talks,
> You'd swear he wanted for his Christmas-box.

2. *recipes:* from Latin *recipe,* take; used by physicians to sign prescriptions (abbreviated Rx). Cf. "This new mode of practice is to draw and frame medicines upon a piece of paper; modelling them into several forms, and contriving them for several purposes; varying *pro re nata,* for every temperament and case, by subtracting and adding this and that variously, as the prescriber fancies" (Everard Maynwaring, *Praxis Medicorum Antiqua & Nova* [1671], p. 91).

4. *the great:* Samuel Johnson similarly complained that Blackmore had "degraded himself by conferring that authority over the national taste, which he takes from the poets, upon men of high rank and wide influence, but of less wit and not greater virtue" (*Lives, 2,* 241).

8. *Christmas-box:* a box, usually of earthenware, in which contributions of money were solicited at Christmas by apprentices, carriers, watchmen, scavengers, and the like, the box being broken when full and the contents shared. Sedley's shaft is double-edged, however, for it also cuts Blackmore down to the level of a common apothecary. These tradesmen custo-

With mangled names old stories he pollutes,
And to the present time past actions suits;   10
Amazed we find, in ev'ry page he writes,
Members of Parliament with Arthur's knights.
It is a common pastime to write ill;
And doctor, with the rest, e'en take thy fill;
Thy satire's harmless: 'Tis thy prose that kills,   15
When thou prescribst thy potions and thy pills.
Go on brave doctor, a third volume write,
And find us paper while you make us sh————.

---

marily presented their bills at Christmastime and this "mean and vile custom of going upon tick till Christmas" was much complained of.

12. *Arthur's bold knights*, in Blackmore's first two epics, bear such half-familiar names as Cutar, Major General John Cutts, baron Cutts of Gowran (I.), M.P. for Cambridgeshire (1693–1702) and Newport, Isle of Wight (1702–07); Erla, Major General Thomas Erle, M.P. for Wareham, Dorset, (1679–98), 1701–18) and Portsmouth, Hampshire (1698–1701); Stannel, Colonel James Stanley, M.P. for Clitheroe, Lancashire (1685–97), Preston, Lancashire (1689–90), and Lancashire (1690–1703); Trelon, Major General Charles Trelawny, M.P. for East Looe, Cornwall (1685–98) and Plymouth, Devonshire (1698–1713); and Vebba, Colonel John Webb, M.P. for Ludgershall, Wiltshire (1695–1713, 1715–24) and Newport, Isle of Wight (1713–15). The first three of these remained solid Whigs, but Trelawny voted to impeach the junto lords and was blacklisted as a Poussineer in 1701, while Webb joined the Tories in the next reign.

17. *a third volume:* Blackmore's next work was known to be in the press when the "Covent Garden wits" were composing their *Commendatory Verses* in December 1699–January 1700 (Thomas Brown, *Occasioned by the News that Sir R—— Bl————'s Paraphrase upon Job Was in the Press, in Commendatory Verses* [1700], p. 8). It was advertised in *The London Gazette*, no. 3580 (29 February–4 March 1700). and a mock-advertisement was obligingly appended to *Commendatory Verses:* "Upon the publishing of *Job* and *Habakkuk,* an heroic poem daily expected, but deferred upon political reasons, new subscriptions will be opened at Will's Coffeehouse in Covent Garden, and all gentlemen, that are willing to subscribe, are desired to send in their quotas."

The Court
(November 1700–March 1701)

Amid the rank proliferation of satire generated by the heat of parties and fertilized by the death of the Licensing Act in 1695, it was almost inevitable that there should appear *A Satire against Satires* (1700) ("When glittering stars around bedeck the sphere"). But here the complaint, probably by Edward Ward, seems superficial and self-pitying: "All satire's vain, and 'tis the poet's curse, / To be despised, and have an empty purse." In *The Court* (15–17), however, the complaint is more general:

> Could ev'ry man, my Damon, be so wise
> Only to meddle where his talent lies,
> Some would not write at all, and many less.

This is one of the passages, moreover, that seem to reply to *The Pacificator*. In the first eighteen lines of the poem, the author has been so successful in creating the illusion that something has gone before, that it is almost impossible to believe that *The Court* is not a reply to some other poem. This other poem, however, has not finally been identified. It can hardly be doubted, however, that the body of the poem, lines 19–62, is an expanded variation of lines 413–21 of *The Pacificator*. The difference between the two passages are instructive. Defoe is simply assigning poets to their "proper talent," "Dryden to tragedy," and so on. The author of *The Court* does the same thing, "To Congreve lofty verse, to Durfy song," but he also interprets "proper talent" in another sense: "Let Ranelagh with paint renew her charms, / And Jeffry's wanton it in Windsor's arms" (49–50).

Yet it is not as an early exemplar of a genre still important but no longer versified—the gossip column—that *The Court* is mainly interesting. The corrupt social and literary world implied by lines 19–62 is only one term of a contrast. In the concluding lines of the poem we are vouchsafed a rare glimpse into another world, the green world that is the repository of all the positive values of Augustan satire. It is these values, moreover, that not only characterize Augustan satire, but distinguish it, for example, from the satire of Donne or Byron. In this ideal world, "Swains . . . are friends" and maidens are "yielding." In the real world, to point the contrast, "Warwick stab[s] his friend" and "nymphs" are "virtuous out of spite." The values of the

616

green world are the stoic values of Virgil's second Georgic, Horace's second epode, and Martial's epigram, "De rusticatione" (2, 90). In *The Court* they are summarized in lines 61 and 62. The goddess of satire is honesty, and the Augustan satirist found her not in the City or at the universities, on the battlefield, or in the inns of court, but in a little village "contiguous to a small, but lofty wood"; "Beneath the shadow of whose spreading trees, / Guarded by cottagers, his goddess sees" (John Tutchin, *A Search after Honesty* [1697], p. 15).

The date of *The Court* can only be approximated. Line 42 refers to *Box* v. *Wells*, which was tried at the King's Bench on 16 November 1700. In two of the MSS the poem is dated "1700." It must have been written, therefore, between 16 November 1700 and 25 March 1701.

Concerning the author there is no evidence at all. What appears to be an attribution to John Tutchin in a paraphrase of *The Court* preserved in Bod. MS. Rawl. poet. D. 361 turns out to be something else. The lines are these:

> Could every man alas! be but so wise,
> Only to meddle where his talent lies; . . .
> Collier would not turn Cato of his age, . . .
> Nor saucy Tutchin daub, nor draw the court.

The last line is more likely to be a reference to Tutchin's arrest for reflecting upon "several great men" in *The Foreigners* (Luttrell, *4*, 676) than an attribution to him of *The Court*.

THE COURT

> Damon forbear, and don't disturb your Muse,
> You can't correct the coxcombs you accuse,
> Some partial judges of their harmless rage
> Out of bravado rashly do engage,
> But many pens, like Wortley Montague   5

3. *rage:* Cf. *The Pacificator*, 8–9: "here's a civil war broke out at home: / Britannia's warlike sons disturb the isle."

5. *Wortley Montague:* Although the exact allusion is lost, the reference is probably to Edward Wortley Montagu (1678–1761). A grandson of Edward, 1st earl of Sandwich, he left Trinity College, Cambridge, in the late 1690s to indulge his literary tastes in London. In 1700 he undertook a grand tour of the Continent, traveling part of the way with Joseph Addison. And although he long served as a Whig M.P. for Huntingdon, Huntingdonshire (1705–13, 1722–34). Westminster (1715–22), and Peterborough, Northamptonshire (1734–61), a lord commissioner of the treasury, and an ambassador to the Ottoman Porte, he "never took any conspicuous part in politics" and is remembered chiefly as the husband of Pope's friend, Lady Mary Pierrepont, whom he married privately in 1712.

Take an affront, and yet beg pardon too.
Others I know, who in their amorous fit,
Blaspheme Parnassus in their bawdy wit.
This aims at satire, and in horrid rhymes
Himself exposes, not the vicious times: 10
He shows his malice, but he cannot bite;
Others strain hard for ev'ry line they write,
And after all the throes they've had, 't'as been
Like a Dutch woman's birth, a souterkin.
Could ev'ry man, my Damon, be so wise   15
Only to meddle where his talent lies,
Some would not write at all, and many less,
Then we might bear the groaning of the press.
    To different Muses, different themes belong:
To Congreve lofty verse, to Durfy song.   20
Let sharp Architectus lampoon the punk,
The bawd, the quiddler, buggerer, and the drunk.
Let Gallus and Catullus court the fair
But Caesar's actions, must be Pindar's care.
Grave Nestor must support the tottering state,   25
And in the council cautiously debate.
Let Lucan soar beyond the common reach,
Let florid Cicero preach, and Zeno teach.
In the black crowd of the litigious hall
Let Holt decide, let Sloan and others bawl.   30
Let critic Dennis from the Frenchman steal,

14. *souterkin:* OED cites John Cleveland, *A Character of a Diurnall-Maker* (1654): "There goes a report of the Holland women, that . . . they are delivered of a sooterkin, not unlike to a rat, which some imagine to be the offspring of the stove."

16. *where his talent lies:* Cf. *The Pacificator*, 412–13: "Let him [Grand Inquisitor of wit] to each his proper talent show."

21. *Architectus:* MSS identify him as "[Christopher] Codrington." "Architectus" may be the word over the etymology of which Codrington once fought a duel. The "lampoon" has not been identified.

22. *quiddler:* a palm-paddler (Othello, II.i.259); OED cites Richard Brome, *The City Wit* (1653): "*Cras.* How does she feel your hand? *Lin.* O, she does so quiddle it, shake it, and gripe it!"

23. *Gallus and Catullus:* Some MSS identify Gallus as "Hopkins." Others also identify Catullus as "Hopkins." Charles Hopkins's amatory verse includes *The History of Love: A Poem* (1695) and *The Art Of Love* (1700). Cf. *The Pacificator*, 169 *n.*,

24. *Caesar:* William III. *Pindar:* Sir Richard Blackmore.

25. *Nestor:* Thomas Herbert, 8th earl of Pembroke. A member of the Privy Council since October 1689, Pembroke was appointed lord president in May 1699.

27. *Lucan:* Samuel Garth.

28. *Cicero:* Gilbert Burnet. *Zeno:* Richard Bentley.

30. *Holt:* See 42 *n. Sloan:* See *Advice to a Painter*, 108 *n.*

Let fools be beaux, whilst wisemen are genteel.
Let Ratcliffe cure the fever, Wall the pox,
Germain and Boucher manage the false box,
Let this one turn a jilt, and that a whore,   35
And Duncombe lavish his ill-gotten store.
Let Cutts be proud of seven and twenty scars,
All got alas! in the Low Country wars,
Let empty Settle not to the bays pretend,

33. *Ratcliffe:* Dr. John Radcliffe: see *A Satire against Wit,* 137 *n. Wall:* James Wall, a barber-surgeon.

34. *Germain:* Sir John Germain (1650?–1718), baronet, was, according to one story, "the son of a private soldier in the Life Guards of William II, Prince of Orange." According to another, "his parents kept an ordinary at Delft." In any case, when he came to England "at the time of the happy Revolution in 1688, he quickly advanced his fortune by being a great gamester." He was "very expert at L'Ombre, the manner of which game is . . . incomparably described by Mr. Pope in his hero-comical poem, entitled *The Rape of the Lock*" (Lucas, p. 212). In 1690 he was charged with "crim. con." with Lady Mary Mordaunt, daughter and heiress of Henry Mordaunt, 2d earl of Peterborough, and wife of Thomas Howard, duke of Norfolk. Even though two witnesses deposed that they found Germain "between a pair of sheets with the duchess" (Luttrell, *2,* 344), the House of Lords twice refused to grant the duke a divorce. Norfolk, therefore, brought suit against Germain for enticement and claimed £50,-000 damages. The jury agreed that Germain was guilty, but found that the duke's loss in the duchess was only 100 marks (Luttrell, *2,* 623–24). *Boucher:* Richard Bourchier, "a plasterer's son, born [c. 1657] in Hartshorn-lane, near Charing Cross, but being not above 16 years old when his parents died . . . he was forced to shift for himself" (Lucas, p. 195). He shifted so well that he once won £500 on a single throw of the dice from John Sheffield, earl of Mulgrave, whose livery he had worn as a footman. On other occasions he won £2500 from King William, 15,000 pistoles from Louis XIV, and £30,000 from Maximilian Emmanuel II, elector of Bavaria. With these winnings he purchased "a very pretty estate near Pershore in Worcestershire," where he was "decently interred" in 1702 (Lucas, pp. 197, 198, 202–03, 206–07). *the false box:* a rigged dice box.

36. *Duncomb:* See *A Satire against Wit,* 234 *n.* and *The True-Born Englishman,* 1101 *n.*

37–38. The implication of these lines is made explicit by the paraphrase in Rawl. poet. D. 361, f. 203: "Let Cutts be proud of 27 scars, / Some gott in Mars, but most in Venus Wars."

39. *Settle:* Elkanah Settle (1648–1724). His first play, *Cambyses King of Persia: A Tragedy,* was produced at Lincoln's Inn Fields about 1667, while he was still an undergraduate at Trinity College, Oxford. He proceeded to London without taking a degree and for a time "spurred boldly on" as Dryden's "rival poet" and laureate of the Whig party, a phase of his career which was climaxed by his appointment as "organizer-in-chief of the pope-burning procession on Queen Elizabeth's birthday (17 November 1680)" *(DNB).* He remained "empty" despite numerous apostasies: in 1681 he published *The Character of a Popish Successor, and What England May Expect of Such a One,* urging James's exclusion from the throne, and four years later he wrote *An Heroic Poem on the Coronation of the High and Mighty Monarch, James II, King of England, etc.* complaining that "twas exclusion Hell's foundation laid." After James's flight he resumed his Whiggism and secured appointment as City poet of London in 1691. His pageants for Lord Mayor's Day in 1692–95 and 1699–1701 are entitled *The Triumphs of London.* The last stage of his career is chronicled in *The Grove: or, The Rival Muses (POAS,* 1707, *4,* 361). Settle's pretensions to the poet-laureateship must have been urged upon the unexpected death of Thomas Shadwell in November 1692. The pun is made possible by the fact that a settle is a long wooden bench, with arms and a high back, and a locker under the seat.

Let Morton rake, and Warwick stab his friend.   40

While worthless Dutchmen get all England's riches

Let Boxe's wife, and hundreds more, turn bitches.

There be grandees, whom 'tis not fit to name

That make it glory to record their shame.

Others transported with the scandal grow,   45

And wed those whores that were proved so.

Portmore and Orkney cupid's fort invade,

And marry what their sovereign princes made.

Let Ranelagh with paint renew her charms,

And Jeffreys wanton it in Windsor's arms.   50

40. *Morton:* James Douglas, 11th earl of Morton (c. 1652–1715), was an impoverished member of the Aberdour, Liddesdale, and Dalkeith branch of the Douglas family. He was both a supporter and pensioner of William of Orange. In June 1704 he was "tried at the Old Bailey for a rape; several of the Scotch nobility appeared in his behalf; and, the prosecution being looked upon as malicious, was acquitted" (Luttrell, *5*, 431). *Warwick:* Edward Rich, earl of Warwick and Holland (1673–1701), was fleshed with hackney coachmen (Luttrell, *3*, 297) and killed his friend Richard Coote in Leicester Fields, following a drunken brawl at Locket's. He was tried in the House of Lords in March 1699 and found guilty of manslaughter, but "acquitted, the statute excusing a peer from being burned in the hand" (Howell, *13*, 939–1032; Luttrell, *4*, 500).

41. *Dutchmen get:* See *Advice to a Painter*, 40 n.

42. *Boxe's wife:* "On Saturday (16 November 1700) was a trial at the King's Bench at *nisi prius*, upon an action brought by Mr. Box (druggist in Cheapside) against Mr. Wells of Hampshire, for lying with the former's wife, and a verdict was given for the plaintiff, and £100 damages; upon which the Lord Chief Justice Holt sent them out again, and then they brought in £60, which his lordship said was too much, considering she was first eloped from her husband" (Luttrell, *4*, 709).

43. *grandees:* the duke of Norfolk and the earl of Macclesfield, according to one MS.

46. *wed those whores:* Sir John Germain married the duchess of Norfolk in September 1701 after the House of Lords had finally granted the duke a divorce the year before. But Anne, countess of Macclesfield, could have had no expectation of marrying Richard Savage, 4th Earl Rivers, the father of her two illegitimate children, after the House of Lords had granted the earl of Macclesfield a divorce in March 1698. In 1700, however, she married Henry Brett, a friend of Colley Cibber and member of the circle at Will's coffeehouse.

47. *Portmore:* In August 1696 Sir David Colyear (c. 1656–1730), 2d baronet, married Catherine Sedley, the only child of Sir Charles Sedley and long the mistress of James II, whom James had created countess of Dorchester in January 1686. In June 1699 Colyear himself was created Lord Portmore and Blackness in the Scottish peerage. *Orkney:* In November 1695 George Hamilton (1666–1737), fifth son of William Douglas, duke of Hamilton, and "much distinguished . . . as a soldier" (Swift, *Prose, 5*, 261), married Elizabeth Villiers, daughter of Sir Edward Villiers, first cousin of Barbara Villiers, and *maîtresse en titre* to William III from the late 1670s to the death of Queen Mary in December 1694. On 3 January 1696 Hamilton was created earl of Orkney in the Scottish peerage.

49. *Ranelagh:* On 11 January 1696 Richard Jones, earl of Ranelagh, married as his second wife Margaret Cecil (1672–1728), the dowager baroness Stawell; he was about 60 and she 24. She is alleged to have cuckolded the earl in "Swan passage . . . near Bloomsbury Square" (*A New Ballad*, BM Add. MS 21094, f. 167).

50. Lady Charlotte Herbert (1676?–1733), daughter of Philip Herbert, 8th earl of Pembroke, married John Jeffreys, 2d baron Jeffreys of Wem, in July 1688, at which time she was "a Papist . . . and said to be worth £70,000" (Luttrell, *1*, 451). Upon the death of her husband, she married Thomas Windsor, 1st viscount Windsor of Blackcastle in August 1703.

May Williams in the horse dung find perfumes,
And hug her coachman in her velvet rooms.
Let some fair nymphs be virtuous out of spite,
Let Thraso brag, but let Achilles fight.
Let Garrat at a bottle spend the day, 55
Let Swan pun on, and Sir George Humble pay.
Let Knipe flog boys, and let Tom Browne translate,
And each be easy in his various fate.
Though men of merit may at theirs repine,
They won't act basely for an Indian mine. 60
Many by avarice, pride, or lust are hurled,
But who commands himself, commands the world.
    Lastly, my Muse, this is not our concern,
For whilst you others teach, yourself should learn.
Damon and I alternative will prove 65
That friendship by the noblest paths does move,
We swains alone are friends, we only love.
By purling rivers, or some grateful shade
We sing the charming and the yielding maid.
Ingenious pens immortalize the brave, 70
Yet rural Muses too their beauties have.
For Virgil's Tityrus has as many charms

51. *Williams:* There is no evidence to identify this Laurentian lady.

54. *Thraso:* Arnold Joost van Keppel, 1st earl of Albemarle; see *Advice to a Painter,* 51 *n.*

55. *Garrat:* probably Sir Samuel Garrard (c. 1651–1725) of Lamer, Hertfordshire, 4th baronet, who succeeded to the baronetcy in January 1701 and became a prominent Tory politician: M.P. for Agmondesham, Buckinghamshire (1701, 1702–10), alderman of Aldersgate ward (1702–22), sheriff (1702–03) and lord mayor of London (1709–10), and president of Bridewell and Bethlehem Hospital (1721–25). By his second wife he had 12 children, of whom 3 survived him. He is "the drunken father" in Defoe, *An Elegy on the Author of the True-Born Englishman* (August 1704), 326–28 (*POAS,* Yale, 7).

56. *Swan:* R. Swan, an habitué of Will's coffeehouse, was an Irishman with a taste for his native whisky. He was also, like Jonathan Swift, a collector and panegyrist of puns (Thomas Brown, *Familiar and Courtly Letters* [1700], p. 257; Edward Ward, *The Secret History of Clubs* [1709], p. 239). John Dennis agreed that "for the management of quibbles and dice, there is no man alive comes near him," but he was also "credibly informed that Will. Urwin has refused to take Conundrums of S———— for Usquebaugh any longer" (*A Pacquet from Wills* [1701], p. 52; reprinted in *The Select Works of Mr. John Dennis,* 2 vols. [1718], *2,* 529). *Humble:* Sir George Humble (c. 1670–1703), of London, 3d baronet, avoided one duel "about gaming" in August 1699 by begging his assailant's pardon, but was killed in another quarrel "at play" in March 1703 at the Blue Posts (Luttrell, *4,* 546; *5,* 278).

57. *Knipe:* Thomas Knipe (1638–1711) was educated at Westminster School and Christ Church, Oxford, whence he graduated B.A. in 1660 and M.A. 1663. In the interval between his degrees he began as an usher at his old school and eventually succeeded the legendary Richard Busby as headmaster in April 1695. He was a strict disciplinarian.

62. *commands himself:* Cf. Horace, *Satires,* II.vii.83: "Quisnam igitur liber? sapiens, sibi qui impriosus."

72. *Tityrus:* Dryden. Tityrus is Virgil's pastoral guise (Eclogues, I, 6–10). Lines 72–73

As when he raised his voice to sing of arms.
But my own censures do myself condemn,
In making others' characters my theme.   75
Then that my crime I may no more pursue,
May you see Cloris smile, and so adieu.
Let our Augustus rule the world in peace,
And may his glory with his hours increase.

---

seem to mean that Dryden is just as effective in his translation of Virgil's pastorals as he was in "the long resounding line" of the *Aeneid*.
  78. *Augustus:* William III.

DANIEL DEFOE

The True-Born Englishman
(1700, 1701)

The etiology of *The True-Born Englishman* is best described by Defoe himself. In August 1700 he recalled, "There came out a vile abhorred pamphlet, in very ill verse, written by one Mr. Tutchin, and called *The Foreigners:* in which the author, *who he was I then knew not,* fell personally upon the king himself, and then upon the Dutch nation; and after having reproached his majesty with crimes, that his worst enemy could not think of without horror, he sums up all in the odious name of *Foreigner*. This filled me with a kind of rage against the book, and gave birth to a trifle which I never could hope should have met with so general an acceptation as it did, I mean, *The True-Born Englishman*" (*An Appeal to Honor and Justice* [1715], p. 6).

Defoe was proud of the unprecedented sale of his "trifle" but doubtful of its literary merit; it was, he said, "far from the best satire that was ever wrote." John Dunton, on the other hand, found it "the finest piece of wit that this age has produced (except the poem called *The Dispensary*)" and this must have been the opinion of thousands of readers who bought the copies that poured from the press.

The flaws of *The True-Born Englishman* were, nevertheless, made public almost immediately. William Pittis, who published *The True-Born Englishman: A Satire Answered* on 1 February 1701 pointed out that the poem is flat and unmusical. "The devil-a-bit of any echo comes from it," he complained.

Measured by Defoe's intentions, however, Pittis's criticism is wholly beside the point. "All along," Defoe insisted in "an explanatory preface," "I have . . . strove rather to make the thoughts explicit, than the poem correct." But this was a mistake; for whatever it may be in propaganda, "directness" is not a virtue in art. By deliberately limiting himself to "pointed truth . . . and down-right English," Defoe evolved a kind of stripped-down poetry of statement that is heard again in Cowper, for example. But by doing so, he cut himself off from the critics of his own age. To gain their approval he would have had to study to "make [his] poem correct," as William Walsh was soon to advise the young Alexander Pope. But this, as noted before, he refused to do. As a result, Lord Halifax had to explain to the duchess of Marlborough that Defoe "has a great deal of wit, [and] would write very well if his necessities did not make him in too much haste to correct."

THE TRUE-BORN ENGLISHMAN

The Introduction

Speak, Satire, for there's none can tell like thee,
Whether 'tis folly, pride, or knavery,
That makes this discontented land appear
Less happy now in times of peace, than war:
Why civil feuds disturb the nation more   5
Than all our bloody wars have done before.
   Fools out of favor grudge at knaves in place,
And men are always honest in disgrace:
The court preferments make men knaves in course:
But they which would be in them would be worse.   10
'Tis not at foreigners that we repine,
Would foreigners their perquisites resign:
The grand contention's plainly to be seen,
To get some men put out, and some put in.
For this our senators make long harangues,   15
And florid members whet their polished tongues.
Statesmen are always sick of one disease;
And a good pension gives them present ease.
That's the specific makes them all content
With any king and any government.   20
Good patriots at court abuses rail,
And all the nation's grievances bewail:
But when the sov'reign balsam's once applied,
The zealot never fails to change his side.
And when he must the golden key resign,   25
The railing spirit comes about again.
   Who shall this bubbled nation disabuse,
While they their own felicities refuse?
Who at the wars have made such mighty pother,
And now are falling out with one another;   30
With needless fears the jealous nation fill,
And always have been saved against their will:
Who fifty millions sterling have disbursed,

25. *golden key:* The lord chamberlain of the king's household wears a gold key as the emblem of his office.

33. *fifty millions sterling:* John Trenchard estimated the cost of the war to be "forty millions of money, and the blood of three hundred thousand men," but modern estimates put the loss of life at 200,000. Charles Davenant's two estimates of the monetary cost, 60 millions and 41 millions, were subject to much ridicule, for "a mistake of 19 millions is no small one" (*Some Remarks on the Bill for Taking, Examining and Stating the Public Accounts* [*1702*], *p. 12*).

To be with peace and too much plenty cursed.
Who their old monarch eagerly undo, 35
And yet uneasily obey the new.
Search, Satire, search, a deep incision make;
The poison's strong, the antidote's too weak.
'Tis pointed truth must manage this dispute,
And downright English Englishmen confute. 40
      Whet thy just anger at the nation's pride;
And with keen phrase repel the vicious tide.
To Englishmen their own beginnings show,
And ask them why they slight their neighbors so.
Go back to elder times and ages past, 45
And nations into long oblivion cast;
To old Britannia's youthful days retire,
And there for true-born Englishmen inquire.
Britannia freely will disown the name,
And hardly knows herself from whence they came: 50
Wonders that they of all men should pretend
To birth and blood, and for a name contend.
Go back to causes where our follies dwell,
And fetch the dark original from Hell:
Speak, Satire, for there's none like thee can tell. 55

Part I

Wherever God erects a house of prayer,
The devil always builds a chapel there:
And 'twill be found upon examination,
The latter has the largest congregation:
For ever since he first debauched the mind, 60
He made a perfect conquest of mankind.
With uniformity of service, he
Reigns with a general aristocracy.
No nonconforming sects disturb his reign,
For of his yoke there's very few complain. 65
He knows the genius and the inclination,
And matches proper sins for ev'ry nation.
He needs no standing-army government;
He always rules us by our own consent:
His laws are easy, and his gentle sway 70

35. *old monarch:* James II.

Makes it exceeding pleasant to obey.
The list of his vicegerents and commanders,
Outdoes your Caesars, or your Alexanders.
They never fail of his infernal aid,
And he's as certain ne'er to be betrayed.   75
Through all the world they spread his vast command,
And death's eternal empire's maintained.
They rule so politic'ly and so well,
As if they were lords justices of Hell.
Duly divided to debauch mankind,   80
And plant infernal dictates in his mind.
     Pride, the first peer, and president of Hell,
To his share Spain, the largest province, fell.
The subtle prince thought fittest to bestow
On these the golden mines of Mexico;   85
With all the silver mountains of Peru—
Wealth which would in wise hands the world undo—
Because he knew their genius was such;
Too lazy and too haughty to be rich,
So proud a people, so above their fate,   90
That if reduced to beg, they'll beg in state,
Lavish of money, to be counted brave,
And proudly starve, because they scorn to save.
Never was nation in the world before,
So very rich, and yet so very poor.   95
     Lust chose the torrid zone of Italy,
Where blood ferments in rapes and sodomy:
Where swelling veins o'erflow with livid streams,
With heat impregnate from Vesuvian flames:
Whose flowing sulphur forms infernal lakes,   100
And human body of the soil partakes.
There nature ever burns with hot desires,
Fanned with luxuriant air from subterranean fires:
Here undisturbed in floods of scalding lust,
Th' infernal king reigns with infernal gust.   105
     Drunk'ness, the darling favorite of Hell,
Chose Germany to rule and rules so well,
No subjects more obsequiously obey,
None please so well or are so pleased as they.
The cunning artist manages so well,   110

79. *lords justices:* Lords justices were appointed each year to rule England during William's visits to the Netherlands.

He lets them bow to Heav'n and drink to Hell.
If but to wine and him they homage pay,
He cares not to what deity they pray,
What god they worship most, or in what way.
Whether by Luther, Calvin, or by Rome,   115
They sail for Heav'n, by wine he steers them home.

    Ungoverned Passion settled first in France,
Where mankind lives in haste and thrives by chance.
A dancing nation, fickle and untrue,
Have oft undone themselves and others, too: 120
Prompt the infernal dictates to obey,
And in Hell's favor none more great than they.

    The pagan world he blindly leads away,
And personally rules with arbitrary sway:
The mask thrown off, plain devil his title stands: 125
And what elsewhere he tempts, he there commands.
There with full gust th' ambition of his mind
Governs, as he of old in Heav'n designed.
Worshipped as God, his paynim altars smoke,
Imbrued with blood of those that him invoke.   130

    The rest by deputies he rules as well,
And plants the distant colonies of Hell.
By them his secret power he maintains,
And binds the world in his infernal chains.

    By Zeal the Irish; and the Rush by Folly: 135
Fury the Dane; the Swede by Melancholy:
By stupid Ignorance the Muscovite:
The Chinese by a child of Hell, called Wit:
Wealth makes the Persian too effeminate:
And Poverty the Tartars desperate: 140
The Turks and Moors by Mah'met he subdues:
And God has giv'n him leave to rule the Jews:
Rage rules the Portuguese and Fraud the Scotch:
Revenge the Pole and Avarice the Dutch.

    Satire, be kind, and draw a silent veil   145
Thy native England's vices to conceal:
Or if that task's impossible to do,
At least be just, and show her virtues too;
Too great the first, alas! the last too few.

    England unknown as yet, unpeopled lay;   150
Happy, had she remained so to this day,
And not to ev'ry nation been a prey.

Her open harbors and her fertile plains,
The merchants' glory these, and those the swains',
To ev'ry barbarous nation have betrayed her,   155
Who conquer her as oft as they invade her.
So beauty guarded but by innocence:
That ruins her which should be her defense.
  Ingratitude, a devil of black renown,
Possessed her very early for his own.   160
An ugly, surly, sullen, selfish spirit,
Who Satan's worst perfections does inherit:
Second to him in malice and in force,
All devil without, and all within him worse.
  He made her first-born race to be so rude,   165
And suffered her to be so oft subdued.
By sev'ral crowds of wand'ring thieves o'errun,
Often unpeopled, and as oft undone.
While ev'ry nation that her pow'rs reduced,
Their languages and manners introduced.   170
From whose mixed relics our compounded breed,
By spurious generation does succeed;
Making a race uncertain and unev'n,
Derived from all the nations under Heav'n.
  The Romans first with Julius Caesar came,   175
Including all the nations of that name,
Gauls, Greeks, and Lombards, and by computation,
Auxiliaries or slaves of ev'ry nation.
With Hengist, Saxons; Danes with Sueno came,
In search of plunder, not in search of fame;   180
Scots, Picts, and Irish from th' Hibernian shore,
And Conqu'ring William brought the Normans o'er.
  All these their barb'rous offspring left behind,
The dregs of armies, they of all mankind;
Blended with Britains who before were here,   185
Of whom the Welsh have blessed the character.
  From this amphibious ill-born mob began
That vain ill-natured thing, an Englishman.
The customs, surnames, languages, and manners
Of all these nations are their own explainers: 190
Whose relics are so lasting and so strong,
They have left a shibboleth upon our tongue;
By which with easy search you may distinguish
Your Roman-Saxon-Danish-Norman English.

The great invading Norman let us know						195
What conquerors in after-times might do.
To ev'ry musketeer he brought to town,
He gave the lands which never were his own.
When first the English crown he did obtain,
He did not send his Dutchmen home again.						200
No reassumptions in his reign were known,
Davenant might there have let his book alone.
No Parliament his army could disband;
He raised no money, for he paid in land.
He gave his legions their eternal station,						205
And made them all freeholders of the nation.
He cantonned out the country to his men,
And ev'ry soldier was a denizen.
The rascals thus enriched, he called them lords,
To please their upstart pride with new-made-words;					210
And Doomsday Book his tyranny records.
    And here begins the ancient pedigree
That so exalts our poor nobility:
'Tis that from some French trooper they derive,
Who with the Norman bastard did arrive:						215
The trophies of the families appear;
Some show the sword, the bow, and some the spear,
Which their great ancestor, forsooth, did wear.
These in the herald's register remain,
Their noble mean extraction to explain.						220
Yet who the hero was, no man can tell,
Whether a drummer or a colonel:
The silent record blushes to reveal
Their undescended dark original.
    But grant the best, how came the change to pass;			225
A true-born Englishman of Norman race?
A Turkish horse can show more history,
To prove his well-descended family.
Conquest, as by the moderns 'tis expressed,
May give a title to the lands possessed:						230
But that the longest sword should be so civil,
To make a Frenchman English, that's the devil.
    These are the heroes that despise the Dutch,
And rail at new-come foreigners so much;
Forgetting that themselves are all derived						235

202. *book*: Charles Davenant, *A Discourse upon Grants and Resumptions* (1700).

From the most scoundrel race that ever lived.
A horrid medley of thieves and drones,
Who ransacked kingdoms, and dispeopled towns.
The Pict and painted Briton, treach'rous Scot,
By hunger, theft, and rapine, hither brought.   240
Norwegian pirates, buccaneering Danes,
Whose red-haired offspring ev'rywhere remains.
Who joined with Norman-French, compound the breed
From whence your true-born Englishmen proceed.
    And lest by length of time it be pretended,   245
The climate may this modern breed have mended,
Wise Providence, to keep us where we are,
Mixes us daily with exceeding care:
We have been Europe's sink, the jakes where she
Voids all her offal outcast progeny.   250
From our fifth Henry's time, the strolling bands
Of banished fugitives from neighb'ring lands,
Have here a certain sanctuary found:
The eternal refuge of the vagabond.
Where in but half a common age of time,   255
Borr'wing new blood and manners from the clime,
Proudly they learn all mankind to condemn,
And all their race are true-born Englishmen.
    Dutch, Walloons, Flemings, Irishmen, and Scots,
Vaudois, and Valtolins, and Huguenots   260
In good Queen Bess's charitable reign,
Supplied us with three hundred thousand men.
Religion, God we thank thee, sent them hither,
Priests, Protestants, the devil and all together:
Of all professions, and of ev'ry trade,   265
All that were persecuted or afraid,
Whether for debt or other crimes they fled,
David at Hackelah was still their head.
    The offspring of this miscellaneous crowd,
Had not their new plantations long enjoyed,   270
But they grew Englishmen, and raised their votes
At foreign shoals of interloping Scots.

260. *Valtolins:* natives of Valtellina, in the present canton of Grisons, Switzerland.
  268. *David at Hackelah:* With about 600 followers, David sought refuge in the mountain of Hachilah from Saul's attempt against his life (1 Sam. 23:9–19).
  272. *interloping Scots:* The attempt of the Company of Scotland Trading to Africa and the Indies to establish a settlement at Darien, in the isthmus of Panama in 1698–99, was greatly resented as a threat to English trade in the Caribbean.

The royal branch from Pict-land did succeed,
With troops of Scots and scabs from North-by-Tweed.
The seven first years of his pacific reign,   275
Made him and half his nation Englishmen.
Scots from the northern frozen banks of Tay
With packs and plods came whigging all away:
Thick as the locusts which in Egypt swarmed,
With pride and hungry hopes completely armed: 280
With native truth, diseases, and no money,
Plundered our Canaan of the milk and honey.
Here they grew quickly lords and gentlemen,
And all their race are true-born Englishmen.

The civil wars, the common purgative,   285
Which always used to make the nation thrive,
Made way for all that strolling congregation,
Which thronged in pious Charles's Restoration.
The royal refugee our breed restores
With foreign courtiers, and with foreign whores: 290
And carefully repeopled us again,
Throughout his lazy, long, lascivious reign,
With such a blessed and true-born English fry,
As much illustrates our nobility.
A gratitude which will so black appear,   295
As future ages must abhor to hear:
When they look back on all that crimson flood,
Which streamed in Lindsey's and Carnarvon's blood:
Bold Strafford, Cambridge, Capel, Lucas, Lisle,
Who crowned in death his father's fun'ral pile.   300

275. Refers to James I.
278. *whigging:* jogging along (*OED* quotes this line).
294. *nobility:* "The extent to which the peerage in 1688 was of Stuart creation is very re-
markable. . . . [Charles II] was responsibile for no fewer than 64 [creations]" (A.S. Turber-
ville, *The House of Lords in the Reign of William III* [Oxford, 1913], p. 2).
298. *Lindsey:* Robert Bertie, 1st earl of Lindsey, killed at the battle of Edgehill, October
1642. *Carnarvon:* Robert Dormer, earl of Carnarvon, was killed at the first battle of Newbury,
September 1643.
299. *Strafford:* Thomas Wentworth, 1st earl of Strafford, was beheaded on 12 May 1641.
Cambridge: James Hamilton, 2d earl of Cambridge, was beheaded on 9 March 1649. *Capel:*
Arthur Capel, Lord Capel of Hadham, was beheaded 9 March 1649 "for his loyalty to King
Charles the First." *Lucas:* Sir Charles Lucas was captured by the parliamentary army at the
siege of Colchester, court-martialed, and shot on 28 August 1648. *Lisle:* Sir George Lisle
suffered the same fate as Lucas. The two heroes are celebrated in Edward Howard, *Caroloiades,
Or, the Rebellion of Forty One. In Ten Books. A Heroic Poem* (1689), pp. 324–26.
300. *fun'ral pile:* cf. *CSPD, 1600–1661,* p. 396: "Mary Lisle . . . is the only survivor of her
family; her two brothers were slain fighting for the late king, and her parents died of grief for
their loss."

The loss of whom, in order to supply
With true-born English nobility,
Six bastard dukes survive his luscious reign,
The labors of Italian Castlemaine,
French Portsmouth, Tabby Scot, and Cambrian,   305
Besides the num'rous bright and virgin throng,
Whose female glories shade them from my song.
    This offspring, if one age they multiply,
May half the house with English peers supply:
There with true English pride they may condemn   310
Schomberg and Portland, new-made noblemen.
    French cooks, Scotch pedlars, and Italian whores
Were all made lords, or lords' progenitors.
Beggars and bastards by his new creation
Much multiplied the peerage of the nation;   315
Who will be all, e'er one short age runs o'er,
As true-born lords as those we had before.
    Then to recruit the Commons he prepares,
And heal the latent breaches of the wars:
The pious purpose better to advance,   320
He invites the banished Protestants of France:
Hither for God's sake and their own they fled,
Some for religion came, and some for bread:
Two hundred thousand pair of wooden shoes,
Who, God be thanked, had nothing left to lose;   325
To Heav'n's great praise did for religion fly,
To make us starve our poor in charity.
In ev'ry port they plant their fruitful train,
To get a race of true-born Englishmen:
Whose children will, when riper years they see,   330
Be as ill-natured and as proud as we:

303–305. *Six bastard dukes:* James Scott, duke of Monmouth and Buccleuch, the son of "Cambrian" Lucy Walter; Charles Fitzroy, duke of Southampton, and George Fitzroy, duke of Northumberland, the sons of "Italian Castlemaine," Barbara Villiers, countess of Castlemaine and duchess of Cleveland; Charles Beauclerk, duke of St. Albans, the son of "Taffy Slut," Nell Gwynne; Charles Lennox, duke of Richmond, the son of "French Portsmouth," Louise de Keroualle, duchess of Portsmouth.

312. *Italian whores:* Presumably the reference includes the duchess of Cleveland and Hortensia Mancini, Duchess Mazarin, the niece of Cardinal Mancini, who momentarily supplanted Portsmouth as Charles's mistress, but neither founded a family nor gained an English title.

327. *poor:* A law of 1662 entitled An Act for the Better Relief of the Poor of this Kingdom (13 & 14 Charles II, c. 12) provided in fact for the more rigorous application of the Elizabethan poor laws.

Call themselves English, foreigners despise,
Be surly like us all, and just as wise.
    Thus from a mixture of all kinds began,
That het'rogeneous thing, an Englishman: 335
In eager rapes, and furious lust begot,
Betwixt a painted Briton and a Scot:
Whose gend'ring offspring quickly learned to bow,
And yoke their heifers to the Roman plough:
From whence a mongrel half-bred race there came,   340
With neither name nor nation, speech or fame.
In whose hot veins new mixtures quickly ran,
Infused betwixt a Saxon and a Dane.
While their rank daughters, to their parents just,
Received all nations with promiscuous lust.   345
This nauseous brood directly did contain
The well-extracted blood of Englishmen.
    Which medley cantonned in a heptarchy,
A rhapsody of nations to supply,
Among themselves maintained eternal wars,   350
And still the ladies loved the conquerors.
    The Western Angles all the rest subdued;
A bloody nation, barbarous and rude:
Who by the tenure of the sword possessed
One part of Britain, and subdued the rest.   355
And as great things denominate the small,
The conqu'ring part gave title to the whole.
The Scot, Pict, Briton, Roman, Dane submit,
And with the English-Saxon all unite:
And these the mixture have so close pursued,   360
The very name and memory's subdued:
No Roman now, no Briton does remain;
Wales strove to separate, but strove in vain:
The silent nations undistinguished fall,
And Englishman's the common name for all.   365
Fate jumbled them together, God knows how;
Whate'er they were, they're true-born English now.
    The wonder which remains is at our pride,
To value that which all wise men deride.
For Englishmen to boast of generation,   370
Cancels their knowledge, and lampoons the nation.
A true-born Englishman's a contradiction,

348. *heptarchy:* the seven kingdoms of the Angles and Saxons in England.

In speech an irony, in fact a fiction.
A banter made to be a test of fools,
Which those that use it justly ridicules.   375
A metaphor invented to express
A man akin to all the universe.
    For as the Scots, as learnéd men have said,
Throughout the world their wand'ring seed have spread;
So open-handed England, 'tis believed,   380
Has all the gleanings of the world received.
    Some think of England 'twas our Savior meant
The Gospel should to all the world be sent:
Since when the blesséd sound did hither reach,
They to all nations might be said to preach.   385
    'Tis well that virtue gives nobility,
Else God knows where we had our gentry;
Since scarce one family is left alive,
Which does not from some foreigner derive.
Of sixty thousand English gentlemen,   390
Whose names and arms in registers remain,
We challenge all our heralds to declare
Ten families which English-Saxons are.
    France justly boasts the ancient noble line
Of Bourbon, Montmorency, and Lorraine.   395
The Germans too their house of Austria show,
And Holland their invincible Nassau,
Lines which in heraldry were ancient grown,
Before the name of Englishman was known.
Even Scotland too her elder glory shows,   400
Her Gordons, Hamiltons, and her Monroes;
Douglas, Mackays, and Grahams, names well known,
Long before ancient England knew her own.
    But England, modern to the last degree,
Borrows or makes her own nobility,   405
And yet she boldly boasts of pedigree:
Repines that foreigners are put upon her,
And talks of her antiquity and honor:
Her Sackvilles, Savilles, Cecils, Delamerts,

378. *as learnéd men have said:* John Cleveland, *The Rebel Scot:* "Had Cain been Scot, God would have changed his doom / not forced him wander but confined him home" (*The Works of Mr. John Cleveland* [1687], p. 41).

390. *Sixty thousand:* Chamberlayne, *Angliae Notitia* (1700, p. 297) puts the number of esquires and gentlemen at "above 6000;"Gregory King estimated 15,000 (Clark, *Later Stuarts,* p. 25).

Mohuns and Montagues, Durases and Veres,   410
Not one have English names, yet all are English peers.
Your Houblons, Papillons, and Lethuiliers,
Pass now for true-born English knights and squires,
And make good senate members, or lord mayors.
Wealth, howsoever got, in England makes   415
Lords of mechanics, gentlemen of rakes.
Antiquity and birth are needless here;
'Tis impudence and money makes a peer.
    Innumerable City knights we know,
From Bluecoat Hospitals and Bridewell flow.   420
Draymen and porters fill the City chair,
And footboys magisterial purple wear.
Fate has but very small distinction set
Betwixt the Counter and the coronet.
Tarpaulin lords, pages of high renown,   425
Rise up by poor men's valor, not their own.
Great families of yesterday we show,
And lords whose parents were the Lord knows who.

411. *peers:* Charles Sackville, earl of Dorset; William Saville, marquis of Halifax; James Cecil, earl of Salisbury; John Cecil, earl of Exeter; Henry Booth, 2d Baron Delamere and 1st earl of Warrington; Charles Mohun, Lord Mohun; Charles Montagu, earl of Manchester; Edward Montagu, earl of Sandwich; Ralph Montagu, earl of Montagu; Louis de Duras, earl of Feversham; Aubrey de Vere, earl of Oxford.

414. *members or lord mayors:* Sir John Houblon (d. 1712), first governor of the Bank of England and master of the Grocers' Company, served as lord mayor of London in 1695. His younger brother, Sir James Houblon (d. 1700), deputy governor of the Bank of England, served the City both as alderman (1692–1700) and as an M.P. (1698–1700). Thomas Papillon (1623–1702) was candidate for mayor in the critical shrievalty election of 1682; he was subsequently elected alderman for Portsoken ward (1689). He was a Whig M.P. for Dover (1673–1681, 1689–1695) and then for London (1695–1700). Sir John Lethuillier (1629?–1719), whose fat wife Pepys "admired so," served as sheriff (1674) and alderman for Cripplegate ward (1676) (Beaven, *2*, 191). He was succeeded in both of these offices by his younger brother, Sir Christopher Lethuillier (d. 1690), who served as alderman for Coleman Street ward (1687–90) and sheriff (1689).

420. "Christ-Church Hospital . . . called by some the Bluecoat Hospital; all the boys and girls being clothed in blue coats, very warm and decent, and provided with all suitable necessaries. . . . Here's almost a thousand poor children, most of 'em orphans, maintained . . . and some of those that have been put to trades, have arrived to the highest dignities in the City, even the praetorial chair hath been proud of being filled with one of these. . . . Bridewell Hospital, or workhouse, is a place where indigent, vagrant and idle people are set to work, and maintained with clothing and diet. . . . To this hospital, divers hopeful and ingenious lads are put apprentices, and prove afterwards honest and substantial citizens" (Chamberlayne, *Angliae Notitia*, 1700, pp. 406–08).

424. *Counter:* The Counters were prisons and there were two of them in London, one on the north side of the Poultry and the other in Wood Street.

425. *Tarpaulin lords:* persons of indifferent origins elevated to the peerage for distinguished naval service.

Part II

The breed's described: now, Satire, if you can,
Their temper show, for manners make the man.   430
Fierce as the Briton, as the Roman brave;
And less inclined to conquer than to save:
Eager to fight, and lavish of their blood;
And equally of fear and forecast void.
The Pict has made 'em sour, the Dane morose;   435
False from the Scot, and from the Norman worse.
What honesty they have, the Saxon gave them,
And that, now they grow old, begins to leave them.
The climate makes them terrible and bold;
And English beef their courage does uphold: 440
No danger can their daring spirit pall,
Always provided that their belly's full.
    In close intrigues their faculty's but weak,
For gen'rally whate'er they know, they speak:
And often their own councils undermine   445
By their infirmity, and not design.
From whence the learned say it does proceed,
That English treasons never can succeed:
For they're so open-hearted, you may know
Their own most secret thoughts, and others' too.   450
    The lab'ring poor, in spite of double pay,
Are saucy, mutinous, and beggarly:
So lavish of their money and their time,
That want of forecast is the nation's crime.
Good drunken company is their delight;   455
And what they get by day, they spend by night.
Dull thinking seldom does their heads engage,
But think their youth away, and hurry on old age.
Empty of all good husbandry and sense;
And void of manners most, when void of pence.   460
Their strong aversion to behavior's such,
They always talk too little, or too much.
So dull, they never take the pains to think;
And seldom are good-natured, but in drink.
    In English ale their dear enjoyment lies,   465
For which they'll starve themselves and families.

430. *manners make the man:* proverbial; the full form is "manners make a man, quoth William of Wickham" (Tilley).
    434. *forecast:* forethought, prudence.

An Englishman will fairly drink as much
As will maintain two families of Dutch:
Subjecting all their labors to the pots;
The greatest artists are the greatest sots.   470
        The country poor do by example live;
The gentry lead them, and the clergy drive.
What may we not from such examples hope?
The landlord is their God, the priest their pope.
A drunken clergy, and a swearing bench,   475
Has giv'n the Reformation such a drench,
As wise men think there is some cause to doubt,
Will purge good manners and religion out.
        Nor do the poor alone their liquor prize,
The sages join in this great sacrifice.   480
The learned men who study Aristotle,
Correct him with an explanation-bottle;
Praise Epicurus rather than Lysander,
And Aristippus more than Alexander.
The doctors too their Galen here resign,   485
And gen'rally prescribe specific wine.
The graduates' study's grown an easier task,
While for the urinal they toss the flask.
The surgeons' art grows plainer ev'ry hour,
And wine's the balm which into wounds they pour.   490
        Poets long since Parnassus have forsaken,
And say the ancient bards were all mistaken.
Apollo's lately abdicate and fled,
And good King Bacchus reigneth in his stead:
He does the chaos of the head refine,   495
And atom thoughts jump into words by wine:
The inspiration's of a finer nature;
As wine must needs excel Parnassus water.
        Statesmen their weighty politics refine
And soldiers raise their courages by wine.   500
Caecilia gives her choristers their choice,
And lets them all drink wine to clear the voice.
        Some think the clergy first found out the way,
And wine's the only spirit by which they pray.
But others less profane than so, agree,   505
It clears the lungs, and helps the memory:

484. *Aristippus:* the drunkard's name for canary.
496. *atom thoughts:* the smallest conceivable particles of idea.

And therefore all of them divinely think,
Instead of study, 'tis as well to drink.
    And here I would be very glad to know,
Whether our Asgillites may drink or no.   510
Th' enlight'ning fumes of wine would certainly
Assist them much when they begin to fly:
Or if a fiery chariot should appear,
Inflamed by wine, they'd have the less to fear.
    Even the gods themselves, as mortals say,   515
Were they on earth, would be as drunk as they:
Nectar would be no more celestial drink,
They'd all take wine, to teach them how to think.
But English drunkards, gods and men outdo,
Drink their estates away, and senses too.   520
Colon's in debt, and if his friends should fail
To help him out, must die at last in jail:
His wealthy uncle sent a hundred nobles,
To pay his trifles off, and rid him of his troubles:
But Colon, like a true-born Englishman,   525
Drank all the money out in bright champagne;
And Colon does in custody remain.
Drunk'ness has been the darling of the realm,
E'er since a drunken pilot had the helm.
    In their religion they are so unev'n,   530
That each man goes his own way to Heav'n.
Tenacious of mistakes to that degree,
That ev'ry man pursues it sep'rately,
And fancies none can find the way but he:
So shy of one another they are grown,   535

510. *Asgillites:* John Asgill (1659–1738), by trade a lawyer and occasional Whig M.P. for Bramber, Sussex (1699–1700, 1702–07), was, like Defoe, an enthusiastic and resourceful projector. He achieved his greatest notoriety in July 1700 when he published *An Argument Proving, That According to the Covenant of Eternal Life Revealed in the Scriptures, Man May Be Translated from Hence into That Eternal Life, without Passing through Death.* Two months later Bishop Burnet ordered all unsold copies to be confiscated, "as containing things of dangerous consequence" (Luttrell, *4*, 691), and Defoe, also responding, as he said, to "the danger . . . to religion," wrote *An Enquiry into the Case of Mr. Asgil's Translation: Showing That 'Tis Not a Nearer Way to Heaven Than the Grave.* This work, however, he suppressed while the sheets were still in the press, probably after he read *The Way to Heaven in a String; Or, Mr. Asgil's Argument Burlesqued,* amusing doggerel that was widely circulated and reprinted (*POAS,* 1704, *3*, 443), and that called into question the seriousness of Asgill's argument. The word "Asgillites" first occurs in this latter work.

521. Colon: character in Samuel Garth's satire on the medical establishment, *The Dispensary,* 1699.

529. *a drunken pilot:* Charles II.

As if they strove to get to Heav'n alone.
Rigid and zealous, positive and grave,
And ev'ry grace, but charity, they have:
This makes them so ill-natured and uncivil.
That all men think an Englishman the devil. 540
    Surly to strangers, froward to their friend;
Submit to love with a reluctant mind;
Resolved to be ungrateful and unkind;
If by necessity reduced to ask,
The giver has the difficultest task: 545
For what's bestowed they awkwardly receive,
And always take less freely than they give.
The obligation is their highest grief;
And never love, where they accept relief.
So sullen in their sorrows, that 'tis known, 550
They'll rather die than their afflictions own:
And if relieved, it is too often true,
That they'll abuse their benefactors too:
For in distress their haughty stomach's such,
They hate to see themselves obliged too much. 555
Seldom contented, often in the wrong;
Hard to be pleased at all, and never long.
    If your mistakes their ill opinion gain,
No merit can their favor reobtain:
And if they're not vindictive in their fury, 560
'Tis their unconstant temper does secure ye:
Their brain's so cool, their passion seldom burns;
For all's condensed before the flame returns:
The fermentation's of so weak a matter,
The humid damps the fume, and runs it all to water. 565
So though the inclination may be strong,
They're pleased by fits, and never angry long.
    Then if good nature shows some slender proof,
They never think they have reward enough:
But like our modern Quakers of the town, 570
Expect your manners, and return you none.
    Friendship, th' abstracted union of the mind,
Which all men seek, but very few can find:
Of all the nations in the universe,
None talk on't more, or understand it less: 575
For if it does their property annoy,

556–57. Cf. *Absalom and Achitophel*, 547–48.

Their property their friendship will destroy.

  As you discourse them, you shall hear them tell
All things in which they think they do excel:
No panegyric needs their praise record;   580
An Englishman ne'er wants his own good word.
His first discourses gen'rally appear
Prologued with his own good name,
He never fails his neighbor to defame: 585
And yet he really designs no wrong;
His malice goes no further than his tongue.
But pleased to tattle, he delights to rail,
To satisfy the lech'ry of a tale.
His own dear praises close the ample speech,   590
Tells you how wise he is; that is, how rich:
For wealth is wisdom; he that's rich is wise;
And all men learned poverty despise.
His generosity comes next, and then
Concludes that he's a true-born Englishman;   595
And they, 'tis known, are generous and free,
Forgetting, and forgiving injury:
Which may be true, thus rightly understood,
Forgiving ill turns, and forgetting good.

  Cheerful in labor when they've undertook it; 600
But out of humor, when they're out of pocket.
But if their belly and their pocket's full,
They may be phlegmatic, but never dull:
And if a bottle does their brains refine,
It makes their wit as sparkling as their wine.   605

  As for the general vices which we find
They're guilty of in common with mankind,
Satire forbear, and silently endure;
We must conceal the crimes we cannot cure.
Nor shall my verse the brighter sex defame;   610
For English beauty will preserve her name.
Beyond dispute, agreeable and fair;
And modester than other nations are:
For where the vice prevails, the great temptation
Is want of money, more than inclination.   615
In general, this only is allowed,
They're something noisy, and a little proud.

  An Englishman is gentlest in command;
Obedience is a stranger in the land:

Hardly subjected to the magistrate; 620
For Englishmen do all subjection hate.
Humblest when rich, but peevish when they're poor;
And think whate'er they have, they merit more.
    Shamwig pretends t' have served the government,
But balked of due reward, turns malcontent, 625
For English Christians always have regard
To future recompenses of reward.
His forfeit liberty they did restore,
And gave him bread, which he had not before.
But true-born English Shamwhig lets them know, 630
His merit must not lie neglected so.
As proud as poor, his masters he'll defy;
And writes a piteous satire 'pon honesty.
Some think the poem had been pretty good,
If he the subject had but understood. 635
He got five hundred pence by this, and more,
As sure as he had ne'er a groat before.
    In bus'ness next some friends of his employed him;
And there he proved that fame had not belied him:
His benefactors quickly he abused, 640
And falsely to the government accused:
But they, defended by their innocence,
Ruined the traitor in their own defense.
    Thus kicked about from pillars unto posts,
He whets his pen against the Lord of Hosts: 645
Burlesques his God and king in paltry rhymes:
Against the Dutch turns champion for the times;
And huffs the king, upon that very score,
On which he panegyricked him before.
    Unhappy England, hast thou none but such, 650
To plead thy scoundrel cause against the Dutch?
This moves their scorn, and not their indignation;
He that lampoons the Dutch, burlesques the nation.
    The meanest English plowman studies law,
And keeps thereby the magistrates in awe: 655

624. *Shamwhig:* John Tutchin (1661?–1707), Whig pamphleteer.
633. *satire 'pon honesty: A Search after Honesty. A Poem by Mr. Tutchin,* dated 1697.
646. *paltry rhymes: The Foreigners.*
    649. *panegyricked him:* In *An Heroic Poem upon the Late Expedition of His Majesty to Rescue England from Popery, Tyranny, and Arbitrary Government* (1689), Tutchin hailed William as "a godlike hero," "our other Moses," the "mighty Nassau" who "conquered by goodness" rather than by might.

Will boldly tell them what they ought to do,
And sometimes punish their omissions too.
    Their liberty and property's so dear,
They scorn their laws or governors to fear:
So bugbeared with the name of slavery,   660
They can't submit to their own liberty.
Restraint from ill is freedom to the wise;
But Englishmen do all restraint despise.
Slaves to the liquor, drudges to the pots,
The mob are statesmen, and their statesmen sots.   665
    Their governors they count such dangerous things,
That 'tis their custom to affront their kings:
So jealous of the power their kings possessed,
They suffer neither power nor kings to rest.
The bad with force they eagerly subdue;   670
The good with constant clamors they pursue:
And did King Jesus reign, they'd murmur too.
A discontented nation, and by far
Harder to rule in times of peace than war:
Easily set together by the ears,   675
And full of causeless jealousies and fears:
Apt to revolt, and willing to rebel,
And never are contented when they're well,
No government could ever please them long,
Could tie their hands, or rectify their tongue.   680
In this to ancient Israel well compared,
Eternal murmurs are among them heard.
    It was but lately that they were oppressed,
Their rights invaded, and their laws suppressed:
When nicely tender of their liberty,   685
Lord! what a noise they made of slavery.
In daily tumults showed their discontent;
Lampooned their king, and mocked his government.
And if in arms they did not first appear,
'Twas want of force, and not for want of fear.   690
In humbler tone than English used to do,
At foreign hands for foreign aid they sue.

---

665. *The mob are statesmen:* Bishop Burnet observed that "though we were falling insensibly into a democracy, we had not learned the virtues, that are necessary for that sort of government" (Burnet, *2*, 247).

679. *No government could ever please:* Cf. *Absalom and Achitophel*, 48.

681–82. *well compared:* Cf. *Absalom and Achitophel*, 45.

692. *for foreign aid they sue:* Cf. *Letter of Invitation to William of Orange*, 30 June 1688: "We

William the great successor of Nassau,
Their prayers heard, and their oppressions saw:
He saw and saved them: God and him they praised; 695
To this their thanks, to that their trophies raised.
But glutted with their own felicities,
They soon their new deliverer despise;
Say all their prayers back, their joy disown,
Unsing their thanks, and pull their trophies down: 700
Their harps of praise are on the willows hung;
For Englishmen are ne'er contented long.
    The rev'rend clergy too! and who'd have thought
That they who had such non-resistance taught,
Should e'er to arms against their prince be brought? 705
Who up to Heav'n did regal pow'r advance;
Subjecting English laws to modes of France.
Twisting religion so with loyalty,
As one could never live, and t'other die.
And yet no sooner did their prince design 710
Their glebes and perquisites to undermine,
But all their passive doctrines laid aside;
The clergy their own principles denied:
Unpreached their non-resisting cant, and prayed
To Heav'n for help, and to the Dutch for aid. 715
The church chimed all her doctrines back again,
And pulpit-champions did the cause maintain;
Flew in the face of all their former zeal,
And non-resistance did at once repeal.
    The rabbis say it would be too prolix, 720
To tie religion up to politics:
The church's safety is *suprema lex*.

---

have great reason to believe we shall be every day in a worse condition than we are, and less able to defend ourselves, and therefore we do earnestly wish we might be so happy as to find a remedy before it is too late for us to contribute to our own deliverance . . . If upon a due consideration of all these circumstances Your Highness shall think fit to adventure upon the attempt, or at least to make such preparations for it as are necessary (which we wish you may), there must be no more time lost." (*EHD*, pp. 120–21).

704. *non-resistance:* A doctrine elaborated by the Anglican clergy in the second half of the 17th century, that since the authority of the king derived solely from God, it could not be resisted even if it violated human law.

705. *to arms:* Henry Compton, bishop of London, one of the seven signers of the letter of invitation to William, accepted a commission as colonel of cavalry in November 1688 and marched into Oxford at the head of his troop. Another militant cleric was George Walker (1618–90), vicar of Lissan, who served as military governor of Londonderry during the siege and was killed at the passage of the Boyne.

710. *their prince:* James II.

And so by a new figure of their own,
Do all their former doctrines disown.
As laws post facto in the Parliament,   725
In urgent cases have obtained assent;
But are as dangerous precedents laid by;
Made lawful only by necessity.
    The rev'rend fathers then in arms appear,
And men of God became the men of war.   730
The nation, fired by them, to arms apply;
Assault their anti-Christian monarchy;
To their due channel all our laws restore,
And made things what they should have been before.
But when they came to fill the vacant throne,   735
And the pale priests looked back on what they'd done;
How English liberty began to thrive,
And Church of England loyalty outlive:
How all their persecuting days were done,
And their deliv'rer placed upon the throne: 740
The priests, as priests are wont to do, turned tail;
They're Englishmen, and nature will prevail.
Now they deplore the ruins they have made,
And murmur for the master they betrayed.
Excuse those crimes they could not make him mend;   745
And suffer for the cause they can't defend.
Pretend they'd not have carried things so high;
And proto-martyrs make for popery.
    Had the prince done as they designed the thing,
Have set the clergy up to rule the king;   750
Taken a donative for coming hither,
And so have left their king and them together,
We had, say they, been now a happy nation.
No doubt we'd seen a blessed Reformation:
For wise men say 't's as dangerous a thing,   755
A ruling priesthood, as a priest-rid king.
And of all plagues with which mankind are cursed,
Ecclesiastic tyranny's the worst.

736. *the pale priests:* "(meaning the nonjurants) . . . were men of such tender consciences, as not to be led by any hopes of gain to take oaths to a prince, who was established in the throne during the life of the king they had sworn to" (*The True-Born Englishman: A Satire, Answered* [1701], p. 57.) Of the entire body of 9743 beneficed clergymen and 28 bishops, only about 400 clergymen and 8 bishops refused to take the oaths of allegiance to William and Mary.

751. *donative:* a gift or present, given formally or officially as a largess or bounty.

  If all our former grievances were feigned,
King James has been abused, and we trepanned;   760
Bugbeared with popery and power despotic,
Tyrannic government, and leagues exotic:
The revolution's a fanatic plot,
William a tyrant, Sunderland a sot:
A factious army and a poisoned nation,   765
Unjustly forced King James's abdication.
  But if he did the subjects' rights invade,
Then he was punished only, not betrayed:
And punishing of kings is no such crime,
But Englishmen have done it many a time.   770
  When kings the sword of justice first lay down,
They are no kings, though they possess the crown.
Titles are shadows, crowns are empty things,
The good of subjects is the end of kings;
To guide in war, and to protect in peace: 775
Where tyrants once commence, the kings do cease:
For arbitrary power's so strange a thing,
It makes the tyrant, and unmakes the king.
If kings by foreign priests and armies reign,
And lawless power against their oaths maintain,   780
Then subjects must have reason to complain.
If oaths must bind us when our kings do ill;
To call in foreign aid is to rebel.
By force to circumscribe our lawful prince,
Is willful treason in the largest sense: 785
And they who once rebel, most certainly
Their God, and king, and former oaths defy.
If we allow no maladministration
Could cancel the allegiance of the nation;
Let all our learnéd sons of Levi try,   790
This eccles'astic riddle to untie:
How they could make a step to call the prince,
And yet pretend to oaths and innocence.
  By th' first address they made beyond the seas,
They're perjured in the most intense degrees;   795
And without scruple for the time to come,
May swear to all the kings in Christendom.
And truly did our kings consider all,

771–72. *Qui cessat regnare cessat judicare,* quoted by Sir Gilbert Dolben in January 1689 during the debate on James II's "withdrawal" (*Cobbett's Parl. Hist., 5,* 37).

They'd never let the clergy swear at all:
Their politic allegiance they'd refuse;   800
For whores and priests do never want excuse.
  But if the mutual contract was dissolved,
The doubt's explained, the difficulty solved:
That kings, when they descend to tyranny,
Dissolve the bond, and leave the subject free.   805
The government's ungirt when justice dies,
And constitutions are nonentities.
The nation's all a mob, there's no such thing
As Lords or Commons, Parliament or king.
A great promiscuous crowd the Hydra lies,   810
Till laws revive, and mutual contract ties:
A chaos free to choose for their own share,
What case of government they please to wear:
If to a king they do the reins commit,
All men are bound in conscience to submit: 815
But then that king must by his oath assent
To postulatas of the government;
Which if he breaks, he cuts off the entail,
And power retreats to its original.
  This doctrine has the sanction of assent,   820
From nature's universal parliament.
The voice of nations, and the course of things,
Allow that laws superior are to kings.
None but delinquents would have justice cease,
Knaves rail at laws, as soldiers rail at peace: 825
For justice is the end of government,
As reason is the test of argument.
  No man was ever yet so void of sense,
As to debate the right of self-defense;

802. *contract:* The question whether there was in fact a contract between king and people was debated in the House of Lords in January 1689 and upon a division, 53 to 46, it was decided that there was (Ralph, *2,* 37). Locke derived all political power "only from compact and agreement, and the mutual consent of those who make up the community" (*Two Treatises of Government* [1690], p. 394).

808–19. These lines are a versification of Locke, *Two Treatises of Government* [1690], pp. 439–40 (hereafter cited as Locke).

813. *case:* outward covering, form.

187. *postulatas:* demands, requirements.

823. *laws superior are to kings:* "For the king's authority [is] given him only by the law" (Locke, pp. 426–27).

826. "The legislative, or supreme authority . . . is bound to dispense justice" (Locke, p. 357).

829. *the right of self-defense:* "It being out of a man's power so to submit himself to another,

A principle so grafted in the mind,   830
With nature born, and does like nature bind:
Twisted with reason, and with nature too;
As neither one nor t'other can undo.
     Nor can this right be less when national;
Reason which governs one, should govern all.   835
Whate'er the dialect of courts may tell,
He that his right demands, can ne'er rebel.
Which right, if 'tis by governors denied,
May be procured by force, or foreign aid.
For tyranny's a nation's term for grief;   840
As folks cry "fire," to hasten in relief.
And when the hated word is heard about,
All men should come to help the people out.
     Thus England groaned, Britannia's voice was heard;
And great Nassau to rescue her, appeared: 845
Called by the universal voice of Fate;
God and the peoples' legal magistrate.
Ye Heav'ns regard: Almighty Jove look down,
And view thy injured monarch on the throne.
On their ungrateful heads due vengeance take,   850
Who sought his aid, and then his part forsake.
Witness, ye Powers! it was our call alone,
Which now our pride makes us ashamed to own.
Britannia's troubles fetched him from afar,
To court the dreadful casualties of war: 855
But where requital never can be made,
Acknowledgment's a tribute seldom paid.
     He dwelt in bright Maria's circling arms,
Defended by the magic of her charms,
From foreign fears, and from domestic harms.   860
Ambition found no fuel for her fire,
He had what God could give, or man desire.
Till pity roused him from his soft repose,
His life to unseen hazards to expose:

---

as to give him a liberty to destroy him; God and nature never allowing a man so to abandon
himself, as to neglect his own preservation" (Locke, pp. 370–91).
    834. *this right:* the right of revolution; cf. "Whenever the legislators endeavor to take away,
and destroy the property of the people, or to reduce them to slavery under arbitrary power
. . . they forfeit the power, the people had put into their hands, for quite contrary ends,
and it devolves to the people, who have a right to resume their original liberty, and, by the
establishment of a new legislative (such as they shall think fit) provide for their own safety
and security, which is the end for which they are in society" (Locke, pp. 441–42).

Till pity moved him in our cause t' appear;   865
Pity! that word which now we hate to hear.
But English gratitude is always such,
To hate the hand which does oblige too much.
    Britannia's cries gave birth to his intent,
And hardly gained his unforeseen assent: 870
His boding thoughts foretold him he should find
The people fickle, selfish, and unkind.
Which thought did to his royal heart appear
More dreadful than the dangers of the war:
For nothing grates a generous mind so soon,   875
As base returns for hearty service done.
    Satire be silent, awfully prepare
Britannia's song, and William's praise to hear.
Stand by, and let her cheerfully rehearse
Her grateful vows in her immortal verse.   880
Loud Fame's eternal trumpet let her sound;
Listen ye distant poles, and endless round.
May the strong blast the welcome news convey
As far as sound can reach, or spirit fly.
To neighb'ring worlds, if such there be, relate   885
Our hero's fame, for theirs to imitate.
To distant worlds of spirits let her rehearse,
For spirits without the helps of voice converse.
May angels hear the gladsome news on high,
Mixed with their everlasting symphony.   890
And Hell itself stand in suspense to know
Whether it be the fatal blast, or no.

Britannia

    "The fame of virtue 'tis for which I sound,
And heroes with immortal triumphs crowned.
Fame built on solid virtue swifter flies,   895
Than morning light can spread my eastern skies.
The gath'ring air returns the doubling sound,
And loud repeating thunders force it round:
Echoes return from caverns of the deep:
Old chaos dreams on't in eternal sleep.   900
Time hands it forward to its latest urn,
From whence it never, never shall return,

---

876. *base returns*: As early as March 1689, William complained to Halifax that "the Commons used him like a dog."

Nothing is heard so far, or lasts so long;
'Tis heard by ev'ry ear, and spoke by ev'ry tongue.
    "My hero, with the sails of honor furled,   905
Rises like the great genius of the world.
By fate and fame wisely prepared to be
The soul of war, and life of victory.
He spreads the wings of virtue on the throne,
And ev'ry wind of glory fans them on.   910
Immortal trophies dwell upon his brow,
Fresh as the garlands he has won but now.
    "By different steps the high ascent he gains,
And differently that high ascent maintains.
Princes for pride and lust of rule make war,   915
And struggle for the name of conqueror.
Some fight for fame, and some for victory.
He fights to save, and conquers to set free.
    "Then seek no phrase his titles to conceal,
And hide with words what actions must reveal.   920
No parallel from Hebrew stories take,
Of godlike kings my similes to make:
No borrowed names conceal my living theme;
But names and things directly I proclaim.
'Tis honest merit does his glory raise;   925
Whom that exalts, let no man fear to praise.
Of such a subject no man need be shy;
Virtue's above the reach of flattery.
He needs no character but his own fame,
Nor any flattering titles, but his name.   930
    "William's the name that's spoke by ev'ry tongue:
William's the darling subject of my song.
Listen ye virgins to the charming sound,
And in eternal dances hand it round:
Your early offerings to this altar bring;   935
Make him at once a lover and a king.
May he submit to none but to your arms;
Nor ever be subdued, but by your charms.
May your soft thoughts for him be all sublime;
And ev'ry tender vow be made for him.   940
May he be first in ev'ry morning thought,

921.ˈ *No parallel:* While he resists the greatest poetical temptation of his day, the tempta-
tion to write in the manner of Dryden's *Absalom and Achitophel,* Defoe cannot eliminate all
traces of this poem from his work; see lines 268, 556–57, 678, 681, 990–91 of the present poem.

And Heav'n ne'er hear a pray'r where he's left out.
May ev'ry omen, ev'ry boding dream,
Be fortunate by mentioning his name.
May this one charm infernal powers affright,   945
And guard you from the terrors of the night.
May ev'ry cheerful glass as it goes down
To William's health, be cordials to your own.
Let ev'ry song be chorused with his name.
And music pay her tribute to his fame.   950
Let ev'ry poet tune his artful verse,
And in immortal strains his deeds rehearse.
And may Apollo never more inspire
The disobedient bard with his seraphic fire.
May all my sons their grateful homage pay;   955
His praises sing, and for his safety pray."
     "Satire return to our unthankful isle,
Secured by Heav'n's regard, and William's toil.
To both ungrateful, and to both untrue;
Rebels to God, and to good nature too.   960
     "If e'er this nation be distressed again,
To whomsoe'er they cry, they'll cry in vain.
To Heav'n they cannot have the face to look;
Or if they should, it would but Heav'n provoke.
To hope for help from man would be too much;   965
Mankind would always tell 'em of the Dutch:
How they came here our freedoms to maintain,
Were paid, and cursed, and hurried home again.
How by their aid we first dissolved our fears,
And then our helpers damned for foreigners.   970
'Tis not our English temper to do better;
For Englishmen think ev'ry man their debtor.
     " 'Tis worth observing, that we ne'er complained
Of foreigners, nor of the wealth they gained,
Till all their services were at an end.   975
Wise men affirm it is the English way,
Never to grumble till they come to pay;
And then they always think their temper's such,
The work too little, and the pay too much.
     "As frighted patients, when they want a cure,   980
Bid any price, and any pain endure:
But when the doctor's remedies appear,
The cure's too easy, and the price too dear.

"Great Portland ne'er was bantered, when he strove
For us his master's kindest thoughts to move.   985
We ne'er lampooned his conduct, when employed
King James's secret councils to divide:
Then we caressed him as the only man,
Which could the doubtful oracle explain:
The only Hushai able to repell   990
The dark designs of our Achitophel
Compared his master's courage to his sense,
The ablest statesman, and the bravest prince.
On his wise conduct we depended much,
And liked him ne'er the worse for being Dutch.   995
Nor was he valued more than he deserved;
Freely he ventured, faithfully he served.
In all King William's dangers he has shared;
In England's quarrels always he appeared:
The revolution first, and then the Boyne;   1000
In both his counsels and his conduct shine.
His martial valor Flanders will confess;
And France regrets his managing the peace.
Faithful to England's interest and her king:
The greatest reason of our murmuring.   1005
Ten years in English service he appeared,
And gained his master's and the world's regard:
But 'tis not England's custom to reward.
The wars are over, England needs him not;
Now he's a Dutchman, and the Lord knows what.   1010
        "Schomberg, the ablest soldier of his age,

987. *divide:* Bentinck served as intermediary, first at the Hague, between the prince of
Orange and the duke of Monmouth, and then (after William learned that Monmouth had de-
clared himself king on 20 June 1685) in London, between the prince and James II. The king
indiscreetly revealed to Bentinck his displeasure with the prince, his son-in-law (Echard,
3, 755, 767).
    989. *oracle:* William of Orange (?).
    990. *Hushai:* Hushai is the friend of David who advises Absalom to "defeat the counsel of
Achitophel" (2 Sam. 15:32–34). In *Absalom and Achitophel* (888–97) he is Laurence Hyde, earl
of Rochester.
    991. *our Achitophel:* James II (?).
    996–97. *deserved . . . served:* Defoe is virtually quoting William's words. In reply to the
Commons' protest against his grant to Portland of crown lands in Wales, the king said, "I
have kindness for my Lord Portland, which he has deserved of me by long and faithful
services" (*CJ, 11,* 409).
    1001. *conduct:* Bentinck commanded a regiment of dragoons at the Boyne in July 1690 and
during eight campaigns in Flanders. He was wounded during the Confederates' defeat at
Landen and distinguished himself on several other occasions.
    1011. *Schomberg:* Friedrich Herman von Schomberg (1615–90) was a German nobleman

With great Nassau did in our cause engage:
Both joined for England's rescue and defense;
The greatest captain, and the greatest prince.
With what applause his stories did we tell?   1015
Stories which Europe's volumes largely swell.
We counted him an army in our aid:
Where he commanded, no man was afraid.
His actions with a constant conquest shine,
From Villa Vitiosa to the Rhine.   1020
France, Flanders, Germany, his fame confess;
And all the world was fond of him, but us.
Our turn first served, we grudged him the command.
Witness the grateful temper of the land.
     "We blame the king that he relies too much   1025
On strangers, Germans, Huguenots, and Dutch;
And seldom does his great affairs of state,
To English counselors communicate.
The fact might very well be answered thus;
He has so often been betrayed by us,   1030
He must have been a madman to rely
On English gentlemen's fidelity.
For laying other arguments aside,
This thought might mortify our English pride,
That foreigners have faithfully obeyed him,   1035
And none but Englishmen have e'er betrayed him.
They have our ships and merchants bought and sold,
And bartered English blood for foreign gold.
First to the French they sold our Turkey fleet,

---

whose mother was English and whose great-grandfather was Sir James Harrington, the political philosopher. He was not only one of the greatest field commanders but also one of the greatest military organizers of his day. His victory over the Spanish at Villa Viciosa (June 1665) completely established the independence of Portugal. He was the last Protestant to be made a marshal of France. He volunteered his services to William of Orange in 1688, was created duke of Schomberg in May 1689, and put in command of all English forces in Ireland. He died leading his troops across the Boyne on 1 July 1690.

1039. *sold our Turkey fleet:* In May 1693 a merchant fleet of 400 to 500 vessels bound for the Levant sailed from Spithead. On the same day Nottingham, the Tory secretary of state, received intelligence that Tourville had sailed from Brest in command of the French grand fleet. Although Nottingham laid this information before the Privy Council, no action was thought necessary. On 17 June Tourville sighted the merchant fleet in Lagos Bay. In the engagement that followed 100 merchant ships, worth about £1,500,000 were lost "and the disgrace of it," as Burnet observed, "was visible to the whole world" (Burnet, 2, 116.) In November 1643 the House of Commons resolved "that, upon examination of the miscarriage of the fleet, and the loss of the Turkey company sustained this summer, this House is of opinion that there hath been a notorious and treacherous mismanagement of the fleet this year."

And injured Talmarsh next at Camaret. 1040
The king himself is sheltered from their snares,
Not by his merit, but the crown he wears.
Experience tells us 'tis the English way,
Their benefactors always to betray.

    "And lest examples should be too remote, 1045
A modern magistrate of famous note,
Shall give you his own history by rote.
I'll make it out, deny it he that can,
His worship is a true-born Englishman,
In all the latitude that empty word 1050
By modern acceptation's understood.
The parish books his great descent record,
And now he hopes e'er long to be a lord.
And truly as things go, it would be pity
But such as he bore office in the City: 1055
While robb'ry for burnt offering he brings,
And gives to God what he has stole from kings:
Great monuments of charity he raises,
And good St. Magnus whistles out his praises.
To City jails he grants a jubilee, 1060

1040. *Talmarsh:* Thomas Tollemache (1615?–94) was one of the two or three most success-ful English military leaders of his day. He commanded one of the regiments that landed with William at Tor Bay and subsequently distinguished himself at Aughrim and Landen. In January 1692, when Marlborough was dismissed, he was promoted to lieutenant-general in his place. In 1694 he was placed in command of a descent upon Brest, in Camarets Bay, the plan for which was known to the French so far in advance that Louis was able to send Vauban to attend to the fortifications (Luttrell, *3*, 328). It is not surprising, therefore, that the operation was a total failure and that Tollemache and almost the entire landing party were killed. Tollemache died believing that he had been betrayed by "the government," *i.e.* by the king's English ministers (Oldmixon, p. 92).

1046. *modern magistrate:* Sir Charles Duncombe.

1052. *great descent:* "His father [was] a haberdasher of hats in Southwark as some say; others that he was steward to Sir Will. Tiringham of Tiringham in Bucks., Knt." (Le Neve, p. 468).

1055. *office in the City:* The line probably refers to the mayoralty election of September 1700: in the poll of liverymen, Duncombe's name stood at the top of the list, but the aldermen voted 14 to 12 to elect a Whig, Sir Thomas Abney.

1057. *gives to God:* The parish church of St. Magnus Martyr was burned down in the great fire and rebuilt. In 1700 Duncombe contributed a clock with a "curious dial." *stole from kings:* In October 1688 Duncombe, while he was serving as a receiver of the customs, "stopped in his hands £60,000 of the king's money, upon account of His Majesty owing him as much" (Luttrell, *1*, 471).

1060. *jubilee:* A jubilee was celebrated in 1700; during this time plenary indulgence could be obtained by a pilgrimage to Rome, the visiting of certain churches there, giving of alms, fasting three days, and the performance of other pious works. During Duncombe's shrievalty, 1699–1700, he released out of prison "above 170 persons that were in for debt" (*The Post Boy*, no. 754, 6–8 February 1700).

And hires huzzas from his own mobile.
"Lately he wore the golden chain and gown,
With which equipped he thus harangued the town."

Sir Charles Duncomb's Fine Speech, Etc.

"With clouted iron shoes and sheepskin breeches,
More rags than manners, and more dirt than riches: 1065
From driving cows and calves to Layton Market,
While of my greatness there appeared no spark yet,
Behold I come, to let you see the pride
With which exalted beggars always ride.
    "Born to the needful labors of the plow,   1070
The cart whip graced me as the chain does now.
Nature and fate in doubt what course to take,
Whether I should a lord or plough-boy make;
Kindly at last resolved they would promote me,
And first a knave, and then a knight they vote me.   1075
What fate appointed, nature did prepare,
And furnished me with an exceeding care.
To fit me for what they designed to have me;
And ev'ry gift but honesty they gave me.
    "And thus equipped, to this proud town I came,   1080
In quest of bread, and not in quest of fame.
Blind to my future fate, an humble boy,
Free from the guilt and glory I enjoy.
The hopes which my ambition entertained,
Were in the name of footboy all contained.   1085
The greatest heights from small beginnings rise;
The gods were great on earth, before they reached the skies.
    "Blackwell, the generous temper of whose mind,
Was always to be bountiful inclined:
Whether by his ill fate or fancy led,   1090
First took me up, and furnished me with bread.
The little services he put me to
Seemed labors rather than were truly so.
But always my advancement he designed;
For 'twas his very nature to be kind.   1095
Large was his soul, his temper ever free;

1088. *Blackwell:* Edward Blackwell was a goldsmith who became the private banker of
Cromwell and then of Charles II, and finally, one of the first public bankers in London,
doing business at the Sign of the Unicorn in Lombard Street. Duncombe began his career
as an apprentice to Blackwell.

The best of masters and of men to me.
And I who was before decreed by Fate
To be made infamous as well as great,
With an obsequious diligence obeyed him,   1100
Till trusted with his all, and then betrayed him.
    "All his past kindnesses I trampled on,
Ruined his fortune to erect my own.
So vipers in the bosom bred, begin
To hiss at that hand first which took them in.   1105
With eager treach'ry I his fall pursued,
And my first trophies were ingratitude.
    "Ingratitude's the worst of human guilt,
The basest action mankind can commit;
Which like the sin against the Holy Ghost,   1110
Has least of honor, and of guilt the most.
Distinguished from all other crimes by this,
That 'tis a crime which no man will confess.
That sin alone, which should not be forgiv'n
On earth, although perhaps it may in Heav'n.   1115
    "Thus my first benefactor I o'erthrew;
And how should I be to a second true?
The public trust came next into my care,
And I to use them scurvily prepare:
My needy sov'reign lord I played upon,   1120
And lent him many a thousand of his own;
For which, great int'rest I took care to charge,
And so my ill-got wealth became so large.
    "My predecessor Judas was a fool,
Fitter to have been whipped, and sent to school,   1125
Than sell a Savior: had I been at hand,
His master had not been so cheap trepanned;
I would have made the eager Jews have found,
For thirty pieces, thirty thousand pound.
    "My cousin Ziba, of immortal fame,   1130

1101. *betrayed him:* When Charles II ordered the Exchequer to stop payments in 1672, Blackwell lost nearly £300,000 and was forced out of business. Duncombe, however, who "was at that time banker to Lord Shaftesbury . . . received a timely warning of the projected closing of the Exchequer . . . and by this means he was enabled to withdraw 'a very great sum of his own,' and £30,000 belonging to the marquis of Winchester, afterwards the first duke of Bolton" (*DNB*, 6, 176).

1118. *public trust:* Duncombe was a receiver of the customs under Charles II and James II, and receiver-general of the excise under William III.

1120. *sov'reign lord:* Charles II.

1130. *Ziba:* "For Jonathan's sake" David restored to Mephibosheth, the crippled son of

(Ziba and I shall never want a name:)
First-born of Treason, nobly did advance
His master's fall, for his inheritance.
By whose keen arts old David first began
To break his sacred oath to Jonathan: 1135
The good old king, 'tis thought, was very loath
To break his word, and therefore broke his oath.
Ziba's a traitor of some quality,
Yet Ziba might have been informed by me:
Had I been there, he ne'er had been content   1140
With half th' estate, nor half the government.

    "In our late revolution 'twas thought strange,
That I of all mankind should like the change:
But they who wondered at it, never knew,
That in it I did my old game pursue: 1145
Nor had they heard of twenty thousand pound,
Which ne'er was lost, yet never could be found.

    "Thus all things in their turn to sale I bring,
God and my master first, and then the king:
Till by successful villainies made bold,   1150
I thought to turn the nation into gold;
And so to forgery my hand I bent,
Not doubting I could gull the government;
But there was ruffled by the Parliament.
And if I 'scaped th' unhappy tree to climb,   1155

Jonathan and grandson of Saul, his grandfather's entire estate, including Ziba, Saul's slave
who had gained his freedom (2 Sam. 9:1–13). Years later, during the revolt of Absalom,
Mephibosheth intended to join David in his flight, but Ziba betrayed him and went off in
pursuit of David with Mephibosheth's asses and provisions (2 Sam. 19:24–28). Catching up
with David on the Mount of Olives, Ziba offered, as his own, Mephibosheth's asses and
provisions, and accepted, as David's reward, Mephibosheth's entire estate (2 Sam. 16:1–4).

    1135. *sacred oath:* David had sworn an oath to show the same kindness to Jonathan's
descendants that he had shown to Jonathan himself (1 Sam. 20:14–19).

    1137. *word . . . oath:* David's "word" to Ziba (1130 *n.*) conflicted with his "oath" to Jona-
than (1135 *n.*) so he set a good precedent for Solomon by dividing Mephibosheth's estate
between Ziba and Mephibosheth (2 Sam. 19:29).

    1145. *old game:* In August 1696 it was reported that "the Dutch are to advance . . .
£300,000 (on the security of these following persons) unto his majesty . . . viz. . . . . Charles
Duncomb." The following March it was reported that "Mr. Duncomb, the banker, has lent
the king £10,000" (Luttrell, *4,* 92, 192).

    1152. *forgery:* In January 1698 Duncombe was charged with "having contrived and
advised the making false endorsements of Exchequer bills (see *Advice to a Painter,* 87 *n.*) and
ordered to be held incommunicado in the Tower. Subsequently, "on examination, and by
the confession of *Charles Duncomb* Esquire," he was expelled from the House and a bill for his
punishment was ordered to be brought in (*CJ, 12,* 63, 78).

    1155. *tree:* the gallows.

'Twas want of law, and not for want of crime.
　　"But my old friend, who printed in my face
A needful competence of English brass,
Having more business yet for me to do,
And loath to lose his trusty servant so,   1160
Managed the matter with such art and skill,
As saved his hero, and threw out the bill.
　　"And now I'm graced with unexpected honors,
For which I'll certainly abuse the donors:
Knighted, and made a tribune of the people   1165
Whose laws and properties I'm like to keep well:
The *custos rotulorum* of the City,
And captain of the guards of their *banditti.*
Surrounded by my catchpoles, I declare
Against the needy debtor open war.   1170
I hang poor thieves for stealing of your pelf,
And suffer none to rob you, but myself.
　　"The king commanded me to help reform ye,

1156. *want of law:* The Commons passed in February 1698 a bill to punish Duncombe for making false endorsements of Exchequer bills. The Lords, however, "after a debate near 3 hours," threw out the bill by a vote of 49 to 48 (Luttrell, *4,* 355; *LJ, 16,* 235). Commons then asked the king to prosecute in the law courts, but when the case was tried in February 1699, Duncombe "of course (was) found not guilty." A retrial in June declared him innocent once more. That night Duncombe treated the jury to "a noble dinner at Locket's ordinary. . . ," and it was rumored he gave them 5 guineas apiece (Luttrell, *4,* 480, 528).

1157. *old friend:* "the devil," according to one MS. Duncombe's "old friend" could not have failed also to suggest Charles Paulet, 6th marquis of Winchester and 1st duke of Bolton (1625?–99) (see 1101 n.), "a man of a profuse expense, and of a most ravenous avarice to support that" (Burnet, *2,* 225). In March 1698, before Duncombe's case came before the House of Lords, "the duke of Bolton brought into the Lords's House Mr. Duncombe's case printed, wherein he sets forth the severity of the bill, and gave every peer one to consider of." Two days later, when the bill was read for the first time, Bolton made a speech against it. Since the final vote closely followed party lines—the Tory leaders, Leeds, Rochester, Nottingham, and Peterborough all spoke against the bill—the vote of Bolton, who was a Whig, was decisive in the 49–48 division (Luttrell, *4,* 351, 355).

1165. *tribune:* Only a week after his acquittal by the court of King's Bench, Duncombe was "without a poll" elected high sheriff of London. It was expected that he would pay the usual fine not to serve, so his decision to accept the post was "a great disappointment to the court of aldermen" (Luttrell, *4,* 530–31).

1167. *custos rotulorum:* The City did not boast of such an official. The *custodes rotulorum* were the principal justices of the peace in the counties (and the liberty of Westminster); they had custody of the rolls and records of the sessions of the peace.

1169. *catchpole:* an under-sheriff, especially a warrant officer who arrests for debt; a bumbailiff.

1170. *needy debtor:* "He was so far from declaring war against needy debtors, that he made even their enemies to be at peace with 'em, and reconciled their creditors to 'em, by assisting those that were insolvent" (*The True-Born Englishman: A Satire Answered* [1701], p. 84).

1173. *The king commanded:* William issued a proclamation in 1698 "ascribing the spread of vice to the magistrates' neglect to enforce the laws, and commanding them 'to be very vig-

And how I'll do't, Miss Morgan shall inform ye.
I keep the best seraglio in the nation,   1175
And hope in time to bring it into fashion.
No brimstone whore need fear the lash from me,
That part I'll leave to Brother Jeffrey.
Our gallants need not go abroad to Rome,
I'll keep a whoring jubilee at home.   1180
Whoring's the darling of my inclination;
A'n't I a magistrate for Reformation?
For this my praise is sung by ev'ry bard,
For which Bridewell would be a just reward.
In print my panegyrics fill the street,   1185
And hired jail-birds their huzzas repeat.
Some charities contrived to make a show,
Have taught the needy rabble to do so:
Whose empty noise is a mechanic fame,
Since for Sir Belzebub they'd do the same."   1190

The Conclusion

Then let us boast of ancestors no more,
Or deeds or heroes done in days of yore,
In latent records of the ages past,
Behind the rear of time, in long oblivion placed.
For if our virtues must in lines descend,   1195
The merit with the families would end:
And intermixtures would most fatal grow;
For vice would be hereditary too;
The tainted blood would of necessity,
Involuntary wickedness convey.   1200
     Vice, like ill nature, for an age or two,
May seem a generation to pursue;
But virtue seldom does regard the breed;
Fools do the wise, and wise men fools succeed.
     What is't to us, what ancestors we had?   1205

---

ilant and strict in the discovery and effectual prosecution and punishment' of all persons
guilty of 'dissolute, immoral, or disorderly practices' " (A. C. Guthkelch, "Defoe's *True-Born
Englishman*," *Essays and Studies by Members of the English Association* 4 [1913]; 150).

1174. *Miss Morgan:* Nothing is known about the lady but her name.

1178. *Jeffrey:* Sir Jeffrey Jeffreys (d. 1709) served as sheriff and was knighted at the same
time as Duncombe. Like Duncombe he was said to be worth £300,000 (Le Neve, p. 470;
Luttrell, *4*, 531).

1205. *What is't to us:* "That question is resolved without any difficulty, for if our ancestors
were good, then the remembrance of their brave actions would excite us to tread in the same
paths of honor; if bad, the reflections on their dishonorable practices would create in us a

If good, what better? or what worse, if bad?
Examples are for imitation set,
Yet all men follow virtue with regret.
　　Could but our ancestors retrieve their fate,
And see their offspring thus degenerate;　　　　　　　　　　1210
How we contend for birth and names unknown,
And build on their past actions, not our own;
They'd cancel records, and their tombs deface,
And openly disown the vile degenerate race:
For fame of families is all a cheat,　　　　　　　　　　　　1215
'Tis personal virtue only makes us great.

Finis

detestation of vice, and make us endeavor to degenerate from 'em" (*The True-Born English-man: A Satire, Answered* [1701], p. 88).

[BEVIL HIGGONS]

The Mourners
(1702)

It had not been difficult to hate the king during his lifetime. His grotesque hook nose, his asthmatic cough, and "ungraceful" laughter—even his bad habit of "folding down of the leaves" of books of devotion which he read—provided ample reasons to dislike him. If the facts were disregarded it was even possible to believe him guilty of filial impiety: "S'il y a quelque justice sur la terre," Voltaire piously affirmed, "il n'appartenait pas . . . au gendre du roi Jacques de le chasser de sa maison."

Since it had been so easy to hate the king during his lifetime it is not surprising that the hatred survived his death. The impression, gained from the title given the following squib when it was reprinted in *POAS,* 1703, that copies were literally strewn in the streets of London is corroborated by *The Observator,* no. 1, (15–18 July 1702).

THE MOURNERS

In sable weeds the beaux and belles appear,
Dismal their out, what e'er their insides are.
Mourn on, you foolish fashionable things,
But mourn your own condition, not the king's;
Mourn for the mighty sums by him misspent,　　　　　5
Those prodigally given, those idly lent;
Mourn for the statues, and the tapestry too,
From Windsor, gutted to aggrandize Loo.
Mourn for the miter long from Scotland gone,

7. *statues, and the tapestry:* A memoir to the States General, dated 24 July/3 August 1702, demanding repatriation of 17 tapestries and 32 paintings—including copies of the Raphael cartoons that had been at Windsor Castle—is preserved in a B.M. MS.

8. *Loo:* William's palace in Scotland.

9. *miter . . . gone:* William and Mary were crowned king and queen of Scotland on 11 May 1689. Since, as Burnet (*2, 23*) says, "the abolishing episcopacy . . . was made a necessary article of the new settlement," an act of the Scottish Parliament abolishing prelacy received the royal assent on 22 July 1689.

The Fall of William III. Engraving by Reinier Vinkeles after a drawing
by Jacobus Buys.

And mourn as much for the union coming on.   10
Mourn for ten years of war and dismal weather,
For taxes, strung like necklaces together,
On salt, malt, paper, cider, lights and leather.
Much of the Civil List need not be said:
They truly mourn who're eighteen months unpaid.   15
If matters then, my friends, you see are so,
Though now you mourn, 't had lessened much your woe
Had Sorrel stumbled thirteen years ago.

10. *union:* In March 1689, only three months after his arrival in London, William recommended a union of the two kingdoms "living in the same island, having the same language, and the same common interest of religion and liberty." On 26 February, only a week before his death, he did "in the most earnest manner" again recommend this matter to the consideration of the House of Commons (Oldmixon, pp. 25, 257). And the very evening before his death "he asked a Privy Councillor by him what the House of Commons had done that day about an union with Scotland" (Luttrell, *5,* 150).

12–13. Taxes on salt, malt, glass, and leather were all imposed for the first time during William's reign. The tax on cider was doubled in 1690.

14. *Civil List:* The nonmilitary items of the national budget, including the civil service, judiciary, diplomatic and consular services, pension lists, royal household and Privy Purse. William died with his Civil List heavily in debt, with more than a year's arrears unpaid on every branch of it.

18. *Sorrel:* the horse whose stumble caused William's fatal fall.

The Golden Age
(1702)

By the middle of the eighteenth century it had become a commonplace to represent the age of Queen Anne as a period of glory that established, in Oliver Goldsmith's phrase, "that excellence which now excites the admiration of Europe." But it is quite surprising to find the same attitude expressed in the present work by an anonymous poet in the first year of Anne's reign.

Since this is a political satire, the poet anticipates this "golden reign"—this second restoration of the Stuarts—wholly in terms of party politics: Iron Age Whigs are to give way to aureate Tories. "The queen had from her infancy," wrote the duchess of Marlborough, "imbibed the most unconquerable prejudices against the Whigs. She had been taught to look upon them all, not only as republicans, who hated the very shadow of regal authority, but as implacable enemies to the Church of England." It was no wonder, the duchess continued, "that as soon as she was seated in the throne, the Tories . . . became the distinguished objects of the royal favor." For the beneficiaries of this favor it was literally a golden age and a note of heady self-congratulation is unmistakable in the tone of this poem.

Nor is it any wonder that the poet should have chosen the fourth eclogue of Virgil, with its riddling images of birth and peace and plenty, as the vehicle for his exultation. Dryden's translation, published in 1697, was available to be plundered for phrases.

What the poet undertook, however, is not another translation, but an imitation. This genre, of which Pope's *Imitations of Horace* and Johnson's *London* are later examples, requires more than translation into the words of another language. It also seeks a modern equivalent for each detail of the ancient prototype; it attempts to restate the classical antitypes in modern terms. The excitement derives from the poet's ingenuity in finding "modern instances": Partridge's almanac for the Sybilline books; Sir Samuel Dashwood, the new lord mayor of London, for C. Asinius Pollio, the new consul of Rome; Whig peculations for *priscae vestigia fraudis*.

But the fit is not perfect: 37-year old Anne was hardly a type of "lovely boy." Since the anonymous poet was so ingenious, one wonders why he was not sufficiently imaginative and daring to find the antitype of the enigmatic, unborn child in an unborn child of Anne rather than in Anne herself. The answer must be that the anonymous poet was a Jacobite. He was looking forward not to the accession of a child of Anne but to the accession of Anne's half-brother, the son of James II, James Francis Edward, whom Louis XIV had already recognized as James III, king of England, Scotland, and Ireland. When Anne became pregnant again in 1703 the Jacobites were confounded.

But neither is the fit imperfect: the messianic boy, with his father's virtues, who was to rule a world at peace, is exactly what the Jacobites hoped would follow "the mighty months" of the reign of Anne.

THE GOLDEN AGE

From the Fourth Eclogue of *Virgil*

Sicilian Muse, thy voice and subject raise,
All are not pleased with shrubs and sylvan lays,
Or if we shrubs and sylvan lays prepare,
Let 'em be such as suit a consul's ear.
Now Merlin's prophecies are made complete,   5
And Lilly's best events with credit meet;
Now banished Justice takes its rightful place,
And Saturn's days return with Stuart's race.
With its own luster now the church appears,
As one year makes amends for fourteen years,   10
And joys succeed our sighs and hopes succeed our fears.
    O goddess, genius of this favorite isle,
On thy own work, this revolution, smile,
Salute the pleasures that come rolling on,
And greet the wonders Heav'n and thou hast done,   15
Worthy the glorious change, inspire our strains,
Now thy own Anna rules, in her own kingdom reigns.
And thou, O Dashwood, by peculiar care,
Reserved till now to fill Augusta's chair,
Behold the mighty months' progressive shine!   20

5. *Merlin's prophecies: Merlinus Liberatus* was the almanac published every year by John Partridge (1644–1715), whose "death" was predicted by Jonathan Swift in 1708.

6. *Lilly's:* William Lilly, astrologer and almanac-maker.

10. *fourteen years:* 1688–1702, the reign of William III.

18. *Dashwood:* Sir Samuel Dashwood, a staunch Tory. He was elected sheriff in September 1683 and served two terms as Member of Parliament for the City. He was defeated in his candidacies for lord mayor in 1698, 1700, and 1701, but upon the accession of Anne he was appointed to the commission for the lieutenancy of London in July 1702 and three months later was finally elected mayor.

See 'em begin their golden race in thine!
Under thy consulship, lo! Vice gives way
And Whigs forever cease to come again in play.
The life of gods the monarch shall partake,
Beloved by gods and men for virtue's sake,   25
As she from heroes sprung, brave acts prefers,
And heroes copy out their fame from hers,
As kingdom's rights she with her own maintains,
And where her injured father governed, reigns.

     Hail, sacred queen! Thy very enemies own   30
Thy lawful claim, and recognize thy throne.
Dissembling statesmen shall before thee stand,
And Halifax be first to kiss thy hand;
Somers shall change his temper with his fate,
And promise duty where he vowed his hate,   35
Seeming for past offenses to atone,
By complementing claims he would postpone;
Had one but lived, that raised him, to his shame,
To let him pack the cards, and win the game.
Wharton shall to St. James's house resort,   40
And leave his master's corpse to make his court;
Stamford quit the practice of his place,

23. *Whigs . . . cease:* The Tory majority in the 5th Parliament of William III had hoped to prevent the Whig junto (Somers, Halifax, and Orford) from ever coming into power again by impeaching them for high crimes and misdemeanors. The Whig majority in the House of Lords, however, dismissed the charges. After the election of July–August 1702 had reinforced their majority in the Commons, the Tories returned to the attack. Almost the first act of the Parliament of Anne was to vote 189–81, upon a motion of Sir Edward Seymour, "that right hath not been done the Commons, upon the impeachments, before the Lords, brought against divers peers in the thirteenth year of His Late Majesty's reign," and to threaten to reopen the impeachment proceedings.

33. *Halifax:* Charles Montagu, created Baron Halifax of Halifax in December 1700, may have kissed the queen's hand for his post of auditor of the Exchequer (which he held for life), but he was struck off the list of Privy Councillors in March 1702.

34. *Somers:* Although dismissed as lord chancellor in April 1700, Somers remained "the life, the soul, and the spirit of his party," and continued to direct its propaganda. As a consequence, he was dismissed not only from the Privy Council, but even from the commission of the peace in March 1702.

38. *one:* William III.

40. *Wharton:* Although he had appointed Wharton to the lucrative post of warden of the royal forests south of Trent in April 1697, William balked at making him secretary of state. As recently as January 1702 Wharton had been made lord lieutenant of Buckinghamshire, but in July 1702 he was removed from this and all other posts.

42. *Stamford:* Thomas Grey, 2d earl of Stamford (c. 1653–1720), was one of the first Whigs suspected of complicity both in the Rye House Plot and in Monmouth's Rebellion. In the next reign he was appointed chancellor of the duchy of Lancaster, among many other offices. In this capacity he laid waste to trees on crown lands and was therefore dismissed from his offices in 1702.

Leave cutting timber down in Enfield chase,
To seek for favor, and prevail for grace.
Old Ranelagh shall thy accession sing,   45
Hoping to serve thee as he servèd the king;
To keep his gridiron while he keeps his life,
And build fresh mansion houses for his wife.
Lions with lambs united shall agree,
And lambs like lions, lions lambs shall be   50
And South with Sherlock hail and bow the knee.
Kennett shall drop his Convocation spleen,
And Atterbury, quarrels with the dean,
To join in our allegiance with the queen.
The churchmen and Dissenters shall combine   55
To pay the tribute due to Stuart's line,
As Presbyters with bishops shall comply,
And bishops shall fling out what Presbyters deny;
Like Lambeth watermen, whose tempers show,
That look one way while they another row.   60
      Yet shall some footsteps of old fraud remain,
And ills be practiced in thy golden reign;
Munden at sea shall in his duty fail,
And Wate and dastard Kirkby turn their tail.

45. *Ranelagh:* As paymaster-general of the army, vast sums of money came into Ranelagh's hands "and God knows where it went; but after the king's death, it was found that twenty two millions sterling was not accounted for" (Ailesbury, *1,* 241). Although not removed from the Privy Council upon Anne's accession, he resigned his post as paymaster-general on 3 December 1702 to avoid a parliamentary inquiry. Subsequently convicted of misappropriation of funds he was expelled from the House of Commons in February 1703. His palatial mansion, painted by Canaletto, was seized for debt.

52. *Kennett:* White Kennett began his political career while an undergraduate at St. Edmund Hall by publishing a Tory pamphlet a few days before the Parliament convened at Oxford in March 1681. In the next reign, however, he came to be called "Weather-cock Kennett" when he opposed the measures of James II. In 1700 he was created D.D. and presented to the rectory of St. Botolph, Aldgate. In the following year he became the archdeacon of Huntingdon, known as "the anti-Convocationist" for maintaining, in his controversy with Atterbury, that "Convocation had few inherent rights of independent action."

53. *Atterbury:* Francis Atterbury began his career as a controversialist while a tutor at Christ Church, Oxford, in 1687 when he published an essay opposing James II's attempt to romanize the university. He took orders the same year and in 1691 was appointed lecturer of St. Bride's, London, and chaplain to William and Mary in 1694. He was one of the Christ Church wits who opposed Richard Bentley in the Phalaris controversy of 1694–98. His *Letter to a Convocation Man* (1697), blaming the rampant immorality of the day partly on the refusal of the king to allow the Convocation to assemble, precipitated an acrimonious controversy with White Kennett, William Wake, and Edmund Gibson.

63. *Munden:* Sir John Munden, Knt., failed to intercept a French squadron between Rochelle and Coruna in May 1702 and was tried at court martial on charges of negligence in July.

64. *Wade and . . . Kirkby:* Richard Kirkby was second in command of the squadron that

Hara at land his country shall abuse,   65
And Bellasis by plund'ring, conquest lose,
While British troops with Ormond at their head
Shall meet with conquest, who from conquest fled,
And Marlborough of William's post possessed,
Reducing Liège, shall France itself invest.   70
Sarum's huge prelate shall before thee preach,
And his dead lord to flatter thee, impeach;
Old dreaming Worcester, once the church's pride,
Shall quit her interest for another side,
Browbeat his clergy, and a chief defame,   75
Spotless as is the blood from whence he came;
And though a prisoner made in dubious times,
Shall now deserve the Tower for real crimes.
'Midst Lords and Commons shall disputes arise,

---

sailed from Jamaica in May 1702 under Vice-admiral John Benbow. Benbow's orders to engage the French fleet which was sighted near Santa Marta in August were not obeyed and in the halfhearted skirmish that resulted, Benbow himself was mortally wounded. Kirkby and Edward Wade, captain of the *Greenwich*, were tried at court martial in Jamaica in October and condemned to be shot for cowardice. The sentence was executed aboard the *Bristol* in Plymouth Sound in 16 April 1703 and brought to an end "the most disgraceful event" in British naval history (*DNB*, 2, 210).

65–67. Ormond captured the undefended villages of Dota and El Puerto de Santa Maria and the small fortress of Santa Catalina, but failed to capture the larger fortress of Matagorda, which dominated the approaches to Cádiz. When discovered that his two immediate subordinates, lieutenant-general Sir Henry Bellasis, Knt. and major-general Sir Charles O'Hara, Knt. were both involved in the looting of El Puerto de Santa Maria, he immediately drew up charges against them. Then, acting on instructions he received the day before the descent on Vigo, he ordered the two officers to be placed under arrest. Upon return of the fleet to England both the officers were removed from their commands for coming ashore at Deal without orders. Bellasis, who had just been reelected M.P. for Durham City, pleaded privilege of Parliament. In court martial proceedings Bellasis was dishonorably discharged from the service, but O'Hara was acquitted and was subsequently created Baron Tyrawley in the Irish peerage.

69. *Marlborough*: William III had appointed Marlborough commander-in-chief of the English forces in the Lowlands in June 1701. A year later the allies responded by giving him sole command of the Confederate army.

70. *Liège*: Marlborough's capture of Liège was reported in London on 23 October 1702.

71. *Sarum's huge prelate*: Gilbert Burnet, bishop of Salisbury.

73. *Worcester*: William Lloyd, the 75-year-old bishop of Worcester, was one of the seven who had dared to oppose James II in 1688. Now, however, he had "browbeat his clergy" to oppose Sir John Pakington for reelection in Worcestershire in July and in November 1702 found himself in danger of being taken into custody for *scandalum magnatum*.

75. *a chief*: Sir John Pakington.

79. *disputes*: Without even hearing the evidence on Lloyd's behalf, the Commons voted unanimously on 18 November 1702 that Lloyd's actions had been "malicious, unchristian, and arbitrary" and addressed the queen to remove him as her lord almoner. Alarmed at these proceedings, the Lords represented to Her Majesty next day that it was the right of every subject to be heard in his own defense, and humbly desired that Lloyd be retained until tried by due course of law. Sir Edward Seymour, however, who had attended the queen with the

And one dissuade what t'other shall advise.   80
Proud Adriatic Orford shall be known
To sink the nation's money for his own,
And fix the courtier's thefts upon the throne.
Funds shall, as if no funds there were, appear,
Millions be giv'n the kingdom's debts to clear,   85
Yet shall we own the millions that we gave,
And pay for what we had not wit to save,
Unless some moths that fret the threadbare state,
Prevent our ruin by their timely fate,
Unless a peer more often accounts keeps,   90
And gives the queen the crop which now he reaps.
But when confirmed in arts of empire grown,
Thou seest thy reign mature, and fixed thy throne,
Both land and sea thy sovereign power shall own.
Fearless of loss, and confident of gain,   95
The merchant shall in safety plough the main;
The lab'ring hind shall cleave the country soil,
And plenty rise and court the farmer's toil.
As every subject sees his wrongs redressed,
Views faction quelled, and anarchy suppressed,   100
And prince and people mutually blessed.

Commons's address, was pleased to inform the House on 20 November that Her Majesty had ordered Lloyd to be removed.

81. *Orford:* Orford commanded the English forces that wintered at Cádiz in 1694–95 and, according to the earl of Hardwicke, "made his fortune there by victualling the fleet." "Adriatic" may allude to Orford's success that winter in bringing the doge of Venice to recognize William III.

82–83. These lines allude to the first of the articles of impeachment drawn up against Orford in May 1701; "Towards the prosecution of [the] war, great sums of money have been given and levied by authority of Parliament; and many debts have been contracted, which remain a very heavy burden upon the people of England; the said earl being then of His Majesty's most honorable Privy Council, but always preferring his private interest to the good of the public, and taking advantage of the ready access he had to His Majesty's person . . . hath procured from His Majesty . . . grants of several manors . . . and also of exorbitant sums of money, to be made to him . . . the profits whereof he now enjoys "(*CJ*, *13*, 520). Orford was removed from the Privy Council in March 1702.

84. *funds:* Despite her "unparalleled goodness" in contributing £100,000 of her own revenue to reduce deficiencies in the funds, Anne had to observe with some concern, in her speech at the opening of Parliament in October 1702, "that the funds given by the last Parliament have . . . fallen short of the sums proposed to be raised by them" and that consequently the deficiencies had increased.

90. *peer:* See 45 *n.*

96. *plough the main:* Cf. "The merchant still shall plough the deep for gain" (*The Fourth Pastoral of Virgil, Englished by Mr. Dryden,* 38).

97. *The lab'ring hind:* Cf. "The laboring hind his oxen shall disjoin" (*The Fourth Pastoral of Virgil, Englished by Mr. Dryden,* 49).

Such be thy reign, the fatal sisters cry,
And such Britannia's future destiny.
　　　　Arise, auspicious queen! the times are come,
When France shall from thy mouth expect her doom;   105
When Providence shall labor in thy cause,
And trembling Spain acknowledge English laws;
Arise, thou bright inspirer of my song,
And vindicate the blood from whence thou'rt sprung.
See the consenting world adore thy fame!   110
Heav'n, earth, and sea confess the justice of thy claim!
See us for thee our vows and prayers employ,
And coming ages smile in hopes of coming joy.
Oh! that this life of mine so long would last,
As I might sing thy future deeds and past,   115
As on thy rising glories I might swell,
And I in verse, as thou in fame, excel!
Not thy own Tate though with thy laurels crowned,
Should touch a sweeter pipe, or give a sweeter sound;
Not favorite Rowe, though Jersey took his part,   120
Should boast more judgment, or reveal more art;
Not Congreve, stocked with all his patron's praise,
Produce a zeal like mine, or equal lays;
Though Congreve Halifax's friend should be,
Congreve, if Halifax were judge, should yield to me.   125
　　　　Begin great queen, the Stuart's steps to tread,
And let thy living worth exceed the dead;
Happiest of princes in this climate born,
Entirely English, above thy enemies scorn,

118. *Tate:* Upon the accession of Queen Anne, Nahum Tate was reappointed poet laureate.

120. *Rowe:* Nicholas Rowe, the dramatist, produced a blank-verse tragedy, *The Ambitious Stepmother,* in December 1700, with a dedication to Edward Villiers, earl of Jersey, the lord chamberlain, and a year later produced a second tragedy, *Tamerlane,* for which Samuel Garth wrote a prologue. This piece, in which history was warped to present a hero of "amiable moderation" who could be identified with William III, was dedicated to the duke of Devonshire and became virtually an article of Whiggish faith. It was "played annually at Drury Lane Threatre on 5 November, the anniversary of William III's landing . . . until 1815" (*DNB, 17,* 341–42). Jersey, retained by Anne in the post of lord chamberlain, would have been most reluctant to "take [the] part" of so violent a Whig as Rowe.

122. *patron's:* Congreve's patron was Charles Montagu, later Lord Halifax, who appointed him in July 1695 to the minor post of commissioner for licensing hackney coaches. Although Congreve may have hurried to court in 1702, as William Pittis claimed (*The Patriots. A Poem* [1702], 9), his patron was then in no position to help him.

129. *Entirely English:* Anne's assurance, in her first address to Parliament on 11 March 1702, three days after the death of the foreigner, William III, that she knew her "heart to be entirely English," "raised a hum from all that heard her" (Trevelyan, *1,* 164). This single phrase,

Thou ne'er wer'st dandled on an Austrian's knee,   130
Nor Hanover stood godfather for thee,
But sprung directly from the British strain,
Where thou first drew'st thy breath, dost there commence thy reign.

---

said to have been inserted in the queen's speech by her uncle, the earl of Rochester, raised the hopes of the Jacobites, thrilled the war party, stiffened the intolerance of the high churchmen, and encouraged a strain of xenophobia that was already flourishing in all strata of English society.

131. *godfather:* Anne's godfather was the high Tory archbishop of Canterbury, Gilbert Sheldon.

133. *first . . . breath:* Anne was born in St. James's Palace on 6 February 1665 and proclaimed queen before the gate of the palace on 8 March 1702.

DANIEL DEFOE

The Spanish Descent
(1702)

The Cádiz expedition of 1702 was the most considerable military adventure that the English had undertaken abroad for more than 100 years, and it left behind an inevitable literary precipitate. "The White Friars Ballad Singers," we are told, "bawl nothing at Shoe-Lane End, and the Porter's Block in Smithfield, but *England's Happiness, or, A New Copy of Verse upon the Taking of the Plate-Fleet, Set to an Excellent New Vigo Tune.*" It is by contrast with such street ballads that Defoe's poem defines itself as literature.

The unexpected failure at Cádiz followed by the even more unexpected success at Vigo supplied a shape to events that Defoe was quick to detect and exploit. His poem begins on the streets, with the first news arriving from Cádiz; then it works its way through the failures and successes of the campaign— with a retrospective glance at the failures and successes of the war of 1689– 97—and ends in St. Paul's Cathedral with a magnificent tableau of queen, Lords, and Commons, drawn up in full regalia singing hymns of thanksgiving.

Running unobtrusively through the ballad and polarizing the scattered details of the poem is the theme of God's Providence: no mortal man could have foreseen that the failure at Cádiz was *necessary* to produce the success at Vigo, for "the vast designs of Fate remain unknown." Just as the Treaty of Ryswick was "imperfect" because it ignored the designs of Providence, so the French at Vigo were helpless because they opposed "Almighty Fate." Thus it is right—both formally and psychologically—that the poem should end in St. Paul's Cathedral with the functionaries of church and state drawn up in ordered ranks and singing praises to the power that brought about the victory.

The Spanish Descent

Long had this nation been amused in vain
With posts from Portugal, and news from Spain,
With Ormond's conquests, and the fleet's success,
And favors from the Moors at Maccaness.
The learned mob bought compasses and scales,   5
And every barber knew the Bay of Cales,
Showed us the army here, and there the fleet,
Here the troops land, and there the foes retreat,
There at St. Maries how the Spaniard runs,
And listen close as if they heard the guns,   10
And some pretend they see them swive the nuns.
    Others describe the Castle and Puntalls,
And tell how easy 'tis to conquer Cales;
Wisely propose to let the silver come,
And help to pay the nation's debts at home.   15
But still they count the spoils without the cost,
And still the news comes faster than the post.
    The graver heads, like mountebanks of state,
Of abdication and revolts debate,
Except a revolution should appear   20
As cheap and easy as it had done here;

3. *Ormond's conquests:* Cf. *The Golden Age*, 65–67 n.

4. *favors from the Moors:* Muley Ismal, the bloodthirsty emperor of Morocco, who had declared war against Spain in June 1702, sent an envoy to Sir George Rooke, commander of the fleet, with assurance of his friendship for the English nation.

11. *swive:* Cf. *Letters from the Living to the Living* [1703], pp. 167–68: "I suppose by this time you have heard strange stories of some part of the soldiery and the nuns: I know not how much the snowball may have gathered in the rolling, but I assure you the devout seraglio had no other usage from us than what I am confident they were well pleased with . . . and therefore, whatever was done to the dishonor of popery, and the glory of the reformed churches, I hope can be thought no evil by a true-blue Protestant."

12. *the Castle and Puntalls:* the castle (Castillo de Matagorda) and puntals (Castillo de San Lorenzo del Puntal), on either side of the bay, controlled the harbor of Cádiz.

14. *silver:* Cádiz was the usual destination of the Plate fleet, which transported the year's production of American silver to Spain, and before the English forces left there it was erroneously reported in London that the Plate fleet was making the best of its way to Cádiz.

17. *proverbial:* The lame post brings the truest news (Tilley, p. 489).

19. *revolts:* John Tutchin had boldly prophesied that great numbers of Spaniards would take advantage of Ormonde's protection to desert the French, "for those people seem only to want an opportunity to declare for the emperor" (*Observator*, no. 1, [2–5 September 1702]). But when Ormonde set up the imperial standard with the arms of the Archduke Charles and issued a declaration exhorting nobility and clergy alike to join him in defending the rights of the Hapsburgs to the throne of Spain, no one took the opportunity to do so.

Bring the revolting grandees to the coast,
And give the duke de Anjou up for lost;
Doom him to France to seek relief in vain,
And send the duke of Austria to Spain;—   25
Canvas the council at Madrid, and find
How all the Spanish courtiers stand inclined; ·
Describe the strange convulsions of the state,
And old Carreroe sacrificed to Fate.
Then all the stage of action they survey,   30
And wish our generals knew as much as they.
　　　Some have their fancies so exceeding bold,
They saw the queens fall out, and heard 'em scold:
Nor is the thing so strange, for if they did,
It was but from Toledo to Madrid.   35
　　　And now the farce is acting o'er again,
The meaning of our mischiefs to explain.
The learnéd mob o'er-read in arms and law,
The cause of their miscarriages foresaw;
Tell us the loitering minutes were misspent,   40
Too long a going, and too few that went;
Exalt the Catalonian garrison,
The new-made works, the platform, and the town;
Tell us it was impossible to land,
And all their batteries sunk into the sand.   45
　　　Some are all banter, and the voyage despise—
For fruitless actions seldom pass for wise—
Tell us 'twas our English politics,
To think to wheedle Spain with heretics.
The disproportioned force they banter too;   50
The ships too many, and the men too few.
　　　Then they find fault with conduct, and condemn
Sometimes the officers, sometimes the men:
Nor scapes his grace the satire of the town;
Whoever fails success, shall fail renown.   55

　　25. *duke of Austria:* The Archduke Charles (1685–1740), second son of the Emperor Leo-
pold I, was proclaimed king of Spain on 19 September 1702 in Vienna.
　　29. *Carreroe:* It was principally Luis Manuel Fernandez de Portocarrero (1635–1709),
archbishop of Toledo and "an old covetous cardinal," who had secured the throne of Spain
for Philippe d'Anjou, but soon after the coronation he "lost much of the esteem which he had
formerly in this court."
　　33. *queens:* The dowager-queen was Maria Ana of Neuburg, the second wife of Carlos II
whom Philippe had caused to be removed to Toledo before his arrival in Madrid. The queen
was the young Maria Luisa of Savoy who married Philippe in October 1701.

Sir George comes in among the indiscreet;
Sometimes the army's censured, then the fleet;
How the abandoned country they destroyed,
And made their early declarations void;
Too hasty proofs of their protection gave,   60
Plundering the people they came there to save;
As if the Spaniards were so plagued with France,
To fly to thieves for their deliverance.
    But amongst all the wisdom of the town,
The vast designs of Fate remain unknown,   65
Unguessed at, unexpected, hid from thoughts,
For no man looked for blessings in our faults.
Mischances sometimes are a nation's good,
Rightly improved, and nicely understood.
    Ten years we felt the dying pangs of war,   70
And fetched our grief and miseries from far.
Our English millions foreign war maintains,
And English blood has drenched the neighboring plains.
Nor shall we blush to boast what all men own,
Uncommon English valor has been shown;   75
The forward courage of our ill-paid men
Deserves more praise than nature spares my pen.
What could they not perform, or what endure,
Witness the mighty bastions of Namur!
We fasted much, and we attempted more,   80
But ne'er could come to giving thanks before,
Unless 'twas when the fatal strife was o'er.
Some secret Achan cursed our enterprise,
And Israel fled before her enemies.
    Whether the poisonous particles were hid   85
In us that followed, or in them that led:
What fatal charm benumbed the nation's sense,

79. *Namur:* The capture of Namur by the armies of Louis XIV in 1692 is celebrated in Boileau's famous *Ode sur la prise de Namur.* When William recaptured the town in August 1695, Prior wrote *An English Ballad,* parodying Boileau's ode, which he reprinted on the facing pages.

83. *Achan:* When they were defeated in a minor skirmish at Ai, Joshua fell to the ground and tore his clothes, regretting that he led the Israelites across the Jordan. Yahweh then explained the reason for the defeat: one Achan, of the tribe of Judah, had appropriated to himself some of the loot from Jericho that belonged to Yahweh (Josh. 7:1–26).

85. *poisonous particles:* The 250 shekels of gold and silver that Achan withheld are called "an accursed thing" in Josh. 7:13. Defoe seems to be making the common Tory charge that the enormous fortunes amassed by war profiteers had made it impossible to gain a clear-cut victory in the last war.

To struggle with Eternal Providence:
Whether some curse, or else some perjured vow,
Or some strange guilt that's expiated now: 90
Was it the pilots who ill steered the state:
Or was it the decisive will of Fate;
'Tis hard to tell; but this too well we know,
All things went backward, or went on too slow;
Small was the glory of our high success,   95
A tedious war, and an imperfect peace;
Peace dearly purchased, and which cost us more
Great kingdoms than we conquered downs before.
    Actions may miss of their deserved applause,
When Heaven approves the men, and not the cause;   100
And well-contrived designs miscarry when
Heaven may approve the cause, but not the men;
Here then's the ground of our expense of blood,
The sword of Gideon's, not the sword of God.
The mighty and the wise are laid aside,   105
And victory the sex has dignified;
We have been used to female conquests here,
And queens have been the glory of the war,
The scene revives with smiles of Providence,
All things declined before, and prosper since;   110
And as if ill success had been entailed,
The posthume projects are the last that failed;
As Heaven, whose works are hid from human view,
Would blast our old designs, and bless our new.
    And now the baffled enterprise grows stale,   115
Their hopes decrease, and juster doubts prevail:

96. *imperfect peace:* The Treaty of Ryswick signed by the English in September 1697 was
"imperfect" because it ignored the problem of who was to succeed the childless Carlos II on
the throne of Spain. As Tutchin said, "That peace of Ryswick was more prejudicial to the
English nation, than was the whole war . . . by that opportunity given the French king of
recruiting his forces, and thereby putting Anjou into possession of the kingdom of Spain"
(*Observator*, no. 1 [29 August–2 September 1702]).
   97–98. *cost us . . . kingdoms:* The reference is to the Partition Treaties of 1698–1700 by
which England divided the vast Spanish empire between France and Austria without taking
anything for herself.
   104. *The sword of Gideon's:* Three hundred Israelites routed a numberless host of Midianites
by blowing trumpets and shouting "the sword of the Lord and of Gideon" (Judg. 7:15–23).
At Cádiz, Defoe implies, the sword of Yahweh remained sheathed.
   112. *posthume projects:* The failure at Cádiz was blamed on its having been proposed by the
late king; the success at Vigo was the first under the new queen. Tutchin expresses the idea of
lines 105–14 much less cryptically: "King William's design upon Cádiz was the occasion of
Queen Anne's destroying the ships at Vigo" (*Observator*, no. 1 [7–11 November 1702]).

> The unattempted town sings victory,
> And scared with walls, and not with men, we fly;
> Great conduct in our safe retreat we show,
> And bravely re-embark when none pursue;   120
> The guns, the ammunition, put on board,
> And what we could not plunder, we restored.
> And thus we quit the Andalusian shores,
> Drenched with the Spanish wine, and Spanish whores.
> With songs of scorn the Arragonians sing,   125
> And loud *Te Deums* make the valleys ring.
>   Uncommon joys now raise the hopes of Spain,
> And Vigo does their Plate fleet entertain;
> The vast galleons deep ballasted with ore,
> Safely reach home to the Galitian shore.   130
> The double joy spreads from Madrid to Rome,
> The English fled, the Silver Fleet come home:
> From thence it reaches to the banks of Po,
> And the loud cannons let the Germans know.
> The rattling volleys tell their short-lived joys,   135
> And roar *Te Deum* out in smoke and noise.
> To Milan next it flies on wings of fame,
> There the young monarch and his heroes came,
> From sad Luzara, and the Mantuan walls,
> To seek new dangers, and to rescue Cales.   140
> His joy for welcome treasure he expressed,
> But grieves at his good fortune in the rest:
> The flying English he had wished to stay,

118. *we fly:* News of the duke of Ormonde's defeat and the fleet's withdrawal from Cádiz on 19 September reached London on 6 October (Luttrell, *5*, 222).

128. *Plate fleet:* Twelve Spanish galleons with a cargo estimated to be worth 60,000,000 pesos and under a French convoy commanded by François Louis de Rousselet, marquis de Chateaurenault, vice-admiral of France, reached Vigo, a port in Galicia, on 22 September 1702.

138. *the young monarch:* Philippe d'Anjou (1683–1704), the second grandson of Louis XIV, was crowned Felipe V of Spain on 21 April 1701, before his 18th birthday. A year later he put himself at the head of the Spanish troops in the French army commanded by Louis Joseph, duc de Vendôme, who was opposing the incursions of Prince Eugene into Italy.

139. *Luzara:* Luzzara, on the banks of the Po, was the scene of the climactic battle in the campaign of 1702 between the forces of France and the empire. To encourage his troops by his presence, the young king of Spain eluded those whom his grandfather had appointed to take care of him and exposed himself to cannon and musket fire. Despite Philippe's efforts, the enemy inflicted 12,000 casualties on the French and Spanish forces and remained master of the field at nightfall. On 17 October Philippe entered Milan, which was then a Spanish possession, and was received with much ceremony. *Mantuan walls:* Philippe did not join the French army until July 1702, a month after Vendôme's appearance in the field with 40,000 troops had forced Prince Eugene to abandon the siege of Mantua.

To crown with conquest one victorious day.
    The priests, in high procession, show their joy,   145
And all the arts of eloquence employ,
To feed his pride of fancied victories,
And raise his untried valor to the skies.
The flattering courtiers his vain mind possess
With airy hopes of conquest and success,   150
Prompt his young thoughts to run on new extremes,
And sycophantic pride his heart inflames.
His native crime springs up, his pulse beats high,
With thoughts of universal monarchy;
Fancies his foreign enemies suppressed,   155
And boasts too soon how he'll subdue the rest.
Princes, like other men, are blind to fate;
He only sees the event who does the cause create.
    From hence through France the welcome tidings fly,
To mock his ancient sire with mushroom joy.   160
Raptures possess the ambitious heads of France,
And golden hopes their new designs advance.
Now they consult to crush the world again,
And talk of rifling Christendom for men.
    New fleets, new armies, and new leagues contrive,   165
And swallow men and nations up alive;
Prescribe no bounds to their ambitious pride,
But first the wealth, and then the world, divide.
Excess of pride to airy madness grows,
And makes men strange romantic things propose: 170
The head turns round, and all the fancy's vain,
And makes the world as giddy as the brain.
Men that consult such weighty things as those
All possible disasters should suppose:
In vain great princes mighty things invent,   175
While Heaven retains the power to prevent:
He that to general mischief makes pretense
Should first know how to conquer Providence.
Such strive in vain, and only show mankind,
How tyrants clothed with power are all inclined.   180
    Meanwhile our melancholy fleet steers home,

170. *strange romantic things:* "Paris, June 26, N.S. The court is daily contriving new methods of raising money to supply the king's urgent occasions . . . and the many edicts lately issued for that purpose being not sufficient, one was published this week, by which the king offers to give the title of gentleman to 200 persons, paying 6000 livres each" (*London Gazette*, no. 3822 [25–29 June 1702]).

Some grieved for past, for future mischiefs some:
Disaster swells the blood, and spleen the face,
And ripens them for glorious things apace.
With deep regret they turn their eyes to Spain,   185
And wish they once might visit her again.
Little they dreamed that good which Heaven prepared;
No merit from below, no signs from Heaven appeared;
No hints, unless from their high-ripened spleen,
And strange ungrounded sympathy within.   190
    The silent duke, from all misconduct free,
Alone enjoys the calm of honesty:
Fears not his journal should be fairly shown,
And sighs for England's errors, not his own.
His constant temper's all serene and clear;   195
First free from guilt, and therefore free from fear.
    Not so the rest, for conscious thoughts become
More restless now the nearer they come home.
The party-making feuds on board begin:
For people always quarrel when they sin.   200
Reflect with shame upon the things misdone,
And shift their faults about from one to one,
Prepare excuses, and compute their friends,
And dread the fate which their desert attends.
Some wish for storms, and curse the wind and sails,   205
And dream, no doubt, of gibbets, and of jails;
Imaginary punishments appear,
And suited to their secret guilts, their fear,
Their hast'ning fate in their own fancies read,
And few, 'tis feared, their innocence can plead.   210
Then their sweet spoils to trusty hands convey,
And throw the rifled gods of Spain away;
Disgorge that wealth they dare not entertain,
And wish the nuns their maidenheads again;
Dismiss their wealth for fear of witnesses,   215
And purge their coffers and their consciences,
Cursing their ill-got trifles, but in vain,
For still the guilt, and still the fears, remain.
    Tell us, ye rabbis of abstruser sense,

193. *journal:* Once back in England, Ormonde demanded a parliamentary inquiry into the miscarriage at Cádiz—or the "Cales farce," as Tutchin called it. The House of Lords subpoenaed Ormonde's journal and those of the other commanders in the subsequent investigation.

199. *feuds on board:* Cf. *The Golden Age*, 65–67 n.

Who jumble fate and fools with Providence;   220
Is this the chosen army, this the fleet,
For which Heaven's praises sound in every street?
Could Heaven provide them one occasion more,
Who had so ill discharged themselves before?
That fleet so many former millions lost,   225
So little had performed, so much had cost:
That fleet, so often manned with knaves before,
That served us all the war to make us poor;
That twice had made their fruitless voyage to Spain,
And saw the straits, and so came home again: 230
Our wooden walls that should defend our trade,
And many a witless wooden voyage have made;
How oft have they been fitted out in vain,
Wasted our money, and destroyed our men,
Betrayed our merchants, and exposed their fleets,   235
And caused eternal murmurs in our streets?
The nation's Genius sure prevails above,
And Heaven conceals his anger, shows his love:
The nation's guardian angel has prevailed,
And on her guardian queen new favors has entailed.   240
　　　Now let glad Europe in her turn rejoice,
And sing new triumphs with exalted voice.
See the glad post of tidings winged with news,
With suited speed the wond'ring fleet pursues:
His haste discerned, increases their surprise,   245
The more they wonder, and the more he flies.
Nor wind, nor seas, proportioned speed can bear;
For Joy and Hope have swifter wings than Fear.
With what surprise of joy they meet the news!
Joys, that to every vein new spirits infuse.   250
The wild excess in shouts and cries appear;
For joys and griefs are all irregular.
　　　Councils of war for sake of forms they call,
But shame admits of no disputes at all:
How should they differ where no doubt can be   255
But if they should accept of victory?

225. *That fleet:* The English fleet entered the Mediterranean twice during the war of 1688–
97. In June 1693 under the command of Sir George Rooke it incurred the disastrous loss of the
Turkey fleet (*The True-Born Englishman,* 1039 *n.*). The next year under the command of Ad-
miral Russell (later Lord Orford), the fleet maneuvered but failed to prevent the French from
safely returning to Toulon and after wintering in Cádiz it was equally unsuccessful in August
1695 in an attempt to recover Palamos from the French.

Whether they should the great occasion take,
Or baffle Heaven, and double their mistake?
Whether the naked and defenseless prize
They should accept, or Heaven and that despise?   260
Whether they should revive their reputation,
Or sink it twice, and twice betray the nation?
Who dare the horrid negative design?
Who dare the last suggest, the first decline?
Envy herself; for Satan's always there,   265
And keeps his councils with the god of war.
Though with her swelling spleen she seemed to burst,
Willed the design while the event she cursed.
  The word's gone out, and now they spread the main
With swelling sails, and swelling hopes, for Spain: 270
To double vengeance pressed where'er they come,
Resolved to pay the haughty Spaniard home:
Resolved by future conduct to atone
For all our past mistakes, and all their own.
New life springs up in every English face,   275
And fits them all for glorious things apace:
The booty some excites, and some the cause;
But more the hope to gain their lost applause.
Eager their sullied honor to restore,
Some anger whets, some pride and vengeance more.   280
  The lazy minutes now pass on too slow,
Fancy flies faster than the winds can blow:
Impatient wishes lengthen out the day;
They chide the loitering winds for their delay.
But time is nature's faithful messenger,   285
And brings up all we wish, as well as all we fear.
  The mists clear up, and now the scout decries
The subject of their hopes and victories:
The wished for fleets embayed, in harbor lie,
Unfit to fight, and more unfit to fly.   290
Triumphant joy throughout the navy flies,
Echoed from shore with terror and surprise.
Strange power of noise! which at one simple sound
At once shall some encourage, some confound.
  In vain the lion tangled in the snare   295
With anguish roars, and rends the trembling air:
'Tis vain to struggle with Almighty Fate;
Vain and impossible the weak debate.

The mighty boom, the forts, resist in vain,
The guns with fruitless force in noise complain.   300
See how the troops intrepidly fall on!
Wish for more foes, and think they fly too soon.
With eager fury to their forts pursue,
And think the odds of four to one too few.
The land's first conquered, and the prize attends;   305
Fate beckons in the fleet to back their friends:
Despair succeeds, they struggle now too late,
And soon submit to their prevailing fate:
Courage is madness when occasion's past,
Death's the securest refuge, and the last.   310
    And now the rolling flames come threat'ning on,
And mighty streams of melted gold run down.
The flaming ore down to its center makes,
To form new mines beneath the oozy lakes.
    Here a galleon with spicy drugs inflamed,   315
In odoriferous folds of sulphur streamed.
The gods of old no such oblations knew,
Their spices weak, and their perfumes but few.
The frighted Spaniards from their treasure fly,
Loath to forsake their wealth, but loath to die.   320
    Here a vast carrack flies while none pursue,
Bulged on the shore by her distracted crew:
There like a mighty mountain she appears,
And groans beneath the golden weight she bears.
Conquest perverts the property of friend,   325
And makes men ruin what they can't defend:
Some blow their treasure up into the air
With all the wild excesses of despair.
Strange fate! that war such odd events should have;
Friends would destroy, and enemies would save: 330
Others their safety to their wealth prefer,
And mix some small discretion with their fear.

299. *The mighty boom, the forts:* The descent upon Vigo was not totally unexpected by "the
united crowns of France and Spain," as they were now described. In August, "Monsieur
Renaud, a French ingenier" had been sent there to fortify the port "against any attempts
that the English and Dutch" might make and as soon as the Plate fleet made harbor, Chateau-
renault ordered a 9-foot thick boom "made up of masts, yards, cables, top-chains and
casks" to be placed across the mouth of the harbor so the ends could be covered by shore
batteries in the forts. After a task force under Ormonde had taken the Castillo de Randa on 11
October and silenced the batteries on the left bank, Thomas Hopsonn, vice-admiral of the
White and second in command under Rooke, broke through the boom in his flagship, the *Tor
Bay*, and cleared a passage for the rest of his squadron.

Life's the best gift that nature can bestow;
The first that we receive, the last which we forego:
And he that's vainly prodigal of blood,   335
Forfeits his sense to do his cause no good.
All desperation's the effect of fear;
Courage is temper, valor can't despair.
    And now the victory's completely gained;
No ships to conquer now, no foes remained.   340
The mighty spoils exceed whate'er was known
That vanquished ever lost, or victor won:
So great, if Fame shall future times remind,
They'll think she lies, and libels all mankind.
    Well may the pious queen new anthems raise,   345
Sing her own fortunes, and her maker's praise;
Invite the nation willing thanks to pay;
And well may all the mighty ones obey.
So may they sing, be always so preserved,
By grace unwished, and conquest undeserved.   350
    Now let us welcome home the conquering fleet,
And all their well-atoned mistakes forget:
Such high success should all resentments drowned,
Nothing but joy and welcome should be found.
No more their past miscarriages reprove,   355
But bury all in gratitude and love;
Let their high conduct have a just regard,
And meaner merit meet a kind reward.
    But now what fruits of victory remain?
To Heaven what praise? What gratitude to man?   360
Let France sing praise for shams of victories,
And mock their maker with religious lies:
But England blessed with thankful hearts shall raise,
For mighty conquests, mighty songs of praise.
    She needs no false pretenses to deceive: 365
What all men see, all men must needs believe.
Our joy can hardly run into excess,

341. *spoils:* Without the loss of a single ship the Confederates captured an entire fleet: 12 Spanish galleons and 15 French men-of-war. The loss of prestige to the united crowns was incalculable, but the loss of plate was not nearly so great as had been feared. A French officer told Rooke that all the king's silver, worth about £3,000,000, had been unloaded and removed to Santiago de Compostella before the English arrived.
345. *anthems raise:* On 3 November Anne appointed a "day of thanksgiving for the good success of Her Majesty's campaign" with the bishop of Exeter to preach in St. Paul's Cathedral "on Thursday next" [12 November].

The well-known subject all our foes confess:
We can't desire more, they can't pretend to less.
    Anne, like her great progenitor, sings praise: 370
Like her she conquers, and like her she prays;
Like her she graces and protects the throne,
And counts the land's prosperity her own:
Like her, and long like her, be blessed her reign,
Crowned with new conquests, and more fleets from Spain.   375
    See now the royal chariot comes amain,
With all the willing nation in her train,
With humble glory, and with solemn grace,
Queen in her eyes, and Christian in her face.
With her, her represented subjects join;   380
And when she prays, th' whole nation says "amen."
    With her, in stalls the illustrious nobles sat,
The cherubims and seraphims of state:
Anne like a comet in the center shone,
And they like stars that circumfere the sun.   385
She great in them, and they as great in her;
Sure Heaven will such illustrious praises hear.
The crowding millions hearty blessings pour:
Saint Paul ne'er saw but one such day before.

376. *the royal chariot:* On 12 November "Her Majesty, habited in purple, wearing her collar, and George, [rode from St. James's palace to St. Paul's] in her body coach drawn by eight horses, in which were also the countesses of Marlborough and Sunderland" (*London Gazette,* no. 3862 [12–16 November 1702]).
    382. *With her . . . nobles sat:* "Her Majesty being entered into the choir, seated herself on her throne of state, which was placed near the west end of the choir, opposite the alter; the peers had seats in the area . . . Commons in the stalls and upper galleries" (ibid.).
    388. *crowding millions:* "The public demonstrations given by the inhabitants of this great and populous City . . . were suitable to so great and solemn an occasion; and the night ended with riging of bells, bonfires, illuminations, and other rejoicings" (ibid.).
    389. *one such day before:* "Queen Elizabeth also, after her great success in ruining King Philip the Second's invincible armada, ordered a day of public thanksgiving for her glorious victory to be solemnized all over the kingdom, and upon the day prefixed, passed herself, attended by a numerous train of nobility and gentry, through the streets of London, hung with blue cloth, to the cathedral of St. Paul, where several of the banners taken in the engagement were placed in view, and there performed the duties of the day" (*Present State of Europe* 13 [November 1702]: 442).

THOMAS BROWN

Upon the Anonymous Author of Legion's Humble Address to the Lords

To That Most Senseless Scoundrel, the Author of Legion's Humble Address to the Lords
(1704)

The most celebrated case in constitutional law to be tried in the reign of Queen Anne was that of Matthew Ashby, a burgess in the town of Aylesbury, Buckinghamshire, who brought an action at common law against the constables of Aylesbury "for having by contrivance fraudulently and maliciously hindered him to give his vote at an election." The original verdict for him was set aside by the court of Queen's Bench and upon a writ of error brought in the House of Lords, Ashby "obtained judgment, to recover his damages for the injury; and afterwards had execution upon that judgment." When five more burgesses in the town of Aylesbury brought actions to recover their damages, they were committed to Newgate by the House of Commons on 5 December 1703 "as having acted . . . in contempt of the jurisdiction, and in breach of the privilege, of that House." Subsequently the Commons declared that the Lords's action in reversing the decision of the Queen's Bench was also "a high breach of the privilege of this House" (*CJ, 14,* 308). Finally, after a series of conferences with the Commons, on 13 March 1704 the Lords drew up a statement of the case on which an address to Her Majesty could be drafted.

The theme of this brief is that the action of the Commons in imprisoning the five Aylesbury burgesses is such that "the most arbitrary governments cannot show more direct instances of partiality and oppression." In *Legion's Humble Address to the Lords,* Defoe calls it "exercising the same arbitrary power they are sent thither to suppress."

Defoe, however, expanded the pamphlet that he published about April 1704 to take in eight points at issue between the two Houses and in each case he decided against "our degenerated representatives," as he called them. Exactly as in January 1703, the machinery of suppression was promptly set in motion: on 29 May 1704 a warrant was issued for the author's arrest, a reward was offered, and Defoe may even have found it necessary to leave London again. On 14 June 1704 an informant told Harley that if Defoe was wanted for writing *Legion's Humble Address to the Lords,* he might be found "at Captain Roger's at the city of Canterbury." The pamphlet must have enjoyed a good sale, for as late as September 1704 "one Sammen, a weaver, a tool of Defoe's," was arrested for dispersing it, but the author was never discovered. This time he enjoyed the protection, not the hostility, of the secretary of state (Luttrell, *5*, 429).

Thomas Brown's two poems are witty attempts to discredit both the author and that "mock authoritative manner," as Swift called it, in which without a snicker Defoe represents the Lords as "the sanctuary and safety of this nation."

UPON THE ANONYMOUS AUTHOR OF
LEGION'S HUMBLE ADDRESS TO THE LORDS

Thou tool of faction, mercenary scribe,
Who preachest treason to the Calveshead tribe,
Whose fruitful head, in garret mounted high,
Sees legions, and strange monsters, in the sky;
Who would'st with war and blood thy country fill,   5
Were but thy power as rampant as thy will:
Well may'st thou boast thy self a million strong,
But 'tis in vermin that about thee throng.

TO THAT MOST SENSELESS SCOUNDREL, THE AUTHOR
OF LEGION'S HUMBLE ADDRESS TO THE LORDS,
WHO WOULD PERSUADE THE PEOPLE OF ENGLAND
TO LEAVE THE COMMONS, AND DEPEND UPON THE LORDS

What demons moved thee, what malicious fiends,
To tempt the people from their surest friends?
Sooner thou might'st embracing floods disjoin,
And make the needle from its north decline:
Or teach the graceful heliotrope to run,   5
A diff'rent motion from th' enlivening sun.
    Our peers have often for themselves rebelled;

2. *preachest*: Cf. *The Reformer Reformed: Or, The Shortest Way with Daniel D'Fooe*, [1703], pp. 4, 6: "the Calves Head Club, of which Mr. D'Fooe is a worthy member . . . Mr. D'Fooe is known to be a preacher at a conventicle."

4. *legions*: Defoe's 1701 *Memorial* (Daniel Defoe, pp. 105–06) was subscribed, "Our name is LEGION, and we are many."

7. *million*: *Legion's Humble Address to the Lords* (1704) was subscribed, "Our Name Is Million, and We Are more."

When did they for the people take the field?
Led not by love, but interest and pride,
They would not let the prince their vassals ride.   10
That pow'r they to themselves reserved alone,
And so through thick and thin they spurred Old Roan.
    To fact and long experience I appeal,
How fairly to themselves they justice deal:
For if my lord, o'erpowered by wine and whore,   15
The next he meets does through the entrails scow'r,
'Tis pity, his relenting brethren cry,
That for his first offense the youth should die:
Come, he'll grow grave; Virtue and he'll be friends,
And by his voting, make the crown amends.   20
'Tis true, a most magnificent parade
Of law, to please the gaping mob, is made.
Scaffolds are raised in the litigious hall,
The maces glitter, and the sergeants bawl.
So long they wrangle, and so oft they stop,   25
The wearied ladies do their moisture drop.
This is the court (say they) keeps all in awe,
Gives life to justice, vigor to the law.
True, they quote law, and much they prattle on her,
What's the result? Not guilty, upon honor.   30
    Should I who have no coronet to show,
Flustered in drink, serve the next comer so,
My twelve blunt godfathers would soon agree,
To doom me, sober, to the fatal tree.
    Besides how punctually their debts they pay,   35
There's scarce a cit in London but can say.
By peep of morn the trusting wretch does rise,
And to His Grace's gate, like lightning flies:
There in the hall this poor believing ass,
With gaping on bare walls seven hours does pass,   40
And so does forty more in the same class.

8. *take the field:* Defoe said that the Lords had "frequently taken arms, and pulled down bloody tyrants; deposing their power, and rescuing [the] country from slavery and oppression" (*Legion's Humble Address to the Lords* [1704], p. 1).

15. *my lord:* Probably Charles Mohun, 4th Lord Mohun.

20. *voting:* Lord Mohun voted against the second bill to prevent occasional conformity in December 1703.

35. *debts:* probably William Cavendish, 1st duke of Devonshire. Devonshire "spoke loud" against the second bill to prevent occasional conformity in December 1703.

38. *gate:* At this time the duke of Devonshire lived in Arlington House(on the present site of Buckingham Palace).

At last my lord, with looks erect and hardy:
"Troth, friends, my tenants have been somewhat tardy:
But for the future, this shall be redressed,
Delays and losses may befall the best.   45
This said, he presses with regardless pride,
Between the opening squadrons on each side:
Calls for his page, then slips into his chair,
And so good gentlemen, you're as you were.
    Cease scribbler then our grandees to defame   50
With feigned encomiums, which they scorn to claim:
What they can challenge by the laws o' th' land,
We freely give, while they no more demand:
But let not in their praise the plot be brought,
Thou know'st the proverb: Nothing due for naught.   55

54. *the plot:* Defoe praised the Lords' "zeal, courage, and fidelity . . . in searching after the deeply laid contrivances of Her [Majesty's] enemies in the late Scotch plot" (*Legion's Humble Address to the Lords* [1704], p. 4).

55. *Nothing due for naught:* perhaps a variant of thank you for nothing.

A Health to the Tackers
(March[?] 1705)

Anne's first Parliament was prorogued on 14 March 1705, and, although the writ for a new election was not signed until 5 April, the Triennial Act required a new election before July 1705 in any case. So *A Health to the Tackers* is probably an election song for the two Tory members for Coventry, Sir Christopher Hales and Thomas Gery. The success of the song as political propaganda can be estimated by guessing how important it may have been in raising the Tory mob that seized the town hall in Coventry, beat up Whigs who attempted to vote, and thus secured large majorities for Hales and Gery.

Besides the tack, the poem mentions another issue raised in the election of 1705. This was the case of *Ashby* v. *White,* which in the previous parliament had polarized not only Tory and Whig, but commoner and peer. The case had begun in January 1701 when Matthew Ashby, a Whig voter in Aylesbury, Buckinghamshire, had been prevented from voting in a parliamentary election by the Tory mayor, William White. Ashby sued White at the assizes on the grounds that he had been denied a legal right. The judge upheld his claim, but White appealed to the court of Queen's Bench, which reversed the judgment. Then, backed by Wharton, the leader of the Whig interest in Aylesbury, Ashby took his case to the House of Lords. There it became a party cause: while the Whig majority in the House of Lords easily set aside the decision of the Queen's Bench, the Tory majority in the Commons denied the jurisdiction of the Lords and insisted that the Commons alone could adjudicate franchise and election disputes. In a show of power the Commons sent Ashby and others who had brought suit against White to prison for breach of privilege.

Tory propagandists seized on the intervention of the Lords in *Ashby* v. *White* as an example of peers interfering in the rights of commoners and this argument appears to have swayed voters. Henry St. John wrote to the duke of Marlborough on 18 May 1705, summarizing election results to date: "Most of the changes I hitherto observed on the lists are against the Tories, and it is not to be conceived what a prejudice they have done their interest in all places by attempting the Tack. There is nothing checks the tide that runs against them, but their opposition to your lordships' proceedings in relation to the Aylesbury business, which is very far from being popular" (Blenheim MS A1-20).

687

A Health to the Tackers

Here's a health to the Tackers, my boys,
    But mine arse for the Tackers about,
May the brave English spirits come in,
    And the knaves and fanatics turn out:
Since the magpies of late are confounding the state,   5
    And would pull our establishments down,
Let us make 'em a jest, for they shit in their nest,
    And be true to the church and the crown.

Let us choose such Parliament men
    As have stuck to their principles tight,   10
And would not their country betray
    In the story of Ashby and White,
Who care not a turd for a Whig or a lord
    That won't see our accounts fairly stated,
For Churchill ne'er fears the address of those peers   15
    Who the nation of millions have cheated.

The next thing advisable is,
    Since schism so strangely abounds,
To oppose ev'ry man that's set up
    By Dissenters in corporate towns,   20
For high church and low church has brought us to no church,
    And conscience so bubbled the nation,
That who is not still for conformity bill
    Will be surely a rogue on occasion.

2. *Tackers about:* On 28 November 1704 when the Commons divided on the question of whether to tack the third bill to prevent occasional conformity to the land tax, about 30 members, according to one Tory account, "hung down their heads and cowardly deserted the cause of their creator" by withdrawing from the House (*The Tackers Vindicated* [1705], p. 4).

3. *come in:* be elected.

5. *magpies:* The Tackers were equally outraged by Whiggish bishops who fouled their own dioceses by voting against the bill to prevent occasional conformity.

14. *accounts fairly stated:* In the last Parliament a bill to continue the commission to audit the public accounts had been lost. On 16 March 1704 the Lords objected to one of the names on the Commons' list and proposed to add two more, but before these differences could be settled Parliament was prorogued on 3 April 1704.

Act of Union

One of the most momentous affairs of state in the whole period 1660–1714 was the union of England and Scotland. Many commentators portray the merging of the two legislatures into the Parliament of Great Britain as the inevitable outcome of a process that began when the two countries were united under one monarch by King James VI and I in 1603. To view the Act of Union of 1707 as a natural consummation, however, is to take undue advantage of hindsight. On the eve of the negotiations that led to it, as Daniel Defoe noted, "the breaches between the two kingdoms rather widened and increased, than tended to close." Indeed at one stage they drifted dangerously close to war.

It was largely to avoid that calamity that the English government set on foot a treaty, and from the start Queen Anne's ministers based their arguments for union almost entirely on the political advantages to be gained by it. In the short run it would heal divisions in the British Isles that could only play into the hands of France and might jeopardize the entire war effort of the Grand Alliance. In the long run it would forestall the possibility of Scotland choosing a monarch other than the Hanoverian successor on Anne's death.

Advocates of union in Scotland tended to stress its economic rather than its political advantages. By 1700 the Scottish economy was showing all the signs of approaching crisis. Scotland's trade with Europe, once the foundation of her commerce, was no longer favorable. French imports in particular were adversely affecting her balance of payments. Scotland had not shared in the general expansion of extra-European trade that occurred in the late seventeenth century. Across the Atlantic Scots were debarred from trading directly with English colonies, while their own colonial projects in Nova Scotia and Darien had proved abortive. The English East India Company was instrumental in bringing about the collapse of a Scottish company designed to exploit commercial possibilities in the Far East. As the pattern of overseas trade shifted against Scotland, trading relations with England assumed more significance in the Scottish economy than ever before.

Where the Scots were prepared to use political blackmail to get economic advantages, the English countered by employing economic pressures to obtain political results. Thus the Security Act was answered by the Alien Act

of 1705. This stipulated that unless the Scottish Parliament repealed the
Security Act, and either recognized the Hanoverian successor or began to
treat for union by Christmas Day 1705, the vital trade in linen and black
cattle would be banned.

The Scottish Parliament turned from confrontation to negotiation, and in
the summer of 1705 asked the queen to appoint commissioners to treat for
union. The English Parliament responded to these overtures by repealing the
Alien Act. Early in 1706 commissioners from both countries were nominated
and by June a treaty was drawn up. It provided for a union of the two Parlia-
ments and a uniform system of customs and excise for Great Britain. Scotland
was to retain its separate legal system and church forever, and its own Privy
Council. A great national debate ensued in pulpit and pamphlet, a debate
that Defoe, as an agent of the English ministers, actively joined in as the
most persuasive advocate of union.

The arguments raised in Scotland by the treaty were rehearsed in the
Edinburgh Parliament when it met to discuss the articles. One of the more
absurd opposition speeches, that of Lord Belhaven, became the butt of
Defoe's wit in *The Vision*. He treated the weightier arguments made on both
sides more seriously and at much greater length in two other poems, *Caledonia*
and *A Scots Poem*.

DANIEL DEFOE

The Vision
(27–28 November 1706)

"The conquest of Scotland," it has been said, "was a project which ambition very naturally suggested to an English king," but it remained for an English queen to realize this ambition (J. L. De Lolme, "An Essay Containing a Few Strictures on the Union of Scotland with England," Daniel Defoe, *The History of the Union*, ed. George Chalmers [1786], p. 4). Edward I failed miserably, after wasting many years of a long reign (1272–1307) in killing Scots. James I in 1604 appointed commissioners from each kingdom to draw up articles for a treaty of union but then abandoned the project for one more compatible with his genius, namely, "to make himself absolute in *Scotland*" (Defoe, *The History of the Union*, pp. 51–53, 717–24). Cromwell succeeded momentarily in imposing a union by force. Charles II in 1666 again appointed commissioners but when they produced a treaty he dismissed them without further notice. William III in March 1689 recommended "uniting both kingdoms into one" and on his deathbed he reminded Parliament that "nothing can contribute more to the present and future peace, security, and happiness, of *England* and *Scotland*, than a firm and entire union between them" (*Leven and Melville Papers*, Edinburgh, The Bannatyne Club, [1843], pp. 2–3; *LJ*, *17*, 50–51).

Anne responded to this in her first speech from the throne by urging Parliament "to consider of proper Methods towards attaining of an Union between *England* and *Scotland*" (*LJ*, *17*, 68). Commissioners were again appointed but negotiations broke down over the issue of trading rights for the Company of Scotland and were adjourned in February 1703. Then, in August 1703, the Scottish Parliament responded by passing the Act of Security, which provided that Anne's successor should be "of the royal line of Scotland and of the true Protestant religion; providing always that the same be not successor to the crown of England" unless England had previously conceded to Scotland "a free communication of trade, freedom of navigation and the liberty of the plantations" (*Acts of the Parliament of Scotland*, 12 vols. [Edinburgh, 1814–75], *11*, 70). The effect would have been to break the union of crowns that had existed since 1603 and to expose England to "the most extreme danger" (James Drake and Henry Pooley, *The Memorial of the Church of England* [1711],

p. 55). Anne momentarily withheld her assent while Harley, her new secretary of state for the northern department, observed that "the succession is to bekept unsettled for a lame arm to beg by" (HMC, *Portland*, *4*, 103).

THE VISION

1.

Come hither ye dreamers of dreams,
Ye soothsayers, wizards and witches,
That puzzle the world with hard names,
And without any meaning make speeches:
    Here's a lord in the north,   5
    Near Edinburgh Forth,
Though little's been said of his name or his worth;
He's seen such a vision, no mortal can reach it,
I challenge the clan of Egyptians to match it.

2.

And first, in the dark it was told him,   10
Which might very well appall us,
That the world was a fighting of old time,
From Nimrod to Sardanapalus;
    That it's all revelation,
    You may pawn your salvation,   15

5. *a lord in the north:* John Hamilton, 2d Lord Belhaven (1656–1708), was one of the Scots nobles who in January 1689 invited William of Orange to take over the government of Scotland. He became a violent and articulate opponent of the union.

9. *Egyptians:* Cf. Joseph as interpreter of dreams in Genesis 40–42.

15. The immediate occasion for *The Vision* was a remarkable speech in Parliament that Defoe heard on Saturday, 2 November 1706. The estates were debating the first article of the Treaty of Union, which was the incorporating article. The debates went on after dark and the clamor outside the Parliament House was so great that violence was feared and the guards were drawn out in readiness. The speech of John Hamilton, 2d Lord Belhaven, was long and emotional. It began with a series of Old Testament-like prophecies of the disasters that would ensue if the kingdoms were united. When Belhaven finished speaking, Patrick Hume, earl of Marchmont and a member of the *Squadrone Volante,* "made a very short return." "He had heard a long speech, and a very terrible one," he said, "but he was of opinion, it required a short answer, which he gave in these words, 'Behold he dreamed, but lo! when he awoke, he found it was a dream' " (Defoe, *The History of the Union,* p. 328). But when the session was finally adjourned, the opponents of union had still prevented the incorporating article from coming to a vote.

Defoe presumably wrote *The Vision* that night, so it could be copied out and distributed among the members before the vote was taken (and the article passed) on the following Monday, 4 November 1706.

For the devil a history gives the relation;
But it's all in the deeps, no mortal can reach it,
We may challenge the clan of Egyptians to match it.

3.

Then Scotland comes next on the stage,
For in visions you must not be nice,   20
And a skip of three thousand years age,
Is nothing where men are concise;
    I name it the rather
    Because you may gather
How that every man is the son of his father;   25
A truth for the future no mortal can doubt,
Whatever they might before he found it out.

4.

But heark, now the wonders begin,
And take care lest the vision should fright ye;
For if it should make you unclean,   30
He has not told you how he would dight ye.
    First the national church,
    Left quite in the lurch,
Was a truckling down to the steeple and porch;
But what is still worse, she's afraid of her friends,   35
So fevers make frantic men hasten their ends.

5.

Was ever such conjuring known,
Or the church so clawed by the steeple;
Nonjurors are her champions grown,
And the prelatists vote for the people.   40
    Protesters appear
    And the Jacques they adhere,

31. *dight*: clean.

32. *the national church*: the Presbyterian church, reestablished in June 1690. It was "left . . . in the lurch" by the Treaty of Union which, by failing to mention religious establishment in either kingdom, aroused fears that the Presbyterian Church of Scotland would end up sleeping in the truckle bed under the Episcopal Church of England in the high bed, or that the Scottish kirk would be governed by 26 bishops in the English Parliament.

34. *a truckling down*: acting subserviently. The phrase is neither dialectal nor Scots, but apparently a coinage of Defoe's. *steeple and porch*: features of Episcopal churches but not of Presbyterian kirks.

35. *her friends*: The "friends" are voters *for* the union, which the Church of Scotland opposed.

42. *Jacques*: Jacobites.

And Antichrist votes the true church to secure,
O Scotland! Was ever such conjuring known,
That the mitre supports the same church pulled her down!   45

6.

Then the nation in sack-cloth appeared,
And the visionist sadly bewailed her;
For mischiefs the like were ne'er heard,
Her privilege of slavery failed her.
 For the mob he complained   50
 That being born chained,
Blessed bondage was lost and damned freedom remained,
So with liberty scared, and afraid to grow rich,
They sued for repentance in a dolorous speech.

7.

And first our amazement t'increase,   55
The soldiers disbanded appear,
Poor drudges put 'prentices to peace,
For want of the blessings of war;
 For though it's in the book,
 Yet the Scripture mistook,   60
When it told us, our swords should to plowshares be broke;
It might be long ago a happiness there,
But it's plain by the vision it's otherwise here.

8.

The merchants are next on the stage,
The enchantment has circled them in;   65
For fear they in wealth should engage,
They resolve they'll never begin;
 The burghs are afraid
 They shall have too much trade,
And the nation to plenty be safely betrayed.   70
So they gravely address, that to keep them secure,
As you find them, you leave them, both foolish and poor.

9.

The next is indeed a sad sight,

45. The line is elliptical but the meaning seems clear: the Episcopalians, disestablished in June 1690, now pretend to be concerned for the security of the Presbyterians who displaced them.

The like on't has rarely been known,
'Twill ruin the country quite,   75
It will never recover its own;
    The plowman's undone,
    From father to son;
For a terrible drawback on corn will come on,
In plenty they'll ship it, be there never so much;   80
And to load us with money, sell all to the Dutch.

10.

O ye virgins! (both sexes) draw near,
And though it's but in spectrum shown,
In sympathy lend us a tear
As the case may some time be your own;   85
    The ladies' condition
    Deserves your compassion;
'Tis very severe to make beauty petition,
Yet here his strange tragedies turned to a jig,
That the men want employments, yet the ladies should beg.   90

11.

Then a crew of old sailors were brought,
At their true benefactors to rail;
That to fight for strange nations were bought
And this will cut off the entail.
    They thought it was hard   95
    The Dutch ships to discard;
And to force the poor Scots their own trade to regard,
For liberty claims a freedom to ill,
And it's hard to get money against a man's will.

12.

And now the exorcist in turn   100
Like a ghost in a circle arises,
Without any tears he can mourn;
He is ecstasies all and surprises;
    But what wildest of all,
    And does strangely appall,   105
Two hours he talked and said nothing at all,
But let drop a few hypocritical tears;
So the crocodile weeps on the carcass she tears.

13.

Then in strange Hebrew words he bewailed ye,
Though the jest was by few understood,   110
Tu quoque mi fili Squadrone,
Or in Scots, *The Parliament's wood.*
    So Caesar they say,
    Cried out in a fray,
When they killed him because he'd his country betray;   115
For Brutus his country's liberty sought;
Was a simile e'er so in happily brought?

14.

Thus he rummaged the histories old,
Like the tale of the bear and the fiddle,
For as 'twas unluckily told,   120
So the story broke off in the middle.
    Some said my lord cried,
    Though others denied;
Which matter of moment it's hard to decide;
But here's a more difficult matter remains,   125
To tell if he showed us less manners or brains.

111. *Squadrone:* The *Squadrone Volante* were moderate members of the country party, headed by John Hay, 2d marquis of Tweeddale, to whom Godolphin had turned to form a government for Scotland in 1704. They proved unable to govern and had to be replaced early in 1705 by the court party, but as a bloc of about 25 members they were able to cast the balance of the contending parties in Parliament in favor of the union. Defoe, however, seems to have believed that Belhaven's thrust was against the government and not against the *Squadrone.* In the *Review,* 6 December 1707, he said, "At last, *this lord* that made *a speech* was for enquiring by *what ways and persons* we were brought into this miserable condition, and where do you think he brought it all to be, *Tu quoque mi Fili Squadrone* . . . which is as much to say, being interpreted by way of equivalent, THE MINISTRY."

112. *wood:* insane.

119. *the tale of the bear and the fiddle:* Cf. Samuel Butler's burlesque poem *Hudibras* in which the hero and his squire, Ralpho, have fantastic encounters with a bear and a one-legged fiddler.

JONATHAN SWIFT

Verses Said to Be Written on the Union
(1707?)

Jonathan Swift was one of those unreconstructed Englishmen whose national prejudices Defoe had failed to remove. For Swift there was only "a certain region, well known to the ancient Greeks, by them called, Σκοtia, or the Land of Darkness, where a religious mania "of the most rank and virulent kind" had been allowed to take root and flourish (*Prose, 1*, 97; *9, 4*).

Union with Scotland, in Swift's view, was "a monstrous alliance," an evil necessity that had been imposed upon England by the wrong management of the earl of Godolphin" in advising the queen to give assent to the Act of Security in August 1704. A recent historian had called it "the greatest of eighteenth-century jobs" (*Scottish Historical Review* 63 [October 1964]: 110).

Although still a Whig and "one that wears a gown"—eager to spend his credit with Somers and Sunderland for the advantage of the Church of Ireland—Swift's opposition to the union was one of the issues which divided him from his Whig friends, for the union was strongly supported by the junto lords. And this, of course, may be one reason he did not publish these verses in 1707.

The poem was published in 1746 when George Faulkner included it in the eighth and last volume of *The Works of Jonathan Swift, D.D.* with "other pieces never before printed."

VERSES SAID TO BE WRITTEN ON THE UNION

> The queen has lately lost a part
> Of her entirely English heart,
> For want of which by way of botch,
> She pieced it up again with Scotch.
> Blessed revolution, which creates   5
> Divided hearts, united states.

---

1. *lately lost a part:* presumably the Anglo-Irish part, which Anne lost in October 1703 by her cold answer to the agitated address of the Irish Parliament for union with England.

See how the double nation lies;
Like a rich coat with skirts of frize:
As if a man in making posies
Should bundle thistles up with roses.   10
Whoever yet a union saw
Of kingdoms, without faith or law.
Henceforward let no statesman dare,
A kingdom to a ship compare;
Lest he should call our commonweal   15
A vessel with a double keel:
Which just like ours, new rigged and manned,
And got about a league from land,
By change of wind to leeward side
The pilot knew not how to guide.   20
So tossing faction will o'erwhelm
One crazy double-bottomed realm.

10. *bundle thistles up with roses:* A thistle and a rose grafted on the same stem are represented on the Scottish lion's shield in the union medal; cf. "We make a mighty difference here [Ireland] between suffering thistles to grow among us, and wearing them for posies" (Swift, *Prose, 2,* 124).

12. *faith or law:* By Articles 18 and 25 of the Treaty of Union, Scotland retained both its own form of "laws concerning private right" and its own established Presbyterian church. Many years later Swift acknowledged that the Scots "were united on their conditions, which . . . they are proud enough to be ashamed of," presumably because he felt that the equivalent of £400,000 they received from the English, according to the treaty, was a bribe (*Correspondence, 2,* 342).

16. *double keel:* Sir William Petty (1623–87), the friend of Hobbes and a founder of the Royal Society, was the first English political economist. He was also a great hobbyist and his favorite project, to which he returned "again and again"—after each failure—was a double-keeled vessel. "It is remarkable that the earlier trials of this class of ship—of which several were built—were more successful than the later" (*DNB, 15,* 1001). Andrew Marvell also made poetical capital out of the project in *The Second Advice,* 241–44.

WILLIAM WALSH

Abigail's Lamentation for the Loss of Mr. Harley

Since the Harley-Godolphin ministry was by design a "moderate" or non-party administration, it was constantly subject to attack from all sides. By 23 October 1707 when the first Parliament of Great Britain convened at Westminster, the hunt was in full cry. The climax of the "year of blunders" came on 31 December when William Gregg, a clerk in Harley's office and a hated Scot, was discovered to be a French spy. Defoe had warned Harley three years before of the deplorable lack of security in the office of the secretary of state, but Harley had done nothing to improve matters and so when Gregg's treasonable correspondence was opened at the post office in Brussels, the Whigs supposed that Harley was involved and demanded his resignation.

Harley was indeed forced to resign in February 1708, but not on account of William Gregg, who is not even mentioned in the present poem celebrating the occasion. Harley's unexpected dismissal and the dramatic fashion in which it was forced upon the queen was a subject that fascinated his contemporaries. William Walsh, however, was in a favored position to speculate upon, if not to solve, the mystery, for he was both a politician and a courtier.

It is remarkable, therefore, that *Abigail's Lamentation for the Loss of Mr. Harley* interprets Harley's "disgrace" as the effect of an unsuccessful struggle with the duke of Marlborough rather than with the duke of Somerset. If Harley's "schemes" had succeeded, "Ormond had been sent to head the war" (line 38) and Marlborough "had been forced to yield" (line 39). Although this is a remarkable anticipation of exactly what happened on 31 December 1711, it is a startling conclusion to be drawn from the events of January–February 1708.

Walsh conceived of his poem as an epic fragment, like something out of Stobaeus: Abigail Masham looks down from "Kensington's high towers" like Helen looking down from the walls of Troy. In sympathy with "the godlike hero's fatal doom" (line 20), the sun itself is obscured by clouds. But Harley and Mrs. Masham are blown up to epic proportion only to suffer mock-epic deflation: "the godlike hero's" coach of state is drawn by mules and Mrs. Masham's brightness is in her nose.

Abigail's Lamentation for the Loss of Mr. Harley,
from the Greek of Homer,
Left Imperfect by Mr. Walsh

Now Phoebus did the world with frowns survey;
Dark were the clouds and dismal was the day,
When pensive Harley from the court returned,
Slowly his chariot moved, as that had mourned;
Heavy the mules before the statesman go,   5
As dragging an unusual weight of woe;
Sad was his aspect, and he waking dreams
Of plots abortive and of ruined schemes;
So some sad youth whose griefs alone survive,
Mourns a dead mistress or a wife alive;   10
Such looks would Russell's funeral triumphs grace,
So Nottingham still looked with such a dismal face.
To Kensington's high towers bright Masham flies,
Thence she afar the sad procession spies,
Where the late statesman doth in sorrow ride,   15
His Welsh supporter mourning by his side;
At which her boundless grief loud cries began,
And thus lamenting, through the court she ran:
    Hither, ye wretched Tories, hither come;
Behold the godlike hero's fatal doom.   20
If e'er you used with ravishing delight
To hear his banter and admire his bite;
Now to his sorrows yield this last relief,
Who once was all your hopes is now your grief.
Had this great man his envied post enjoyed,   25
Tories had ruled and Whigs had been destroyed.
Harcourt the mace, to which he long aspired,

---

11. *Russell's funeral triumphs:* One of the greatest triumphs of William Russell, the under-taker in Cheapside, was the funeral of Walsh's friend, John Dryden (*POAS*, Yale *6*, 206–08).

12. *dismal:* Nottingham's nickname.

13. *bright:* "Bright" is used here to mean, not the opposite of "dismal," but "flaming red," in allusion to Abigail's countenance. Her face was so disfigured that she was called "Car-bunconella" and "that pimplefaced bitch" (*Letter Books of John Hervey, 1st Earl of Bristol,* 3 vols. [Wells, 1894], *1*, 294; Holmes, p. 214).

16. *Welsh supporter:* Sir Thomas Mansell, who quit his post as comptroller of the household when Harley was removed.

27. *Harcourt:* Sir Simon Harcourt, attorney general (April 1707–February 1708), was to have been lord chancellor in Harley's projected ministry.

Had now possessed, and Cowper had retired;
And Sunderland his post been forced to quit,
Which St. John had supplied with spritely wit.   30
Sage Hanmer (passing court employments by)
Had ruled the coffers, Tories to supply.
Gower had shined with rich Newcastle's seal,
And Harley's self, to show his humble zeal,
Had been contented with that trifling wand,   35
That now does mischief in Godolphin's hand.
Our fleet secure had been Rooke's tender care,
And Ormond had been sent to head the war.
Blenheim to Radnor had been forced to yield,
And Cardiff cliffs obscured Ramillia's field.   40

28. *Cowper:* The incumbent lord chancellor was Lord Cowper, whose appointment by Godolphin on October 1705 had been opposed by Harley.

29. *Sunderland:* Roger Coke "was told by a considerable Tory, but about four days before the discovery was publicly made, that the earl of Sunderland was to be out of his secretary's place such a day, he being the person they resolved to begin with" (*A Detection of the Court and State of England,* ? vols. [1719], *3,* 323–24).

30. *St. John:* Henry St. John was designated as secretary of state in both accounts of Harley's projected ministry which Addison sent to Lord Manchester (Addison, *Letters,* pp. 91, 95). *spritely wit:* When Swift met Stella in November 1710, Swift told him, "I think Mr. St. John the greatest young man I ever knew; wit, capacity . . . quickness of apprehension . . . admirable conversation" (*Journal, 2,* 401).

31. *Hanmer:* Sir Thomas Hanmer was a "True Church" Tory, a Tacker, and a member of the October Club. But he also became the leader of the Whimsicals, who criticized the peace in 1713 and emerged as Hanoverian Tories. In the Parliament of 1714 Hanmer was speaker. He was also something of a scholar. In *The Dunciad, 4,* 105, he is discovered in the act of laying his edition of Shakespeare at the feet of Dulness.

32. *ruled the coffers:* Addison could not remember what post Harley intended for Hanmer, but this line makes it sound like chancellor of the Exchequer.

33. *Gower:* Sir John Leveson-Gower was a Tory M.P. for Newcastle-under-Lyme from 1692 to March 1703, when he became one of the four—"the violentest of the whole party" (Burnet, *2,* 344)—who were raised to the peerage to create a majority in the House of Lords. He was also a Privy Councillor (April 1702-May 1707) and chancellor of the duchy of Lancaster (1702–06). *Newcastle:* John Holles, duke of Newcastle (1662–1711), was the Protestant patron to whom Dryden dedicated *The Spanish Fryar* (1681). Harley secured his appointment as lord privy seal and three days later he was sworn of Her Majesty's Privy Council. It was Newcastle, Harley's friend, who at last pressed the queen to part with him on 10 February 1708.

35. *wand:* the lord treasurer's staff of office.

37. *Rooke:* Ever since Rooke's dismissal in 1705, his friends had sought a suitable post for him, and Sir Cloudesley Shovel's death in October 1707 seemed to have created such an opening. But since Walsh made a similar joke in *The Golden Age Restored* (*POAS,* Yale, *6,* 494), there may be no substance to the insinuation that Harley intended to make Rooke admiral of the fleet.

39. *Blenheim:* After the battle of Blenheim in August 1703, the queen rewarded Marlborough by giving him the royal manor of Woodstock, on which Blenheim Palace began to be built in June 1705. *Radnor:* Harley sat in Parliament as the member for New Radnor, Wales, from March 1690 to May 1711, when he was elevated to the peerage.

40. *Cardiff cliffs:* Harley's country place.

WILLIAM CONGREVE

Jack Frenchman's Defeat
(6–15 July 1708)

After the disasters of the year before, the allies were desperate for success in 1708. Success came, almost by accident, at the battle of Oudenarde. This was no set piece in the theater of war, but an improvised drama. Marlborough's willingness to commit his troops to fight with their backs to an impassable river—or to commit them at all after two days of forced marches—and his consummate skill in deploying them once they were committed, paid off again. After cavalry skirmishes in the morning, the two armies drew up in the hedgerows and orchards a mile north of Oudenarde in the late afternoon of 30 June / 11 July 1708, and the killing went on until dark. The first estimates of 6000 French soldiers killed and another 4000 captured were, for once, too low. Only the darkness prevented Vendôme's army from being surrounded and annihilated. "If it had pleased God that we had had one hour's daylight more at Oudenarde," Marlborough wrote to Godolphin, "we had, in all likelihood, made an end of this war" (Coxe, *2*, 273).

What made the battle such a popular success in England was the fact that five princes of the blood were engaged in it. Two of these, John William, prince of Orange-Nassau and stadholder of Friesland, and George Augustus, heir to the electoral prince of Hanover and the future George II of England, particularly distinguished themselves. But two grandsons of Louis XIV and James Francis Edward, the pretended prince of Wales, were supposed to have run away.

JACK FRENCHMAN'S DEFEAT

Being an Excellent New Song to a Pleasant Tune Called
"There was a Fair Maid in the North-Country,
Come Tripping Over the Plain, etc."

> Ye Commons and Peers,
> Pray lend me your ears,
> I'll sing you a song if I can;
> How Louis le Grand
> Was put to a stand,
> By the arms of our gracious Queen Anne.

5

How his army so great
Had a total defeat,
Not far from the River of Dender;
    Where his grandchildren twain   10
    For fear of being slain,
Galloped off with the popish pretender.

    To a steeple on high
    The battle to spy,
Up mounted these gallant young men;   15
    But when from the spire
    They saw so much fire,
They most gallantly came down again.

    Then a horseback they got
    Upon the same spot,   20
By the advice of their cousin Vendôme;
    O Lord! cried out he
    To young Burgundy,
Would your brother and you were at home.

    Just so did he say,   25
    When without more delay
Away the young gentry fled;
    Whose heels for that work
    Were much lighter than cork,
But their hearts were more heavy than lead.   30

    Not so did behave
    Young Hanover brave
In this bloody field I'll assure ye;

9. *Dender:* Lessiness, on the Dender, a tributary of the Scheldt, and about 15 miles from Oudenarde, which the allies had only occupied the night before, was the point from which the advance guard of Marlborough's army moved out at 1:00 A.M. on the morning of 30 June / 11 July 1708.

10. *grandchildren twain:* Two of Louis XIV's grandchildren, the eldest, Louis, duc de Bourgogne (1682–1712) and Charles, duc de Berry (1686–1714), were present at the battle. The duc de Bourgogne, in fact, shared command of the French army with Louis Joseph, duc de Vendôme.

13. *steeple:* The French princes and the English pretender observed the battle from a mill. As the story was told later, the pretender "made a campaign in Flanders, where by the help of a telescope, he saw the Battle of Oudenarde, and the Prince of Hanover's horse shot under him; being posted on a high tower, with two French princes of the blood" (Addison, *The Freeholder,* 23 April 1716).

21. *advice;* What Vendôme actually said to the princes was even more insulting than Congreve imagined: "Eh bien! s'écria-t-il, Messieurs, je vois bien que vous le voulez tous; il faut donc se retirer! Aussi bien, ajouta-t-il en regardant Mgr. le duc de Bourgogne, il y a longtemps, Monseigneur, que vous en avez envie" (Saint-Simon, *2,* 1903). *cousin:* Vendôme was a second cousin of the half-blood once removed of the duc de Bourgogne.

When his war horse was shot
He mattered it not,   35
But fought it on foot like a fury.

While death flew about
Aloud he called out
Hoh! You chevalier of St. George.
If you'll neither stand   40
By sea nor by land,
Pretender, that title you forge.

Thus firmly he stood
As became that high blood,
Which runs in his veins so blue;   45
This gallant young man,
Being kin to Queen Anne,
Did as were she a man, she would do.

What a racket was here,
(I think 'twas last year)   50
For a little ill fortune in Spain;
When by letting 'em win,
We have drawn the putts in
To lose all they are worth this campaign.

Though Bruges and Ghent   55
To Monsieur were lent,
With interest he soon shall repay 'em;
While Paris may sing
With her sorrowful king,
De Profundis instead of Te Deum.   60

From their dream of success,
They'll awaken we guess
At the noise of great Marlborough's drums.
They may think if they will
Of Almanza still,   65
But 'tis Blenheim wherever he comes.

39. *chevalier of St. George:* The captured French general to whom Marlborough had
inquired about the pretended prince of Wales explained that in the French army he was
known simply as the chevalier de Saint-Georges.

41. *By sea:* In the intended invasion of March 1708, the pretender was prevented by bad
weather and bad planning from reaching Scotland.

47. *kin:* George Augustus was Anne's second cousin once removed.

53. *putts:* silly fellows.

55. *Bruges and Ghent:* The French had recaptured Ghent and Bruges only a week before
Oudenarde.

O Louis perplexed,
What general's next?
Thou hast hitherto changed 'em in vain:
    He has beat 'em all round,   70
    If no new ones are found,
He shall beat the old over again.

    We'll let Tallard out
    If he'll take t'other bout;
And much he's improved let me tell ye,   75
    With Nottingham ale
    At every meal,
And good pudding and beef in his belly.

    As losers at play
    Their dice throw away,   80
While the winner he still wins on:
    Let who will command,
    Thou hadst better disband,
For old Bully, thy doctors are gone.

69. *changed:* Louis XIV's commander in the Lowlands from 1702 to 1706 was François de Neufville, duc de Villeroi (1644–1730). After his defeat at Ramillies he was dismissed and replaced by Vendôme.

73. *Tallard:* Louis XIV's commander at Blenheim was still a prisoner in Nottingham castle.

84. *doctors:* As well as physicians (here imagined to have given up Louis XIV's case as hopeless), "doctors" are false dice.

[ARTHUR MAINWARING]

A New Ballad
(February–July 1708)

One copy of *A New Ballad* is endorsed, "The ballad the duchess of Marlborough mentions." And it is further possible that the duchess may have been coached for her performance by the author himself, for Arthur Mainwaring is known to have sung ballads to his own accompaniment on the harpsichord "with becoming impudence" (Blenheim MS E27).

Whoever he was, the author took as his model for *A New Ballad* an old ballad by Thomas Deloney entitled *A Mourneful Dittie on the Death of Faire Rosamond* that was first published in *Strange Histories* (1607) and frequently reprinted.

Mainwaring became the duchess's informant, adviser, coconspirator, collaborator, confidant, and accompanist on the harpsichord. It was this relationship that made it possible for *A New Ballad* to reflect the duchess of Marlborough's attitudes so exactly. And it was this relationship that propelled Mainwaring into the role of Swift's main antagonist in the propaganda battles of the last years of the reign.

A New Ballad

To the Tune of "Fair Rosamund"

Whenas Queen Anne of great renown
    Great Britain's scepter swayed,
Besides the church, she dearly loved
    A dirty chambermaid.

Oh! Abigail that was her name,   5
    She starched and stitched full well,
But how she pierced this royal heart,
    No mortal man can tell.

However, for sweet service done
    And causes of great weight,   10

706

Her royal mistress made her, Oh!
    A minister of state.

Her secretary she was not,
    Because she could not write,
But had the conduct and the care   15
    Of some dark deeds at night.

The important pass of the back stairs
    Was put into her hand;
And up she brought the greatest rogue
    Grew in this fruitful land.   20

And what am I to do, quoth he,
    Oh! for this favor great?
You are to teach me how, quoth she,
    To be a slut of state.

My dispositions they are good,   25
    Mischievous and a liar;
A saucy proud ungrateful bitch,
    And for the church entire.

Great qualities! quoth Machiavell,
    And soon the world shall see   30
What you can for your mistress do,
    With one small dash of me.

In counsel sweet, Oh! then they sat,
    Where she did griefs unfold,
Had long her grateful heart oppressed,   35
    And thus her tale she told:

From shreds and dirt in low degree,
    From scorn in piteous state,
A duchess bountiful has made
    Of me a lady great.   40

Such favours she has heaped upon
    This undeserving head,
That for to ease me from their weight,
    Good God, that she were dead!

14. *could not write:* Nothing seems to be known about Mrs. Masham's education, but she could in fact write. Some of her letters to Harley are preserved.

28. *for the church:* Mrs. Masham was deeply imbued with the maxims of the high church party and did not hesitate to interfere in appointments to episcopal sees.

Oh! let me then some means find out,   45
    This teasing debt to pay.
I think, quoth he, to get her place
    Would be the only way.

For less than you she must be brought,
    Or I can never see   50
How you can pay the boons received
    When you were less than she.

My argument lies in few words,
    Yet not the less in weight;
And oft with good success we use   55
    Such, in affairs of state.

Quoth she, 'tis not to be withstood;
    I'll push it from this hour;
I will be grateful, or at least
    I'll have it in my power.   60

Quoth he, since my poor counsel gains
    Such favor in your eye,
I have a small request to make,
    I hope you won't deny.

Some bounties I, like you, have had   65
    From one that bears the wand,
And very fain I would, like you,
    Repay them if I can.

Witness ye Heavens! how I wish
    To slide into his place;   70
Only to show him countenance
    When he is in disgrace.

Oh! would you use your interest great
    With our most gracious queen,
Such things I'd quickly bring about   75
    This land hath never seen.

Give me but once her royal ear,
    Such notes I'll in it sound,
As from her sweet repose shall make
    Her royal head turn round.   80

66. *the wand:* Lord Treasurer Godolphin's staff of office.

He spoke, and straightway it was done,
    She gained him free access.
God long preserve our gracious queen,
    The Parliament no less!

Now from this hour it was remarked   85
    That there was such resort
Of many great and high divines
    Unto the queen's fair court,

Mysterious things that long were hid,
    Began to come to light;   90
And many of the church's sons
    Were in a zealous fright.

'Twas said, with sighs and anxious looks,
    A general abroad
Had won more battles than their friends,   95
    The French, could well afford;

That so much money had been sent
    Such needless things t'advance,
It sure was time, as in reigns past,
    Some now should come from France.   100

At last they spoke it out and said,
    'Twas of the last import,
That there should be a thorough change
    In army, fleet, and court.

For wicked Johnny Marlborough   105
    So madly pushed things on,
That should he unto Paris go
    The church was quite undone.

The wise and pious queen gave ear
    To this devout advice,   110
And honest sturdy Sunderland
    Was whipped up in a trice.

Avast! cried out the admiral;

87. *high divines:* Harley's influence began to be suspected in April 1707 when Anne privately admitted two high churchmen to her closet to kiss hands for the bishoprics of Exeter and Chester while the Whigs were being assured that low churchmen would be preferred.

    111. *Sunderland:* Sunderland, the only junto Whig in the Godolphin ministry, was to have been the first to be dismissed.

    113. *the admiral:* George, prince of Denmark, the queen's consort, lord high admiral of

No-near, you rogues, no-near!
Your ship will be amongst the rocks,   115
   If at this rate you steer!

With that the man that kept the cash
   Slipped in a word or two,
Which made an old acquaintance think
   This game would never do.   120

He but one eye had in his head,
   But with that one he saw
These priests might bring about his ears
   A thing we call club-law.

He on his pillow laid his head,   125
   And on mature debate
With that, and with his wife, resolved
   To play a trick of state:

Like Dr. Burgess much renowned,
   Of one he did take care;   130
Then slipped his cloak and left the rest
   All in most sad despair.

The consequence of this was such.
   Our good and gracious queen,
Not knowing why she e'er went wrong.   135
   Came quickly right again.

England. The prince was easily drawn into Harley's scheme by being told that he had too small a share in the government but he was just as easily intimidated by George Churchill, the younger brother of the duke of Marlborough, to urge the queen to drop Harley in order to avoid a convulsion in the state.

114. *No-near:* a command to the helmsman to come no closer to the wind.

119. *old acquaintance:* Charles Talbot, 1st duke of Shrewsbury (1660–1718), had been Godolphin's ministerial colleague and horse-racing crony in the last reign. He had played an active part in the revolution and was twice William's secretary of state (1689–90, 1694–1700), but now he was without office, having spent the years 1700–06 abroad, mainly in Italy. Both Marlborough and Harley had sought his support for the ministry, against the Whig junto, and had been favorably received. But lines 121–32 imply that when Harley sought to displace Godolphin, Shrewsbury abandoned him. Subsequently, when Godolphin failed to find a place for Shrewsbury in the reshuffled cabinet that he had put together with the junto, Shrewsbury changed his mind again and in 1710 by sole interest of Harley he was made lord chamberlain. In September 1713 he was appointed lord lieutenant of Ireland, and Anne on her deathbed in July 1714 made him her lord treasurer to succeed Harley.

121. *one eye:* The text implies that even with one eye Shrewsbury could see that Harley's scheme would have required "club-law," physical force as contrasted with argument.

129. *Dr. Burgess:* Daniel Burgess (1645–1713) was the most celebrated Presbyterian minister in London. His defection from the established church had already become proverbial.

However, taking safe advice
   From those who knew her well,
She Abigail turned out of doors,
   And hanged up Machiavell.   140

Leviathan
(June–July? 1709)

The seventeenth century had witnessed a great debate about the origin and nature of civil government. Traditionalists, like Sir Robert Filmer, argued from the Bible and from history seen through biblical glasses, that all authority derived from God and that patriarchal monarchy was the form of government most acceptable to God. A corollary of this concept of indefeasible hereditary right was the Doctrine of Passive Obedience or Non-Resistance, that it was sinful to resist the Lord's anointed upon any pretext whatsoever.

Opposed to this religious view was a secular theory that civil government originated in a contractual arrangement for the security and benefit of the governed. In the *Leviathan* Hobbes conceived of government as an agreement between interest groups to obey a ruler who was not party to the contract but whose function was to see that it was enforced. John Locke, on the other hand, made the ruler into one party to the contract with the ruled as the other party. Unlike Hobbes's absolute monarch, Locke's constitutional monarch was bound by the terms of the contract.

This debate survived the Revolution of 1688, although the traditionalists had to exercise considerable ingenuity to square their theories with the facts of history. Some argued that God had manifested his displeasure with the head of the Stuart dynasty by transferring his blessing to James's eldest daughter and his nephew, her husband. Others maintained that there had been no resistance in 1688, that James had voluntarily abdicated and that the crown had passed to Mary by the laws of primogeniture. This, of course, required a refusal to believe in the legitimacy of the son born to James's wife in June 1688, but such incredulity was widespread, among Tories as well as Whigs. And the notion of indefeasible hereditary right actually took on a new lease of life when James died in September 1701 and his daughter Anne succeeded as queen in March 1702.

Along with a new interest in divine right theories came a new insistence upon Passive Obedience and Non-Resistance. Henry Sacheverell became the most notorious, but Offspring Blackall, bishop of Exeter, was a more intelligent advocate. Political power, Blackall argued, must derive from God,

"For there is no power but of God," as St. Paul said, and "Whosoever there-
fore resisteth the power, resisteth the ordinance of God" (Rom. 13:1–2).
The magistrate's power, Blackall said, in a fine Platonic image, is "a ray or
portion of the divine authority and power . . . communicated to him by
God" (*The Divine Institution of Magistracy, and the Gracious Design of its Institu-
tion* [1709], p. 6). The magistrate, Blackall pointed out quite correctly, could
not derive his power from the people, for the people never had it (p. 8).

When Blackall's sermon was published by royal command, Benjamin
Hoadly felt compelled to write a reply. Hoadly was the most ambitious pro-
pagandist for the contractual theory of kingship. Blackall came back with
The Lord Bishop of Exeter's Answer to Mr. Hoadly's Letter (1709), ridiculing
Hoadly's imaginary states of nature and nonexistent original contracts. The
present poem catches Hoadly in the act of composing a reply to *The Lord
Bishop of Exeter's Answer.*

In form the poem is a hymn, in fact a mock Calf's-Head-Club hymn. As
such it celebrates not God but the mob, "that crooked serpent" from whom in
republican theory all power is derived, "Leviathan, our God and King"
(line 57). In this new application of the Biblical symbol, Leviathan is no
longer the absolute monarch of Hobbes's book, "The Multitude . . . united
in one person," but "The Multitude" itself, the monster-mob taking power
into its own hands. And finally, of course, the poem is another example, like
The Shortest-Way with the Dissenters and *A Tale of a Tub,* of a work of total
irony, meaning at every point the opposite of what the words say.

Leviathan, or A Hymn to Poor Brother Ben

To the Tune of "The Good Old Cause Revived"

Why now so melancholy, Ben?
What, stabbed to death by Blackall's pen?
Invoke old Hobbes and snarl again.

What, freezing nigh the Arctic Pole
Rouse, rouse thy sad dejected soul,   5
Here's Tom of Bedlam with a bowl.

Then wake, and clear the fatal cup,
'Twill cheer thy drooping spirits up;
'Tis Faction's bowl, leave not a cup.

Title. The Good Old Cause: the parliamentary side in the civil wars. By taunting Hoadly for
his "zeal for that [Good Old] Cause," Blackall was accusing him of being a crypto-republi-
can.

Oh, bravely drink! For this I'll raise   10
Thy name aloft in Milton's lays,
And Tindal's rights shall sound thy praise.

Why howl the dogs? From whence this sound?
Why dance the golden tripods round?
And what is it moves the solid ground?   15

Chorus

Great Ben with sacred rage is blessed,
He foams, he swells, he is compressed,
The god sits heavy on his breast.

Hence, hence, ye mitred priests, away,
All ye who blind obedience pay   20
To royal monarchs' princely sway.

Thou, mob, our sovereign lord, appear,
With unpolluted feet draw near,
And sit in thy imperial chair.

Thou equal to the gods above,   25
And scarce inferior unto Jove,
Through thee we are, we live, and move.

Thou art the universal pole;
Round thee all other powers roll,
And thou dost actuate the whole.   30

From thee all magistracy springs;
Thou giv'st the sacred rule to kings,
And at thy nod they're useless things.

What though they style themselves divine,
And would succeed by right of line,   35
There is no law on earth but thine.

To whom thou list thou giv'st the crown,
To Charles or Nol, to prince or clown;
And who sets up, may tumble down.

Thou bid'st them act the people's good;   40

11. *Milton's lays:* Milton continued to be regarded as a republican—even Whiggish—poet,
particularly after 1698 when John Toland published *A Complete Collection of the Historical,
Political, and Miscellaneous Works of John Milton.*

13. *Why howl the dogs?:* Hoadly is about to be represented as a sibyl, or priestess of Apollo,
and dogs bark and tripods dance and earth quakes at the expected approach of the deity.

But if they rule not as they should,
With glory thou may'st let them blood,

Like thy bold sires in forty-eight,
Who necked their prince (a worthy fate!)
For tyrannizing o'er the state.   45

That prince, by title Charles the First,
Of all the race of kings the worst,
Nor pious, great, nor good, nor just.

Therefore thy sires could not him save,
But sent him headless to the grave;   50
Such honor all the saints shall have.

And if, like them, thou wilt fulfill
Our sovereign lord the people's will,
Thou must dethrone or stab the ill.

Then thus great Salters-Hall shall ring;   55
Thus, thus the Calf's-Head-Club shall sing,
Leviathan, our god and king.

56. *Calf's-Head-Club :* This club, of which John Milton was supposed to have been one of the
founders, met on 30 January to perform a kind of republican black mass to celebrate the
execution of Charles I. The ceremonies included the singing of republican hymns.

To the Tune of "Ye Commons and Peers"
(March 1710?)

When the news reached Sunderland on the night of 28 February 1710 that the mob was burning down meeting houses and threatening worse violence, he went immediately to the queen, who empowered her principal secretary of state to call out her horse- and foot-guards to disperse the rabble. Inevitably several of the mob were killed. "We are now come to fresh paradoxical circumstances," as one Tory observed, "that while the rabble are pulling down houses out of zeal for passive obedience, the vile tools of the most arbitrary ministry that ever nation groaned under are rending their throats in defense of forcible resistance."

Another irony was the fact that Lord Sunderland was the most republican member of the ministry. It was he who told Swift (*Prose, 7, 9*) that he "hoped to see the day, when there should not be a peer in England." Yet his action in suppressing the riots was so arbitrary that the captain of the guards demanded to have his orders in writing.

To the Tune of "Ye Commons and Peers
Pray Lend Me Your Ears
I'll Cut 'Em All Off If I Can."

> Sacheverell the learnéd,
> Of wise men discernéd,
> Had fairly got off with the peers,
> But the bishops were cullied,
> And all the lords bullied,
> And none but poor ladies in tears.   5
>
> Oh, England awake!
> Thou has played thy last stake
> And must part with old Paul to the Romans;

9. *Paul to the Romans:* In the controversy over the origins of civil government, Rom. 13:1–2 was a crucial text: "For there is no power but of God," it said. On the other hand the vio-

Both he and St. Peter,   10
In spite of my meter,
Must yield to a vote of the Commons.

When the mob gets up next,
Without canon or text,
To ding down those men of resistance;   15
Then Harry the doctor
Will prove a good proctor
And well you deserve his assistance.

You must trust to your guards,
Who their pay and rewards   20
Will value above reputation;
Then late you'll recall
Poor Peter and Paul,
When an army commands all the nation.

In vain you cry out   25
And keep such a rout
'Gainst Louis, the pope, and pretender;
'Tis obedience to laws
Must keep up the cause
Of the church and her glorious defender.   30

Then sure 'tis a jig
For the court to turn Whig
On a mystical point of expedience,
Whilst (O monstrous story!)
The mob turns Tory   35
And preacheth up Passive Obedience.

---

lence of the London mob, which went on from pulling down conventicles to plundering
private houses, charging the horse guard, and threatening to attack the Bank of England,
demonstrated "the ill consequences of the doctrine advanced by the Whigs of the original of
government's being from the people" (Hearne, *2, 355*).

10. *St. Peter:* Peter's epistles were frequently cited in support of Non-Resistance and Pas-
sive Obedience.

14. *Without canon or text:* without the authority of the Bible or the laws of the church.

31. *a jig:* a joke.

32. *court to turn Whig:* Anne attended most sessions of the Sacheverell trial incognito. Since
no one was neutral, Anne, by not supporting Sacheverell, appeared to be against him, and
thus the court, on the "mystical" grounds of expedience—i.e., the unstated advice of un-
named "friends"—appeared to "turn Whig."

On the Sentence Passed by the House of Lords on Dr. Sacheverell
(March 1710?)

It was generally expected that the sentence against Sacheverell would be severe. The Whigs had threatened to "roast" him, and once he was found guilty by the House of Lords on 20 March they hoped to make good their threat by getting the peers to agree to four punishments. First, he was not to preach for seven years. Second, he was not to be preferred during that period. third, he was to be imprisoned in the Tower for three months and to be bound over on good behavior for seven years. Finally, his sermons were to be burned by the common hangman.

When the first of these four resolutions was put to the House of Lords on 21 March, the term of the doctor's enforced silence was reduced from seven to three years, to the government's consternation. It was even more galling when the second proposal was defeated. Seeing the way the tide was going the government withdrew the third motion, and the fourth was carried. As Boyer put it, "As soon as it was known abroad what a mild sentence the Lords had resolved to pass upon Dr. Sacheverell, his friends, who looked upon it rather as an absolution than a condemnation . . . could not forbear expressing their joy" (Boyer, *Annals,* 1710, pp. 330–31).

The Whigs were flabbergasted, since on paper they had control of the Upper House. As Marlborough asked his wife, "How were these Lords influenced to be for Sacheverell: duke of Northumberland, duke of Hamilton, earl of Pembroke, earl of Suffolk, bishop of Chichester, Lord Berkeley, earl of Northesk, earl of Wemyss, Lord Lexington? I should have thought all these would have been on the other side" (Coxe, *3,* 27). The answer to the duke's question, as the following poem suggests, was that Anne had changed her mind. At the outset of the impeachment she told Burnet "that it was a bad sermon, and that he deserved well to be punished for it" (Burnet, *2,* 543). On 27 February, however, she informed Sir David Hamilton "that there ought to be a punishment, but a mild one . . . and that his impeachment had been better let alone" (Hertfordshire R.O. MS, Hamilton Diary). The wavering lords, therefore, were not inspired by clemency, as the poem asserts, so much as by self-interest.

Hail, pious days! thou most propitious time,
When hated moderation was a crime,
When sniv'ling saints were cropped for look of grace,
And branded for a conventicle face,
Whole floods of gore distained the guilty years,   5
Noses ragou'd, and fricassees of ears;
When rampant Laud the church's thunder threw,
His sacred fury no distinction knew:
The people suffered and the priesthood too.
   But now behold the bright inverted scene,   10
Mercy returns in a forgiving queen:
Her senate's anger burns in milder fires,
Proud of that clemency which she inspires.
Calmly they try their enemy professed,
And though they damn the doctrine, save the priest;   15
On the deluded tool look mildly down,
And spare the factious pedant for the gown.
So when in sullen state, by peasants bound,
The gen'rous lion walks his thoughtful round,
Should some small cur his privacy invade,   20
And cross the circle which his paws had made,
Fired with disdain, he hurls his eyes below,
But loath to grapple with so mean a foe,
Bestrides him shivering with inglorious fear,
And pisses on the wretch he scorns to tear.   25

1. *time:* the eleven years' personal rule of Charles I from 1629 to 1640.

2. *hated moderation was a crime:* During the 1630s Archbishop Laud set the stamp of Arminianism on the Anglican church by asserting that episcopacy was *jure divino,* insisting upon complete conformity to official orthodoxy and by suppressing any challenge to it. This policy had much in common with the ideals of the high church men of Anne's reign. They hated moderation, with its leniency to dissent, and looked back nostalgically to the days of Laud.

15. *damn the doctrine:* In speaking to the first article of impeachment, Sir Joseph Jekyl said, "My lords, as that doctrine of unlimited Non-Resistance was implicitly renounced by the whole nation in the revolution, so diverse acts of Parliament afterwards passed expressing the renunciation" (*The Tryal of Dr. Henry Sacheverell* [1710], p. 49).

The Old Pack
(March? 1710)

The idea for this rollicking song came from the practice of giving hunting dogs political names. "You shall not meet with a pack of hounds," Defoe said, "but you may hear the Huntsman cry, 'Hark Tory, to him high-church, pox of that Whig, he's meer cur'," (*Review*, Vol. 7, Preface [1711], sig. A2v.).

The House of Commons, in which the Whigs had such a large majority that there were "few, very few, of the true English breed," (line 25), is reduced to a pack of hounds (line 33). The owner of the pack is that well-known sportsman, Lord Godolphin (line 38). Benjamin Hoadly is "the huntsman" (line 41) and "the leaders" (line 34) of the pack are the 20 members of the committee to impeach Henry Sacheverell of high crimes and misdemeanors. While the hunt is in full cry it is interrupted by the rabble: "Take heed," they say, "Sure the Devil's your leader, and you hunt for confusion" (lines 52–54). Perhaps for this reason, but the point is not made explicit, the pack is now put up for sale. The speaker in the poem is an auctioneer, whose huckster chant is imitated in the strong anapaestic rhythm of the verse and the insistent repetition of the refrain.

THE OLD PACK

Come ye old English huntsmen that love noble sport,
Here's a pack to be sold and staunch dogs of the sort;
Not Sir Sewster nor Chetwynd can match our fleet hounds
For breaking down fences or leaping o'er bounds;
Some are deep-mouthed and speedy, some mad, blind, and lame,   5
Most yelpers and curs, but all fit for the game.
　　Then to horse, loyal hearts, lest the round-heads deceive ye,
　　For they have the dogs, and are riding tantivy.

3. *Sewster nor Chetwynd:* Sir Sewster Peyton and Walter Chetwynd were the queen's Masters of the Buck and Stag Hounds.
4. *breaking down fences:* This phrase would suggest levelers to a contemporary reader, since the original levelers got their name from destroying fences around enclosures.
8. *tantivy:* full tilt. The expression had originally been applied by Whigs to Tory churchmen who were accused of riding "tantivy to Rome."

There's Atheist and Deist, and fawning Dissenter,
There's Republican sly and old long-winded Canter;   10
There's Heresy, Schism, and mild Moderation,
That's still in the wrong for the good of the nation;
There's Baptist, Socinian, and Quaker with scruples,
Till kind toleration linked 'em all in church-couples.
    Then to horse, etc.   15

Some were bred in the camp, and some dropped in the fleet,
Under bulks some were littered and some in the street;
Some are good harmless curs, without tooth or claw,
Some were whelped in a shop and some runners at law;
Some were poor wretched curs, mongrels, starters and setters,   20
Till dividing the spoil they put in with their betters.
    Then to horse, etc.

A few, very few, of the true English breed,
Whose noses are good and of excellent speed;
But what's a fine mouth to oppose every throat,   25
Where number and noise quite drown the sweet note?
If he hits of a fault or runs the scent right,
Honest Tory is worried for a rank Jacobite.
    Then to horse, etc.

Five hundred stout dogs are a brave pack to run,   30
But the leaders in chief are but old forty-one;
On hot burning scent, when they open their throats,
Then trail a court-place, how the staunchest change notes!
Though no horn nor voice can their fury control,
Yet to the White Staff they hunt all under bole.   35
    Then to horse, etc.

Cries the huntsman, Ben Hoadly, dear dogs I'm a knave,
But you're all sovereign curs, and your prince is your slave;
This my writings will prove, stole from Prynne, Nye, and Peters,
That all free-born dogs may fall on the betters: 40
Then away on that scent, 'tis the old game and good,
While peers have fat haunches, and kings royal blood.
    Then to horse, etc.

17. *bulks:* the coverings of basement steps.
30. *five hundred:* approximate membership in the House of Commons.
31. *forty-one:* the year in which the civil war began.
35. *White Staff:* the official emblem of the lord treasurer.
39. *Prynne:* William Prynne (1600–69), a Presbyterian pamphleteer who lost his ears for writing against the hierarchy in the reign of Charles I. *Nys:* Philip Nye (1596?–1672) was an

A stout orthodox doctor fell first in the wind;
The pack opened their throats, in hopes mob would ha' joined;   45
By a strong passive scent they ran him full speed,
'Till the rabble cried out, You're too rank there—Take heed;
What, o'erleap the church-pales and break through constitution?
Sure the devil's your leader and you hunt for confusion!
    Then to horse, etc.   50

At the head of the pack stupid William's commanding,
Who's of quality breed, by his deep understanding;
If to dull worthless whelps we may titles afford,
His merits confess him a dog of a lord;
Those crafty old curs that despise the poor tool,   55
Yet only for luck's sake they hunt with a fool.
    Then to horse, etc.

There's blasphemy Jack that was stripped by Oak Royal,
The republican whelp of a sire that was loyal;
With gaol-birds and whores to plantations he crossed,   60
Till the sharper retrieved what the bubble had lost;
Now in hopes of a place, he still yelps and impeaches,

---

independent divine. Among his writings which Hoadly is here accused of plagiarizing was an
Exhortation to the Taking of the Solemn League and Covenant, 1644. *Peters:* Hugh Peters (1598–
1660) was Cromwell's chaplain and was executed as a regicide in 1660.

41. *the old game:* the Good Old Cause of the English revolutionaries.

44. *doctor:* Sacheverell.

49. *confusion:* "The truth is, the great fundamental principle of the Whigs, is confusion"
(*Most Faults on One Side* [1710], p. 23). Sacheverell gave this book "gilded and neatly covered
to several members of Parliament" (*A Vindication of the Faults on Both Sides* [1710], p. 34).

51. *William:* Lòrd William Powlett (d. 1729) was one of the 20 members chosen by the
Commons to be managers of the Sacheverell trial.

58. *Jack:* John Dolben (1662–1710) was a Whig M.P. *stripped by Oak Royal:* The Royal Oak
was a lottery in which Dolben lost heavily.

59. *a sire that was loyal:* Dolben was the son of John Dolben, archbishop of York (d. 1686).

60. *to plantations he crossed:* Dolben attempted to retrieve his fortunes in the West Indies.

61. *sharper retrieved:* "By the gift of persuasion, which he had paid dearly for, he got into the
good graces of a fair lady with a very great fortune, who, in process of time, was married to
him, and as an access to her beauty, endowed him with all of her bodily goods. This was such
a hit, as repaired the breaches of a broken estate" (*The Life and Adventures of John Dolben,* p. 7).
Dolben continued to gamble even after the recuperation of his finances to such an extent that
his uncle, who had intended to leave him £5,000, wrote into his will that "being unwilling to
have it thrown away at gaming-houses . . . I give J. Dolben no legacy" (ibid., pp. 8–9).

62. *impeaches:* It was Dolben who first complained to the House of Commons on 13 Decem-
ber 1709 about Sacheverell's sermons (Boyer, *Annals,* 1710, p. 221). Next day the Commons
ordered him to "go to the Lords, and at their bar, in the name of all the common of Great
Britain, impeach the said Doctor Henry Sacheverell of high crimes and misdemeanors; and
acquaint the Lords, that this House will, in due time, exhibit articles against the said Dr.
Henry Sacheverell" (*CJ, 16,* 241).

Though your pert forward cur oft himself overreaches.
   Then to horse, etc.

There's Wolf the rapacious, old Bluster and Thunder,   65
Sir Peter the grim and the late Speaker Blunder;
For your dull heavy curs love to mount in a chair,
Though like monkeys that climb they expose their parts bare;
And Jackal the ill-looked, who trains up newcomers,
And still speaks in season, for his wit comes from Somers.   70
   Then to horse, etc.

There's Hackum and Brass for their deep mouths renowned,
Because empty skulls have a great strength of sound;
Send Hackum to Spain, what great feats he'll achieve,
And his conduct's enough to make senates believe;   75
And young Brass of Corinth can never deceive ye,
For he pays off the Cause just as well as the navy.
   Then to horse, etc.

How honor and honesty dogs can unite,
For their dear country's sake, they'll steal, plunder, and bite;   80
Themselves and their whelps they enrich for its good,
And make monarch's great by shedding their blood;
Yet so eager for game, the white staff take away,

---

65. *Wolf:* Thomas, Lord Coningsby (1656?–1729), a Whig M.P. for Leominster from 1689 to 1710. He declined to stand in 1710, possibly fearing that as a manager of the Sacheverell trial he would not be reelected. He was an insatiable place-hunter. *old Bluster and Thunder:* Sir John Hawles (1645–1716), oldest of the managers, known for his peevish disposition.

66. *Peter:* Sir Peter King (1669–1734), whose legal expertise was as significant as his politics in his selection as a manager of the Sacheverell trial. A leading country Whig, he was a defeated candidate for the speakership in 1708. *late Speaker Blunder:* John Smith (1655–1723), who obtained the chair and held it until 1708, when he became chancellor of the exchequer. His "blunder," it may be supposed, was his decision to serve on the committee to impeach Sacheverell, which probably cost him the speakership.

69. *Jackal:* Sir Joseph Jekyll (1663–1738) was a leading spokesman for the junto in the lower house and helped to sponsor the articles of impeachment.

70. *Somers:* Jekyll married Elizabeth, sister of Lord Somers.

72. *Hackum:* James Stanhope (1673–1721), another leading country Whig, who eventually became the only serious rival to Walpole within the party. *Brass:* Robert Walpole (1676–1745), the future prime minister. *for their deep mouths renowned:* Stanhope and Walpole were regarded as being among the ablest orators in the House of Commons.

74. *send Hackum to Spain:* Stanhope, who had been on an embassy to Charles III in 1706, returned to Spain in 1710 and won victories at Almenara and Saragossa in September, but was defeated and captured at Brihuega in December and remained a prisoner of war until 1712.

76. *Brass of Corinth:* Corinthian brass was a symbol of effrontery and shamelessness.

They'd hunt down Volpone for a rank beast of prey.
　　Then to horse, etc.   85

Then Tory, poor Tory, never hope to prevail,
You are beat from the pack with a stone at your tail;
Go learn to plead conscience when you cheat, lie, and cant,
And plunder the public with the looks of a saint;
If you'd join the old set, with new principles fit ye,   90
Stick at nothing that's base, you'll be of the committee.
　　Then to horse, etc.

84. *Volpone:* Godolphin.

JONATHAN SWIFT

The Virtues of Sid Hamet, the Magician's Rod
(12–14 October 1710)

Swift arrived in London on 7 September 1710 empowered to negotiate re-
mission of the first fruits and twentieth parts, a tax of about £1200 a year
that the Irish clergy paid into the English treasury. He was still "much
inclined to be what they called a Whig in politics" (Swift, *Prose, 8,* 120) and
hoped to use his acquaintance with the junto lords to secure this benefaction
for the Church of Ireland. But he found himself in the midst of a ministerial
revolution in which it seemed that "every Whig in great office will, to a
man, be infallibly put out" (Swift, *Journal, 1,* 7).

Within two days of his arrival in London, he called upon Lord Godolphin,
with whom he had discussed this matter in June 1708. It was only a courtesy
call, for Swift could not have expected much help from a cast courtier. Swift
had been offended by Godolphin on the occasion of their first interview when
Godolphin very cynically implied that the price of taking off the first fruits
and twentieth parts was the support of the clergy for repeal of the Test Clause
in Ireland, which Swift and 99 percent of his fellow churchmen felt "would
level the Church Established with every sniveling sect in the nation" (Swift,
Prose, 6, 130). On that occasion, with Godolphin at the height of his power,
Swift could only bow and take his leave. But to be received with coldness by
a politician out of power put very different ideas into Swift's head. It "has
enraged me so, I am almost vowing revenge," he told Esther Johnson (Swift,
Journal, 1, 6).

Three days later at the St. James's coffeehouse Swift ran into another
Whig, Charles Bodvile Robartes, second earl of Radnor, and "talked treason
heartily against the Whigs, their baseness and ingratitude. And I am come
home rolling resentments in my mind and framing schemes of revenge: full
of which (having written down some hints) I go to bed" (*Journal, 1,* 13).

One of these "hints" became *The Virtues of Sid Hamet, the Magician's Rod.*

By 14 October the verses had been published and were being "cried up to
the skies." People "think nobody but Prior or I could write them," Swift
boasted to the ladies in Dublin.

THE VIRTUES OF SID HAMET, THE MAGICIAN'S ROD

The rod was but a harmless wand,
While Moses held it in his hand,
But soon as e'er he laid it down,
'Twas a devouring serpent grown.
    Our great magician, Hamet Sid,   5
Reverses what the prophet did;
His rod was honest English wood,
That senseless in a corner stood,
Till metamorphosed by his grasp,
It grew an all-devouring asp;
Would hiss, and sting, and roll, and twist,   10
By the mere virtue of his fist:
But when he laid it down, as quick
Resumed the figure of a stick.
    So to her midnight feasts the hag   15
Rides on a broomstick for a nag,
That, raised by magic of her breech,
O'er sea and land conveys the witch;
But, with the morning dawn, resumes
The peaceful state of common brooms.   20
    They tell us something strange and odd,
About a certain magic rod,
That, bending down its top, divines
Whene'er the soil has golden mines:
Where there are none, it stands erect,   25
Scorning to show the least respect.
As ready was the wand of Sid
To bend where golden mines were hid;
In Scottish hills found precious ore,
    Achilles' scepter was of wood,

Title. The Magician's Rod: the staff of Lord Treasurer Godolphin, which, on 29 May 1711, was given to Harley.

2. *Moses:* "And the Lord said unto [Moses], What is that in thine hand? And he said, A rod. And he said, Cast it on the ground, and it became a serpent" (Exod. 4:2–3).

3. *laid it down:* The phrase means "resigned his office," but as Swift knew, Godolphin had not resigned; he had been dismissed.

5. *Hamet Sid:* This nickname for Sidney Godolphin is borrowed from Sidi Hamet Benengeli, "the first author" of *Don Quixote,* to whom Cervantes attributes the original work in Arabic.

29–30. Swift gives further currency to the rumor that Godolphin had "lavished away near a million sterling, to bring about the union; with no other design than to retrieve a false step [advising the queen to give her assent to the Act of Security], for which he might have lost his head" (*An Essay towards the History of the Last Ministry and Parliament,* [1710], p. 47).

Where none e'er looked for it before; 30
And, by a gentle bow, divined
How well a cully's purse was lined:
To a forlorn and broken rake,
Stood without motion, like a stake.
    The rod of Hermes was renowned 35
For charms above and under ground;
To sleep could mortal eyelids fix,
And drive departed souls to Styx.
That rod was just a type of Sid's,
Which, o'er a British senate's lids, 40
Could scatter opium full as well,
And drive as many souls to hell.
    Sid's rod was slender, white, and tall,
Which oft he used to fish withal:
A place was fastened to the hook, 45
And many a score of gudgeons took;
Yet, still so happy was his fate,
He caught his fish and saved his bait.
    Sid's brethren of the conj'ring tribe
A circle with their rod describe, 50
Which proves a magical redoubt
To keep mischievous spirits out:
Sid's rod was of a larger stride
And made a circle thrice as wide,
Where spirits thronged with hideous din, 55
And he stood there to take them in.
But, when th' enchanted rod was broke,
They vanished in a stinking smoke.

40. *British senate:* Godolphin undertook to control both houses of Parliament by systematic bribery.

45. *Place:* About 20 place-holders in *A List of Gentlemen That Are in Offices, Employments, etc.,* Cambridge, [1705] had been appointed by Godolphin. After the union, 20 to 25 percent of the House of Commons, called "the Queen's servants," were expected to vote with the ministry. In the House of Lords the figure was between 40 and 50 percent.

48. Cf. "They blame [Harley] for his slowness in turning people [Whigs] out; but I suppose he had his reasons" (Swift, *Journal, 1,* 298). Surely the reason is that an unfilled post can secure the votes of half a dozen hopeful candidates, whereas only one can be gained by filling it.

55. *spirits thronged:* Defoe observed that the scores of Scots who came to London after the union "gaping for preferment . . . served only to make the *English* jealous and uneasy" (*An Essay at Removing National Prejudices against a Union with Scotland,* part I [1706], p. 7).

59. *Achilles' scepter:* The scepter on which Achilles swore his awful oath in the *Iliad I* was

Like Sid's, but nothing near so good;   60
Though down from ancestors divine
Transmitted to the hero's line,
Thence, through a long descent of kings,
Came an heirloom, as Homer sings,
Though this description looks so big,   65
That scepter was a sapless twig:
Which, from the fatal day when first
It left the forest where 'twas nursed,
As Homer tells us o'er and o'er,
Nor leaf, nor fruit, nor blossom bore.   70
Sid's scepter, full of juice, did shoot
In golden boughs and golden fruit,
And he, the dragon never sleeping,
Guarded each fair Hesperian pippin.
No hobby-horse, with gorgeous top,   75
The dearest in Charles Mather's shop,
Or glittering tinsel of May-Fair,
Could with this rod of Sid compare.
   Dear Sid, then why were thou so mad
To break thy rod like naughty lad?   80
You should have kissed it in your distress,
And then returned it to your mistress,
Or made it a Newmarket switch,
And not a rod for thy own breech.
   But since old Sid has broken this,   85
His next may be a rod in piss.

Agamemnon's. Hephaistos had made it for Zeus, and it descended to Agamemnon through
Pelops, Atreus, and Thyestes.
   66–70. Swift virtually translates lines 234–37 of *Iliad I*.
   76. *Charles Mather:* a toy seller in Fleet Street.
   77. *May-Fair:* an annual fair held near Hyde Park.
   83. *a Newmarket switch:* Godolphin was attending the races at Newmarket in April 1710
when Anne made the first move toward replacing his ministry by appointing Shrewsbury as
her lord chamberlain.
   86. *a rod in piss:* "a prospective punishment, scolding" (Partridge).

ARTHUR MAINWARING

An Excellent New Song Called "Mat's Peace"
(1711)

The making of the peace of Utrecht was the most momentous event in ths last years of Anne's reign. Harley had come to power in 1710 with a definite policy of cutting through the Gordian knot of the war. His predecessors had been accused of failing to end hostilities because of an unreasonable insistence that Louis XIV should assist the allies in removing his own grandson from the throne of Spain. After the Battle of Almanza in April 1707 it became increasingly clear that Charles III's title was almost entirely nominal and that the attempt to make it real was doomed. Hopes revived in September 1710 when Stanhope rallied the allied forces in Spain and actually got to Madrid. But they were forever dashed in December when he was defeated and captured at Brihuega. Harley had probably already decided to cut his losses and to reach agreement with France on the basis of recognizing the Bourbon claimant as king of Spain.

Since such a policy required an abandonment of allied war aims, initial moves had to be made in secret. Private negotiations were opened between the British and French ministries through the mediation of the earl of Jersey and the Abbé Gaultier. These unofficial talks developed to a stage where the discussion of preliminary articles for a treaty could be arranged in the summer of 1711.

Accordingly, in July 1711 Matthew Prior was sent secretly to Paris to discuss peace terms with the marquis de Torcy, the French foreign minister. In these talks the British government agreed to recognize Philip V as king of Spain, and to partition the rest of the Spanish Empire between him and the archduke Charles. Although Prior had an audience with Louis XIV, who assured him of his eagerness for peace, the French refused to commit themselves immediately, but sent him back to England accompanied by Nicolas Mesnager, who was authorized to negotiate preliminaries.

Prior's journey remained a secret until his return to England with Mesnager. When he landed at Deal, however, he was discovered by the vigilance of John Macky, the customs officer. Macky intercepted the men at Canterbury and immediately reported his discovery to the duke of Marlborough and the earl of Sunderland, who warned their friends at home and abroad that clandestine moves for peace were afoot. St. John was furious and dismissed Macky, but it was too late. The news of "Mat's Peace" was out. The government tried in vain to throw a smokescreen over the whole affair by getting Swift to compile an almost entirely fictitious account of Prior's visit in which Swift conveyed the impression that the government had insisted not only on the cession of Spain to Charles III by Philip V, but that the French should help bring about the transfer.

An Excellent New Song Called "Mat's Peace," or The Downfall of Trade

To the Good Old Tune of "Green-sleeves"

The news from abroad does a secret reveal,
Which has been confirmed both at Dover and Deal,
That one Mr. Matthew, once called plain Mat,
Has been doing at Paris the Lord knows what.
But sure what they talk of his negotiation,   5
Is only intended to banter the nation:
For why have we spent so much treasure in vain.
If now at the last we must give up Spain,
    If now we must give up Spain?

Why so many battles did Marlborough win?   10
So many strong towns why did he take in?
Why did he his army to Germany lead,
The crown to preserve on the emperor's head?
Why does he the honor of England advance?
And why has he humbled the monarch of France   15
By passing the lines and taking Bouchain,
If now at the last we must give up Spain,
    If now we must give up Spain?

Our stocks were so high and our credit so good
(I mean all the while our late ministry stood),   20
That foreigners hither their money did send,

12. *army to Germany:* Marlborough took the allied forces to the Danube and fought the Battle of Blenheim in 1704 to rescue the emperor.

16. *Bouchain:* Marlborough's last military victory in September 1711 was the capture of Bouchain, a citadel on the Scheldt, after a siege lasting twenty days.

19. *stocks:* Between 1707 and 1710 bank stock never fell below par. *credit:* On 22 February 1709 the Bank of England "opened their books for a new subscription of £2,200,000 towards next years taxes, and in 5 hours the whole was subscribed; a 5th part of which was paid down, and a great deal more offered to be subscribed, but refused" (Luttrell, *6,* 410).

And bankers abroad took a pleasure to lend.
But though all the service was duly supplied,
And nought was embezzled or misapplied,
By all that wise management what shall we gain,   25
If now at the last we must give up Spain,
   If now we must give up Spain?

We made this alliance, as well it is known,
That Austria's great house might recover their own:
King Charles is part of this kingdom possessed,   30
And Bouchain would quickly fright France from the rest.
For sure the whole nation by this time must know,
The way to Madrid is by Paris to go;
But why have we made such a glorious campaign,
If now at the last we must give up Spain,   35
   If now we must give up Spain?

All treaties with France may be sung or be said,
Tomorrow they'll break what today they have made;
And therefore our senate did wisely address
That none should be made while they Spain did possess.   40
The queen too to them did last sessions declare,
That Spain ought to be their particular care:
But speeches, addresses and senates are vain,
If now at the last we must give up Spain,
   If now we must give up Spain.   45
     By giving up Spain, we give up all our trade;

29. *Austria . . . might recover their own:* The Grand Alliance stipulated for the Austrian Hapsburgs "the procuring an equitable and reasonable satisfaction to His Imperial Majesty for his pretension to the Spanish succession" (*EHD, 8,* 873).

30. *part:* By 1711 the Austrian archduke Charles had obtained possessions in Italy and the Netherlands.

31. *the rest:* Philip V was in effective control of all Spain except Catalonia and the West Indies.

39. *senate . . . address:* On 19 December 1707 the House of Lords resolved "That no peace can be honorable or safe, for Her Majesty and her allies, if Spain and the Spanish West Indies be suffered to continue in the power of the House of Bourbon" (*LJ,* 18, 393).

41. On 25 November 1710 the queen used the following expression in her speech at the opening of Parliament: "The carrying on the war in all its parts, but particularly in Spain, with the utmost vigor, is the likeliest means, with God's blessing, to procure a safe and honorable peace for us and all our allies" (*Cobbett's Parl. Hist., 6,* 928).

46. *give up . . . our trade:* The war aim of "No peace without Spain" became the policy of the Grand Alliance in 1703 when Portugal joined on condition that the Bourbons should be ousted from the Iberian peninsula. Consequent to the Portuguese's adhering to the alliance the English signed a very favorable commercial treaty with them, whereby they obtained port wine and bullion in exchange for cloth. This is the trade that the Whigs held would be jeopardized by the peace preliminaries recognising Philip V as king of Spain.

In vain would they tell us a treaty is made
For yielding us forts in the distant South Seas,
To manage our traffic with safety and ease.
No lies are too gross for such impudent fellows,   50
Of forts in the moon as well they might tell us;
Since France at her pleasure may take them again,
If now at the last we must give up Spain,
If now we must give up Spain.

Some lords were impeached for a famous partition,   55
Which kept the allies in far better condition;
For then of raw silk we were only bereft,
But now neither silver nor gold will be left.
If that treaty then did impeachment require,
Sure this calls at least for the rope or the fire;   60
Since British had never such cause to complain,
If now at the last we must give up Spain,
    If now we must give up Spain.

When Petticum to Paris did openly go,
What doubts and what jealousies did we not show: 65
How loudly did we against Holland exclaim,
Yet surely our statesmen are now more to blame.
For how can they think our allies will not fire
At privately sending that Machiavel Prior,
Who richly deserves to be whipped for his pain,   70
If now at the last we must give up Spain,
    If now we must give up Spain?

Since matters stand thus, I am sorely afraid,
Whenever this scandalous peace shall be made,
Our senate for Cato will quickly decree   75
Some punishment worse than a sting of a bee.
Poor Mat in the pillory soon will be seen
For Mortimer too, Oh! well had it been
That he in his hole had been pleased to remain,
If now at the last we must give up Spain,   80
    If now we must give up Spain.

48. *forts in the distant South Seas:* To make the peace acceptable to the business community
the new or Harley ministry held out hopes of profitable trade with Spanish colonial posses-
sions. The actual concessions wrested from Spain in the Assiento and commercial treaties of
1713 were disappointing to the City. Not only were forts not obtained in the Pacific, but the
English were not allowed to trade directly with the Spanish East Indies, and could only deal
with Spain's American possessions.

55. *lords were impeached:* In 1701 four Whig lords were impeached by the House of Com-
mons for allowing William III to negotiate the partition treaties of 1698 and 1700, without
consulting his Privy Council or Parliament.

The Procession
(November 1711)

To celebrate the 153d anniversary of the accession of Queen Elizabeth on 17 November 1558, the the Whigs planned a public spectacle unequaled since the great pope-burning processions of November 1679, 1680, and 1681, which had been directed by the first earl of Shaftesbury.

The pageant of 1711 appropriated many features of Shaftesbury's procession including "six beadles with Protestant flails" and introduced striking innovations such as "twenty four bagpipes marching four and four, and playing the memorable tune of *Lillibullero*."

Swift explained the whole thing to Stella on 17 November: "The Whigs designed a mighty procession by midnight, and had laid out a thousand pounds to dress up the pope, devil, cardinals, Sacheverell, etc., and carry them with torches about, and burn them . . . but they were seized last night by order from the secretary [Dartmouth]. . . . The militia was raised to prevent it, and now, I suppose, all will be quiet" (Swift, *Journal*, *2*, 415–16). All was indeed quiet and there was no celebration for the Protestant queen.

THE PROCESSION: A NEW PROTESTANT BALLAD

To an Excellent Italian Tune

Let's sing the new ministry's praise
   With hearts most thankful and glad,
For the statesmen of these our days
   Are the wisest that ever we had.

But not to wander too far   5
   In the maze of their endless merit,
I'll give you an instance most rare
   Of their vigilance, wisdom, and spirit.

They heard on Queen Bess's birthday
   The 'prentices had an intent   10
Th' old Protestant gambol to play,
   Which churchmen, they thought, should prevent.

The frolic, it seems, was no less
  Than to carry about in procession
A pope in ridiculous dress   15
  And to burn it by way of diversion.

Besides these turbulent folk
  (Than their ancestors much more uncivil)
To their pageant had added the joke
  Of a Perkin and eke of a devil,   20

With cardinals, Jesuits, friars,
  A cartload together at least,
Intended to crown their bonfires,
  A very unseas'nable jest.

For sure there could be no sense,   25
  When a peace is coming upon us,
T' affront such a powerful prince
  As the pope; why it might have undone us.

Then if the most Christian king
  Should have taken it ill at our hand,   30
Such a very unmannerly thing
  Might have put the peace to a stand.

The Jacobites next, to be sure,
  Would have risen to defend their master;
And who could have told where a cure   35
  Could be found for such a disaster?

Besides it would bear a doubt,
  Whether burning the pope and the devil
Might not be designed to flout
  At high-church and Dr. Sacheverell.   40

Furthermore in these days of sin,

12. *churchmen, they thought, should prevent:* "The court," Swift said, "apprehensive of a design
to inflame the common people, thought fit to order that the several figures should be seized
as popish trinkets; and the guards were ordered to patrol for preventing any tumultuous
assemblies" (*Prose, 7,* 28). But "it appeared very strange, that a popular rejoicing so grateful
to this Protestant City, which was never attempted to be quashed but in King James the
Second's reign, should at this juncture, be interrupted" (Boyer, *Annals,* 1712, p. 279).
  20. *Perkin:* the pretender.
  29. *most Christian king:* The style and title of the kings of France included the phrase, "Rex
Christianissimus."

'Twas feared by folks that were hearty,
A numerous mob might have been
Even raised for the devil and's party.

'Twas therefore expedient found									45
To send the footguards on the scout,
To search all the suburbs around,
And find the bold pageant out.

They took it, and as it was fit,
A magistrate wise and great										50
The criminals straight did commit,
That the law might determine their fate.

Then for fear of a rescue by night,
At which we should all have been troubled,
'Twas ordered (and sure that was right)								55
That the guards should be everywhere doubled.

Besides that no harm might come nigh us,
The bands so well trained were drawn out,
And as long as those heroes stand by us
The devil himself we may rout.										60

What though some people did sneer,
And call 'em the pope's life guard;
They stood to their arms and their beer
All night, and kept watch and ward.

So God save our gracious queen,										65
And her ministers every one,
And he that don't say amen,
Is a churl, and may let it alone.

The Hanover house God preserve,
And blast the pretender's hope,										70
The Protestant cause let's serve,
And give to the devil the pope.

50. *A magistrate:* The "magistrate" was the secretary of state, William Legge, the newly created earl of Dartmouth.
51. *The criminals:* the wax figures found in a house off Drury Lane.
58. The trained bands were the militia of the City of London and the county of Middlesex.

JONATHAN SWIFT

An Excellent New Song
(6 December 1711)

Daniel Finch, second earl of Nottingham, was the leading Anglican layman of his day. His defection to the Whigs in November 1710 was not only a surprise in itself, but it tied together an outstanding event of the early years of Anne's reign—the triple failure of the Tories to pass a bill against occasional conformity—and the outstanding event of the last years of the reign—the enactment of the Treaty of Utrecht.

Although he had done nothing to bring down the Godolphin ministry, Nottingham expected to share with Harley and Shrewsbury in the spoils. And although he was violently opposed to Harley's "wild and unwarrantable scheme of balancing parties," as he called it, he expected to be included in this scheme (Horwitz, p. 228). Early in the session of November 1710–June 1711 his opposition took the form of demands for criminal prosecution of the late ministers, which ingratiated him with the October Club Tories just organizing themselves in the House of Commons.

Harley made three attempts, short of taking him into the government, to regain Nottingham's support. The first, in February 1711, ended with Nottingham's walking out of the meeting muttering strange threats that "if we did not act in concert with the Whigs, we should soon find the effects of our good-nature" (Burnet, *6*, 37 *n.*). The second, in October 1711, was a letter, to which Nottingham returned a very chilly answer. Soon after this, Oxford learned the meaning of Nottingham's threat: he had joined with the Whigs to bring down the ministry on the question of peace without Spain.

Oxford responded by proroguing Parliament to give the Scots lords more traveling time. Then he made a third attempt to engage Nottingham in the court interest but was again rebuffed. Oxford also begged the queen to "speak to a certain lord who was looked upon as dubious" (Swift, *Prose, 2,* 147). Then, counting the pensionary lords who "were only kept in awe by fear of offending the crown" (ibid., *7,* 17), he concluded that he had a majority of ten in the House of Lords and decided not to ask for a further prorogation.

At the last minute Oxford caused to be inserted in *The Post Boy*, 6 December 1711, the following public notice:

Where a very tall, thin, swarthy complectioned man, between 60 and 70 years of age, wearing a brown coat, with little sleeves and long pockets, has lately withdrawn himself from his friends, being seduced by wicked persons to follow ill courses, these are to give notice, that whoever shall discover him, shall have 10s. reward; or if he will voluntarily return, he shall be kindly received by his friends, who will not reproach him for past follies, provided he give good assurances, that, for the future, he will firmly adhere to the Church of England, in which he was so carefully educated by his honest parents.

At the last minute Oxford hinted to Swift at dinner that he wished a ballad made on Nottingham. Swift sent off to the printer the next day "the ballad, two degrees above Grubstreet" (Swift, *Journal*, 2, 430–31). In this work of pure imagination and a few facts supplied by Oxford and Dartmouth, Swift not only brings to life the second earl of Nottingham, but writes the speech that he delivered the next day in the House of Lords.

An Excellent New Song, Being the Intended
Speech of a Famous Orator against Peace

An orator dismal of Nottinghamshire,
Who has forty years let out his conscience to hire,
Out of zeal for his country, and want of a place,
Is come up, vi et armis, to break the queen's peace.

1. *dismal:* "So they call him from his looks" (Swift, *Journal*, 2, 430).

2. *forty years:* Finch entered Parliament in a by-election for the borough of Great Bedwin, Wiltshire, in February 1673. Before the election he took care to provide a new town hall for Great Bedwin (Horwitz, p. 7).

3. *want of a place:* Although rumors had made him secretary of state in June, first lord of the admiralty in September, and lord privy seal in December 1710, Nottingham had been carefully excluded from Harley's "balanced" government. "Upon the earl of Rochester's decease [21 May 1711], he conceived that the crown would hardly overlook him for president of the council: and deeply resented that disappointment. But the duke of Newcastle lord privy seal dying some time after [15 July 1711], he found that office was . . . disposed of to [John Robinson] the bishop of Bristol" (Swift, *Prose*, 7, 16). Harley thought he was an "old woman" (Horwitz, p. 222) and he was "disagreeable personally to the queen" (Bolingbroke, *1*, 281). Since he had been out of office since May 1704 (when Harley replaced him as secretary of state), he was "as sour and fiercely wild as . . . anything . . . that has lived long in the desert" (*HMC, Portland, 5*, 119).

4. *vi et armis:* with force and arms. *the queen's peace:* "the general peace and order of the

He has vamped an old speech, and the court to their sorrow,   5
Shall hear him harangue against Prior tomorrow.
When once he begins, he never will flinch,
But repeats the same note the whole day, like a finch.
I have heard all the speech repeated by Hoppy,
And, mistakes to prevent, I have obtain'd a copy.   10

THE SPEECH

Whereas, notwithstanding, I am in great pain,
To hear we are making a peace without Spain;
But, most noble senators, 'tis a great shame
There should be a peace, while I'm not in game.
The duke showed me all his fine house; and the duchess   15
From a closet brought out a full purse in her clutches:
I talked of a peace, and they both gave a start;
His Grace swore by—, and Her Grace let a f—t:
My long old-fashioned pocket was presently crammed;
And sooner than vote for a peace I'll be d—ned.   20
But some will cry, turncoat, and rip up old stories,
How I always pretended to be for the Tories:
I answer; the Tories were in my good graces,
Till all my relations were put into places.

---

realm as provided for by law" (*OED*, s.v. "peace," sb. 9b.). In the context, however, "the queen's peace" meant a treaty with France on the basis of the six preliminary articles that Prior had brought back from France in August 1711 and that had been printed in *The Post Boy*, 13–16 October 1711. Since Somerset was industriously spreading the rumor that the preliminary articles were not acceptable to the queen, it was important by this phrase to suggest that they were. And now, or shortly hereafter, "The queen's peace" became a favorite Tory toast.

5. *an old speech:* On 19 December 1707 Nottingham had opened an attack in the House of Lords on the Godolphin ministry for the failures in Spain.

8. *finch:* Nottingham's family name.

9. *Hoppy:* Hoppy may be Edward Hopkins (1675–1736), an M.P.

15. *The duke:* Swift imagines that Nottingham's recruitment to Whiggery took place at Blenheim. Actually it took place in London during an interview with Marlborough and Godolphin.

16. *a full purse:* Cf. "The earl of Nottingham became a convert for reasons already mentioned. Money was distributed where occasion required" (Swift, *Prose, 7,* 108).

24. *relations were put into places:* A disappointed candidate for the bishopric of Carlisle in June 1703 complained that Lord Nottingham "lays his hand on all church preferment. His brother, his chaplains, and his favorites are all taken care of". Nottingham had already succeeded in getting his brother, Henry Finch, promoted to the deanery of York, and his "favorites," Humphrey Prideaux and William Nicolson to the deanery of Norwich and to the bishopric of Carlisle (Luttrell, *5,* 164, 171). More recently, two of his nephews, the earl of Dartmouth and Sir Thomas Benson, had been appointed secretary of state and lord of the treasury, respectively. His friend John Annesley, 4th earl of Anglesey, had been appointed paymaster of Ireland, and a prebendal stall at Canterbury had been added to his brother's

But still I'm in principle ever the same,   25
And will quit my best friends, while I'm not in game.
    When I and some others subscribed our names
To a plot for expelling my master King James;
I withdrew my subscription by help of a blot,
And so might discover, or gain by the plot: 30
I had my advantage, and stood at defiance,
For Daniel was got from the den of the lions.
I came in without danger; and was I to blame?
For rather than hang, I would be not in game.
    I swore to the queen that the prince of Hanover   35
During her sacred life, should never come over:
I made use of a trope; that an heir to invite,
Was like keeping her monument always in sight.
But when I thought proper, I altered my note;
And in her own hearing I boldly did vote,   40
That Her Majesty stood in great need of a tutor,
And must have an old, or a young coadjutor:

---

benefices. In June 1711, his nephew, Heneage Finch, had been made master of Her Majesty's jewel house, his indigent cousin, Charles Finch, earl of Winchilsea, was put at the head of the new commission for trade and plantations, an office worth £1500 a year and another "favorite," John Ward, was made a Welsh judge. Finally, in July 1711, his son-in-law, Sir Roger Mostyn, was made paymaster-general of the marines (Boyer, *History*, pp. 500, 514–15). By this time St. John could hope that "his relations are so well provided for, that . . . he ought to be contented" (Bolingbroke, *1*, 281).

  27. *subscribed our names:* Nottingham had been approached in June 1688 to join the conspiracy to send an invitation to William of Orange to seize the English throne. "Upon the first proposition [he] entertained it, and agreed to it. But at their next meeting he said he had considered better of that matter" (Burnet, *1*, 764) and his name is not included among the "Immortal Seven" who signed the invitation in cipher. His own account of this episode, written many years later, says nothing about a blotted signature: "This was the greatest difficulty that ever I was plunged into in my whole life. . . . I was indeed asham'd to quit the Company who had admitted me into their Secrets and on the other hand I did not dare to proceed in an affair of which the next step would be high treason" (PRO Finch, S. Political Papers 148, p. 10, quoted in Horwitz, p. 52).

  35. *swore to the queen:* While he was still secretary of state (May 1702–May 1704), Nottingham told the queen, according to Lord Dartmouth, "that whoever proposed bringing over her successor in her life-time, did it with a design to depose her" (Burnet, *5*, 227*n*.).

  37–38. The italicization of these lines may indicate that they are the *ipsissima verba* of Nottingham in his interview with the queen (35 *n*. above). Since Dartmouth was an intimate friend of Swift, he may have provided the quotation.

  39. *altered my note:* Having made these assurances to the queen while he was secretary of state, Nottingham turned around in November 1705, after he had been dismissed, and voted to invite the dowager electress of Hanover to reside in England (Horwitz, p. 205).

  40. *in her own hearing:* "The queen heard the debate, and seemed amazed at the behaviour of some, who when they had credit with her . . . had possessed her with deep prejudices against it" (Burnet, *2*, 430). Dartmouth records that "This made an impression upon the queen to Lord Nottingham that could never be overcome" (Burnet, *5*, 227*n*.).

For why; I would fain have put all in a flame,
Because, for some reasons, I was not in game.

Now my new benefactors have brought me about,   45
And I'll vote against peace, with Spain, or without:
Though the court gives my nephews, and brothers, and cousins,
And all my whole family, places by dozens;
Yet since I knew where a full purse may be found,
And hardly pay eighteenpence tax in the pound: 50
Since the Tories have thus disappointed my hopes,
And will neither regard my figures nor tropes;
I'll speech against peace while Dismal's my name,
And be a true Whig, while I'm not in game.

46. *against peace, with Spain, or without:* Oxford recognized that "the outcry against a peace at this time is raised by the art and cunning of some who are against any peace" (HMC, *Portland, 5,* 120).

49. *full purse:* Swift believed that "Nottingham had certainly been bribed" (*Journal, 2,* 432).

50. *eighteenpence tax in the pound:* This is intended to outrage Tory squires who were paying the wartime tax on their estates of four shillings, or forty-eight pence, in the pound.

52. *figures nor tropes:* Nottingham indeed lived up to expectations. In his speech he referred to France, "our enemy" as "a loose card" that we ought not "to be put to our trumps" to take (HMC, *Lords,* n.s., *9,* 369).

[WILLIAM SHIPPEN]

The Character of a Certain Whig
(31 December 1711)

The genre of this poem is announced in its title. It is a "character" of Thomas Wharton, fifth baron, first earl, and eventually (February 1715) first marquess of Wharton. Its announcement as a character probably should imply that it will not be impartial, that it will have a theme. The second expectation is fulfilled in Wharton's "joined contradictions" (line 4), a theme carefully built up in lines 5–17 to achieve a climax in line 18 in the image of the sane madman.

THE CHARACTER OF A CERTAIN WHIG

Industrious, unfatigued in faction's cause,
Sworn enemy to God, his church, and laws,
He dotes on mischief for dear mischief's sake,
Joins contradictions in his wond'rous make;
A flattering bully and a stingy rake;   5
Joins depth of cunning with excess of rage,

1. *faction's cause:* Wharton's energy as a Whig election manager may be judged from the following: hearings at a trial in Yorkshire in which Wharton was defendant opened at ten o'clock in the morning on 7 May 1708 and the court sat all night. "As soon as the judge began to summon up the evidence to the jury, [Wharton] left the court, went into his coach and six horses, and ordered his coachman to drive him directly to Woburn [his seat in Buckinghamshire] where he got up about twelve at night, and rose at five next morning, set out at six for Malmesbury, where, having rode thirty miles of the way a-horseback, he arrived at night. The next day was the election of members for that borough, which he managed with that dexterity and dispatch as to carry it for both of his friends [Henry Mordaunt and Thomas Farrington], and on the morrow took coach for London" (*Memoirs of the Life of the Most Noble Thomas, Late Marquess of Wharton* [1715], pp. 43–44).

2. *enemy to God:* "As long as he was talked of," Wharton was called "an atheist grafted on a Presbyterian" (Burnet, *5*, 228 *n.*). In 1680 Wharton was arrested and fined £1000 for desecrating Gloucester Cathedral. In December 1705, during a debate in the House of Lords when Wharton ridiculed the idea that the church was in danger, the old duke of Leeds stood up and said, "If there were any that had pissed against a communion table, or done his other occasions in a pulpit, he should not think the church safe in such hands. Upon which Lord Wharton was very silent for the rest of the day" (Burnet, *5*, 236 *n*).

Lewdness of youth with impotence of age;
Descending, though of race illustrious born,
To such vile actions as a slave would scorn.
A viceroy once, by unpropitious fate, 10
The rule and the robber of the state,
His dignity and honor he secures
By oaths, profaneness, ribaldry, and whores;
Kisses the man whom just before he bit,
Vends lies for jests and perjury for wit 15
To great and small alike extends his frauds,
Plund'ring the crown and bilking rooks and bawds;
His mind still working, mad, of peace bereft,
And malice eating what the pox has left;
A monster whom no vice can bigger swell, 20
Abhorred by Heaven and long since due to Hell.

8. *race illustrious:* Although the Whartons appear to have been at Wharton [Westmorland] since the time of Edward I [1272–1307], the pedigree begins with Thomas Wharton who was M.P. for Appleby, 1436–37.

10. *viceroy:* The "unpropitious fate" that let Wharton rule and rob Ireland was the death on 28 October 1708 of Prince George, the royal consort. In her grief Anne was unable to hold out any longer against the junto's demands for a post for Wharton, and on 15 November 1708 she allowed him to kiss her hand as the lord lieutenant of Ireland. Wharton also "urged his active star" by blackmailing Godolphin. Then, during the short time he was in Ireland (April–September 1709, May–August 1710), he was able to steal at least £45,000 (Swift, *Prose, 3,* 181). According to another source he found over £70,000 in the Irish treasury upon his arrival in Dublin and "left but 29 shillens and 6 pence" after his departure (BM Add. MS 31143, f. 595).

15. *lies:* "Are you such a simpleton," Wharton said, "as not to know that a lie well believed is as good as if it were true?" (Burnet, *5,* 228 *n.*).

[ARTHUR MAINWARING]

The Queen's Speech
(December 1711?)

The following song is a remarkably close parody in a difficult stanza form of the queen's words at the opening of the second session of her fourth Parliament on 7 December 1711. But more remarkable is the great economy of means used to generate irony in the poem. The humble non sequitur, as in "By which" (line 12) and "therefore" (line 21), produces very sophisticated ironical effects. The slight mistake of saying "ally" (line 10) for "enemy" seems to generate a disproportionately large ironic jolt. And introduction of such stubborn words as "pain" (line 11) and "ruin" (line 34) into the bland and windy discourse of governments is sharply reductive.

The discourse here parodied was one of the most important that Anne had to make. She and her servants were now irreversibly committed to peace on terms that had been negotiated, separately and secretly, with the enemy. They "were willing," therefore, in James Macpherson's words which are not without their own ironies, "to have some account of the progress of that important measure to lay before the two houses, when they should first assemble. The speech with which the queen opened the session was more suitable to the known design of her servants, than in itself sincere" (James Macpherson, *Original Papers, Containing the Secret History of Great Britain from the Restoration to the Accession of the House of Hanover*, 1775, 2, 506).

As soon as Anne had spoken her part, taken off her royal robes, and come back to the House of Lords incognito to hear the debate and possibly, by her presence, to moderate it, Lord Nottingham was launched into a long and labored speech. He was moving that a clause be inserted in the usual address of thanks for the queen's speech, "That no peace can be safe or honourable to Great Britain or Europe, if Spain and the West Indies are to be allotted to any branch of the House of Bourbon" (*LJ, 19*, 336). Five hours later Nottingham's clause had been carried in the affirmative by a vote of 61–55, and the Oxford ministry and peace without Spain were both in high jeopardy.

743

THE QUEEN'S SPEECH

To the Tune of "Packington's Pound"

As soon as I could I have called you together,
Though twice I've prorogued you, since first you came hither,
My council, 'tis true, who with France have been treating,
Were somewhat in pain, when they thought of your meeting.
  But since it is known,   5
  Our Commons have shown
A decent regard to French coin, and our own,
To take your advice I'm no longer afraid,
Concerning a peace which already is made.

The French, our allies, their concurrence express,   10
The Indies and Spain for themselves to possess;
By which I establish your freedom and laws,
The Protestant church, and the Hanover cause.
  By this too your trade
  So large will be made,   15
That in future times it of me shall be said;
For such loyal people my love was no other,
Than that of a tender affectionate mother.

2. *twice . . . prorogued:* After the usual series of prorogations during the summer, Parliament was twice prorogued after most of the peers and members had returned to London in the fall, once on 13 November and again on 27 November 1711.

3. *council:* Yet another prorogation was proposed at a meeting of the Privy Council on the night of 5 December, "but some members . . . having represented the fears and jealousies which such an adjournment, after so many prorogations, might create in the minds of the people," the proposal miscarried (Boyer, *History,* p. 525). *France:* The preliminary articles were signed for France by the Comte de St. Menager on 27 September 1711 and published in *The Post Boy,* 13–16 October 1711. A great outcry went up when it was learned that Spain and Spanish America had been abandoned to Louis XIV's grandson and that the only guarantee that the two crowns would not be united under a Bourbon Monarch was Louis XIV's bona fides, which was already a joke.

8. *advice:* Although the conduct of foreign affairs was still the exclusive prerogative of the crown, there was also a tradition that war was declared and peace concluded with the advice and consent of Parliament.

10. *The French, our allies:* This is a daring transposition to create a shocking phrase, for France had been the enemy since Louis XIV declared war in 1689 and Englishmen had died fighting Frenchmen only three months before in the siege of Bouchain. What Anne actually said was, "Our allies (especially the States General), whose interest I look upon as inseparable from my own, have, by their ready concurrence, expressed their entire confidence in me" (*LJ, 19,* 335). The emperor, as the Hapsburg claimant to the Spanish throne, was in fact vehemently opposed to the congress, and the Austrian ambassador had protested against the preliminary articles so violently that he had been declared persona non grata and expelled.

Queen Anne's Entirely English Heart, the reverse of an accession medal
executed by John Croker.

The princes and states that engaged in the war,
I wisely have left of themselves to take care;   20
And therefore our friendship sure never can cease,
But all will unite for securing the peace.
   And since as you find
   The French are so kind,
To take the poor lot that for them is designed,   25
I hope none will envy Great Britain or me
The glory of making such terms as you see.

All former abuses I now will redress
And hang up the men that have served with success;
This notice I give you, that you may confound   30
All those that have made me so great and renowned;
   And this I propose
   To show all my foes,
That we are a people most unanimous;
So may God direct you in your wise consultations,   35
To ruin these happy and flourishing nations.

28–31. The queen declared her intention "to correct and redress such abuses as may have crept into any part of the administration during so long a war." Although the poet may not have known that they were ready to proceed against Marlborough, General William Cadogan, and Rober Walpole, he did know that a commission for examining the public accounts had been voted during the previous session and that six of the seven commissioners were members of the October Club.

32–36. "I cannot conclude," the queen said, "without earnestly recommending to you all unanimity and that you will carefully avoid everything which may give occasion to the enemy to think us a people divided amongst ourselves, and consequently prevent our obtaining that good peace of which we have such reasonable hopes and so near a view. I pray God direct your consultations to this end, that, being delivered from the hardships of war, you may become a happy and a flourishing people."

JONATHAN SWIFT

The Fable of Midas
(14 February 1712)

Harley had tried twice to salvage Marlborough for a moderate ministry and had failed both times. And St. John predicted correctly what would be the result: "The moment he leaves the service and loses the protection of the court, such scenes will open as no victories can varnish over" (Bolingbroke, *1,* 81). But even before Harley's second attempt, Swift had begun, presumably with the ministry's consent, his own attack on Marlborough in *The Examiner,* 23 November 1710. This was followed up by *The Examiner* of 8 February 1711 in which Marlborough, in the guise of Crassus the triumvir, was accused of "that odious and ignoble vice of covetousness" (Swift, *Prose, 3,* 84). These attacks, however, were tempered by praise for Crassus's "gracefulness," "understanding," and "subduing of his anger."

But Marlborough's understanding seems to have failed him when he came home from the victorious campaign of 1711 to throw himself into frantic and discreditable attempts to overturn the Oxford ministry. His vote against the peace preliminaries on 7 December 1711 sealed his fate. *The Fable of Midas* is unqualified in its monumental scorn.

The disgrace of Marlborough was one of the most difficult decisions taken by the Oxford ministry. It could not fail to have dangerous repercussions both at home and abroad. That the scheme succeeded may be attributed partly to an effective propaganda campaign. Oxford, who believed that in propaganda the only defense is a good offense, was delighted with *The Fable of Midas,* according to Swift (*Journal, 2,* 488).

Midas, we are in story told,
Turned everything he touched to gold:
He chipped his bread, the pieces round
Glittered like spangles on the ground:
A codling e'er it went his lip in,   5
Would straight become a golden pippin:
He called for drink, you saw him sup
Potable gold in golden cup.
His empty paunch that he might fill,
He sucked his vittles through a quill: 10
Untouched it passed between his grinders,
Or't had been happy for gold finders.
He cocked his hat, you would have said
Mambrino's helm adorned his head.
Whene'er he chanced his hands to lay,   15
On magazines of corn or hay,
Gold ready coined appeared, instead
Of paltry provender and bread:
Hence we are by wise farmers told
Old hay is equal to old gold;   20
And hence a critic deep maintains,
We learned to weigh our gold by grains.
     This fool had got a lucky hit,
And people fancied he had wit:
Two gods their skill in music tried,   25
And both chose Midas to decide;

5. *codling:* a variety of cooking apple.

14. *Mambrino's helm:* Mambrino is a pagan king in *Orlando Furioso* whose golden helmet is acquired by Rinaldo. Don Quixote took possession of a barber's basin under the delusion that it was the helmet of Mambrino.

17. *Gold ready coined:* Marlborough too turned bread into gold. The commissioners of public accounts reported to the House of Commons on 21 December 1711 that between 1702 and 1711 Antonio Alvarez Machado and Sir Solomon Medina paid Marlborough £62,000 for the contract to supply bread to the army (*CJ, 17,* 15–16).

21. *critic deep:* The one cited by *OED* is Robert Recorde, *The Ground of Artes* (1565), p. 202: "the least portion of weight is commonly a grain, meaning a grain of . . . wheat, dry, and gathered out of the middle of the ear."

25. *Two gods:* "In a musical contest between Apollo and Pan, Midas decided for the latter, whereupon Apollo changed his ears to those of an ass, which the king attempted to conceal beneath a high Phrygian cap" (Swift, *Poems, 1,* 156). The allegory requires the two gods to be Oxford (Apollo) and Godolphin (Pan). Marlborough "decreed" against Oxford "and gave it" for Godolphin in February 1708.

He against Phoebus' harp decreed,
And gave it for Pan's oaten reed:
The god of wit to show his grudge,
Clapped asses' ears upon the judge,   30
A good pair, erect and wide,
Which he could neither gild nor hide.
        And now the virtue of his hands
Was lost among Pactolus sands,
Against whose torrent while he swims,   35
The golden scurf peels off his limbs:
Fame spreads the news, and people travel
From far, to gather golden gravel;
Midas, exposed to all their jeers,
Had lost his art, and kept his ears.   40
        This tale inclines the gentle reader,
To think upon a certain leader,
To whom from Midas down, descends
That virtue in the fingers' ends:
What else by perquisites are meant,   45
By pensions, bribes, and three percent?
By places and commissions sold,
And turning dung itself to gold?
By starving in the midst of store,
As t' other Midas did before?   50
        None e'er did modern Midas choose,
Subject or patron of his Muse,
But found him thus their merit scan,
That Phoebus must give place to Pan.

46. *three percent:* Besides the kickback on the bread contracts, Marlborough had a warrant to deduct not 3 percent but $2\frac{1}{2}$ percent from the pay of foreign troops on the English establishment without any accounting therefor. From 1701 to 1711 this amounted to £282,366 9s. 7d., and Marlborough defended the arrangement on the ground that it did "not properly relate to the public accounts, being a free gift of the foreign troops" (Boyer, *Annals,* 1712, 277, 279, 283).

47. *commissions sold:* The poem anticipates the charges made by Earl Poulet on 28 May 1712 during the debate on the restraining orders. Ormonde, Poulet said, "was not like a certain general, who led troops to the slaughter, to cause a great number of officers to be knocked on the head in battle, or against stone walls, in order to fill his pockets, by disposing of their commissions" (*Cobbett's Parl. Hist.,* 6, 1137).

49. The duke was parsimonious as well as avaricious. "This mean passion of that great man operated very strongly in him in the very beginning of his life, and continued to the very end of it." On one occasion when he won sixpence at picquet, he insisted upon being paid even though this meant changing a guinea, on the ground that he needed the change for a sedan chair. The loser "did at last get change, paid the duke his sixpence, observed him a little after he left the room, and declares that (after all this bustle that had been made for his sixpence) the Duke actually walked home" (Spence, *1,* 163–64).

He values not the poet's praise,   55
Nor will exchange his plumbs for bays:
To Pan alone rich misers call,
And there's the jest, for Pan is all:
Here English wits will be to seek,
Howe'er, 'tis all one in the Greek.   60
     Besides, it plainly now appears,
Our Midas too has asses' ears;
Where every fool his mouth applies,
And whispers in a thousand lies;
Such gross delusions could not pass,   65
Through any ears but of an ass.
     But gold defiles with frequent touch,
There's nothing fouls the hands so much:
And scholars give it for the cause,
Of British Midas' dirty paws;   70
Which while the senate strove to scour,
They washed away the chemic power.
While he his utmost strength applied,
To swim against this pop'lar tide,
The golden spoils flew off apace,   75
Here fell a pension, there a place:
The torrent, merciless, imbibes
Commissions, perquisites, and bribes,
By their own weight sunk to the bottom;
Much good may it do 'em that have caught 'um.   80
And Midas now neglected stands,
With asses' ears, and dirty hands.

56. *plumbs:* A plumb was a cant word for £100,000.

73. *utmost strength applied:* Swift evidently believed in the reality of the Plunket Plot, a new version of the Popish Plot, by which Marlborough was to seize power after assassinating Oxford, taking the queen into custody, and burning London. A more plausible story is that Marlborough's "conduct, since his arrival from Holland [18 November 1711], was full of offense and liable to suspicion. . . . He threw his whole weight into the scale against the ministry. He caballed with Buys. He courted Bothmar. He herded with the discontented of all nations. Neglecting that government of his passions, for which he had been admired by the world, he fell into all the impotencies of rage and resentment, upon every party-debate. He left to the queen her choice of two alternatives: To stop the progress of the peace, to dismiss the ministry, and to dissolve the Parliament; or to rid herself of a person, who from a servant, was likely to become a tyrant. She determined to adopt the latter measure" (Macpherson, *Secret History of Great Britain, 2,* 512–13).

[WILLIAM SHIPPEN]

Pasquin to the Queen's Statue
(*January 1715?*)

The twentieth of January 1715 "being appointed as a thanksgiving for King George's safe arrival and his quiet taking possession of these kingdoms," Mr. Atkinson of Queen's College, Oxford preached a flattering sermon on the text, "By me kings reign and princes decree justice" (Hearne, 5, 18). But the application of the text was false, for George I reigned not by God but by two acts of Parliament.

It is only fair that the Jacobites have the last word on the subject of the Hanoverian succession, for they stood to be the chief losers by it. The Whigs, who had carefully cultivated Georg Ludwig since 1701, could hope a dynastic revolution and the impending election would return them to power. The moderate Tories, one of whose leaders, Sir Thomas Hanmer, had been speaker in the Parliament that had been dissolved only fifteen days before, and another of whose leaders, the admirable Shrewsbury, had been lord treasurer until October 1714, could hope for a share of power in a nonpartisan government, but the Jacobites had nothing to hope for.

Their frustration is expressed in a large body of verse and prose of which *Pasquin to the Queen's Statue* is a good example. "Nothing could be grosser," Horace Walpole recalled, "than the ribaldry that was vomited against the sovereign and the new court, and chanted even in their hearing about the public streets" (*Reminiscences Written by Mr. Horace Walpole in 1788*, ed. Paget Toynbee [Oxford: Clarendon Press, 1924], p. 30). *Pasquin to the Queen's Statue* supplies good evidence that Horace Walpole's memory was not at fault.

Pasquin to the Queen's Statue at St. Paul's, During the Procession, January 20, 1714

Behold he comes to make thy people groan,
And with their curses to ascend thy throne;
A clod-pate, base, inhuman, jealous fool,

Title. Pasquin: The archetypal pasquinade is a dialogue between Pasquin and another statue found in the Campo Martio and christened Marforio. *the queen's statue:* In this poem the other statue is that of Queen Anne by Francis Bird, erected in front of St. Paul's, facing

Explanation of the figures:
1. Britannia
2. France
3. America
4. Ireland

The Statue of Our Sovereign Lady QUEEN ANNE, being of y.e finest Marble, erected in Honour of Her Majesty at the West end of S.t PAUL'S CATHEDRALL London.

Printed & Sold by Henry Overton at y.e whiteHorse with out New gate London

The statue of Queen Anne by Francis Bird, erected in 1712 in St. Paul's Yard.

The jest of Europe and the faction's tool.
Heaven ne'er heard of such a right divine,   5
Nor earth e'er saw a successor like thine:
For if in sense or politics you failed,
'Twas when his lousy long succession you entailed.
   Let the ungrateful wretch think what you've done
For all his beggared race and bastard son.   10
See his mock daughter and her offspring shine
In all those blazing brilliants that were thine:
Drunk with incestuous lust, the cunning jilt
Pretends religion to conceal her guilt.
Kings could not draw her from her brother's bed;   15

Ludgate Hill. "A public statue in London," it has been said. "needs to be very bad to attract to its demerits any special attention" (*DNB*, *2*, 535), but Anne's statue provided the occasion for the following popular verses:

> Brandy Nan, brandy Nan,
> You're left in the lurch
> With your face to the gin shop,
> And your back to the church.

2. *curses:* What these were may be inferred from the demonstrations upon the coronation of George I. In Bristol a mob kicked out the bonfires, "crying, Down with the Roundheads, God bless Dr. Sacheverel." In Birmingham the cry was "Down with the Whigs." The Reading mob was even more explicit, crying, "No Hanover . . . no foreign government" (Abel Boyer, *The Political State of Great Britain, 60* vols. [London, 1711–40], *8*, 363, 367–68).

3. *clod-pate:* "The king's character may be comprised in very few words, In private life he would have been called an honest blockhead." (*The Letters and Works of Lady Mary Wortley Montagu*, ed. John Stuart-Wortley, Lord Wharncliffe, 3 vols. [1837], *1*, 107. *inhuman, jealous:* "Whether guilty or not (and no known evidence of her guilt exists, except in a correspondence of disputable authenticity), the electoral Princess Sophia Dorothea was accused of a criminal intrigue with Count Philip von Königsmark, a Swedish adventurer . . . in the Hanoverian military service . . . Against the princess . . . sentence of divorce was pronounced on the ground of malicious desertion, and she was detained a prisoner at Ahlden, near Celle, till her death, 3 November 1726." (*DNB*).

10. *bastard son:* Doubts about the legitimacy of Prince George Augustus were raised by the allegations of his mother's liaison with Königsmark in 1694 and with Cosmo III de' Medici, grand duke of Tuscany.

11. *mock daughter:* The daughter of George I, Sophia Dorothea, did not come to England because she had married in 1705 the crown prince of Prussia, who succeeded as Friedrich Wilhelm I in 1713. The context makes it clear that George's "mock daughter" is his daughter-in-law, Caroline of Anspach (1683–1737), who married Prince George Augustus in 1705. George I called her "Cette Diablesse" (Walpole, *Reminiscences,* p. 27).

14. *Pretends religion:* Caroline refused in 1703 to marry Archduke Charles, later Emperor Charles VI, on the grounds that she could not abandon her Protestant faith.

15. *brother:* Caroline's brother, Wilhelm Friedrich, was born in 1685. When their father died in 1686, the children were taken to live first in Eisenach, and then, when their mother married the elector of Saxony in 1692, to Dresden, where manners and morals are said to have been "extraordinary." Upon the death of their mother in 1696 the children lived in Berlin with their guardians, the elector of Brandenburg and his wife, Sophia Charlotte of

Till he was slain, she would not yield to wed.
See how her henpecked stripling struts with pride,
To George alone in little sense allied:
With headpiece framed miraculously thin,
All brush without and emptiness within.   20
See his fantastic air and foreign mien,
His awkward gesture, and affected grin,
Which apish Bullock imitates in vain.
  Had you, great queen, ne'er broke the nation's laws
And wronged your brother and your brother's cause,   25
Ne'er by the Hell-born faction been dismayed,
By fools deluded, or by knaves betrayed,
Brunswick a petty prince had still remained,
By mercenary troops his court maintained,
And over slaves and German boobies reigned,   30
On leeks and garlic still regaled his taste,
In dirty doulas shirts and fustian dressed,
Been once a month from bugs and lice made clean,
The only free-born subjects of his reign.
  Was it for this your ashes are abused,   35

Hanover. Upon the death of Sophia Charlotte in 1704, Caroline and her brother lived in
Triesdorf until her marriage in September 1705 to George Augustus of Hanover, which she
made conditional upon Wilhelm Friedrich's approval.

17. *henpecked:* Caroline's "first thought on her marriage was to secure to herself the sole
and whole direction of her spouse" and George Augustus remained entirely under the
government of his wife until her death in 1737. Even when he became king he was taunted
in a popular rhyme: "You may strut, dapper George, but 'twill all be in vain, / We know
'tis Queen Caroline not you does reign." *stripling:* This may refer to George's small stature.
When a dwarf was presented at court, George "Rejoiced to see within his court / One shorter
than himself" (*The Seven Wise Men* ["Seven Sages in our happy Isle are seen"] 17). *pride:*
"His pride told him that he was placed above constraint . . . and he looked on all the men
and women that he saw as creatures he might kick or kiss for his diversion; and, whenever he
met with any opposition in those designs, he thought his opposers insolent rebels to the will
of God" (*The Letters and Works of Lady Mary Wortley Montagu, 1,* 117).

18. *To George . . . allied:* Since George Augustus believed in his mother's innocence and on
one occasion at least tried to force his way past the guards to see her, and since he had been
invited in 1711 to live in England without the knowledge, or against the inclination of George
I, he was always at odds with George I. In January 1718 the king ordered the prince and his
family to remove themselves from St. James's Palace.

24. *broke the nation's laws:* Anne broke the law of primogeniture by succeeding to the throne
to the exclusion of the male heir.

26. *the Hell-born faction:* the Whigs.

35. *ashes are abused:* Anne's death was openly celebrated by the Whigs: "Ipswich August
14 [1714]. Although we are deeply concerned for the loss of the queen we can't forbear giving
some account of the indecent and disrespectful behavior of our Whigs upon the news of the
death of the queen which was the 2d instant. The next morning orders were sent to the church
wardens to ring their bells . . . so that we had ringing in most churches all day long" (Exeter
City Library MS City Records, Ancient Letters 471).

Your servants libeled and the peace accused?
You to the church distributed your store,
Gave to the distressed, the innocent, and poor:
But now your vast revenue's all bestowed
On punks at home and managers abroad.   40
Legions of pimps, and whores they scarce can score,
Infest this island and the land devour,
But this insatiate brood still gape for more,
More than for native kings was e'er decreed,
But beggars horsed will to the devil speed.   45
Pigburgh and Kilmanseck, the modest toast,
Will soon have pensions at the nation's cost
Beyond what Portland or what Orkney boast.

36. *peace accused:* The attack on the Treaty of Utrecht was kept up in lampoons and in such pamphlets as Steele's *The Importance of Dunkirk Considered* (September 1713), The *Crisis* (January 1713), and *The French Faith Represented in the Present State of Dunkirk* (July 1714).

37. *to the church:* On the day after her birthday in 1704 Anne gave to the church the "entire revenues from tenths and first fruits, appropriated to the crown in 1534, and amounting to between £16,000 and £17,000 a year" (*DNB, 1,* 453). Through the intervention of Harley, Swift obtained the same favor for the Church of Ireland in February 1711 (Swift, *Journal, 1,* 185).

40. *punks:* Cf. *The Blessings Attending George's Accession and Coronation,* (n.p., n.d.):

> Hither he brought . . .
> . . . himself, his pipe, close-stool and louse;
> Two Turks, three W—es, and half a dozen nurses:
> Five hundred Germans, all with empty purses.

At the time of his death in 1727 it was said that George I was quite rotten and eat up with whoring" (Hearne, *9,* 332)

46. *Pigburgh:* the countess of Lippe and Picquebourg, one of the ladies of the princess of Wales. *Kilmanseck:* Sophia Charlotte, Countess von Platen and Hallermund, and *jure mariti* Baroness von Kielmansegge (c. 1673–1725), whom "time and very bad paint had left without any of the charms which had once attracted him," arrived in London in September 1714 with George I. This "was enough to make her called his mistress, or at least so great a favorite that the whole court began to pay her uncommon respect" (*The Letters and Works of Lady Mary Wortley Montagu, 1,* 109, 111). What Horace Walpole chiefly remembered was her great bulk—she became known as the Elephant and Castle—and the paint: "two acres of cheeks spread with crimson, an ocean of neck that overflowed and was not distinguished from the lower part of her body, and no part restrained by stays" (Walpole, *Reminiscences,* p. 30).

47. *soon have pensions:* The prophecy was generously fulfilled. Kielmansegge had "two gallons of beer a day for herself and servants in 1714. In June 1715 she requested and was given four and a half gallons; by April 1717 she had twelve barrels a month, increased on 17 April to fourteen, and on 6 June to sixteen. Her allowance of sherry, claret, bread and candles grew correspondingly." By 1718 it was decided to give her £3000 a year and a kitchen in lieu of board and other allowances (J. M. Beattie, *The English Court in the Reign of George I,* [Cambridge University Press, 1967], p. 80).

48. *Portland:* William III lavished such grants on his favorite, Willem Bentinck, earl of Portland, that he made him "the richest subject in *Europe*" (Macky, *Memoirs of John Macky,* p. 62). *Orkney:* William settled on his mistress, Elizabeth Villiers, in May 1695 nearly all of the Irish estates of King James III, said to be worth £25,995 13s. a year. She then married her cousin, George Hamilton, who was created earl of Orkney in January 1696.

But since on knavish models George is split,
By Townshend cullied and by Churchill bit,   50
Take it from me that his destruction's sure,
Nor can his ill-got monarchy endure,
For when known villains at the helm preside,
And kings against themselves with faction side,
When impious rage against the church they boast,   55
Her sons oppressed, the constitution lost,
Then soon abandoned by the rabble rout,
Despised and hissed and trampled under foot,
A king becomes a vile detested name
And quits his life as well as crown with shame.   60
Be this that bold usurping upstart's fate,
Who on another's throne would fain look great,
Sworn to maintain, yet laughs at all the laws,
And by tyrannic rule supports his cause:
By redcoats and by arms enforcing sway,   65
By hungry bloodhounds and by birds of prey.
He said, and straight the cursed usurper's soul,
Like Aetna heaved; his eyeballs wildly roll:
Such is his rage and so the monster stares,
When the dread ghost of Königsmark appears.   70

50. *Townshend:* Charles Townshend, 2d viscount Townshend (1675–1738), and Horace Walpole's brother-in-law, signed the notorious Barrier Treaty with the Dutch in October 1709. In February 1712 he was accused in Parliament of exceeding his instructions and voted an enemy to his country. But through his friendship with Hernstorff, Bothmar, and Robethon, the Hanoverian managers abroad, he was appointed George I's first secretary of state in September 1714. *Churchill:* Upon Anne's death, Marlborough hastened to reach England before the king arrived and was "received with great expressions of joy from the people" (*The Flying Post,* 5 August 1714). Upon George's arrival, one of his first acts was to sign a warrant reinstating Marlborough as captain general of the forces, master general of the ordnance, and colonel of the first regiment of foot guards. But the old leaven of avarice still worked within him and his demands for more and more finally disgusted even some Whigs.

51. *destruction's sure:* One of the mistresses of George I refused to come to England, "fearing that the people of England, who, she thought, were accustomed to use their kings barbarously, might chop off his head in the first fortnight" (*The Letters and Works of Lady Mary Wortley Montagu, 1,* 108).

55. *against the church:* George I, a Lutheran, knew that most of the lower clergy of the Church of England, by promoting indefeasible hereditary right, had opposed the Hanoverian succession. So he did not favor the church. In December he issued directions signed by Townshend that commanded, among other things, that the clergy not intermeddle in any affairs of state.

70. *Königsmark:* Philipp Christoph, count of Königsmark (1665–94) was a Swedish soldier of fortune who fought bulls in Spain, murdered or procured the murder of Thomas Thynne of Longleat, and became the lover or the supposed lover of Sophia Dorothea, the electoral princess of Hanover. When George Ludwig heard the rumors, he ordered Königsmark "to quit his dominions the next day. The princess, surrounded by women too closely connected

And Mahomet and Mustapha prepare
To stem by force his madness and despair.

with her husband, and consequently enemies of the lady they injured, was persuaded by them to suffer the count to kiss her hand before his abrupt departure; and he was actually introduced by them into her bedchamber the next morning before she arose. From that moment he disappeared, nor was it known what became of him, till on the death of George I, on his son the new king's first journey to Hanover, some alterations in the palace being ordered by him, the body of Königsmark was discovered under the floor of the electoral princess's dressingroom" (Walpole, *Reminiscences,* p. 21).

71. *Mahomet and Mustapha:* The two Turks whom Georg Ludwig had captured in 1686 fighting for the emperor and who had become his most trusted body servants accompanied him to England. The suspicion that they had strangled Königsmark fed the rumors that the king "keeps two Turks for abominable purposes" (BM Add. MS 47028, p. 14).

72. *madness:* There were also rumors that George was "frantic often times and walks about in his shirt" (ibid.).

WORKS FREQUENTLY CITED

Ailesbury: *Memoirs of Thomas, Earl of Ailesbury, Written by Himself.* 2 vols. London, 1890.

Aubrey: John Aubrey. *Brief Lives.* Ed. Andrew Clark. 2 vols. Oxford, 1898.

Beaven: Alfred B. Beaven. *The Aldermen of the City of London.* 2 vols. London, 1908–13.

Biographia Britannica: Biographia Britannica: Or, The Lives of the Most Eminent Persons. 6 vols. in 7. London, 1747–66 (2d ed. Ed. Andrew Kippis et al. 5 vols. London, 1778–93).

Bolingbroke: *Letters and Correspondence, Public and Private, of the Right Honourable Henry St. John, Lord Visc. Bolingbroke.* 4 vols. London, 1798.

Boyer, *Annals:* Abel Boyer. *The History of the Reign of Queen Anne, Digested into Annals.* 11 vols. London, 1703–13.

Boyer, *History:* Abel Boyer. *The History of the Life and Reign of Queen Anne.* London, 1722.

Brown, *Shaftesbury:* Louise Fargo Brown. *The First Earl of Shaftesbury.* New York, 1936.

Browning, *Danby:* Andrew Browning. *Thomas Osborne, Earl of Danby and Duke of Leeds.* 3 vols. Glasgow, 1944–51.

Bryant: Arthur Bryant. *King Charles II.* London, 1934.

Buckingham: *The Works of George Villiers, Second Duke of Buckingham.* 3d ed. 2 vols. London, 1715.

Burnet: *Bishop Burnet's History of His Own Time: With the Suppressed Passages of the First Volume, and Notes by the Earls of Dartmouth and Hardwicke, and Speaker Onslow.* 6 vols. Oxford, 1823.

Chamberlayne, *Angliae Notitia:* Edward Chamberlayne. *Angliae Notitia: Or, The Present State of England.* 19 vols. London, 1669–1704.

Chappell: William Chappell. *Popular Music of the Olden Time.* 2 vols. London, 1855–59.

CJ: *The Journals of the House of Commons.*

Clarendon: Edward Hyde, earl of Clarendon. *The Life of Edward Hyde, Earl of Clarendon, Lord High Chancellor of England, and Chancellor of the University of Oxford in Which Is Included a Continuation of His History of the Grand Rebellion.* 2 vols. Oxford, 1857.

Clark, *Later Stuarts:* George N. Clark. *The Later Stuarts.* Oxford, 1949.

Clarke, *James II:* J.S. Clarke. *The Life of James II.* 2 vols. London, 1816.

Cobbett's Parl. Hist.: *Cobbett's Parliamentary History of England.* 36 vols. London, 1806–20.

Coxe: William Coxe. *Memoirs of the Duke of Marlborough.* Rev. ed. Ed. John Wade. 3 vols. London, 1847–48.

CSPD: *Calendar of State Papers, Domestic Series, 1660–1702.* Ed. Mary E. Greene et al. 38 vols. London, 1860–1964.

CTP: *Calendar of Treasury Papers, 1557–1728.* Ed. Joseph Redington. 6 vols. London, 1868–89.

Dalrymple: Sir John Dalrymple, Baronet. *Memoirs of Great Britain and Ireland.* 3d ed. 3 vols. London, 1790.

Dennis, *Critical Works:* *The Critical Works of John Dennis.* Ed. Edward N. Hooker. 2 vols. Baltimore, Md., 1939–43.

Dennis, *Works:* *The Select Works of Mr. John Dennis.* 2 vols. London, 1718.

Dering: *The Parliamentary Diary of Sir Edward Dering, 1670–1673.* Ed. B. D. Henning. New Haven, Conn., 1940.

DNB: *The Dictionary of National Biography.* Ed. Sir Lesile Stephen and Sir Sidney Lee. 22 vols. New York, 1949–50.

D'Oyley: Elizabeth D'Oyley. *James, Duke of Monmouth.* London, 1938.

Dryden, *Poems:* *The Poems of John Dryden.* Ed. James Kinsley. 4 vols. Oxford, 1958.

EB: *Encyclopedia Britannica.* 13th ed. 32 vols. London and New York, 1926.

Echard: Laurence Echard. *The History of England from the Restoration of King Charles the Second to the Conclusion of the Reign of King James the Second.* 3 vols. London, 1707–18.

EHD: *English Historical Documents, 1660–1714.* Ed. Andrew Browning. London, 1953.

Ellis Correspondence: George Agar Ellis. *The Ellis Correspondence, 1686–1688.* 2 vols. London, 1707–18.

Essays of John Dryden. Selected and edited by W. P. Ker. 2 vols. Oxford, 1900.

Evelyn: *The Diary of John Evelyn.* Ed. Esmond S. deBeer. 6 vols. Oxford, 1955.

Feiling, *Foreign Policy:* Keith Feiling. *British Foreign Policy, 1660–72.* London, 1930.

Feiling, *Tory Party:* Keith Feiling. *A History of the Tory Party, 1640–1714.* 2d ed. Oxford, 1950.

Foxcroft: *A Supplement to Burnet's History of My Own Time.* Ed. Helen C. Foxcroft. Oxford, 1902.

Fraser, *Intelligence of the Secretaries of State:* Peter Fraser. *The Intelligence of the Secretaries of State and Their Monopoly of Licensed News, 1660–1688.* Cambridge, 1956.

GEC: George E. Cokayne. *The Complete Peerage*. Ed. V. Gibbs et al. 13 vols. London, 1910.

Gramont, *Memoirs:* Anthony Gramont. *Memoirs of Count Gramont*. Ed. Allan Fea. London, 1906.

Grey: Anchitell Grey. *Debates of the House of Commons from the Year 1667 to the Year 1694*. 10 vols. London, 1769.

Hatton Correspondence: Correspondence of the Family of Hatton, Being Letters Chiefly Addressed to Christopher, First Viscount Hatton, 1601–1704. Ed. E. M. Thompson. 2 vols. London, 1878.

Hearne: *Remarks and Collections of Thomas Hearne*. Ed. C. E. Dobel et al. 11 vols. Oxford, 1884–1918.

HMC: Historical Manuscripts Commission Reports.

Holmes: Geoffrey Holmes. *British Politics in the Age of Anne*. New York, 1967.

Horwitz: Henry Horwitz. *Revolution Politics: The Career of Daniel Finch, Second Earl of Nottingham, 1647–1730*. Cambridge, 1968.

Howell: *A Complete Collection of State Trials*. Ed. Thomas B. Howell. 33 vols. London, 1816–26.

Kennett: White Kennett. *A Complete History of England*. 3 vols. London, 1706–19.

Kenyon: John P. Kenyon. *Robert Spencer, Earl of Sunderland, 1641–1702*. London, 1958.

Lane: Jane Lane. *Titus Oates*. London, 1949.

Le Neve: *Le Neve's Pedigrees of the Knights*. Ed. George W. Marshall. London, 1873.

L'Estrange, Roger. *The History of the Plot*. London, 1679.

L'Estrange, Roger. *Notes upon Stephen College*. London, 1681.

LJ: The Journals of the House of Lords.

Luttrell: Narcissus Luttrell. *A Brief Historical Relation of State Affairs from September 1678 to April 1714*. 6 vols. Oxford, 1857.

Macaulay: Thomas Babington Macaulay. *The History of England from the Accession of James II*. Ed. Charles H. Firth. 6 vols. London, 1913–15. (Vols. paginated consecutively.)

Macdonald: Hugh Macdonald. *John Dryden: A Bibliography of Early Editions and of Drydeniana*. Oxford, 1939.

Margoliouth: *The Poems and Letters of Andrew Marvell·*. Ed. H. M. Margoliouth. 2d ed. 2 vols. Oxford, 1952.

Milward: John Milward. *The Diary of John Milward, Esq.: Member of Parliament for Derbyshire, September 1666 to May 1668*. Ed. Caroline Robbins. Cambridge, 1938.

Neal, Daniel. *The History of the Puritan or Protestant Nonconformists from the Reformation, 1517, to the Revolution of 1688*. 4 vols. London, 1732–38.

North: Roger North. *Examen*. London, 1740.

Noyes: *The Poetical Works of Dryden.* Ed. G. R. Noyes. 2d ed. Cambridge, Mass. 1956.

OED: Oxford English Dictionary. Ed. Sir. J. H. Murray et al. 13 vols. Oxford, 1933.

Ogg, *Charles II*: David Ogg. *England in the Reign of Charles II.* 2 vols. Oxford, 1956.

Ogg, *James II*: David Ogg. *England in the Reign of James II and William III.* 2d ed. Oxford, 1957.

Oldmixon: John Oldmixon. *The History of England during the Reigns of King William and Queen Mary, Queen Anne, King George I.* London, 1735.

Oldmixon, *Life of Maynwaring:* John Oldmixon. *The Life and Posthumous Works of Arthur Maynwaring, Esq.* London, 1715.

Osborne, *Advice-to-a-Painter Poems:* Mary Tom Osborne. *Advice-to-a Painter Poems, 1633–1856, An Annotated Finding List.* Austin, Texas, 1949.

Osborn MSS: Manuscripts of James M. Osborn, deposited in the Yale University Library.

Partridge: Eric Partridge. *A Dictionary of Slang and Unconventional English.* 4th ed. London, 1956.

Pepys: Samuel Pepys. *Diary.* Ed. Henry B. Wheatley. 10 vols. New York, 1942.

Pinto, *Enthusiast in Wit:* Vivian de Sola Pinto. *Enthusiast in Wit: A Portrait of John Wilmot, Earl of Rochester, 1647–1680.* Lincoln, Nebr., 1962.

Pinto, *Poems by Rochester:* Vivian de Sola Pinto. *Poems by Rochester.* London, 1953.

Pinto, *Sedley:* Vivian de Sola Pinto. *Sir Charles Sedley, 1639–1701: A Study in the Life and Literature of the Restoration.* London, 1927.

Pollock: Sir John Pollock. *The Popish Plot: A Study in the History of the Reign of Charles II.* Cambridge, 1944.

Ralph: James Ralph. *The History of England during the Reigns of King William, Queen Anne, and King George the First.* 2 vols. London, 1744–46.

Ranke: Leopold von Ranke. *A History of England Principally in the Seventeenth Century.* 6 vols. Oxford, 1875.

Reresby: Sir John Reresby. *Memoirs and Selected Letters.* Ed. Andrew Browning. Glasgow, 1936.

Scott-Saintsbury: Walter Scott and George Saintsbury. *The Works of John Dryden.* 18 vols. Edinburgh, 1882–93.

Somers' Tracts: A Collection of Scarce and Valuable Tracts, Selected from . . . Private Libraries: Particulary that of . . . Lord Somers. Ed. Sir Walter Scott. 13 vols. London, 1809–15.

Spence: Joseph Spence. *Observations, Anecdotes, and Characters of Books and Men Collected from Conversation.* Ed. James M. Osborn. 2 vols. Oxford, 1966.

Strype: John Stowe. *A Survey of the Cities of London and Westminster*. Ed. John Strype. 2 vols. London, 1720.

Swift, *Correspondence*: *The Correspondence of Jonathan Swift*. Ed. Harold Williams. 5 vols. Oxford, 1963–65.

Swift, *Journal*: Jonathan Swift. *Journal to Stella*. Ed. Harold Williams. 2 vols. Oxford, 1948.

Swift, *Poems*: *The Poems of Jonathan Swift*. Ed. Harold Williams. 3 vols. Oxford, 1937.

Swift, *Prose*: *The Prose Writings of Jonathan Swift*. Ed. Herbert Davis. 13 vols. Oxford, 1939–62.

Tedder: Arthur W. Tedder. *The Navy of the Restoration from the Death of Cromwell to the Treaty of Breda: Its Work, Growth, and Influence*. Cambridge, 1916.

Tilley: *A Dictionary of the Proverbs in England in the Sixteenth and Seventeenth Centuries*. Ed. Morris P. Tilley. Ann Arbor, Mich., 1950.

Trevelyan: George Macaulay Trevelyan. *England under Queen Anne*. 3 vols. London, 1930.

Turner: F. C. Turner. *James II*. London, 1948.

Vernon: *Letters Illustrative of the Reign of William III from 1696 to 1708 Addressed to the Duke of Shrewsbury by James Vernon*. Ed. G. P. R. James. 3 vols. London, 1841.

Vieth: David M. Vieth. *Attribution in Restoration Poetry*. New Haven, Conn., 1963.

Walpole, *Noble Authors*: Horace Walpole. *A Catalogue of the Royal and Noble Authors of England, with Lists of Their Works*. 2 vols. London, 1759.

Weekly Pacquet: Henry Care. *Weekly Pacquet of Advice from Rome*. London, 1679–83.

Wilson, *All the King's Ladies*: J. Harold Wilson. *All the King's Ladies: Actresses of the Restoration*. Chicago, 1958.

Wilson, *The Court Wits*: J. Harold Wilson. *The Court Wits of the Restoration: An Introduction*. Princeton, N.J., 1948.

Wood, *Athenae Oxonienses*: Anthony à Wood. *Athenae Oxonienses. An Exact History of All the Writers and Bishops Who Have Had Their Education in the University of Oxford. To Which Are Added the Fasti, or Annals of the Said University*. Ed. Philip Bliss. 4 vols. London, 1813–20.

Wood, *Life and Times*: *The Life and Times of Anthony Wood*. Ed. Andrew Clark. 5 vols. Oxford, 1891–1900.

INDEX OF FIRST LINES

GENERAL INDEX

ITALICIZED PAGE NUMBERS REFER TO FOOTNOTES.